PRACTICAL LAW OFFICE MANAGEMENT

WEST LEGAL STUDIES

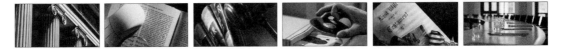

Options.
Over 300 products in every area of the law: textbooks, CD-ROMs, reference books, test banks, online companions, and more – helping you succeed in the classroom and on the job.

Support.
We offer unparalleled, practical support: robust instructor and student supplements to ensure the best learning experience, custom publishing to meet your unique needs, and other benefits such as West's Student Achievement Award. And our sales representatives are always ready to provide you with dependable service.

Feedback.
As always, we want to hear from you! Your feedback is our best resource for improving the quality of our products. Contact your sales representative or write us at the address below if you have any comments about our materials or if you have a product proposal.

Accounting and Financials for the Law Office • Administrative Law • Alternative Dispute Resolution • Bankruptcy • Business Organizations/Corporations • Careers and Employment Civil Litigation and Procedure • CLA Exam Preparation • Computer Applications in the Law Office • Contract Law • Court Reporting • Criminal Law and Procedure • Document Preparation • Elder Law • Employment Law • Environmental Law • Ethics • Evidence Law • Family Law • Intellectual Property • Interviewing and Investigation • Introduction to Law Introduction to Paralegalism • Law Office Management Law Office Procedures Legal Nurse Consulting • Legal Research, Writing, and Analysis • Legal Terminology • Paralegal Internship • Product Liability • Real Estate Law • Reference Materials • Social Security Sports Law • Torts and Personal Injury Law • Wills, Trusts, and Estate Administration

---

West Legal Studies
5 Maxwell Drive
Clifton Park, New York 12065-2919

For additional information, find us online at:
www.westlegalstudies.com

THOMSON
DELMAR LEARNING

PRACTICAL LAW OFFICE MANAGEMENT

Third Edition

Brent Roper, J.D., MBA

THOMSON

DELMAR LEARNING

Australia • Canada • Mexico • Singapore • Spain • United Kingdom • United States

THOMSON

DELMAR LEARNING

WEST LEGAL STUDIES

Practical Law Office Management, 3E

by Brent D. Roper

Vice President, Career Education Strategic Business Unit:
Dawn Gerrain

Acquisitions Editor:
Shelley Esposito

Senior Product Manager:
Melissa Riveglia

Editorial Assistant:
Melissa A. Zaza

Director of Production:
Wendy A. Troeger

Content Project Manager:
Matthew J. Williams

Director of Marketing:
Wendy E. Mapstone

Marketing Channel Manager:
Gerard McAvey

Marketing Coordinator:
Jonathan Sheehan

Cover Design:
Joe Villanova

Cover Images:
Steve Cole/Getty Images
JG Photography/Alamy
Janis Christie/Getty Images
Nick Koudis/Getty Images
Chad Baker/Getty Images

Library of Congress Cataloging-in-Publication Data:

Roper, Brent D.
  Practical law office management / Brent D. Roper.—3rd ed.
     p. cm.—(West legal studies series)
  Includes bibliographical references and index.
1. Law offices—United States. I. Title.
II. Series.
KF318.R66 2006
340.068—dc22
                                    2006013158

NOTICE TO THE READER

To the wife of my youth,
Shirley Phelps-Roper

BRIEF CONTENTS

CONTENTS

2 LEGAL ADMINISTRATION AND TECHNOLOGY   51

4   CLIENT RELATIONS AND COMMUNICATION SKILLS   201

6   CLIENT TRUST FUNDS AND LAW OFFICE ACCOUNTING   363

7   CALENDARING, DOCKET CONTROL, AND CASE MANAGEMENT   445

PREFACE

Another class, another boring textbook. Right? Wrong! Law office management is a dynamic subject and a great class. It will make you a better legal assistant. You will learn about real-life problems you will encounter on the job and how to deal with them successfully. You will understand how important it is to perform quality work for clients. You will learn methods for improving your communication skills and your ability to work with clients successfully. You will be shown how to track and bill your time correctly, and how to use your time effectively. There are explanations throughout the book about how to avoid ethical problems that may come up. Law office management is anything but boring.

The goal of *Practical Law Office Management* is to educate legal assistant students regarding law office management procedures and systems. Law firms, as well as legal assistants themselves, must have good management skills to survive in today's competitive marketplace. This text is written for the student who wants to understand effective law practice management techniques and systems whether or not he or she will go on to become a law office administrator.

This text is not intended to be an "armchair" text on the theories and principles of management, nor is it a text on how to set up a law office. Rather, this text presents a practical discussion of law office management from a legal assistant's view.

The information presented is national in scope and assumes no prior knowledge of management or the legal field. Sociology, theories, and jargon are kept to an absolute minimum. To present a flavor of how a real law office operates, step-by-step explanations, "how-to" tips, practical charts, recent trends in law office management and software, and many practical ideas on law office management from the legal assistant's perspective are provided. Information is presented in a manner that encourages students to think independently and to learn by participating.

This book, among other things, will explain what management generally expects of legal assistants, and will present good law office systems and practical information about law office management.

Legal assistants must learn to manage themselves in addition to performing their normal duties. This book will help the student manage him- or herself in addition to teaching basic law office systems, such as timekeeping and billing, docket control, financial management, file and library management, technology, and more. If the student takes the time to learn the management systems in this book, he or she will perform tasks more efficiently, with greater accuracy, and with less work. Sound too good to be true? That is what good management is all about.

A book on law office management has inherent limitations because there are many different management styles, techniques, and philosophies, depending on the size and type of firm (e.g., small, medium, and large firms, corporate legal departments, etc.), location of the firm (urban, rural, east, west), and so forth. In addition, law office management is such a diverse area that most people cannot agree on all the topics that should be covered. In light of these inherent problems, a vast and varied amount of information from many different angles is presented.

Ethics

The importance of ethics is stressed throughout the text. Assuring a high ethical standard in the law office is a major function of law office management. It is very important to your career that you be educated regarding ethical issues and adopt a high ethical standard as a way of life. Every chapter in the text has an in-depth section on ethics. In "Chapter 3—Ethics and Malpractice," the codes of ethics for both the National Association of Legal Assistants (NALA) and the National Federation of Paralegal Associations (NFPA) are included. Ethical related cases also appear at the end of most chapters. The cases discuss major ethical points covered in the chapter in real life, actual settings. As much as possible, the cases involve legal assistants.

Organization of Text

The text is organized into nine chapters. Chapter 1 is an introduction to the legal environment, including a discussion of the members of the legal team in most law offices, and information about the different sizes and types of law practices and law firm governance. Chapter 2 is a broad introduction to law office management and includes coverage of 11 major areas regarding the topic. However, from Chapter 2 onward, the chapters stand on their own and do not depend on the preceding chapter(s). Thus, instructors can assign the chapters in whatever order they believe is appropriate.

Changes to the Third Edition

The third edition of *Practical Law Office Management* offers major enhancements over the second edition. The text has been completely updated to reflect current management practices and technological advances. Some of the more significant changes include the following:

- The total number of chapters has been reduced from 10 to 9. This was possible because the organization of the text has been greatly enhanced. The organization was completely reworked, and a couple of chapters were combined. The organization is now tighter and makes more sense.
- All kinds of exercises were added to the text. The text now has more kinds and types of practice hands-on exercises than any other law office management text I am aware of. These include law office management software tutorials (for time and billing, trust accounting, docket control, ethics/conflicts of interest, and client relationships), Excel tutorials, On the Web Exercises (for every chapter), projects (for every chapter), thought-provoking questions and exercises (for every chapter), excellent Web Links (for every chapter), great ethical cases included at the end of most chapters (many of which are new), Suggested Reading (for every chapter), and a new section entitled "Test Your Knowledge." The text really tries to be *practical* and hands on and offers the student many learning opportunities.

- A demonstration version of the software product ProLaw is packaged with the text. ProLaw is a time and billing, trust accounting, financial management and docket control/case management program, among other things. One of the real problems with packaging demonstration software with a textbook is that the author and publisher of the textbook cannot control the software product or manufacturer. Software manufacturers sometimes give poor support to our adopters, put limitations on the demonstration version, or make other changes that are detrimental to our adopters. We are delighted that ProLaw, a Thomson-owned company, the publisher of this text, is providing a demonstration version of their program. We believe that this will greatly enhance our ability to provide a solid software product with top-of-the-line software support for our adopters.
- Additional ethical cases have been added to the text. Whenever possible, the cases involve actual legal assistants in the facts of the cases. Most of the cases involve truly interesting fact patterns and present excellent learning opportunities for students.
- Hands-on exercises for Microsoft Excel were added to Chapter 5, Legal Timekeeping and Billing; and to Chapter 6, Client Trust Funds and Law Office Accounting. All of the exercises are law-office-management based and give the student experience with building practical spreadsheets regarding these important topics. The exercises are fun and full of learning opportunities.
- A new chapter on legal marketing was added near the end of the text.
- Chapter 2, Legal Administration, was added to the text. This chapter is a holistic view of law office management and is broken down into 11 separate areas. It gives students a broad "30,000-foot view" of law office management and provides an excellent framework for the rest of the book.
- Most of the charts and graphs in the text have been updated and are current.
- The text continues to have a strong ethical base. Ethics is covered in every chapter. Many of the exercises also have an ethical foundation. All of the ethics citations have been updated to include revisions the American Bar Association has recently made to the *Model Rules of Professional Conduct.*
- Coverage of technological advances has been added to every chapter.
- PowerPoint presentations for each chapter have been added for instructors in the Online Companion.

Special Features

- Strong, practical coverage of ethics throughout the text
- Ethics cases regarding law office management topics in most chapters
- Citations to the *Model Rules* including recent updates
- Quotes from practicing legal assistants throughout the text
- Hands-on exercises and software for ProLaw
- Introductions that "set the stage" for each chapter
- Up-to-date charts, figures, and graphs to illustrate concepts
- Key terms/concepts defined in the margin
- List of Internet sites by topic for each chapter

- List of suggested reading for each chapter
- Expanded discussion questions and exercises at the end of each chapter
- Chapter objectives listed for each chapter
- Practical suggestions on how to succeed as a legal assistant and avoid problems
- "On the Web" exercises for each chapter
- Projects for each chapter
- Microsoft Excel tutorials for two chapters
- PowerPoint Presentations for Institutes for each chapter in the Online Companion

Supplements

Several supplements are available for use with the text, including an instructor's manual and software.

- **Instructor's Manual with Test Bank**   West Legal Studies has provided a downloadable Instructor's Manual online at *http://www.westlegalstudies.com*, in the Instructor's Lounge under "Resources." The Instructor's Manual is designed to save the instructor time in organizing and preparing for class. Written by the author of the text, it includes outlines, teaching objectives, discussion ideas, transparency masters, and a test bank.
- **Computerized Test Bank**   The Test Bank found in the Instructor's Manual is also available in a computerized format on CD-ROM. The platforms supported include Windows™ 3.1 and 95, Windows™ NT, and Macintosh. Features include:
  - Multiple methods of question selection
  - Multiple outputs—that is, print, ASCII, and RTF
  - Graphic support (black and white)
  - Random questioning output
  - Special character support
- **Web page**   Come visit our Web site at *http://www.westlegalstudies.com*, where you will find valuable information specific to this book such as hot links and sample materials to download, as well as other West Legal Studies products.
- **Westlaw**®   West's on-line computerized legal research system offers students "hands-on" experience with a system commonly used in law offices. Qualified adopters can receive 10 free hours of Westlaw®. Westlaw® can be accessed with Macintosh and IBM PC and compatibles. A modem is required.

Software Tutorials and Hands-On Exercises

The text accommodates legal assistant programs that have access to computers by including software tutorials at the end of many of the chapters. However, these are simply an added feature and computer use is completely optional. This text can be used fully by legal assistant programs that choose not to use computers.

The software tutorials included in the text are completely interactive and allow the student hands-on experience with the software programs. In addition, all of the tutorials are specifically related to law offices and legal applications so the student not only learns how to operate the software, he or she also learns how to use it in a law office. An educational version of ProLaw is provided free of charge for schools adopting the text. ProLaw is a full-featured legal software program that includes functionality in:

- Legal timekeeping and billing
- Trust accounting
- Docket control
- Conflict of interest
- Client relationship management

Step-by-step exercises are included in the text for each of these areas, along with exercises for Microsoft Excel regarding client trust funds/budgeting, timekeeping, and billing.

To the Student

Law office management is exciting and ever changing. It is my hope that you will find this book useful as a reference tool in your professional career and that you will use some ideas in it to climb the ladder of success. Remember that just because you graduate from a paralegal program, you do not get to start at the top. Everyone has to start at the bottom and work his or her way up. I started as a runner/clerk and worked up from there. Do not be surprised or disappointed if you start in an entry-level job. The experience you will gain is priceless, and through hard work and determination, you will move up more quickly than you think, and you will be better for it because you will have earned it. Also remember to help your coworkers. You will not be able to succeed without their help. Treat them like you would like to be treated, put the interests of your law office ahead of your own, and you will go far.

If you have an interesting idea, have solved some problem in law office management, or just have a story to tell and you would not mind me using it as an example in a subsequent edition of this book, please do not hesitate to contact me. I am always interested in learning from you. I wish you the best of luck in your endeavors. Brent Roper, 3640 Churchill Road, Topeka, KS 66604.

Acknowledgments

One of my favorite parts of writing a book is getting to thank the people who helped me put it together. To all the people who have worked on this project: thank you for all of your help.

REVIEWERS   Thank you to the reviewers of this third edition for their time and suggestions for improving the text.

Linda Delorme
Olympic College, Bremerton, Washington

Konnie Kustron
Eastern Michigan University, Ypsilanti, Michigan

Paula Sinopoli
Mississippi Gulf Coast Community College, Gulfport, Mississippi

Judith Sturgill
North Central State University, Mansfield, Ohio

PRACTICING LEGAL ASSISTANTS   A special "thank you" goes to the following practicing legal assistants who provided information and quotations for this text. It was a pleasure to include their real-life experiences herein.

Lenette R. Pinchback, CLA
Andrea L. Blanscet, CLA
Vanessa Beam, CLAS
Linda Rushton, CLA

WEST   A special thanks goes to the wonderful people at West, including Shelley Esposito, Acquisitions Editor; Brian Banks, Editorial Assistant; Melissa Riveglia, Senior Product Manager; and Matthew Williams, Content Project Manager. Without their long hours and help, this book would not have been possible. They are a wonderful team of people to work with.

Other

- Without my daughter, Megan Phelps-Roper, this book would not have been possible. She has helped in many capacities, including testing and helping me with all of the Hands-on Exercises.
- James Publishing, publishers of Legal Assistant Today, 3520 Cadillac Ave, Suite H, Costa Mesa, CA 92626, (714) 755-5450.
- The American Bar Association (ABA), that was, as always, extremely helpful in providing superb information and source material.
- Bill Statsky, who has unselfishly helped me develop my ideas and thoughts as a writer. Bill also provided me with a library of source material.
- A special thanks goes to my wife, Shirley Phelps-Roper, and children, Samuel, Megan, Rebekah, Isaiah, Zacharias, Grace Elizabeth, Gabriel, Jonah, Noah, and Luke, who put up with my long hours and hectic schedule, and who also desperately wanted to see their names in print again. Without the love and cooperation of my family, I never could have seen this project through.

Brent D. Roper
3640 Churchill Road,
Topeka, KS 66604

Please note that the Internet resources are of a time-sensitive nature and URL addresses may often change or be deleted.

Contact us at westlegalstudies@delmar.com

THE LEGAL TEAM, LAW PRACTICES, AND LAW FIRM GOVERNANCE

Chapter Objectives

After you read this chapter, you should be able to:

- Discuss the titles and duties of each member of the legal team.
- Explain the trends in legal assistant salaries.
- Discuss the different types of law practices.
- Identify alternative law office organizational structures.

The law firm was more than 40 years old and was well established in the legal community. Recently, however, the firm had moved to a particularly high-rent building and decided to spend substantially more on technology than it had originally planned; as a result, expenses were exploding and the firm was burdened with expensive debt. Employee turnover was growing, and productivity and client billings were down. Governance of the firm was bureaucratic and unresponsive to business demands. The firm had refused to hire professional administrators, and partners were fighting among themselves. The firm had no marketing strategy and new clients were not coming to the firm; the organization had grown dependent on two large clients for most of its business. Unexpectedly, one of the clients moved its business to a competing law firm. The client stated that it was not pleased with the quality of legal services it was receiving, so it moved to another firm who had worked hard to obtain their business.

Management decided that a bold move was necessary to save the firm. A legal management consulting firm was hired. A number of professional legal administrators were hired to run the business. The firm adopted a new governance structure that was streamlined and decisive. Clients were interviewed to see how the firm's services could be improved. Analysis was conducted to discover niche markets the firm could expand into and a carefully constructed marketing plan was implemented. The idea of merging with a stronger law firm that was a good "fit" was explored. Detailed budgets were developed to help control expenses and project income. All of the partners and administrators participated in creating a long-term, strategic business plan. Discussions were held with the staff to explore ways to increase retention, revenues, and productivity while trimming costs. While the firm still had a long way to go, it was on its way to recovery.

Law offices are organizations that provide legal services to clients, but they are fundamentally a business. Like any business, their function is to make money, operate at a profit, and earn money for their owners. This chapter introduces you to the legal team members who provide services to clients and management to a law office; salary trends of legal assistants; different types of law practices that operate in the legal field; and various organizational structures used by law firms.

legal team
A group made up of attorneys, administrators, law clerks, librarians, legal assistants, secretaries, clerks, and other third parties. Each provides a distinct range of services to clients and has a place on the legal team.

THE LEGAL TEAM

In a law office, many people make up the legal team. The **legal team** consists of attorneys, administrators, law clerks, librarians, legal assistants, secretaries, clerks, and other third parties (see Figure 1-1). Each person provides a distinct range of

Figure 1-1 The Legal Team

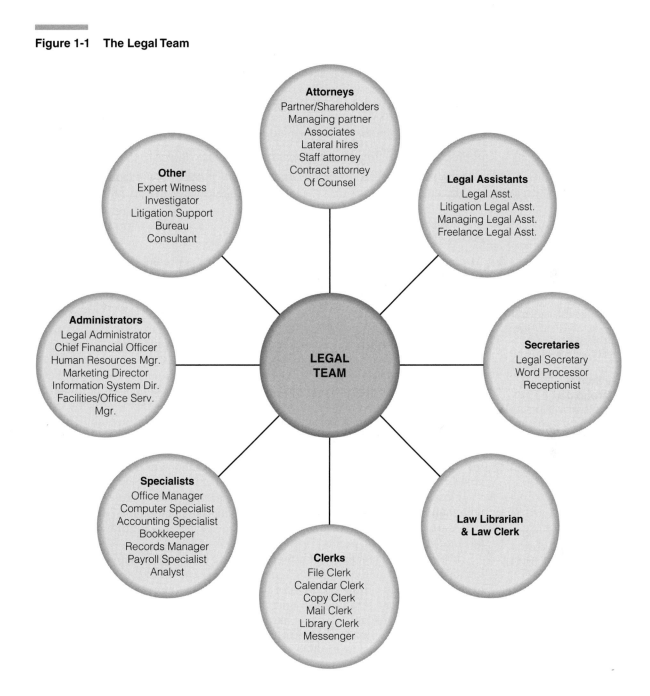

services to clients, and each has his or her place on the legal team. The positions and job duties in any law office depend on the type and size of the office. A list of job titles and a general description of common duties and responsibilities are provided in this section. It should be noted that job titles are just that—they are "titles" only. Attorneys and law office administrators are far more impressed with a person's actual performance than with a job title.

> *Treat everyone, from the senior partner to the mail delivery person, with the same degree of respect and courtesy due any member of the legal team.*[1]

Attorney

Attorneys counsel clients regarding their legal rights, represent clients in litigation, and negotiate agreements between clients and others. Depending on the size of the law office, attorneys may also have administrative duties. There are several kinds of attorneys.

PARTNER/SHAREHOLDER   A **partner** or **shareholder** is an attorney-owner in a private law practice who shares in its profits and losses. In the partnership form of business, an owner of the business is called a partner. In the corporate form of business, an owner is called a shareholder. Partners and shareholders serve primarily the same purpose; it is only the legal structure that is different. For simplicity, "partner" will be used to refer collectively to partners and shareholders, but "shareholder" could also have been used.

Partners attend partnership meetings and vote in the management decisions of the firm. Partners must also make monetary contributions to the firm if the need arises. Partners are sometimes called "equity partners," since they share in the profits or losses of the firm. To become a partner, an attorney must either be an attorney who founded the firm or be voted into the position by the existing partners. Typically, partners do not receive a "salary" but may receive a periodic draw, which is an advance against future profits.

In some firms, a **managing partner** is chosen by the partnership to run the firm and make administrative decisions and set policies. The managing partner reports to the partnership on the progress of the firm. Managing partners are typically elected to serve for a set amount of time, such as one or two years. Depending on the size of the firm, a managing partner may spend part or all of his or her time on management duties. In smaller law offices, a managing partner will practice law in addition to running the firm, while in large firms, managing the practice is typically a full-time job.

ASSOCIATE ATTORNEYS   An **associate attorney** does not have an ownership interest in the law firm and does not share in the profits. The associate is only an employee of the firm who receives a salary and has no vote regarding management

attorneys
Licensed professionals who counsel clients regarding their legal rights, represent clients in litigation, and negotiate agreements between clients and others.

partner or shareholder
An owner in a private law practice who shares in its profits and losses.

managing partner
An attorney in a law firm chosen by the partnership to run the firm, make administrative decisions, and set policies.

associate attorney
Attorney who is a salaried employee of the law firm, does not have an ownership interest in the firm, does not share in the profits, and has no vote regarding management decisions.

decisions. Associates can be hired directly out of law school or come from other firms. Associates who are hired from other firms are known as lateral hires or lateral hire associates. Associates who are candidates for a future partnership are said to be on a partnership track. An associate is usually with the firm between 5 and 10 years before he or she is a candidate for a partnership position, depending on the size of the firm. In large metropolitan firms, the time may be longer. An associate passed over for partnership may or may not leave the firm to practice elsewhere. Sometimes, to keep good associate attorneys who have nevertheless been passed over for partnership, the firm creates a position known as a nonequity partner. A **nonequity partner** does not share in the profits or losses of the business but may be included in some aspects of the management of the firm and may be entitled to other benefits not given to associates. A **staff attorney** is another type of associate. A staff attorney is an attorney hired by a firm with the knowledge and understanding that he or she will never be considered for partnership. Finally, a **contract attorney** is an associate attorney who is temporarily hired by the law office for a specific job or period. When the job or period is finished, the relationship with the firm is over.

OF COUNSEL   The **"of counsel"** position is a flexible concept but generally means that the attorney is affiliated with the firm in some way, such as a retired or semi-retired partner. "Of counsel" attorneys lend their names to a firm for goodwill and prestige purposes, in order to attract additional clients and business to the firm. An "of counsel" attorney may be paid on a per-job basis or may be an employee of the firm. He or she does not usually share in the profits of the firm. The "of counsel" arrangement is also used when an attorney is considering joining a firm as a partner and wants to work on a trial basis first.

nonequity partner
One who does not share in the profits or losses of the firm but may be included in some aspects of management and may be entitled to certain benefits.

staff attorney
An attorney hired by a firm with the knowledge and understanding that he or she will never be considered for partnership.

contract attorney
An attorney temporarily hired by the law office for a specific job or period. When the job or period is finished, the relationship with the firm is over.

of counsel
An attorney affiliated with the firm in some way, such as a retired or semiretired partner.

> *Not only are more firms beginning to see the essential role of administrators, and are delegating to them more and more administrative functions, but there is an accelerating trend toward actually giving them power in addition to their authority.*[2]

Legal Administrators

Legal administrators are usually found in medium and large firms, although they are beginning to be used in small firms as well. Law office administrators are responsible for some type of law office administrative system such as general management, finance and accounting, human resources, marketing, or computer systems. Legal administrators are typically nonattorneys who have degrees in business or related fields or who have been promoted through the ranks. Legal administrators have a broad range of power to make management decisions with the approval of the partnership. Most report directly to a committee or a partner.

Legal administrators draft annual budgets, prepare and interpret management reports, supervise the fiscal operations of the business, hire and fire support staff,

legal administrator
Person responsible for some type of law office administrative system, such as general management, finance and accounting, human resources, marketing, or computer systems.

and are responsible for implementing effective systems. In short, legal administrators are managers hired to relieve partners or managing committees of management burdens. Experienced legal assistants are sometimes promoted to administrative positions; administration can be a positive career move for legal assistants with good management skills. An excellent source of information regarding law office administration is the Association of Legal Administrators (ALA) [http://www.alanet.org].

Legal administrators come in a variety of types and with a range of titles. In smaller firms, they may have a generalist title and a wide range of duties (see Figure 1-2). In larger firms, there may be an administrator for each specific business function in the law practice, such as chief financial officer, human resources manager, marketing director, information systems director, facilities and office services manager, and so forth. A legal administrator may attend partnership or committee meetings, direct the accounting and billing functions, hire and terminate staff, make purchasing decisions, and much more.

Legal Assistants

legal assistants
A distinguishable group of persons who assist attorneys in the delivery of legal services. They have knowledge and expertise regarding the legal system and substantive and procedural law that qualifies them to do work of a legal nature under the supervision of an attorney.

Legal assistants, also known as paralegals, are a distinguishable group of persons who assist attorneys in the delivery of legal services. Through formal education, training, and experience, legal assistants have knowledge and expertise regarding the legal system and substantive and procedural law that qualify them to do work of a legal nature under the supervision of an attorney.[3] This definition is used by the National Association of Legal Assistants (NALA), but it is not the only one in use today. Figure 1-3 shows four separate definitions for a legal assistant or paralegal as defined by the American Bar Association (ABA), National Federation of Paralegal Associations (NFPA), National Association of Legal Assistants (NALA), and American Association for Paralegal Education (AAfPE). The terms *legal assistant* and *paralegal* often are used interchangeably, with no difference in meaning. This text, as well as the ABA, NFPA, and NALA, uses these terms interchangeably (see Figure 1-3). However, in some parts of the country, and in some legal organizations, there are various distinctions between the two terms. A 2004 NALA survey found that 30 percent of participants were referred to as legal assistants by their employers, while 62 percent were called paralegals.

With the steady growth of the legal assistant profession, legal assistants have become an integral part of modern law practice.[4]

The ABA Standing Committee on Legal Assistants recently stated

As we approach [and enter] the 21st century, one of the highest priority goals of the American Bar Association is to increase access to legal services. . . . One of the most effective ways to improve access to legal services is through the expanded utilization of well-qualified legal assistants who, with proper training and supervision, can be delegated work that would otherwise have to be done by a lawyer.[5]

Summary of Responsibilities

Manages the planning and business functions, as well as the overall operations of a law office. Reports to the managing partner, management committee, or chairperson of the board, and participates in management meetings. In addition to general responsibility for financial planning and controls, personnel administration, and systems and physical facilities, the legal administrator identifies and plans for the changing needs of the organization, shares responsibility with the appropriate partners or owners for strategic planning, practices management and marketing, and contributes to cost-effective management throughout the organization.

Whether directly or through a management team, the legal administrator is responsible for much or all of the following:

Financial Management

Including planning, forecasting, budgeting, variance analysis, profitability analysis, financial reporting, general ledger accounting, rate determination, billing and collections, cash flow control, banking relationships, investment, tax planning, tax reporting, trust accounting, payroll, pension plans, and other financial management functions.

Human Resource Management

Including recruiting, selection, training and development, performance evaluation, salary administration, employee relations, motivation, counseling, disciplining, discharging, benefits administration, workers' compensation, personnel data systems, job design, resource allocation, and other human resource management functions for the legal, paralegal, and support staff.

Systems Management

Including systems analysis, operational audits, cost/benefit analysis, computer systems design, programming and systems development, information services, records management, library management, office automation, document construction systems, information storage and retrieval, telecommunications, litigation support, legal practice systems, and other systems management functions.

Facilities Management

Including space planning and design, purchasing, inventory control, reprographics, records storage, reception/switchboard services, telecommunications, mail, messenger, and other facilities management functions.

As a member of the organization's management team, the legal administrator manages and/or contributes significantly to the following:

General Management

Including strategic and tactical planning, business development, risk management, quality control, organizational development, firm planning processes, and other general management functions.

Practice Management

Including lawyer recruiting, lawyer training and development, legal assistant supervision, work product, quality control, professional standards, substantive practice systems, and other practice management functions.

Marketing

Including management of client profitability analysis, forecasting of business opportunities, planning client development, marketing legal services, and enhancing the firm's visibility and image in the desired markets.

**Figure 1-2
Legal Administrator
Job Description**

Source: Association of Legal Administrators

Organization	Definition of Legal Assistant or Paralegal
American Bar Association (ABA)	"A legal assistant or paralegal is a person, qualified by education, training, or work experience, who is employed or retained by a lawyer, law office, corporation, governmental agency, or other entity, and who performs specifically delegated substantive legal work for which a lawyer is responsible." *ABA Standing Committee on Legal Assistants. Reprinted with permission.*
National Federation of Paralegal Associations (NFPA)	"A paralegal/legal assistant is a person qualified through education, training, or work experience to perform substantive legal work that requires knowledge of legal concepts and is customarily, but not exclusively, performed by a lawyer. This person may be retained or employed by a lawyer, law office, governmental agency or other entity or may be authorized by administrative, statutory, or court authority to perform this work." *Reprinted with permission of NFPA.*
National Association of Legal Assistants (NALA)	"Legal assistants, also known as paralegals, are a distinguishable group of persons who assist attorneys in the delivery of legal services. Through formal education, training, and experience, legal assistants have knowledge and expertise regarding the legal system and substantive and procedural law which qualify them to do work of a legal nature under the supervision of an attorney." *Reprinted with permission of the National Association of Legal Assistants. www.nala.org, 1516 S. Boston #200, Tulsa, OK 74119*
American Association for Paralegal Education (AAfPE)	"Paralegals perform substantive and procedural legal work as authorized by law, which work, in the absence of the paralegal, would be performed by an attorney. Paralegals have knowledge of the law gained through education, or education and work experience, which qualifies them to perform legal work. Paralegals adhere to recognized ethical standards and rules of professional responsibility." *Reprinted with the permission of the National Association for Paralegal Education.*

The ABA has also recognized the contribution of legal assistants to the legal profession by creating an associate membership category for them, which allows them to participate in relevant activities and join sections and divisions of the ABA. Many state and county bar associations also allow legal assistants to participate as associate members in their organizations. Legal assistants have two of their own national professional associations—NFPA and NALA—among others that they may join. Figure 1-4 shows NALA's home page. Both NALA and NFPA offer legal assistants many resources and benefits.

Although legal assistants may perform many tasks, they are strictly prohibited from giving legal advice to clients, from representing clients in court proceedings, from accepting client cases, and from setting a fee in a matter. This is covered in more detail in Chapter 3.

A "traditional" legal assistant works under the direct supervision of an attorney and is accountable to that attorney. There are also other "nontraditional" legal assistants, including freelance, contract, and independent legal assistants, also called *legal technicians*. A **freelance** or **contract legal assistant** works as an independent

**freelance/contract
legal assistant**
Works as an independent
contractor with
supervision by and/or
accountability to an
attorney; is hired for a
specific job or period.

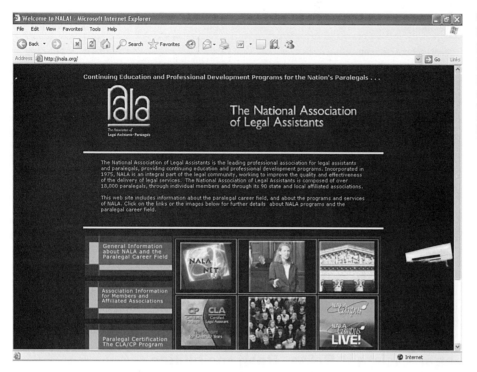

Figure 1-4
Home page of the NALA Web site

Reprinted with permission of the National Association of Legal Assistants, http://www.nala.org, 1516 S. Boston, # 200, Tulsa, OK 74119.

contractor with supervision by and/or accountability to an attorney. These legal assistants are self-employed and market and sell their services to legal organizations on a per-job basis. While they work under the supervision of an attorney, they may do so off-site and for a number of attorneys or legal organizations at the same time.

> *I like the freedom of movement and being able to be my own boss and set my own hours [as a freelance legal assistant]. I'm not restricted to a set schedule, though of course I set appointments with the attorneys or their clients. I can come and go as I please. The client's [i.e., the law firm's] only concern is that I get the work done. I charge an hourly rate, which the law firms bill to their clients. It's a win/win situation.—A freelance legal assistant[6]*

Independent legal assistants, or **legal technicians,** provide services to clients in regard to a process in which the law is involved and for whose work no lawyer is accountable.[7] Legal technicians assist in providing "self-help services to the public." Because they do not work under the auspices of an attorney, they are often accused of ethical misconduct and subject to statutes against the unauthorized practice of law; this is discussed in detail in Chapter 3.

Some larger legal organizations have **legal assistant managers** who oversee the legal assistant program at the firm and are responsible for administering all firm

independent legal assistant
Provides services to clients in which the law is involved, but is not accountable to a lawyer.

legal assistant manager
Oversees a legal assistant program in a legal organization, including preparing work plans, hiring, training, and evaluating legal assistants.

Response	Percent	Responses
High school diploma	18%	242
Associate degree	33%	436
Bachelor's degree	44%	578
Master's degree	5%	69
Ph.D.	1%	6

Source: National Association of Legal Assistants, 2004 National Utilization and Compensation Survey Report, Table 1.4, General Education Degree Attained

policies pertaining to legal assistants. The firm's legal assistants report either directly or indirectly to the legal assistant manager. Legal assistant managers develop work plans and standards, prepare staffing plans and bill rates, recruit and hire, provide training and development, monitor workloads, and conduct evaluations of the legal assistants.

A recent survey by the National Association of Legal Assistants found that more than 80 percent of respondents had earned some kind of college degree (see Figure 1-5). Both NFPA and NALA have voluntary certification exams, and some states offer certifications as well.

Legal Assistant Roles, Responsibilities, and Employment

People unfamiliar with the legal profession might assume that legal assistants spend a great deal of time in court. This is a common misconception. No matter what kind of law a law office practices, a considerable amount of a legal assistant's time is spent researching background information, plowing through reams of files, summarizing depositions, drafting pleadings and correspondence, and organizing information. It is not always exciting, but it is essential work in every case; often, the facts gathered, researched, and presented determine a case's outcome. Many of the legal assistant's duties don't involve a courtroom, such as preparation of wills, real estate closing transactions, drafting discovery, and preparation of business corporation papers.

Defining the work legal assistants do is not an easy task, given the wide variety and versatility of the profession. Figure 1-6 shows some of the more frequent duties legal assistants perform. Notice that assisting at trial is the lowest on the chart. Although there is diversity among legal assistant job duties, nearly all legal assistants spend a considerable portion of their time drafting documents and communicating either in writing or orally. A majority of the legal assistants responding to the survey in Figure 1-6 draft letters and case correspondence, work with and manage files and cases, calendar and keep track of case deadlines, work with computer systems, draft pleadings and formal court documents, work on miscellaneous office matters, and work with clients on a daily basis.

Most legal assistants practice in a particular area of the law. Figure 1-7 shows the areas in which legal assistants most frequently practice. Notice in Figure 1-7 that 45 percent of the legal assistants surveyed indicated that they specialized

Duty	Daily	Weekly	Monthly	Rarely	Total Responses*
Draft correspondence	74%	18%	5%	4%	1214
Case management	72%	18%	6%	4%	1036
Calendar deadlines	63%	21%	6%	10%	1079
Automation systems/ computers	56%	16%	12%	17%	936
Draft pleadings	46%	30%	11%	13%	994
Assist with client contact	44%	25%	17%	15%	1096
Office matters	44%	21%	14%	21%	991
General, factual research	40%	37%	17%	7%	1134
Document analysis/ summary	36%	32%	19%	13%	993
Court filings	33%	33%	13%	21%	950
Investigation	26%	31%	23%	21%	882
Personnel management	22%	13%	13%	53%	606
Client/witness interviews	14%	26%	24%	36%	871
Train employees	13%	0%	25%	50%	708
Legal research	12%	25%	31%	33%	996
Prepare/attend closings	8%	9%	18%	65%	509
Law library maintenance	4%	7%	16%	74%	528
Deposition summaries	2%	10%	28%	60%	730
Prepare/attend depositions	2%	16%	32%	50%	672
Assist/attend mediations	1%	6%	27%	67%	528
Assist at trial	1%	2%	19%	79%	743

(Respondents were asked to skip the item if their work does not require the duty)

Figure 1-6
Legal Assistant Duties

Source: National Association of Legal Assistants, 2004 National Utilization and Compensation Survey Report, Table 2.16, Functions and Duties/Frequencies

in civil litigation. Litigation provides many employment opportunities for legal assistants.

In addition to practicing in many different areas of the law, legal assistants are employed in different kinds of legal organizations (see Figure 1-8). Close to three-fourths of all legal assistants work in private law offices. Figure 1-8 also shows that about 63 percent of the legal assistants surveyed worked in relatively small firms with 10 or fewer attorneys. The size of the law office has an effect on the job duties and salaries of legal assistants. In small law offices, legal assistants usually compose and draft their own documents on a computer and do their own secretarial tasks. In larger firms, legal assistants may supervise secretarial personnel or share secretary staff with other legal professionals. Figure 1-8 shows that about 46 percent of all legal assistants are supervised by an attorney and about 43 percent are supervised by an administrator, manager, or department head. Another interesting fact shown in Figure 1-8 is that as the number of attorneys in firms increase, the ratio of attorneys to legal assistants goes down dramatically. In a sole practitioner's office, the ratio of attorneys to legal assistants is 0.7:1, but in a firm with more than 100 attorneys, the ratio is 5:1.

Legal Assistant Compensation

Figure 1-9 contains a national survey of legal assistant compensation. This survey found that the average compensation for all legal assistants was $46,862/year. The

**Figure 1-7
Legal Assistant
Specialty Areas of
Practice**

Source: National Association
of Legal Assistants, 2004
National Utilization and
Compensation Survey Report,
Table 2.20, Specialty Areas of
Practice by Number of
Responses

Specialty Areas	Percent of Respondents Selecting the Specialty	Number of Respondents
Civil litigation	45%	648
Corporate	29%	421
Personal injury	26%	372
Contracts	24%	351
Real estate	23%	337
Administrative/government/public	19%	273
Probate/estates	18%	263
Trusts and estates	18%	259
Office management	17%	245
Insurance	17%	241
Employment/labor law	17%	239
Medical malpractice	16%	232
Bankruptcy	15%	216
Collections	13%	188
Products liability	13%	185
Family law	13%	183
Intellectual property	12%	170
Worker's compensation	12%	166
Banking/finance	11%	152
Criminal	10%	137
Mergers/acquisitions	9%	134
Tax	8%	108
Environmental law	7%	103
Securities/antitrust	7%	98
Oil and gas	5%	74
Legislative lobbying	5%	74
Social Security	5%	71
Energy/utility	5%	70
Immigration	5%	68

survey found that legal assistants in tax intellectual property, securities/antitrust, and corporate law departments receive higher compensation on average than do legal assistants in other areas of practice. The survey also found that 1) legal assistants with more experience earned higher pay than those with less experience, 2) legal assistants working in the far west and New England/eastern areas earned higher compensation than those working in other areas of the U.S., and 3) legal assistants working in smaller firms tended to make less money than legal assistants working in large law firms (see Figure 1-9).

**Fair Labor
Standards Act**
Federal law that sets
minimum wage and
overtime pay requirements
for employees.

EXEMPT v. NONEXEMPT   The **Fair Labor Standards Act (FLSA)** is a federal law that sets minimum wage and overtime pay requirements for employees. It requires that overtime pay (one-and-one-half times their normal rate) be paid to employees who work in excess of 40 hours per week. Employees do not need to be

Employer	Percent	Respondents
Private law firm	69%	928
Corporation	14%	182
Public sector/government	8%	101
Insurance company	2%	26
Self-employed	2%	21
Nonprofit organization	1%	17
Bank	1%	16
Court system	1%	15
Health/medical	1%	8

**Figure 1-8
Legal Assistant
Employment
Statistics**

Source: National Association of Legal Assistants, 2004 National Utilization and Compensation Survey Report, Table 2.1, Type of Employer

Number of Attorneys	Percent	Respondents
1 (sole practitioner)	15%	174
2–5	31%	372
6–10	17%	201
11–20	14%	168
21–50	13%	153
50–100	7%	71
More than 100	4%	46

Source: National Association of Legal Assistants, 2004 National Utilization and Compensation Survey Report, Table 2.10, Number of Attorneys in Firm

Supervised by	Percent	Respondents
One or more attorneys	46%	611
Office administrator/manager	31%	409
Legal assistant manager	6%	75
Department head	6%	17
No supervision (or other)	6%	77
General counsel	4%	51
Management committee	2%	21

Source: National Association of Legal Assistants, 2004 National Utilization and Compensation Survey Report, Table 2.8, Overall Supervision of Support Staff

Number of Attorneys	Ratio of Attorneys to Legal Assistants
1	.7
2–5	1.4
6–10	1.8
11–15	2.4
16–20	3
21–40	3
41–60	2.7
61–100	4.2
More than 100	5

Source: National Association of Legal Assistants, 2004 National Utilization and Compensation Survey Report, Table 2.11, Ratio of Attorneys to Legal Assistants

Figure 1-9
Legal Assistant
Compensation Survey

By Years of Legal Experience	Average Total Compensation	Respondents
1–5 years	$35,434	139
6–10 years	$43,433	238
11–15 years	$47,624	268
16–20 years	$48,752	291
21–25 years	$51,796	148
Over 25 years	$51,985	194
All years	$46,862	

Source: National Association of Legal Assistants, 2004 National Utilization and Compensation Survey Report, Table 4.7, Annual Salary and Compensation by Total Years of Legal Experience

By Region	Average Total Compensation	Respondents
Far West	$55,760	150
New England/East	$51,479	44
Southwest	$47,709	274
Southeast	$45,460	527
Great Lakes	$44,415	89
Plains States	$42,694	128
Rocky Mountains	$43,609	72

Source: National Association of Legal Assistants, 2004 National Utilization and Compensation Survey Report, Table 4.11, Annual Salary and Compensation by Region

By Practice Area	Average Total Compensation (Greater than 40% of time in practice area)	Respondents
Tax	$61,379	9
Intellectual property	$60,326	48
Securities/antitrust	$55,940	24
Corporate	$53,217	118
Employment/labor law	$50,639	62
Contract	$49,276	83
Environmental law	$47,820	16
Civil litigation	$46,405	387
Criminal	$45,789	34
Probate	$45,467	91
Real estate	$45,372	113
Administrative/government/public	$44,577	89
Bankruptcy	$44,555	44
Personal injury	$44,174	173
Insurance	$43,917	94

Source: National Association of Legal Assistants, 2004 National Utilization and Compensation Survey Report, Table 4.14, Total Compensation by Specialty Area Greater than 40% of Time

Number of Attorneys	Average Total Compensation	Respondents
1	$45,569	189
2–5	$45,893	396
6–10	$45,092	220
11–15	$45,366	132
16–20	$47,088	56
21–25	$48,713	51
26–30	$54,247	40
31–40	$44,569	50
41–50	$53,084	28
51–75	$49,896	27
76–100	$53,397	49
More than 100	$56,014	47

Figure 1-9
(Continued)

Source: National Association of Legal Assistants, 2004 National Utilization and Compensation Survey Report, Table 4.13, Annual Salary and Compensation by Number of Attorneys

---

Paralegals and legal assistants are projected to grow faster than the average for all occupations through 2012. Some employment growth stems from law firms and other employers with legal staffs increasing hiring paralegals to lower the cost and increase the availability and efficiency of legal services. . . . Despite projections of fast employment growth, competition for jobs should continue as many people seek to go into this profession; however, highly skilled, formally trained paralegals have excellent employment potential.

Bureau of Labor Statistics, U.S. Dept. of Labor, Occupational Outlook Handbook, 2004–2005 Edition.

---

paid overtime if they fall into one of the four "white-collar" exemptions: executive, administrative, professional, or outside sales. If an employee is **exempt,** he or she is not required to be paid overtime wages. If an employee is **non-exempt,** he or she is required to be paid overtime wages. According to a recent survey of legal assistants, 52.2 percent of respondents indicated that they were classified as "exempt" by their employers and were not paid overtime wages.

The issue of whether legal assistants should be exempt or nonexempt is hotly debated. The United States Department of Labor, which administers the FLSA, has long taken the position that legal assistants are nonexempt and are thus entitled to overtime pay for hours worked in excess of 40 per week because their "duties do not involve the exercise of discretion and independent judgment required by the regulations" (see Wage & Hour Opinion Letters [available at http://www.dol.gov/esa/whd/opinion/opinion.htm] dated March 20, 1998; February 19, 1998; April 13, 1995; February 10, 1978). As recently as 2005 (see Wage & Hour Opinion Letter

exempt
The employee is not required to be paid overtime wages over 40 hours per week.

nonexempt
The employee is required to be paid overtime wages (time and a half) over 40 hours per week.

dated January 7, 2005, FLSA2005-9), the Department of Labor stated that a legal assistant was not exempt from the FLSA even if the legal assistant possessed a four-year degree, had a paralegal certificate, had taken continuing legal education classes, and had been practicing as a legal assistant for 22 years. The Department relied on section 541.301(3)(7), which states that "[p]aralegals and legal assistants generally do not qualify as exempt learned professionals because an advanced specialized academic degree is not a standard prerequisite for entry into the field. Although many paralegals possess general four-year advanced degrees, most specialized paralegal programs are two-year associate degree programs from a community college or equivalent institution."

The advantage of this long-held position by the Department of Labor is that if a legal assistant is deemed non-exempt, then he or she is entitled to overtime pay, which can be an attractive benefit. Unfortunately, the ruling arguably diminishes the profession by holding that it is not of a prestigious enough nature to warrant exempt status. The Department of Labor's rulings have been widely criticized because they fail to take into account the recent practice and utilization of legal assistants, the recognized status of the profession, legal assistants' advanced education and continuing legal education, the substantive duties they perform, and the degree to which legal assistants exercise discretion and independent judgment in the performance of the job.[8] In 1994, a jury in the case of *Riech v. Page & Addison, P.C.*, (Case No. 3-91-CV-2655-P in the United States District Court, Northern District of Texas, Dallas Division) found that the legal assistants at the Page & Addison law firm were exempt from overtime requirements. Nevertheless, the Department of Labor did not change its general position on the matter. Interestingly, a rather large number of law firms still do not pay overtime compensation to legal assistants, even after the many rulings of the Department of Labor on the subject; according to Figure 1-10, only 38 percent of firms always pay overtime compensation for legal assistants.

> *Paralegals being classified as exempt or nonexempt is a double-edged sword. Being nonexempt protects the paralegal from working "associates on partner track" hours (i.e., large numbers of hours), especially in a cost-minded firm (and what firm is not cost-minded nowadays?). However, paralegals are striving to be recognized as "professionals" and most professionals are exempt employees.*
>
> —Linda L. Rushton, CLA

The Judicial System's Recognition of the Legal Assistant Profession

The United States Supreme Court case of *Missouri v. Jenkins*, 491 U.S. 274, 109 S.Ct. 2463, 105 L.Ed. 2d 229 (1989), established that the legal assistant profession had come of age. In that case, the plaintiff was successful on several counts under a

Do You Receive Overtime Compensation?	Percent	Respondents
Always paid	38%	468
Sometimes paid	7%	85
Never paid	37%	467
Compensatory time off	19%	231

Figure 1-10
Legal Assistant Overtime Compensation

Source: National Association of Legal Assistants, 2004 National Utilization and Compensation Survey Report, Table 2.4, Overtime Compensation

federal statute in a civil rights lawsuit and was attempting to recover attorney's fees from the defendant. The federal statutory language allowed the prevailing party to recover "reasonable attorney's fees" from the adverse party. The plaintiff argued for the right to recover the time that both attorneys and legal assistants had spent working on the case. The defendant argued that legal assistant time was not "attorney's fees." Alternatively, the defendant argued that if required to pay for legal assistant time, the amount should be about $15 an hour, a representation of the overhead costs to the firm of a legal assistant.

The Court found that legal assistants carry out many useful tasks, and that "reasonable attorney's fees" refers to a reasonable fee for work produced, whether by attorneys or legal assistants, and could be compensable as long as the work was not of a clerical nature. The Court also found that under the federal statute, legal assistant time should be compensable at the prevailing market rates. The Court noted that the prevailing rate at that time for legal assistants in that part of the U.S. was about $40 an hour and held that the plaintiff was entitled to receive that amount for legal assistant hours expended on the case. This important case defined a legal assistant position not as a secretarial or clerical position but as a professional, fee-generating profession.

Former Chief Justice Warren Burger stated that the "expanded use of well-trained assistants, sometimes called 'paralegals,' has been an important development. The advent of the paralegal enables law offices to perform high quality legal services at a lower cost. Possibly we have only scratched the surface of this development."

While *Missouri v. Jenkins* was a landmark decision for legal assistants, the case involved a federal court interpreting a specific federal statute, the Civil Rights Act. Because fee questions occur in many different situations, it is possible for a court under a different statute to reach a different conclusion. Since *Missouri v. Jenkins*, many federal and state courts have allowed for recovery of legal assistant billable hours [see *Baldwin v. Burton*, 850 P.2d 1188, 1200-01 (Utah 1993), *Cooper v. Secretary of Dept. of Health and Human Services*, No. 90-608V, 1992 WL 63271 at 3(Cl. Ct. March 11, 1992), *Consolo v. George*, 58 F.3d 791 (1st Cir. 1995), *Department of Transp., State of Fla. v. Robbins & Robbins, Inc.* 700 So. 2d 782, Fla. App. 5 Dist. (1997), *Guinn v. Dotson* (1994) 23 Cal. App. 4th 262, *In re Mullins*, 84 F.3d 459 (D.C. Cir. 1996), and *Taylor v. Chubb Group of Insurance Companies*, 874 P.2d 806 (Ok. 1994). *Role Models American, Inc. v. Brownlee*, 353 F.3d 962 (C.A.D.C., 2004)].

> *The recognition by the courts that legal assistants are income-producing members of the professional legal service delivery team, that they perform substantive legal tasks under the supervision of the attorney, and that their fees are property included as a component in an award of attorney fees has done much to increase the status of the legal assistant profession.*[9]

Legal Assistant Profitability for Law Offices

The use of legal assistants is a financially profitable proposition and represents a win-win situation for both the law office and client. Law offices charge clients for legal assistant time. Legal assistant billing rates are substantially more than the salaries law offices pay them, so law offices make a profit by billing legal assistant time. In addition, clients are typically very willing to pay for legal assistant time because the billable rate is substantially less than what an attorney would charge to do the same work.

> *To remain competitive, lawyers need to acknowledge that they are overqualified for much of what they do. . . . It is through the expanded use of legal assistants that lawyers can remain profitable while meeting current client demands.*[10]

Office Manager

office manager
Manager who handles day-to-day operations of the law office, such as accounting, supervision of the clerical support staff, and assisting the managing partner.

Office managers are typically found in smaller firms. They handle day-to-day operations of the law office, including such activities as timekeeping and billing, supervision of the clerical support staff, assisting the managing partner in preparing a budget, and making recommendations with regard to changes in systems and purchases. Office managers typically do not have degrees in business. They are usually not given as much decision-making power as administrators and, unlike administrators, usually assist a managing partner in managing the law office. Nonetheless, good office managers are important to the survival of smaller firms. Experienced legal assistants are sometimes promoted into office manager positions.

Law Clerk

law clerk
A law student working for a law firm on a part-time basis while he or she is finishing a law degree. Law clerk duties revolve almost exclusively around legal research and writing.

A **law clerk** is usually a student who works for a law firm on a part-time basis while he or she is finishing a law degree. Law clerk duties revolve almost exclusively around legal research and writing. Law clerks perform research, write briefs and motions, and prepare memorandums of law.

Law Librarian

A **law librarian** conducts legal research using both computerized and manual methods; acquires and preserves library materials; is an expert in legal and nonlegal research methods/tools; advises attorneys and legal professionals on legal research methods; maintains, classifies, indexes, and stores library materials; manages the library/legal research budget and may coordinate the use of electronic resources, such as Westlaw, LexisNexis, and other services.

law librarian
A librarian is responsible for maintaining a law library, conducting legal research, and managing library resources.

Legal Secretaries

Legal secretaries provide a variety of services to attorneys and legal assistants. Typical duties include preparing documents, composing routine correspondence, proofreading, reading and routing mail, scheduling appointments, organizing material, filing, answering the phone and screening calls, faxing, copying, responding to e-mails, responding to clients, and other tasks. Figure 1-11 shows that about 60 percent of legal assistants have limited or full access to secretarial support. Secretaries include legal secretaries, receptionists, and word processing secretaries. Competent legal secretaries have highly specialized skills and perform many services for law firms. Legal secretaries, like legal assistants, have their own local, regional, state, and national associations. It is not uncommon for a person to start employment with a law office as a legal secretary and work his or her way up to legal assistant, office manager, or another position. Receptionists are commonly found in all law offices, and their duties include answering the phone, greeting clients, opening the mail, and making photocopies. Word processing secretaries are commonly found in larger law offices. They type, format, and produce documents using word processing software.

It is not uncommon for friction to exist between legal assistants and secretaries. Problems may occur in law offices where there are no clear descriptions of job duties, where legal assistants are required to do some clerical or administrative work, and where secretaries perform higher-level research or case management from time to time. This blurring of the lines sometimes causes confusion about who is supposed to do what; when this happens, pressure is added to the working relationship. Some secretaries also resent legal assistants performing higher-level work than they themselves are allowed to perform. In addition, some secretaries refuse or resist performing clerical work for legal assistants because they view legal assistants

legal secretaries
Employees who provide assistance and support to other law office staff by preparing documents, composing correspondence, scheduling appointments, and performing other tasks.

Secretarial Assistance	Percent	Respondents
Have personal secretary	4%	45
Share secretary with one or more attorneys	28%	365
Share secretary with one or more legal assistants	4%	57
Have limited access to a secretary (perform some of own secretarial duties)	21%	269
Have access to word processing staff or secretarial pool	6%	72
No secretarial service	39%	503

**Figure 1-11
Secretarial Support
Provided to Legal
Assistants**

Source: National Association of Legal Assistants, 2004 National Utilization and Compensation Survey Report, Table 2.2, Kinds of Secretarial Assistance Provided

as peers. In any case, legal assistants and secretaries must work together as members of the same team. They must put the needs of the team first and always support their coworkers, because eventually they will need their help.

> *Get along with the secretaries. You work together. They do not work [exclusively] for you. They are a great ally, but an even greater road block if you get in their way. Give them respect.*[11]

Clerks

clerks
Employees who provide support to other staff positions in a variety of miscellaneous functions.

Clerks provide support to other staff positions in a variety of functions. Law offices may have a wide variety of clerks, including mail clerks, copy clerks, file clerks, process servers, messengers, calendar clerks, and billing clerks. Much of their work involves data entry and physically handling files and documents.

Other Legal Team Members

expert witness
A person who has technical expertise in a specific field and agrees to give testimony for a client at trial.

A variety of other people and organizations make up the legal team. Other team members may include expert witnesses, investigators, litigation support bureaus, and consultants. An **expert witness** is a person who has technical or scientific expertise in a specific field and agrees to give testimony for a client at trial. Professional investigators are sometimes hired to gather facts and evidence regarding a case. Litigation support service bureaus may be used in cases that have hundreds or thousands of documents to organize and records to computerize for trial. Specialists may also be hired, such as computer specialists, accountants, bookkeepers, records managers, payroll specialists, and analysts. Some large firms employee analysts who are experts in their fields, such as biologists, chemists, and others. These analysts advise the firm and their clients on extremely complex cases. Law offices use business, marketing, and other types of consultants to give them advice on how to run their operation efficiently. Law offices may also use temporary or permanent staffing firms and may outsource jobs, projects, or services as needed, including copying, mail services, and records management.

TYPES OF LAW PRACTICES

To a certain extent, how law office management operates depends on the type of law office. Therefore, it is necessary to review the different types of law practices and their functional effect on management. Usually, people think of the private law firm as the only type of law practice, but there are others, including corporate law, government, and legal service practices.

Corporate Law Practice

Some businesses, including large corporations, banks, retailers, manufacturers, transportation companies, publishers, insurance companies, and hospitals, have their own in-house legal departments. Attorneys employed by a corporate law department are often referred to as "in-house counsel." In a corporate legal department, attorneys and legal assistants have just one client: the business itself. However, some corporate legal departments see each division or department in the corporation as an individual client for whom they must provide quality legal services.

Corporations with their own legal departments are generally large, with millions of dollars in assets. Unlike private law firms, a corporate legal department is not involved in many administrative functions, such as accounting, since the corporation itself provides these services. Corporate legal departments do not record billable hours, since all costs are covered by the corporation. However, corporate legal departments must still budget, track, and plan activities, and they are responsible for the overall efficiency of their department. Corporate law departments handle a variety of legal concerns in such areas as contracts, labor relations, employee benefits, federal tax laws, intellectual property, environmental law issues, Security Exchange Commission (SEC) filings, general litigation, real estate law, and workers' compensation claims, among others.

> *The benefits of working for a corporation are really great. There is a lot of responsibility. . . . There is more opportunity for upward mobility within the company, since you can contribute your legal skills in other areas, such as sales and marketing. . . . The stress level is lower—it is not as frantic as at a law firm.*[12]
>
> —A corporate legal assistant

Most corporate legal departments are too small to handle all the legal needs of the corporation, so the law departments hire private law firms that specialize in the additional areas they need. This is sometimes referred to as having "outside counsel." The chief attorney for a corporate legal department is called the **general counsel.** The general counsel, in addition to having legal duties, may also be the corporate secretary. The general counsel typically reports to the chief executive officer and interacts closely with the board of directors of the corporation. Many corporate law departments have practice groups that specialize in certain areas, such as litigation, regulatory work, taxes, contracts and intellectual property work, and more.

Staffing in corporate legal departments includes secretaries, legal assistants, law clerks, administrators, and attorneys (see Figure 1-12). Most corporate legal departments employ one or more legal assistants. The job duties a legal assistant performs in a corporate legal department are similar to those performed in other

general counsel
The chief for a corporate legal department.

**Figure 1-12
Corporate Law
Department
Organizational
Chart**

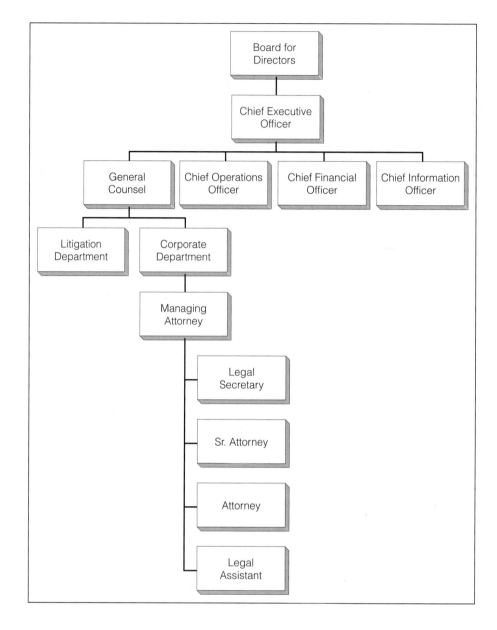

types of practices and may include preparing deposition summaries, performing legal research, and drafting documents. Like legal assistants in private law firms, legal assistants in corporate legal departments might also specialize in specific areas, such as litigation, real estate, or business law.

Government Practice

Government attorneys, like corporate attorneys, have just one client. In most local, state, and federal agencies, a legal department represents the interests of *each* particular agency. Government attorneys representing agencies or governmental bodies may be involved in contract law, bankruptcy law, tax law, employment law, property law, and environmental law, to name a few. Each state also has an attorney general's office; the attorney general operates as the state's chief law enforcement officer and attorney. In many instances, when a state or state agency is sued, the attorney general's office represents the state. In addition, many other types of government attorneys exist, including local district and city attorneys, state attorney generals, and U.S. attorneys.

In many ways, practicing for the government is similar to practicing for a large corporation. Government attorneys, like corporate attorneys, do not record billable hours and are not responsible for as many management duties as are their counterparts in private law firms. Government practices differ from corporate legal department practices in that politics plays a role; government attorneys and legal assistants are also paid according to their civil service classification. Staffing for government legal departments consists of secretaries, investigators, legal assistants, law clerks, and attorneys. The job duties of legal assistants in government practices vary depending on the area of practice, and these duties may be tested in various civil service exams that are a prerequisite to hiring.

Recently I started working for a government contractor after spending my entire career at private law firms. The biggest advantage of being in the government/corporate environment is that the pressure of achieving a certain amount of billable hours every month is no longer there. Also, the attorneys in the corporate and government environment seem to be more laid back than attorneys in private practice.

—Linda L. Rushton, CLA

Legal Services Offices

A **legal services office,** sometimes called a legal clinic or legal aid office, is a not-for-profit law office that receives grants from the government and private donations to pay for representation of disadvantaged persons who otherwise could not afford legal services. In some cases, legal services offices or clinics are operated by law schools, bar associations, or other nonprofit entities as a public service to the community. Clients pay little or no fees for legal services. Legal services offices typically represent the disadvantaged in areas relating to child support, child custody, disability claims, bankruptcies, landlord-tenant disputes, and mental health problems. Staffing for legal services offices includes secretaries, legal assistants, law clerks, and

legal services office
A not-for-profit law office that receives grants from the government and private donations to pay for representation of disadvantaged persons who otherwise could not afford legal services.

attorneys. In legal services practices, legal assistants may be used fairly extensively and are usually given a wide variety of tasks because their use is cost effective. Legal services offices typically handle civil matters, while government public defenders' offices handle criminal matters for low-income clients.

> *After 10 years of work at the Vermont Legal Aid, I seem to have accumulated cases that never close, clients that never stop calling. . . . "Can I run this by you?" So why does this work still seem fresh and new to me? Perhaps because no day is like any other. . . .*
>
> *[A recent case of] helping [a] client through her housing crisis was a team effort, and that is a real benefit of working in this office.*[13]

Private Law Practices

The most common way that attorneys practice law is in a private law firm (see Figure 1-13). A private law practice is a firm that generates its own income by representing clients. Private law firms, like any business, are operated to make a profit

Figure 1-13
Percent of Attorneys by Practice Type/Size

Practice Type	Percent
Private practice	74%
Government	8%
Corporate/private industry	8%
Retired/inactive	5%
Judiciary	3%
Education	1%
Legal Aid/public defender	1%
Private Association	1%

Source: *The Lawyer Statistical Report,* American Bar Foundation, 2004 Edition

Private Practitioners

Practice Type	Percent
1	48%
2–5	15%
6–10	7%
11–20	6%
21–50	6%
51–100	4%
More than 100	14%

Source: *The Lawyer Statistical Report,* American Bar Foundation, 2004 Edition

for their owners. Private law firms represent a variety of clients and come in all shapes and sizes, from the sole practitioner to international megafirms.

The terminology is somewhat arbitrary, and may depend on the relative size of your community, but, for this text, a small firm is a law office that has fewer than 20 attorneys; a medium-size firm usually has from 20 to 75 attorneys; and a large firm can employ from 75 to hundreds of attorneys. There are also megafirms that employ between 500 and 1000 attorneys or more. Private practices, no matter the size, have their own unique styles, methods, clients, cultures, and ways of doing things. As of 2005, there were 1.1 million attorneys in the U.S., according to the American Bar Association. Figure 1-13 shows the types and sizes of practices they join.

For over two years, I have worked for a sole legal practitioner. I am the only paralegal in the office and am directly involved in almost everything that transpires in our office. . . . My input is not only heard, but utilized. I have no billing quotas. While we do keep close track of billable hours, I don't have to justify every minute of my workday. . . .[14]

—A sole practitioner's legal assistant

Sole Practitioner

A sole practitioner is an attorney who individually owns and manages the practice. Anyone who works for the attorney is considered an employee. Sole practitioners sometimes hire another attorney as an employee, who is not entitled to any share of the practice's profits. Although the sole practitioner has the advantage of freedom and independence, he or she is also ultimately responsible for all, or nearly all, of the legal work and management duties of the law office. It is important that overhead costs stay as small as possible, if the sole practitioner is to succeed. Overhead costs are expenses incurred month after month and include such things as rent (thus the term "overhead"), utilities, the lease of equipment (such as copiers and computers), and support staff salaries. These are costs incurred whether the attorney is serving one client or 100. Sole practitioners typically have small offices with a very small law library.

Sole practitioners are typically generalists, meaning they handle a wide variety of cases, such as probate, family law, criminal law, and personal injury. The sole practitioner typically refers a case outside of his or her area of expertise to another attorney who is skilled in that matter. Sole practitioners need good management skills for their practice to survive. This may pose a problem, because management duties take the sole practitioner away from the actual practice of law, which is the activity that brings in the money. Figure 1-13 shows that nearly half of all attorneys in the U.S. are sole practitioners.

Staffing can include a secretary, legal assistant, law clerk, and possibly an associate attorney; these positions may even be part time. Legal assistants working in a sole practitioner's office enjoy a great deal of responsibility and diversity in their jobs. Duties include conducting legal research, drafting pleadings and discovery materials, word processing, and interviewing witnesses. Because sole practitioners are generalists, their legal assistants work in many areas of the law. In a solo practice, the legal assistant has the opportunity to learn firsthand about law office management and to perform management functions.

Law Firms

Law firms have two or more attorneys in practice together. There are 47,563 law firms in the U.S. (not counting sole practitioners), according to the American Bar Association. While there is not as much freedom as in sole practice, law firms do not incur as much risk. If a sole practitioner becomes ill, loses a large client, or faces other such catastrophes, the sole practitioner's income may be endangered. These problems may be alleviated in law firms, because more than one attorney is available. Law firms are usually categorized as small, medium, or large.

> The [small] size of the law office contributes to the fact that we, as paralegals, are appreciated for more than just our clerical or organizational skills. At times we do research or writing that an associate might do at a larger law office.[15]
>
> —Small law firm legal assistant

THE SMALL LAW FIRM   The small firm usually has fewer than 20 attorneys. Notice in Figure 1-13 that nearly 76 percent of all attorneys in the U.S. practice as either a sole practitioner or in a small firm. Most small firms have a staff member—such as an office manager or an administrator—who helps with the day-to-day operations of the business. However, a partner or managing partner is usually responsible for major management decisions such as hiring, firing, distributing profits, and setting salaries. Small firms usually concentrate in a few areas of the law but may also have attorneys who are general practitioners.

boutique firm
A small law office that specializes in only one or two areas of the law.

A small law office that specializes in only one or two areas of the law is sometimes called a **boutique firm.** The boutique firm normally has several attorneys who practice in the same specialty. Legal assistants who work for boutique firms also usually become specialists in that particular area of the law.

Disadvantages that hinder small firms include cash-flow problems, the lack of time to recruit, hire, and train new staff, little time for management, and long hours.

Staffing positions include clerks, secretaries, legal assistants, office managers, law clerks, and attorneys. Small firms offer legal assistants a relatively large variety of tasks to perform.

THE MEDIUM-SIZE FIRM   The medium-size firm usually has from 20 to 75 attorneys. Typically, medium-size firms are organized into subject-area departments. Medium-size firms differ from small firms in that most medium-size firms have professional administrators who manage many aspects of the business. Administrators usually report to a managing partner or a committee that has overall management responsibilities. Medium-size firms typically have multiple offices, and it is not uncommon for them to have sophisticated computer systems. Staffing often consists of administrators, law librarians, receptionists, secretaries, legal assistants, law clerks, and attorneys. Legal assistants in medium-size firms have a more structured existence than in smaller firms; the diversity of duties and areas of practice are not as broad. However, the legal assistant may learn a particular area of law in greater depth. In addition, the internal structure and lines of communication are more intense and more important than in small firms, where colleagues tend to be more familiar with one another.

A [mega lawfirm] is an incredible place to work. I'm allowed to do whatever I want to take on. . . . The longer I'm here, the more opportunity there is to take on a bigger piece of the process.

—Legal assistant in a 1000+ attorney firm.[16]

The resources at a large firm are greater than smaller firms. There will be a number of experienced legal assistants to whom an entry-level legal assistant can turn to for a mentor. In addition, there will be more variety of law practiced by the attorneys; therefore, when an issue arises which is not your practice group's specialty, another attorney or practice group in the firm can handle the situation instead of referring it out of the firm.

—Linda L. Rushton, CLA

THE LARGE FIRM   The large firm has between 75 and several hundred attorneys. A few large firms, sometimes called "megafirms," have 500 to 1000 or more attorneys. Most large firms have practice groups or departments. A large firm might

**Figure 1-14
Large Law Firm
Administrative
Staff Positions**

Accounts payable clerk	Law librarian
Accounts receivable clerk	Legal secretary/administrative assistant
Analyst	Library specialist
Bookkeeper	Litigation support specialist
Chief financial officer	Mail clerk
Controller	Messenger/driver
Computer specialist	Payroll specialist
Copy room clerk	Proofreader
Credit/collections manager	Purchasing manager
Data processing operator	Purchasing clerk
Director of marketing	Receptionist
Docket clerk	Records/file manager
Employee benefits manager	Recruiter
Equipment manager	Risk manager
Facilities manager	Trainer
File room clerk	Time and billing assistant
Human resource manager	Word processor
Legal administrator	Word processing supervisor
Legal assistant manager	

have 15 or more different practice groups, including antitrust, bankruptcy, environmental, estate planning, intellectual property, international, labor/employment law, litigation, patents, trademarks, copyright, property, and tax. The internal structure of these firms is more similar to the structure of business corporations than to other types of law firms. Staffing in large firms typically includes various classes of legal assistants, law clerks, and attorneys, in addition to the positions shown in Figure 1-14. Large firms often have large corporations as clients. Many have offices throughout the U.S., and some have international offices. Large firms also tend to have resources such as large law libraries, a word processing department, and extensive, technologically advanced computer systems connecting all their offices for information exchange.

Disadvantages encountered by large firms include recruiting and retaining good employees in the vital areas of the practice, getting departments to communicate and work together, and controlling the bureaucracy itself. Large law firms usually employ a large number of legal assistants and treat them formally and professionally, requiring them to attend department meetings, assist attorneys in depositions, and travel as needed. The physical space occupied by a large firm is more lavish than in small and medium-size firms, usually occupying several floors in a large office building.

Plaintiff/Defense Firms

Private law practices may categorize themselves as either more or less plaintiff or defense oriented, no matter what the size of the law office. Plaintiff-oriented firms, as the name implies, represent clients who bring claims against others. Plaintiff-oriented firms tend to be smaller, not as well funded, and have fewer employees than defense-oriented firms. Cash flow in plaintiff firms may not be as stable as in defense-oriented firms because, in many cases, they take clients on a contingency fee basis; that is, the law office recovers fees for the case only if it wins.

Defense-oriented firms, on the other hand, have the luxury of billing defendants—who are typically businesses—according to the time spent on the case. This gives defense-oriented firms a more stable cash flow, enabling them to hire more personnel, purchase advanced equipment, and spend more on litigation services, such as hiring expert witnesses and taking as many depositions as needed. Nonetheless, effective management is needed in both plaintiff- and defense-oriented firms.

No matter the type of legal organization, good management, including sound financial management, cost-efficient hiring and training of personnel, efficient use of equipment, and overall leadership, is important.

Law Firm Mergers and Acquisitions

Law firm mergers are commonplace in the U.S. legal market. Law firms merge for different reasons. A law firm might merge as a growth strategy, in order to quickly expand their personnel and client base. A law firm might merge in order to create a presence in a new geographic area or to move into a new practice specialty. A law firm might merge in order to create a national or international practice. A law firm might also merge if it is financially weak or if key partners have left or are retiring, as a way to save what's left of the practice. Law firm mergers can be complicated for a number of reasons, including conflict of interest problems (if the firms are representing different parties in a legal action), law office culture differences, staffing issues, financial resources, client satisfaction, computer compatibility, political power struggles, and other issues. Nonetheless, they occur regularly among private law practices throughout the U.S.

Geographic Service Areas

In years past, a law firm operated in a single location, and the office typically attracted clients within a limited geographic area around that location. That model no longer works in the current legal marketplace. The Internet, sophisticated computer networks that can tie offices together from across the country or around the world, and large, multi-office law firms have changed that paradigm. Many law firms have developed a geographic strategy regarding business expansion and how they define where and what their marketplace and client base will be. Geographic service strategies include: local, statewide, regional/multi-state, national, international, and industry specific. When considering law practices, size is just one factor; it is also important to take geographic and business strategy into account, along with where they see themselves going in the short and long terms. Geographic and business strategy are also important in that they play a significant part in how firms are managed and operated, and these issues can cause a great deal of disagreement and problems between the owners of a firm who may not see eye to eye on these issues.

Law Practice Organization Structures

Law practices have different organization or management structures. Private law practices are managed by a powerful managing partner, by all partners, or by committees. Corporate and government law practices have either a centralized or decentralized management structure.

Legal Forms of Private Law Firms

Management structures of law firms are affected by the firm's legal status. A law firm can be formed as a sole proprietorship, partnership, corporation, or, in some states, a limited liability company. Before the management structure of law offices can be considered, the legal status of those law offices must be explained.

SOLE PROPRIETORSHIP   In a sole proprietorship, the proprietor, in this case an attorney, runs the business, receives all profits, and is personally responsible for all losses and liabilities of the law office. However, a sole proprietorship is a distinct type of legal structure, and a sole practitioner does not have to use the sole proprietorship form; many sole practitioners are incorporated.

PARTNERSHIP   The partnership's legal structure allows two or more attorneys to associate themselves together and to share in the profits or losses of the business. Many group practices use this structure. When a law office is established as a partnership, the founding attorneys are usually named as partners. As growth takes place, the partnership may hire additional associate attorneys.

All the partners are jointly and severally liable for the actions of the firm. This means if one partner commits malpractice and injures a client, each partner may be held individually or jointly responsible. Partners are also personally liable for the debts of the partnership. Partnerships typically use committees to make policy decisions, and partners meet regularly to discuss partnership business.

PROFESSIONAL CORPORATION   The professional corporation allows a single shareholder or a group of shareholders from the same profession, such as attorneys, to join together to share in the outcomes of a business. When a law office is established as a professional corporation, the founding attorney or attorneys receive shares in the business. As in a partnership, associates are not owners and are only paid a salary. Shareholders can vote to offer additional shares of the business to associates and expand the ownership of the law firm. All attorneys are employees of the corporation and are paid a salary. Besides a salary, shareholders are also paid a dividend. The amount of the dividend depends on the profitability of the corporation and on the number of shares owned. Shareholders are not personally responsible for the debts of the professional corporation. The corporate form requires the election of officers and a board of directors.

LIMITED LIABILITY COMPANY   The limited liability company (LLC) is a hybrid form of legal structure; it is a combination of the corporate and partnership forms. The LLC form of structure is valid in many states. The main advantage of an LLC is that it allows for limited personal liability of company debts for its owners (like a corporation), but is treated like a partnership for income tax purposes.

Private Law Firm Management Structures

The type of management or governing structure used to manage the business aspect of the firm is the choice of the firm itself, but the legal structure of the business may dictate some of that management structure. For example, a corporation—by law—must have a board of directors. Many law practices struggle with the problem of determining who runs the firm and who has the final say on firm decisions. Possible management structures include one powerful managing partner, rule by all partners/shareholders, and rule by management committee or board.

THE POWERFUL MANAGING PARTNER   In a **powerful managing partner** management structure, a single partner manages the firm. The managing partner is responsible for day-to-day operations of the partnership, while partners vote on major firm decisions (see Figure 1-15). The managing partner may have a specific term of office. In some firms, the position is rotated among the practicing partners. In many firms, the managing partner spends anywhere from 60 to 100 percent of his or her time on management responsibilities. This form allows other partners to spend more time practicing law, but it places the managerial duties on one partner and reduces the managing partner's time to practice law. The powerful managing partner structure is autocratic: power rests with only one person. In some cases, the other partners may feel that they are without a voice in the management of the firm.

    The strong managing partner structure works well in small- to medium-sized law practices where the managing partner is well-regarded and well-liked; makes sound business decisions so that the firm is profitable and stable; is an effective delegator, leader, and manager; and where the practice is not expanding rapidly. One benefit of this structure is that decisions are made relatively quickly and decisively because the power principally lies with one person. The managing partner structure tends to break down, however, when the managing partner makes an unpopular decision, when there is not enough partner oversight to satisfy the other

powerful managing partner
A management structure in which a single partner is responsible for managing the firm.

Figure 1-15   Powerful Managing Partner Structure

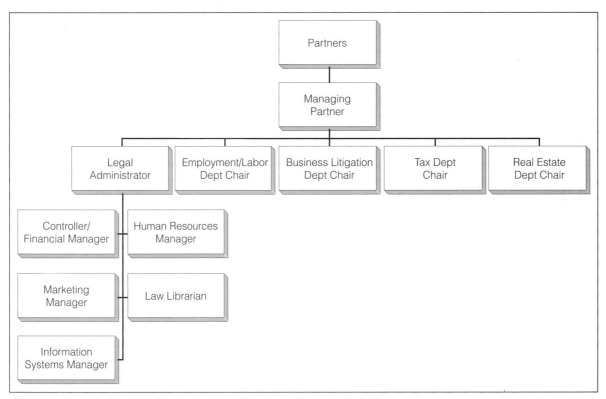

partners, when the firm is not profitable, or where there is substantial conflict or questions about the direction of the firm.

> *Smaller firms tend to favor a democratic form of governance. Typically, every partner votes on every management decision. As firm size increases, it soon becomes obvious that this system is too cumbersome to be practical once a firm reaches . . . 12 to 15 partners.*[17]

**rule by all partners/
shareholders**
A management structure in which all partners/shareholders are included in decisions that affect the firm.

RULE BY ALL PARTNERS/SHAREHOLDERS   **Rule by all partners/shareholders** is a management structure in which all partners/shareholders make decisions that affect the firm (see Figure 1-16). All the partners or shareholders meet whenever management policies or decisions need to be made. This is a democratic structure, since all the partners have a say in firm decisions and policies. Although this structure allows partners/shareholders involvement in all decisions of the firm, as the

Figure 1-16 Rule by All Partners/Shareholders

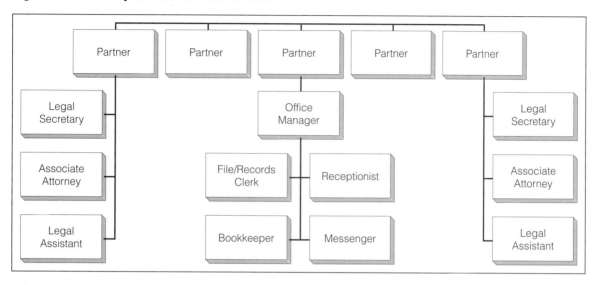

number of partners/shareholders increases, the effectiveness of the group may decrease; a larger group may foster indecision and a lack of direction.

> *The most common arrangement for mid-size firms is governance by a committee, variously called the executive committee, the management committee, the policy committee, or some equivalent. The committee members serve, in effect, as delegates for the rest of the partners.*[18]

RULE BY MANAGEMENT COMMITTEE/BOARD The **rule by management committee/ board** management structure uses a committee structure to make management decisions for the firm (see Figure 1-17). Committees are made up of 5 to 10 members depending on the size of the firm, and are typically composed of partners or shareholders. Common committees include the library committee, automation or technology committee, finance committee, and personnel committee. These committees usually report to a management or executive committee. If the committee gets too large, the actions of the committee slow down greatly and can hamper the effectiveness of the firm. Participation on a committee can be based on simple interest by a partner or shareholder, a seniority system, or an election or representation system, depending on how the firm wants to organize the committee selection process. A representation system, for example, is where a practice group (such as an employment and labor law practice group) elects or selects a chair, and that chair then represents the whole group on the executive or management committee. Committee systems are typically used in medium to large law firms.

rule by management committee/board
Management structure that uses a committee structure to make management decisions for the firm.

Figure 1-17   Rule by Management Committee Structure

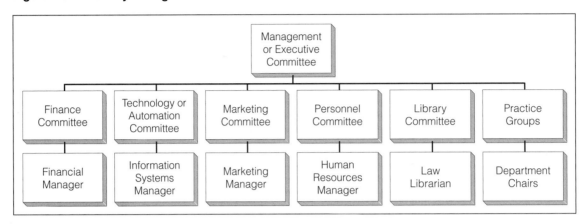

Corporate, Government, and Legal Aid Organization Structures

Corporate and government law practices have different organizational and management structures than private law firms. Corporate law departments can be centralized or decentralized. In the past, many—but not all—were centralized, meaning they were usually located in the firm's corporate headquarters but provided legal services to the whole company. Many government practices take a decentralized approach; most state and federal agencies have their own legal departments that provide legal services only to that particular agency. Like most private law firms, corporate and government practices can have different divisions within the practice, such as litigation or labor law. Although many corporate departments are centralized and many government practices decentralized, the choice depends on the type, size, and dynamics of the organization.

The management structure of corporate and government practices is dependent upon the corporation's or agency's own organizational structure as well. Many corporate and government departments have a general counsel responsible for the overall management of the department (see Figure 1-17). The power of the general counsel is similar to that of the powerful managing partner in private law firms. However, the power is diluted, since the general counsel must still act under the auspices of the overall corporate structure or of the legislative or other public body in the government practice.

Legal services practices, because they are usually nonprofit corporations, are overseen by a board of directors (see Figure 1-18). The board of directors might be made up of law professors, attorneys in private practice, judges, and other interested persons. The board usually hires an executive director who is responsible for the day-to-day operations of the practice. The executive director has attorneys, legal assistants, clerical staff, and administrators who report to him or her.

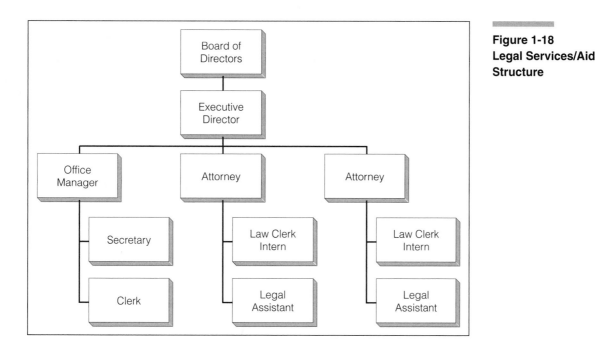

**Figure 1-18
Legal Services/Aid
Structure**

SUMMARY

Many people make up the legal team in a law office, including attorneys, administrators, legal assistants, law librarians, legal secretaries, and clerks, among others. An attorney is a licensed professional who counsels clients regarding their legal rights. A partner or shareholder is an attorney-owner in a private law practice. A managing partner is an attorney who runs the firm in some law practices. An associate attorney is a paid employee of the law firm who does not, however, share in the profits of the business. An "of counsel" attorney is a lawyer who is affiliated with a law practice in some way, such as being semi-retired, or who is paid by the firm on a per-job basis.

A legal administrator is responsible for a certain type of law office administrative system, such as general management, human resources, finance and accounting, marketing, or computer systems. Legal administrators typically have degrees in business or related fields.

Legal assistants are a distinguishable group of persons who assist attorneys in the delivery of legal services. They have knowledge and expertise regarding the legal system and substantive and procedural law that qualifies them to do work of a legal nature under the supervision of an attorney. The Department of Labor has consistently found that legal assistants are nonexempt under the Fair Labor Standards Act and are thus entitled to overtime pay (one- and-one-half times their normal rate) for work in excess of 40 hours per week.

Law librarians conduct legal research, acquire and preserve library materials, advise attorneys and legal assistants on research strategies, classify and index materials, and maintain the law firm library.

Law practices include corporate law departments, government practices, legal service/aid practices, and private law firms. Corporate legal departments are found in large corporations and are usually headed up by a general counsel, the attorney responsible for the in-house legal services provided to the company.

Government law practices includes attorneys who work in local, state, and federal agencies, as well as in state attorney general offices, and criminal prosecutors who work in all levels of government, among others.

Legal services/aid offices provide legal services to disadvantaged persons who otherwise could not afford it. Legal services/aid offices are nonprofit organizations and are funded by government and private donations.

Most attorneys practice in private law offices; approximately 48 percent of all attorneys are sole practitioners who own and manage their own law practices. Law firms come in all sizes, including small firms with fewer than 20 attorneys, medium-sized firms with 20 to 75 attorneys, and large firms with 75 to as many as 1000 attorneys. Many practices distinguish themselves as either plaintiff or defense firms, and law firm mergers are commonplace in the U.S. legal market. Through business strategy and technology, law firms can have different geographic service areas, including clients who are local, statewide, regional/multistate, national, international, or industry specific.

Law firms can take different legal forms, including a sole proprietorship, partnership, professional corporation, or limited liability company. Law firms can also use different governance structures, including a powerful managing partner structure, rule by all partners/shareholders, or rule by management committee.

HELPFUL WEB SITES

ORGANIZATION	DESCRIPTION	INTERNET ADDRESS
American Association for Paralegal Education	Association for legal assistant educators. Contains position papers on the legal assistant profession and information on how to find quality paralegal programs to attend.	http://www.aafpe.org
American Bar Association (ABA)	Association for attorneys. The site contains a large amount of information and publications relevant to individuals working in the legal profession.	http://www.abanet.org
ABA Law Practice Today	ABA site devoted to law practice management issues and concerns, including management publications, articles and resources.	http://www.abanet.org/lpm
ABA Standing Committee on Paralegals	ABA site devoted to the use of legal assistants in legal organizations. Contains publications, articles, and other useful information for legal assistants.	http://www.abaparalegals.org

ORGANIZATION	DESCRIPTION	INTERNET ADDRESS
American Bar Association—Market Research Page	ABA site devoted to links to other sites regarding research, statistics, and information about the legal profession.	http://www.abanet.org/marketresearch/resource.html
Association of Legal Administrators	National association for legal administrators. Contains resources and information related to law office management and legal administration.	http://www.alanet.org
Findlaw—Find a Lawyer site	Internet legal resource related to finding lawyers. Contains a database and links to attorney and law firm Web sites nationwide.	http://lawyers.findlaw.com
International Paralegal Management Association	International association for legal assistant managers. Contains resources for legal assistant managers and general information related to legal assistants.	http://www.paralegalmanagement.org
Legal Assistant Today	National magazine for legal assistants. The Web site has limited information, but the magazine itself is full of extremely useful and practical information for legal assistants.	http://www.legalassistanttoday.com
National Association of Legal Assistants	National association for legal assistants. Contains many resources for legal assistant students and practicing legal assistants. Includes articles, utilization surveys, and other helpful information.	http://www.nala.org
National Federation of Paralegal Associations	National association for legal assistants. Contains extensive links for practicing legal assistants.	http://www.paralegals.org

SUGGESTED READING

1. *Law Practice* magazine, published by the American Bar Association Law Practice Management Section [http://www.abanet.org/lpm].

2. *Legal Assistant Today* magazine, published by James Publishing [www.legalassistanttoday.com].

3. *Model Guidelines for the Utilization of Paralegal Services,* American Bar Association, 2004 [http://www.abanet.org/legalservices/paralegals/downloads/modelguidelines.pdf].

4. *National Association of Legal Assistants' [Annual] Utilization and Compensation Survey,* National Association of Legal Assistants [http://nala.org/Survey_Table.htm].

5. Munneke, G. A., & Davis, A.E. (2003). *The essential form book—comprehensive management tools.* American Bar Association.

6. Grella, T. C., & Hudkins, M. L. (2004). *The lawyer's guide to strategic planning.* American Bar Association.

KEY TERMS

associate attorney
attorneys
boutique firm
clerks
contract attorney
expert witness
Fair Labor Standards Act (FLSA)
exempt
nonexempt
freelance/contract legal assistants
general counsel
independent legal assistant
law clerk
law librarian
legal administrators

legal assistants
legal assistant manager
legal secretaries
legal services office
legal team
managing partner
nonequity partner
"of counsel"
office manager
partner or shareholder
powerful managing partner
rule by all partners/shareholders
rule by management committee/board
staff attorney

TEST YOUR KNOWLEDGE

Test your knowledge of the chapter by answering these questions.

1. What is the difference between a partner or shareholder and an associate attorney?
2. Partners are sometimes called _____ partners because they share in the profits and losses of the firm.
3. What are the duties of a managing partner?
4. What is a lawyer called who is a salaried employee and does not have an ownership interest or share profits in the law firm?
5. An associate is usually with a firm between 5 and ____ years before being a candidate for a partnership position.
6. A _____ partner does not share in the profits or losses of the firm but may be included in some aspects of management of the firm and be entitled to certain benefits.
7. What is a temporary associate attorney who is hired for a specific job or period called?

8. An attorney affiliated with a firm in some way, such as being retired or semiretired from the firm, may have the designation "of _____."
9. Legal administrators are usually found in _____ and _____ -sized law firms.
10. Name three areas of responsibility for a legal administrator.
11. True or false: a legal assistant can become an associate member of the American Bar Association.
12. A distinguishable group of persons who assist attorneys in the delivery of legal services are called _____.
13. Legal assistants who work as independent contractors but are still supervised and report to an attorney are called _____.
14. True or false: drafting correspondence is the number one duty of most legal assistants.
15. True or false: most legal assistants attend depositions and trials.

16. True or false: the number one specialty area for legal assistants is civil litigation.
17. Nearly 69 percent of all legal assistants are employed in what type of law practice? a) private, b) government, c) corporate, d) legal services/aid practice
18. According to the United States Department of Labor, are legal assistants exempt or non-exempt under the Fair Labor Standards Act?
19. Why is the United States Supreme Court case of *Missouri v. Jenkins* important to the legal assistant profession?
20. Office managers are usually found in _____ -sized law firms.
21. The four types of law practices are _____, _____, _____, and _____.
22. The head lawyer of a corporate law department is called a _____.
23. A not-for-profit law office that receives grants from the government and private donations to represent disadvantaged persons or people who cannot afford legal services is called a _____.
24. The majority of attorneys in the U.S. work in _____ practice.
25. Approximately 48 percent of all attorneys work in this size law office.
26. A small law office that specializes in only one or two areas is sometimes called a _____ firm.
27. Private law practices have four options from which to choose their legal status. A sole proprietorship is one; what are the other three?
28. A management structure in a private law firm where one partner is responsible for managing the firm is called a _____.
29. The three types of management structures for private law firms are _____, _____, and _____.

On the Web Exercises

1. Legal Assistant Compensation In this exercise, you will research average or median compensation for paralegals or legal assistants at different experience levels. You can even see market salary for a given city and state on a few sites. Complete the table below for paralegals in your city and state (if the site will allow it) based on the different levels of experience. Collect data from three different sources (this may or may not be possible). If you cannot get data specific for your city, either use regional information, if available, or national data. Likewise, if you can't get the exact experience levels that the table reflects, simply record what you can find. Use the "notes" section of the table to cite any irregularities or anything you need to clarify. The object of this exercise is to get rough estimates of salary levels.

Start your research at http://www.salary.com. Note: information on that site is free as long as you don't customize the data (which is not necessary for this exercise). If possible, try to get data that includes base pay and bonus pay (this is sometimes called "total compensation"). Print a copy of the results, showing the total compensation (if possible) for each search. Complete the table below or enter the table into a word processor. Include the name of the source of the data and the year the survey is dated, if a date is given. Turn in your table, your printed search results, and a short analysis of what you found. What did you find? Were you surprised by any of the results? How did the results from the different sources compare? Below are possible sources to research.

Possible Paralegal Salary Web Sites

Web Site	Description
http://www.salary.com	Contains salary data by city and state for hundreds of jobs.
http://nala.org/Survey_Table.htm	National Association of Legal Assistants—National Utilization and Compensation Survey Report (see compensation section). If the link does not work, try going to http://www.nala.org and then to "General Information," "The Paralegal Profession," "Current Survey Info." Alternatively, at the "Search This Site" command, try typing in "National Utilization and Compensation Survey" and then click on "Survey Report."
http://www.altmanweil.com/	Altman Weil Pensa publishes an annual survey called "The Paralegal Compensation Survey." The full survey is sold, but they often have sample pages or press releases that contain a summary of their report. After going to http://www.altmanweil.com in the "search" field type: "Paralegal Compensation Survey" and then select articles related to paralegal compensation.
http://www.paralegals.org	This is the site for the National Federation of Paralegal Associations. They regularly publish national compensation data for paralegals. Try going to the home page, click on "Site Search," and then type "compensation" to locate their compensation and benefits report.
http://www.google.com, http://www.yahoo.com, or other general search engines	Try searching for "paralegal compensation" or related terms. You may pull up other sites or newspaper articles with relevant data.

Paralegal or Legal Assistant Total Compensation (Average or Median Salary)

City: _____ State: _____

Years of Experience	Source 1 Name of Source:_____ Date of Data:	Source 2 Name of Source:_____ Date of Data:	Source 3 Name of Source:_____ Date of Data:
Paralegal 0–2 yrs	$_____	$_____	$_____
Paralegal 2–5 yrs	$_____	$_____	$_____
Paralegal 5–8 yrs	$_____	$_____	$_____
Paralegal 8+ yrs	$_____	$_____	$_____
Notes:			

2. Law Firm Web Sites In this exercise, you will find three law firm Web sites on the Internet, review them, and research information about the firms. Start your research by going to http://lawyers.findlaw.com or to www.findlaw.com and clicking on the "Find Lawyers" button. Click on "Law Firms" and then select any city or state you would like. You do not need to select a specialty. Then, click "Search." Alternatively, you can use any general search engine, such as http://www.google.com or http://www.yahoo.com, to search for law firms. Try to find three law firms, such as a solo practitioner, a small- to medium-size firm (2 to 75 lawyers), and a large law firm (75 or more attorneys). View the "Profile" on Findlaw, go to the firm's Web site, and complete the table below or enter the table into a word processor. If you have difficulty finding large law firms, try using a general search engine to search for "large law firm."

Question	Law Firm 1	Law Firm 2	Law Firm 3
Web address			
Law firm name			
What is the total approximate number of attorneys in the entire firm?			
What is the total number of offices the firm has?			
What is the geographic service area for the firm (local, state, regional, national, or international)?			
What is the number of practice areas the firm has?			
List a few of the main practice areas in which the firm specializes.			
What is the firm's legal structure (if listed)? (e.g., sole proprietorship, partnership, professional corporation [PC], or limited liability company [LLC])			
What kind of attorneys does the firm have ("of counsel," partner, associate, etc.)?			
In addition to marketing information, does the site contain resources, articles, or other information clients or members of the public might find helpful?			

3. **Legal Service/Aid Offices** In this exercise, you will find a legal services/aid office near you. Start by going to http://www.lsc.gov and clicking on the map of the U.S. Click on your state and find the closest legal services offices. Go to the office's Web site, if there is a link to it. Alternatively, you can use a general search engine to search for "(state name) legal services aid office." Refer to the office's Web site to learn about their mission, the total number of attorneys, what kind of matters the office handles, the funding level of the office, and other general information. Type a one-page summary of what you found.

PROJECTS

1. **Compare and Contrast Legal Assistant Definitions** Conduct an in-depth analysis and write a report on what a legal assistant or paralegal does, according to the 1) American Bar Association, 2) National Legal Assistant Association, 3) National Federation of Paralegal Associations, and 4) American Association for Paralegal Education. Compare the definitions. What are the similarities and differences? Consider the nature of the group and the interests they represent. Does this influence how they define what a legal assistant does? Go behind the definitions and look at the functions and tasks that legal assistants actually perform, according to each group. What kind of activities do they say that legal assistants should perform? Are there any caveats or limitations on the duties? Which organization's definition do you like best, and why?

2. **Legal Assistants—Exempt or Nonexempt under the Fair Labor Standards Act** Research and write an in-depth report regarding the question of whether legal assistants/paralegals are exempt or nonexempt under the Fair Labor Standards Act (FLSA). Your report should, at a minimum, include answers to the following questions.

- What is the FLSA?
- What is the difference between an exempt and a nonexempt employee?

- What are the so-called "white collar" exemptions to the FLSA?
- What is the position of the United States Department of Labor regarding the exemption status of legal assistants under the law, and why?
- What positions do the national paralegal/legal assistant associations take on the matter?
- What is your opinion regarding this matter?

There is a tremendous amount of information on the Fair Labor Standards Act. Starting points for research on this subject include: the National Association of Legal Assistants [http://www.nala.org], the National Federal of Paralegal Associations [http://www.paralegals.org], the United States Department of Labor FLSA compliance page [http://www.dol.gov/dol/compliance/comp-flsa.htm], and the United States Department of Labor FLSA Opinion Letters [http://www.dol.gov/esa/whd/opinion/opinion.htm] (see January 7, 2005, FLSA2005-9). If you have access to Westlaw, LexisNexis, or case law, you may also find these resources helpful in researching this issue.

QUESTIONS AND EXERCISES

1. Compare and contrast *Missouri v. Jenkins*, 491 U.S. 274, 109 S.Ct. 2463, 105 L.Ed. 2d 229 (1989) and *Role Models American, Inc. v. Brownlee*, 353 F.3d 962 (C.A.D.C., 2004), which allowed recovery of legal assistant fees, with *Joerger v. Gordon Food Service, Inc.*, 224 Mich.App. 167, 568 N.W.2d 365 (Mich.App., June 13, 1997), which did not allow recovery.

2. You are a new legal assistant in an eight-attorney law firm. Your supervising attorney has instructed you to give clerical work to a legal secretary named Pat. Pat has been with the firm for many years and considers herself to have as much legal experience as any legal assistant. She has made it perfectly clear that she will not peaceably make copies for you or help you in any way with any clerical work. Pat does not bill clients for her time, but you must. You are required to bill 1,750 hours annually. You know that you are not allowed to record billable hours for time you spend doing clerical work. You are responding to a Request for Production of Documents in a case in litigation, and you estimate that it will take five hours to copy the documents. How would you handle the matter?

3. You are in your last semester of school, about to graduate with a legal assistant degree, and you plan to begin looking for a job. Government practice would give you job security; a corporate law department would be interesting and provide opportunities for advancement; a legal aid office would give you the feeling that you were helping others; a private law office would be exciting and fast-paced; and being a freelance legal assistant would let you be your own boss. What type of job would you select, and why?

4. Interview two legal professionals in your area. Find out about their jobs and the firms that they practice in, such as: how many attorneys each firm has, what practice areas they specialize in, what types of jobs/positions are included in their "legal team," whether or not they use legal assistants in their practice (and if so, what tasks the legal assistants perform), what the legal structure of the firm is (e.g., partnership, professional corporation, etc.), how the firm is managed, and what type of clients the firms serve or target. Prepare a report regarding your findings.

NOTES

1. Murray, T. I. (1998, May/June). The unwritten rules: Survival in a law firm, *Legal Assistant Today*, 12. Reprinted courtesy of *Legal Assistant Today* magazine. For subscription information, call (714) 755-5450, or visit http://www.legalassistanttoday.com.
2. Quoted from Richard, L., Dr. (1996). *How firms manage.* Newtown Square, PA: Altman Weil, Inc.
3. National Association of Legal Assistants (NALA). Reprinted with the permission of the National Association of Legal Assistants, 1516 S. Boston, #200, Tulsa, OK. [http://www.nala.org].
4. American Bar Association. (2004). *The legal assistant's practical guide to professional responsibility* (2nd ed.), xi. Reprinted by permission.
5. American Bar Association Standing Committee on Legal Assistants. (1997). *Guidelines for the approval of legal assistant education programs.* Reprinted by permission.
6. Milano, C. (1993, May/June). Salary survey results. *Legal Assistant Today*, 68. Reprinted with permission from *Legal Assistant Today* magazine.
7. National Federation of Paralegal Associations (NFPA). Courtesy of National Federation of Paralegal Associations.
8. Rodriguez, X. (2000, March) Paralegal overtime: Yes, no, or maybe? An update. *Texas Bar Journal,* 267.
9. Brittain, V. K. (2000). Evidence required to prove the validity of legal assistant fees as a compensable component of attorney fee awards, *Texas Bar Journal, 63*(No. 3), 262.
10. Greene, A. (1993). *Leveraging with legal assistants* (p.vii). American Bar Association. Reprinted by permission.
11. Murray, T. I. (1998, May/June). The unwritten rules: Survival in a law firm. *Legal Assistant Today*, 12. Reprinted courtesy of *Legal Assistant Today* magazine. For subscription information, call (714) 755-5450, or visit http://www.legalassistanttoday. com.

For subscription information, call (714) 755-5450 or visit http://www.legalassistanttoday.com.

12. Milano, C. (1993). Salary survey results. *Legal Assistant Today*, 71. Reprinted courtesy of *Legal Assistant Today* magazine. For subscription information, call (714) 755-5450, or visit http://www.legalassistanttoday.com.

13. Printed with permission of Vermont Bar Association. Bauer, J. C. (1993). *Vermont Bar Journal and Law Digest, 19*(No. 2), 20.

14. A sole practitioner's legal assistant. (1993, March/April). Am I the only small-firm paralegal? *Legal Assistant Today,* 15. Reprinted courtesy of *Legal Assistant Today* magazine. For subscription information, call (714) 755-5450, or visit http://www.legalassistanttoday.com.

15. Small law firm legal assistant in Kerley, P. N. (1992, July/August). High-profile criminal defense cases attract top paralegals. *Legal Assistant Today*, 33. Reprinted courtesy of *Legal Assistant Today* magazine. For subscription information, call (714) 755-5450, or visit http://www.legalassistanttoday.com.

16. Levy, D. (2001). Paralegal with a twist. *Legal Assistant Today*, 64. Reprinted courtesy of *Legal Assistant Today* magazine. For subscription information, call (714) 755-5450, or visit http://www.legalassistanttoday.com.

17. Quoted from Richard, L., Dr. (1996). *How firms manage.* Newtown Square, PA: Altman Weil, Inc.

18. Quoted from Richard, L., Dr. (1996). *How firms manage.* Newtown Square, PA: Altman Weil, Inc.

ANSWERS TO TEST YOUR KNOWLEDGE

1. A partner/shareholder is an owner of the law firm, while an associate is an employee of the firm and does not share in its profits or losses.
2. Equity
3. Manage or run the operation of the law firm
4. An associate attorney
5. Ten
6. Nonequity
7. Contract attorney
8. Counsel
9. Medium, large
10. General management, finance and accounting, human resources, marketing, and computer systems
11. True
12. Legal assistants
13. Freelance/contract legal assistants
14. True
15. False
16. True
17. a) Private
18. Nonexempt
19. The Unites States Supreme Court recognized that legal assistants could bill for their time at the prevailing market rate.
20. Smaller
21. Private, government, legal services/aid, corporate
22. General counsel
23. Legal services/aid office
24. Private
25. Sole practitioner
26. Boutique
27. Professional corporate, partnership, limited liability company
28. Managing partner or powerful managing partner
29. Managing partner, rule by all partners/shareholders, by management committee

CASE REVIEW

William Dowsing Davis III v. Alabama State Bar, 676 So.2d 306 (1996).

676 So.2d 306
(Cite as: 676 So.2d 306)

Supreme Court of Alabama.
William Dowsing DAVIS III
v.
ALABAMA STATE BAR.
Dan Arthur GOLDBERG
v.
ALABAMA STATE BAR.
1940686, 1940687.
Jan. 19, 1996.
Rehearing Denied March 15, 1996.

MADDOX, Justice.

Two attorneys appeal from Alabama State Bar disciplinary proceedings. They challenge the sufficiency of the evidence presented at their disciplinary hearing, claiming that the disciplinary proceeding was nothing more than a "witch-hunt" that they say the Bar conducted because it did not approve of the attorneys' advertising practices. They further challenge the penalties imposed as being too severe.

The Alabama State Bar Disciplinary Board found William Dowsing Davis III and Dan Arthur Goldberg to be violating Rule 1.1, Alabama Rules of Professional Conduct (failure to provide competent representation); Rule 1.4(a) and (b) (failure to keep clients reasonably informed and failure to reasonably explain a matter so as to permit a client to make an informed decision); Rule 5.1 (failure to make reasonable efforts to ensure that the lawyers in their firm conformed to the Rules of Professional Conduct); Rule 5.3(b) (failure to ensure that the activities of a nonlawyer under an attorney's supervision are compatible with professional standards); Rule 5.5(b) (providing assistance to a person engaging in the unauthorized practice of law); Rule 8.4(a) (violation of the Rules of Professional Conduct through the acts of another); Rule 8.4(d) (engaging in conduct prejudicial to the administration of justice); and Rule 8.4(g) (engaging in conduct that adversely reflects on a lawyer's fitness to practice law). Both of the attorneys were suspended from the practice of law for 60 days.

The record before this Court is voluminous. Several former and present attorneys and secretaries of these attorneys' firm testified at the disciplinary hearing. Several clients of the firm also testified.

These two attorneys were the sole partners in the law firm of David & Goldberg. The firm spent approximately $500,000 annually on advertising, primarily television advertising, and the advertising attracted a large number of clients. As a result of this large expenditure and the volume of clients produced by the advertising, the attorneys implemented several policies, described below, designed to minimize expenses and maximize profits.

The Bar presented evidence, for example, that David and Goldberg allowed nonlawyer secretaries to provide legal services. It was also shown to be common practice at the firm for secretaries to interview clients and prepare legal filings, especially bankruptcy petitions. Evidence also indicated the nonlawyer staff members gave clients legal advice, such as "informing" clients of the differences between Chapter 7 and Chapter 13 bankruptcy. One former associate attorney testified that it was the firm's practice that attorneys would not interview or have any contact with the client before the first scheduled court appearance.

There was further testimony that these two attorneys imposed unmanageable caseloads on associate attorneys, many of whom were inexperienced. Some associate attorneys, for example, maintained caseloads of nearly 600 active cases. Former associates testified that because of the sheer volume of cases, the amount of time that could be spent on each case was so limited as to make it ***308** impossible for them to adequately represent their clients. At the hearing before the Disciplinary Board, the attorneys' own expert witness on Social Security law, Charles Tyler Clark, testified that the Social Security caseload, as described by a former associate of the firm, could not have been adequately handled by the one attorney assigned to it.

There was testimony that the firm had an inadequate supply of filing cabinets for case files and that files were simply stacked in various parts of the office, including the employees' break room and the hallway near the bathrooms. The evidence further tended to show that associate attorneys were given the barest of support staffs and that this fact, coupled with the huge volume of cases imposed upon the associates, created a situation in which files were mishandled, resulting in harm to the interests of clients.

The harm resulting from what could be described as a practice of the firm is best illustrated in the testimony of a former client, Brenda Marie Wood. Her husband, Douglas Wayne Wood, suffers from acute peripheral neuropathy and is dying. He was awarded Social Security disability benefits, but did not begin receiving his payments until eight months after he was supposed to. Mr. and Mrs. Wood saw a David & Goldberg television commercial that promised that the firm would "cut through the Social Security red tape" and get its clients' Social Security benefits fast. Because of the statement made in the advertisement, Mr. Wood hired the firm of David & Goldberg in October 1991 to represent him is his claim for past-due benefits. The firm lost Wood's file three times, and each time Wood was required to fill out a new set of forms. Wood was continuously assured by the firm's staff that his claim had been filed, when in fact it had not been. In February 1992, Wood received a letter from the firm informing him that the deadline for filing the claim had passed, and that it was too late to file his appeal.

The associates employed by Davis & Goldberg were also subjected to policies that interfered with their adequate and professional representation of their clients. These policies included the imposition of time limits or restrictions on the amount of time that they could spend with clients and on cases; the

imposition of a quota system that required associates to open a specified number of files in a certain time period; and the imposition of a policy requiring associates not to return the phone calls of existing clients, so that the attorneys could free more time to sign new clients.

[1][2] The appellants contend that the Bar did not meet its burden of proof as to the allegations against them. The standard of review applicable to an appeal from an order of the Disciplinary Board is "that the order will be affirmed unless it is not supported by clear and convincing evidence or misapplies the law to the facts." Noojin v. Alabama State Bar, 577 So.2d 420, 423 (Ala. 1990), citing Hunt v. Disciplinary Board of the Alabama State Bar, 381 So.2d 52 (Ala. 1980). We disagree with the attorneys' claims that the evidence was insufficient. In fact, the evidence presented amply showed that the two attorneys, in an effort to turn over a huge volume of cases, neglected their clients and imposed policies on associate attorneys that prevented the attorneys from providing quality and competent legal services. The evidence more than met the clear and convincing standard, and the Board's findings that these lawyers had violated the Rules of Professional Conduct are due to be affirmed.

[3] Even though we affirm the findings that these lawyers had violated the Rules of Professional Conduct, we elect to address their argument that the disciplinary proceeding amounted to a "witch-hunt" conducted because the Bar does not approve of the firm's advertising practices. We reject this contention. Instead, we find that the Disciplinary Board properly fulfilled its role of being a guardian of the image of the legal profession, and, thus, acted as a guardian of the profession itself. [FN1] We cannot find, as the ***309** attorneys ask us to find, that the Bar was conducting a "witch-hunt." In fact, there was evidence that the Bar examined the attorneys' advertising practices; it could have found that their advertisements were misleading, specifically in that the attorneys did not provide the quality legal service advertised. The Disciplinary Board heard evidence that one specific advertisement was misleading as it related to a United States Supreme Court ruling on the availability of Social Security benefits. Even the

appellants' expert witness testified that the advertisement could have been misleading under certain circumstances.[FN2]

FN1. Justice O'Connor described the need for such protection in her dissent in Shapero v. Kentucky Bar Ass'n, 486 U.S. 466, 488–89, 108 S.Ct. 1916, 1929–30, 100 L.Ed.2d 475 (1988):

"One distinguishing feature of any profession, unlike other occupations that may be equally respectable, is that membership entails an ethical obligation to temper one's selfish pursuit of economic success by adhering to standards of conduct that could not be enforced either by legal fiat or through the discipline of the market. There are sound reasons to continue pursuing the goal that is implicit in the traditional view of professional life. Both the special privileges incident to membership in the profession and the advantages those privileges give in the necessary task of earning a living are means to a goal that transcends the accumulation of wealth. That goal is public service, which in the legal profession can take a variety of familiar forms. This view of the legal profession need not be rooted in romanticism or self-serving sanctimony, though of course it can be. Rather, special ethical standards for lawyers are properly understood as an appropriate means of restraining lawyers in the exercise of the unique power that they inevitably wield in a political system like ours."

FN2. During the cross-examination of Charles Tyler Clark at the Bar disciplinary hearing, the following testimony was presented:

"MR. KENDRICK: This tape that we just listened to on the commercial, the last part of it, if I wrote it down correctly, says, 'Remember, no fee unless we collect. If you received a notice from Social Security or think you were wrongfully denied benefits, call David & Goldberg.'

Now, if somebody just listened to the last half of that tape, they wouldn't have [an] idea that they were talking about children's denial of Social Security benefits, would they?

"MR. NORTH: Mr. Chairman, I object to the last half of the tape. The tape as a whole.

"THE CHAIRMAN: I understand. But I'll let him answer the question, I understand the tape.

"MR. KENDRICK: If somebody walked in the room and turned the TV on and only caught the last half of it, they wouldn't understand that those cases were limited to children—denial of children's benefits, would they?

"MR. TYLER: That would be correct."

[4] This Court recognized that attorneys have a First Amendment right to engage in various forms of commercial speech. [FN3] We uphold the discipline imposed upon these attorneys, but we are not upholding it because they advertised; rather, we uphold it because the advertising was misleading in that the attorneys did not provide what they said they would provide. False and misleading advertising by attorneys can, and probably has, greatly harmed the public's perception of the legal profession, at a time when the public's confidence in attorneys has diminished. Indeed, the vast majority of those in the legal profession think advertising is harmful to the image of attorneys. [FN4]

FN3. This Court recognizes—and has ruled consistently with the United States Supreme Court regarding—the constitutionality of attorney advertising that is not "false, deceptive, or misleading." Zauderer v. Office of Disciplinary Counsel, 471 U.S. 626, 638, 105 S.Ct. 2265, 2275, 85 L.Ed.2d 652 (1985); also see Bates v. State Bar of Arizona, 434 U.S. 881, 98 S.Ct. 242, 54 L.Ed.2d 164 (1977), and Alabama State Bar Ass'n v. R.W. Lynch Co., 655 So.2d 982 (Ala. 1995).

FN4. In a Gallup poll conducted in November 1993 for the ABA Journal, 87% of the attorneys polled stated that they think legal advertising has harmed the public image of attorneys.

James Podgers, ABA Journal, Feb. 1994, 66–72.

Justice O'Connor warned in her dissent in Shapero v. Kentucky Bar Assn, 486 U.S. 466, 108 S.Ct. 1916, 100 L.Ed.2d 475 (1988), that the advertising practices of some attorneys, similar to those practices followed by these two attorneys, will "undermine professional standards" by giving an attorney "incentives to ignore (or avoid discovering) the complexities that would lead a conscientious attorney to treat some clients' cases as anything but routine." [FN5] 486 U.S. at 486, 108 S.Ct. at 1928. (For further discussion of *310 Justice O'Connor'' dissent, see notes 1 and 5.)

FN5. Justice O'Connor went on to state:

"[B]ecause lawyers must be provided with expertise that is both esoteric and extremely powerful, it would be unrealistic to demand that clients bargain for their services in the same arm's-length manner that may be appropriate when buying an automobile or choosing a dry cleaner."

486 U.S. at 489–90, 108 S.Ct. at 1930.

Evidence was presented that these two attorneys placed advertisements that were false and misleading. There can be no constitutional right to advertise in a false and misleading way. The evidence tends to show that these two attorneys' ethical violations were caused by their advertising practices and desire to turn over a huge volume of cases. The harm caused by this practice seems apparent.

Additionally, this Court finds no error or abuse in regard to the sanction the Board imposed, a 60-day suspension of the licenses of Davis and Goldberg. The violations were serious, and we cannot hold that the Board acted improperly in imposing the punishment. Consequently, the orders of the Disciplinary Board are affirmed.

In their application for rehearing, the attorneys argue that in its opinion of December 15, 1995, the Court erred in upholding the disciplinary sanctions based solely on allegations of misleading of false advertising. They are apparently referring to the Board's acquittal as to the charge of violating Rule 7.1, Alabama Rules of Professional Conduct. The Court affirmed the Disciplinary Board's numerous findings of violations of ethical rules, but did not address the Board's acquittal of the alleged violation of Rule 7.1, Instead, the Court addressed the attorneys' contention that the Disciplinary Board had conducted a "witch-hunt" against them because the Board did not approve of their advertising policies.

However, the Disciplinary Board found the attorneys in violation of Rule 8.4(g), which states: "It is professional misconduct for a lawyer to . . . (g)Engage in any other conduct that adversely reflects on fits fitness to practice law."

As we have stated earlier, much evidence was presented at the disciplinary hearing that proved that the attorneys' advertising practices and the procedures and policies adopted by Davis & Goldberg adversely affected the attorneys' ability to practice law in the manner required by the Rules of Professional Conduct. Further, Rule 8.4(g) is broad enough to require that attorney advertisements be honest and accurate and that an attorney's practice of law centered around such heavy advertisement be professional and competent as generally required by the Rules of Profession Conduct.

The evidence presented to the Disciplinary Board showed that Davis & Goldberg advertised that the firm provided legal services of a very high standard, but that the firm's representation of its clients failed to meet the high standard presented in its advertising. This evidence of a failure on the part of Davis & Goldberg to do what was promised in its advertisements, taken with the evidence regarding harmful policies and practices adopted by the firm in response to the fact that a large number of clients were attracted to the firm by its advertising practices, is more than sufficient to support the Board's finding that the attorneys violated Rule 8.4(g).

1940686 and 1940687—OPINION OF DECEMBER 15, 1995, WITHDRAWN; OPINION SUBSTITUTED; APPLICATION OVERRULED; AFFIRMED.

HOOPER. C.J., and HOUSTON, KENNEDY, INGRAM, and BUTTS, JJ., concur.

EXERCISES

1. Why was the court overly concerned with the two attorneys' business plan "designed to minimize expenses and maximize profits"?

2. Referring to Figure 1-13, analyze what the attorneys did correctly and incorrectly in terms of the responsibilities of law firm management.

3. How could the attorneys have corrected their management strategy?

4. Why was the court not convinced of the attorneys' "witch-hunt" theory but instead focused on the attorneys' clients?

5. Can an associate attorney or legal assistant reasonably maintain quotas of nearly 600 active cases each?

6. The two attorneys asserted that their non-lawyer staff were simply "informing" clients about differences in the law. Why did the court not agree with their conclusion? Do you agree or disagree with the court? Explain your response.

LEGAL ADMINISTRATION AND TECHNOLOGY

After you read this chapter, you should be able to:

- Distinguish between practice management and administrative management.

- Identify the functions of legal administration.

- Define total quality management.

- List and explain major federal employment laws.

- Discuss what a staff manual is and why it is important.

- Explain the purpose of strategic planning.

- Describe what disaster planning is.

- Discuss major technology issues in law offices.

Effective legal administration is an indispensable part of any law office no matter the size. The list of responsibilities is seemingly never ending . . . managing, planning, people, technology, systems, equipment, marketing, leading, finances, policies, buildings, and more. The trick is not to be successful in one or two areas, but to have a team in place that can do them all well.

The past two decades have brought lawyers [and legal assistants] new technology tools that have revolutionized the way lawyers [legal assistants,] and law firms work. While contracts are still drafted, disputes still mediated, and lawsuits still tried in court, technology has radically changed our methods and practices. . . . Law firms that recognize and embrace these changes are the ones most likely to thrive and succeed in an increasingly competitive industry.

Source: Amiel, P. (2005, July). Top down technology: A large firm's example. *Texas Bar Journal 68*(7), 589.

LEGAL ADMINISTRATION PRINCIPLES

This chapter covers the full spectrum of law office management and legal administration principles. These terms are used interchangeably. Legal administration is complex and broad in scope. Some legal administration topics will be covered in more detail in later chapters while others will only get brief coverage in this chapter.

There was a time when legal administration was viewed as unimportant. Attorneys viewed management responsibilities as something that got in the way of providing legal services to their clients. In truth, some of this view still prevails. This is why a competent legal assistant, able to take over some responsibilities in legal administration, is a valuable member of the legal team. Today, the highly competitive nature of the legal field and the need to control costs make legal administration an important topic. While many might think that management is more important in very large firms than in small law firms or corporate legal departments, this is not the case. Good management skills are equally important in every type of legal practice if the practice is going to be successful in serving clients, providing quality jobs for its employees, operating efficiently, and producing profits for its partners or shareholders.

During the last 25 years, there has been a computer and automation revolution that has forever changed legal administration. Before that, law offices were generally unconcerned with computers, word processing, computerized accounting and billing, mobile computing, the "paperless office," the Internet, e-mail, and much more. Now, virtually every aspect of legal administration is computerized in some way. Law offices have spent hundreds of millions of dollars to implement these new technologies.

Dispelling a Myth

A particular myth about attorneys needs to be dispelled. Many people assume that attorneys automatically make good managers. In truth, however, it is generally agreed that many lawyers are not very good managers.[1] Although lawyers have gone to school to learn about practicing law, most have no management skills or training. Practicing law and practicing management take very different skills. In fact, there is an adage that says "The best system for law office management is the system that involves the lawyers least."[2] Although attorneys may realize that management is important, that does not necessarily mean they are proficient at it. As you read this chapter, keep in mind that many attorneys practicing today have never taken a course like this one. Although national and local bar associations have put emphasis on training attorneys in management skills, they still have quite far to go. Because of the general lack of management training for attorneys, legal assistants with good management skills can be very useful to law firms.

In today's medium- and larger-size firms, the situation is alleviated somewhat with the use of professional administrators. Unfortunately, most smaller firms do not have the resources to hire administrators and must rely on attorneys, legal assistants, and other staff members to deal with problems as well as their other duties. Given the increasing competitiveness of the legal market, effective legal administration will be a prime concern for law firms for years to come.

Why Legal Assistants Need to Know Legal Administration

Good legal administration affects legal assistants, attorneys, and other law office staff alike. Firms that are unsuccessful in legal administration must close, merge, or even lay off staff. The operating costs of running a law office are extremely high, and legal assistants depend on the viability of the law office for their economic survival. Management affects everyone in the practice. Legal assistants benefit from good management because well-managed practices run with fewer problems and crises, work flows smoothly, billings and client payments are received in a timely manner, appointments and deadlines are met, ethical problems are taken seriously, staff members are adequately compensated, staff are adequately trained to perform their jobs, and there is less stress.

Practicing good management is hard; it takes time and teamwork, but it is well worth the effort. Some signs of poor management include frustrated and unhappy staff members and clients, daily "crises," reduced attorney effectiveness, higher costs, low employee job satisfaction, high employee turnover, increased use of employee sick leave, and low staff morale. From the legal secretary to the law clerk to the legal assistant to the attorney, everyone has a stake in the action. In short, effective management is good for everyone and should be practiced by all.

Figure 2-1
Practice Management v.
Administrative
Management

Practice, Case, or Substantive Management
- What type of <u>cases</u> should we specialize in?
- Which <u>cases</u> should we accept?
- How will <u>case</u> files be organized?
- How will documents for each <u>case</u> be indexed for retrieval later?
- What form files will need to be created for each type of <u>case</u>?

Administrative, or Office, Management
- Purchasing equipment and supplies for the <u>law office</u>
- Hiring and evaluating law <u>office staff</u>
- Sending out invoices for the <u>law office</u>
- Managing the finances and profitability of the <u>law office</u>
- What administrative structure is the most efficient for the <u>law office</u>?

Practice Management v. Administrative Management

practice management
Management decisions about how a law office will practice law and handle its cases.

There are two major aspects of managing a law office: practice management and administrative management. **Practice management (i.e., substantive or case management)** refers to management decisions about how a law office will practice law and handle its cases (see Figure 2-1). Practice management decisions include determining the general types of cases the law office will specialize in, how many cases the law office should accept in a given area, and which clients should be accepted or rejected. Practice management is sometimes called "case management" or "file management" because this type of management centers on managing and controlling client files and client cases.

The cases and clients a law office takes on directly affect the profitability of the firm. If a law office undertakes to represent a number of client cases that do not generate any profits because the client does not pay, the contingency case is lost, or the fees received are unexpectedly low, the economic effects on the law office are quite harmful. Also, if law office staff do not manage and organize cases effectively, then there may be poor-quality legal services, reduced profitability, unhappy clients, and ethical complaints.

administrative management
Management decisions relating to operating or managing a law office, including financial and personnel matters.

Administrative management (i.e., office management) refers to management decisions relating to operating or managing a law office, including financial and personnel matters. This text largely covers administrative management topics, but some practice management areas are also introduced.

FUNCTIONS OF LEGAL ADMINISTRATION

management
The administration of people and other resources to accomplish objectives.

Management is the administration of people and other resources to accomplish objectives. In private law practices, the primary objective of management is to provide efficient, high-quality legal services that please clients while earning a reasonable profit for the firm. In a corporate or government legal department,

Figure 2-2   The Functions of Legal Administration

where generating a profit is not applicable, the objective of management is to provide efficient, high-quality legal services to its client at a reasonable cost.

The functions of legal administration (see Figure 2-2) include practice management, leadership, controlling, financial management, human resources management, planning, marketing management, organization/policies/systems, facilities management, office services management, and technology or information systems management. Each of these areas will be discussed in this chapter. Two areas, financial management and marketing, have one or more chapters devoted to them later in the text, so they are only introduced in this chapter. All of these functions are essential to successful legal administration regardless of the size of the office. The people who perform these tasks vary, depending on the management structure of the firm; it could be a sole practitioner, a managing partner with the help of an office manager, committees with the help of professional administrators, or all of the partners or shareholders in a firm.

PRACTICE MANAGEMENT

As defined earlier, practice management refers to management decisions about how a law firm will practice law and provide legal services to clients. In the end, every law practice must be able to provide their clients with prompt, competent, and courteous legal services that satisfy and add value to the client, and that are priced at a cost that clients are willing to pay. Law firms are service providers, and if clients do not receive quality legal services, they *will* go somewhere else to get them; it is currently easier than ever to do so, given the intense level of competition in the legal marketplace. A firm's lifeblood is the ability of management to prudently choose the type of clients it services, to keep existing clients, and to gain new clients for the future. To do this, law firms must define what practice areas and clients to focus on, what legal services they will provide to those clients, and what practice systems and resources they will need to provide those services to the clients. Every firm must deal with these types of practice management issues.

> *To "hardwire" clients to your firm, they cannot be taken for granted. That means learning everything possible about clients—their expectations of the firm, their business, and their plans for growth.*[3]
>
> *A conviction that the client's need must be placed above everything else is apparent in successful firms.*[4]

Defining the Law Firm's Practice

Every law practice must define who it is they will serve. Figure 2-3 shows fundamental questions that every law practice must answer and basic decisions that management will need to make. Most of these questions must be answered by the firm's owners. None of the questions are easy, and all of them will dramatically affect who the firm will serve and how it will provide services to its clients. There are two basic and important practice management maxims to understand: 1) the practice of law is so broad that even megafirms with 1000 or more attorneys cannot possibly practice in all areas or subspecialties of the law, and, therefore, specialization is absolutely required; and 2) successful law practices do not take all of the clients or cases that come to them. Successful law practices weed out good clients from bad clients and strong cases from poor ones. Not all clients are created equal; some clients are easier to work with than others. Some clients have financial resources to pay for legal services, and some do not. Some clients are honest and trustworthy, and some are not. A successful law firm will decide which clients are right for them. Likewise, some cases have true merit to them and some are frivolous or without legal foundation. Again, successful law firms and attorneys are able to decide which cases are the best for them and which ones to refuse.

Even the largest full-service firms tend to be "best available" in a relatively small number of key practice areas. The vast majority of firms compete in a limited number of substantive practice areas or industry sectors. . . . Today well-focused specialists are winning the [legal] marketplace wars. . . . Trying to be all things to all people is never a good strategy.[5]

Defining the Law Firm's Services

Once a law firm has decided upon areas of practice and which clients to serve, it must decide and define what services will be provided. For example, if a solo practitioner has decided to practice in the general area of decedent estates, that person must decide whether he or she will 1) draft trusts, 2) advise clients on complex tax issues, 3) perform estate planning, 4) draft wills (including whether to write only simple wills or to draft complex wills involving millions of dollars in assets), 5) probate estates, and so forth. The law firm must decide what specific services they are willing to provide and what services they should refer to other attorneys or decline to take because they lack particular expertise. The answers to these questions are important to the practice management of every firm.

Defining the Law Firm's Practice System Needs

Once the firm has decided which clients they want to serve and what services they want to provide, the firm must then determine what types of practice systems are needed to provide and implement those services. Law firms have nearly endless choices regarding the types of practice systems and tools they can use to provide legal

Who are our primary clients (businesses, individuals, governments)?
What market segments will we serve?
What legal services will we provide?
What resources will be needed to provide those services?
What services do our clients need or want? What will we need to add or delete in order to be successful?
What types of cases do we want to take? What is the long-term projection for those cases?
In what legal areas will we specialize? Should we focus on area subspecialties?
How many practice areas will we have? How many can we do well with the resources we have?
Who will champion the practice areas and lead their development?
Should we focus on providing services to an industry?
What geographic area will we serve?
How will we attract clients?
How will we assure that the clients receive quality services?
How will we hold on to the clients (what will be our basis for competition to differentiate our services from the next firm)?

**Figure 2-3
Practice
Management—
Defining the Law
Firm's Practice**

Practice Systems	Choices
Document preparation	Pen/paper, typewriter, word processor
File/records management	File cabinets, computer/paperless office
Legal research	State or county law libraries, personal collection of books, Westlaw, LexisNexis, CD-ROMs
Docket control	Paper calendars, computer calendars (Outlook), legal docket control, full case management
Specialty-specific software	Word processors and general tools or costly but efficient and sophisticated specialty software
Litigation support	Manual methods, computerized litigation support programs, outsourcing to litigation support vendors, e-discovery
Computer systems	Stand-alone systems, hardwired network systems, wireless networks, Internet, intranet, extranet, desktop computers, laptop computers, PDAs
Communication systems	Telephone systems, voice mail, mobile phones, e-mail, e-filing

services to clients. Figure 2-4 contains some examples of different practice systems and options that are available. Technology had virtually no role in how law was practiced 25 years ago; at that time, technology mainly impacted "back office" functions, such as timekeeping, billing, and administrative systems. This is no longer the case. Attorneys and legal assistants use practice management technology every day in the practice of law. There is almost no area of law practice that has not been profoundly changed by technology. For more than 200 years, lawyers exclusively used files and file cabinets for records management. Now, many law firms have moved to "paperless offices," where all documents coming into or going out of the firm are scanned and saved in an electronic format for later retrieval without a hard copy. Likewise, legal research has taken the same route. Law books that take up large amounts of expensive space and quickly become outdated have mostly been replaced with CD-ROMs or electronic services such as Westlaw, LexisNexis, the Internet, and others. Law practices must also provide practice systems that set standards for such things as ethics, internal law practice policies for providing service, and quality.

Quality and Total Quality Management

Ensuring that clients receive quality legal services is one of the most important practice management responsibilities of any law firm partner or administrator. There simply is no substitute for having a quality product, particularly in the legal field.

> *We know exactly what we want in a product or a service, whether it is legal services, a car, or a hamburger and fries: it's quality. Quality is not an accident of nature, nor a gift to the lucky; rather, it is the product of a well-managed organization.* We *decide whether ourselves or our organization will have quality as its standard.*[6]

What Is TQM?

> Clients will most often identify a "quality product" as the [single] most important expectation of their law firm.[7]

Some might say that total quality management is outdated and has little to do with a legal organization or a practicing legal assistant. Others would say that quality never goes out of style. Because legal organizations must provide quality legal services to stay in business and please clients—whether a megacorporation in litigation, an ordinary person needing a will, or a corporate legal department—that quality must always be the object of focus for a law firm. Legal organizations provide quality legal services through their staff, including their legal assistants. There will always be a market for legal assistants who look out for the client and provide quality legal services. Quality is what distinguishes poor or average legal assistants from exceptional ones. There is also a strong connection between quality and loyalty when it comes to clients. When a client is receiving quality legal services, he or she is usually willing to pay a higher price for those services and has no reason to look elsewhere for a different service provider.

> Why would a client risk moving his or her business to another firm (and have to pay to educate that firm on his or her business) when his or her current firm, current attorneys, and current legal assistants provide outstanding quality legal services that always meet or exceed his or her expectations?

Total quality management (*TQM*) is a management philosophy that is based upon knowing the needs of each client and allowing those needs to drive the legal organization at all levels of activity, from the receptionist to the senior partner. From the outset of this book, you have been introduced to the importance of meeting client needs and providing quality legal services to clients. TQM is just an expansion on this basic idea. The TQM philosophy of allowing clients' needs to drive an organization, instead of the other way around, was taught to major Japanese corporations in the 1950s by W. Edwards Deming.

The TQM philosophy focuses on the idea that businesses should compete based on the quality of the service that is provided, as opposed to price or other factors. Figure 2-5 shows the difference between management decisions based on client needs and those based on what is easiest for the law practice to provide.

total quality management
Management philosophy of knowing the needs of each client and allowing those needs to drive the legal organization.

**Figure 2-5
Product-Centered v.
Client-Centered
Philosophies in a
Law Office**

Product-Centered Philosophy	Client-Centered Philosophy
1. Inner forces control the law office.	Client forces control law office decision making.
2. Emphasis is on short-run productivity.	Emphasis is on long-range planning for quality and client satisfaction.
3. Law office decisions are forced upon clients.	Law office decisions are made based on client input and meeting clients' needs.
4. Law office provides services they already have.	Law office develops new services and modifies existing services based on clients' needs.
5. Law office provides services but does not survey clients to ensure satisfaction.	Law office surveys clients before, during, and after services are rendered to ensure client satisfaction and makes appropriate changes based on clients' needs.
6. Law office focuses on short-term profitability and financial success.	Law office focuses on long-range profitability by putting the priority on meeting clients' needs and providing quality legal services.

What Are Specific TQM Philosophies?

TQM has many nuances and subtleties, but there are several main points to the TQM philosophy.

1. **Management has an overriding duty to ensure that the firm provides quality legal service.** Management must make decisions based on how the decision will affect the quality of the legal services being provided. The distribution of firm assets, including purchases, contracts, and staff employees, must be viewed from the client's perspective and be based on how these decisions will affect the *quality* of the services the firm provides. Likewise, when a legal assistant makes a decision or participates in making a decision about a case, he or she must view that decision in terms of how the decision will affect the quality of legal services, such as deciding what copy service, litigation support bureau, or software to use.
2. **Quality service involves every person in the firm, and everyone must be involved and committed.** Providing quality services begins and ends with everyone. It encompasses the idea of putting dedication and commitment into everything that is done; it requires integrating quality methods into the daily work routine of every member of the staff; and it begins with every person taking pride in his or her work.
3. **Quality service is based not on management's or our own perception of quality, but on the perceptions of the client.** In the end, the only person who is going to bring business back to the firm, or refer your services to other businesses, is the client. Therefore, only the client's perception of

> *I am a firm believer that the quality of work personally reflects on the parale-gal, and I take my work very personally. I know that my name will be at-tached to everything I do, so I strive to be as perfect as possible, not to say that I do not make mistakes because I am human. Attorneys are perfection-ists and any work performed by the legal assistant should be as thorough and complete as possible. Attorneys also count on the legal assistant to be detail-orientated; therefore, the work needs to reflect that as well. Of course, the quality of work rises as the legal assistant gains experience. For an entry-level legal assistant, my advice would be to ask questions and do not stop asking questions, even when you gain experience.*
>
> —Linda Rushton, CLA

quality is what counts. Because it is the client's opinion that counts, firms must regularly poll or survey their clients to find out what they are doing right, what they are doing wrong, and how they can provide better services to the client. This can be done by interviewing current clients and mailing out client surveys when matters have been resolved, but it is the client's opinions that motivate the firm to change. For a TQM policy to be effective, the firm must be willing to *listen* to the client and to institute *change* to meet the needs of the client. Keep in mind that client needs are constantly chang-ing, so to keep up, the firm must also be willing to change.

> *I used to work for an attorney who was absolutely maniacal about proofread-ing work products and I used to think she was just being "Type A." As I have progressed in my career, I have learned that there is nothing more irritating than picking up a document that has just been sent out in the mail to find that it is pathetically inadequate in grammar and spelling. Remember, whatever you do it reflects on you, your boss, your firm, and your client.*
>
> —Andrea Blanscet, CLA

As a practicing legal assistant, you do not have to wait until the end of a case or matter to ask a client whether or not he or she is pleased with the services you are providing or if there is anything else you can do to be of assistance. Clients will not always volunteer that kind of information; you may have to ask.

4. **Quality service depends on the individual's, the team's, and ultimately the organization's performance.** In the end, the client will judge the quality of a firm's job based on his or her experience. Thus, everyone involved must be committed to the idea of quality and must be able to share in the

financial or other types of benefits the firm receives. TQM eliminates the "we v. they" mentality and rewards all members of the team who contribute. TQM uses project teams to identify and solve problems and increase efficiency.

As a legal assistant, it is crucial that you work as a team member with the other legal professionals on a client's case. If you see another team member struggling, about to make a mistake, or unable to complete a task in a timely fashion, you have to be willing to help.

> *One of the most important qualities a staff member can have is the self-confidence to raise an issue when he or she believes an error has been made without feeling threatened about retaliation.*[8]

5. **Improve systems constantly.** Along with assuring high-quality services, there is also a focus on increasing performance and productivity by constantly improving the systems and ways in which services are provided. This may include purchasing technology, rethinking the ways in which work is performed or routed, removing repetitive tasks, or taking further actions that will increase productivity and efficiency. This is a vigorous process that never ends.

What Are the Benefits of the TQM Philosophy?

The TQM philosophy offers many benefits.

- **Increased client satisfaction**—The ultimate benefit is that clients are satisfied beyond their expectations, and, based on this satisfaction, they will entrust all their legal services and refer new clients to the firm.
- **Unity among the management, attorneys, and staff**—TQM breaks down the barriers among competing groups in a law practice by focusing everyone on the same goal (unity of purpose) and by allowing all involved to share in the profits of the business. This can be done by awarding bonuses, giving awards, or recognizing outstanding performance. The "we v. they" mentality is a thing of the past.

> *What is the legal assistant's role in delivering and assuring quality legal services? The legal assistant must accept responsibility for taking the initiative to do what needs to be done to resolve problems and extend first-rate service to the customer (the attorney and the . . . client).*[9]

- **Seek to continuously improve performance and productivity**—TQM seeks to improve the quality of legal services to clients by increasing staff efficiency and productivity, not just once or twice a year, but constantly, in order to improve the system. This involves all members of the staff checking the quality of their own work, learning advanced technologies, and doing whatever is necessary to provide the client with the best service.

How Is TQM Implemented?

TQM can be implemented by hiring professional consultants to develop systems for obtaining client feedback and to educate staff members on total quality management techniques.

Some law firms include a TQM policy in their staff manual. For example, the American Bar Association publishes a sample manual; the sample policy on total quality management states:

> *The firm is committed to Total Quality Management (TQM), a philosophy that focuses on providing the highest quality service tailored to our individual clients' needs in the most cost-efficient manner. The policies associated with TQM encompass both professional and support staff personnel and pervade every stage of the work process. _____ is the individual in charge of overseeing the Firm's quality management program. Suggestions and questions regarding this program should be directed to _____ at extension _____. Law Office Policy and Procedures Manual*, Wert and Hatoff, American Bar Association, p. 62.

To a lesser degree, TQM also can be implemented by reading about the subject, by simply accepting the principles of TQM, by being responsive to client needs, and by recognizing the effect management decisions have on the quality of the legal services being provided. In effect, TQM serves as a reminder that quality services are what everything else in the firm depends on.

LEADERSHIP

Another function of legal administration is leadership. **Leadership** is the act of motivating or causing others to perform and achieve objectives. Effective leaders inspire others; they set a clear mission, vision, and goals for an organization, and they provide direction and guidance. Good leaders are forward thinking, set clear objectives, measure results, inspire trust, are innovators, and make quality decisions. For any law firm or practice to be truly successful, quality leadership must exist, whether it be from the partnership, a managing partner, legal administrators, committees, or other individuals or groups. Figure 2-6 shows a more complete list of effective leadership practices in a law office.

leadership
The act of motivating or causing others to perform and achieve objectives.

**Figure 2-6
Effective Law Office
Leadership**

Effective Law Office Leadership

Establishes a vision of a positive and successful future for the law practice.
Enlists others in generating the firm's mission statement, goals and objectives.
Develops a written strategic plan incorporating the input, values, and ideas of others.
Anticipates what can go wrong and acts proactively.
Acts consistently to support the legal team in carrying out the firm's mission.
Stresses goal attainment in day-to-day activities.
Rewards team members based on their achievements of goals and objectives.
Reports and tracks goal attainment data at partnership and law firm meetings.
Shows confidence in and respect for all legal team members.
Defuses rumors by keeping all legal team members informed of matters that are relevant to them or the practice.
Never represents facts or divulges information given in confidence.
Insists that all team members have strong ethics and high integrity.
Is trusted by others in the practice.
Creates a supportive environment for learning, coaching, and developing staff; takes interest in team members as human beings; and is not overly critical of mistakes.
Takes time to listen to others, no matter who they are, and makes a concerted effort to be responsive.
Effectively communicates with team members so that they are given continuous, specific feedback regarding progress toward their goals and clearly know what is expected of them.
Consistently makes difficult decisions without procrastinating and seeks appropriate input from others.

CONTROLLING

controlling
The process of determining whether the law practice is achieving its objectives, holding stakeholders accountable for their goals and making strategy adjustments as necessary so the firm achieves its objectives.

Controlling is the process of determining whether the law practice is achieving its objectives, holding stakeholders accountable for their goals, and making strategy adjustments as necessary so the firm achieves the objectives. Management must determine whether the law office is achieving its short- and long-range goals. Management must also make stakeholders accountable for meeting objectives and should assist in adjusting strategies so goals can be met. Exercising control is a fundamental aspect of management; this is done via. financial audits, budgets v. actual reporting, operational audits, risk management, analysis of financial reports, and the progress tracking of short- and long-range plans.

FINANCIAL MANAGEMENT

financial management
The oversight of a firm's financial assets and profitability to ensure overall financial health.

Financial management is the oversight of a firm's financial assets and profitability to ensure overall financial health. Financial management is important in any business; a business that does not earn a profit will quickly cease to exist. There are many different aspects of the financial management of a law firm. Timekeeping and billing, which include tracking time spent on clients by attorneys and legal assistants and billing clients, is a particularly crucial area, as is trust accounting, which entails the ethical responsibilities of keeping track of client monies paid but not yet earned by the firm. Budgeting and tracking firm expenses, revenue, and profitability, as well as making payments (accounts payable) and tracking firm receipts (accounts receivable), are also important to the overall success of the firm. Other areas of financial management include setting billing and hourly rates, purchasing high-quality goods and services at the least expensive cost, tracking the assets of the firm (including equipment and furniture), properly investing firm monies that are not currently being used, having a good relationship with a bank to secure loans as necessary, tracking tax liabilities, and having proper insurance to protect the firm's assets, payroll, and cash flow. Chapters 5 and 6 cover these topics in detail.

HUMAN RESOURCES MANAGEMENT

Human resources management refers to hiring, evaluating, compensating, training, and directing law office personnel. While law firms use technology to serve clients more efficiently, for the most part, legal services are delivered to clients by a firm's staff. Therefore, the quality management of that staff is of great concern to most law offices. Firms must recruit, select, and hire staff who are trained and competent in their areas of expertise. Managers must also effectively evaluate staff to let them know how they are doing in terms of meeting the expectations of their jobs, and coach and counsel staff if there are performance problems. Firms must provide compensation and benefits that will appropriately reward and motivate staff so that they are able to retain the employees they have. Furthermore, the staff must be trained regarding changes in the law, technology, and client needs. The firm must also direct staff and periodically review its organizational structure, job designs, and how services are provided to clients, in order to make adjustments that ensure effectiveness.

human resources management
Hiring, evaluating, compensating, training, and directing law office personnel.

The Hiring Process

At some point in your career, you may be required to hire someone, such as a legal secretary, another legal assistant, or a clerk. It is important that you hire the right individual for the job the first time. A poor hiring decision can cost a law office thousands of dollars in wasted salary, training expenses, time, and potential malpractice problems. In addition, if the right person is not hired the first time, the firm must hire another individual and incur the cost of advertising and training all over again.

The hiring process is fairly detailed. Typically, a detailed job description is drafted, ads are placed in newspapers (or recruitment is started), resumes and employment applications are analyzed, candidates are interviewed, references are checked, and a final selection is made.

WRITING JOB DESCRIPTIONS   The first step in the hiring process is to write a detailed job description (see Figure 2-7) that explains the duties of the position. If an

**Figure 2-7
Sample Litigation
Legal Assistant Job
Description**

Job Description

JOB TITLE: **LEGAL ASSISTANT** (Litigation)

EXEMPT:	Non-Exempt	**GRADE LEVEL:**	10
DIVISION:	Legal	**LOCATION:**	Headquarters
DEPARTMENT:	Litigation		
INCUMBENT:			
REPORTS TO:	Attorney		
PREPARED BY:	Antonio Brown	**DATE:**	January 2006
APPROVED BY:	Susan Smith	**DATE:**	January 2006

SUMMARY:

Under supervision of an attorney, provides a broad range of professional and technical duties related to litigation. Performs factual investigations including gathering documents, researching records, and interviewing witnesses/clients. Works with the supervising attorney and client to prepare and answer discovery documents in draft form. Prepares deposition summaries, witness summaries, and case chronologies or timelines. Manages and organizes litigation files and exhibits. Prepares drafts of pleadings and correspondence. Conducts legal research as needed. Manages the computerized litigation support for each case as needed.

ESSENTIAL DUTIES AND RESPONSIBILITIES (and other duties as assigned):

1. Performs factual investigations including gathering, analyzing, and organizing documents such as medical records, police records, birth and death records, motor vehicle records, incorporation records, and other documents using a variety of sources including the Internet, government agencies, and other contacts. Compiles and summarizes data as necessary. Conducts interviews with clients and witnesses as needed. Works with expert witnesses as needed.
2. Performs a variety of tasks related to discovery under the supervision of an attorney including preparing drafts of interrogatories, requests for admissions, and requests for production of documents. Works with the attorney and client to prepare and coordinate drafts of discovery responses. May prepare drafts of deposition questions, coordinate deposition scheduling, and prepare case chronologies and timelines as necessary. Prepares deposition and witness summaries.
3. Organizes and maintains litigation files, prepares trial notebooks, and assists in organizing, maintaining, and indexing trial exhibits. Performs case management, docketing, scheduling, and planning as needed.
4. Conducts drafts of legal research memorandums using the Internet, Westlaw, LexisNexis, CD-ROM databases, and the law library as needed.
5. Prepares drafts of a variety of litigation-related legal documents under the supervision of an attorney including pleadings, motions, discovery documents, and general correspondence.
6. Reviews, analyzes, organizes, and indexes discovery documents and all case-related documents, including managing the computerized litigation support for each case.

MINIMUM EDUCATION AND EXPERIENCE:

Bachelor's degree (B.A.) from four-year college or university (major: legal assistance); or one to two years of related experience; and/or training or equivalent work experience.

LICENSES/CERTIFICATIONS REQUIRED:

Paralegal certificate

KNOWLEDGE, SKILLS, AND ABILITIES REQUIRED:

Knowledge of the principles and procedures of legal research. Strong interpersonal and communication skills and the ability to work effectively with a wide range of constituencies in a diverse community. Skill in the use of personal computers and related software applications. Ability to draft legal documents, such as pleadings, legal responses, affidavits, position statements, and briefs. Ability to develop and maintain recordkeeping systems and procedures. Database management skills. Ability to gather and organize legal evidence. Knowledge of litigation and civil procedure helpful. Knowledge of planning and scheduling techniques. Skill in organizing resources and establishing priorities. Ability to maintain confidentiality of records and information. Excellent customer service skills required.

REASONING ABILITY:

Ability to define problems, collect data, establish facts, and draw valid conclusions. Ability to interpret an extensive variety of legal instructions in different areas of the law and deal with several abstract and concrete variables.

LANGUAGE ABILITY:

Ability to read, analyze, and interpret legal documents. Ability to write legal documents and legal/business correspondence. Ability to effectively present information and respond to clients, attorneys, witnesses, opposing counsel, and the general public.

Figure 2-7
(Continued)

employer does not know what the new hire is going to do, there is no way he or she can recognize the best person for the position. A detailed job description lets the employer match the strengths of candidates to the particular position that is being filled. Job descriptions also help the employee to understand his or her role in the firm and what will be expected. Most job descriptions include a job title, a summary of the position, a list of duties, and minimum qualifications that the new employee must have.

ADVERTISING AND RECRUITING   After a detailed and accurate job description is drafted, organizations begin the actual hiring process. This includes either promoting from within the organization or recruiting candidates from outside the organization. The process of recruiting candidates can include the use of newspaper advertisements, candidate interviews at specific schools or institutions, employment agencies and search firms, professional associations, the Internet, or candidate referrals from the organization's own employees.

EMPLOYMENT APPLICATIONS AND RESUMES   Once an employer has drafted a detailed job description and advertised the position, the next step is to review the employment applications or resumes received.

In many cases, an organization will receive a resume first and subsequently have the individual fill out a formal application for employment. An application for employment is a good idea, because resumes are inconsistent and may not provide all the information needed to make a quality decision.

Employment applications must comply with legal requirements and may not ask for information that the employer is not entitled to have, such as information regarding race, religion, or age.

INTERVIEWING   Once resumes and employment applications have been analyzed and the field of candidates narrowed, the next step is the interview process. The interview is typically the most dynamic part of the hiring process. This is the point where the interviewer decides which applicant is the most qualified and will "fit" with the organization. Below are some general insights regarding interviews.

Screen Applicants to be Interviewed   A common problem that occurs during the interview is the discovery that a candidate who looked good on paper is, in fact, a bad "fit" for the organization. In this case, the whole interview is a waste of both the employer's and the applicant's time. One way to avoid this is to conduct a casual phone screen of all applicants. By asking some salient questions over the phone, an interviewer can determine whether it is appropriate to have the applicant come in for a formal interview.

Ensure That All Interviews are Consistent   It is extremely important that all interviews conducted for a position are done consistently. The interviewer must make sure that all candidates are asked the same questions and that all candidates are treated fairly. If interviews are not performed consistently, an interviewer may be giving preference or special treatment to one candidate over another. The more consistent the interview is, the less likely an organization will be susceptible to a discrimination complaint.

The Interviewer Should Talk Less and Listen More   The interviewer should talk as little as possible. Any time the interviewer is talking, he or she is giving up the opportunity to hear from the candidate, which is the whole purpose of the interview. Interviewers should avoid filling in pauses or completing sentences for candidates.

Ask Open-Ended and Behavioral-Based Questions   Most questions in interviews today are open-ended in that no specific answer is hinted at or suggested by how the interview question is asked. The applicant must decide how to answer the question. For example, a typical open-ended question might be "Can you review your work experience for me and tell me how it prepares you for the position you have applied for?" A behavioral-based question is another type often asked in interviews; this type of question asks the candidate to provide a specific example from his or her past. For example, a typical behavioral-based question is "Can you tell me about a time you had a particularly difficult legal ethics problem and how you handled it?" Many organizations use behavioral-based questions because it is more difficult for an applicant to rehearse these answers beforehand. Good interviewers will ask candidates a variety of open-ended and behavioral-based questions that call for concrete examples relating to the candidate's personality, job history, education, and experience related to the potential job.

Avoid Discriminatory Questions   Particular caution should be used when deciding what interview questions to ask. There are many questions that should be avoided because they might be considered discriminatory (see Figure 2-8). Figure 2-8 is not an all-inclusive list, as many states and local governments have additional antidiscrimination laws. As a rule, if a question is not directly relevant to the position or job performance, an interviewer should not ask it. There is no reason to take unnecessary risks. Personal or family-related questions should be avoided; the

Race/Color/Religion/Sex
Any question that is related to a candidate's race, color, religion, sex, national origin, age, disability, sexual orientation, or veteran status

Name/Marital Status
- What was your maiden name?
- Have you ever used another name?
- Are you married? (permissible after hiring)

Ancestry
- Where were you born?
- Where does your family come from?

Residence
- How long have you lived at this address?
- Do you own your house?

Family/Personal
- How many children do you have?
- How will you provide child care?
- Are you pregnant?

Credit/Financial
- Have you ever filed for bankruptcy?
- Have your wages been garnished?

Age
- What is your date of birth? (permissible after hiring)
- When did you graduate from elementary or high school?

Organizations
- What organizations do you belong to? (You can ask this if you instruct them to delete organizations related to race, religion, color, disability, age, and so forth.)

Religion
- What church do you belong to?

Medical
- Are you disabled or taking medication regularly? (You can ask whether they have the ability to perform the essential functions of the job.)

Figure 2-8
Interview Questions that Should *Not Be* Asked

problem with most personal questions is that they relate to the applicant's race, color, religion, sex, national origin, age, or disability. Many city statutes and ordinances prevent discrimination on the basis of sexual orientation, so questions related to this should be avoided as well.

REFERENCE CHECKS   Once the employer has narrowed the list to two or three final candidates, the only thing left to do is check references. Checking references is an important part of the hiring process and should never be left out. Researchers have found that nearly 30 percent of all resumes contain exaggerated statements or misstatements about education or employment history. In addition, employers have been held liable for negligent hiring. **Negligent hiring** is when an employer hires an

negligent hiring
Hiring an employee without sufficiently and reasonably checking the employee's background.

employee without sufficiently and reasonably checking the employee's background. In one case, an apartment complex was found liable after a new manager used a passkey to enter an apartment and rape a tenant. The apartment complex had failed to check the new manager's references and reasonably investigate the person's background for felony convictions, fighting, and other criminal activity. Thus, references should always be checked, and gaps in employment and other indicators of problematic behavior should be investigated.

The following are some tips on how to get good information when performing reference checks.

Call Past Employers/Supervisors Typically, the most relevant information an employer can gather is from the candidate's last employer or supervisor. Call these people first. Although some will refuse to give out any information for fear of being sued for defamation if they say something negative, many will still answer your questions. A way around this problem is to ask potential candidates to sign a release or waiver that allows the past employer to talk to you openly and freely without fear of being sued for defamation. Ask specific questions about the candidate's dates of employment, job duties and responsibilities, quality and quantity of work, disciplinary problems, work attitude, communication skills, dependability, ability to be a team player, and reason for leaving. Also ask whether the former employer would rehire the person.

Call Institutions/Schools If a candidate lists graduation from a school or institution, call the school and confirm it. This usually does not take a great deal of time. This is seldom done and many candidates claim that they have finished degrees when, in fact, they have not.

Call Character References Last Candidates only give potential employers character references who will give them a glowing recommendation. Expect this, but ask specific questions as well.

Fair Credit Reporting Act
Federal legislation that governs the use of consumer reports in all employment decisions.

Fair Credit Reporting Act The **Fair Credit Reporting Act** is federal legislation that governs the use of "consumer reports" in all employment decisions. "Consumer reports" are defined very broadly and include reference checks, education checks, credit history reports, and criminal background checks, when an employer hires a third party to conduct these checks. If an employer conducts these checks personally, compliance with the Fair Credit Reporting Act is not required; however, if a third party is used, the organization must comply. The employer must give prior written notice to the applicant before procuring the consumer report, and obtain prior written authorization by the applicant before obtaining the consumer report. Before "adverse action" is taken against the applicant (such as not hiring the applicant based on the consumer report), the applicant must be provided with a copy of the report and notified of his or her legal rights.

Performance Evaluations

Timely performance evaluations are a strong human resource development technique. Employees need to know—on a regular basis—what they are doing right and where they need to improve. Performance evaluations allow employees to know where they stand and help them to grow and progress. A performance evaluation should not be viewed as a heavy object with which to beat or threaten employees, but rather as a part of the process of working toward a common goal.

If done correctly, evaluations can strengthen ties with employees by allowing them to participate in the evaluation process. In the end, a well-defined evaluation process can make the organization more efficient. Employee evaluations should be conducted privately, and, when possible, the evaluation itself should be given to the employee before meeting so that he or she is prepared to talk about the evaluation and its findings. The evaluation should always be performed in writing and should be kept in the employee's personnel file.

EVALUATIONS SHOULD BE DONE REGULARLY Evaluations should be done on a regular basis in order to be effective. Some offices evaluate employees quarterly, biannually, or annually. Quarterly or biannually evaluations are recommended, because criticism or praise usually has more effect soon after an incident has happened.

EVALUATIONS SHOULD BE OBJECTIVE AND MATCH RATINGS WITH PERFORMANCE
Evaluations should be based on objective performance by an employee and not on any personal likes or dislikes of the employer. It is particularly important to match ratings with performance and to always remain fair. It is also important that employers communicate with employees on a regular basis and take a "hands-on" approach to knowing whether or not employees really deserve a certain rating. Using objective criteria and actual examples of the employee's performance will help in this process. Examples of how the employee earned an "excellent" or "average" performance rating will help identify what he or she is doing correctly or incorrectly.

ELICIT OPEN COMMUNICATION AND SET MUTUAL GOALS FOR IMPROVEMENT
Any evaluation method must allow the employee to participate in the process by communicating how he or she feels about the evaluation, including what he or she likes or dislikes and what both parties can do to help solve problems. There must be a give-and-take relationship in the evaluation process to make it work. One technique is to ask the employee how he or she feels the year went: what went right or wrong? Let him or her do the talking. This will put the employee at ease and will let the person feel that he or she has taken part in the process. Setting realistic goals to solve any problems also helps to communicate what is expected of the employee in the future. One way of doing this is by having both the employer and the employee set certain goals.

COACHING TECHNIQUE—ONGOING EVALUATION One way to help an employee succeed in his or her job is to coach and counsel him or her on a daily, ongoing basis. The **coaching technique** focuses on the positive aspects of the employee's performance and explores alternative ways to improve performance. Most people are more willing to listen to advice from a "friend" who is interested in their well-being than from a disinterested and heavy-handed "boss." The coaching technique is

coaching technique
Counseling that focuses on the positive aspects of the employee's performance and explores alternative ways to improve his or her performance.

**Figure 2-9
The Coaching
Technique**

1. Event—Describe exactly what happened; do not be negative, just state the facts.
2. Effect—Describe the impact of the event, including who or what was adversely affected and why; be specific. Let the employee know why the behavior should be changed.
3. Advice—Describe exactly how the employee can improve performance in the future.
4. Remind—Emphasize that you believe the employee is competent and that this was just a lapse.
5. Reinforce—Monitor the employee's performance. If the employee corrects the mistake, let the person know that he or she is doing it right. Reinforce the positive change he or she made.

borrowed from sports, where a coach works with an individual to overcome deficiencies through counseling and by explaining any problems to the person.

The coaching technique works best when the supervisor has had direct experience in the employee's position. This allows the supervisor to give concrete tips, examples, information, and opinions that the employee can use. Employees typically are more willing to accept advice if the supervisor has been in the same position. When discussing areas that need improvement, try not to be judgmental, but instead give advice on exactly how to correct a deficiency. This technique is especially useful when an employee lacks knowledge about a situation. One of the most positive aspects of the coaching technique is that it does not place blame on the employee; the employee is able to retain his or her self-esteem, which can be lost when an employee is simply reprimanded. Figure 2-9 explains how the coaching technique works. The coaching technique is not a substitute for a regular evaluation, but it is a technique for helping an employee be successful in his or her job.

GENERAL PERFORMANCE EVALUATION FORM   Figure 2-10 contains a general performance evaluation form that could be used for many law office support jobs. This type of evaluation is straightforward and quick to prepare. However, the checklist is not job specific and does not allow a great deal of interaction on the part of the employee. If possible, the employee should be allowed to make comments and be an active participant in the evaluation process.

GOAL SETTING AND MANAGEMENT BY OBJECTIVES (MBO)   Another type of performance system is based on goal setting, also commonly referred to as "management by objectives" (see Figure 2-11). In a **management by objectives** (MBO) performance program, the employee and employer agree upon the employee's goals at the beginning of the evaluation period. Target dates for reviewing the employee's progress toward the goals, and a determination for how it will be decided if the goals were achieved or not, are also included in the objectives. An accomplishment report is prepared detailing which goals were accomplished, and rewards or incentives are given for meeting the goals. For example, a goal might be to reduce non-billable hours by 5 percent or increase billable hours by 50 hours during the fourth quarter.

management by objectives
A performance program in which the individual employee and the employer agree on goals for the employee.

**LEGAL ASSISTANT
PERFORMANCE EVALUATION**

Name: _____   Title: _____

Evaluation Type: Probation   Six-Month   Annual   Special: _____

Date: _____   Evaluation Period: _____

Evaluate the staff member's performance using the following rating criteria and make comments as necessary:

Rating: Description:

5   **Outstanding:** Employee's performance is exceptional and far exceeds normal expectations.

4   **Above Average:** Employee's performance is very good and exceeds expectations.

3   **Average:** Employee performs to normal expectations of the position.

2   **Below Average:** Employee's performance falls below acceptable levels from time to time.

1   **Unacceptable:** Employee's performance is completely unacceptable.

1.   Competence in the Law Office

_____   a. Is technically competent in all areas of work.
_____   b. Other staff members have confidence in and trust the employee's work.
_____   c. Continuously strives to learn and expand his/her competence level.

Comments: _____
_____
_____

2.   Quality of Work

_____   a. Is accurate in all work.
_____   b. Is thorough and complete in all work.
_____   c. Takes pride in work.
_____   d. Work is consistently of high quality.

Comments: _____
_____
_____

3. Dependability

_____   a. Highly dependable.
_____   b. Work is always turned on time.
_____   c. Can be counted on in a crisis.
_____   d. Works independently without need of supervision.

Comments: _____
_____
_____

**Figure 2-10
Legal Assistant
Performance
Evaluation**

Figure 2-10
(Continued)

4. Work Habits/Attitude

_____ a. Has excellent work habits.
_____ b. Has a positive and enthusiastic attitude.
_____ c. Acts as a team player.
_____ d. Gets along with other staff members and supervisors.
Comments: _____
_____
_____

5. Communication/Relationships

_____ a. Treats clients professionally.
_____ b. Treats other staff members professionally.
_____ c. Can write effectively.
_____ d. Has good grammar skills.
_____ e. Listens effectively.
_____ f. Can make self understood orally.
Comments: _____
_____
_____

6. Judgment

_____ a. Makes sound judgment calls.
_____ b. Exercises appropriate discretion.
_____ c. Intelligently arrives at decisions.
_____ d. Thinks through decisions.
Comments: _____
_____
_____

7. Initiative

_____ a. Accepts new assignments willingly.
_____ b. Takes on new responsibilities without being asked.
Comments: _____
_____
_____

General Comments: _____
_____
_____

Employee's Strengths: _____
_____
_____

Areas That Need Improving: _____
_____
_____

OVERALL RATING: **Outstanding Above Average Average Below Average Unacceptable**

Employee Comments: _____
_____
_____

Supervisor Signature: _____   Employee Signature: _____

Date: _____   Date: _____

Employee signature only verifies that this evaluation has been discussed and does not indicate agreement with the evaluation.

EMPLOYEE SELF-APPRAISAL:

A. What were your achievements this year?

B. List any goals you would like to achieve next year.

C. What strengths do you have in performing this position?

D. What areas do you think you can improve upon?

E. What can your supervisor do to help you reach your goals?

F. Overall, how would you rate your own performance level?

Figure 2-10
(Continued)

---

1. Employee and supervisor agree on the employee's major performance objectives for the coming period, including target dates for accomplishing each part of them.
2. Employee and supervisor agree on how the objectives will be measured and how it will be decided if the objectives have been met.
3. Employee and supervisor meet periodically to discuss the employee's progress toward meeting the goals.
4. An accomplishment report is prepared at the end of the period, stating which objectives were met or not met.
5. Awards or incentives are given, depending on whether the objectives were met.

Figure 2-11
Management by
Objectives Process

Compensation and Benefits

Another aspect of human resources management is paying law practice employees and providing them with benefit packages. Most firms set compensation for positions based on the "market salary" for the job in the marketplace. Some firms may be "above market" while others are "below market." To determine the appropriate compensation and benefits for a position, law practices will consider job description and the education and experience requirements, and will use the average market salary as a benchmark (see Figure 1-7 for legal assistant salary data). According to a 2005 survey, approximately two-thirds of all legal assistants receive an annual bonus in addition to base pay. An average annual bonus for a legal assistant is roughly between $2,500 and $3,500. Many firms also offer benefit packages to attract and retain legal assistants. According to the 2005 survey, 88 percent received some form of health insurance, 80 percent received some kind of retirement benefit, 68 percent received life insurance, 65 percent had professional association dues paid by their employer, and 57 percent received some form of dental coverage.

Training and Development

Some law practices offer training and development opportunities for new professional staff, including legal assistants. This is usually offered in large law firms where a structured development program is instituted. Specific learning experiences are planned and progress is measured. In many small to medium firms, little training is provided, and new legal assistants learn through experience. Many firms, of all sizes, offer continuing education programs to staff. Some of these may be offered through in-house training programs within large firms or by sending staff to external continuing education programs at the firms' expense in small- to medium-sized firms. According to the 2005 survey, approximately 62 percent of legal assistants receive some kind of continuing education benefits from their employer.

Personnel Policies

personnel handbook
A manual that lists the formal personnel policies of an organization.

One of the most useful things a law office of any type can do to effectively manage its human resources is to create a comprehensive and up-to-date personnel handbook. A **personnel handbook** (sometimes called an employee handbook) lists the formal personnel policies of an organization. Personnel handbooks (1) establish formal policies on personnel matters so staff members will know what to expect of management and what management expects of them regarding personnel issues; (2) establish a standard so that all employees are treated fairly and uniformly; and (3) help to protect the law office if it is involved in litigation regarding personnel matters and to avoid government-compliance problems.

Current Personnel Law Issues

Personnel-related issues are highly regulated and often litigated. The following is a sampling of some of the more important areas related to federal personnel/labor law. Figure 2-12 contains a summary of federal employment laws.

Law	Description
Family and Medical Leave Act of 1993	Provides that eligible employees be allowed up to 12 work weeks of unpaid leave within any 12-month period for a) the birth, adoption, or placement of a child for foster care; b) the care of a child, spouse, or parent with a serious health condition; and c) the employee's own serious health condition.
Civil Rights Act of 1991	Relaxes the burden of proof in discrimination claims and allows for greater recovery of damages.
Civil Rights Act of 1964	Prohibits discrimination against employees on the basis of race, color, religion, sex, or national origin. The Equal Employment Opportunity Commission (EEOC) was established to enforce this law.
Americans with Disabilities Act of 1990 (ADA)	Prohibits employers from discriminating against persons with disabilities in several different areas.
Age Discrimination in Employment Act of 1967 (ADEA) (Amended 1978)	Prohibits employers from discriminating against persons age 40 or more on the basis of their age unless age is a bona fide occupational qualification.
Equal Pay Act of 1963	Prohibits employers from basing arbitrary wage differences on gender.
Fair Labor Standards Act of 1938	Sets minimum wage and maximum basic hours of work for employees, and requires overtime pay for nonexempt employees.

Figure 2-12
Partial List of Federal Employment-Related Laws

Employment-At-Will Doctrine

The **employment-at-will doctrine** states that an employer and employee freely enter into an employment relationship, and that either party has the right to sever the relationship at any time without reason. If an employee is covered by a union collective-bargaining agreement, employment contract, or civil service regulations, the employment-at-will doctrine does not apply, and the employer must comply with the terms of the contract or regulations. Employment-at-will typically happens when an employee works for an employer without any type of written agreement or reference to how long the employee will work. For example, suppose a law office hired a legal secretary in an employment-at-will state. The legal secretary did good work, but the firm subsequently changed its mind and decided that it did not need the extra position and terminated the secretary. This would be perfectly acceptable, and the secretary would have no basis for a lawsuit against the law office. For another example, suppose that the legal secretary gets a better-paying job at another law office and quits without giving notice. This also would be acceptable under employment-at-will status.

Organizations should be careful when drafting their personnel handbook to state that the policies therein are not a contract or that employees will be retained for a certain amount of time. For example, an employer should not include language such as "If you do your work satisfactorily, you will always have a job here." If a court finds that the employer gave the expectation to an employee that he or

employment-at-will doctrine
Doctrine that states that an employer and employee freely enter into an employment relationship, and that either party has the right to sever the relationship at any time without reason.

she would have a job forever (as long as the work were satisfactory), or that the policies in the personnel handbook were a type of contract, this would upset the normal expectation of employment-at-will. Personnel handbooks should contain a simple employment-at-will statement, typically near the front, that states the following:

> Employment-At-Will
> It is understood that these personnel policies and any other firm document do not constitute a contract for employment, and that any person who is hired may voluntarily leave employment upon proper notice, and may be terminated by the firm any time and for any reason.

In addition, some employers require employees to sign a statement like the one above, or they place the statement on the employment application form.

The employment-at-will doctrine does, of course, have limitations. Courts have found that at-will employees may have legal rights against employers, even though the employer is supposed to be able to terminate the employee without any reason. Instances include when the employer violates public policies, such as firing an employee for filing a workers' compensation claim, firing an employee for refusing to commit perjury, or terminating an employee to avoid paying retirement benefits or sales commissions. Other instances include terminating an employee based on discrimination or terminating an employee when the employer promised to retain the employee as long as the employee did a good job. Thus, although employment-at-will is a doctrine that works in favor of employers, it is by no means absolute. Some states even limit the employment-at-will doctrine by statute, so any organization should be familiar with its own state laws.

When employment-at-will is not in effect, or if there is an employment contract in place, the typical standard is "just cause." An employment contract is a contract between the employer and an employee, setting forth the terms and conditions of the employment relationship. "Just cause" means that before an employer can terminate an employee, the employer must have a just, reasonable cause to do so. Just cause can include many things, such as violating the company's rules and regulations, insubordination, and dishonesty.

The Family and Medical Leave Act of 1993

Family and Medical Leave Act of 1993 (FMLA)
Legislation that allows employees in certain circumstances to receive up to 12 workweeks of unpaid leave from their jobs for family or health-related reasons.

The **Family and Medical Leave Act of 1993 (FMLA)** applies to employers with 50 or more employees and provides that eligible employees be allowed up to 12 workweeks of unpaid leave within any 12-month period for (a) the birth or adoption of a child or placement of a child for foster care; (b) the care of a child, spouse, or parent with a serious health condition; and (c) the employee's own serious health condition. To be eligible for FMLA, an employee must have one year of service with the organization and have worked at least 1,250 hours in the last year. The FMLA requires that an employee granted leave under the act be returned to the same position held before the leave or be given one that is equivalent in pay, benefits, privileges, and other terms and conditions of employment. The employee also is entitled to health care benefits during the leave. The purpose of the FMLA is to assist workers to better balance the demands of the workplace with the needs of their families.

Fair Labor Standards Act

The Fair Labor Standards Act sets minimum wage and maximum hours of work for employees. It also requires that overtime pay (one- and-one-half times their normal rate) be paid to employees who work in excess of 40 hours a week. Employees do not need to be paid overtime if they fall into one of the four "white-collar" exemptions: executive, administrative, professional, or outside sales.

If an employee is exempt, it means that he or she is not required to be paid overtime wages. If an employee is nonexempt, it means that he or she is required to be paid overtime wages. Whether legal assistants are exempt or nonexempt is a hotly debated issue (see Chapter 1 for a detailed discussion).

Equal Employment Opportunity

Equal employment opportunity requires employers to make employment-related decisions without arbitrarily discriminating against an individual. This is a statement that is often seen in want ads, employment applications, and other employment-related documents. Federal laws, including the **Civil Rights Act of 1964,** prohibit employers from discriminating against employees or applicants on the basis of race, color, national origin, religion, or gender. The **Americans with Disabilities Act of 1990 (ADA)** prohibits employers from discriminating against employees or applicants with disabilities (see the following section on the ADA). The **Age Discrimination in Employment Act of 1967** prohibits employers from discriminating against employees and applicants on the basis of age where the individual is 40 or older. The **Equal Pay Act of 1963** prohibits employers from paying workers of one sex less than the rate paid an employee of the opposite sex for work on jobs that require equal skill, effort, and responsibility and that are performed under the same working conditions. There are several other federal laws that legislate in this area. Most of the laws cited here make it unlawful for an employer to arbitrarily discriminate against employees or applicants.

Every personnel handbook should have a policy stating the law office's position on equal employment opportunity, such as:

Equal Employment Opportunity Statement
It is the policy of the firm to apply recruiting, hiring, promotion, compensation, and professional development practices without regard to race, religion, color, national origin, sex, age, creed, handicap, veteran status, or any other characteristic protected by law.

An exception to equal employment opportunity is when age, sex, or religion is a **bona fide occupational qualification** (BFOQ). A BFOQ means that to perform a specific job adequately, an employee must be of a certain age, sex, or religion. A BFOQ does not apply to race or color; an example of a BFOQ would be for a position as a Catholic priest. The employer could reasonably discriminate against

---

equal employment opportunity
Concept that requires employers to make employment-related decisions without arbitrarily discriminating against an individual.

Civil Rights Act of 1964
Legislation that prohibits employers from discriminating against employees or applicants on the basis of race, color, national origin, religion, or gender.

Americans with Disabilities Act of 1990 (ADA)
Legislation that prohibits employers from discriminating against employees or applicants with disabilities.

Age Discrimination in Employment Act of 1967
Legislation that prohibits employers from discriminating against employees and applicants on the basis of age when the individual is 40 or older.

Equal Pay Act of 1963
Legislation that prohibits employers from paying workers of one sex less than the rate paid an employee of the opposite sex for work on jobs that require equal skill, effort, and responsibility and that are performed under the same working conditions.

bona fide occupational qualification
An allowable exception to equal employment opportunity; for example, for an employee to perform a specific job, the employee must be of a certain age, sex, or religion.

non-Catholics because the candidate must believe in and have knowledge of the Catholic religion in order to qualify. In general, BFOQs have been narrowly construed by most courts, and there are few positions in a law office—if any—that would qualify.

Americans with Disabilities Act

The Americans with Disabilities Act of 1990 (ADA), among other things, makes it unlawful to discriminate in employment against qualified applicants and employees with disabilities. Under the ADA, a person has a "disability" if he or she has a physical or mental impairment that substantially limits a major life activity, such as seeing, hearing, breathing, speaking, walking, performing manual tasks, working, or learning. This does not include a minor impairment of short duration, such as a broken limb, infection, or sprain. An individual with a disability also must be qualified to perform the essential functions of the job, with or without reasonable accommodation; that is, the applicant or employee must be able to satisfy the job requirements, including education, experience, skills, and licenses, and be able to perform the job. The ADA does not interfere with an employer's right to hire the best-qualified applicant but simply prohibits employers from discriminating against a qualified applicant or employee because of his or her disability.

reasonable accommodation
Accommodating a person with a disability, which may include making existing facilities readily accessible, restructuring the job, or modifying work schedules.

The ADA also requires that employers "reasonably accommodate" persons with disabilities. An employer must make **reasonable accommodation** for a person with a disability, which may include making existing facilities readily accessible, restructuring the job, or modifying work schedules. The ADA provides that individuals with disabilities have the same rights and privileges in employment as employees without disabilities. For example, if an employee lounge is in a place inaccessible to a person using a wheelchair, the lounge might be modified or relocated, or comparable facilities might be provided in a location that would enable the individual to take a break with coworkers. Persons who have been discriminated against because of a disability can receive back-pay damages, reinstatement, punitive damages, and other remedies.

Sexual Harassment

sexual harassment
Unwelcome sexual advances, requests for sexual favors, and other verbal or physical conduct of a sexual nature that create an intimidating, hostile, or offensive working environment. Figure 2-13 contains a sample antiharassment policy.

Sexual harassment includes unwelcome sexual advances, requests for sexual favors, and other verbal or physical conduct of a sexual nature that creates an intimidating, hostile, or offensive working environment.

Many people typically think of sexual harassment as a male supervisor sexually coercing a female subordinate in order for her to keep her position or to be promoted. Sexual harassment is much broader than this, however. Sexual harassment can include unwelcome sexual jokes, inappropriate sexual remarks, inappropriate e-mails, innuendos, insults, leering, subtle forms of pressure for sexual activity, vulgar or indecent language, sexual propositions, displaying sexually oriented photographs, and unwelcome and inappropriate touching, patting, and pinching.

ANTIHARASSMENT

We are strongly committed to the principle of fair employment, and it is our policy to provide employees a work environment free from all forms of discrimination. In recognition of each person's individual dignity, harassment of employees will not be tolerated.

Unwelcome harassment is verbal or physical conduct by an employee or any individual (including customers, vendors, or suppliers) that denigrates or shows hostility or aversion toward an employee and/or his or her relatives, friends, or associates because of his or her race, color, sex, religion, age, national origin, handicap or disability, veteran status, sexual orientation, or other status protected by law, and which

1. has the purpose or effect of creating an intimidating, hostile, abusive, or offensive working environment.
2. has the purpose or effect of unreasonably interfering with an individual's work performance.
3. otherwise adversely affects an individual's work performance.

This includes acts that are intended to be "jokes" or "pranks" but that are hostile or demeaning with regard to race, color, religion, gender, national origin, age, handicap or disability, veteran status, sexual orientation, or other status protected by law.

As part of this antiharassment policy, no employee or any other individual (including customers, vendors, or suppliers) may sexually harass any employee. Sexual harassment includes unwelcome sexual advances, sexual jokes or comments, requests for sexual favors, or other unwelcome verbal or physical conduct of a sexual nature. This policy is violated when

1. submission to such conduct is made, either explicitly or implicitly, a condition of employment.
2. submission to or rejection of such conduct is used as a basis for employment-related decisions such as promotion, discharge, performance evaluation, pay adjustment, discipline, work assignment, or any other condition of employment or career development.
3. such conduct otherwise unreasonably interferes with work performance or creates an intimidating, abusive, or offensive working environment, even if it leads to no adverse job consequences.

Any employee who has a question, concern, or complaint of discrimination, including harassment based on race, color, sex, religion, age, national origin, handicap or disability, veteran status, sexual orientation, or other protected status, is encouraged to bring the matter to the immediate attention of his or her supervisor or manager. If for any reason the employee would feel uncomfortable discussing the situation with his or her supervisor or manager, or if he or she feels further discussion is needed, the employee should contact the human resources manager.

All reports of inappropriate conduct will be promptly and thoroughly investigated, and we ensure that any improper conduct will cease immediately and corrective action will be taken to prevent a recurrence. Any employee who violates this policy will be subject to the full range of disciplinary action, up to and including termination of employment. We will inform the complaining employee of the resolution of the complaint as appropriate.

All complaints will be treated confidentially to the extent practical for an effective resolution. No employee will suffer adverse employment consequences as a result of making a good faith complaint or taking part in the investigation of a complaint. An employee who knowingly alleges a false claim against a manager, supervisor, or other employee or individual will be subject to the full range of disciplinary action, up to and including termination of employment. (1/2006)

**Figure 2-13
Antiharassment
Policy**

Sexual harassment does not have to involve a subordinate and a supervisor; it also can take place between persons at the same job level. Sexual harassment can involve clients as well; it has been reported that clients sometimes sexually harass law office staff. The law office has as a duty to investigate a client harassing a staff member, since the law office may be liable if it does not take appropriate action to protect its employees. Finally, although the majority of sexual harassment cases involve male employees harassing female employees, women, also have been accused of sexually harassing male subordinates. Regardless of who is involved, the employer is responsible for taking corrective action.

Paralegal managers play a key role in preventing harassment by communicating policies and keeping the door open to complaints . . . "[W]e need to convey to legal assistants that we are sensitive to the situation and to assure them that they do not need to tolerate harassment. . . . The way to preempt problems down the road is to develop policies which prohibit sexual harassment, then communicate the policies to employees. Firms with a policy in place are less likely to face litigation because people have a place to go and feel as though they will be treated fairly."[10]

PLANNING

planning
The process of setting objectives, assessing the future, and developing courses of action to achieve these objectives.

Planning is the process of setting objectives, assessing future needs, and developing a course of action to achieve the objectives. Planning is the road map for meeting the firm's goals. Law firms should have short-range and long-range plans or goals. A short-term plan for a law office might include increasing profitability by 10 percent, while a long-term plan might include opening additional offices in other cities or expanding the practice into new legal areas. Without a plan, the law office goes about its business with no real direction. Successful law practices only happen with careful planning and the execution of good management decisions.

> *The simple fact is that most law offices do not plan for the future. They wait for the future to come get them; then they get pulled into it kicking and screaming. These [firms] are the victims of change; they never truly succeed; they never quite get out of the rut.*[11]

Why Legal Assistants Need to Learn to Develop Plans

As a legal assistant's career expands, he or she will be given more complex assignments, duties, and tasks. As the complexity of assignments increases, the ability to develop and execute plans is crucial. The following are some plans that legal assistants may prepare:

- Budgets for a legal assistant department
- Case budgets for a particular case (i.e., how much the law office will expend to bring a case to trial)

- Case plans (in conjunction with a supervising attorney), including which witnesses need to be deposed; which interrogatories, requests for production, and requests for admissions need to be issued, and to whom; which experts need to be hired; which strategies the office should pursue; what further investigation needs to be conducted, and so forth.
- Large projects, such as developing a litigation-support database in cases that have thousands of documents (legal assistants and others must plan how the documents will be entered into the computer, what program, service bureau, or technique will be the most successful, and so forth)
- Administrative projects that require planning, including computerizing a law office's time and billing system from a manual system, implementing a computerized docket control system, or setting up a new filing system or law library
- The office's mission statement and some strategic plans (in small law offices)
- Their own career plans (where they want to be in two to five years and how they are going to get there)

Planning skills are very important for a paralegal. One of the keys to good planning is to be organized and proactive. Learn how the attorney does things and stay a step ahead of him or her. If you know a deadline is coming up on the calendar, go to the attorney early to see what you can do to assist him or her. Do not wait for the attorney to come to you because the attorney has many other things to focus on. Poor planning leads to last minute work and rushes. Some things will come up at the last minute that cannot be avoided, but try to limit those occurrences by planning ahead and being prepared.

—Linda Rushton, CLA

The Mission Statement and Strategic Plans

A mission statement is a particular type of plan. The **mission statement** is a general, enduring statement of the purpose or intent of the law practice. It is a plan or vision stating what the firm is about and what are its goals and objectives. It puts forth the fundamental and unique purpose that sets it apart from other firms, identifies the firm's scope, and explains why it exists. For examples, see the mission statements in Figure 2-14.

All law practices need a vision: they need to know where they have been and where they are going. They need to have a few guiding principles and philosophies

mission statement
A general, enduring statement of the purpose or intent of the law practice.

**Figure 2-14
Law Office Mission
Statements**

Large law firm	The mission of the Davis, Saunders, & Lavely law firm is to deliver high-quality legal services to business clients nationwide through personalized, value-added service and a strict adherence to the highest ethical standards.
Corporate law department	The KGLPE law department seeks to offer the corporation the best legal services available while keeping costs to a minimum. The law department will utilize four divisions: labor, environmental, litigation, and general business. The use of in-house staff will be maximized. Only matters of vital importance to the corporation will be contracted out. The other departments of the corporation will be defined as our "clients". Our clients will be given the same high-quality legal services as provided by outside counsel. Our clients will be surveyed on an annual basis, and we will obtain a 90 percent average approval rating.
Small law firm	Woodson and Stetson is a full-service, client-centered law firm. Our goal is to provide outstanding, responsive services to our clients at a reasonable cost. We represent clients as we ourselves would want to be represented. We use a team approach to provide legal services to our clients, including lawyers, paralegals, and office associates to ensure a professional level of response to our clients' needs.

that motivate and determine the direction of the firm. The mission statement represents the foundation for priorities and all other plans. If the firm you work for has a mission statement, memorize and use it. Every idea, new client, new employee, equipment purchase—everything you do should be judged by whether it advances the mission of the firm. If it does not advance the mission, then it may not be right for the firm.

Mission statements may include when the firm began, who founded the firm, the philosophy of the founder(s), the nature of the practice (areas of experience and expertise), the geographic service area, the departments in the practice, the philosophies toward costs, income, growth, technology, client services, and personnel, and who the firm's clients are. Mission statements are not static; they should be changed and updated as long as everyone in the firm understands the change. A mission statement is a vision that keeps the firm headed in the right direction. Without one, a law practice may spend a considerable amount of time never knowing where it is headed.

Strategic planning has always been important, but the present circumstances make it imperative for law offices to consider strengths and weaknesses, evaluate the competition, and devise a game plan that will set the course to the future.

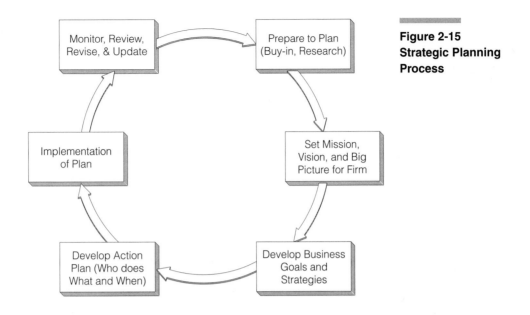

**Figure 2-15
Strategic Planning
Process**

Strategic planning is the process of determining the major goals of a firm and then adapting the courses of action and allocating resources necessary to achieve those goals. Figure 2-15 shows a diagram of the strategic planning process. For instance, a strategic plan may include expanding a firm's practice into additional areas of the law, such as adding a tax or labor law department. Before you can sell a legal service to someone, though, you must have a buyer; that is, you should not focus on what you want to sell but rather on what the buyer or the client wants to buy. Strategic plans usually answer the questions contained in Figure 2-16.

strategic planning
Determining the major goals of a firm and then adopting the courses of action necessary to achieve those goals.

[In successful firms there is a] constant action or movement toward objectives. . . . Standing still is viewed as stagnating or losing ground to competitors. There exists a general perception that if the firm is not continually evaluating its position, problems, or opportunities, movement toward the goals might not exist. The old adage, "If it ain't broke, don't fix it," is ignored. [Successful] law offices realize that there are always better ways to accomplish goals.[12]

Figure 2-16
Key Questions a Law
Office Strategic Plan
Should Answer

Who are our clients and what legal services will we provide? (see all of the questions regarding practice management in Figure 2-3)

Who will manage the firm? Is our governing structure still adequate? Evaluate the current methods used to set and implement firm policy.

Assess the effectiveness of the executive committee, managing partner, planning committee, compensation committee, and legal administrator.

What are the general goals of the firm? Rank them in order of importance.

What new geographic area of the country/world will we enter?

What sources of finance will we use?

Will we rent or purchase office space and equipment?

What kind of technology and systems will we use to provide our legal services to clients?

What marketing channels will we use to attract clients?

How will we achieve continual growth?

What was the firm's growth rate over the past three years? Can the projected growth rate for the next three years be established with any degree of certainty?

Does the firm have established bill rate requirements for legal staff? Are they adequate or should they be revisited?

What is the capability of the firm to meet its future needs within existing practice areas? Which areas need improvement?

What is the culture of the firm? Does it suit the firm well?

What kinds of insurance will we need to purchase (health, disability, life, malpractice)?

How many employees will we need and in what positions?

Should we use alternatives to permanent staff such as temporary workers, contract workers, or should we use outsourcing techniques?

How will we recruit, train, and retain the right people for our firm?

Will the firm merge with another firm to obtain a competitive advantage?

Environmental Analysis—Consider demographic, political, and economic factors when considering strategic planning. How will these factors affect how the firm will serve the clients?

Industry Analysis—Consider the legal environment as a whole, including surveys of other law firms, average profit margins, growth rates, costs, etc. How does the firm compare to industry averages?

Competitive Analysis—Who are the firm's major competitors? What are their strengths and weaknesses? What are your competitors' business strategies?

Internal Analysis—Compare your strategies with those of your major competitors, and compare your strengths and weaknesses to those of your competitors.

Determine Threats and Opportunities—Consider what new markets are the most attractive for the firm and then analyze the firm's competitive position in the marketplace, identify any threats that competitors may have, and identify opportunities resulting from market conditions or a competitor's weakness.

Ideas on How to Plan Effectively

The following are some ideas on how to plan effectively.

- **Gather timely, relevant information.** It is axiomatic that, without good information, you cannot possibly make an effective plan. Too many times, people make plans based on faulty information. Gathering timely and relevant information is one of the most important things you can do to make sure your plan will succeed. You can gather information from public libraries, law libraries, the Internet, Westlaw, LexisNexis, the American Bar Association (ABA), local, state, and national bar associations, law office surveys, consultants, other firms, and historical records from your own firm. Good information is a key to making good decisions.

- **Write all plans.** Goals and plans should be in writing as constant reminders of where you are supposed to be headed.

- **Involve everyone in the planning process.** Always ask for comments from anyone who would be affected by the plan. You want to build a consensus so that everyone will have input into the plan and will support it when it comes time to implement it. People promote plans that they perceive as being their own, either in part or as a whole. This is the "ownership" concept. Soliciting input from others opens the lines of communication and allows all firm members to feel that they have a stake in the action, that their thoughts are important, and that they are needed. When you are involving others in the process, do not judge their suggestions; listen to them and consider them. Your job is to facilitate communication and to provide a nonthreatening environment in which everyone can participate.

- **Stick to the plan.** It takes an amazing amount of patience to stick to a plan and follow through with what you started. It does a firm little good to make a detailed and wonderful plan and then scrap it two months later. It takes commitment from everyone involved to give the plan a chance to succeed.

- **Recognize that planning is a continuous process.** Planning is a continuous process of making improvements; it is not a one-time effort in which you develop a plan and then never revisit it. If all you do is make a plan and never follow it up or monitor it, you have wasted the firm's time.

- **Monitor the plan and communicate the results to others.** Always monitor the progress of the plan. One way to do this is to make a timeline or Gantt chart to track the expected progress over time. A **Gantt chart** is a plan or timeline of the projected begin and end dates of a project. A Gantt chart breaks a large project down into specific jobs or items that must be accomplished. As an item is finished, it can be marked completed (see Figure 2-17). Gantt charts are also good at simplifying and communicating complicated projects. Most people find charts more reader friendly than straight text.

Gantt chart
A plan or timeline of the projected begin and end dates of a project.

Figure 2-17   A Gantt Chart

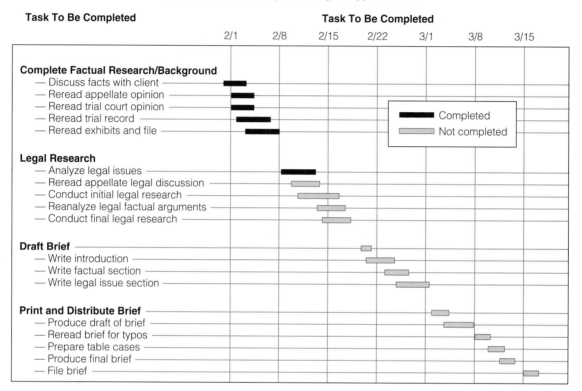

Gantt Chart Re: Drafting and Filing an Appellate Brief

Periodically, you should check the progress of the project to determine whether the plan needs to be revised or completely overhauled to accomplish its objectives. One way to do this is to hold monthly planning meetings or to otherwise communicate the progress of the plan to others by keeping them informed about how the project is going. If possible, you want to build into the plan quantifiable means to show others that the plan is working as expected and that resources are not being wasted.

MARKETING MANAGEMENT

marketing
The process of educating consumers on the quality legal services that a law office can provide.

Marketing is the process of educating consumers about the legal services the law office provides. It is not enough to simply service existing clients. Law firms, like other businesses in a competitive environment, must continue to bring in new business in order to grow and survive. Marketing has become an important element of management in today's law office. Marketing efforts include market research, discovering and developing a market niche regarding a client need that has previously been unrecognized or unmet, creating a "brand" name for the firm so that it is recognized by potential clients, and advertising efforts through brochures, word-of-mouth/referrals, networking, television, radio, and the Internet. Chapter 7 contains a full chapter on legal marketing.

ORGANIZING, POLICIES AND SYSTEMS

Organizing is the process of arranging people and physical resources to carry out plans and accomplish objectives. Effective legal administrators create order through setting policy and creating effective systems for accomplishing tasks. A **system** a consistent or organized way of doing something. A system allows you to create a set procedure for doing something as opposed to dealing with activities or problems in an ad hoc manner. Without a system, each time a legal service or an administrative function is performed, the person performing the task would rely solely on his or her memory to complete the task. Productivity and accuracy suffer when staff must recreate processes each time a task is done. By developing a system, staff members can take advantage of the experience and expertise of others in the law office. A system collects experience and expertise and passes it on to others. Systems preserve the procedures that have worked successfully in the past, but must be reviewed periodically to allow for future evolution. Systems guarantee quality because the same mistakes are not made twice.

Systems can be used for both substantive tasks and administrative tasks. A **substantive task** is a task that relates to the process of actually performing legal work for clients. An **administrative task** (or a business-related task) is one that relates to the internal practices and duties involved with operating or managing a law office.

Substantive systems include using form files, checklists, and detailed instructions to standardize many types of legal tasks. Certain areas of the law are particularly suitable for systems because of their routine nature, including: bankruptcy, divorces, adoptions, probate, estate planning, and workers' compensation.

Administrative tasks such as docket control, timekeeping and billing, purchasing, and human resource management can also be set up using an established system of procedures. A staff manual establishes administrative policies and procedures and documents how things will be accomplished administratively.

organizing
The process of arranging people and physical sources to carry out plans and accomplish objectives.

system
A consistent or organized way of doing something.

substantive task
A task that relates to the process of actually performing legal work for clients.

administrative task
A task relating to the internal practices and duties involved with operating or managing a law office.

Law Practice Policies and Procedures— the Staff Manual

Read and digest any staff manual provided.

You should know what it says and keep it updated as new policies are published. Despite the comments you may hear describing the manual as out of date, it will give you a good overview of office policies. And if the firm bothered to publish the manual, it obviously was important to someone involved in the firm's future, as well as yours. So until you are advised otherwise by someone in authority, presume that the manual states the rules.[13]

One of the main systems is a law office staff manual, also called a policy and procedures manual. The purpose of a staff manual is to set out in writing the standing policies and procedures of a law office. The types of policies covered by the staff manual depend on the office, but they can range from personnel policies and how files will be maintained to how letters and pleadings will be formatted (see Figure 2-18). Staff manuals establish and document an efficient and cost-effective way of handling the day-to-day operations of the firm. The manual allows everyone to operate under the same procedures and to quickly find consistent answers to common questions. Without a staff manual, each person develops his or her own particular method for accomplishing tasks. Law offices need uniformity so that elements are not missed or forgotten. Staff manuals can be used to guarantee each client the same high-quality legal services, every time.

In order for . . . staff to provide the quality service that clients require, you need to communicate to them your office and personnel policies and procedures in a clear, effective manner. A staff manual is a necessity to convey . . . policies efficiently and accurately.[14]

Staff manuals are particularly helpful when training new employees. New employees can immediately get a feel for how the firm operates and what procedures are to be followed just by reading the manual. This makes the orientation process quicker and less difficult. The idea that staff manuals are only needed in large firms is a misconception. Small law offices, legal aid offices, and government and corporate law departments need written procedures as well.

A small law office I know recently suffered a real crisis. The office had a law office manager that virtually ran all of the systems and procedures for the whole office. She handled all accounting and money transactions, staff payroll, billing, computer use and computer passwords, the firm's form files, everything. Unfortunately, she suffered an unexpected heart attack. She was the only one in the office that knew how all the systems worked. It took the rest of the staff months to piece everything together and the office itself really suffered.[15]

Section 1

Departments and Committees

1.1 Departments According to Principal Areas of Law
1.2 Committees

Section 2

Office Policies

2.1 Diversity
2.2 Equal Opportunity Employer
2.3 Policy on Sexual Harassment
2.4 Americans with Disabilities Act of 1990 (ADA)
2.5 The Family and Medical Leave Act of 1993
2.6 Code of Personal and Professional Conduct
2.7 Office Hours
2.8 Overtime
2.9 Quality Management/Client Relations
2.10 Weekly Time Report
2.11 Professional Attitude
2.12 Personal Appearance

Section 3

Personnel Policies and Benefits

3.1 Employee Classifications
3.2 Recruitment and Hiring
3.3 Training
3.4 Probation or Trial Period
3.5 Compensation

Section 4

Preparation of Correspondence, Memoranda, and Legal Documents

4.1 Letter Construction
4.2 Memoranda
4.3 Drafts
4.4 Legal Opinion Letters
4.5 Legal Documents

Section 5

Office Security and Emergency Procedures

5.1 Emergency Procedures
5.2 Medical Emergencies, Work Injuries, or Accidents
5.3 Data Protection
5.4 Disaster Planning and Recovery

Section 6

Financial Management

6.1 Timekeeping Records
6.2 Receipts
6.3 Disbursements
6.4 Petty Cash
6.5 Billing Procedures
6.6 Trust Account

**Figure 2-18
Partial Law Office
Staff Manual—Table
of Contents**

Source: Adapted from Wert, R., & Hatoff, H. (2004). *Law office policy and procedures manual* (4th ed., p. iii). American Bar Association.

Figure 2-18
(Continued)

Section 7

File System

7.1 Removal of Files from the Record Room
7.2 The File Opening Form and Worksheet
7.3 Opening a New File
7.4 Returning Files to the Record Room
7.5 Closing Files
7.6 Form Files

Section 8

Technology

8.1 Policy on the Use of Technology
8.2 Handling Computer Crashes
8.3 Dealing with Computer Viruses
8.4 Training
8.5 Word Processing
8.6 Network
8.7 Docket/Calendar Software
8.8 Time/Billing Software
8.9 Fax/Modems/Internet
8.10 LexisNexis/Westlaw
8.11 Security

Section 9

Library

9.1 The Function and Use of the Library
9.2 Location
9.3 The Librarian
9.4 Library Organization and Functions
9.5 Use by Non-Firm Personnel
9.6 Library Copies of the Firm's Work Product
9.7 Client Charges

What Systems or Subjects are Included in the Staff Manual?

Figure 2-18 contains a list of systems that are often found in staff manuals. Staff manuals usually cover such items as how the office is organized, ethical and confidentiality policies, personnel-related policies, the use of office equipment, and office procedures for opening new files. Staff manuals can be adapted to the needs of the specific law practice. In general, if management has to reiterate a policy more than once or twice on a matter of importance, the policy should be put in writing.

policy
A specific statement that sets out what is or is not acceptable.

procedure
A series of steps that must be followed to accomplish a task.

Drafting Policies and Procedures

Staff manuals can contain both policies and procedures. Although the concepts are similar, they also are very different from each other. A **policy** is a specific statement that sets out what is or is not acceptable (see Figure 2-13). A **procedure** is a series of steps that must be followed to accomplish a task. Some firms have separate manuals for policies and procedures. All policies and/or procedures should be detailed, accurate, and succinct; procedures should be clearly stated, easy to read, and should assign specific responsibilities, stating *who* is responsible for the tasks. In addition, whenever possible, a due date also is included so that staff members know exactly *when* items are due. When writing policies and procedures, a balance should be struck between having too many details (i.e., overregulating) and having too few. The aim is not to make a bureaucratic, detail-ridden manual, but to have a usable, practical guide.

Staff Manuals from an Ethics Perspective

Staff manuals also are important from an ethical point of view. The manual allows management to draft policies that will deter ethical violations. For instance, a common ethical problem is neglect of client matters. A manual can address this by stating which person is responsible for keeping the calendar, how items will be put on the calendar, and what steps will be taken to avoid missing the deadline. In addition, the staff manual can be used to set out policies on ethical situations, such as the need for strict confidentiality of client information.

Staff Manuals on the Law Office Intranet

An **intranet** is an internal information distribution system based on Internet technology. In short, it is a private "Internet" that is used only by law firm staff. When the staff manual is on an intranet, it is immediately accessible to all staff with access to a computer; it can be updated electronically; and it can save thousands of dollars in reduced paper and copying costs.

intranet
An internal information distribution system used only by a law firm staff.

> *The intranet is a good resource, especially in a large firm. It helps to get information to a large group of people who may be scattered across the nation in different office locations. I have always found the firm directory to be very helpful. Other helpful postings include computer information, such as when the computer system will be shut down for maintenance, or maps for the clients to find the office.*
>
> —Linda Rushton, CLA

An intranet can also be used to provide information related to

- Accounting and billing—Access to client time/billing records, firm accounting policies, and accounting forms
- Law library resources—Access to form files, brief banks, CD-ROM products, Westlaw, LexisNexis, and links to many legal sites on the Internet

- Human resources and benefits—Human resource information, including job openings, compensation plans, legal postings, benefit plans, and links to benefit-provider sites
- Continuing legal education—Information related to upcoming CLE seminars, and links to local and national bar associations
- Client tracking—Client directories, matter lists, contact information, matter numbers, and other client-related information
- Practice areas—Separate pages can be created for each of a firm's departments and specialties. Each specialty can have information specifically related to that area of the law, including Internet links to government regulations and statutes, case law, discussion groups, and resources developed by the firm itself to assist practitioners.

FACILITIES MANAGEMENT

facilities management
encompasses planning, designing, controlling, and managing a law office's building or office space.

Facilities management encompasses planning, designing, controlling, and managing a law office's building or office space. Facilities management includes a variety of subject areas, such as: property acquisition, moves/construction/remodeling, space planning/office design/furniture, parking, cleaning/maintenance/grounds, common areas, environmental considerations (lighting, electrical, climate, and plumbing), and security/safety/disaster recovery.

Property Acquisition

Property acquisition refers to acquiring space in which the law office will be housed, including purchasing a building/property or leasing office space. Property acquisition is an important and expensive proposition for any law office, whether it is a large law firm looking for a long-term lease for a number of floors in a downtown office building (to be near business clients) or a sole practitioner who concentrates on family law and might purchase a house or small building near a residential area. Depending on the office, the practice may want to be on public transportation routes, accessible from major highways, and other such considerations.

Moves/Construction/Remodeling

Facilities management also includes moving from one location to another, constructing a whole new office from scratch, or constructing/remodeling existing office space to meet new needs or demands. All of these areas include a great deal of planning and organizing.

Space Planning/Office Design/Furniture

Office space is important for many reasons; office space and decor help define the law office's image. The facility should be functional and practical, and it should work for the particular law office's structure and needs.

One of the first aspects of space planning that must be considered is the organization of the law office. Law office management must decide upon the needs of the office. For example, management must decide whether practice groups will be grouped together or apart; whether computers, files, and other equipment will be centralized or decentralized; what types of offices are needed (e.g., number and size of conference rooms, kitchen area, and separate postage and copy areas); and whether the office will need to expand in the near future. An effective way of determining needs is to survey the staff members, ask them what they think they need, and then use that information in the planning process. Some offices, especially medium- to larger-sized offices, hire consultants and architects to help with these as well as other issues.

Furniture should not only project an office's image but also provide sufficient work surfaces, be comfortable and usable, and efficiently use the space within the law office. There are thousands of different styles of furniture, including traditional (wood and plastic laminate); contemporary (wood, metal, and laminate); high-tech (glass, wood, and metal); and ergonomic (laminate, wood, and metal).

Many law offices use system furniture or module design, including movable partitions or panels, and work surfaces, file cabinets, and drawers that attach to the partitions instead of interior walls. The panels typically have electric cabling that runs through the bottom of each for electrical outlets. In this way, law offices can be completely flexible and use their space more wisely than ever before. The major disadvantages of interior landscaping are increased noise and decreased privacy. Interior landscaping has gained in popularity because of the increased cost of office space; minimizing the amount of space a law office uses reduces rent and maintenance costs.

Some studies have shown that the most negative feature of interior landscaping is not the increased noise but the lack of personal privacy, especially when short partitions that allow people to see over the top are used, and when the entryways face out, allowing others to see into the work space.

CORRELATION BETWEEN SPACE AND COST Any law office administrator will tell you that there is a direct correlation between the amount of office space needed and the cost. Office space has become increasingly more expensive, especially in metropolitan areas. Lease payments represent a large overhead expense, which can put pressure on cash flow because it is a fixed cost, meaning that it is incurred every month without relation to whether the office is having a good month, financially speaking. Thus, offices have struggled to become physically smaller and more compact and to use the space they have wisely.

Parking

Adequate parking for both employees and clients should be taken into consideration when choosing office space. Poor parking is a common complaint of law offices in downtown business districts.

Cleaning/Maintenance/Grounds

Facilities management also includes having the facility cleaned (typically through a cleaning service), repairing or replacing items that break, and being responsible for the office grounds, including lawn care, snow removal, and more.

Common Areas

Facilities management may also include being responsible for common areas in the office, such as the waiting room, kitchen areas, conference rooms, bathrooms, and storage rooms, to name a few.

Environmental Considerations

Environmental considerations include a variety of important topics, such as lighting, electrical, climate, and plumbing. Depending on the size of the office and the number of employees, each of these areas can be extremely technical and involve government standards, and many are operated by sophisticated computer systems. Many offices hire a facilities management company to provide maintenance and other services regarding environmental matters.

Security and Workplace Violence

> *Looking for a law firm or a lawyer's office? It can be easily identified by a dignified sign on the building's directory and outside the office suite's door. Inside, seated behind a desk, a receptionist greets visitors. She asks the guest's business and leaves to get him a cup of coffee. . . . He now has access to all of the firm's attorney and staff offices merely by strolling down the hall. This is not an unusual scenario [in small law offices]; it is one you may recognize from your own office, and one that may kill you.*[16]

Law office security and safety is an extremely important aspect of facilities management. Tragically, violence to attorneys, legal assistants, court personnel, and other legal professionals happens quite frequently. Disgruntled clients assault all kinds of law offices all over the country, from the rural solo practitioner to large downtown law firms in skyscrapers.

On July 1, 1993, Gian Luigi Ferri, a disgruntled client, entered the lobby of the law offices of Pettit & Martin, on the 34th floor of a downtown office building in San Francisco. He brought with him a number of automatic and semi-automatic guns. He reportedly walked through the offices, killing at random. The shooting spree left the gunman and eight others dead.

There are many ways to provide security, including installing security systems, limiting access to private areas of the office using locked and secure doors that open only with security cards, installing locking doors with buzzers at reception areas, hiring security guards, installing security cameras, issuing identification and/or building passes, and limiting elevator service after certain hours. Law offices simply cannot afford to ignore the security issues that face them. Figure 2-19 lists suggestions for tightening security. The type of security you use depends on the size of the firm, the type of building, and many other factors.

**Figure 2-19
Strengthening Law
Office Security**

- **Never allow free access throughout your office**—The golden rule of security is to **never** allow people free access throughout your office. Access to your office can be limited by restricting points of entry. If you are in a small building, lock the back door and do not allow the public to use it. Require the public to use the front door and have a receptionist there at all times, monitoring the entrance with a panic button that will contact the police or others in the case of an emergency.

  If your office is in a highrise building, security stations and/or a receptionist can be posted at the entrance to the building or your suite.
- **Limit the public to a waiting room with a locked door to inner offices**—A good way to limit access to your office is to secure your waiting room. Simply put, the door from your waiting room to your inner offices should be locked and have a buzzer installed. By having a locked door to your inner offices, you restrict access and require the visitor to check in with the receptionist. This is similar to many doctor's offices, where a receptionist sits behind a sliding window and sounds a buzzer that enables the visitor to enter the internal part of the office.
- **Issue security badges**—Another way to limit access in larger offices is to issue security cards or badges to personnel, and to require visitors to check in and be issued a visitor badge.
- **Use security cards**—Many offices use electronic locked doors that use a keyless entry system. If a person does not have a security card, he or she cannot open the locked door.
- **Monitor entrances**—Entrances to the building or suites should be monitored, when possible, by using security cameras, buzzers, security guards, keyless entry systems, or other such methods.
- **Remind staff about security issues and issue policies**—Always remind staff about the importance of security issues, and draft policies regarding security issues. Always be prepared.
- **Train staff members on security issues**—Whenever possible, staff members should be trained regarding safety awareness and security issues.
- **Large buildings may install metal detectors**—Metal detectors may be installed in large offices.

Law offices also need formal policies on security and workplace violence issues, such as the following:

Doors
The doors from the reception area to the interoffice corridors are to be locked at all times.

Admission of Visitors and Strangers
At no time shall persons other than employees of the Firm be allowed to roam at will, unescorted, through our offices. . . . If you encounter strangers in our offices who are unescorted and do not satisfactorily identify themselves, please advise the receptionist, or, if it is after hours, contact the Police if such persons' refuse to identify themselves or leave.

Source: Wert, & Hatoff. (2004). *Law office policy and procedures manual* (p. 147). American Bar Association.

Workplace Violence
It is the policy of the firm to expressly prohibit any acts or threats of violence by any party against any employee in or about the firm's facilities or elsewhere at any time. The firm takes a zero-tolerance policy toward any type of workplace violence. It is the commitment of the firm

1. *To provide a safe and healthy work environment.*
2. *To take prompt remedial action against anyone who engages in any threatening behavior or acts of violence or who uses any abusive or threatening language or gestures on the firm's premises or while on firm business.*
3. *To take appropriate action when dealing with employees, former employees, or visitors to the firm's facilities who engage in such behavior. Action may include disciplinary action including termination, notifying the police, and prosecuting violators of this policy to the maximum extent of the law.*
4. *To prohibit employees, former employees, and visitors, other than law enforcement personnel, from bringing firearms or other weapons onto the firm's premises.*

SAFETY   Safety issues include ensuring the building has a sprinkler system, fire alarms, emergency power/lighting, fire escapes, and similar features. All law offices should also have an evacuation plan and policies in their firm's staff manual regarding what to do in case of a fire, earthquake, or bomb threat. A policy should be in place regarding what to do in the instance of a medical emergency, work injury, or accident. It is also prudent for the law office to have safety related items such as bandages, gauze, and related items on hand. Larger offices may have oxygen and more advanced medical supplies as well. Occasional fire drills (and related drills) are also prudent and advised.

DISASTER RECOVERY PLANNING   Disaster recovery planning also tends to fall under the scope of facilities management. All law offices should have a disaster recovery plan in place that can be implemented in the case of a disaster. The

disaster recovery plan includes information on how the office will rebuild and recover from a total disaster. Copies of the disaster recovery plan should be kept off-site. It is important to have information and plans in place that can be implemented at a moment's notice.

Typical information contained in a disaster recovery plan would include the following:

- Who is in charge of overseeing implementation of the disaster recovery operation? What key individuals make up the disaster recovery team, and what are their functions and responsibilities? Who will be contacted, and how? Where is the designated meeting place (and an alternative) if the whole facility is unavailable?
- What services/areas/departments have been determined as vital to the recovery operation? What are the steps, components, and alternative strategies for making each area/department operational? What will each department require in terms of resources (computers, minimal office space, desk, chairs, information, etc.) to be operational? All of this must be put in writing, and a copy should be maintained off-site.
- How do firm personnel obtain information and instructions on what to do when a disaster happens?
- Where are important papers and computer backup data located? Important documents should always be maintained off-site in the case of a disaster. These include copies of leases; names, addresses, and phone numbers of all staff; bank account information; copies of insurance policies; a listing of all clients, including contact information for the client and opposing counsel in cases; complete firm-wide inventory list (computers, furniture, art, library books, fixtures, etc.); disaster recovery plans for each department; and computer backup tapes.
- In the case of a disaster, what vendors and companies have been identified in advance who can help to assist with restoration, and who are the contact people for these vendors?

If you wait until the disaster occurs to start planning, it's too late. By that time, you could lose everything. If everything *is* lost, can the firm recover? Can the law office continue as a business? What are the ethical problems with losing everything related to a client's case? If a law office of any size loses everything in a disaster, there is a good chance that it will not be able to recover; that's why disaster recovery planning is so important.

disaster recovery plan
A disaster recovery plan includes information on how the law office will rebuild and recover from a total disaster.

OFFICE SERVICES MANAGEMENT

Office services management refers to a number of internal systems and services in a law office. Office service responsibilities include management of the mail room, copiers and copy facility, file/records management (discussed in Chapter 9), telecommunications (including telephone systems, voice mail, fax machines, and video conferencing), among others.

office services management
It refers to the administration of a number of internal systems and services in a law office. These include mail, copy, fax, and telecommunication services, among others.

Mail Room

Medium and large law offices have mail rooms that manage and sort incoming mail. They also weigh and place postage on mail with either a postage meter device or electronic means. They may also coordinate overnight delivery services. In small law offices, a clerk, receptionist, or legal secretary may perform these services.

Copy Machines

Copy machines are a staple of every law office, regardless of size or type. Law offices must routinely copy documents for internal files, clients, courts, opposing counsel, and others. While the delivery of documents through electronic means is popular, there is no end in sight for the copier's usage. It is not uncommon, even in a solo practitioner's office, to make tens of thousands of copies a year. Some larger offices have a centralized copy center or department that has its own staff. Other law offices have one or more self-serve copy machines located throughout the office. Some offices have both a centralized department, which handles large documents, and self-serve copy machines for smaller jobs.

As an alternative to the high cost of purchasing and maintaining copy machines, some law offices outsource this function to a vendor. The vendor provides the copy machine, maintenance, supplies, and personnel. In many cases, the vendor is given office space and provides these services on-site.

BILLING FOR CLIENT COPIES   Making sure that clients are properly billed for copies made for their case can be problematic, given the larger number of cases and copies. Some offices have staff members complete expense slips detailing which client the copies were made for, how many copies were made, and why. Some copy machines allow the user to enter a client identification number, which then tracks the number of copies to be billed to each client, while other machines use client copy cards to calculate the number of copies.

File/Records Management

Law offices of all types must have an effective file/records management system that allows the practice to store, track, and retrieve information about cases in a logical, efficient, and expeditious manner. File/records management is covered in detail in Chapter 9.

Telecommunications

Telecommunications is a rapidly evolving area that has many aspects important to law offices. Among these are telephone systems, voice mail, fax machines, and video conferencing.

TELEPHONE EQUIPMENT   Telephones are vital to any law office because they are the means by which staff members communicate with clients, opposing counsel, courts, witnesses, and one another.

Telephone systems for law offices can cost from $1,000 to $100,000 or more, depending on the number of phone stations and outgoing lines needed.

VOICE MAIL   Voice mail is a computerized telecommunications system that stores and delivers voice messages. Callers are able to leave a detailed message directly, without going through a secretary or other individual where messages can be distorted or miscommunication can take place. An individual can then retrieve his or her messages—either on- or off-site—by dialing his other "mailbox." Voice mail is available 24 hours a day, so clients can leave messages for people even when the office is not open. Voice mail is an integral part of many law offices.

FAX MACHINES   Fax machines are used by most law offices. Fax machines allow a user to electronically transmit a document's image to a receiving fax machine at another location, which prints the document that was sent. Fax machines are easy to operate and come in hundreds of styles with many features. Some fax machines work in conjunction with a computer system and allows a user to fax a document, such as a word processing file, from his or her computer.

Faxes have become so accepted in the legal community that many courts allow documents to be faxed if the documents are not more than 10 to 15 pages long.

FAXES AND CONFIDENTIALITY   Faxes should be sent very carefully because an improper or misdirected fax transmission can lead to breach of client confidentiality, loss of attorney-client privilege, and legal malpractice. All fax cover pages for law offices should have some kind of confidentiality disclaimer on them, such as the following:

> CONFIDENTIALITY NOTICE—This fax message contains legally confidential and privileged information intended for the sole use of the individual(s) or organizations named above. If you are not the intended recipient of this fax message, you are hereby notified that any dissemination, distribution, or copy of this message is strictly prohibited. If you have received this fax in error, please notify us immediately by telephone and return this fax to us by mail.

Other precautions that can be taken to ensure fax information stays confidential include assuring that everyone using the fax machine knows how to use it correctly; making sure that everyone operating the fax machine understands that a misdirected fax can destroy client confidentiality and the attorney-client privilege and can result in charges of malpractice; and requiring the sender to check to make sure the material has been received.

> *In a pending asbestos case being heard in the Circuit Court for Baltimore, Maryland, a temporary secretary for one of the defense firms pushed the wrong precoded telephone number button on the fax machine's automatic dialer and mistakenly sent a top secret report on the psychological profiles of prospective jurors to the opposing side. The plaintiff's counsel, in return, shared the report with the other plaintiffs' firms. As a result, Judge Marshall Levin felt compelled to dismiss all 51 jurors selected for the nation's largest consolidation of asbestos personal injury cases (9,032 plaintiffs and 10 defendants). In his oral opinion, Judge Levin said that, because the defense firm did not take reasonable precautions to prevent the mistake, the plaintiffs' attorneys know the inner most thinking of the defense counsel.*[17]

TELECOMMUNICATIONS AND CLIENT CONFIDENTIALITY   Client confidentiality should always be considered when dealing with phone systems. This is especially true considering the amount of time that legal assistants spend on the phone. Users should never broadcast client names over the law office's intercom/paging system; users should also be very careful about who is in the room when a client's case is being discussed on the phone. Conversations on mobile phones, particularly those that include confidential or sensitive information, should be limited, if possible. Some radios/scanners have the ability to pick up these frequencies.

Video Conferencing

Video conferencing allows users in remote sites to see and hear one another via a monitor and speaker using telephone lines, computer equipment, and a camera. Medium- and larger-size law offices may have these internally. Smaller law offices can use a vendor for video conferencing. Video conferencing may be used internally to connect remote offices for a meeting and, on occasion, may be used for depositions, among other things.

TECHNOLOGY AND INFORMATION SYSTEMS MANAGEMENT

It is difficult to overestimate the impact that technology has had on the practice of law in the last 20 years. Technology, computers, networks, mobile computing, and information systems in general have completely changed the way that legal professionals practice law and run a law office business. There is virtually no aspect of how legal services are delivered to clients and how a law office is operated that has not been affected. While technology has greatly increased productivity and efficiency, enhanced systems for communicating, and made researching and finding information easier and more accessible, all this has come at a price. Many law offices, large and small, struggle to keep up with technology advancements and with finding the money and resources to continue to enhance their technology. Recent surveys found that, on average, solo practitioners spend approximately $2,063 on technology annually, small firms spend between $3,000 and $5,000 per attorney, medium-size firms spend approximately $17,700 per attorney, and large law firms spend an average of $25,800 per attorney. The commitment to and reliance on technology at medium and larger firms are substantial.

> *Clients who have mastered technology in their businesses have required their law firms to be technologically advanced. Many firms have been forced to meet the challenges, regardless of their inclination and whether or not the necessary funds were in the budget.*[18]

Most law offices, even small ones, must now have dedicated staff to support the myriad of computer systems in a typical law practice. Most medium and large firms must have a host of computer professionals including a chief information officer, who are solely responsible for the firm's technology. Figure 2-20 shows a partial list of common technology in law offices. The list grows every year as new technology is introduced.

> *Today, we have an IT budget of approximately 4 percent of our annual revenues and an IT staff of 30 supporting more than 150 software applications used by more than 900 users in 11 offices worldwide.*[19]

Legal Assistants and Technology

> *Keeping abreast of the latest changes in technology and online information resources will continue to be extremely important for our [legal assistant] profession . . . the ability to find information quickly and then analyze, sort, and pare it down into a more manageable, useful format will [always] be in high demand.*[20]

**Figure 2-20
Partial List of Typical
Technology in a Law
Office**

Hardware (and Software) Used by Technical Staff	Software Used by Legal Professionals or Administrators	Telecommunications
Desktop or laptop computer, monitor, speakers, storage devices, and mouse for every staff member	Word processing	Internet
Networked or stand-alone printer	Spreadsheet	Intranet
Networked or stand-alone color printer	Database	Extranet
Multifunction printer (printer, fax, scanner, copier)	Presentation	Westlaw/LexisNexis/other online service
Local network servers, cards, wireless, etc.	E-mail	Instant messaging
Wide-area network servers	Internet browser	Blogs
Laptop computers	Docket control/calendar	
PDAs (personal digital assistants, handheld computers)	Litigation support	
Mobile phones	Time and billing	
Scanner	Accounting	
Operating system software on every computer, laptop, and handheld device	Case management	
Virus protection software	Document assembly	
Digital projector	Document management	
Digital camera	Electronic discovery	
Digital video camera	Knowledge management	
Portable printer	PDF creation	
Firewall	Scanning/optical character recognition	
Central storage devices	Speech recognition	
Tape backup	Trial presentation	
Digital printers	Legal-specific programs	
Computerized telecommunication equipment	Graphic/illustration programs	
Computerized security systems	Project management	
Web design/development software	Citation checking	
Web site management	Conflict checking	
Document sharing software	Transcript/deposition management	
Portable hard drives	Contact management	
Remote access software		

	Daily	Weekly	Occasionally	Never
CD-ROM	14.3%	20.5%	54.3%	11.0%
E-mail	97.8%	0.4%	0.9%	0.9%
Handheld computer (PDA)	11.6%	2.8%	6.0%	79.5%
Internet	95.1%	4.4%	0.4%	0.0%
Laptop computer	12.8%	7.8%	28.9%	50.5%
Multimedia equipment	7.0%	5.6%	54.4%	33.0%
Scanner	20.8%	27.6%	36.7%	14.9%
Video conferencing	0.5%	2.8%	35.3%	61.5%
Wireless phone	27.4%	6.4%	24.2%	42.0%
Software				
Accounting	24.5%	8.0%	14.6%	52.8%
Calendar/docket	60.6%	8.7%	12.5%	17.1%
Case management	31.6%	11.5%	18.7%	38.3%
Client relationship management	15.0%	5.8%	12.1%	67.0%
Document assembly	27.8%	10.5%	11.0%	50.7%
Document management	42.7%	7.0%	10.8%	39.0%
Electronic discovery	8.6%	9.0%	23.3%	59.0%
Knowledge management	14.4%	5.4%	14.4%	65.8%
Legal online service	22.3%	19.5%	29.3%	28.8%
Litigation support	15.5%	11.7%	19.7%	53.1%
PDF creation	26.9%	23.1%	20.8%	29.2%
Practice management	9.2%	4.9%	12.1%	73.8%
Scanning/OCR	22.9%	27.1%	29.4%	20.6%
Speech recognition	0.0%	0.5%	4.3%	95.2%
Time and billing	47.2%	6.5%	6.9%	39.4%
Trial presentation	2.3%	7.2%	34.4%	55.5%
Word processing	92.7%	5.5%	1.4%	0.5%

Figure 2-21
How Legal Assistants Use Technology at Work

Source: Hughes, R. (2005, May/June). Peering into the future. *Legal Assistant Today,* 58.

Figure 2-21 shows the results of a 2005 survey regarding how practicing legal assistants are using technology in the workplace. The survey shows that e-mail, the Internet, word processing, calendar/docket control, and time and billing programs are used the most on a daily basis. The survey found that more than 90 percent of the legal assistants surveyed worked in a law office with networked computers. Interestingly, the survey found the nearly 60 percent of the legal assistants surveyed provided input into the technology decisions that were made at their firms.

Hardware

The selection of currently available computer hardware is overwhelming. Law offices can choose from many different types of computer hardware and manufacturers, depending on the type of operation and objectives they have. Options include desktop, laptop, handheld, wireless, and mobile technology. Figure 2-22 shows that small law firms have access to much of the same technology as large firms; this is largely due to the wide selection of available hardware and the fact that computer technology prices continue to fall.

Mobile computing is also changing the way legal professionals practice. Legal assistants and attorneys have nearly constant access to their firms and information via networks, wireless technology, and the Internet. Legal professionals can access

Figure 2-22
Computer Hardware
Used in Law Offices
by Attorneys

Source: 2003 ABA Legal
Technology Resource Center
Survey Report, Law Office
Technology, ABA 2004, p. 115.
Reprinted by permission.

	NUMBER OF LAWYERS AT ALL LOCATIONS					
	TOTAL	**1**	**2–9**	**10–49**	**50–99**	**100 OR MORE**
Cellular/wireless phone	79.5%	78.6%	89.3%	75.4%	70.6%	72.2%
Desktop computer	76.2%	95.2%	72.0%	79.7%	70.6%	58.3%
Handheld/personal digital assistant (PDA)	46.4%	45.2%	46.7%	37.7%	52.9%	61.1%
Notebook/laptop computer	53.1%	47.6%	54.7%	49.3%	47.1%	66.7%
Server	31.4%	19.0%	41.3%	29.0%	35.3%	27.8%
Digital projector	13.8%	11.9%	5.3%	20.3%	29.4%	13.9%
Digital still camera	25.5%	28.6%	36.0%	23.2%	23.5%	5.6%
Digital video camera	11.3%	14.3%	16.0%	8.7%		8.3%
Inkjet printer	30.1%	28.6%	40.0%	31.9%	17.6%	13.9%
Laser printer (b&w)	56.1%	57.1%	50.7%	56.5%	47.1%	69.4%
Laser printer (color)	12.6%	2.4%	5.3%	17.4%	35.3%	19.4%
Multifunction printer	27.2%	33.3%	25.3%	27.5%	17.6%	27.8%
Portable printer	7.5%	2.4%	10.7%	4.3%		16.7%
Flatbed scanner	19.2%	28.6%	18.7%	15.9%	23.5%	13.9%
Portable or handheld scanner	1.3%		2.7%	1.4%		
Sheetfed scanner	14.6%	16.7%	8.0%	18.8%	17.6%	16.7%
Firewall	28.0%	42.9%	33.3%	17.4%	17.6%	25.0%
CD-ROM drive	49.8%	57.1%	58.7%	52.2%	23.5%	30.6%
CD-ROM jukebox or tower	5.9%	2.4%	5.3%	8.7%		8.3%
CD-R drive	22.2%	33.3%	25.3%	18.8%	11.8%	13.9%
CD-RW drive	23.4%	47.6%	28.0%	15.9%	5.9%	8.3%
DVD drive	19.7%	28.6%	24.0%	13.0%	11.8%	16.7%
DVD recorder	5.4%	16.7%	5.3%	1.4%		2.8%
Portable hard drive	5.0%	7.1%	5.3%	2.9%		8.3%
Tape backup drive	7.9%	11.9%	12.0%	4.3%		5.6%
Zip or super disk drive	11.7%	26.2%	13.3%	7.2%		5.6%

data from the courthouse, their homes, the road, and nearly anywhere in the world. Court-bound lawyers ccan now take entire cases with them on a laptop, including pleadings, transcripts of arguments and proceedings, court records, depositions, discovery, and millions of documents, all accessible and ready to be retrieved.

Software

The hours spent stuffing overnight mail envelopes with legal documents have been replaced with a push of a button sending hundreds of pages of documents instantly to multiple recipients over the globe; our trial exhibits are in multimedia form, displayed to judges and juries over flat-panel monitors; and millions of pages of documents are stored on laptops wirelessly networked together in the courtroom, available to our trial team for instant access and display.[21]

Law offices have a wide selection of software that includes general business and productivity programs, general legal programs (such as time and billing), and legal programs designed for a specific type of practice (such as software designed for professionals practicing in the area of taxes). Figure 2-23 shows some widely available programs that are being used in many law offices. As in Figure 2-22's hardware survey, notice that many small law offices have access to much of the same software as large firms.

ELECTRONIC MAIL Electronic mail is the single most used software application by legal professionals (see Figures 2-21 and 2-23).

| | NUMBER OF LAWYERS AT ALL LOCATIONS | | | | | |
	TOTAL	1	2–9	10–49	50–99	100 OR MORE
Accounting	23.9%	51.4%	23.2%	16.9%	6.7%	15.2%
Antivirus	59.2%	83.8%	60.9%	47.5%	60.0%	48.5%
Case management	24.4%	13.5%	33.3%	25.4%	33.3%	12.1%
Citation checking	31.9%	16.2%	42.0%	30.5%	40.0%	27.3%
Conferencing	16.4%	10.8%	7.2%	10.2%	20.0%	51.5%
Conflict checking	24.4%	13.5%	26.1%	22.0%	33.3%	33.3%
Contacts	62.4%	56.8%	59.4%	57.6%	66.7%	81.8%
Customer relationship management (CRM)	20.2%	16.2%	26.1%	22.0%	13.3%	12.1%
Databases	16.4%	18.9%	13.0%	15.3%	20.0%	21.2%
Docket/calendaring (not rules based)	19.7%	21.6%	23.2%	20.3%	20.0%	9.1%
Docket/calendaring (rules based)	6.1%	13.5%	5.8%	3.4%	6.7%	3.0%
Document assembly (generic)	30.5%	32.4%	31.9%	27.1%	26.7%	33.3%
Document assembly (specialized)	10.3%	21.6%	8.7%	5.1%		15.2%
Document management	25.4%	10.8%	17.4%	25.4%	20.0%	60.6%
Document sharing	27.7%	16.2%	26.1%	30.5%	20.0%	42.4%
E-mail	81.7%	83.8%	81.2%	86.4%	53.3%	84.8%
Employee monitoring	2.8%		2.9%	1.7%	13.3%	3.0%
Encryption	6.6%	8.1%	5.8%	3.4%	13.3%	9.1%
Fax	62.4%	67.6%	60.9%	62.7%	46.7%	66.7%
Firewall	24.4%	48.6%	24.6%	13.6%	20.0%	18.2%
Groupware	23.5%	5.4%	17.4%	35.6%	26.7%	33.3%
Instant messaging	15.5%	16.2%	21.7%	8.5%	20.0%	12.1%
Integrated desktop	30.0%	29.7%	31.9%	32.2%	13.3%	30.3%
Knowledge management	7.0%	5.4%	5.8%	3.4%	6.7%	18.2%
Litigation support	11.7%	2.7%	7.2%	15.3%	26.7%	18.2%
Presentation	32.4%	21.6%	24.6%	30.5%	53.3%	54.5%
Project management	8.5%	8.1%	8.7%	5.1%	26.7%	6.1%
Redlining	40.4%	40.5%	29.0%	42.4%	40.0%	60.6%
Remote access	46.5%	29.7%	33.3%	52.5%	53.3%	78.8%
Scanning images	27.7%	29.7%	20.3%	32.2%	53.3%	21.2%
Scanning text (OCR)	28.6%	29.7%	21.7%	33.9%	33.3%	30.3%

Figure 2-23
Computer Software Used in Law Offices by Attorneys

Source: 2003 ABA Legal Technology Resource Center Survey Report, Law Office Technology, ABA 2004, pp. 164–165. Reprinted by permission.

(Continued)

Figure 2-23
Computer Software
Used in Law Offices
by Attorneys
(Continued)

	NUMBER OF LAWYERS AT ALL LOCATIONS					
	TOTAL	1	2–9	10–49	50–99	100 OR MORE
Specialized practice	19.2%	16.2%	30.4%	11.9%	26.7%	9.1%
Spreadsheets	46.0%	48.6%	39.1%	47.5%	60.0%	48.5%
Time and billing	45.5%	35.1%	40.6%	52.5%	73.3%	42.4%
Time entry	37.1%	32.4%	33.3%	42.4%	53.3%	33.3%
Transcript/deposition management	8.9%	5.4%	4.3%	10.2%	20.0%	15.2%
Trial presentation	4.7%	2.7%	1.4%	5.1%	20.0%	6.1%
Voice recognition	5.6%	10.8%	8.7%	3.4%		
Web browser	62.9%	59.5%	63.8%	61.0%	40.0%	78.8%
Web site Design/development	6.6%	10.8%	5.8%	6.8%		6.1%
Web site management	5.2%	10.8%	4.3%	5.1%		3.0%
Word processing	70.9%	78.4%	69.6%	67.8%	80.0%	66.7%

Electronic mail (e-mail) allows users to send and receive messages using a computer. When an Internet account is opened, the user is given an e-mail address and can then send and receive messages. Hundreds of millions of people use e-mail to communicate every day.

There are many advantages to using e-mail: messages can be sent, almost instantaneously, nearly anywhere in the world; e-mail is very inexpensive (the cost of an Internet account); word processing, sound, and graphic files can be attached to e-mail messages; messages can be sent, read, and replied to at the user's convenience; e-mail prevents telephone tag; messages can be sent to groups of people at the same time; users can get their messages from anywhere; and messages can be saved, tracked, and managed electronically. A common client complaint is that legal professionals are often very busy and hard to reach. E-mail allows legal professionals and clients to communicate with one another quickly and conveniently.

E-Mail in the Legal Environment

E-Mail is now a major means of communicating with clients, other attorneys, and courts, and most legal assistants use e-mail in their jobs every day. E-mail is being used in legal organizations for everything from routine correspondence to billing, newsletters, and filing court papers (see Figure 2-24). Most clients now demand e-mail access to their lawyers and legal assistants. The security of e-mail has long been a concern to legal professionals, but in a recent survey, 63 percent of legal organizations indicated that they now send confidential or privileged communications/documents to clients via e-mail. The issue of security can be handled a number of ways, including requiring clients to provide oral or written consent to sending confidential information via e-mail, adding a confidentiality statement at the end of all e-mails, using encryption software, or simply not using e-mail to send confidential documents. In addition, new uses of e-mail arise often; the service of process by e-mail has even been approved by a few courts.

Figure 2-24 How E-mail is Being Used in Legal Organizations

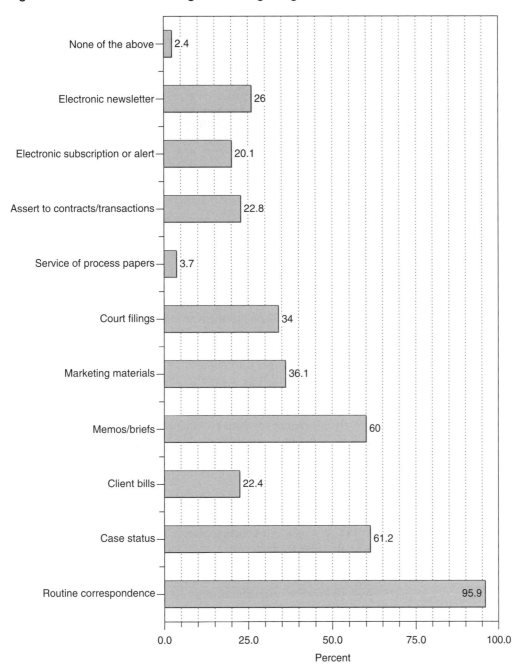

2003 Legal Technology Survey Report—Law Office Technology American Bar Association, 2004, p.107

E-Mail Encryption and Digital Signatures

Because e-mail can pass through many network servers before it reaches its destination, it is subject to being read by system administrators, hackers, or others. E-mail is often considered to be more like a postcard than a sealed letter in this respect. Some legal organizations use encryption software to protect confidential e-mails sent to others. Encryption software is used to lock e-mail so that it can be opened only by the intended recipient.

Business E-Mail Etiquette and Tips   Most people are familiar with e-mail. However, there is a difference between using e-mail for personal use and business use. In business, you must be very careful about your e-mail usage. Below are important tips for using e-mail in a law office setting.

- *Be succinct and clear, and use short paragraphs*—Whenever possible, keep your e-mails short and to the point. You should be as clear as possible in your messages so the reader does not have to ask for clarification regarding something you wrote. Use paragraphs liberally. Long paragraphs are hard to read on a computer screen, and it is easy to lose your place, particularly if you have to scroll up and down the message.
- *Spell-check and reread your e-mails*—Most e-mail programs have a spell-check function; use it whenever possible. Many users send e-mails full of spelling and grammar errors that may change the meaning of the message. Before sending your e-mails, reread them to make sure they make sense. Remember, you will be using e-mail to correspond with clients, so it shouldn't be sloppy.
- *Be careful to treat e-mail as business correspondence*—E-mails cannot be retrieved once they are sent. They are written records that are kept by the recipients, so be extremely careful about what you send and make sure that you can live with the message. When in doubt, do not send it. Also, remember that the recipient cannot see your body language or interpret your tone, so be careful how you phrase things.
- *If a message is unclear, ask for clarification*—If you are unsure about a message someone has sent you, ask for clarification and do not assume you know the answer.
- *Be careful of "Reply All"*—Sometimes users get e-mail with 20 other people copied on it. If the user selects "Reply," only the sender of the original e-mail will get a response, but selecting "Reply All" will send a reply to all 20 of the other recipients. Far too often, a user intends to send a personal message to the sender of the e-mail and mistakenly selects "Reply All." Before you select "Reply All," make sure you really want to send your e-mail to everyone on the original message.
- *Do not use e-mail to communicate with clients regarding sensitive information*— Since Internet e-mail can pass through many network servers where the e-mail can be read, it is probably better not to use e-mail at all for communicating with clients about sensitive information; if in doubt, always ask the client first.
- *Double-check the recipient of your e-mail*—Often users intend to send e-mail to one person and accidentally select the wrong person. Always double-check the e-mail address to make sure you entered the correct one.

- *Limit each e-mail message to one topic*—It is difficult to decide where to file multiple-topic e-mails, and it is sometimes difficult to follow up on them. There could be multiple follow-up actions buried in one e-mail.
- *Always password-protect word processing and other documents sent to clients*—By password-protecting documents, you add some degree of security to the attachment with minimal effort.

Problems with E-Mail   While e-mail is inexpensive and convenient, it is not perfect. Keep the following considerations in mind when using e-mail.

- *Do not assume that an e-mail was read just because you sent it*—Like any other form of written communication, e-mail can be lost, unopened, or accidentally deleted.
- *E-mail relies on computer technology that fails from time to time*—E-mail works only if the computer networks, telephone lines or other technology, and the recipient's computer hardware and software are working correctly. If any of these fail, your message will not reach the recipient.
- *Be careful what you say in e-mails, since they can be forwarded to others*—The nature of an e-mail is that it can be easily forwarded to another person. For example, you may send an e-mail to X about Y, and X can immediately forward it to Y.
- *E-mail security can be breached*—As noted before, e-mail is not necessarily confidential, and e-mail security can be breached in many ways, including the following:
  - Leaving confidential e-mails open on your computer screen for others to read over your shoulder
  - Leaving your office for lunch or a break while signed into your e-mail program
  - Printing e-mails that others can find (such as at a network printer)
  - Using a password such as "password" or names of family members that would be easy for others to guess

E-Mail Errors

It is important to be careful when using e-mail. Errors can happen several different ways and may result in malpractice claims against the legal organization. Some common errors include the following:

- *Sending an ill-conceived e-mail to a client or others before it is carefully considered*—Unlike a letter placed in the outgoing mailbox that can be retrieved a few hours later, once the user presses the "Send" button, e-mail is gone.
- *Sending e-mail to unintended parties*—It is easy to use the "Reply All" command to send a private message to a group of people unintentionally, or to click on the wrong e-mail address. Depending on the content of the message, errors like these can damage a client's case, particularly when e-mail is sent to the opposition.
- *Sending the wrong attachments*—Since files can be sent as attachments to e-mails, it is particularly important to ensure that the correct file is attached. It is easy to attach the wrong file to an e-mail that might be devastating to a

client's case. This can be avoided by opening the file after it is attached to the e-mail to make sure it is the correct one.

- *Typing errors*—Typing errors, such as leaving words out, can substantially change the meaning of a sentence. For example, in a client e-mail you might intend to type "We don't recommend that you do this," but instead you type "We recommend that you do this." While you have left only one word out, that word could be crucial to how the client proceeds.

E-Mail Confidentiality

As discussed earlier, confidentiality while using e-mail to communicate with clients is an important issue. The *ABA Model Rules of Professional Conduct* generally state that an attorney cannot reveal information about a client's matter unless the client consents to it.[22] The ABA Ethics Committee looked at the confidentiality of e-mail exchanges between attorneys and clients and concluded that an attorney can communicate with clients over e-mail without encryption. The Ethics Committee stated that e-mail affords users a reasonable standard of expectation of privacy, similar to that of a telephone call, and that unencrypted e-mail could be used to communicate with a client.

However, the ABA also found that an attorney had a duty to consider the sensitivity of the issue being communicated, what it would mean to the client's representation if the communication were disclosed, and the relative security of the contemplated means of communication. Arguably, the ABA wants legal professionals to use a common sense standard when using e-mail or other forms of communication with clients. If communication with a client is highly sensitive, then the legal professional should check with the client about whether a more secure form of communication is warranted.

Practical considerations for using e-mail ethically include the following:

- Having a policy for the legal organization regarding the use of e-mail and how it will be used to communicate with clients
- Consulting clients about what type of information they want to communicate via e-mail, how often the client receives or responds to e-mail, and other information about the particulars of the client's specific e-mail system or habits
- Making sure the e-mail addresses are accurately entered so that client communication is not sent to others by mistake
- Sending a test e-mail to a client to ensure the right e-mail address is being used
- Adding a confidentiality statement to all client e-mails—this is similar to statements accompanying many fax cover pages that state that the information is intended solely for the recipient and any third party who receives it should immediately forward it or destroy it
- Not using e-mail at all for particularly sensitive information

WORD PROCESSING/SPREADSHEETS/DATABASE MANAGEMENT/PRESENTATION SOFTWARE　　Word processing, spreadsheets, databases, and presentation software are some of the most commonly used software by legal professionals. They are used to draft documents and correspondence, make financial calculations and projections, track and organize documents, and present information to fact finders.

DOCKET CONTROL/CALENDARING/CASE MANAGEMENT   Docket control, calendaring, and case management are covered in detail in Chapter 7; these programs are generally used to track, organize, and manage the many appointments and deadlines in a law office.

TIME AND BILLING   Timekeeping and billing software automate the process of tracking a timekeeper's billable hours, billing clients, and posting payments to a client's account. Timekeeping and billing is covered in detail in Chapter 5.

DOCUMENT MANAGEMENT   **Document management software** organizes, controls, distributes, and allows for extensive searching of electronic documents typically in a networked environment. Document management software allows a legal organization to file documents electronically so they can be found by anyone in the organization, even when there are hundreds of users spread across offices throughout the country. Document management software goes far beyond the file management capabilities in operating system software. It is the electronic equivalent of a filing room with rows and rows of filing cabinets. If a legal organization is going to move to a "paperless office," the office will have to have a document management program to manage the electronic files. Document management software also provides for extensive searching capabilities and allows users to add a profile of every document that can be easily searched on later.

document management software
Organizes, controls, distributes, and allows for extensive searching of electronic documents, typically in a networked environment.

DOCUMENT ASSEMBLY   **Document assembly software** creates powerful standardized templates and forms. Instead of having to open an existing client's word processing document and edit it for a new client, it allows the user to create a template than can be used over and over. Document assembly programs have more powerful commands and capabilities than templates found in word processing programs.

document assembly software
Creates powerful standardized templates and forms

LITIGATION SUPPORT   Litigation support software organizes, stores, retrieves, and summarizes information that is gathered in the litigation of a lawsuit. Litigation support programs are powerful database management programs that have been designed specifically for litigation. They can store thousands and even millions of records, search for and retrieve the requested records, summarize and track important case information, and much more.

> *For paralegals, electronic discovery is changing the way they work in terms of how they search, sort, gather, view and produce documents. . . . The majority of cases and other legal matters involving document discovery now incorporate some form of electronic discovery and legal assistants often are heavily involved in the process.*
> *Legal Assistant Today,* May/June 2005, p. 61.

ELECTRONIC DISCOVERY   Electronic discovery programs have the ability to store, search, and retrieve electronic documents in a case, such as e-mails, word processing files, spreadsheets, and other attachments and electronic data produced during discovery. For 200 years, documents have been produced as hard copy, but this is no longer the case. In many legal matters, the parties need the ability to search, sort, track, and organize electronic data. People communicate via e-mail, attachments, and electronic files, and legal professionals need a way to search this information to find data that will assist them in representing their clients.

LEGAL-SPECIFIC SOFTWARE   Legal-specific software includes programs developed for a legal specialty area. For example, an attorney who practices criminal law might purchase a program that automates and tracks information about criminal cases. The software might track each individual criminal count against a defendant, automate the scheduling of the case, automate documents in the case (such as witness lists), track restitution, track evidence, and much more.

TRIAL SOFTWARE   Trial software assists litigators in preparing for and presenting information to a jury or fact finder. They can work closely with automated courtrooms where judges and juries have computer screens in front of them to receive evidence. The programs typically provide sophisticated presentation graphics features, outline and organize information that will be presented to the fact finder, and include the ability to organize information by legal issue; organize, track, and display trial exhibits; and generate and display complex timelines.

Telecommunications

> *High-speed, large-bandwidth connections that link our offices to each other and to the Internet allow for convenient, instant sharing of documents and files among lawyers and clients and also make video conferencing a practical reality. E-mail transmissions, with attachments of documents, have largely replaced correspondence files. . . . Correspondence and documents received by a lawyer are scanned and stored with other electronic files in electronic file cabinets and other sophisticated database management tools. . . . All of our offices have wireless connectivity so our lawyers can take their laptops with them as they move among offices or to conference rooms and remain linked to our firm network.*[23]

LAW OFFICE WEB SITES   Many law offices now have home pages on the Internet; in fact, a recent survey showed that more than 70 percent of U.S. law offices have Web sites. Most offices use the Web site for marketing information, but some are expanding the content to include such things as client intake questionnaires, real-time consulting with prospective clients, and self-help information and research. Some firms have in-house staff and a variety of computer programs to design, develop, and host their own sites, while others outsource these tasks.

INTERNET ACCESS   Nearly all law offices provide access to the Internet. Notice in Figure 2-21 that 95 percent of the legal assistants surveyed indicated that they used the Internet on a *daily* basis. Law offices use the Internet for a variety of purposes, including factual research, legal research (including access to Westlaw and LexisNexis), purchasing, marketing, communicating with clients, and much more. With this access comes a host of security issues, such as hackers, viruses, spyware, and so forth.

INTRANET   As defined earlier, an intranet is an internal distribution system used only by a law firm staff. It disseminates information to internal staff using a Web browser and the look and feel of the World Wide Web. An intranet provides information to internal users in the same way the Internet provides information to the public. Typical information a firm might include on its intranet site includes office policies and procedures, links to law-related Web sites, training material, contact lists, links to form files or brief banks, and much more.

EXTRANET   An **extranet** is a network designed to provide, disseminate, and share confidential information with clients. A client with a Web browser can access the law practice's extranet, go through security and ID/password protections, and access his or her case plans, documents, strategies, billing information, and other data.

extranet
A network designed to provide, disseminate, and share confidential information with clients.

LEGAL WEBLOGS   A weblog, or "blog," is a Web site with information contained in posts that are arranged in reverse chronological order. Blogs resemble diary or journal entries in a notebook, and they can contain links to other Web sites or articles. There are many law-related blogs on the Internet, including specific blogs on certain type of law, such as immigration or taxes.

SUMMARY

Legal administration is important to the survival of every law practice. Legal administration covers the following subject matters: practice management, leadership, controlling, financial management, human resources management, planning, marketing, organization/policies/systems, facilities management, office services management, and technology or information services management.

Practice management refers to management decisions regarding how a law office will practice law and handle cases. Administrative management refers to management decisions regarding how a firm will operate as a business, such as how it will handle financial or human resources matters.

Practice management decisions include defining the law office's practice (what cases it will take), services, and the practice systems necessary to provide legal services to clients. Another aspect of practice management is the quality of services that it provides to clients. Total quality management is a management philosophy that is based on knowing the needs of each client and allowing those needs to drive the legal organization. This includes the ideas 1) that management has the duty to make sure the firm provides quality legal services to clients, 2) that quality service involves every person in the firm, 3) that clients determine what constitutes "quality services," 4) that quality depends on individual, team, and organizational performance, and 5) that there is a focus on constantly improving services.

Leadership is the act of motivating or causing others to perform and achieve objectives. Controlling is the process of determining whether the law practice is achieving its objectives, holding stakeholders accountable for their goals, and making strategy adjustment so the firm achieves its objectives. Financial management is the oversight of the firm's financial assets and profitability to ensure overall financial health.

Human resources management refers to hiring, evaluating, compensating, training, and directing law office personnel. Important federal employment laws include the Family and Medical Leave Act, the Fair Labor Standards Act, the Civil Rights Act of 1964, the Americans with Disabilities Act, and the Age Discrimination in Employment Act, among others.

Planning is the process of setting objectives, assessing the future, and developing courses of action to achieve the objectives. Marketing is the process of educating consumers on the quality of legal services that a law office can provide. Organizing is the process of arranging people and physical resources to carry out plans and accomplish objectives. A system is a consistent way of performing a task. A policy is a specific statement that sets out what is or is not acceptable. A procedure is a series of steps that must be followed to accomplish a task. A law office staff manual contains the firm's policies and procedures related to legal and administrative work.

Facilities management includes planning, designing, controlling, and managing a law office's building or office space. Facilities management includes areas such as: property acquisition, moves/construction/remodeling, space planning/office design/furniture, parking, cleaning/maintenance/grounds, common areas, environmental considerations (lighting, electrical, climate, and plumbing), security, safety, and disaster recovery planning. Maintaining a secure and safe environment is an extremely important aspect of facilities management. Locked doors, security systems, limited access to interior halls, security passes, and other initiatives help to keep a law office secure. A disaster recovery plan includes information on how the office will rebuild and recover from a disaster.

Office services management refers to internal systems and services in a law office. The services include management of the mail room, copiers and copy facilities, file/records management, and telecommunications (including telephone systems, voice mail, fax machines, and video conferencing).

Technology has had a large and continual impact on how legal professionals practice law. Law offices have a myriad of choices when it comes to computer hardware and software. Electronic mail is used more by legal professionals on a daily basis than any other application. Other applications that legal professionals use include docket control, time and billing, document management, document assembly, litigation support, electronic discovery programs, and others. Telecommunication services that legal professionals use include law office Web sites, Internet access, intranets, extranets, and legal blogs.

HELPFUL WEB SITES

ORGANIZATION	DESCRIPTION	INTERNET ADDRESS
ABA Law Practice Today	ABA site devoted to law practice management and legal administration.	http://www.abanet.org/lpm
ABA Legal Technology Resource Center	ABA site devoted to technology. Includes resources and articles.	http://www.abanet.org/tech/ltrc/home.html
Alabama State Bar—Law Office Management Assistance Program	Articles on a variety of law office management topics, including a disaster recovery kit.	http://www.alabar.org/lomap/

ORGANIZATION	DESCRIPTION	INTERNET ADDRESS
Association of Legal Administrators	National association for legal administrators. Contains resources and information related to law office management and legal administration.	http://www.alanet.org
Law Office Computing magazine	Excellent magazine, but limited information online. The site has good links to manufacturers that offer law office software.	http://www.lawofficecomputing.com
Law Technology News	Excellent periodical for legal technology issues. Good white papers on technology issues.	http://www.lawtechnews.com and http://www.law.com/jsp/ltn/whitepapers.jsp
Maryland State Bar Association—Law Practice Management Assistance	The site has a wide variety of law office management topics, including a number of articles and excellent resources.	http://www.msba.org/departments/loma/articles/index.htm
New Jersey State Bar Association—Law Office Management Articles	Articles on a variety of law office management topics.	http://www.njsba.com/law_office_manage/index.cfm?fuseaction=articles
New York State Bar Association	The site is extremely in-depth and has a collection of some of the best law office management related articles and information on the Internet. The articles are also arranged by folders according to subject matter.	http://www.nysba.org/Content/NavigationMenu/Attorney_Resources/Practice_Management/Practice_Management.htm
South Carolina Bar— Practice Management Section	The site has a wide variety of law office management topics, including a number of articles and excellent resources.	http://www.scbar.org/pmap/resources.asp
State Bar of Georgia— Law Practice Management Articles	Articles on a variety of law office management topics.	http://www.gabar.org/programs/law_practice_management/law_practice_management_program_articles/
State Bar of New Mexico— Law Office Management Site	Miscellaneous law office management and legal administration topics and links.	http://www.nmbar.org/Template.cfm?Section=Law_Office_Management1

SUGGESTED READING

1. American Bar Association. (2004). *American Bar Association legal technology surveys*.

2. Schultz, & Schultz. (2005). *The complete guide to designing your law office*. American Bar Association.

3. *Law Office Computing* magazine, published by James Publishing [http://www.lawofficecomputing.com].

4. Wert, & Hatoff. (2004). *Law office policy & procedures manual* (4th ed.). American Bar Association.

5. *Law Practice* magazine, published by the American Bar Association Law Practice Management Section [http://www.abanet.org/lpm].

6. *Law Technology* News periodical [http://www.lawtech-nologynews.com].

7. Grella, T. C. & Hudkins, M. L. (2005). *Strategic planning for lawyers and law firms: Defining, setting, and achieving your firm's goals*. American Bar Association.

8. Munneke, G. A., & Davis, A. E. (2003). *The essential form book—comprehensive management tools*. American Bar Association.

9. Grella, T. C., & Hudkins, M. L. (2004). *The lawyer's guide to strategic planning*. American Bar Association.

KEY TERMS

administrative management
administrative task
Age Discrimination in Employment
  Act of 1967
Americans with Disabilities Act of 1990
bona fide occupational qualification
Civil Rights Act of 1964
coaching technique
controlling
disaster recovery plan
document assembly software
employment-at-will doctrine
document management software
equal employment opportunity
Equal Pay Act of 1963
extranet
facilities management
Fair Credit Reporting Act
Family and Medical Leave Act of 1993
financial management
Gannt chart

human resources management
intranet
leadership
management
management by objectives
marketing
mission statement
negligent hiring
office services management
organizing
personnel handbook
planning
policy
practice management
procedure
reasonable accommodation
sexual harassment
strategic planning
substantive task
system
total quality management

TEST YOUR KNOWLEDGE

Test your knowledge of the chapter by answering these questions.

1. _____ management refers to management decisions related to how a law office practices law and handles its cases.

2. _____ management refers to management decisions related to operating a law office including financial and personnel matters.

3. Three basic practice management questions that must be considered are a) what clients will the law office serve? b) what services will be offered to the client? and c) _____.

4. True or false: It is generally recognized that a good law office strategy is to practice in all areas and subspecialties.

5. List the 11 functions of legal administration.

6. _____ is a management philosophy that is based upon knowing the needs of each

client and allowing those needs to drive the legal organization.

7. What distinguishes poor legal assistants from exceptional ones?

8. The quality of provided legal services is best determined by the _____.

9. What is the act of motivating or causing others to perform and achieve objectives called?

10. What is the process of determining whether the law practice is achieving its objectives, holding stakeholders accountable for their goals, and making strategy adjustments as necessary so the firm achieves the objectives, called?

11. Setting hourly billing rates, tracking firm assets, and budgeting are responsibilities regarding _____ management.

12. What is hiring, evaluating, compensating, training, and directing law office personnel called?

13. The _____ technique is taken from sports, focuses on the positive aspects of the employee's performance, and explores alternative ways to improve his or her performance.

14. What employment doctrine states that both the employee and employer are free to enter and sever the employment relationship at any time without reason?

15. Describe the Family and Medical Leave Act of 1993.

16. What law prohibits employers from discriminating against people with a disability?

17. Define sexual harassment.

18. _____ is the process of setting objectives, assessing the future, and developing courses of action to achieve these objectives.

19. _____ is a general, enduring statement of what the purpose or intent of the law practice is about.

20. What is marketing?

21. A manual that governs the policies and procedures of law office is called a _____.

22. What is the type of management that is responsible for property acquisition, moves, space planning, and design, parking, and security?

23. A plan that describes how the law office will react to a catastrophe is called a _____.

24. What type of management is responsible for the mail room, copy room, and records/file management?

25. Name three problems or errors that can occur when using e-mail.

26. The "paperless office" is associated with what type of computer program?

ON THE WEB EXERCISES

1.   Compare, contrast, and print out mission statements for three law offices. Some firms may call them core values, firm philosophy, or a purpose statement. Some firms include the purpose of their firm or their mission in a general introductory statement; . large firms typically include this on their Web site. To start, you may want to go to a general search engine like http://www.google.com or http://www. yahoo.com and search for "global law firms" or "large law firms." The Findlaw site, http://www. findlaw.com, has features that allow users to search for lawyers and law firm Web sites as well. The Chicago Committee on Minorities in Large Law Firms is another site to try [http://www. chicagocommittee.org/MemberFirms.cfm?ShowAll= yes]; this site lists approximately 50 large firms

(and links to their Web sites) that are members of their organization.

2.   Research law-related blogs on the Internet. Find five legal blogs including at least one on either law office technology or law practice management or administration. Print a few pages of the blogs you find and write a paragraph explaining each site. Start by going to http://www.blawg.org or to a general search engine, such as http://www.google. com or http://www. yahoo.com, and typing "legal blog."

3.   Using the sites listed in the Web Links section of this chapter, or a general search engine, find checklists and helpful sites regarding moving a law office.

4. Using the sites listed in the Web Links section of this chapter, or a general search engine, find resources, information, and checklists that would assist an attorney in opening a new law practice.

5. Use a general search engine to find job descriptions for a legal secretary, legal assistant or paralegal, attorney, legal administrator, and law librarian.

6. The chapter states that successful law practices do not take all of the clients or cases that come to them, and that they carefully select the ones that are profitable and right for them. Using the sites contained in the Web Links section of this chapter, research articles on how to weed out undesirable clients and cases.

PROJECTS

1. Research and write an in-depth report on disaster recovery plans. Obtain a minimum of five different resources. Information covered in the report should include why they are important, which major sections or areas a disaster recovery plan has, how they are used, and information related to why disaster recovery plans are particularly important in law offices. In addition, write a disaster recovery plan for yourself (e.g., if your apartment or residence were to catch fire and everything you had was destroyed).

2. Assume that you have been asked by an attorney who is starting a new law practice to prepare a detailed list of computer hardware and software that he or she might need. The attorney will be a general practitioner and will employ him or herself, a legal secretary, and you as the legal assistant. Compile a detailed list, including pricing and some background on why each item is necessary.

3. Research and write a detailed report on total quality management. At a minimum, the report should include who is credited with developing it, where it originated and became popular, what specific ideologies it includes, and how it can be implemented in any business, including a law office.

4. Research and write a one-page detailed summary on each of the following federal employment laws: Civil Rights Act of 1964, Family and Medical Leave Act, Americans with Disabilities Act, and Age Discrimination in Employment Act. At a

minimum, include why the law was passed, major provisions of the law, what agency is responsible for enforcing it, and other relevant information about it.

5. Research and write a report on law office security and workplace violence. Include some history of the subject, including major tragedies like the 1993 Pettit & Martin shootings and others. Include what law offices can do to limit their exposure to security problems.

6. Group Project: Opening a Law Office
Your group will act as the Law Practice Management Committee of Brayton and James Attorneys at Law, a new firm specializing in corporate and insurance law that expects to begin practicing law this year.

Your job as the Law Practice Management Committee is to put together a strategic management plan for the first year of operation. Great care should be taken in preparing the plan, since this will guide your firm for the first year of operation and will also be given to your bank to secure financing. You are to submit one copy of the strategic management plan, which will be reviewed for accuracy, completeness, and logic. Each member of your group will receive a grade. You will also evaluate each other regarding the work done on the project.

The Brayton and James law office will have two partners and two associate attorneys. The partners expect to make $100,000 a year, and associates expect to make $70,000 a year. You must determine what other staff will need to be hired and at what pay rate. You have no budgetary constraints.

Your strategic management plan should include the following sections:

A. **Physical location of the building:** You must choose an actual office site for the business. You will need private offices for each of the attorneys and appropriate office space for the other staff. You will also need a reception area, library, and conference room. You must give a narrative description of the office site and include cost (leased or purchased) and justification as to why this site was chosen.

B. **Layout of the office and furniture:** You must decide how the office interior will be laid out. A layout of the office should be provided, including a narrative description of each office and its accompanying furniture, and an explanation as to why the office was laid out in the particular manner.

C. **Technology/equipment:** Appropriate technology/equipment should be researched. Assume the attorneys want to purchase all new equipment typically found in a law office, including computers, software, printers, Internet access, fax machine, copiers, and so forth. A narrative description of the items to be purchased (and the cost) should be included, as well as the justification for the purchase.

D. **Staff employment:** Explain what additional staff positions will be needed to support the two partners and two associates. Draft job descriptions for each of the positions.

E. **Law library:** An appropriate library for insurance and corporate law must be purchased. Please explain what will be purchased, why, and the cost.

F. **Budget:** A detailed budget should be included for both income and expenses (see Chapter 6). Please indicate the billing rates and hours to be billed for the partners, associates, and any legal assistants hired (see Chapter 5). The rates and hours should reflect the common market rates and hours for the area. When considering expenses do not forget to add 25 percent to associate and staff salaries to cover fringe benefits. The budget should provide the partners with the income they expect and include the typical expenses found in most law offices.

QUESTIONS AND EXERCISES

1. Interview an attorney and get answers to the following questions:. What is the mission of his or her firm? How does he or she define his or her practice? Who are his or her primary clients? What primary services does he or she provide? What practice systems does he or she use to support the legal services provided to clients?. Does he or she prefer practice or administrative management?

2. Many business professionals believe that it is easier to find and keep a long-term customer than it is to constantly find new customers. Think of a product or service to which you are very loyal (brand of car, shoe, computer, printer, bike, clothes, etc.). How long have you been loyal to the brand or product? Why are you loyal to it? Does it have to do with the quality of the product? How much money have you given to the brand or product because of your loyalty? Could you have gone to a competitor? Why didn't you? Can you see how this same philosophy applies to the practice of law? Why is providing quality services to clients important?

3. Assume that you are a new legal assistant in a sole practitioner's office. The attorney has asked you to sit in with her to interview a legal secretary. She has asked you to draft a job description, and 15 interview questions. Use the Internet or other resource to do this. What things would you be looking for in a candidate?

4. Write a mission statement for yourself. What is important to you? What are your goals and objectives? Develop a five-year strategic plan for

yourself. Where do you see yourself in five years? What will you have to do to reach your goals and objectives?

5. In reviewing Figure 2-21, were you surprised to see the extent to which legal assistants use computers in their jobs? What conclusions can you draw from Figure 2-21 regarding legal assistant computer use?

6. Call a realtor in your area that handles commercial property and ask about the price range or the average square foot cost for office space in your area. Assume a solo practitioner with several staff would need 600 square feet, a small firm would need 2500 square feet, and a medium-sized firm would need 10,000 square feet; what would be the annual cost for each size of office in your area? For example, if the going rate were $30 per square foot of office space, and you had an office with 1,000 square feet, the annual lease would be $30,000 ($30 × 1,000 = $30,000).

NOTes

1. Reed, R. C. (1988). *Managing a law practice: The human side* (p. 3). American Bar Association. *Citing Law Office Economics & Management* (Summer 1977).
2. Ibid.
3. A law firm consultant in Clay, T., & Maddock, C. (1999, January/February). The 12 deadly management sins. *Pennsylvania Lawyer*. Reprinted by permission.
4. Clay, T. S. (1988). Profile of a successful law firm. In *The law firm management guide* (p. A-15). Pennsylvania, PA: Altman Weil. Reprinted with permission from Altman Weil, Inc.
5. McKenna, P. J. (2000, November/December). The case for selective focus: If you're not special, you're dead. *Law Practice Management*. 49.
6. Manahan, E. C. (1992, Fall). Deciding to train for quality service. *Cornerstone, 14*(2), 11.
7. Clay, T., & Maddock, C. (1999, January/February). The 12 deadly management sins. *Pennsylvania Lawyer*.
8. Nelson, A. M. (1999, October). Work with support staff to promote quality. *Wisconsin Lawyer*. Reprinted with permission of the October 1999 *Wisconsin Lawyer*, the official publication of the State Bar of Wisconsin.
9. Wahl, D. C. (1992, Spring). Managing for quality. *The LAMA Manager,* 21. Reprinted with the permission of the Legal Assistant Management Association.
10. Perry, P. M. (1992, July/August). Sexual harassment. *Legal Assistant Today* 66. Copyright 1992, James Publishing, Inc. Reprinted with permission from *Legal Assistant Today* magazine. For subscription information, call (714) 755-5450, or visit http://www.legalassistanttoday.com.
11. Munneka, G. A. (1991). *Law practice management* (p. 570). St. Paul, MN: West Publishing Group.
12. Clay, T. S. (1988). Profile of a successful law firm. In *The law firm management guide* (p. A-15). Pennsylvania, PA: Altman Weil. Reprinted with permission from Altman Weil, Inc.
13. Greene, R. (1992). *Making partner* (p. 3). American Bar Association. Reprinted by permission.
14. Wert, & Hatoff. (2000). *Law office policy and procedures manual* (4th ed.). American Bar Association.
15. Kurzman, R. G., & Gilbert, R. *Paralegals and successful law practice*. Institute for Business.
16. Mathis, K. Violence in the workplace: Protecting your law office. Retrieved from American Bar Association (General Practice, Solo & Small Firm Section).
17. Bentzen, M. P., & Brandon-Brown, E. A. (1993, Winter). Are you sure your fax transmissions are confidential? *ABA Law Practice Management Publication Network 1*(3). Reprinted with permission.
18. Greene, A. G. (2005). *The lawyer's guide to increasing revenue* (p. 89). American Bar Association.

19. Amiel, P. H. (2005, July). Top down technology: A large firm's example. *Texas Bar Journal 68*(7), 589.

20. Anderson, C. (1999, January/February). Technology trends. *Legal Assistant Today*, 52.

21. Amiel, P. H. (2005, July). Top down technology: A large firm's example. *Texas Bar Journal 68*(7), 589.

22. American Bar Association. *ABA Model Rules of Professional Conduct*, 1.6 Confidentiality of Information.

23. Amiel, P. H. (2005, July). Top down technology: A large firm's example. *Texas Bar Journal 68*(7), 589.

ANSWERS TO TEST YOUR KNOWLEDGE

1. Practice
2. Administrative
3. What practice systems are needed to provide the agreed-upon legal services to the client?
4. False
5. Practice management, leadership, controlling, financial management, human resources management, planning, marketing management, organization/policies/systems, facilities management, office services management, technology management
6. Total quality management
7. The quality of their work
8. Client
9. Leadership
10. Controlling
11. Financial
12. Human resources management
13. Coaching
14. Employment-at-will
15. Generally applies to employers with 50 or more employees and employees with at least one year of service who worked at least 1,250 hours in the last year. The law provides for 12 weeks of unpaid leave annually for 1) the birth or adoption of a child, b) the care of a child, spouse, or parent, or 3) the employee's own serious health condition.
16. Americans with Disabilities Act
17. Unwelcome sexual advances, requests for sexual favors, and other verbal or physical conduct of a sexual nature that create an intimidating, hostile, or offensive working environment.
18. Planning
19. Mission statement
20. The process of educating consumers on the quality legal services that a law office can provide.
21. Staff manual or policies and procedures manual
22. Facilities management
23. Disaster recovery plan
24. Office services
25. Technology can fail, what you say can be easily forwarded to others, e-mail security can be breached, once e-mail is sent it cannot easily be retrieved, e-mail can be sent to unintended parties, incorrect attachments can be accidentally sent, typing errors can occur.
26. Document management

CASE REVIEW

Bednar v. CT Corporation, 2003 WL 23571819 (D.Minn.)

West's Minnesota Jury Verdict Reports

Thomas Bednar worked for CT Corporation System as a customer specialist. CT is a nationwide legal document service company. The company offers various services to attorneys and law firms, and has offices in several states. There are approximately 300 customer specialists employed by CT. Until August of 2002, the customer specialists were compensated on a salary or "exempt" basis, and as such, were ineligible for overtime pay for any hours worked in excess of 40 hours per week. After August 2002, customer service specialists were reclassified as non-exempt. In 2003, Bednar filed a class action complaint again CT in a Minnesota federal district court, alleging the classification of customer specialists as exempt violated the federal Fair Labor Standards Act, 29 U.S.C. 207(a)(1) and various state wage and hour laws. The complaint sought reimbursement for unpaid overtime, liquidated damages, and an award of attorney's fees and costs. The parties agreed to settle the case on December 15, 2003 for a total payment not to exceed $2,825,000, including attorney's fees. Under the terms of the settlement agreement, each member of the class who chose to participate in the settlement would receive back overtime pay based on the actual excess hours that individual worked, in addition to a payment of $4,066. The additional payment was deemed to cover any potential state law violations, liquidated damages and various other damages.

Questions

1. Were you surprised that this FLSA violation happened to a company that works in the legal industry and works with attorneys and law firms every day?

2. Notice in this case that it was only *after* the defendants figured out that they had wrongly misclassified the customer service specialists—and, in fact, corrected the matter—that the plaintiffs discovered the error and filed the class action to recover damages when they were misclassified. Is that fair?

3. Notice also that what may have started as one person, Thomas Bednar, having a single claim against the defendant turned into a full-blown class action costing the firm $2.8 million dollars in damages alone. Did it surprise you how much the case was settled for and how quickly it was litigated?

CASE REVIEW

Smith v. Chrysler Financial Corporation, 101 F.Supp.2d 534 (E.D. Mich. 2000).

101 F.Supp.2d 534

(Cite as: 101 F.Supp.2d 534)

United States District Court,

E.D. Michigan, Southern Division

Karen SMITH, Plaintiff,

v.

CHRYSLER FINANCIAL CORPORATION,
Chrysler Corporation,
James Kozik and Allan Ronquillo,
jointly and severally, Defendants.

No. 97-CV-60309-AA.

May 30, 2000.

I.

Background

Plaintiff Karen Smith filed a First Amended Complaint on November 12, 1999 alleging she and Jessica Framer were employed by defendant CFC as paralegal, ***537** and were supervised by CFC's then Assistant General Counsel James Kozik. Plaintiff alleges Kozik made repeated sexual advances and comments to Farmer. Plaintiff alleges that, once others reported Kozik's misconduct to CFC, Kozik retaliated against her by recommending that she receive only marginal pay raises, and by denying her certain performance reviews. Plaintiff alleges she thereafter filed a confidential sexual harassment complaint with CFC's Sexual Harassment Committee on August 12, 1996, which determined after an internal investigation that there was "reason to believe" Kozik had committed sexual harassment. Plaintiff initially filed a sex discrimination lawsuit in state court on October 15, 1996. Six days later, on October 21, 1996, she was removed from her CFC paralegal position by CFC's then General Counsel Allan Ronquillo and was transferred to a non-paralegal position away from CFC paralegal positions by current CFC General Counsel Christopher Taravella. Smith alleges hostile work environment sexual harassment (Count I) and retaliation and reprisal (Count II), each in violation of Title VII of the Civil Rights Act of 1964, 42 U.S.C. §2000e et seq.

III.

Motions for Summary Judgment

A.

Standard of Review

Federal Rule of Civil Procedure 56(c) empowers the court to render summary judgment "forthwith if the pleadings, depositions, answers to interrogatories and admissions on file, together with the affidavits, ***540** if any, show that there is no genuine issue as to any material fact at that the moving party is entitled to judgment as a matter of law." See FDIC v. Alexander, 78 F.3d 1103, 1106 (6th Cir.1996). The standard for determining whether summary judgment is appropriate is " 'whether the evidence presents a sufficient disagreement to require submission to a jury or whether it is so one-sided that one party must prevail as a matter of law." Winningham v. North Am. Resources Corp., 42 F.3d 981, 984 (6th Cir.1994) (citing Booker v. Brown & Williamson Tobacco Co., 879 F.2d 1304, 1310 [6th Cir.1989]). The evidence and all inferences therefrom must be construed in the light most favorable to the nonmoving party. Matsushita Elec. Indus. Co., Ltd. v. Zenith Radio Corp., 475 U.S. 574, 587, 106 S.Ct. 1348, 89 L.Ed.2d 538 (1986); Enertech Elec., Inc. v. Mahoning County Comm'r, 85 F.3d 257, 259 (6th Cir.1996); Wilson v. Stroh Cos., Inc., 952 F.2d 942, 945 (6th Cir.1992).

If the movant establishes by use of the material specified in Rule 56(c) that there is no genuine issue of material fact and that it is entitled to judgment as a matter of law, the opposing party must come forward with "specific facts showing that there is a genuine issue for trial." First Nat'l Bank v. Cities Serv. Co., 391 U.S. 253, 270, 88 S.Ct. 1575, 20 L.Ed.2d 569 (1968); see also Adams v. Philip Morris, Inc., 67 F.3d 580, 583 (6th Cir.1995). The nonmoving party cannot rest on its pleadings to avoid summary judgment, but must support its claims with probative evidence. Kraft v. United States, 991 F.2d 292, 296 (6th Cir.), cert, denied, 510 U.S. 976, 114 S.Ct. 467, 126 L.Ed.2d 419 (1993); Anderson v. Liberty Lobby, Inc.,

477 U.S. 242, 248, 106 S.Ct. 2505, 91 L.Ed.2d 202 (1986).

B.

Plaintiff's Motion for Summary Judgment as to Liability Only

Plaintiff moves for summary judgment as to liability only, as to the Title VII retaliation claims only, proffering: (1) Ronquillo's and CFC Human Resource Manager Linda Rumshlag's testimony that Smith was transferred out of her CFC paralegal position on October 21, 1996 because she filed a discrimination lawsuit and; (2) CFC Associate General Counsel Tracy Hackman's testimony that Smith has not since been considered for a paralegal position because of plaintiff's state and federal lawsuits.

Defendants counter that plaintiff has misconstrued the testimony, and assert that the reason plaintiff was reassigned and is not now eligible to occupy a paralegal position is for the protection of corporate security, to wit defendants' fear that a disgruntled plaintiff Smith will leak confidential and sensitive legal information. Defendants also assert plaintiff was transferred out of her paralegal position, and is currently ineligible for a paralegal position, consistent with her professional and ethical duty to eliminate conflicts of interest; defendants maintain plaintiff cannot properly represent her former client and employer CFC while, at the same time, she is suing them.

[7] To demonstrate a prima facie case of unlawful retaliation under Title VII, the plaintiff must prove: (1) she engaged in protected activity; (2) the exercise of protected rights was known to the defendant; (3) the defendant thereafter took adverse employment action against the plaintiff, or subjected the plaintiff to severe or pervasive retaliatory harassment by a supervisor, and; (4) a causal connection between the protected activity and the adverse employment action or harassment. Morris v. Oldham County Fiscal Court, 201 F.3d 784, 792 (6th Cir.2000). If the plaintiff establishes a prima facie case, the burden of production shifts to the defendant employer to articulate a legitimate, nondiscriminatory reason for its actions. Id. at 793. The plaintiff then bears the burden ***541** of demonstrating that

the proffered reason was not the true reason for the employment decision. Id.

[8] Construing the pleadings and evidence in a light most favorable to defendants CFC and Chrysler, the evidence in the record presents a sufficient disagreement as to CFC's true motivations for transferring plaintiff out of her paralegal position on October 21, 1996, and for continuing to refuse to consider her for other CFC paralegal positions that the issue of CFC's true motivation for these employment decisions must be submitted to a jury. Winningham, 42 F.3d at 984. The proffered testimony of Ronquillo, Rumshlag, Hackman, and Travella demonstrates, as plaintiff argues, that plaintiff was transferred out of her CFC paralegal position, and is not currently considered eligible for a CFC paralegal position, as a direct result of the sex discrimination lawsuits she filed and continues to pursue. Defendant does not dispute that filing a sex discrimination lawsuit against an employer constitutes an exercise of activity protected by Title VII. What remains to be decided by a jury, however, is whether defendant CFC retaliated against plaintiff for filing and maintaining the lawsuits, or whether CFC legitimately reasoned that plaintiff posed a potential threat to corporate security if she occupied a paralegal position while her lawsuits remained pending. The "only effect of the employer's nondiscriminatory explanation is to convert the inference of discrimination based upon the plaintiff's prima facie case from a mandatory one which the jury must draw, to a permissive one the jury may draw, provided that the jury finds the employer's explanation 'unworthy of belief." Manzer v. Diamond Shamrock Chemicals Co., 29 F.3d 1078, 1083 (6th Cir.1994). Plaintiff now bears the burden of proving that the defendants' proffered reasons are simply unworthy of belief given plaintiff has never before leaked confidential client information, and has not threatened to leak such information. Oldham County, 201 F.3d at 793. Evidence in the record construed in a light most favorable to the defendants nonetheless indicates that CFC attempted, albeit briefly, to build a "firewall" between plaintiff and her access to confidential CFC information before plaintiff was transferred, lending support to the proffered legitimate reason of protecting corporate security. Construing this and other evidence in light most fa-

vorable to the defendants, the issue of CFC's true motivation remains for the jury to decide.

The court notes that the defendants' more recent argument that plaintiff was transferred due to ethical considerations is not supported by the proffered testimony; the court is not cited to any deposition testimony by Ronquillo, Rumshlag, Hackman, or Taravella, or any other agent of CFC or Chrysler, who has testified to date that plaintiff was removed from her paralegal position, and is no currently eligible for a paralegal position, because plaintiff cannot ethically occupy the position as a legal professional. The issue is not whether a legitimate reason exists, but whether CFC and Chrysler relied upon a legitimate reason for their challenged employment decisions. Nonetheless, the true causal connection between plaintiff's transfer from her paralegal position and her tiling of sex discrimination lawsuits, as well as the nondiscriminatory justification proffered by defendants, should be submitted to a jury. Plaintiff's motion for partial summary judgment as to liability only, as to her retaliation claims only, must therefore be denied. Winningham, 42 F.3d at 984.

C.

Defendants' Motions for Summary Judgment

i.

Defendants move for summary judgment of plaintiff's retaliation claims predating August 12, 1996—the alleged hostile work environment created by Kozik, an alleged retaliatory January 1996 performance *542 appraisal, and an alleged retaliatory April 4, 1996 low salary increase—arguing the court lacks subject matter jurisdiction over these claims because they are broader than the claims plaintiff made in her May 14, 1997 Charge of Discrimination submitted to the EEOC. Defendants also argue references made in plaintiff's complaint regarding comments about "African-Americans" and "physically disabled employees" are likewise outside the scope of the Charge of Discrimination.

Plaintiff's EEOC Charge of Discrimination, set forth in an EEOC form, reads:

> I began employment for CFC's Legal Department in May, 1989.

I performed my job duties in an exemplary manner and regularly received merit raises based upon my performance. My supervisor was CFC's Assistant General Counsel and was responsible for my merit raises, performance reviews, job assignments and positions with CFC's Legal Department.

At various times while the Assistant General Counsel supervised me, he subjected me to demeaning and harassing remarks and behavior intended to denigrate myself and/or women in general. After I reported his conduct to CFC's General Counsel, his illegal misconduct continued and he vowed to "get rid of" and retaliate against those CFC employees he suspected reported his conduct to General Counsel.

On or about August 12, 1996, I filed a confidential sexual harassment complaint with CFC's Sexual Harassment Committee pursuant to CFC's sexual harassment policy. In response to my complaint, CFC and Chrysler purportedly conducted a thorough investigation into my sexual harassment claim.

On September 16, 1996, CFC and Chrysler provided the harasser [sic] with a promotion from CFC to Chrysler's Legal Department. On October 15, 1996, I filed a lawsuit against the Defendants alleging, inter, violations of the Elliott-Larsen Civil Rights Act (ELCRA). On or about October 21, 1996, in response to filing a lawsuit alleging violations of the ELCRA, CFC demoted and/or involuntarily transferred me to a different, non-paralegal position at a location away from CFC's headquarters.

I believe that I have been wrongfully sexually harassed, based on my sex, female, and demoted, in retaliation for reporting sexual harassment and for filing a lawsuit, in violation of Title VII of the Civil Rights Act of 1964, as amended.

As to the alleged cause of discrimination, plaintiff checked the boxes in the form titled "sex" and "retaliation." Describing the dates of discrimination, plaintiff wrote "unknown" for the "earliest" date, "ongoing" for the "latest" date, and checked the box "continuing action."

[9][10] This court enjoys jurisdiction over claims explicitly filed in the EEOC charge as well as claims that were reasonably expected to grow out of the charge. See Abeita v. TransAmerica Mailings, Inc., 159 F.3d 246, 254 (6th Cir.1998) (Citing Ang v. Procter & Gamble Co., 932 F.2d 540, 544-45 [6th Cir.1991]). Construing the pleadings and evidence in a light most favorable to plaintiff Smith, plaintiff's pre-August 12, 1996 sexual harassment and retaliation claims can reasonable and fairly be read as growing out of the broad allegations set forth in her Charge of Discrimination, which begin with the date May 1989, allege subsequent misconduct and threats of retaliation, continue through to August 12, 1996 and the filing of the internal confidential sexual harassment complaint, and continue further through plaintiff's October 21, 1996 transfer from her paralegal position, all allegations consistent with an alleged "continuing action." The court need not apply a "liberal construction" applicable to pro se claimant's in reaching this conclusion. See Ang, 932 F.2d at 546. As to plaintiff's allegations in this lawsuit regarding comments made about "African-Americans" and "physically disabled employees," plaintiff is not alleging ***543** race or disability discrimination claims, and thus, the court has not improperly exercised jurisdiction over such claims. Defendants are not entitled to summary judgment based on lack of subject matter jurisdiction. Winningham, 42 F.3d at 984.

ii.

Defendants move for summary judgment of plaintiff's claims pre-dating August 16, 1996 arguing any such claims are untimely because they arose more than 300 days prior to June 12, 1997, or August 16, 1996, the date the EEOC first filed plaintiff's charge with Michigan's "deferral agency" the Michigan Department of Civil Rights or, in the alternative, 300 days prior to April 23, 1997, or July 2, 1996, the date the EEOC first received plaintiff's April 22, 1997 letter.

[11] Generally under 42 U.S.C. § 2000e-5(e)(1) and 42 U.S.C. § 2000e-5(c) of Title VII, no charge may be filed with the EEOC until 60 days have elapsed from the time a charge is filed with a local state agency having the authority to administer state civil rights laws that prohibit unlawful employment practices.

The purpose of this 60-day deferral period is "to give States and localities an opportunity to combat discrimination free from premature federal intervention." Equal Employment Opportunity Commission v. Commercial Office Products Co., 486 U.S. 107, 110–11, 108 S.Ct. 1666, 100 L.Ed.2d 96 (1988). Mohasco Corp. v. Silver, 447 U.S. 807, 100 S.Ct. 2486, 65 L.Ed.2d 532 (1980) held that, consistent with this deferral period, a complainant must either file a charge with the state agency, or have the EEOC refer the charge to the state agency, within 240 days of the alleged discriminatory event. See Commercial Office Products, 486 U.S. at 111, 108 S.Ct. 1666 (citing Mohasco, 447 U.S. at 814 n. 16, 100 S.Ct. 2486 [1980]). However, if the EEOC enters into work sharing agreements with a state agency authorized to enforce state employment discrimination laws, and the state waives the Title VII statutory 60 day deferral period, the state's investigation is considered "terminated," and a claimant may file a discrimination charge directly with the EEOC within 300 days after the alleged discriminatory conduct—even if the claimant has not filed a timely state charge. Commercial Office Products, 486 U.S. at 124–25, 108 S.Ct. 1666. See also Janikowski v. Bendix Corp., 823 F.2d 945, 947 (1987) ("In states such as Michigan, which have their own laws forbidding age discrimination, a plaintiff must file a claim of ADEA violation 'within 300 days after the alleged unlawful practice occurred.'"). Consequently, plaintiff's claims based on discriminatory conduct that occurred 300 days before the EEOC received plaintiff's April 23, 1997 Charge of Discrimination, being claims based on conduct that occurred on or after July 2, 1996, are timely as a matter of law.

[12] Further, plaintiff may also pursue pre-July 2, 1996 hostile work environment and retaliation claims pursuant to the "continuing violation" doctrine. Plaintiff has produced evidence indicating Kozik made sexually hostile remarks to former co-employee Jessica Farmer within plaintiff's working environment after July 2, 1996, specifically, on July 25, 1996, August 13, 1996, and August 16, 1996. A confidential memo regarding harassment/fear of retaliation was allegedly submitted to CFC on August 12, 1996, and Kozik was not removed from the work environment until August 16, 1996. Otherwise time-barred unlawful discriminatory acts may be actionable if, as here, the plaintiff can establish a continuous pattern discrimination throughout her term of employment that continued into the EEOC charge-filing period. See Held v. Gulf Oil Co., 684 F.2d 427, 430 (6th Cir.1982) ("[s]ince [the evidence] supports a finding that discriminatory acts continued throughout her period of employment, the plaintiff's action is not time barred"). See also Hull v. Cuyahoga Valley Joint Vocational School District Board of Education, 926 F.2d 505, 510–11 (6th Cir.1991) (stating "there are important ***544** policy reasons not to require a discrimination suit be filed at the first instance of discrimination or not at all."). Defendants are not entitled to summary judgment based on the asserted untimeliness of plaintiff's claims. Winningham, 42 F.3d at 984.

iii.

Defendants move for summary judgment of plaintiff's claims post-dating August 16, 1996 arguing: (1) plaintiff cannot prove that she suffered an objective, material adverse employment action as a result of other transfers from the CFC paralegal position to Discount Supervisor, to Receptionist, and on to her current position as a Bankruptcy Specialist/Supervisor because plaintiff cannot prove she has lost any pay or benefits; (2) plaintiff cannot prove she suffered emotional damages after October 12, 1997 when she was promoted to the position of Bankruptcy Specialist/Supervisor, and; (3) plaintiff has not rebutted defendants' legitimate reasons for her transfer out of the paralegal position.

[13][14][15] On October 28, 1996, plaintiff was transferred to the position of Discount Supervisor in CFC's Troy, Michigan office, where she worked until March 1997 when she took a medical leave of absence. Upon her return to work on July 5, 1997, she was assigned a position as a Receptionist. In October 1997, plaintiff was transferred to her current position as a Bankruptcy Specialist/Supervisor. A tangible employment action includes reassignment to a position with "significantly different responsibilities." Burlington Industries, Inc. v. Ellerth, 524 U.S. 742, 761, 118 S.Ct. 2257, 141 L.Ed.2d 633 (1998). In determining whether an employment action was materially adverse, and thus actionable, a court

should consider such factors as a demotion evidenced by a decrease in wages or salary, a less distinguished title, a material loss of benefits, significantly diminished responsibilities, or other indices unique to the situation. See Kocsis v. Multi-Care Mgt., Inc., 97 F.3d 876, 886 (6th Cir.1996) (cited in Burlington Industries, 524 U.S. at 761, 118 S.Ct. 2257). A plaintiff's subjective personal preferences are insufficient to prove an actionable adverse employment action. See Brown v. Brody, 199 F.3d 446, 455 (D.C.Cir.1999).

[16] Plaintiff Smith has produced evidence that her transfer from her position as a CFC paralegal to Discount Supervisor, and then to the position of Receptionist, resulted in changes a professional to clerical positions, resulted in a less distinguished title, significantly diminished her job responsibilities, and resulted in the loss of a private office. Although plaintiff may have been required to work as a Receptionist on her return from medical leave because the Discount Supervisor position had been filled, it must be remembered that plaintiff was initially transferred to the Discount Supervisor position by CFC. The court also concludes that, in construing the evidence in a light most favorable to plaintiff, a jury could further conclude that the transfer from the CFC paralegal position to the current Bankruptcy Specialist/Supervisor position likewise represents a tangible adverse employment action accompanied by objective loss. The increase in actual and potential pay and benefits is not dispositive, especially in this unique situation involving several job transfers. See Kocsis, 97 F.3d at 886. The court is not prepared to find that plaintiff cannot recover post-October 1997 emotional damages solely because she now occupies a position that pays better than the paralegal position she occupied on October 27, 1996. The issue of plaintiff's damages, and the defendants mitigation of same, should be submitted to the jury.

As pointed out in Section III, B, supra, plaintiff Smith may rebut the proffered legitimate reasons of corporate security and potential ethical breaches by showing: (1) the reasons have no basis in fact; (2) these reasons did not actually motivate the challenged decisions, or; (3) the reasons are insufficient to motivate the transfer decision. See Manzer, 29 F.3d at 1084. ***545** Defendants are not entitled to summary judgment based on the absence of an actionable adverse employment action, an inability to prove post-October 12, 1997 emotional damages, or an inability to rebut defendants' proffered reasons for the employment decisions made. Winningham, 42 F.3d at 984.

iv.

[17][18][19] Defendants move for summary judgment of plaintiff's hostile work environment claims arguing plaintiff has not plead requisite severe and pervasive conduct, nor does plaintiff allege she was the target of Kozik's sexual advances. A hostile work environment claim requires proof that the discrimination is so severe or pervasive as to alter the conditions of the plaintiff's employment. See Oldham County, 201 F.3d at 790; Hafford v. Seidner, 183 F.3d 506, 512 (6th Cir.1999) (quoting Meritor Sav. Bank, FSB v. Vinson, 477 U.S. 57, 67, 106 S.Ct. 2399, 91 L.Ed.2d 49 [1986]) (deciding issue of race discrimination). In order to prove a prima facie hostile environment claim, the plaintiff must establish five elements: (1) she is a member of the protected class; (2) she was subjected to unwelcome harassment; (3) the harassment was based on sex; (4) the harassment had the effect of unreasonably interfering with her work performance by creating an intimidating hostile or offensive work environment and (5) the existence of employer liability. Seidner, 183 F.3d at 512.

> In determining whether an environment is one that a reasonable person would find hostile or abusive and that the plaintiff in fact did perceive to be so, courts look at all of the circumstances, including: [T]he frequency of the discriminatory conduct; its severity; whether it is physically threatening or humiliating, or a mere offensive utterance; and whether it unreasonably interferes with an employee's work performance.

Harris [v. Forklift Sys. Inc.], 510 U.S. [17,] 23, 114 S.Ct. 367, 126 L.Ed.2d 295; Abeita v. TransAmerica Mailings, Inc., 159 F.3d 246, 251 (6th Cir.1998). "A recurring point" in the Supreme Court's opinions is that" 'simple teasing,' offhand comments, and isolated incidents (unless extremely serious) will not amount to discriminatory changes in the 'terms and conditions of employment'" and that "conduct must be extreme to amount to a change in the terms and conditions of employment." Faragher v. City of Boca Raton, 524 U.S. 775, 785–86, 118 S.CT. 2275, 2283–84, 141 L.Ed.2d 662 (1998) (citations omitted).

Seidner. 183 F.3d at 512–13. See also Oldham County, 201 F.3d at 790. Isolated incidents and remarks do not give rise to Title VII liability unless they are extremely serious because Title VII is not a "general civility code." Faragher, 524 U.S. at 781, 118 S.Ct. 2275.

[20] To determine if an abusive work environment existed, the court must apply a two part totality of the circumstances test, requiring an analysis under both an objective reasonable person standard and a subjective standard. Seidner, 183 F.3d at 512.

> Conduct that is not severe or pervasive enough to create an objectively hostile or abusive work environment—an environment that a reasonable person would find hostile or abusive—is beyond Title VII's purview. Likewise, if the victim does not subjectively perceive the environment to be abusive, the conduct has not actually altered the conditions of the victim's employment, and there is no Title VII violation.

Harris, 510 U.S. at 21–22, 114 S.Ct. 367. A court must review the work environment as a whole because, under certain circumstances, a hostile work environment may be proven by establishing the cumulative effect of related acts of abuse. See Williams v. General Motors Corp., 187 F.3d 553, 563 (6th Cir.1999).

[21] Construing the pleadings and available evidence in a light most favorable *546 to plaintiff Smith, the issue of whether plaintiff was subjected to an actionable sexually hostile work environment must be submitted to the jury. The fact the Kozik's alleged sexual comments were not directed at plaintiff is relevant to the determination of whether an objectively hostile work environment existed, but is not dispositive. See Oldham County, 201 F.3d at 790. See also Jackson v. Quanex Corp., 191 F.3d 647, 660 (6th Cir.1999) (rejecting view that harassment, to be actionable, must be aimed at the plaintiff); Equal Opportunity Commission v. Ohio Edison, 7 F.3d 541 (6th cir.1993) (Title VII prohibits discrimination against an employee who "opposes any practice" unlawful under Title VII). As determined in Section III, C, ii, supra, the "continuing violation" doctrine permits plaintiff to pursue her hostile work environment claims based on all of Kozik's alleged harassment, including any pre-July 2, 1996 conduct. Consistent with this determination, and reviewing plaintiff's work environment as a whole, including pre-July 2, 1996 conduct, this record does not preclude Smith's claims that Kozik's conduct in the CFC work environment went beyond simple teasing, offhand comments, or isolated incidents directed at paralegal Farmer. The court awaits full development of the work environment at trial. Defendants are not entitled to summary judgment based on plaintiff's asserted inability to prove she was subjected to a sufficiently severe or pervasive sexually hostile conduct. Winningham, 42 F.3d at 984.

IV.

Conclusion

For the reasons set forth above, defendants CFC's and Chrysler's motion to compel arbitration is hereby DENIED. Plaintiff Smith's motion for partial summary judgment as to liability only is hereby DENIED. Defendants CFC's and Chrysler's motions for summary judgment are hereby DENIED.

IT IS ORDERED.

END OF DOCUMENT

EXERCISES

1. If the Assistant General Counsel, in fact, made repeated sexual advances and comments about others to the paralegal, do you believe this constitutes sexual harassment?

2. Based on the facts of the case, do you believe the defendants transferred the paralegal based on their belief that she would leak confidential and sensitive information or because the paralegal filed a sexual harassment lawsuit?

3. Did you agree with the court that the paralegal's transfer to clerical positions could indeed be construed as "adverse employment action"?

4. Did you generally agree or disagree with the decision?

ETHICS AND MALPRACTICE

Chapter Objectives

After you read this chapter, you should be able to:

- Define what the unauthorized practice of law is and list factors that are used to determine whether a legal assistant is "practicing law."

- Discuss the voluntary ethical codes established by national legal assistant associations.

- Explain the attorney-client privilege and to whom it applies.

- List guidelines that will prevent legal assistants from accidentally revealing confidential client information.

- Explain what a conflict of interest is and what a law office can do to limit conflict of interest problems.

- Discuss what an "Ethical Wall" is and when it applies.

The Johnson & Smith law firm primarily handled bankruptcy cases. The firm employed two attorneys, several legal assistants, and clerical staff. The bankruptcy trustee considered the firm to be a "high-volume filer," filing an average of 77 cases per month (nearly 1,000 per year). The firm's standard practice in handling cases was for a legal assistant to:

- hold an initial consultation meeting with the client, without an attorney present.

- discuss with the client the bankruptcy chapters available.

- assist the client in deciding which, if any, chapter proceedings should be filed.

- consult an attorney if a client had a question he or she could not answer

and relay the attorney's response back to the client.

- ask the client to complete a questionnaire.

- review the questionnaire.

- prepare the bankruptcy papers to be filed.

- meet with the client again (without an attorney present) for the purpose of having the client sign the papers.

In most instances, unless the client specifically requested to meet with an attorney, the client's first contact with the attorney was at the meeting of creditors. The court found that the legal assistants performed many services that constituted the unauthorized practice of law. Adapted from *In re Pinkins*, 213 B.R. 818 (Bankr.E.D. Mich.1997), included at the end of this chapter.

WHY ARE ETHICS AND MALPRACTICE IMPORTANT?

The importance of high ethical standards and of following your state's ethical rules cannot be overemphasized. Clients and attorneys must have total confidence that a legal assistant understands the many ethical problems that might arise in the practice of law and that the legal assistant's ethical judgment is clear. Ethical problems routinely encountered by legal assistants include unauthorized practice of law questions, conflict of interest problems, and confidentiality problems. Unethical behavior of a legal assistant can cause an attorney to lose a case, destroy client confidence in the entire law office, or lead a client to dismiss the attorney. Unethical behavior on the part of a legal assistant could lead to sanctions, fines, and disciplinary action against the attorney, and can cost a legal assistant his or her job. It also could result in damaging publicity for the law office and may even lead to criminal charges being filed against the attorney. Consequently, legal assistants must know how to work through and solve tough ethical problems.

A legal assistant must perform careful, high-quality work in everything he or she does. An error can be very costly and can subject an attorney or law office to a malpractice claim. Malpractice occurs when an attorney's or law office's conduct does not meet the professional standard for the area and injures a client. Malpractice claims can result in a law office being liable for thousands of dollars of damages to injured clients. Legal assistants must clearly understand how malpractice occurs and how it can be prevented.

> *Every day, paralegals run into minor or major roadblocks and are faced with situations requiring professional or ethical judgment. The consequences of ignoring or walking away from the sometimes subtle, fine, gray line can have serious ramifications and aftermath.*[1]

LEGAL ETHICS AND PROFESSIONAL RESPONSIBILITY

Legal ethics is an increasingly important and difficult topic for legal assistants in every type of law practice. There are many treatises that cover this topic in depth. This section will cover ethics only from a legal assistant's perspective and will give insight into common ethical problems likely to arise.

Ethics is an important topic not only because a law office or attorney can be disciplined for violating ethical rules but also because legal ethics bears on whether quality legal services are being provided to clients. If a law office or its employee engages in unethical conduct, the reputation of the office will be affected and clients will lose confidence in it. The unethical behavior does not necessarily have to be directly detrimental to the client or the client's case. If a client senses that the attorney or legal assistant is acting unethically toward an adversary, the client may suspect that the attorney or legal assistant could be guilty of the same type of practice toward her. The issues of trust and ethics are closely related and bear directly upon the attorney and client relationship.

When clients lose confidence, they may move their business to another law office, cease referring new clients to the law office, or even sue. Nearly 70 percent of all new business a law office receives comes from referrals. When a client takes business elsewhere, it has an immediate as well as a long-term effect on the firm, since that source of revenue is also gone for future years. In short, legal ethics has a direct bearing on the law office's bottom line and on the long-term success of the firm. Thus, legal assistants and attorneys have both an incentive and a duty to act ethically and to develop systems that stress the importance of legal ethics on a daily basis.

> *Legal ethics is becoming increasingly complex for lawyers and legal assistants alike. With greater accountability to clients, increased mobility for all law firm personnel, and a growing demand to improve the image of the legal profession, it is essential to keep abreast of current developments in ethics and to adhere to professional standards.*[2]

Figure 3-1
Example of Ethical
Violation and
Subsequent Ethical
Proceedings
Against an Attorney

The facts:	An attorney represented a client who was selling a piece of real estate. It was agreed that the attorney's fees would be $6,500. After completing the sale, the proceeds of the sale were placed into the attorney's trust account (i.e., a holding account for client funds). The attorney paid some proceeds to the client, withdrew $14,000 for himself, would not provide an accounting of the funds to the client, and would not respond to many messages left by the client.
The client:	The client, becoming increasingly frustrated with the attorney, calls the local courthouse and asks how to complain about the conduct of the attorney. The client is told to send a letter of complaint to the state's disciplinary administrator in the state's judicial branch. The client is told that the letter should clearly explain who the attorney was and exactly what happened. The client then sends the letter.
The disciplinary administrator:	The state's disciplinary administrator receives the client's letter. The administrator determines that if everything the client says is true, the attorney may have violated Supreme Court Rule 4-1.5 for his state, which says that "an attorney shall not charge an illegal or clearly excessive fee." The administrator sends a letter to the attorney asking for his side of the story but never receives a reply.
Investigation:	The disciplinary administrator then refers the matter to the State Bar's Investigation Committee, which investigates the matter, including interviews with both the client and the attorney. The Committee, after a full investigation, recommends that formal charges be filed before the state's bar court to discipline the attorney.
State's bar court/state's supreme court:	The disciplinary administrator files formal charges and prosecutes the attorney for the ethical violations before the state's bar court, an arm of the state's supreme court. A hearing or trial is held where both sides present their evidence. The bar court determines that the attorney violated Rule 4-1.5 and disciplines the attorney by suspending him from the practice of law for two years, and orders him to pay restitution to the client.

Ethical Standards for Attorneys

ethical rule
A minimal standard
of conduct.

An **ethical rule** is a minimal standard of conduct. An attorney may not fall below the standard without losing his or her good standing with the state bar. Attorneys who violate ethical rules may be disciplined; discipline for unethical conduct may include permanent disbarment from practicing law, temporary suspension from practicing, public censure, private censure, or an informal reprimand. Figure 3-1 shows a procedural example of ethical rules at work. The client initiates the inquiry in most instances of attorney misconduct, typically by sending a letter of complaint to the state's disciplinary administrator. The state disciplinary administration is in charge of enforcing the state's professional licensing standards for attorneys.

It is estimated that about one disciplinary complaint is filed for every 10 lawyers each year. The important thing with disciplinary complaints is not to win the war, but rather to avoid the battle.[3]

Ethics has had a long-standing place in the American legal system. In 1908, the American Bar Association (ABA), a voluntary association of attorneys, adopted the Canons of Professional Ethics. In 1969, the ABA updated and expanded the canons into the *Model Code of Professional Responsibility.* The *Model Code* was updated in 1983 and is now called *Model Rules of Professional Conduct.*

In the late 1990s, the ABA convened the Ethics 2000 Commission on evaluation of the rules of professional conduct to undertake a comprehensive review and rewrite of the *Model Rules;* in 2002, the ABA adopted the newly revised *Model Rules* after several years of work and 50 days of open meetings, including numerous public hearings and free debate.

Today, nearly all states base their ethical rules on the ABA *Model Rules.* Attorneys in each state are regulated by their individual state bar association and state court system. Although state courts are free to create their own rules of conduct for attorneys, most simply modify either the ABA *Model Code* or ABA *Model Rules* to reflect the specific ethical conditions in their own states. For this text, the ABA *Model Rules* is most often cited, even though some states still model their ethical/disciplinary rules on the older ABA *Model Code.*

Model Code of Professional Responsibility/ Model Rules of Professional Conduct
Self-imposed ethical standards for ABA members, but they also serve as a prototype of legal ethic standards for state court systems.

Attorney Ethical Rules Not Directly Applicable to the Legal Assistant

State canons of ethics, the *Model Code of Professional Responsibility,* or the *Model Rules of Professional Conduct* do not apply directly to legal assistants, but to attorneys only. However, attorneys can be disciplined for the acts of their staff members, including legal assistants, because attorneys have the duty to adequately supervise their staffs (see Figure 3-2).

The American Bar Association's Model Rules of Professional Conduct *and the rules of the various state bar associations are more than a list of ethical dos and don'ts. They are a strategic plan that addresses our relationship [as legal professionals] with clients, the courts, government, and . . . lawyers.*[4]

This section of the *Model Rules* is important to legal assistants because it requires attorneys to ensure that their staff members operate within the bounds of these rules. Figure 3-3 is a summary of case where a law office was sued for malpractice and the attorney was suspended from practice because of the unethical acts

RULE 5.3 RESPONSIBILITIES REGARDING NONLAWYER ASSISTANTS

With respect to a nonlawyer employed or retained by or associated with a lawyer:

(a) a partner, and a lawyer who individually or together with other lawyers possesses comparable managerial authority in a law firm shall make reasonable efforts to ensure that the firm has in effect measures giving reasonable assurance that the person's conduct is compatible with the professional obligations of the lawyer;

(b) a lawyer having direct supervisory authority over the nonlawyer shall make reasonable efforts to ensure that the person's conduct is compatible with the professional obligations of the lawyer; and

(c) a lawyer shall be responsible for conduct of such a person that would be a violation of the Rules of Professional Conduct if engaged in by a lawyer if:

    (1) the lawyer orders or, with the knowledge of the specific conduct, ratifies the conduct involved; or

    (2) the lawyer is a partner or has comparable managerial authority in the law firm in which the person is employed, or has direct supervisory authority over the person, and knows of the conduct at a time when its consequences can be avoided or mitigated but fails to take reasonable remedial action.

Comment

[1] Lawyers generally employ assistants in their practice, including secretaries, investigators, law student interns, and paraprofessionals. Such assistants, whether employees or independent contractors, act for the lawyer in rendition of the lawyer's professional services. A lawyer must give such assistants appropriate instruction and supervision concerning the ethical aspects of their employment, particularly regarding the obligation not to disclose information relating to representation of the client, and should be responsible for their work product. The measures employed in supervising nonlawyers should take account of the fact that they do not have legal training and are not subject to professional discipline.

[2] Paragraph (a) requires lawyers with managerial authority within a law firm to make reasonable efforts to establish internal policies and procedures designed to provide reasonable assurance that nonlawyers in the firm will act in a way compatible with the Rules of Professional Conduct. See Comment [1] to Rule 5.1. Paragraph (b) applies to lawyers who have supervisory authority over the work of a nonlawyer. Paragraph (c) specifies the circumstances in which a lawyer is responsible for conduct of a nonlawyer that would be a violation of the Rules of Professional Conduct if engaged in by a lawyer.

of a paralegal. If a legal assistant is found to be acting unethically, especially when there is a pattern and practice of doing so, the attorney has an affirmative duty to remedy the situation, even if that means terminating the legal assistant's employment. Thus, there are many incentives for legal assistants to act ethically and to comply with the same rules as attorneys. In addition, this rule ensures that an attorney cannot avoid the ethical rules and accomplish an unethical act by delegating or allowing a staff member to do it.

So, although a legal assistant cannot be disciplined by state regulatory bodies for violating state ethical rules, he or she would be held accountable by the attorney who hired or supervised him or her. Legal assistants must understand and abide by any ethical rules governing the conduct of attorneys.

In April, the owners of Asphalt Engineers met with Robert Walston, a legal assistant with Lee and Peggy Galusha, doing business as Galusha, Ltd., a private law firm. Asphalt Engineers told Walston that they wanted to file liens against real property involved in three construction jobs for which they had not been paid. They also requested that lawsuits foreclosing those liens be filed, if necessary. At trial, the owners of Asphalt Engineers testified that they believed Walston was an attorney. Walston requested and received a retainer payment from Asphalt Engineers. A lien was filed on one of the projects, but not on the other two. The project where the lien was filed was settled.

In June of the same year, Walston requested and received an additional retainer fee. Although Walston indicated that liens had been filed on the remaining two projects, none actually were. The time for filing both liens expired. Before Asphalt Engineers discovered that the two liens had not been filed, they brought forth another project for Walston to file a lien on; again, no lien was filed.

The court found that neither of the Galushas had ever met with Asphalt Engineers and that the Galushas allowed Walston, a nonlawyer, to provide legal advice to Asphalt Engineers, failed to file and foreclose liens, failed to adequately supervise Walston, and failed to prevent Walston from actually practicing law, among other things. Subsequently, a jury awarded Asphalt Engineers more than $75,000 in actual damages, attorneys' fees, and punitive damages against the Galusha law firm. In addition, Lee Galusha faced ethical proceedings for failing to adequately supervise the legal assistant and for failing to adequately perform legal work for a client. Lee Galusha was subsequently suspended from the practice of law and eventually was disbarred.

Figure 3-3
Attorneys Liable for Unethical Acts of Legal Assistant

Source: See *Asphalt Engineers, Inc. v. Galusha*, 770 P.2d 1180 (160 Ariz. 134, 1989).

In addition to the possible effect upon a legal assistant's continued employment, a breach of ethics may require payment of monetary damages to an opposing party. The legal assistant's failure to conform to ethical standards also may result in specific, demonstrable harm to the client, when, for example, the ethical breach consists of disclosure of confidential information, taking a position in conflict with that of the client, practicing law without a license, or performing professional work in a negligent manner.[5]

Voluntary Ethical Codes Established by Legal Assistant Associations

Legal assistants remain largely unregulated. There are, however, self-imposed, *voluntary* ethical standards set out by national or local legal assistant associations. Both the National Association of Legal Assistants (NALA) and the National Federation of Paralegal Associations (NFPA) have adopted ethical canons for their members. Figures 3-4 and 3-5 show the codes of ethics for both associations. Legal assistants cannot be disciplined for not following such voluntary codes. However, following such a code will help the legal assistant avoid ethical problems.

**Figure 3-4
National Association
of Legal Assistants,
Inc. Code of Ethics
and Professional
Responsibility**

Reprinted with the permission
of Legal Assistants, 1516 S.
Boston, #200, Tulsa.
www.nala.org. Copyright 1975:
revised 1979, 1988, 1995.

NALA Code of Ethics and Professional Responsibility

A legal assistant must adhere strictly to the accepted standards of legal ethics and to the general principles of proper conduct. The performance of the duties of the legal assistant shall be governed by specific canons as defined herein so that justice will be served and goals of the profession attained. (See *Model Standards and Guidelines for Utilization of Legal Assistants,* Section II.)

The canons of ethics set forth hereafter are adopted by the National Association of Legal Assistants, Inc., as a general guide intended to aid legal assistants and attorneys. The enumeration of these rules does not mean there are not others of equal importance although not specifically mentioned. Court rules, agency rules and statutes must be taken into consideration when interpreting the canons.

Definition: Legal assistants, also known as paralegals, are a distinguishable group of persons who assist attorneys in the delivery of legal services. Through formal education, training and experience, legal assistants have knowledge and expertise regarding the legal system and substantive and procedural law, which qualify them to do work of a legal nature under the supervision of an attorney.

Canon 1.   A legal assistant must not perform any of the duties that attorneys only may perform nor take any actions that attorneys may not take.

Canon 2.   A legal assistant may perform any task which is properly delegated and supervised by an attorney, as long as the attorney is ultimately responsible to the client, maintains a direct relationship with the client and assumes professional responsibility for the work product.

Canon 3.   A legal assistant must not: (a) engage in, encourage, or contribute to any act which could constitute the unauthorized practice of law; and (b) establish attorney-client relationships, set fees, give legal opinions or advice or represent a client before a court or agency unless so authorized by that court or agency; and (c) engage in conduct or take any action which would assist or involve the attorney in a violation of professional ethics or give the appearance of professional impropriety.

Canon 4.   A legal assistant must use discretion and professional judgment commensurate with knowledge and experience but must not render independent legal judgment in place of an attorney. The services of an attorney are essential in the public interest whenever such legal judgment is required.

Canon 5.   A legal assistant must disclose his or her status as a legal assistant at the outset of any professional relationship with a client, attorney, a court or administrative agency or personnel thereof, or a member of the general public. A legal assistant must act prudently in determining the extent to which a client may be assisted without the presence of an attorney.

Canon 6.   A legal assistant must strive to maintain integrity and a high degree of competency through education and training with respect to professional responsibility, local rules and practice, and through continuing education in substantive areas of law to better assist the legal profession in fulfilling its duty to provide legal service.

Canon 7.   A legal assistant must protect the confidences of a client and must not violate any rule or statute now in effect or hereafter enacted controlling the doctrine of privileged communications between a client and an attorney.

Canon 8.   A legal assistant must do all other things incidental, necessary, or expedient for the attainment of the ethics and responsibilities as defined by statute or rule of court.

Canon 9.   A legal assistant's conduct is guided by bar associations' codes of professional responsibility and rules of professional conduct.

NATIONAL FEDERATION OF PARALEGAL ASSOCIATIONS, INC.
MODEL CODE OF ETHICS AND PROFESSIONAL RESPONSIBILITY
AND GUIDELINES FOR ENFORCEMENT

PREAMBLE

The National Federation of Paralegal Associations, Inc. (NFPA) is a professional organization comprised of paralegal associations and individual paralegals throughout the United States and Canada. Members of NFPA have varying backgrounds, experiences, education and job responsibilities that reflect the diversity of the paralegal profession. NFPA promotes the growth, development and recognition of the paralegal profession as an integral partner in the delivery of legal services.

In May 1993 NFPA adopted its Model Code of Ethics and Professional Responsibility (*Model Code*) to delineate the principles for ethics and conduct to which every paralegal should aspire.

Many paralegal associations throughout the United States have endorsed the concept and content of NFPA's *Model Code* through the adoption of their own ethical codes. In doing so, paralegals have confirmed the profession's commitment to increase the quality and efficiency of legal services, as well as recognized its responsibilities to the public, the legal community, and colleagues.

Paralegals have recognized, and will continue to recognize, that the profession must continue to evolve to enhance their roles in the delivery of legal services. With increased levels of responsibility comes the need to define and enforce mandatory rules of professional conduct. Enforcement of codes of paralegal conduct is a logical and necessary step to enhance and ensure the confidence of the legal community and the public in the integrity and professional responsibility of paralegals.

In April 1997 NFPA adopted the Model Disciplinary Rules (*Model Rules*) to make possible the enforcement of the Canons and Ethical Considerations contained in the NFPA *Model Code*. A concurrent determination was made that the *Model Code of Ethics and Professional Responsibility,* formerly aspirational in nature, should be recognized as setting forth the enforceable obligations of all paralegals.

The *Model Code* and *Model Rules* offer a framework for professional discipline, either voluntarily or through formal regulatory programs.

§1. NFPA MODEL DISCIPLINARY RULES AND ETHICAL CONSIDERATIONS
1.1 A PARALEGAL SHALL ACHIEVE AND MAINTAIN A HIGH LEVEL OF COMPETENCE.
1.2 A PARALEGAL SHALL MAINTAIN A HIGH LEVEL OF PERSONAL AND PROFESSIONAL INTEGRITY.
1.3 A PARALEGAL SHALL MAINTAIN A HIGH STANDARD OF PROFESSIONAL CONDUCT.
1.4 A PARALEGAL SHALL SERVE THE PUBLIC INTEREST BY CONTRIBUTING TO THE IMPROVEMENT OF THE LEGAL SYSTEM AND DELIVERY OF QUALITY LEGAL SERVICES, INCLUDING PRO BONO PUBLICO SERVICES.
1.5 A PARALEGAL SHALL PRESERVE ALL CONFIDENTIAL INFORMATION PROVIDED BY THE CLIENT OR ACQUIRED FROM OTHER SOURCES BEFORE, DURING, AND AFTER THE COURSE OF THE PROFESSIONAL RELATIONSHIP.
1.6 A PARALEGAL SHALL AVOID CONFLICTS OF INTEREST AND SHALL DISCLOSE ANY POSSIBLE CONFLICT TO THE EMPLOYER OR CLIENT, AS WELL AS TO THE PROSPECTIVE EMPLOYERS OR CLIENTS.
1.7 A PARALEGAL'S TTTLE SHALL BE FULLY DISCLOSED.
1.8 A PARALEGAL SHALL NOT ENGAGE IN THE UNAUTHORIZED PRACTICE OF LAW.

Figure 3-5
NFPA Model Code of Ethics and Professional Responsibility
Courtesy of National Federation of Paralegal Associations.

Criminal Statutes Regarding the Unauthorized Practice of Law

There are criminal statutes in nearly every state that provide sanctions for non-lawyers who engage in "practicing law," which usually includes providing legal advice to the public or representation of a client in a court of law.

There is no direct regulation of legal assistants, but they are indirectly regulated through state ethical standards for attorneys, nonbinding legal assistant association ethical standards, and criminal statutes barring nonattorneys from practicing law.

THE UNAUTHORIZED PRACTICE OF LAW

Most states have a criminal statute that prohibits a layperson from practicing law. The reason behind such a statute is to protect the general public from individuals who are not qualified to give legal advice because they do not have the proper educational training, have not passed the bar exam, or are not fit to practice law. In Florida for example, an unauthorized practice violation results in a third-degree felony charge and up to a $5,000 fine.

Besides criminal prohibitions, there are ethical prohibitions as well. Rule 5.5 of the ABA *Model Rules of Professional Conduct* prohibits an attorney from assisting a person who is not a member of the bar in an activity that would constitute the unauthorized practice of the law. This rule draws a line that legal assistants cannot cross. A legal assistant is permitted to assist an attorney as long as the activity does not, in itself, constitute "practicing law."

The real question is: at what point does one actually "practice law"? The ABA, as well as most states, has been unwilling to give a specific definition of exactly what the "practice of law" is, preferring to consider the matter on a case-by-case basis.

> *Simply put, legal assistants may conduct any law-related services at which they are competent, provided they do not engage in the "unauthorized practice of law." The unauthorized practice of law (UPL) is the practice of law by someone who does not hold a current law license.*[6]

While what constitutes the practice of law is established by each jurisdiction, Figure 3-6 explains what types of actions are typically referred to in court decisions as the "practice of law;" Figure 3-6 also defines "other work" in a law office. Notice in Figure 3-6 that there are many other professional duties that a legal assistant can perform that do not constitute the practice of law.

"Practice of Law"	"Other Work" in a Law Office
Giving legal advice	Obtaining facts from a client
Representing clients in court proceedings	Communicating information to the client
	Interviewing witnesses
Performing legal analysis and preparing legal documents	Performing limited legal research to assist an attorney with legal analysis
Evaluating a case and selecting an appropriate course of action	Obtaining documents
	Preparing drafts of requests for production of a document
Accepting or rejecting a case	Preparing drafts of interrogatories
Setting a fee	Preparing drafts of responses to requests for production of documents
Sharing a fee with an attorney	Preparing drafts of responses to interrogatories
	Preparing drafts of pleadings
	Preparing correspondence
	Organizing documents and evidence
	Preparing case chronologies
	Preparing deposition summaries
	Preparing exhibit lists
	Organizing and tracking deadlines
	Conducting factual research on the Internet
	Designing/entering litigation support database
	Working w/e-discovery requests/software
	Preparing presentations

Figure 3-6
The "Practice of Law" Versus "Other Work" in a Law Office[7]

Giving Legal Advice

Legal assistants may not directly advise a client regarding a legal matter. Courts usually apply three tests to determine whether, in fact, legal advice has been given.

- **Did the advice given require legal skill or knowledge?[8]** Generally, the question is whether or not the advice entails specific legal knowledge or skill.

The temptation to give legal advice is a challenge that almost every legal assistant encounters daily. During the span of a career, legal assistants become quite familiar with certain practice areas. They learn the answers to many common client questions. It can be very tempting to respond to a client's inquiry when one believes that he or she knows the answer . . . the legal assistant should refer the question to the lawyer with a statement such as "That's a question you should discuss with the lawyer."[9]

- **Was the person advised of his or her legal rights?**[10] This question centers around whether or not a client was specifically advised of his or her legal rights of what the law is or is not regarding a specific issue. While it is true that a legal assistant cannot advise a client of his or her rights without a UPL violation, most courts allow a legal assistant to consult with an attorney regarding a legal question and then convey the attorney's answer to the client. In this instance, the legal assistant is simply a conduit between the client and the attorney. As long as the legal assistant does not advise the client or convey separate thoughts or legal analysis of his or her own, he or she is not giving legal advice.[11] However, when legal assistants do convey legal advice to a client on the behalf of an attorney, it should be clearly stated that the attorney is the source of the information.

For example, in *In re Houston*, 127 N.M. 582, 985, P.2d 752 (N.M. 1999), clients came to an attorney's office when a van they had recently purchased had serious mechanical problems that the dealer refused to repair. The firm filed a lawsuit against the dealer. Approximately 18 months later, the car dealer filed for bankruptcy. The law firm received the bankruptcy notice, but never told the clients. The clients discovered the bankruptcy from someone else and called the law firm. The attorney's legal assistant handled the call and told the clients that the bankruptcy would not affect the case. The clients were never told that their claim could be lost if a discharge was entered in bankruptcy without an objection to discharge being granted for their claim. After the bankruptcy was closed, the district court dismissed the clients' claim as barred by the discharge in bankruptcy. At no time, from when the clients initially came to the law firm until just before the case was dismissed, did the clients meet with an attorney. The legal assistant gave legal advice specifically related to the effect of bankruptcy on the clients' case. The advice required legal skill and knowledge, arguably included advising the clients of their rights (the conclusion that the clients did not need to do anything because the bankruptcy would have no effect). In addition, the court found that having a legal assistant conduct all meetings with the clients, during which the clients' objectives and the means for pursuing them were discussed and decided, raised serious questions regarding the unauthorized practice of law. The attorney was suspended for 18 months. In another case, the Oregon state attorney general's office is presuming a $25,000 fine for an unauthorized practice of law validation of a paralegal. The unauthorized practice of law violation is for "continued possession of immigration law materials in his business office, representation to consumers of expertise of special knowledge about immigration matters, and use of the Internet to provide information related to immigration matters to consumers."

Avoiding the unauthorized practice of law (UPL) is probably the "finest line" any paralegal is asked to walk. Even experienced paralegals are not always sure how to handle situations involving insistent clients demanding an answer right now, or that acquaintance or family member who just needs some "friendly advice." If you are not sure if the activity you are about to undertake or the answer you are about to give constitutes UPL, the best rule of thumb is not to do it. It is much easier to say to someone. "I'll have to get back to you," or "Let me check with [supervising attorney/employer]," or "I really can't answer that question because I am not an attorney, but I will be happy to find out for you" than it is to find yourself facing charges for UPL and the very real possibility that you will never again be able to work in the legal field in any capacity.

—Lenette Pinchback, CLA

- **Is the advice not normally given by a nonlawyer as part of another business or transaction?**[12] Many professionals, such as tax accountants and real estate brokers, work in legal areas where they may regularly give law-related advice in the ordinary course of their job. This type of general advice usually does not amount to the practice of law.

Misrepresentation of Status

Another factor sometimes at issue regarding the giving of legal advice is whether or not the person giving the information to the client or third party clearly identified himself or herself as a legal assistant. Unless otherwise told, a client may rightly assume that he or she is talking to an attorney when, in fact, he or she is not. In such instances, the client may rely on the information from the legal assistant as legal advice. If a client is misled to believe that a legal assistant is an attorney, the client will expect the legal assistant to be able to take certain actions to advance his or her case that the legal assistant may either be insufficiently knowledgeable to undertake or expressly prohibited from taking.[13] To avoid misunderstandings, legal assistants should always disclose their status as a legal assistant and nonlawyer. Notice in Figure 3-3 that the NALA Code of Ethics and Professional Responsibility, Canon 5, states that "A legal assistant must disclose his or her status as a legal assistant at the outset of any professional relationship with a client, attorney, a court or administrative agency or personnel thereof, or a member of the general public."[14]

Representing Clients in Court Proceedings

Legal assistants generally cannot appear in federal or state courts or legal proceedings, such as a deposition, on behalf of a client; the rights and interests of the parties are more fully safeguarded with licensed attorneys who have extended training. However, some administrative agencies do allow a legal assistant to appear on behalf of a client. Some federal and state agencies require nonlawyers to satisfy certain requirements before appearing before them, while others do not. Some jurisdictions allow legal assistants to make limited appearances, such as in uncontested matters and small claims court. A legal assistant should carefully check the rules of his or her jurisdiction before making an appearance in a proceeding.

Performing Legal Analysis and Preparing Legal Documents

Legal assistants cannot draft legal documents such as wills, briefs, motions, pleadings, or contracts without the supervision of an attorney. Legal assistants routinely draft these types of documents; the distinction is that they do so properly under the direction and supervision of a member of the bar. The attorney is ultimately responsible for the legal documents; legal documents affect the legal rights of clients and parties and therefore require the oversight of an attorney. As long as a legal assistant is actively working under the supervision of an attorney, and the attorney maintains a relationship with the client, the legal assistant may interview witnesses or prospective clients, perform legal research, draft pleadings and briefs, and investigate the facts of cases without being accused of the unauthorized practice of law.

> *A legal assistant working for a lawyer in compliance with this rule can prepare documents without fear of UPL violations. It is the obligation of the legal assistant and lawyer to make sure the work product is reviewed by the lawyer before it is filed with a court or agency or shown to a client or third party.*[15]

Evaluating a Case, Selecting or Rejecting a Case, and Selecting an Appropriate Course of Action

The act of evaluating a fact pattern, applying it to the law, considering possible courses of action based on that factual and legal analysis, and working with the client to strategize the best outcome for the client is reserved exclusively for an attorney. It is a fundamental duty of practicing law for an attorney to perform these functions. Legal assistants may, of course, participate in this process, but they must do so under the auspices of an attorney. Also, the act of accepting or rejecting the representation of a client is usually reserved by an attorney, because the process includes the evaluation of the case and the potential giving of legal advice to the client. In *Cincinnati Bar Association v. Bertsche,* 84 Ohio St.3d 170, 702 N.E.2d 859 (Ohio 1998), an attorney allowed a legal assistant to operate a satellite office without adequate supervision. The legal assistant interviewed clients, obtained information, prepared documents, operated bank accounts, secured signings of bankruptcy petitions and other documents, and presumably (though not specifically stated) accepted cases (given that it was a satellite office). From time to time, the attorney would visit the office, interview clients, and oversee the signing of documents. The court concluded that the attorney's delegation of such matters to the legal assistant and his lack of supervision over that assistant violated a disciplinary rule regarding a lawyer not neglecting an entrusted legal matter.

Setting a Fee and Sharing a Fee

Legal assistants are not allowed to set legal fees or directly share in the fees.[16] A legal assistant can provide information regarding fees to a client at the attorney's direction, but the legal assistant should be careful to explain that the setting of the fee was done by the attorney. Rule 5.4(a) of the ABA *Model Rules of Professional Conduct* specifically states that lawyers may not share fees with nonlawyers.

In *In re Soulisak*, 227 B.R. 77 (E.D. Va. 1998), a lawyer and a nonlawyer worked together to provide legal services in bankruptcy cases. In addition, they agreed to split the legal fees. The agreement was to charge bankruptcy clients $650: $400 was paid to the attorney, and $250 was paid to the nonlawyer to cover paralegal, clerical, and operating expenses. The court found that the nonlawyer provided many of the services to the clients, thereby committing a UPL violation. The court also found the fee agreement to be improper fee sharing.

Legal Technicians, Freelance Legal Assistants, and the Unauthorized Practice of Law

Recently, a new class of legal assistants, sometimes called "legal technicians," has emerged. What separates **legal technicians** from legal assistants is that they market their services directly to the public and do not work under the supervision of an attorney. Bar associations across the country have argued that since legal technicians do not work under the supervision of a licensed attorney but represent clients directly, they clearly violate criminal statutes regarding the unauthorized practice of law. Legal technicians argue that they simply provide forms that have been written by attorneys and help the clients fill in the forms. Cases are being decided on this issue on a case-by-case matter, but many courts have limited or greatly restricted what services legal technicians can provide.

legal technicians
People who market their legal services directly to the public.

Freelance legal assistants were defined in Chapter 1 as self-employed legal assistants who market and sell their services to law offices on a per-job basis. Freelance legal assistants are less likely to be accused of the unauthorized practice of law, since they are supposed to be acting under the supervision of an attorney. However, in instances where the freelance legal assistant is removed from the attorney, and where supervision is limited or nonexistent, unauthorized practice of law problems can occur.

How to Avoid the Unauthorized Practice of Law

- **Always have your work approved by a supervising attorney.** No matter how routine a legal document is, an attorney should always review it. Remember, a legal assistant can do many types of activities as long as they are done under the supervision of an attorney, so take advantage of this and get everything approved. Never let an attorney approve your work without reading it. If the attorney says, "I do not have time to review it; I'll sign it and you just send it out, I trust you," bring the document back at another time or find a tactful way to suggest to him or her that the document needs to be approved the right way.

- **Never let clients talk you into giving them legal advice.** Most legal assistants never intend to give a client legal advice. However, it is easy to give in when a client presses you. This is usually because the attorney is unavailable and the client "needs an answer now." Legal advice might include telling the client what he or she should or should not do, answering a legal or statutory question, or telling the client what defense or legal argument he or she should make. Tell the client that you are a legal assistant and cannot give legal advice, but that you will either have the attorney call the client directly or you will talk to the attorney and call the client with the attorney's advice. If a legal assistant does give legal advice and things go wrong, for any reason, many clients will not hesitate to turn on you and say that they relied on your advice; this is why this issue is so critical. What a legal assistant can do is provide general broad information or the procedural aspects of the matter and suggest that the client seek the advice of an attorney.
- **Do not start sentences with "You should" or "I think."** When you hear yourself say "You should" or "I think," stop and realize that you are probably about to give legal advice. Again, it's not worth the risk.

> They (clients) sometimes think they can call you and get the same advice they get from the attorney, and unless you have cleared things with your attorney, you are really getting yourself in hot water if you tell them, "Yeah, you don't have to do this, just do that. . . . "Well, that's legal advice. . . . [17]

- **Always clearly identify yourself as a legal assistant.** When you talk to clients or send letters out on law office or company letterhead, *always* identify yourself as a legal assistant. It is very easy for a client to say "Well I thought he was an attorney" to a disciplinary administrator or in a malpractice case.

  Never represent to others, either directly or indirectly, that you are an attorney. Legal assistants are allowed to have business cards and sign letters on the law practice letterhead in many states, as long as the title of "legal assistant" or "paralegal" is included.
- **Management should develop ethical guidelines and rules.** From a management perspective, law office managers should publish rules regarding the unauthorized practice of law, tell staff members what they can and cannot do, and provide a policy on the responsibilities of supervising attorneys.
- **Management should make periodic checks of ethical standards.** It is not enough to simply establish rules and then never monitor them to see if they are being followed. Occasionally, management must monitor its staff regarding compliance with law practice rules and state guidelines to ensure compliance. Management should keep staff members up-to-date on changes or

clarifications in ethical standards by circulating recent ethical opinions. Publications of legal assistant associations also report on recent ethical opinions. When appropriate, these should be called to the attention of management for general circulation. Another option is for law office management to hold workshops or seminars on ethics. Attorneys, legal assistants, and staff members should be constantly reminded about ethics.

COMPETENCE AND DILIGENCE

The drafters of the ABA Model Rules *chose to give competence the most prominent place in the body of legal ethics rules. It is the very first rule, Model Rule 1.1. This positioning makes sense, because competence is necessary in every matter a lawyer or legal assistant handles and in each step in the delivery of legal services.*[18]

Legal assistants and attorneys must perform legal services in a competent and diligent manner. The *Model Rules'* Rule 1.1 (see Figure 3-7) states that an attorney must be competent in order to represent the client; that is, he or she must reasonably know the area of law that the client needs representation in and, assuming the attorney does know the area of law, that he or she takes the preparation time to become familiar with the case in order to represent the client adequately.

The purpose of this rule is to ensure that an attorney does not undertake a matter that he or she is not competent in, and to ensure that the attorney has had "adequate preparation." The amount of adequate preparation depends on the type of legal matter the client has; major litigation will require far more preparation time than, say, the amount of time it takes to prepare a will. A legal professional should not undertake to represent a client if he or she does not have the skill or preparation time necessary to do so. Legal assistants must have a basic understanding of the law in each area in which they are working. Additionally, they must be able to analyze, organize, and prepare the factual and legal data obtained to perform their job competently.

The legal assistant should be able to write clearly and effectively. The legal assistant must understand the goals, manner of, and organization of documents needed in the lawyer's practice, as well as the style and tone necessary for correspondence to clients and others. Although the lawyer ultimately will review all documents, the [legal] assistant should strive for perfection in the initial preparation. In this way, there will be less chance of an error.[19]

**Figure 3-7
ABA Model Rules
of Professional
Conduct—Rule 1.1**

RULE 1.1 COMPETENCE

A lawyer shall provide competent representation to a client. Competent representation requires the legal knowledge, skill, thoroughness and preparation reasonably necessary for the representation.

Comment:

Legal Knowledge and Skill

[1] In determining whether a lawyer employs the requisite knowledge and skill in a particular matter, relevant factors include the relative complexity and specialized nature of the matter, the lawyer's general experience, the lawyer's training and experience in the field in question, the preparation and study the lawyer is able to give the matter and whether it is feasible to refer the matter to, or associate or consult with, a lawyer of established competence in the field in question. In many instances, the required proficiency is that of a general practitioner. Expertise in a particular field of law may be required in some circumstances.

[2] A lawyer need not necessarily have special training or prior experience to handle legal problems of a type with which the lawyer is unfamiliar. A newly admitted lawyer can be as competent as a practitioner with long experience. Some important legal skills, such as the analysis of precedent, the evaluation of evidence, and legal drafting, are required in all legal problems. Perhaps the most fundamental legal skill consists of determining what kind of legal problems a situation may involve, a skill that necessarily transcends any particular specialized knowledge. A lawyer can provide adequate representation in a wholly novel field through necessary study. Competent representation can also be provided through the association of a lawyer of established competence in the field in question.

[3] In an emergency a lawyer may give advice or assistance in a matter in which the lawyer does not have the skill ordinarily required where referral to or consultation or association with another lawyer would be impractical. Even in an emergency, however, assistance should be limited to that reasonably necessary in the circumstances, for ill-considered action under emergency conditions can jeopardize the client's interest.

[4] A lawyer may accept representation where the requisite level of competence can be achieved by reasonable preparation. This applies as well to a lawyer who is appointed as counsel for an unrepresented person. See also Rule 6.2.

Thoroughness and Preparation

[5] Competent handling of a particular matter includes inquiry into and analysis of the factual and legal elements of the problem, and use of methods and procedures meeting the standards of competent practitioners. It also includes adequate preparation. The required attention and preparation are determined in part by what is at stake; major litigation and complex transactions ordinarily require more extensive treatment than matters of lesser complexity and consequence. An agreement between the lawyer and the client regarding the scope of the representation may limit the matters for which the lawyer is responsible. See Rule 1.2(c).

Maintaining Competence

[6] To maintain the requisite knowledge and skill, a lawyer should keep abreast of changes in the law and its practice, engage in continuing study and education and comply with all continuing legal education requirements to which the lawyer is subject.

Model Rule 1.3 requires that an attorney act with a reasonable degree of diligence and promptness in pursuing the client's case. Further insight is found in the comment to the rule:

> A client's interests can be adversely affected by the passage of time or the change of conditions; in extreme instances, as when a lawyer overlooks a statute of limitations, the client's legal position may be destroyed. Even when the client's interests are not affected in substance, however, unreasonable delay can cause a client needless anxiety and undermine confidence in the lawyer's trustworthiness.

The comment to this rule also notes that attorneys should carry through to conclusion all legal matters undertaken for a client unless the relationship is properly and clearly terminated. The purpose of this rule is to ensure that attorneys put forth reasonable effort and diligence in representing a client. Attorneys and legal assistants cannot adequately represent the interests of clients if they ignore the case, if they are lazy and do not work the case, or if they negligently handle the case.

> *Knowing my mistake could cost the attorneys I work for their license to practice law causes a great deal of stress. However, that knowledge is simultaneously beneficial because it causes me to be more careful, pay great attention to detail, and always strive to increase efficiency and effectiveness in my work [as a legal assistant].*[20]

Attention to detail is an extremely important skill for a legal assistant to possess. Figure 3-8 provides examples of how legal assistants failed to perform competently—not by failing to know the law, but rather by being disorganized or failing to pay attention to details.

Confidentiality and the Attorney-Client Privilege

Another basic ethical concept is that of client confidentiality. **Client confidentiality** refers to the need to keep information exchanged between a client and law office staff, including attorneys and legal assistants, confidential. In addition to the ethical rules of maintaining client confidences, there is a rule of evidence, generally called the attorney-client privilege, that an attorney or legal assistant may invoke to avoid revealing the secrets of a client. The purpose of both the privilege and the ethical rules is to ensure that clients can consult with their attorneys without the fear that such statements will be passed to others or used against them later. If clients knew that what they told their attorney could be repeated to others, clients would be reluctant to tell their attorneys the truth. The attorney-client privilege and the ethical rules on confidentiality complement one another to achieve the same end.

client confidentiality
Keeping information exchanged between a client and law office staff confidential.

**Figure 3-8
Legal Assistants
Failing to Act Compe-
tently and Diligently**

Legal Assistants Sued for Negligence

Unsupervised legal assistants engaged in the unauthorized practice of law:

When she represented three clients regarding their auto accident claims, the legal assistant's negligence was the proximate cause of clients' injuries, and attorneys and paralegal were jointly and severally liable for damages.

Tegman, et al., v. Accident: Medical, investigations, 107 wash. App 868, 30 p. 3d 8.

Legal Assistant Fails to File Document, Leads to Dismissal of Case

See *Ortiz v. Gavenda,* 590 N.W.2d 119 (Minn. 1999).

Israel Ortiz was severely injured on September 24, 1993 when the motorcycle he was driving collided with a truck driven by Bryan Gavenda and owned by Gavenda's employer, Frito Lay, Inc. Israel Ortiz died from those injuries on December 11, 1993. On June 6, 1995, his widow, Frances Ortiz (Ortiz), served a complaint on Gavenda and Frito Lay (collectively Gavenda) asserting a wrongful death claim and seeking damages as the trustee for the heirs of Israel Ortiz. Gavenda's answer to the complaint denied liability and alleged that Ortiz's claim "failed to comply with the provisions of Chapter 573 of Minnesota Statutes"—the chapter governing wrongful death actions.

On November 15, 1995, Ortiz signed a petition to have herself appointed trustee for the next of kin of her deceased husband as required by Minn. Stat. § 573.02, subd. 3 (1998). Although the petition and an accompanying consent and oath form were properly signed and duly notarized, a legal assistant for Ortiz's attorney inadvertently failed to submit the documents to the court and, as a consequence, Ortiz was not appointed trustee. The mistake went unnoticed when Ortiz's complaint was filed with the Anoka County District Court on December 6, 1995. The oversight came to light and Ortiz filed her petition to be appointed trustee on January 8, 1997, but by then more than three years had elapsed since her husband's death. The Minnesota Supreme Court dismissed the action due to the document not being filed on time by the legal assistant.

Legal Assistant Loses Complaint on Desk and Costs Employer Half Million Dollars

A legal assistant working for a corporation received a complaint on her desk regarding a wrongful termination lawsuit. Apparently, the legal assistant was gone the day the complaint arrived, and it was laid on her desk. The legal assistant did not find the complaint until approximately 38 days later. Under state law, there is a 20-day deadline for responding, and the judge granted the plaintiff a default judgment in the amount of $562,489. The defendant corporation appealed the judge's decision, but higher courts refused to reverse it, and the judgment against the company stood.

Source: *Legal Assistant Today,* January/February 1999, 24.

Legal Assistant's $92 Million Error

A legal assistant at Prudential mistakenly left off the last three zeros on a mortgage used to secure a $92,885,000 loan made by Prudential to a company that filed for bankruptcy. Because of the mistake, Prudential had a lien for only $92,885; the error left Prudential's lien $92,792,115 short.

Source: William Statsky. (1992). *Introduction to paralegalism.* St. Paul, MN: West Publishing.

The Attorney-Client Privilege
Rule of Evidence

Generally, the **attorney-client privilege** precludes the disclosure of confidential communications between a lawyer and a client by the lawyer. Thus, if a criminal defendant confessed a crime to his attorney, the attorney-client privilege prevents the prosecutor from calling the attorney to the stand to testify about the confession. In addition, courts have applied the attorney-client privilege to legal assistants.

> *It has long been held that the [attorney-client] privilege applies . . . to members of the bar, of a court, or their subordinates. . . . Examples of such protected subordinates would include any law student, paralegal, investigator, or other person acting as the agent of a duly qualified attorney under circumstances that would otherwise be sufficient to invoke the privilege.*
>
> —8 Wigmore, Evidence Section 2301 (McNaughton Rev. 1961).

Source: Dabney v. Investment Corp. of America, 82 F.R.D. 464, 465 (E.D. Pa. 1979).

attorney-client privilege
A standard that precludes the disclosure of confidential communications between a lawyer and a client by the lawyer.

For the privilege to be invoked, the communication must have been made in confidence between the client and the attorney for the purpose of obtaining legal advice.

> *A fundamental principle of the lawyer-client relationship is that a lawyer will not disclose a client's confidential information. This cornerstone of legal representation enables a client to speak freely without fear that embarrassing or legally damaging information will be revealed. . . . Lawyers or legal assistants may inadvertently waive the privilege if they share the information with a third person to whom the privilege does not extend, remove incriminating evidence from its original position, or divulge secrets to a court under a mistaken belief that disclosure is required. Waiver of the privilege means that the information can be admitted into evidence against the client at trial.*[21]

Ethical Prohibitions on Revealing
Client Communications

There are several ethical rules regarding attorneys preserving client communications, including Rule 1.6 of the ABA *Model Rules of Professional Conduct.* Rule 1.6 states that an attorney cannot reveal information relating to the representation of a client unless the client has consented to the release of information.

Canon 7 of the NALA *Code of Ethics and Professional Responsibility* (see Figure 3-4 and section 1.5 of NFPA's *Model Code of Ethics and Professional Responsibility* (see Figure 3-5), although not enforceable, prohibit legal assistants from revealing client confidences.

> *I used to work in a very small town where everyone knew everyone else's business. My mother-in-law would ask me every day how my day went and did I work on any interesting cases. After a few too many short answers indicating my day was fine without offering any "juicy details," she and I got into a very large fight about why I would never talk to her. Once I explained that I was not allowed to discuss the "juicy details," we got along just fine and she never asked again.*
>
> —Andrea Blanscet, CLA

Again, the purpose of these ethical rules is to encourage clients to be completely honest with their attorneys. Note that there are many nuances regarding the attorney-client privilege and ethical rules, however, including some exceptions to the rules.

Legal assistants have an absolute duty to preserve the confidences and communications of clients. All information must be kept confidential and should not, under any circumstances, be revealed in casual conversations with anyone outside the workplace. In addition to the moral and ethical reasons for not disclosing client communications, there also is the issue of quality service to the client. If a client learns that his or her communications have been revealed to outside sources, by whatever means, even if it is by accident, the client may lose confidence in the entire firm. If a client cannot trust his or her attorney, the client will quickly move on to another firm. If confidential information gets out, it could actually compromise the client's case.

How to Avoid Confidentiality Problems

- **Resist the temptation to talk about what goes on in the office, whether or not it is client related.** There is always a temptation to talk about office politics and other office matters with people outside the firm. Resist this temptation. If you do this, it will only make it easier to talk about client-related matters. Consider that you are a professional and that both your firm and your clients demand anonymity.
- **Only talk about client matters to office personnel on a need-to-know basis.** Never go around your office talking about a client's case to employees who do not have a reason to know about it. You must get in the habit of keeping information to yourself. Why tell someone about client-related matters, even if it is a fellow employee, unless he or she needs to know for some legitimate reason? Even if you are talking to someone who has a need to know, avoid doing so in public places, such as waiting rooms, elevators, and restaurants, where your conversation can be overheard.

Discussing a client's case with a friend or relative may be tempting. . . . Discussing cases may seem harmless if the names of the parties are changed or shielded. However, talking about cases, even innocently, is a breach of client confidentiality. Client information must never be discussed outside of the firm. . . . One never knows who may be acquainted with a client or with someone connected with a case or who may overhear a conversation. Concealing names will not be enough to protect confidential information if the listener (or someone else) can put all the pieces together. Revealing the information could result in a lost case, a malpractice suit, and a disciplinary action against the lawyer.[22]

- **Never discuss the specific facts or circumstances of a client's case with anyone, not even friends or relatives.** There is a specific temptation to talk with friends and relatives about interesting cases you have worked on, because you trust them. However, many client secrets have been unwittingly revealed by friends and relatives who have repeated information they never should have been told. The statement "I promise I won't tell anyone" does not work. People do tell. Former girlfriends or boyfriends may reveal knowledge you told them in order to spite you. Mothers, fathers, brothers, sisters, or friends may inadvertently reveal a confidence you told them that gets back to the client, adverse party, or a member of your law office. When this happens, you will hear about it one way or another, and the repercussions can be severe. Do not take the chance: it is simply not worth losing a client or a job. You should not even reveal the fact that an individual is or may be a client of your law office.
- **Always clear your desk of other case files when meeting with clients.** If case files are left in the open, other clients can read the files and access confidential information. Be very careful with any case files taken away from the law office.

If you get a call from someone outside the office asking for information about the case you're working on, always check with an attorney before divulging information. Don't even admit that your firm represents a particular client unless you're absolutely sure that is public information. Never, ever give out the names of your witnesses, or even divulge that you have witnesses, if opposing counsel calls. (In cases where there is a rule requiring you to do so, check with the attorney first.)[23]

**Figure 3-9
Law Office
Confidentiality
Policy**

5.9.2 Confidential Nature of Client Matters

All matters relating to any clients or office matters are completely confidential. Nothing that occurs in the office should be discussed with family, friends, other clients, or anyone else. Particular care should be taken with papers that are transmitted in the office. Papers should not be examined and matters should not be discussed in public places such as restaurants, lobbies, or elevators, where other persons can peruse such papers or overhear conversations. Particular care should be exercised in commuter trains, buses, or any public area where much law office talk still continues to be overheard on a daily basis. Even after a case has become a matter of public notice by virtue of its having been filed in court or reported in the press, assume that it is still confidential and do not discuss it publicly.

Staff members should be careful, even in the office, not to leave confidential papers in open or public areas, nor should they leave computer monitors on in places where they can be easily seen by passersby. It is the policy of the firm not to use a client's name for the purpose of surveys or in materials that are prepared to describe the firm without the permission of the billing lawyer(s).

The paper shredder located in _____ should be used for confidential material that must be destroyed; however, such material should not be destroyed without the prior approval of the billing lawyer(s). The use of a confidentiality notice or facsimile (telecopier) transmissions should also be considered as appropriate. Likewise, care must be exercised in dealing with all computer disks, tapes, and other media that contain privileged material.

Care should be taken when dealing with vendors as well. A confidentiality agreement may exist between the firm and a vendor or potential vendors making proposals to the firm.

- **Do not take phone calls from other clients when meeting with a client.** Taking phone calls from other clients while a client is in your office can expose confidential information. Be aware of who is in your office when talking about confidential information on the phone, and, when possible, keep your door closed when meeting or talking with clients.
- **Management must create policies and systems to ensure confidentiality.** Law office managers also have a duty to create systems that ensure confidentiality. Some of these systems may include locking file cabinets that contain client files, limiting access to client files on a need-to-know basis, requiring files to be checked out, having law office policies on client confidentiality, and developing procedures to ensure that the confidential information of clients is maintained (see Figure 3-9). Most law offices limit staff members from revealing to persons outside the office that a particular individual is being represented; even revealing the names of clients can give the appearance that the law office does not take confidentiality seriously. Although there is an affirmative ethical duty to maintain client confidentiality, there is also the potential for malpractice liability for firms that violate confidentiality. Under a legal malpractice theory, if a law office (through its employees) reveals client confidences, accidentally or intentionally, it could be legally liable to the client for damages that result.
- **Be careful when responding to discovery requests.** Many times, legal assistants are involved in responding to discovery document requests. It is

important that all confidential files (including electronic files) are labeled and identified appropriately, that each piece of documentation that is to be submitted to the opposing party is carefully reviewed to ensure that confidential client information is not given out, and that such information is discussed with the supervising attorney.

- **Be particularly careful when using fax machines, e-mail, mobile telephones, and related services.** There have been many instances where confidential information conveyed over these media has been inadvertently revealed to others. It is particularly easy to accidentally reveal confidential information via fax machine and e-mail.

  Faxes should be sent very carefully. An improper or misdirected fax transmission can lead to breach of client confidentiality. All fax cover pages for law offices should have some kind of confidentiality disclaimer on them. The confidentiality of e-mail is also a concern. From the client's perspective, there are many advantages to using e-mail to communicate with legal professionals. The problem with e-mail was addressed in Chapter 2.

CONFLICT OF INTEREST

The exponential growth of law firms, particularly during the last decade, has spawned an increasing number of conflict of interest issues. As firms expand and their client rosters increase, so does the potential that new engagements will create conflicts with the interest of present or former clients.[24]

Conflict of interest problems are an important ethical concept. A **conflict of interest** occurs when an attorney or legal assistant has competing personal or professional interests with a client's case that would preclude him or her from acting impartially toward the client.

Conflict of interest problems typically occur when

- an attorney or legal assistant has a personal, financial, or other interest in a case.
- the attorney or legal assistant is a substantial witness in the case.

When a staff person who is coming from another law firm accepts a position . . . we conduct a conflict screening with the former firm and, if appropriate, we set up an information barrier within the firm.[25]

- a law office, attorney, or legal assistant sometime in the past represented a client who is now an adverse party in a current case.
- an attorney and a client enter into business together.

conflict of interest
A competing personal or professional interest that would preclude an attorney or legal assistant from acting impartially toward the client.

- when an attorney is asked to advocate a position on behalf of a client that is contrary to the position of another of the firm's clients (an issue conflict).
- law firm mergers or acquisitions occur.
- legal professionals change jobs/firms.

If, for instance, an attorney represented a husband and wife in a legal action and then, several years later, the husband approaches the attorney to sue the wife for divorce, the attorney has a conflict of interest problem because he had at one time represented both parties. Not only would he have a question as to which client he should be loyal to, but the attorney may have during the first representation been privy to confidences and secrets of the wife that could be used in the divorce case against her.

Rule 1.7 of the ABA *Model Rules of Professional Conduct* states that an attorney cannot represent a client if the attorney has a conflict of interest. According to Rule 1.7, a conflict exists if an attorney's representation of one client directly and adversely affects another client. The rule allows the attorney to represent the clients where the attorney is able to provide competent representation of each client, it is not prohibited by law, both clients give informed written consent, and the attorney is not representing both parties in the same litigation where the parties are asserting claims against each other.

Most case law in this area presumes that if a firm has represented both parties in the past, there is an actual conflict of interest. It is not necessary to prove that confidences and secrets were exchanged during the first representation. Usually, but not always, when an actual conflict of interest occurs, the whole firm, not just the attorney involved, is prohibited from entering the case.

Rule 1.8 of the *Model Rules of Professional Conduct* also speaks to the conflict of interest issue. It states, among other things, that attorneys cannot enter into business transactions with a client that is adverse to the client unless a number of specific conditions are met. Rule 1.8 also prohibits an attorney from using information related to the representation of a client to the disadvantage of the client unless the client has given informed consent. Under the rule, generally, attorneys cannot solicit substantial gifts from clients as well.

Attorneys and legal assistants should be loyal to their clients and have no alternative motives that might influence their independent professional judgment to represent the clients. Figure 3-10 provides a few more examples of conflict of interest problems.

As noted before, there are different types of conflicts, including an issue conflict. In an issue conflict, an attorney or firm takes different positions on the same issues for different clients. The *Model Rules* generally prohibits this; however, if each client gives an informed consent, then the firm can most likely continue representing the clients. Also, if the legal matters are in different jurisdictions and the firm reasonably believes neither party will be adversely affected, then most likely the firm can continue representing the clients.

Conflict Checking

Because law offices and attorneys typically represent a large number of clients, it is often difficult for them to remember every client. As a result, it is possible for an

- Using Client Information to Harm the Client
  An ambitious associate attorney regularly defends the X insurance company. Client comes into attorney's office and wants to sue X insurance company for a major personal injury claim, not knowing that the attorney has represented the company before. Attorney, in an effort to help X insurance company, intentionally lets the statute of limitations run and then pays the client $2,500 from his own pocket, telling him that the insurance company settled. Attorney had a clear duty to tell the client of his conflict of interest. Attorney was disbarred and the law firm was sued for malpractice.
- Financial Interest
  Attorney is an employee of the county government's water district. Attorney uses his position of authority to influence the water board's decision to purchase a piece of land that he owns through a partnership. Attorney also delays $300,000 of sewer connection fees to another of his pieces of land until after the sale of land is completed to a third party. Attorney had a clear conflict of interest in both cases. Attorney was suspended for two years for the practice of law and pled guilty to using his official office to influence a governmental decision.

Figure 3-10
Conflict of Interest Examples

Before any new file can be opened, a conflicts check must be undertaken. Such conflicts check will be completed before requesting an internal file number from the accounting department.

No new file may be opened if such search discloses any potential conflict with any past or present client or adverse party. Any such conflict should be immediately reported to the responsible attorney. A log of each conflicts check will be maintained. Anyone opening a new file for a new client or new litigation matter without conducting the conflicts check will be subject to disciplinary action.

Figure 3-11
Sample Conflict of Interest Policy[26]

attorney to have a conflict of interest but simply not remember the former client. Thus, it becomes the responsibility of management to ensure that before new cases are taken, a conflicts check takes place. A written policy regarding conflict checking is prudent (see Figure 3-11).

Many law offices maintain a list of all their former clients and adverse parties so that when a new case is being considered as to whether it should be accepted, the firm will routinely check this list to ensure that there are no conflict of interest problems.

Most law firms now use a computer program to search for conflicts; some firms use a computerized database program to do conflict checking. A database program is application software that stores, searches, sorts, and organizes data. When using a database, it is advantageous to include the client's date of birth or social security number, otherwise a misspelled name may not be picked up by the program. Some accounting, billing, docket control, and case management programs can also be used to perform conflicts checking. Figure 3-12 shows a simple conflict of interest database design, and Figure 3-13 shows some case-specific conflict of interest designs. If a firm practices in a certain area, a more specific design would be beneficial.

Some insurance companies that issue malpractice insurance to attorneys also require that, before the policy is written, the firm has and consistently uses a conflict-checking device.

**Figure 3-12
Simple Conflict of
Interest Database**

Last Name	First Name	Social Security	Adverse Party	Type of Case	Date
Allen	Alice	515722404	Hays, Jonathan	Personal injury	1/15/91
Allen	Mariam	093342872	Cox Construction	Contract	12/01/92
Barney	Larry	023234912	Barney, Cindy	Divorce	1/08/88
Johnson	Donald	505235682	Beckwith, Eric	Real estate	8/02/90
Kitchen	Jennifer	093239832	State	Admin.\law	10/06/91
Hall	Electric	235648905	Den, Robert	Collection	3/16/92
Winslow	Harriet	452239423	—	Adoption	6/7/91

**Figure 3-13
Fields to Track in a
Case-Specific Conflict
of Interest System**

Type of Legal Matter	Fields to Track
Administrative law	• Adverse party • Counsel • Investigator • Witnesses
Bankruptcy	• Debtor(s) • Creditor(s) • Other interested parties • Counsel
Corporate	• Owner(s) • Officers • Partners • Shareholders • General counsel • Affiliates/subsidiaries
Criminal	• Defendant(s) • Prosecutor • Victim(s) • Witnesses • Experts
Estates, trusts, probate	• Testator • Heirs • Children • Spouse • Trustee • Conservator • Power of attorney • Personal representative • Beneficiaries • Counsel
Family law	• Spouse • Children • In-laws • Counsel • Guardian
Litigation	• Client • Adverse parties • Witnesses • Expert • Insurer

Type of Legal Matter	Fields to Track
Real estate	• Buyer
	• Seller
	• Agent
	• Counsel
Workers' compensation	• Client
	• Employer
	• Insurer
	• Health care provider
Other	• Firm lawyers
	• Firm legal assistants
	• Spouses/parents/siblings
	• Employees
	• Current/past clients
	• Prospective clients

Figure 3-13
(Continued)

The Ethical Wall

Although it is the general rule that courts tend to disqualify a whole firm when a conflict of interest problem arises, some courts have carved out an alternative to disqualification. The alternative is called the **Ethical Wall,** which occurs when a firm effectively isolates the legal assistant or attorney with a conflict of interest from having anything whatsoever to do with the case, thus creating an Ethical Wall around him or her (see excerpts of the *Lamb v. Pralex* opinion in Figure 3-14). This is typically done by instructing staff members not to talk to the attorney in question about the case, not to disclose any information acquired at the previous firm, and limiting any access the attorney might have to the files of the case by locking file cabinets and placing passwords on computer files.

Ethical Wall
Term for a technique used to isolate the legal assistant or attorney with a conflict of interest from having anything to do with a case.

If the Ethical Wall is erected and the court agrees, it will limit disqualification to the legal assistant or attorney. Not all courts accept the Ethical Wall theory. Again, it would be the duty of management to ensure that the office locks up the files, and to segregate the attorney or legal assistant with the conflict from the rest of the staff. Law offices must also effectively limit access to computers and client data files to build an effective Ethical Wall.

Legal Assistant Conflict of Interests

Many courts have extended the conflict of interest issue to legal assistants as well as attorneys. Conflict of interest problems usually occur when a legal assistant changes employment. For instance, in *In re Complex Asbestos Litigation,* a legal assistant worked for a law firm defending major asbestos litigation claims. He worked with discovery documents, was a part of the defense team for three years, and attended defense strategy meetings. Subsequently, he was hired by a firm representing asbestos plaintiffs. The defendants moved to disqualify the plaintiff's attorney because

Figure 3-14
A Case Upholding the
Ethical Wall Theory

Lamb v. Pralex, 333 F.Supp.2d
361 (2004 D. Virgin Islands)

The plaintiff in this case is represented by Lee J. Rohn (Rohn) of the Law Offices of Lee J. Rohn. Defendants are represented by Kevin Rames, Esq. (Rames) of the Law Offices of Kevin Rames. This motion revolves around Eliza Combie (Combie), who worked as a paralegal at the Rames law office from October 30, 2000 to March 26, 2004. Her work at Rames' office involved working with several litigation matters, including this case. On March 26, 2004, Combie began work with the Rohn law firm. During Combie's interview with Rohn, they discussed the possible conflicts raised by Combie's possible employment. Combie was told should she accept employment with the Rohn firm, she would be barred from contact with those cases. Rohn states that on Combie's first day of work with Rohn, she submitted the list of cases. The list was circulated to all employees and a memo informing employees to refrain from discussing those cases in her presence was circulated and posted in common areas of the office. Combie and Rohn state that no one in the office has discussed any of the relevant matters with Combie. They also state that Combie is locked out of the electronic files and does not work in close proximity to them or to Rohn.

Rames invokes ABA Rules of Professional Conduct 5.3, 1.9, 1.16, and 1.10 to argue that Rohn and the entire law firm must be disqualified because during Combie's previous employment with Rames, she obtained confidential information regarding pending matters which she may divulge to Rohn. The Court is satisfied that the procedures employed by Rohn's office to shield Combie from the files supports a finding that any information obtained at the Rames law firm will not be disclosed. It is important that nonlawyer employees have as much mobility in employment opportunity consistent with the protection of clients' interests. To so limit employment opportunities that some nonlawyers trained to work with law firms might be required to leave the careers for which they have been trained would disserve clients as well as the legal profession.

In light of the foregoing, disqualification is not warranted. In addressing ethical problems created by nonlawyers changing employment from a law firm representing one party to a law firm representing an adverse party, courts must fashion rules which strike a balance between the public policy of protecting the confidentiality of attorney-client communications and a party's right to representation by chosen counsel. Accordingly, any restrictions on the nonlawyers' employment should be held to the minimum necessary to protect confidentiality of client information. The Court finds that plaintiff's counsel has rebutted the presumption of improper disclosure by presenting evidence of the "Chinese Wall" ["or Ethical Wall"] implemented in that regard. Accordingly, disqualification is not warranted and the defendants' motion will be denied at this time.

---

of the legal assistant's conflict of interest (he had knowledge of confidential information gained over several years). The motion was granted by the court.

Legal assistants should be ready to answer questions about their previous employers when interviewing for jobs to avoid conflict of interest problems. The ABA Committee on Ethics and Professional Responsibility recently issued an opinion regarding this matter, which states the following:

> A law office that hires a nonlawyer employee, such as a paralegal, away from an opposing law office may save itself from disqualification by effectively screening the new employee from any participation in the case the two firms have in common.

The legal assistant should be alert to situations that might present a potential conflict of interest as a result of information gained in past employment and should disclose any questionable situation to the employer.

I accepted a [legal assistant job] offer from another law firm, unaware that the attorneys on both sides knew about a potential conflict of interest. When I switched law firms, the former firm's client expressed major concern over the fact that I was now employed by the law firm representing his opponent. I was put behind an Ethical Wall and could hardly walk anywhere within the firm without having to shut my eyes and ears or look the other direction. Then one morning . . . a senior partner announced that I would be sent home for two weeks until the firm could get a conflict waiver from the other party. My new law firm would continue to pay my salary and benefits, but no one had any idea what was to follow. Finally, after 16 weeks, the conflict waiver was granted. Do not take any chances with potential conflict of interest matters. Be sure to find out before you accept a job offer what the firm's policy is if a conflict of interest arises. [27]

How Legal Assistants can Avoid Conflicts of Interest

- **When changing jobs, bring up the issue of potential conflicts in the interview.** Tell the firm whom you have worked for and what types of cases you have worked on. It is better to deal with potential conflict problems up front than for an employer to hire you and then find out there are problems.
- **Be absolutely honest about your past.** Do not hide or deceive employers about potential conflict of interest problems. Honesty is always the best policy.
- **If you later find out you may have a conflict, immediately inform your supervising attorney or legal assistant manager and do not have anything to do with the case.** If you find out after you have been hired by a new firm that you may have a conflict problem, immediately raise the issue with your supervising attorney. Do not volunteer information to the new firm regarding the matter. If you can, approach your former employer and ask for an informed and express written waiver giving consent for you to work for the other firm. Verbal consent is hard to prove, so get it in writing.
- **Management must ensure that conflict of interest problems are checked.** It is also the duty of management to ensure that employees are not hired who have substantial conflict of interest problems, or if they do have such problems, that the firm knows about them up front. For instance, management might want to add a question to its employment form that asks potential employees to state any conflict problems, in addition to establishing the conflict checking system mentioned earlier.

Resolving Ethical Problems

There is nothing easy about resolving an ethical problem. Typically, ethical issues are complex and messy; they are rarely "black and white." However, the following ideas can help you deal with ethical problems.

I took a job in a 10-lawyer firm in a big city. . . . I soon sensed an undercurrent of shady activities by some of the lawyers. My way of dealing with it at the time was to terminate my employment. I got another job and left. I never discussed it with anyone. When you make your own decision in an ethical dilemma, you have to live with its aftermath. . . . At the time, I was not mature enough to handle such a sensitive situation . . . I would [now] try to work through the problem with my employer because you don't leave problems behind. Your next employment situation will bring other problems. We need to learn how to deal with them to become better practitioners and better people.[28]

- **Talk to your legal assistant manager or supervising attorney regarding ethical problems.** When you encounter an ethical problem, the first thing you should do is to talk to someone else about it to get a different perspective. Typically, this will be your legal assistant manager or supervising attorney. However, this is sometimes hard to do when the supervising attorney is the one asking you to do something you think is unethical or if the attorney is him- or herself doing something unethical. One way to approach the issue is to discreetly ask the attorney if he or she thinks this might be a problem; it is important not to be accusatory, but to simply inquire into the issue and to present your point as objectively as possible. You always have the option, no matter how difficult, to say no to the attorney if he or she asks you to do something that you know is unethical. Also, be sure to check your firm's personnel policy manual. Ethical problems and procedures for handling them are sometimes covered in this type of manual.

If there is something that does not feel right, then do not do it. There is nothing wrong with going up the chain of command to obtain clarification of whether something is ethical or not. If it involves an attorney, go to the managing partner or office administrator. If it involves another staff member, go to human resources. It is better to "check" on the situation rather than let it go. If the dilemma is too great and nothing is done to resolve the issue, there is nothing wrong with seeking other employment and working with another group who are more ethically compatible with you.

—Linda Rushton, CLA

- **Talk to another attorney or legal assistant in the firm regarding ethical problems.** If you have a hard time talking to your supervising attorney about an ethical problem, talk to another attorney, legal assistant, or ethics committee, if the firm has one. It is important when dealing with ethical problems to take counsel with others, to bounce ideas off others, and to talk about them. Other people may have more experience than you and might have previously dealt with a similar situation. When talking to another attorney in the firm, use the same non-accusatory approach. Be sure that you are talking to a person you can trust for sincere advice on how to handle the situation; you do not want to be perceived as spreading rumors or stirring up trouble. In larger firms, you also have the option of asking to be transferred.

- **Join a professional legal assistant association.** Professional associations offer a good way to share information and experiences with others, including information about ethical problems. Most professional legal assistant organizations provide guidance on ethical concerns. Use these resources to help you solve your ethical problem.
- **Be familiar with the ethical rules of your state.** It is always a good idea to have a copy of the ethical rules used in your jurisdiction and to review them from time to time.
- **Subscribe to legal assistant periodicals that cover ethical issues.** Many national legal assistant publications routinely carry articles on ethical concerns. Some even have a regular column on the issues of ethics. This kind of timely information can be helpful when dealing with ethical problems.

Unfortunately, we are all faced with decisions regarding ethical matters on a daily basis, both in our professional and personal lives. In the professional realm, not all ethical dilemmas are created by clients. Many unethical situations are created by the very person we should be able to count on for support and advice regarding ethics: our supervising attorney. Whether it be "padding" of time entries, attorneys "stealing" time entries from you or other staff members for work the attorney did not perform in order to bill a higher fee, being asked by your supervising attorney to make a statement or undertake some action that you feel is morally or ethically incorrect, or any number of other unethical situations, quite often your conscience must be your guide. If/when you feel uncomfortable about a situation, your first recourse should always be to speak privately with your supervising attorney. Sometimes it is enough to simply state, "I do not feel comfortable doing that." In most instances, you will find that your supervising attorney will have much more respect for you for having the courage to stand up for your personal and professional ethical beliefs. If this is not the case and more drastic steps are needed, again, your conscience must be your guide. I have communicated with other paralegals who have gone so far as to resign a position over ethical dilemmas. However, this is quite rare. Discussion usually solves the problem.

—Lenette Pinchback, CLA

1. Know the ethical rules governing attorneys. If you understand when attorneys are vulnerable to charges of unprofessional conduct, you will be better able to help them avoid such charges.
2. Know the ethical rules governing paralegals. At the start of your paralegal career, promise yourself that you will adhere to rigorous standards of professional ethics, even if these standards are higher than those followed by people around you.
3. Never tell anyone who is not working on a case anything about that case. This includes your best friend, your spouse, and your relatives.
4. Assume that people outside your office do not have a clear understanding of what a paralegal or legal assistant is. Make sure that everyone with whom you come in contact (clients, attorneys, court officials, agency officials, the public) understands that you are not an attorney.
5. Know what legal advice is and refuse to be coaxed into giving it, no matter how innocent the question asked of you appears to be.
6. Never make contact with an opposing party in a legal dispute, or with anyone closely associated with that party, unless you have the permission of your supervising attorney and of the attorney for the opposing party, if the latter has one.
7. Don't sign your name to anything if you are not certain that what you are signing is 100 percent accurate and that the law allows a paralegal to sign it.
8. Never pad your time sheets. Insist that what you submit is 100 percent accurate.
9. Know the common rationalizations for misrepresentation and other unethical conduct:
   • It's always done.
   • The other side does it.
   • The cause of our client is just.
   • If I don't do it, I will jeopardize my job.
   Promise yourself that you will not allow any of these rationalizations to entice you to participate in misrepresentation or other unethical conduct.
10. If what you are asked to do doesn't feel right, don't proceed until it does.

Suppose a paralegal, in the interest of job preservation, decides to engage in unethical or illegal activity that has been ordered by an attorney. At what point does that paralegal become liable criminally or civilly for such acts? . . . . Nothing at all would insulate the paralegal [from criminal prosecution if the acts are illegal]. Whether the individual is an attorney or a paralegal, the criminal liability is the same. We indict judges and we indict lawyers. There is no reason to believe we will not indict paralegals.

—Robert P. Cummins, member of the ABA's Standing Committee on Lawyers Professional Responsibility[30]

- **Report ethical violations to the state bar association as a last resort.** If you have tried to work out an ethical problem to no avail, you always have the option of reporting the violation to the state bar association. This is a very difficult decision to make because you may lose your job as a result. Ethical problems are not easy to deal with, and you must be able to live with whatever decision you make.
- **When considering ethical questions, think conservatively.** When you are faced with a hard ethical question, be conservative and do what you know is right, no matter how much it may hurt. Figure 3-15 contains a list of ethical "commandments" that may guide you in this direction.
- **Do not ignore the ethical problem.** A common way to handle ethical problems is to simply ignore them and hope they will go away. Unfortunately,

this approach rarely works. In many instances, it simply makes the situation worse. For example, if you see a staff person charging time to a client's case when he or she is not working on that case, it is better to bring the issue to the forefront right away than wait for him or her to do the same to 20 clients. Ethical problems are better handled when they first occur as opposed to letting them fester and become far more complicated.

ANSWERS TO COMMON LEGAL ASSISTANT ETHICAL QUESTIONS

The following are answers to other common legal assistant ethical questions. The answers are based on general statements of law, but an answer may be different depending on your particular jurisdiction.

- **May legal assistants have business cards and may their names appear on law firm stationery?** In many states, the answer is yes. For business cards, care must be taken to ensure that the nonlawyer status of the cardholder is displayed prominently on the card. Regarding firm stationery, the name of the legal assistant(s) must be set apart from the lawyers' names, and the legal assistant's title must be shown clearly. Some firms print lawyers' names on one side of the stationery and print legal assistants' names on the other.
- **May a legal assistant sign letters prepared on firm stationery?** Yes, provided (1) the letter contains no direct legal advice or opinions, and (2) the legal assistant's status is shown clearly. The best practice is to include the title "Legal Assistant" or "Legal Assistant to X" directly below the typed name in the signature block of the letter.
- **May a legal assistant discuss fee ranges with a client on a preliminary basis, leaving the final discussion and decision to the supervising attorney?** All discussions related to fees must be deferred to the attorney. Even when a firm uses an internal fee schedule, it generally serves as a guideline only. It is solely the attorney's responsibility to measure the situation presented by each case and to set the fee.
- **How often and in what way must a legal assistant identify his or her nonlawyer status?** There is no single, correct way to identify the legal assistant's status. It seems prudent to do so at the beginning of all telephone conversations and at the beginning of every initial conference with a client or witness. For example, regarding a telephone call, one might say, "Hello. This is Jack Samson, Jane Mitchell's legal assistant." If it appears that the other party thinks the legal assistant is a lawyer, that impression should be corrected right away. The issue is not how often identity must be clarified to comply with the rules, it is how often identity should be clarified to protect the legal assistant from charges related to the unauthorized practice of law.
- **May a legal assistant counsel a close friend or a relative about a legal matter when the friend or relative knows that the legal assistant is not a lawyer and when the legal assistant is not paid for the advice?** Other than suggesting that the friend or relative see a lawyer, the legal assistant cannot

give advice or comment in any way that may be taken as a legal opinion. The problem arises most frequently at family dinners, parties, and other social events. Friends and relatives can create an extremely uncomfortable situation. Whether the legal assistant is paid or not is irrelevant; legal advice cannot be given by the legal assistant under any circumstances.

legal malpractice
Possible consequence when an attorney's or law office's conduct falls below the standard skill, prudence, and diligence that an ordinary lawyer would possess or that is commonly available in the legal community.

MALPRACTICE AND MALPRACTICE PREVENTION

Legal malpractice occurs when an attorney's or law office's conduct in representing a client falls below the standard skill, prudence, and diligence that an ordinary lawyer would possess or that is commonly available in the legal community.

Figure 3-16 lists the most common types of errors that result in a malpractice claim being filed. Notice in Figure 3-16 that substantive errors account for 56 percent

Figure 3-16
Profile of Legal Malpractice Claims, 1996–1999

Source: *Profile of Legal Malpractice Claims, 1996–1999,* published by the American Bar Association Standing Committee on Lawyers' Professional Liability. Reprinted with permission.

Type of Alleged Error	1996–1999	1996–99
ADMINISTRATIVE	**NUMBER**	**PERCENT**
Failure to calendar properly	2,201	7.03
Procrastination in performance/follow-up	1,551	4.95
Failure to file document (no deadline)	481	1.54
Failure to react to calendar	398	1.27
Clerical error	390	1.25
Lost file/document evidence	125	0.40
Subtotal	**5,146**	**16.43**
SUBSTANTIVE		
Failure to know/properly apply law	6,858	21.90
Failure to know/ascertain deadline	4,772	15.24
Inadequate discovery/investigation	1,921	6.13
Conflict of interest	1,602	5.12
Planning error (procedure choice)	1,004	3.21
Error in public record search	829	2.65
Failure to understand/anticipate tax	491	1.57
Error in mathematical calculation	150	0.48
Subtotal	**17,627**	**56.29**
CLIENT RELATIONS		
Failure to obtain consent/inform client	3,724	11.89
Failure to follow client's instruction	1,231	3.93
Improper withdrawal of representation	916	2.93
Subtotal	**5,871**	**18.75**
INTENTIONAL WRONG		
Malicious prosecution/abuse of process	1,282	4.09
Fraud	661	2.11
Libel or slander	368	1.18
Violation of civil rights	360	1.15
Subtotal	**2,671**	**8.53**
TOTAL	**31,315**	**100.00**

1. Gather factual information from the client to determine the basis of any legal claim and immediately determine and track when the statute of limitations takes effect.
2. Give the client a copy of the written fee agreement specifying the terms of employment and the basis of the attorney's fees in the case.
3. Conduct a thorough conflict of interest check before the client's case is accepted and immediately notify the client in writing if a conflict or a potential conflict is discovered.
4. Investigate the facts of the client's case and the law regarding the case diligently and promptly.
5. Keep the client informed regarding the status of his or her case by providing routine status reports; always inform the client of all developments that might affect the client's rights; and ask for his or her participation throughout the case.
6. Charge a reasonable and fair fee for services performed and provide the client with clear and detailed accounting of the basis for the fees charged.
7. Carefully and thoroughly proofread all documents and e-mails before they go out for mistakes and, whenever possible, send a copy of the document to the client for his or her approval and review.
8. Immediately tell the client of problems or mistakes as they happen and offer solutions.
9. Do not overestimate the firm's capacity to take on cases outside its expertise and always determine whether there is sufficient time to handle the matter properly.
10. Provide the client with written notice upon the attorney's withdrawal from representation (obtain court approval in matters involving litigation) and promptly provide the client with his or her file and other property he or she is entitled to.

Figure 3-17
Ten Ways to Prevent
Legal Malpractice

of malpractice claims and that failure to know or properly apply the law represented the most common reason for all malpractice claims.

If a mistake is found, never offer excuses such as "My secretary must have misplaced it, "The photocopy clerk didn't duplex the pages as I had asked," or "The attorney shouldn't have waited so long to make the assignment." Just fix it. Identify the problem, figure out what went wrong, figure out how to avoid the problem in the future, and solve it. It doesn't matter whose "fault" it is. In an equal team, everyone has an equal responsibility for getting the job done right.[31]

Figure 3-17 also provides some excellent suggestions for helping to avoid costly malpractice claims. Engagement and disengagement letters are another way to avoid malpractice claims. Clients sometimes think attorneys are representing them when, in fact, they are not. Law offices should always send an engagement letter or contract that clearly sets out when a case is taken, what the firm is going to do, and on what the fees will be based.

In addition, law offices should routinely send out disengagement letters for any type of case or legal matter, even if the only thing the law office did was to

**Figure 3-18
Disengagement
Letters**

Example 1: Disengagement Letter—New Client Where Case Was Not Accepted

Subject: Potential Claim of Client v. Johnson

Dear Client:

Thank you for coming in to our office on Tuesday, November XX, 200, regarding your legal matter. We are interested in your concerns and appreciated the opportunity to meet with you. However, after further consideration we have decided to decline representation of your interests in the captioned matter.

We have not made a legal opinion as to the validity or merits of your case. You should be aware that any action in this matter must be filed within the applicable statute of limitations. We suggest that you consult with another attorney concerning your rights in this matter.

Again, we will not be representing you in the captioned matter and are closing our file.

Thank you again, and we wish you the best.

Kindest Regards,

Example 2: Disengagement Latter Following Representation

Subject: *Client v. Johnson*

Dear Client:

Thank you for allowing us the opportunity to serve you regarding the captioned matter. The case is now closed. We are closing our files and taking the case out of our active file drawers, in that our work in the matter is finished. We will be sending our file to storage shortly. If you would like evidence or other material that you have provided to us returned, please give me a call so I can get it to you.

We are interested in knowing how you feel about the quality of legal services you received from our firm. We would appreciate it if you would complete the enclosed client survey questionnaire. We are always interested in knowing how we can serve you better in the future.

Again, the captioned case is now closed, and we greatly enjoyed representing your interests.

If you have any questions, please feel free to give me a call.

Kindest Regards,

---

meet with the client in an initial interview (see Figure 3-18). The purpose of the disengagement letter is to clearly set out in writing that the attorney-client relationship was not formed or has ended. A client may not understand that the firm, is not pursuing the matter, then come back months or even years later claiming that the attorney committed malpractice against him or her by not following up on the case.

SUMMARY

An ethical rule is a minimal standard of conduct. An attorney may not fall below the standard without losing his or her good standing with the state bar. The *Model Rules of Professional Conduct* are ethical rules for attorneys that are promulgated by the American Bar Association. Ethical rules for attorneys do not apply directly to legal assistants. However, attorneys can be disciplined for the acts of their staff, including legal assistants. In addition, legal assistants themselves can lose their jobs and face criminal charges and fines for practicing law without a license, among other things, so it is important that legal assistants act in an ethical manner.

Attorneys are directly responsible for the acts of their legal assistants and under the *Model Rules* must make reasonable efforts to ensure that their conduct is compatible with the ethical rules. Legal assistants have two national associations that they may belong to, the National Association of Legal Assistants and the National Federation of Paralegal Associations. Both associations have voluntary model codes of ethics for legal assistants.

All states have statutes regarding the unauthorized practice of law by nonlawyers. Legal assistants that "practice law" can be criminally charged under these statutes. Legal assistants are prevented from giving legal advice. The factors involved in making this determination include 1) whether advice given requires legal skill or knowledge, 2) whether the person was advised of his or her legal rights, and, 3) whether the advice is not normally given by a non-lawyer as part of another business or transaction (such as a tax consultant). A legal assistant also may not misrepresent his or her status so that others believe that he or she is an attorney; the legal assistant must clearly state his or her title and that he or she is not an attorney. Legal assistants may not

represent clients in court proceedings, perform legal analysis and prepare legal documents (without supervision of an attorney), set or share a fee, or evaluate a case regarding whether to accept or reject it.

Attorneys—and, therefore, legal assistants—are required to act in a competent manner for their clients. They must reasonably know and understand the area of the law they are working in and they must adequately prepare for the representation of the client. Attorneys and legal professionals must also act diligently, including acting promptly and without undue delay.

Attorneys and legal assistants are required to maintain client confidentiality. The duty of confidentiality is an important part of the client-attorney relationship; the attorney-client privilege is a part of that relationship. The privilege precludes the disclosure of confidential communications between a lawyer and a client by the lawyer. The privilege also extends to legal assistants.

Attorneys and legal assistants are prohibited from representing a client where they have a conflict of interest. A conflict of interest is a competing personal or professional interest that would preclude an attorney or legal assistant from acting impartially toward the client. An "Ethical Wall" is a technique used to isolate the legal assistant with a conflict of interest from having anything to do with a case; the Ethical Wall can sometimes be erected so that an entire firm does not have to be disqualified from representing a client because of the conflict with one staff member, such as a legal assistant.

Legal malpractice occurs when an attorney's conduct in representing a client falls below the standard skill, prudence, and diligence that an ordinary lawyer would possess or that is commonly available in the legal community.

Helpful Web Sites

Organization	Description	Internet Address
American Bar Association (ABA) Center for Professional Responsibility	The site has a number of excellent resources regarding ethics, including the full version of the *Model Rules of Professional Conduct,* summaries of ABA ethical opinions, and more.	http://www.abanet.org/cpr/home.html
ABA Standing Committee on Paralegals	ABA site devoted to the use of legal assistants in legal organizations. Contains publications, articles, and other useful information for legal assistants, including the ABA *Model Guidelines for the Utilization of Paralegal Services.*	http://www.abaparalegals.org
American Legal Ethics Library	Excellent online resource for ethics-related information and articles.	http://straylight.law.cornell.edu/ethics/
California State Bar	State bar site with a number of state and national resources related to ethics.	http://www.calbar.ca.gov/state/calbar/calbar_generic.jsp?cid=10128
Colorado Bar Association—Ethics area	State bar site with a number of state and national resources related to ethics.	http://www.cobar.org/group/index.cfm?category=1607&EntityID=CETH
FindLaw—Ethics and Professional Responsibility practice area	The site has a number of resources, articles, and links to a variety of ethics issues.	http://www.findlaw.com/01topics/14ethics/index.html
Legal Assistant Today	National magazine for legal assistants. The Web site has limited information but the magazine itself is full of useful articles, including ethical issues related to legal assistants.	http://www.legalassistanttoday.com
LegalEthics.com	An excellent site for updated cases and information related to legal ethics.	http://www.legalethics.com/
MegaLaw Ethics and Professional Liability section	The site has a number of resources, articles, and links to a variety of ethics issues.	http://www.megalaw.com/top/ethics.php
Michigan State Bar	State bar site with a number of state and national resources related to ethics.	http://www.michbar.org/opinions/ethicsopinions.cfm

ORGANIZATION	DESCRIPTION	INTERNET ADDRESS
National Association of Legal Assistants	National association for legal assistants. Contains many resources for legal assistants, including ethics-related articles and model ethics rules.	http://www.nala.org
National Federation of Paralegal Associations	National association for legal assistants. Contains many resources for legal assistants, including ethics-related articles and model ethics rules. The site also has a page related to ethics.	http://www.paralegals.org or http://www.paralegals.org/displaycommon.cfm?an=1&subarticlenbr=330

SUGGESTED READING

1. *The Legal Assistant's Practical Guide to Professional Responsibility* (2nd ed.), American Bar Association, 2004.

2. *Model Guidelines for the Utilization of Paralegal Services,* American Bar Association, 2004 [http://www.abanet.org/legal-services/paralegals/downloads/modelguidelines.pdf].

3. *Annotated Model Rules of Professional Conduct*, American Bar Association (current edition).

4. *Attorney-Client and Attorney Work Product Privileges: Their Application to Paralegals,* National Federation of Paralegal Associations [http://www.paralegals.org/displaycommon.cfm?an=1&subarticlenbr=372].

5. Kaufman, K. (2004). *Legal ethics.* Clifton Park, NY: Thomson/Delmar Learning.

6. *Model Code of Ethics and Professional Responsibility*, National Federation of Paralegal Associations [http://www.paralegals.org/displaycommon.cfm?an=1&subarticlenbr=133].

7. *NALA Code of Ethics and Professional Responsibility*, published by the National Association of Legal Assistants [http://www.nala.org/stand.htm].

8. *NALA Model Standards and Guidelines for Utilization of Legal Assistants,* published by the National Association of Legal Assistants [http://www.nala.org/stand.htm].

9. Schneeman, A. (2000). *Paralegal ethics.* St. Paul, MN: West Publishing Group.

10. *The Ethical Wall—Its Application to Paralegals*, National Federation of Paralegal Associations [http://www.paralegals.org/displaycommon.cfm?an=1&subarticlenbr=388].

KEY TERMS

ABA *Model Code of Professional Responsibility*
ABA *Model Rules of Professional Conduct*
attorney-client privilege
client confidentiality
conflict of interest

ethical rule
Ethical Wall
legal malpractice
legal technicians

TEST YOUR KNOWLEDGE

Test your knowledge of the chapter by answering these questions.

1. Explain what the ABA *Model Rules of Professional Conduct* are.
2. True or false: An attorney can be disciplined for the acts of his or her legal assistant.

3. True or False: Under the *Model Rules,* an attorney does not have to make reasonable efforts to ensure that a legal assistant's conduct is compatible with the professional obligations of the attorney.

4. True or false: Legal assistants must comply with the model codes of ethics from the two major national legal assistant associations.
5. True or false: In most states, you can go to jail for the unauthorized practice of law.
6. List five things that a legal assistant cannot do without being accused of the unauthorized practice of law: _____, _____, _____
   _____, _____.
7. What are three factors that are considered in determining whether a legal assistant gave legal advice to a client?
8. What is a legal technician?
9. What does "competent representation" require, according to the *Model Rules?*
10. According to *Model Rule* 1.3, "a lawyer shall act with reasonable _____ and promptness in representing a client."
11. The standard that precludes the disclosure of confidential communications between a lawyer and a client by the lawyer is called the
    _____.
12. According to *Model Rule* 1.6, "a lawyer shall not reveal information related to the representation of a client unless the client _____."
13. A conflict of interest occurs when _____
    _____.
14. True or false: Even if a conflict of interest exists, if the affected clients give informed consent, confirmed in writing, the attorney can represent the parties (subject to the provision in the rule).
15. A technique used to isolate a legal assistant or attorney with a conflict of interest from having anything to do with a case is called an
    _____.
16. When an attorney's conduct in representing a client falls below the standard skill, prudence, and diligence that ordinary attorney would possess, it is called _____.

ON THE WEB EXERCISES

1. Using a general search engine, such as http://www.google.com or http://www.yahoo.com, search for all of the lawyer disciplinary agencies for the 50 states. A number of them have Web sites. Visit five of the Web sites and compare what kind of information is available to clients that are having difficult with an attorney.

2. Visit three state bar association sites on the Internet and compare the information on ethics for each one. Several sites are listed in the Web Links section of this chapter and also in Chapter 2. Alternatively, you can search for state bar associations using http://www.google.com or http://www.yahoo.com. Most of the disciplinary administrator sites found in exercise number one use the state bar association site as well, so if you completed that assignment, you should have already found most of them.

3. Visit the NALA and NFPA sites on ethics that are listed in the Web Links section of this chapter. What kind of information do they offer, and is it helpful?

4. Visit several state bar association sites and find articles on conflicts of interest, confidentiality, malpractice, and competence.

5. Visit the FindLaw, MegaLaw and American Legal Ethics Library sites listed in the Web Links section. Compare the research materials available for each.

PROJECTS

1. Go to the Web site http://www.legalethics.com. The site is usually updated regularly and features a number of current ethics-related cases. Read one of the current cases on the Web site and prepare a report that summarizes the case and the justification that the court gave for its decision.

2. Write a comprehensive report that compares and contrasts the NALA and NFPA codes of ethics.

In the report, explain which code you thought was better, and why. Also discuss how the sections on confidentiality and conflict of interests compare with the ABA's *Model Rules.* Were the sections similar to the *Model Rules* or not?

3. Write a report regarding legal assistants and the unauthorized practice of law; use a minimum of four resources. Discuss what legal assistants can and cannot do, and why. Start your research at the national legal assistant associations. Many of the state bar associations also have articles and resources regarding this issue.

4. Read the case of *Tegman v. Accident & Medical Investigations*, 107 Wash.App. 868, 30 P.3d 8, (2001) at the end of the chapter. Also, read the appeal at 150 Wash. 2d 102, 75 P.3d 497 (2003). Write an in-depth report on the case, including a detailed summary of the facts, what the lower court held, what the Washington Supreme Court held, why there was a dissenting opinion, and what you think legal assistants should learn from the case.

QUESTIONS AND EXERCISES

1. You are a legal assistant in the real estate section of a corporate law department. Your company is a large retailer that owns thousands of small retail outlets across the country. You process the leases, review the contracts, and coordinate lease payments with the accounts payable department to make sure the proper lease payments will be made. By the time the lease gets to you, the contract has been reviewed by the attorneys. Typically you assume that the description of the property is accurate, even though you could pull the full file to confirm the description. This is the way that it has always been done. What are your thoughts regarding the adequacy of the description of the property? Is this a good policy? What is the risk if the property description is not accurate? Does it change your answer if your supervising attorney thinks that you are in fact reviewing the contract for accuracy and completeness?

2. You are a legal assistant at a law firm that is representing a company in the process of negotiating a deal to merge with a competitor. You inadvertently mention the possibility of the merger to your father. Without your knowledge, your father purchases a large sum of stock in the company you represent, knowing that when the merger becomes public, the price of the stock will substantially rise. Several months after the transaction, your father gives you a check for $5,000 and explains how he made the money. He tells you that he only did it for your benefit. Disregarding the criminal statutes that have been violated, how would you handle the situation and how could the problem have been avoided?

3. You work for a government agency and are responding to a plaintiff's request for production of documents. One of the requests specifically asks for any notes or memoranda arising out of the facts of the case. In one of the boxes of material the agency has collected on the matter, you find a particularly incriminating memorandum that will virtually win the case for the plaintiffs if it is produced. What do you do?

Assume you go to your supervising attorney about the matter. The attorney responds that he or she will take care of the matter and thanks you for your diligent work. Several months go by and you are now working on preparing the case for trial. You quickly realize that the document was never produced to the plaintiffs. How would you resolve this situation?

4. You are working on a client's case when the client's accountant calls and asks you for information about the client. You have worked with this particular accountant before and know the accountant is trustworthy. Is there any problem with revealing the information to the accountant? How would you handle it?

5. Your law office just signed an agreement to represent a famous athlete in contract negotiations with his team. A reporter from *Sports Illustrated* calls and asks if your firm is representing the athlete. You read *Sports Illustrated* all the time and are impressed that one of its reporters called your firm. In fact, you are caught off guard by the question. Being typically honest and forthright, you begin to answer. What is your answer?

6. You are a new legal assistant right out of school. You take the first job offered to you, at a small firm that is poorly run and not very well respected in the legal community. You work at the firm for only a month and quit. You apply for another position at a different firm and decide not to mention the employment at the small firm, as it was for only a month. You sign the employment application form knowing that it says if you are found to have lied on the application form, you could be terminated. You are subsequently hired by the new firm. Later, you find out the two firms have a highly publicized case they are litigating against each other. What do you do?

7. As a legal assistant in a medium-size law office, you have access to all the resources of the firm, including copy machines, telephones, e-mail, and the postage meter. While the firm's staff manual states that the firm's equipment will only be used for firm business, you notice that the other legal assistants frequently use the copier, envelopes, and postage machine for personal use. When you ask one of the other legal assistants in the firm about it, the legal assistant says, "Don't worry about it. Everyone does it." How would you handle the situation?

8. Your law office represents a nonprofit corporation. The executive director of the nonprofit corporation calls you when your supervising attorney is out of the office. The executive director states that an employee is demanding overtime pay, since she worked more than 40 hours last week, and is saying that if she is not paid overtime, she will immediately file a wage-and-hour complaint with the appropriate state agency. The attorney will not be in the office the whole week but may call in. You recollect from previous experience that the Fair Labor Standards Act generally states that employees should receive overtime pay for hours worked in excess of 40 hours a week, though you are not sure about exceptions to the rule. The executive director presses you and says that he absolutely has to have an answer immediately and

that if your firm cannot respond to emergencies, then maybe he will take his business elsewhere. How would you resolve the situation? Give options.

9. As a legal assistant for a legal aid office, one of your jobs is to screen clients. You routinely see new clients and report the facts of each client's case to one of the attorneys. The attorneys then decide which cases they have time to take on. On Monday, a client comes into your office. The client has no money but appears to need an attorney. The client advises you that she has been sued and needs legal counsel to represent her for a hearing in the state district court on Friday at 10:00 A.M. before Judge Smith. From your experience, you are sure the attorneys do not have the time to accept this case. After listening to the client, you respectfully tell her that you do not think the office will be able to represent her. The client then leaves and you prepare a memo to the attorneys. The attorneys subsequently decide not to handle the matter and file is closed.

On Friday at 10:15 A.M., the office receives a phone call from Judge Smith. Judge Smith tells your receptionist that an attorney from your office has five minutes to get over to her courtroom to represent the client or she (Judge Smith) will hold the office/ attorneys in contempt of court and levy a fine against the office. Apparently, the client told Judge Smith that she had met with a representative from the legal aid office and had told the representative about the hearing. It was the client's understanding that an attorney from the legal aid office would represent her. Explain how this matter could have been avoided.

10. You notice one of your fellow legal assistants at the legal aid office where you work routinely using fake names and misrepresenting herself when tracking down witnesses or trying to serve subpoenas. Is this unethical or just uncouth? Analyze the situation using either the NALA or NFPA code of ethics.

11. You are a legal assistant for a sole practitioner. You have been working on a motion that has to be filed by 4:30 P.M. At 4:10 P.M., you hand the completed motion to the attorney. The attorney signs the motion and hands it back to you and asks you to copy it and file it. How would you handle this situation? List your options.

NOTES

1. Heller, N. B. (1992, October). "Dealing with ethical dilemmas—can you sleep at night?" *On Point* (Newsletter of the National Capital Area Paralegal Association), 1. Printed with the permission of Nancy B. Heller, paralegal.

2. American Bar Association. (2004). *The legal assistant's practical guide to professional responsibility* (2nd ed, p. xii). Reprinted by permission.

3. Foonberg, J. (2004). *How to start and build a law practice* (p. 564). American Bar Association.

4. Foonberg, J. (2004). *How to start and build a law practice* (p. 524). American Bar Association.

5. American Bar Association. (2004). *The legal assistant's practical guide to professional responsibility* (2nd ed, p. 5). Reprinted by permission.

6. Ibid., p. 25.

7. Adapted from Green, A. G. (1993). *Leveraging with legal assistants*. American Bar Association. Reprinted by permission.

8. American Bar Association. (2004). *The legal assistant's practical guide to professional responsibility* (2nd ed., p. 27). Reprinted by permission.

9. Ibid., p. 8. Reprinted by permission.

10. Ibid. Reprinted by permission.

11. Ibid. Reprinted by permission.

12. Ibid. Reprinted by permission.

13. Ibid., p. 31. Reprinted by permission.

14. *NALA code of ethics and professional responsibility*, National Association of Legal Assistants. Reprinted with the permission of the National Association of Legal Assistants, 1516 S. Boston, #200, Tulsa. http://www.nala.org. Copyright 1975; revised 1979, 1988, 1995.

15. American Bar Association. (2004). *The legal assistant's practical guide to professional responsibility* (2nd ed., p. 30). Reprinted by permission.

16. Ibid., p. 17.

17. Tokumitsu, C. (1991, November/December). "How to avoid the top 10 mistakes paralegals make on the job," *Legal Assistant Today*, 34. Reprinted courtesy of *Legal Assistant Today* magazine. For subscription information, call (714) 755-5450, or visit http://www.legalassistanttoday.com.

18. American Bar Association. (2004). *The legal assistant's practical guide to professional responsibility* (2nd ed., p. 49). Reprinted by permission.

19. Ibid., p. 51. Reprinted by permission.

20. (2003, September/October). Determination and courage. *Legal Assistant Today, 33.*

21. American Bar Association. (2004). *The legal assistant's practical guide to professional responsibility* (2nd ed., pp. 61, 63). Reprinted by permission.

22. Ibid., p. 71. Reprinted by permission.

23. Murray, T. I. (2001). The unwritten rules: Survival in a law firm. *Legal Assistant Today*, May/June 1998, p. 13. Reprinted courtesy of *Legal Assistant Today* magazine. For subscription information, call (714) 765-5450 or visit http://www.legalassistanttoday.com.

24. Flom, J. H., & Lerner, J. J. (1991, March). Lawyer's conflicts. *Law Practice Management*, 28. Printed with the permission of Nancy B. Heller, paralegal.

25. Nelson, A. M. (1999, October). Work with support staff to promote quality. *Wisconsin Lawyer*. Reprinted with permission of the October 1999 *Wisconsin Lawyer*, the official publication of the State Bar of Wisconsin.

26. *Law Office Policy and Procedures Manual*, 4th ed., 2000, American Bar Association. Reprinted by Permission.

27. Oder, S. L. (1992, May). Reprinted in part from the *Los Angeles Paralegal Association Reporter*.

28. Milano, C. (1992, March/April). Hard choices: Dealing with ethical dilemmas on the job," *Legal Assistant Today*, 72, 78, 79. Reprinted courtesy of *Legal Assistant Today* magazine. For subscription information, call (714) 755-5450 or visit http://www.legalassistanttoday.com.

29. Statsky, W. (1992). *Introduction to paralegalism* (p. 264). Saint Paul, MN: West Publishing Co.

30. Perry, P. M. (1993, March/April). Should you rat on your boss? *Legal Assistant Today*, 66.

31. Murray, T. I. (1998, May/June). The unwritten rules: Survival in a law firm. *Legal Assistant Today*, 12. Reprinted courtesy of *Legal Assistant Today* magazine. For subscription information, call (714) 755-5450 or visit http://www.legalassistanttoday.com.

Answers to Test Your Knowledge

1. Self-imposed ethical standards for ABA members, but they also serve as a prototype of legal ethic standards for state court systems. Nearly all states base their ethical rules on either the *Model Rules* or *Model Code*.
2. True
3. False
4. False
5. True
6. Give legal advice, represent clients in court, perform legal analysis (without supervision of an attorney), prepare legal documents (without supervision of an attorney), evaluate a case, accept or reject a case, set a fee, or share a fee with an attorney.
7. Did the advice given require legal skill or knowledge, was the person advised of his or her legal rights, and was the advice not normally given by a nonlawyer as part of another business or transaction?
8. A person who markets their legal services directly to the public but who does not work under the supervision of an attorney.
9. Legal knowledge, skill, thoroughness, and preparation reasonably necessary for the representation.
10. Diligence
11. Attorney-client privilege
12. Gives informed consent
13. An attorney or legal assistant has competing personal or professional interests with a client's case that would preclude him or her from acting impartially toward the client.
14. True
15. Ethical Wall
16. Legal malpractice

Case Review

Tegman v. Accident & Medical Investigations, 107 Wash.App. 868, 30 P.3d 8 (2001).

Court of Appeals of Washington,
Division 1.

Maria TEGMAN, Linda Leszynski and Daina Calixto, Respondents,

v.

ACCIDENT & MEDICAL INVESTIGATIONS, INC., a Washington corporation, Richard McClellan and Jane Doe McClellan, individually and as husband and wife, and the marital community composed thereof; Joy A. Brown and John Doe Brown, individually and as husband and wife, and the marital community composed thereof; Michael D. Hoyt and John Doe Hoyt, individually and as husband and wife, and the marital community composed thereof; James P. Bailey and Jane Doe Bailey, individually and as husband and wife, and the marital community composed thereof; Camille H. Jescavage and John Doe Jescavage, individually and as husband and wife, and the marital community composed thereof, Defendants,

Deloris M. Mullen and John Doe Mullen, individually and as husband and wife, and the marital community composed thereof; Lorinda S. Noble and John Doe Noble, individually and as husband and wife, and the marital community composed thereof, Appellants.

Nos. 45837-0-I, 45885-0-I, 45886-8-I, 46085-4-I.

Aug. 13, 2001.

PUBLISHED IN PART

BECKER, A.C.J.

When a paralegal performs legal services with knowledge that there is no supervising attorney responsible for the case, the paralegal will be held to an attorney's standard of care. Attorneys have a duty to keep ***872** their clients informed about material developments in their cases. The trial court found that Deloris Mullen, a paralegal, and Lorinda Noble, an attorney, while employed by a nonlawyer who represented accident victims, breached this duty and caused harm to the plaintiffs when they failed to advise them of the risk involved with allowing a nonlawyer to settle their cases. We affirm the judgments.

The trial court's findings of fact present the following account of the events surrounding this dispute. Between 1989 and 1991, plaintiffs Maria Tegman, Linda Leszynski, and Daina Calixto were each injured in separate and unrelated automobile accidents. After their accidents, each plaintiff retained G. Richard McClellan and Accident & Medical Investigations, Inc. (AMI) for legal counsel and assistance in handling their personal injury claims. McClellan and AMI purported to represent each plaintiff in seeking compensation from insurance companies for their injuries. Each plaintiff signed a contingency fee agreement with AMI, believing that McClellan was an attorney and AMI a law firm. McClellan has never been an attorney in any jurisdiction.

McClellan and AMI employed Camille Jescavage and Lorinda Noble, both licensed attorneys. ****12** Jescavage and Noble learned that McClellan entered into contingency fee agreements with AMI's clients and that McClellan was not an attorney. They settled a number of cases for AMI, and learned that McClellan processed settlements of AMI cases through his own bank account. Noble resigned from AMI in May 1991, after working there approximately six months. In July 1991, McClellan hired Deloris Mullen as a paralegal. Mullen considered Jescavage to be her supervising attorney though Jescavage provided little supervision. Jescavage resigned from AMI in the first week of September 1991. McClellan told Mullen that her new supervising attorney would be James Bailey. Mullen did not immediately contact Bailey to confirm that he was her supervising attorney. He later told her he was not. While at AMI, Mullen worked on approximately 50–60 ***873** cases, including those of plaintiffs Tegman, Leszynski, and Calixto. Mullen was aware of some of McClellan's questionable practices and knew that there were substantial improprieties involved with his operation. Mullen stopped working at AMI on December 6, 1991, when the situation became personally intolerable to her and she obtained

direct knowledge that she was without a supervising attorney. When she left, she did not advise any of the plaintiffs about the problems at AMI. After Mullen left, McClellan settled each plaintiff's case for various amounts without their knowledge or consent, and deposited the funds in his general account by forging their names on the settlement checks. In 1993, Calixto, Leszynski, and Tegman each individually sued McClellan, AMI, Mullen, and Jescavage. Tegman also sued Noble. Their complaints sought damages on various theories. The cases were consolidated. Discovery took place between 1993 and 1998. In the interim, McClellan pleaded guilty to mail fraud in United States District Court in 1997 and was sentenced to two years imprisonment. Also, this court affirmed a judgment by the same trial court in another case where McClellan settled a client's case without authorization and stole the proceeds. Bullard v. Bailey, 91 Wash.App. 750, 959 P.2d 1122 (1998). That judgment apportioned 20-percent fault to attorney James Bailey who, like Noble and Jescavage, had associated himself with AMI and failed to warn his clients of McClellan's improprieties. In the present matter, the court entered summary judgment against McClellan and AMI on the issue of liability. After a six-day trial, the court held Mullen, Noble, and Jescavage liable for negligence and legal negligence, and awarded damages. Only Mullen and Noble appealed. Their appeals have been consolidated.

STANDARD OF REVIEW

[1] An appellate brief must include argument in support of issues presented for review, together with citations to ***874** legal authority. *See* RAP 10.3(a)(5). Assignments of error not argued in a brief are deemed abandoned. Valley View Industrial Park v. City of Redmond, 107 Wash.2d 621, 630, 733 P.2d 182 (1987); Pappas v. Hershberger, 85 Wash.2d 152, 153, 530 P.2d 642 (1975). Accordingly, we review only those assignments of error that are supported by argument in appellants' briefs. [2] Our review of a trial court's findings of fact and conclusions of law is a two-step process. We first determine whether the trial court's findings of fact were supported by substantial evidence in the record. Landmark Development, Inc. v. City of Roy, 138 Wash.2d 561, 573, 980 P.2d 1234 (1999). Substantial evidence is evidence which, viewed in the light most

favorable to the party prevailing below, would persuade a fair-minded, rational person of the truth of the finding. State v. Hill, 123 Wash.2d 641, 644, 870 P.2d 313 (1994). If the findings are adequately supported, we next decide whether those findings of fact support the trial court's conclusions of law. Landmark Development, 138 Wash.2d at 573, 980 P.2d 1234.

PARALEGAL NEGLIGENCE

[3] Mullen, a paralegal, contends the court erred in finding her negligent. To establish the elements of an action for negligence, a plaintiff must show: (1) the existence **13 of a duty owed, (2) breach of that duty, (3) a resulting injury, and (4) a proximate cause between the breach and the injury. Iwai v. State, 129 Wash.2d 84, 96, 915 P.2d 1089 (1996). [4] Nonattorneys who attempt to practice law will be held to the same standards of competence demanded of attorneys and will be liable for negligence if these standards are not met. Bowers v. Transamerica Title Insurance Company, 100 Wash.2d 581, 586-89, 675 P.2d 193 (1983); Hogan v. Monroe, 38 Wash.App. 60, 65, 684 P.2d 757 (1984) (realtor who drafted addendum that substantially altered the rights of property buyers held to the standard of care of a reasonably prudent attorney). *875 In Bowers, sellers sold property to buyers who had persuaded a nonattorney escrow agent to prepare an unsecured promissory note in favor of the sellers. After the deed was delivered to the buyers, the sellers learned the significance of the fact that the note was unsecured. They discovered that the buyers had departed for places unknown after using the property as security for a substantial loan. The sellers sued the escrow agent and obtained summary judgment on liability for negligence. Our Supreme Court affirmed, holding the escrow agent to an attorney's standard of care. The escrow agent breached a duty to inform the sellers of the advisability of obtaining independent counsel. Bowers, 100 Wash.2d at 590, 675 P.2d 193. That duty was owed because the escrow agent, by preparing the closing documents, was engaging in the practice of law. [5] The "practice of law" clearly does not just mean appearing in court. In a larger sense, it includes "legal advice and counsel, and the preparation of legal instruments and contracts by which legal rights are secured." In re Droker and Mulholland, 59 Wash.2d 707, 719, 370 P.2d 242 (1962). See also Bowers, 100

Wash.2d at 586, 675 P.2d 193; Washington State Bar Assn v. Great West. Union Fed. Savings & Loan Assn, 91 Wash.2d 48, 54, 586 P.2d 870 (1978); State v. Hunt, 75 Wash.App. 795, 801–02, 880 P.2d 96 (1994). [6] Mullen contends that her status as a paralegal precludes a finding that she was engaged in the practice of law. She argues that a paralegal is, by definition, someone who works under the supervision of an attorney, and that it is necessarily the attorney, not the paralegal, who is practicing law and owes a duty to the clients. Her argument assumes that she had a supervising attorney. The trial court's determination that Mullen was negligent was dependent on the court's finding that Mullen knew, or should have known, that she did not have a supervising attorney over a period of several months while she was at AMI. "Had Mullen been properly supervised by an attorney at all times during her employment with AMI, plaintiffs presumably *876 would have no case against her. Rather, her supervising attorney would be responsible for any alleged wrongdoing on her part."[FN1]

> FN1. Court's Memorandum Decision Following Trial, at 24.

[7] [8] We agree with the trial court's observation. The label "paralegal" is not in itself a shield from liability. A factual evaluation is necessary to distinguish a paralegal who is working under an attorney's supervision from one who is actually practicing law. A finding that a paralegal is practicing law will not be supported merely by evidence of infrequent contact with the supervising attorney. As long as the paralegal does in fact have a supervising attorney who is responsible for the case, any deficiency in the quality of the supervision or in the quality of the paralegal's work goes to the attorney's negligence, not the paralegal's. In this case, Mullen testified that she believed James Bailey was her supervising attorney after Jescavage left. The court found Mullen was not justified in that belief. Mullen assigns error to this finding, but the evidence supports it. Mullen testified that she had started to distrust McClellan before he informed her that Bailey would be her supervising attorney. Mullen also testified that she did not contact Bailey to confirm that he was supervising her. Bailey testified at a deposition that he did not share Mullen's clients and she did not consult him regarding any of her ongoing

cases. He also said that one of the only conversations he remembers having with **14** Mullen with respect to AMI is one where he told her that he was not her supervising attorney after she raised the issue with him. This testimony amply supports the trial court's finding that Mullen was unjustified in her belief that Bailey was her supervising attorney. [9] In *Hunt,* a paralegal appealed a criminal conviction for the unauthorized practice of law based on his conduct in running a claim settlement company. Among other things, Hunt failed to inform his clients of his activities, did not inform clients of the full amount of settlements, reached *877 settlements without consulting his clients, and filed incomplete or improper documents in court. In a constitutional challenge to the unauthorized practice of law statute, RCW 2.48.180, Hunt argued that his status as a paralegal prevented a finding that he was engaged in the practice of law. The Court of Appeals disagreed and affirmed his conviction: "It is the nature and character of the service performed which governs whether given activities constitute the practice of law, not the nature or status of the person performing the services." Hunt, 75 Wash.App. at 802, 880 P.2d 96 (citing in part, WSBA, 91 Wash.2d at 54, 586 P.2d 870). As in *Hunt*, Mullen's status as a paralegal did not preclude the trial court from concluding that Mullen had engaged in the practice of law. [10] Contrary to Mullen's argument, such a conclusion does not require evidence that the paralegal called herself an attorney, entered appearances, or charged fees. Mullen testified that she negotiated settlements on behalf of the plaintiffs. She sent a letter rejecting, without Tegman's knowledge, a settlement offer made to Tegman. She continued to send out demand and representation letters after Jescavage left AMI. Letters written by Mullen before Jescavage's departure identify Mullen as a paralegal after her signature, whereas letters she wrote after Jescavage's departure lacked such identification. Even after Mullen discovered, in late November 1991, that Bailey was not her supervising attorney, she wrote letters identifying "this office" as representing the plaintiffs, neglecting to mention that she was a paralegal and that no attorney was responsible for the case. This evidence substantially supports the finding that Mullen engaged in the practice of law. [11] Mullen contends that she cannot be

held liable for negligence because the statute that prohibits the unauthorized practice of law was not in effect at the time she worked for AMI. The trial court dismissed the plaintiffs' claims that were based on the alleged statutory violation, but this does not prevent Mullen from being liable on the negligence claim. Under *Bowers,* the duty arises from the *878 practice of law, not from the statute. [12] Mullen points out that an attorney-client relationship is an element of a cause of action for legal malpractice. Daugert v. Pappas, 104 Wash.2d 254, 704 P.2d 600 (1985). The trial court did not find that she had an attorney-client relationship with any of the plaintiffs, and she contends that as a result it is illogical to hold her to the standard of care of an attorney. Mullen, because she is not an attorney, could not have attorney-client relationships. Nevertheless, as *Bowers* demonstrates, a layperson can logically be held to the standard of care of an attorney in a negligence action. The duty arises from the attempt to engage in the practice of law rather than from the professional status of the defendant. The trial court, covering all bases, held Mullen liable both for negligence and legal negligence. While the "legal negligence" label may have been incorrect, any such error is immaterial because the negligence theory produces the same result and, as the trial court observed, for practical purposes the allegations are the same. [13] Accordingly, we conclude the trial court did not err in following *Bowers* and holding Mullen to the duty of an attorney. The duty of care owed by an attorney is that degree of care, skill, diligence, and knowledge commonly possessed and exercised by a reasonable, careful, and prudent lawyer in the practice of law in Washington. Hizey v. Carpenter, 119 Wash.2d 251, 261, 830 P.2d 646 (1992). [14] Mullen challenges, as unsupported by the evidence, the trial court's key finding **15** as to the duties that Mullen owed and breached. The court found that the standard of care owed by an attorney, and therefore also by Mullen, required her to notify the plaintiffs of: (1) the serious problems concerning the accessibility of their files to persons who had no right to see them, (2) the fact that client settlements were not processed through an attorney's trust account, but rather McClellan's own account, (3) the fact that McClellan and AMI, as nonlawyers, had no right to enter *879 into contingent fee agreements with clients and receive contingent fees, (4) the fact that McClellan was, in fact, engaged in the unlawful practice of law, and that, generally, (5) the clients of McClellan and AMI were at substantial risk of financial harm as a result of their association with AMI. Mullen breached her duty to her clients in all of these particulars. [FN2]

> FN2. Finding of fact 101. This same finding was made under number 80 in the Leszynski and Calixto cases.

The finding rests on the testimony of attorney Charles Nelson Berry III, an expert witness for the plaintiffs. The trial court found Berry's testimony to be "thoughtful and well-considered" and significantly, unrebutted. [15] [16] Mullen argues that the finding must be stricken because Berry improperly derived the standard of care from the Rules of Professional Conduct. In testifying that an attorney's conduct violated the legal standard of care, an expert witness may base an opinion on an attorney's failure to conform to an ethics rule, and may testify using language found in the Rules of Professional Conduct, as long as the jury is not led to believe that the ethical violations were actionable. Hizey, 119 Wash.2d at 265, 830 P.2d 646. Berry's testimony, phrased in terms of breach of the standard of care, stayed within this constraint. We conclude the finding is supported by substantial evidence. Accordingly, the trial court did not err in concluding that Mullen was negligent. [17] [18] The trial court's findings on damages, unchallenged by Mullen on appeal, are verities. See Cowiche Canyon Conservancy v. Bosley, 118 Wash.2d 801, 808, 828 P.2d 549 (1992). Mullen does, however, challenge the trial court's findings on proximate cause. Like the defendant attorney in Bullard v. Bailey, 91 Wash.App. 750, 959 P.2d 1122 (1998), she essentially contends this element is unsupported because McClellan's improper settlement of the cases would have caused the plaintiffs' damages regardless of her failure to warn them. She emphasizes that by the time she left AMI, the plaintiffs had already signed invalid contingency fee agreements with McClellan and that he was well on his way to converting their funds. [19] [20] *880 Proximate cause consists of two elements: cause in fact and legal causation. Bullard, 91 Wash.App. at 755, 959 P.2d 1122. Cause in fact is the "but for" consequence of the injury. Bullard, 91 Wash.App. at

755, 959 P.2d 1122 (citing Seattle v. Blume, 134 Wash.2d 243, 251, 947 P.2d 223 [1997]). It is a matter of what has in fact occurred and is generally for the trier of fact to decide. Bullard, 91 Wash.App. at 755, 959 P.2d 1122. As in Bullard, we conclude the trial court did not err in its determinations of proximate cause. All three plaintiffs testified that they hired McClellan and AMI to legally represent them and believed that McClellan was an attorney whom they trusted and relied upon to handle their respective claims. They found out that he was not an attorney only after their claims had been settled. Mullen did not advise any of the plaintiffs that McClellan was not a lawyer; that AMI was not a law firm; that she, as a paralegal, had no real supervision; or that client funds did not go through a trust account. These omissions by Mullen sufficiently link her to the plaintiffs' later injury to establish cause in fact. See Bullard, 91 Wash.App. at 757, 959 P.2d 1122. It was reasonable for the trial court to infer that if Mullen had properly advised the plaintiffs of the problems at AMI, more likely than not they would have withdrawn their cases from AMI in time to avoid being harmed by McClellan's fraudulent acts. **16 [21] [22] Legal causation turns on a policy question of how far the consequences of a defendant's acts should extend. Blume, 134 Wash.2d at 252, 947 P.2d 223. Whether legal liability adheres depends on "mixed considerations of logic, common sense, justice, policy, and precedent." Hartley v. State, 103 Wash.2d 768, 779, 698 P.2d 77 (1985). Mullen contends that her connection to the plaintiffs' injuries is too remote because she did not render direct legal advice and that it is unjust to hold her, an employee paralegal, responsible for the criminal, intentional acts of her employer. The Bullard court rejected a similar argument asserted by Bailey, an attorney who allowed himself to become associated with McClellan: *881 Under the circumstances presented, particularly McClellan's financial difficulties, unlawful legal practice, and Bailey's failure to correct Bullard's misapprehensions, ordinary human experience should have led Bailey to expect Bullard would suffer some harm at McClellan's hands, regardless whether it was the precise harm suffered. Bullard, 91 Wash.App. at 759, 959 P.2d 1122. Although Mullen was a paralegal, she is held to an attorney's standard of care because she worked on the plaintiffs' cases during a period of several months when she had no supervising attorney. The fact that she did not render legal advice directly does not excuse her; in fact, her failure to advise the plaintiffs of the improper arrangements at AMI is the very omission that breached her duty. Under these circumstances it is not unjust to hold her accountable as a legal cause of the plaintiffs' injuries. As all the elements of negligence have been established, we affirm the judgment against Mullen.

JOINT AND SEVERAL LIABILITY

[23] The trial court entered judgment against Mullen and Noble, McClellan, and AMI jointly and severally for compensatory damages. These amounts were $15,067.25 for Tegman, $27,362 for Leszynski, and $25,000 for Calixto. The court entered judgment against McClellan and AMI for substantial additional sums, including attorney fees, for criminal profiteering and Consumer Protection Act violations. Mullen and Noble object to being held jointly liable for the compensatory damages. They ask that the judgments be revised so that they are responsible for only that portion of the compensatory damages corresponding to the percentages of fault the trial court attributed to them. The trier of fact, in all "actions" involving fault of more than one "entity", must "determine the percentage of the total fault which is attributable to every entity which caused the claimant's damages". RCW 4.22.070(1). Citing *882 this statute, the trial court determined that Mullen was 10 percent at fault in each of the three cases; attorney Jescavage was 10 percent at fault in each of the three cases; and Noble was five percent at fault in Tegman's case. The court determined that McClellan and AMI had the remaining percentages in each case. The court then concluded that each of the plaintiffs was not at fault, and held all defendants jointly as well as severally liable in accordance with the statute: (b) If the trier of fact determines that the claimant or party suffering bodily injury or incurring property damages was not at fault, the defendants against whom judgment is entered shall be jointly and severally liable for the sum of their proportionate shares of the claimants total damages. RCW 4.22.070(1)(b). [24] Mullen and Noble argue that under this statute, the court should not have apportioned their fault with McClellan under this statute because he was an intentional tortfeasor and

the term "fault" in the statute does not include intentional conduct. They rely on Welch v. Southland Corp., 134 Wash.2d 629, 952 P.2d 162 (1998). In *Welch*, an unknown assailant robbed the plaintiff as he was leaving a convenience store owned by defendant Southland. The complaint alleged that Southland was negligent in failing to maintain a safe premises for its business invitees. The store asserted, as an affirmative defense, that under RCW 4.22.070(1) any **17 fault on the store's part should be apportioned with the intentional acts of the unknown assailant. The trial court ruled that a negligent defendant is entitled to the benefit of the comparative fault statute, and that the jury would be permitted to attribute comparative fault to the unknown assailant—an "empty chair" entity. The potential effect of this ruling, as Southland readily acknowledged, was to make Southland liable for only its own percentage of the damages instead of being held jointly liable for all the damages. This was because the assailant was not a defendant, and joint liability arises only among defendants "against whom judgment is entered." RCW 4.22.070(1)(b). The *883 Supreme Court reversed, holding that intentional acts are not included in the statutory definition of "fault" in the contributory and comparative fault statutes, and, thus, a negligent tortfeasor is not entitled to apportion liability to an intentional tortfeasor. Intentional torts are "part of a wholly different legal realm" from the apportionment mechanism provided in RCW 4.22.070(1). Welch, 134 Wash.2d at 635, 952 P.2d 162 (quoting Price v. Kitsap Transit, 125 Wash.2d 456, 464, 886 P.2d 556 [1994]). The judgment as entered by the trial court in this case did not violate the statute or *Welch*, because the court treated the action against McClellan and AMI as functionally separate from the action against Mullen, Noble, and Jescavage. The court held McClellan solely liable on the causes of action alleging intentional conduct. The court held Mullen, Noble, and Jescavage solely liable on the causes of action alleging negligence. Because the plaintiffs were free of fault, the court properly held the three negligent tortfeasors jointly as well as severally liable for the total compensatory damages caused by their negligence. That joint liability by the three negligent tortfeasors was the correct result is indicated by the result in *Welch*, which left Southland exposed to liability for the entire damage sustained by the plaintiff. The difference from *Welch* is that in this case, the plaintiffs did make the intentional tortfeasor a defendant in the same suit, and did obtain entry of a judgment against him. This is not a distinction that leads to diminished liability for the negligent tortfeasors. The trial court's apportionment of "fault" to the intentional tortfeasor did not lead to a different result for Mullen and Noble as far as their joint liability is concerned than if the plaintiffs had sued them in a completely separate lawsuit, and it did not have any effect on the recovery of the fault-free plaintiffs. At most it affected the percentages of fault as between the defendants, an issue we need not evaluate as it has not been raised. Any error in the court's decision to apportion "fault" to McClellan has caused no prejudice so far as the issue of **884* joint liability is concerned, and therefore is not reversible. Noble argues that reversal is necessary because the trial court failed to segregate the damages between the intentional tort and negligence claims. She relies on Honegger v. Yoke's Washington Foods, 83 Wash.App. 293, 921 P.2d 1080 (1996). *Honegger* was a personal injury case brought by a shoplifter who was injured when the store's employees aggressively pursued him and committed assault and battery. The trial court refused the plaintiff's request to segregate damages caused by the employees' intentional conduct from damages caused by negligence, including the plaintiff's contributory negligence. The plaintiff appealed from a relatively small judgment. A new trial was found necessary because there had been no allocation of damages between intentional tort and negligence claims. As a result, it was not possible to determine on what basis the jury reached the amount awarded as damages: The verdict could have been an award for damages sustained solely as the result of the assault and battery, or could reflect other injuries. The jury could have concluded all the damages resulted from the employees' actions, since Mr. Honegger was trying to escape further injury. Since we do not know the basis of the award and how it may have been compromised by the contributory negligence instruction, the entire matter needs to be retried. Honegger, 83 Wash.App. at 298-99, 921 P.2d 1080. The problem identified by the *Honegger* court does not exist in this case. The judgment separately sets forth the awards to the ***18* plaintiffs arising from McClellan's criminal profiteering and Consumer Protection Act violations, and holds

only McClellan and his firm responsible for these sums. [FN3] Mullen and Noble are jointly liable with McClellan only for compensatory damages. The trial court measured **885* the compensatory damages caused by Mullen and Noble's negligence in exactly the same way as the compensatory damages caused by McClellan's intentional conduct: the value of the settlements the plaintiffs would have received if their claims had been handled by a competent attorney. Noble has not pointed out any basis upon which the trial court, as finder of fact, could have segregated the damages with greater precision.

FN3. The judgment summary in Tegman's case, for example, provides in pertinent part as follows:

"Name of Plaintiff/ Judgment Creditor:		Maria **Tegman**
"Attorney for Judgment Creditor:		Gregory D. Lucas Lucas & Lucas, P.S.
"Judgment Debtors:		Deloris Mullen Lorinda Sue Noble Camille Jescavage G. Richard McClellan and **Accident & Medical Investigations, Inc.** ("AMI")
"Base Judgment Amount:	$15,067.25	(All defendants)
"Criminal Profiteering:	50,000.00	(McClellan & AMI only)
"Consumer Protection Damages:	10,000.00	(McClellan & AMI only)
	- - - - - - -	
"Judgment Amount:	$75,067.25	

"Interest Rate: 12% per annum from the date hereof until paid.

"Statutory Attorneys' Fees:	$ 125.00	(All defendants)
"Attorneys' Fees:	$79,218.50	(McClellan & AMI only)"

The judgments are affirmed.

- - - - - - -

NOTE: This decision was appealed to the Supreme Court of Washington, en banc, see 150 Wash. 2d 102, 75 P.3d 497 (2003). The Court held that the attorney was not jointly and severally liable for the intentional acts of the legal assistant.

EXERCISES

1. Did it surprise or bother you that the attorneys and the legal assistant were all working for a nonattorney?

2. Why did the court find that Mullen, the legal assistant, was not working under the supervision of an attorney? What did Mullen do wrong and what should she have done? What difference did it make in this case?

3. The court was very critical of the legal assistant. Why was the court so disturbed by the behavior and actions of the legal assistant? Do you think it was justified?

4. What did Mullen specifically do that the court found was the unauthorized practice of law?

5. Were you surprised that Mullen, as a legal assistant, was held to an attorney's standard of care once she began the authorized practice of law?

6. Why was the plaintiff able to pursue the claim against Mullen?

CASE REVIEW

In re Pinkins, 213 B.R. 818 (Bankr. E.D. Mich.1997),

213 B.R. 818
(Cite as: 213 B.R. 818)
United States Bankruptcy Court,
E.D. Michigan,
Southern Division.

In re Darain PINKINS, Walterine Jones, Charles & Shirley Daberkoe, Angela Hall, Pamela Fields, Maretta Roberson, Glenn Peeples, Rahman & Chantay

Harmon, Sabrina Sanders, Phyllis Dunson, Tammy Trombley, Barbara Ellis, Darris

Finney, D'Anyai Asaki, Luis & Denise Sierra, Lashawn & Angela Taylor, Theresa

Singletary, Sandra Asberry, Ralph Knox, Leon Smith, Junotia Robertson, Debtors.

Bankruptcy Nos. 97-40722, 97-40965, 97-42032, 97-42576, 97-42719, 97-42790,

97-42791, 97-42885, 97-43062, 97-43162, 97-13353, 97-43356, 97-43414, 97-43419,

97-43494, 97-43661, 97-43664, 97-44060, 97-44160, 97-44241, 97-44564.
Oct. 14. 1997.

*819 Julie Lesser, Royal Oak, MI, for Debtors.

David Wm. Ruskin, Southfield, MI, Trustee

MEMORANDUM OPINION

STEVEN W. RHODES, Chief Judge.

This matter is before the Court on the Chapter 13 Trustee's objections to fee applications submitted by the Castle Law Office of Detroit, P.C. in 21 cases. The Court conducted a hearing on the objections on August 21, 1997. Because most of the objections relate to all of the fee applications, the Court will address them in one consolidated opinion.

I. Introduction

The Castle Law office ("Castle") handles primarily Chapter 13 bankruptcy cases. The firm employs attorneys Julie Lesser and Terri Weik, and several legal assistants and clerical staff members. The Trustee's office considers Castle a "high volume filer," filing an average of 77 cases per month since January 1997. (Transcript of August 21, 1997 hearing [Tr.] at 36.) Castle's standard practice [FN1] in handling initial consultations with clients was that the client met with a legal assistant, who discussed with the client the available chapters and assisted the client in deciding which, if any, chapter proceedings the client should file. If the client had a question and requested an answer from an attorney, the legal assistant would personally ask the attorney and relate the answer back to the client. The client would not meet with ***820** an attorney. The assistant gave a questionnaire to the client to fill out and return. The assistant then reviewed the questionnaire and prepared the papers to be filed. The client then returned to sign the papers, again meeting with a legal assistant, rather than an attorney. In most instances, unless the client had specifically requested to meet with an attorney, the client's first contact with the attorney was at the meeting of creditors.

> FN1. The Court is aware that the law firm has since modified some of its procedures. However, this opinion addresses the procedures in effect at the time the fees in question were generated.

The Trustee's primary fee objection is that the firm's clients did not meet with an attorney prior to the meeting of creditors. The Trustee's concern in this respect is that the legal assistant is giving legal advice and acting without direct supervision of an attorney. The Trustee also objects to the similarity of time entries on the fee applications and the lack of detail. The Trustee raises further objections in specific cases in which the fees charged exceed the agreed-upon fees, and in cases which were dismissed at or before confirmation and Castle submitted an application for the full amount of the fees.

II. Unauthorized Practice of Law

A.

[1] Michigan law governs whether Castle legal assistants engage in the unauthorized practice of law. In re Bright, 171 B.R. 799, 802 (Bankr.E.D.Mich.1994) (no federal law regulating the extent to which nonlawyers may appear before the bankruptcy court; Michigan law applies). Mich. Comp. Laws Anno. § 600.916 provides in pertinent part:

> It is unlawful for any person to practice law, or to engage in the law business, or in any manner whatsoever to lead others to believe that he is authorized to practice law or to engage in the law business, or in any manner whatsoever to represent or designate himself as an attorney and counselor, attorney at law, or lawyer, unless the person so doing is regularly licensed and authorized to practice law in this state.

M.C.L.A § 600.916; M.S.A. 271A.916.

[2][3] The statute does not identify the activities that constitute the practice of law. Accordingly, "[t]he formidable task of constructing a definition of the practice of law has largely been left to the judiciary." State Bar v. Cramer, 399 Mich. 116, 132, 249 N.W.2d 1 (1976) (citing Comment, Lay Divorce Firms and the Unauthorized Practice of Law, 6 J.L. Reform 423, 426 [1973]). The courts should construe the term with the purpose of the statute in mind, which is to protect the public. Cramer, 399 Mich, at 134, 249N.W.2d 1.

In Cramer, the issue before the court was whether a nonlawyer selling "Do-It-Yourself Divorce Kits" was engaged in the unauthorized practice of law. The court held that it does not constitute the unauthorized practice of law for a nonlawyer to provide or sell standard forms and general instructions for completing the forms, or to provide typing services. Cramer, 399 Mich, at 136, 249 N.W.2d 1. However, the court stated, "[t]o the extent that defendant provides personal advice peculiar to [the client's particular legal situation], she is engaged in the 'unauthorized practice of law.' " Id. at 138, 249 N.W.2d 1.

In Bright, the bankruptcy court addressed whether the services provided by a paralegal constituted the unauthorized practice of law. The paralegal specialized in preparing divorce kits, but also assisted debtors in preparing Chapter 7 bankruptcy forms. The practice of the paralegal in that respect was to collect data from the debtor, decide where information should be placed on the forms, and add language to the standard forms not dictated by the debtor. The paralegal also stated that she responded to questions from debtors regarding the interpretation and definition of terms, referred debtors to specific pages of reference books in response to questions, and provided information about local procedures and requirements. She also consulted an attorney when a legal question arose and related the response back to the debtor. Bright, 171 B.R. at 800–01. The court noted that there had been no cases in Michigan specifically dealing with the unauthorized practice of law in the bankruptcy setting and looked to bankruptcy cases in other jurisdictions that have attempted to define what constitutes the unauthorized practice of law in the bankruptcy context. Id. at 802. Courts have held that the following activities constitute the practice of law in other jurisdictions:

*821 (I) Determining when to file bankruptcy cases. In re Herren, 138 B.R. 989, 995 (Bankr.D.Wy0.1992).

(2) Deciding whether to file a Chapter 7 or a Chapter 13. Arthur, 15 B.R. at 54[6] [In re Arthur. 15 B.R. 541 (Bankr.E.D.Pa.1981)].

(3) Filling out or assisting debtors in completing forms or scheduled. In re Glad, 98 B.R. 976, 978 (9th Cir. BAP 1989); In re McCarthy, 149 B.R. 162, 166 (Bankr.S.D.Cal.1992); Herren, 138 B.R. at 993–4; In re Webster, 120 B.R. 111, 113 (Bankr.E.D.Wis.1990); In re Bachmann, 113 B.R. 769, 773–4 (Bankr.S.D.Fla.1990); In re Calzadilla, 151 B.R. 622, 625 (Bankr. S.D. Fla. 1993).

(4) Solicitation of financial information and preparation of schedules. Herren, 138 B.R. at 994; In re Grimes, 115 B.R. 639, 643 (Bankr. D.S.D.1990).

(5) Providing clients with definitions of legal terms of art. Herren, 138 B.R. at 995.

(6) Advising debtors which exemptions they should claim. McCarthy, 149 B.R. at 166–7; Herren, 138 B.R. at 995; Webster, 120 B.R. at 113.

(7) Preparing motions and answers to motions. McCarthy, 149 B.R. at 166; Webster, 120 B.R. at 113.

(8) Advising debtors on dischargeability issues. Arthur, 15 B.R. at 54 [6].

(9) Advising debtors concerning the automatic stay. Arthur, 15 B.R. at 54 [6].

(10) Habitual drafting of legal instruments for hire. Arthur, 15 B.R. at 54[6].

(11) Correcting "errors" or omissions on bankruptcy forms. In re Calzadilla, 151 B.R. at 625.

(12) Advising clients as to various remedies and procedures available in the bankruptcy system. In re Calzadilla, 151 B.R. at 625.

Bright, 171 B.R. at 802-03.

[4] This Court finds that the legal assistants of Castle perform many services that constitute the unauthorized practice of law. First, legal assistants explain to prospective clients the difference between Chapter 7 and Chapter 13. (Tr. at 15.) They are thus defining and explaining concepts and legal terms of art.

Second, Lesser stated that approximately 33 percent of prospective clients who come to their office for an initial consultation are given other suggestions as to how to resolve their problems without filing bankruptcy. (Tr. at 15.) Because these prospective clients meet only with a legal assistant at the initial consultation, the Court infers that the legal assistant makes the determination that bankruptcy is not the best choice for this particular individual and advises the client of other options. The rendering of advice peculiar to a client's particular situation is specifically prohibited by Cramer, 399 Mich, at 138, 249 N.W.2d I.

Third, it appears that the assistant helps the client determine whether to file Chapter 7 or Chapter 13. Although Lesser testified that the client makes the choice (Tr. at 151), Lesser also later stated that the decision "by the client and the initial consultant" (Tr. at 16) is immediately reviewed by an attorney. Regardless of that review, the assistant's participation in this important decision constitutes the prohibited practice of law.

Fourth, if the legal assistant is not comfortable answering a specific question, or if the client is not comfortable with the advice given by the legal assistant, the legal assistant asks the attorney what the advice should be and relates that information back to the client. (Tr. at 17.) The primary concern with this practice is that the legal assistant uses his or her own judgment to decide which questions to refer to an attorney and which questions to attempt to answer themselves. There is also a chance that the assistant will not properly phrase the question to the attorney or will not communicate the advice properly to the client. Moreover, and most importantly, the client is entitled to the professional judgment of the attorney.

Lesser stressed that the legal assistants employed by the Castle law firm are very well trained, and that the legal services, although not provided by an attorney, are of the highest quality. (Tr. at 20.) This argument misses the point. Legal assistants are not authorized to practice law.

*822 B.

A number of the Michigan Rules of Professional Conduct provide further guidance on this issue. Michigan Rules of Professional Conduct 5.5 states in part:

A lawyer shall not:

****

(b) assist a person who is not a member of the bar in the performance of activity that constitutes the unauthorized practice of law.

The Comment to Rule 5.5 states, "[l]imiting the practice of law to members of the bar protects the public against rendition of legal services by unqualified persons."

Michigan Rules of Professional Conduct 5.3—Responsibilities Regarding Nonlawyer Assistants—states in part:

With respect to a nonlawyer employed by, retained by, or associated with a lawyer:

(a) a partner in a law firm shall make reasonable efforts to ensure that the firm has in effect measures giving reasonable assurance that the person's conduct is compatible with the professional obligations of the lawyer;

(b) a lawyer having direct supervisory authority over the nonlawyer shall make reasonable efforts to ensure that the person's conduct is compatible with the professional obligations of the lawyer; . . .

The Comment to Rule 5.3 stresses that the "measures employed in supervising nonlawyers should take account of the fact that they do not have legal training and are not subject to professional discipline."

Michigan Rules of Professional Conduct 1.1 states:

A lawyer shall provide competent representation to a client. A lawyer shall not:

(a) handle a legal matter which the lawyer knows or should know that the lawyer is not competent to handle, without associating with a lawyer who is competent to handle it;

(b) handle a legal matter without preparation adequate in the circumstances; or

(c) neglect a legal matter entrusted to the lawyer.

Michigan Rules of Professional Conduct 2.1 states:

In representing a client, a lawyer shall exercise independent professional judgment and shall render candid advice. In rendering advice, a lawyer may refer not only to the law, but to other considerations such as moral, economic, social and political factors that may be relevant to the client's situation.

The Comment to Rule 2.1 indicates that the "client is entitled to straightforward advice expressing the lawyer's honest assessment."

[5] An issue similar to the one before the Court was addressed in State Bar of Michigan Ethics Opinion RI-128, April 21, 1992. [FN2] There, an attorney inquired as to whether his legal assistant could meet with a prospective client, collect information from the client, and forward the information to the attorney, at which point the attorney would prepare the required documents for signing without ever meeting with the client. The Standing Committee on Professional and Judicial Ethics examined the rules cited above and stated,

FN2. Although ethics opinions are not binding on state or federal courts, they do provide guidance in resolving issues of professional responsibility. Upjohn Co. v. Aetna Cas. & Sur. Co., 768 F. Supp. 1186, 1214 (W.D. Mich. 1990).

Taken as a whole, the recurrent theme found in these [ ] rules and comments is that a lawyer's expertise and judgment are an integral part of the service provided to a client. While legal assistants may behave in a very professional manner while interacting with clients and carrying out the multitude of other duties they perform on a regular basis, the fact of the matter is that a legal assistant has not received the extensive, in-depth legal training which is required of a lawyer. Without such training, it is possible, perhaps even likely, that a legal assistant, having the only interaction with the client, may not spot an issue or issues that could make a difference in the drafting or representation provided.

RI-128. The Committee further stated that "it is impossible to see how the legal assistant, being the only contact with the law office, could refrain from giving legal advice. ***823** Certainly, any client will have questions regarding legal advice, and if the lawyer is not directly interacting with the client, any advice must be delivered through the legal assistant." RI-128.

[6] Michigan Rules of Professional Conduct 1.4(b), which provides that a "lawyer shall explain a matter to the extent reasonably necessary to permit the client to make informed decisions regarding representation," also infers that it is the lawyer who is communicating with the client. In most instances, clients of the Castle law firm did not meet with an attorney until the meeting of creditors. An attorney cannot adequately represent a client consistent with the Michigan Rules of Professional Conduct without meeting with the client before filing the case.

C.

In Bright, the court stated that under the Michigan Rules of Professional Conduct, a lawyer is not adequately supervising a nonlawyer if:

> (1) the lawyer does not know of the existence or content of meetings between the nonlawyer and the client;

> (2) the lawyer relies solely on the nonlawyer as intermediary, neglecting to meet directly with the client; or

> (3) the lawyer fails to use his independent professional judgment to determine which documents prepared by the nonlawyer should be communicated outside the law office.

Bright, 171 B.R. at 805.

[7] Lesser stressed that an attorney reviews the file at every step. Specifically, after the initial consultation, an attorney reviews the initial consultation paperwork and determines if the appropriate chapter has been selected. (Tr. at 16.) The attorney reviews the petition and plan. The attorney selects the exemptions. (Tr. at 19.) After the client signs the petition, the attorney makes a final review of the papers and signs them. However, even if the attorney is as personally involved with the file as Lesser suggests, this does not obviate the need for direct client contact. Although it is not improper for attorneys to delegate certain matters to nonlawyer members of their staff, lack of contact or a direct relationship with the client precludes proper delegation. In re Stegemann, 206 B.R. 176, 179 (Bankr. C.D. 111.1997).

[8] A further problem arises from Castle's practice of having the legal assistant sign client retention letters. The agreement is purportedly entered into by the client and the attorney. However, the attorney does not sign the client retention letter. (See Ex. I.) This issue was addressed by the Standing Committee on Professional and Judicial Ethics in Op 113. There, the lawyer was prohibited from allowing a nonlawyer employee to sign a client retention letter. The Committee reasoned that since court rules (MCR 2.114) require a lawyer to sign all pleadings, and retention letters are equally important, a nonlawyer may not handle retention letters. See Ethics and Legal Assistants, 71 Mich. BJ. 826 (August 1992).

D.

[9] Various sanctions are available in situations, such as this, involving the unauthorized practice of law. Courts have enjoined the unauthorized practice of law, disgorged fees, denied fees, fined the service provider, and ordered the service provider to pay the bankruptcy trustee's reasonable attorney fees. See Bright, 171 B.R. at 807 (citations omitted). The Court finds under the circumstances of these bankruptcy cases that it is appropriate to deny all fees for the work of legal assistants. The Court cannot award fees for unauthorized and unlawful services.

III. Fees Charged in Excess of Fee Agreement

[10] The Trustee raised objections in the following cases where the amount of the fee application was: greater than the agreed upon fees: Darain Pinkins, 97-40722; Tammy Trombley, 97-43353; Charles & Shirley Daberkoe, 97-42032; and Barbara Ellis,

97-43356. Lesser explained that the initial fee agreement covered only limited services and, in certain circumstances, additional services were required. The retainer agreement states that the $1,200 fee covers: 1) prefiling consultations, 2) creditor calls, 3) preparation and filing of original petition, 4) attorney representation at meeting of creditors, and 5) attorney representation at one confirmation *824 hearing. The retainer does not include attorney representation in any court action filed in conjunction with the petition, including adversary proceedings and motions. (See Ex. 1.) Following a review of the fee applications, the Court is satisfied that Castle has charged additional fees only in situations where services were provided that were not included in the initial fee agreement. Accordingly, this objection is overruled.

IV. Fees for Dismissed Cases

[11] The Trustee objects to Castle charging the full fee in the following cases that were dismissed at or before confirmation: Walterine Jones, 97-40965; Angela Hall, 97-42576; D'Anyai Asaki, 97-3419; and Darain Pinkins, 97-40722. The Trustee questioned whether there was a benefit to the estate in light of the fact that the cases were dismissed. Lesser argued that the dismissals in question were the fault of the debtor and in such instances the law firm should be compensated for the services they provided.

Section 330(a)(3) provides that in determining the amount of reasonable compensation, all relevant factors are to be considered, including:

> (C) whether the services were necessary to the administration of, or beneficial at the time at which the service was rendered toward the completion of, a case under this title.

11 U.S.C. § 330(a) (3) (C).

The Trustee has focused on the subsequent dismissal of the case in his objection to these fees, without identifying any specific charges which he considers objectionable. Because the standard for determining reasonableness considers the fees "at the time at which the service was rendered," it is not appropriate to merely object to the total amount because the case was subsequently dismissed. Lesser argues that in each case in question, the dismissal

was the result of actions of the debtor. If any actions by the attorney had contributed to the dismissal, then a reduction in fees would be warranted. However, the Court finds no indication of that in these cases and accordingly this objection is overruled.

V. Services of Clerical Personnel

[12] Castle included in its fee applications expenses for the services of clerical personnel, including the following: Opening of file (file preparation/organization of paperwork, entering client into system); Court preparation for filing; Filing of petition; and Copying of plan/POS to creditors and Trustee. These charges should not be billed separately to clients, but should be included in office overhead. As noted by this Court in In re Woodward East Project, Inc., 195 B.R. 372 (Bankr. E.D. Mich. 1996), "it is the normal practice of attorneys in this district that the expenses of . . . clerical services are part of an attorney's office overhead, and are not billed separately to clients." Id. at 377; see also In re Westwood Asphalt, 45 B.R. 111 (Bankr. E. D. Mich. 1984); In re Bank of New England Corp., 134 B.R. 450 (Bankr.D.Mass.1991), aff'd 142 B.R. 584 (D.Mass.1992). Accordingly, expenses for clerical services are not permitted and are disallowed.

VI. Similarity of Time Entries and Insufficiency of Detail

The Trustee objected that each of the 21 fee applications stated the same amount of time for the same type of service. Lesser stated that the firm did not keep contemporaneous time records, and that the fee applications were reconstructed from memory and from reviewing the files. (Tr. at 22–23.)

The Trustee also objected to the lack of specificity of the time records. This lack of specificity necessarily resulted from Castle's initial failure to keep contemporaneous time records and the reconstruction of time records after the fact.

[13] The failure to maintain contemporaneous time records affects the reliability of the records, In re Dawson, 180 B.R. 478, 480 (Bankr. E.D.Tex. 1994), and, although it does not automatically result in the denial of all fees, it does justify a reduction in the fees requested, in re Evangeline Refining Co., 890 R2d 1312, 1326–27 (5th Cir.1989). Without an opportunity to review actual time records, it is

impossible for the Court to determine whether any particular time entry is reasonable.

[14][15][16] Additionally, the description of services provided in the reconstructed fee applications is lacking in detail, making it difficult for the Court to determine if the fees requested are reasonable. Local Bankruptcy *825 Rule 3.03(a)(12)(C) requires the time statement to "describe with particularity the services rendered." Entries such as "Signing Appointment 45 min." or "Phone call to client re: insurance 15 min." fail to adequately describe the services rendered. A fee application which sets forth with specificity the exact nature of the services rendered, the time expended, and the expenses incurred is a prerequisite to making a determination that the services were necessary and reasonable. In re Meyer, 185 B.R. 571, 574

(Bankr. W.D. Mo. 1995). The Court "will not indulge in extensive labor and guesswork to justify a fee for an attorney who has not done so himself." In re Taylor, 66 B.R. 390,393 (Bankr.W.D.Pa.1986); see also J. F. Wagner's Sons Co., 135 B.R. 264, 267 (Bankr.W.D. Ky.1991). The Court finds that a 20-percent reduction in remaining fees is warranted due to Castle's failure to keep contemporaneous time records and resultant lack of detail in their reconstructed time records.

VII. Conclusion

In summary, the Court denies all fees requested for the services of legal assistants and clerical personnel. The Court further reduces the remaining fees for the services of the attorneys by 20 percent. After those deductions, the allowable fees in each case are as follows:

Case Name	Case Number	Amount Requested	Amount allowed
Pinkins	97-40722	$1,500.00	$863.32
Jones	97-40965	$1,200.00	$730.00
Daberkoe	97-12032	$1,500.00	$706.66
Hall	97-42576	$1,200.00	$550.00
Reids	97-42719	$1,200.00	$573.34
Roberson	97-42790	$1,200.00	$436.67
Peeples	97-42791	$1,200.00	$610.00
Harmon	97-42885	$1,200.00	$526.66
Sanders	97-43062	$1,200.00	$570.00
Dunson	97-43162	$1,200.00	$573.34
Trombley	97-43353	$1,400.00	$740.00
Ellis	97-43356	$1,600.00	$806.67
Finney	97-43414	$1,200.00	$516.00
Asaki	97-43419	$1,200.00	$580.00
Sierra	97-43494	$1,200.00	$563.34
Taylor	97-43661	$1,200.00	$566.67
Singletary	97-43664	$1,200.00	$490.00
Asberry	97-44060	$1,200.00	$493.33
Knox	97-44160	$1,000.00	$506.66
Smith	97-44241	$1,200.00	$616.66
Robertson	97-44564	$1,200.00	$466.66

An order regarding the allowed fees will be entered in each case.

END OF DOCUMENT

EXERCISES

1. What were the main factors listed by the court that persuaded them that the services performed by the legal assistants violated the unauthorized practice of law statutes?

2. Regarding the decision of a client to either file under Chapter 7 or Chapter 13 bankruptcy, suppose the legal assistants argued that they were simply giving information to the client that the client could have gotten from the Internet, in a book, or at the bankruptcy clerk's office, and that therefore their conduct did not violate UPL statutes. Evaluate their argument.

3. The attorney for the Castle Law Office argued that the legal assistants were very well trained, and that, while they were not attorneys, their legal services were of the highest quality. Is this a strong argument? How much legal analysis did the court spend on this argument?

4. The attorney for the Castle Law Office argued that, even though an attorney did not meet with clients directly, an attorney did, in fact, review every legal document that each legal assistant prepared and therefore there could be no UPL violation. How did the court handle this argument? Whose argument did you find more persuasive: the court's or the Castle Law Office's? Why?

5. The court concluded that the legal assistants should not have been allowed to sign the client retention letter (i.e., the letter agreeing to represent the client) for the Castle Law Office. What issues are raised by this fact? How did the court handle the matter?

6. For each issue raised by the court regarding the unauthorized practice of law by the legal assistants, what new procedural system would you put in place in the Castle Law Office to allow for correction?

PROLAW—CONFLICT OF INTEREST CHECKING

BASIC LESSONS

Number	Lesson Title	Concepts Covered
Lesson 1	Introduction to ProLaw	Understanding the ProLaw interface
Lesson 2	Entering Contacts	Adding new contacts
Lesson 3	Conflict of Interest Searching	Using the Quick Find and Conflicts functions to perform conflict of interest searches.

WELCOME TO JOHNSON AND SULLIVAN

Welcome to Johnson and Sullivan! We are an active and growing firm with four attorneys and two legal assistants. As you know, you have been hired as a legal assistant intern. We are very happy to have you on board; we can certainly use your help.

At Johnson and Sullivan we use computer systems extensively, so it is necessary that you have a basic understanding of our system. We currently use ProLaw, a comprehensive legal-specific program that has many functions. ProLaw automates the practice and management side of operating a law firm. ProLaw features include timekeeping and billing, accounting, trust accounting, docket control, case management, and many others.

In this lesson, you will focus on entering new contacts into ProLaw and learn how to do basic conflict of interest checking. We pride ourselves on being an extremely ethical firm; before we take any new matter we run an extensive conflict of interest search, so it is important that you know how to do this. We know you want to begin using ProLaw immediately, so there is only a short "Getting Started" section that you should read before getting on the computer.

GETTING STARTED

Introduction

Throughout these exercises, information you need to type into the program will be designated in several different ways.

- Keys to be pressed on the keyboard will be designated in brackets, in all caps and bold type (i.e., press the [ENTER] key).

- Movements with the mouse will be designated in bold and italics (i.e., *point to File on the Menu Bar and click the mouse*).
- Words or letters that should be typed will be designated in bold and enlarged (i.e., type **Training Program**).
- Information that is or should be displayed on your computer screen is shown in the following style: **Press ENTER** to continue.

Lesson 1: Introduction to ProLaw

In this lesson, you will load ProLaw and be introduced to the Contacts and Matters functions as an example of the basic interface of the program.

1. Load Windows. To load ProLaw, *click on the* Start *button, point with the mouse to* Programs *or* All Programs, *then point to* ProLaw Evaluation *and point and click on* **PROLAW.**
2. You should now have the **ProLaw** window displayed, including the Daily Docket calendar for the current day on your screen.
3. *Point and click on the maximize icon at the top right of the* ProLaw *window* (it is just to the left of the red "X" and looks like two layered squares. If you point to an icon with your mouse for more than a second, the icon title will be displayed.)
4. Notice that there is a column of icons on the left edge of the screen. These icons give you access to ProLaw's major functions; they include Contacts, Matters, Events, Files, Transactions, Journals, Ledger, and Reports.
5. Below is a table showing the purpose of each function in ProLaw.

ProLaw Icon/Function	Purpose
CONTACTS	Contains contact information for all clients, parties, attorneys, judges, etc. It is an electronic address book. Conflict of interest searches can also be performed using this function.
MATTERS	Contains detailed information about every case/client matters. This includes billing information, notes about the case, related contacts, related matters, and settlement information, among others.
EVENTS	Allows the user to run queries for a specific set of docket entries and print docket reports.
FILES	Allows the user to check files in and out and report on the location and status of physical file folders.
TRANSACTIONS	Allows the user to create time entries, run cost recovery imports, edit pre-bills, and produce statements.
JOURNALS	Allows the user to enter checks, cash receipts, reconcile accounts, and produce financial reports.
LEDGER	Allows the user to view client billing and payment history, statement images, and unbilled statements.
REPORTS	Allows the user to produce and print a wide variety of reports.

6. *Point and click with the mouse on* Contacts. The Contacts window is now displayed.

7. *Point and click with the mouse on* Quick find, located in the View section of the Shortcuts pane. *In the* Search for *field press the* **[BACKSPACE]** key. This will clear the field and search for all contacts in the database. Press the **[ENTER]** key.

8. Press the **[DOWN ARROW]** cursor key or *use the mouse* to scroll down through all of the contacts. Notice that the database is already populated with information.

9. *Scroll back until you find the entry for* Adam Schnieder, which is located near the bottom of the list. *Point and double-click on* Adam Schnieder.

10. Notice that the **Adam Schnieder—Contact** window is now displayed. You can now see the contact information for Adam Schnieder including name, class (i.e., type of entry; in this case, "client"), address, phone number, etc.

11. In the **Adam Schnieder—Contact** window, *point and click on the* Close *icon (the red "X" located in the upper-right corner of the window) to close this window.*

12. The "Contacts" window should now be displayed. *Point and click on "Recent"* (under "Shortcuts" and "View"). Notice that only the entry for Adam Schnieder is listed. The Recent command contains a list of your most recently used contacts.

13. In the Contacts window, *point and click on the* Close *icon (the red "X" located in the upper-right corner of the window) to close this window.*

14. You should now be back where you started at the **Daily Docket** screen.

15. *Point and click with the mouse on* **Matters.** The **Matters** window is now displayed.

16. *Point and click with the mouse on* Quick find, if it is not already displayed (located in the **View** section of the **Shortcuts** pane), hit the **Search** for field, press the **[BACKSPACE]** key. This will clear the field and search for all matters in the database. Press the **[ENTER]** key.

17. In the Matters window, *point and click with the mouse on the* maximize *icon at the top right corner of the window.* (located just to the left of the Close icon; it looks like two layered squares). This will allow you to see additional columns.

18. Press the **[DOWN ARROW]** cursor key or *use the mouse* to scroll down through all of the matters.

19. *Point and double-click with the mouse on the first entry* (Matter ID 1000-001—Maguire, Robert, Maguire—Chapter 7).

20. The 1000-001—**Matter** window should now be displayed. Notice that there are a number of tabs in the window, including General, Notes, Billing, Related Contacts, and others. *Point and click on each of these tabs.* Then, close the 1000-01—Matter window by *pointing and clicking on the* Close *icon.*

21. The **Matters** window should now be displayed. *Point and click on* Recent (located in the "View" section of the "Shortcuts" pane). Notice that only the "Maguire, Robert—Maguire—Chapter 7" matter is listed.

22. *In the* Matters *window, point and click on the* Close *icon to close this window.*

23. You should now be back where you started at the Daily Docket screen.
24. This concludes Lesson 1. To exit ProLaw, *point and click on the* Close *icon in the* ProLaw *window to close the program.* Alternatively, you *may point and click on* File *on the menu bar and then click on* Exit.

Lesson 2: Entering Contacts

In this lesson, you will enter several new contacts into ProLaw.

1. Load Windows. To load ProLaw, *click on the* Start *button, point with the mouse to* Programs *or* All Programs, *point to* ProLaw Evaluation, *and then point and click on* **PROLAW.**
2. You should now have the **ProLaw** window displayed on your screen, including the **Daily Docket** calendar for the current day.
3. *Point and click with the mouse on* Contacts. The Contacts window is now displayed. You should see the entry for Adam Schnieder displayed under Recent.
4. *Point and click with the mouse on the* Add Item *icon on the toolbar* (the toolbar is located just under the menu bar at the top of the screen; the **Add Item** icon looks like a file folder with a sun over it and is at the far left of the toolbar). The **New Contact** window with an empty record should now be displayed.
5. The cursor should be in the Company field. Press the [**TAB**] key to go to the Full Name field. Type **James Lund** and then press the [**TAB**] key. The cursor should now be in the Class field. Notice that ProLaw automatically enters "James" in the Salutation field.
6. With the cursor in the Class field, *point and click with the mouse on the down arrow of the drop-down box at the right edge of the field.* Using the cursor keys *or the mouse, scroll down to* Expert Witness *and point and click on it.* Expert witness should now be shown in the Class field.
7. Press the [**TAB**] key to go to the Salutation field. Type **Jim** and press the [**TAB**] key.
8. *Point and click with the mouse in the blank field under the* General *tab.* This is where the mailing address goes.
9. Type **2301 McGee** and then press the [**ENTER**] key.
10. Type **Culver City, CA 94063.**
11. *Point and click with the mouse on* Edit *on the Menu Bar at the top of the screen and then on* Address Detail. You can now see how ProLaw has entered the data into the address database. *Point and click with the mouse on the* green checkmark *in the* Address Detail *window.*
12. *Point and click with the mouse on the down arrow of the drop-down box at the right edge of the field and point and click on* Mailing.
13. You are now ready to enter phone numbers for Mr. Lund. Find the white box under Phone Number. *Point and click with the mouse on the* Add item *icon (i.e., a blue folder with a sun on it) to the right of "Phone Number, Ext., Type, Main?"* (Please note that there are three Add item icons on the screen; select the one to the right of **Phone Number.**) When you select the Add item icon, you are now allowed to type a phone number.
14. Type: **415-599-7000** and then press the [**TAB**] key four times.

15. The cursor should now be in the phone number field directly under the number you just entered. Type: **415-599-7010** and then press the **[TAB]** key twice.

16. The cursor should now be in the Type field. *Point and click with the mouse on the down arrow of the drop-down box in the* Type *field. Point and click on the* Fax *option* and then press the **[TAB]** key twice.

17. The cursor should now be in the phone number field directly under the fax number you just entered. Type **jlund@expert.com** and then press the **[TAB]** key three times. Notice that ProLaw automatically recognized it as an e-mail address.

18. *Point and click with the mouse on the* Notes *tab* (located just to the right of the General tab). This is where you can enter notes about the contact.

19. In the large white box on the left, type: **Mr. Lund's specialty is engineering/construction as it relates to cement and structural loads. We have used Mr. Lund on several occasions and he is outstanding.**

20. *Point and click with the mouse on the* Custom *tab.* In this database, you can enter the Social Security Number of the person. Type: **505-66-9899.**

21. To save the new contact, *point and click with the mouse on* File *on the Menu Bar, and then on* Save (notice that there is a greencheck mark next to it). Alternatively, you could *point and click on the green checkmark on the toolbar.*

22. *Close the* James Lund—Contact *window.*

23. To confirm that Mr. Lund has been correctly entered, *point and click with the mouse on* Quick Find *in the* Contact *window.* In the Search for field, type: **Lund,** hit Search by field, and choose **Last Name** from the list in the drop-down box. Press **[ENTER].**

24. Notice that the record for Mr. Lund is retrieved.

25. *Point and click with the mouse on* Lund *in the* Search for *field* and then press **[BACKSPACE]** to delete it.

26. *Point and click with the mouse on the* Add item *icon on the toolbar at the top left of the window* (located just under "File" on the Menu Bar; it looks a file folder with a sun on it). The **New Contact** window with an empty record should now be displayed.

27. You are now ready to enter some additional contacts on your own. Enter the following contact information:

Field	Data to be Entered
Full Name	**June Hill**
Class	**Judge**
Salutation	**Judge Hill**
General	**Orange County Courthouse**
	4500 Main
	Montgomery, NY 12549
Description (which defaults to "Home")	**Mailing**
Phone Number	**202-456-6444**
E-mail	**jhill@co.orange.nv.us**
Notes	Judge Hill is a stickler for court rules and is extremely conservative in her opinions.

Field	Data to be Entered
Full Name	**Rebekah Wason**
Class	**Accountant**
Salutation	**Rebekah**
General	**2743 North 8th Ave**
	Denver, CO 80204
Description (which defaults to "Home")	**Mailing**
Phone Number	**303-962-8852**
E-mail	**rlw@acctusa.com**
Notes	Rebekah is an experienced accountant whose specialty is corporate accounting.

Field	Data to be Entered
Company Name	
Full Name	**Linda Lewis**
Class	**Attorney**
Salutation	**Linda**
General	**6532 132nd St, NW**
	Detroit, MI 23432
Description (which defaults to "Home")	**Mailing**
Phone Number	**323-234-6566**
Fax Number	**323-234-6566**
E-mail	**llewis@lewisatty.com**
Notes	Linda advises us on complex Indian gaming issues from time to time.

28. This concludes Lesson 2. To exit ProLaw, *click on the* Close *icon in all ProLaw windows.* Alternatively, you may *point and click on* File *on the Menu Bar and then click on* Exit.

Lesson 3: Conflict of Interest Searching

In this lesson you will conduct conflict of interest searches in ProLaw.

1. Load Windows. To load ProLaw, *click on the* Start *button, point with the mouse to* Programs *or* All Programs, *point to* ProLaw Evaluation, *and then point and click on* **PROLAW.**
2. You should now have the ProLaw window displayed on your screen, including the Daily Docket calendar for the current day.
3. *Point and click with the mouse on "Contacts."*
4. *Point and click with the mouse on* Quick find. In the Search for field, press the [**BACKSPACE**] key until it is empty. Press the [**ENTER**] key.

5. You are now ready to conduct conflict of interest searches in ProLaw. You have been asked to conduct a conflict search regarding the potential claim of Valerie Little. Ms. Little would like a divorce from her husband, Jimmy Lund.

6. *Point and click with the mouse on* Conflicts (located in the View section of the Shortcuts pane on the left side of the screen). The cursor is now blinking next to "Names" under the heading "Conflicts."

7. Type: **Lund [ENTER]**
   Little [ENTER]

8. *Point and click with the mouse on the* Start Query *icon* (located just to the right of the Names field; it looks like a file folder with a magnifying glass in the middle of it).

9. Notice that ProLaw retrieves the record for "Linda Blunder." ProLaw returns any name that contains "Lund," so "B<u>lund</u>er" is returned.

10. Notice also that "James Lund" is returned. You initially did not think of "James Lund," an expert that the firm uses from time to time, as "Jimmy Lund." You ask your potential client, Valerie Little, for her husband's social security number; sure enough, she says it is 505-66-9899. Notice that this is the exact number your conflict search has returned. This is a significant conflict and most likely will keep the firm from representing Valerie Little.

11. Press the **[BACKSPACE]** key to clear the Names field.

12. You have been asked to conduct a conflict search regarding a potential claim of Timothy Handley. Mr. Handley was involved in a five-car accident on a busy highway. Mr. Handley was rear-ended by a number of cars that were going too fast, which created a five-car pile up. The drivers of the other cars were John Gable, Gina Saprano, Duane Fuller, and Todd Hoyt.

13. Enter the last names of all of the drivers in the **Names** field and execute the search.

14. Notice that Gina and Victor Saprano are returned. *Point and double-click with the mouse on* **Gina Saprano.** Notice that she is the spouse of a client, Victor Saprano. This may or may not be a problem in that **FKA** ("formerly known as") is selected as the class; it is possible that they are divorced, but this is a significant issue that needs further follow-up.

15. In the Gina **Saprano—Contact** window, *point and click on the* Close *icon.*

16. You have been asked to conduct a conflict search regarding a potential claim of William Kearns. Mr. Kearns is a correctional officer at a maximum-security prison. Mr. Kearns was attacked and severely injured on the job. He is considering claims against his attackers and prison management for ineffective security and OSHA violations. His attackers were David Smith and Mark Mclcher. The warden of the facility is Wayne Pritchard.

17. Enter the last names of the potential client and potential defendants in the Names field and execute the search.

18. Notice that David Smith is returned. Notice that Mr. Smith is listed as a potential client. It is possible that, prior to his incarceration, Mr. Smith came to the firm for representation. This may or may not be a problem, since "David Smith" is a common name and it may not be the same person, but this is a significant issue that needs further follow-up.

19. This concludes Lesson 3. To exit ProLaw, *click on the* Close *icon in all ProLaw windows.* Alternatively, you may *point and click on* File *on the Menu Bar and then click on* Exit.

This concludes the ProLaw Conflict of Interest Checking Hands-On Exercises.

For additional resources, visit our Web site at www.westlegalstudies.com

CLIENT RELATIONS AND COMMUNICATION SKILLS

After you read this chapter, you should be able to:

- Discuss factors that will promote effective client relationships.
- Discuss ways to communicate effectively.
- Identify communication barriers.
- Explain the importance of good listening skills.
- Identify the pros and cons of using groups to make decisions.
- Discuss the characteristics of a leader.

A client hired an attorney to file a petition. At that time, the client paid the attorney $650. Over the next five months, the client made approximately 25 telephone calls to the attorney. The attorney failed to return all of the client's calls. The attorney asked an independent legal assistant to prepare a draft of the petition. The legal assistant prepared a draft of the petition and then made 26 attempts to reach the attorney by telephone and by pager, but the attorney failed to respond. The attorney did not pay the legal assistant for the work on the petition, did not review the petition, and did not provide legal services to the client. The attorney was disbarred.[1]

***

Over a two-and-a-half-year period, an attorney failed to perform legal services in 38 client matters. Of the 38 matters, the attorney was charged and found culpable in 33 cases of failure to competently perform legal services, 27 cases of failure to communicate, 30 cases of failure to refund unearned fees, 5 cases of aiding others in the unauthorized practice of law, 2 cases of failure to maintain client funds in trust, 2 cases of improper withdrawal, and 1 case of failure to comply with a court order. The attorney's clients were significantly harmed. Some of her clients suffered financial losses, and others suffered stress, loss of sleep, and loss of time because of the attorney's misconduct. The attorney was disbarred.[2]

***

A sole practitioner lost a court case after months of preparation and weeks of trial. The attorney had been representing one of her best corporate clients who had paid her faithfully each month during litigation. The attorney did not relish the thought of visiting the owner of the company. When she did, she was stunned. The client offered his condolences and expressions of support. During the course of the litigation, the attorney and all the members of the attorney's staff had kept the client fully informed of everything that was transpiring in the case. The client knew that the attorney and her staff had worked hard on the case and how intent they had been on winning. He also knew that he had been treated fairly and that the attorney and the staff had acted honestly and ethically in representing his interests. While winning would have been better, the client felt well served.[3]

WHY DO LEGAL ASSISTANTS NEED TO FOSTER GOOD CLIENT RELATIONSHIPS AND COMMUNICATE EFFECTIVELY?

Fostering positive client relationships and communicating effectively with others is an important aspect of practice management and is an absolute necessity for legal assistants to be successful. Customer service and satisfaction are very important to the practice of law, especially considering the number of law offices and the fierce competition that exists. Legal assistants who mishandle client relationships by not putting the client first will cause clients to go elsewhere for legal services. Nearly every task a legal assistant performs requires communication skills such as writing correspondence, drafting briefs, interviewing clients and witnesses, and legal research/writing. The ability to effectively exchange ideas and information with others is an essential part of being a legal assistant.

This section will present an overview of ethical duties to clients and a basic but practical explanation of communication, and will give you some ideas for how communication skills can be improved. Also included in this section are related communication topics such as leadership qualities, the advantages and disadvantages of working with groups, and how to conduct client interviews.

> *Establish a good relationship with a client early by showing him or her respect, listening, and being responsive to his or her needs. If you tell a client that you will get back to him or her, do so, even if you are only telling him or her that you are still working on solving the issue and do not have an answer. If you promise a client that you will send him or her something, stop what you are doing and send it. Offer to help the client while always keeping in mind that you cannot give answers to specific legal questions and the need to avoid the unauthorized practice of law. A paralegal can be accommodating to a client without having to worry about unauthorized practice of law issues.*
>
> —Linda Rushton, CLA

ETHICAL DUTY TO COMMUNICATE WITH CLIENTS

While much of this chapter covers how to provide clients with excellent customer service as it relates to providing quality legal services, there is also a strong ethical duty regarding the need to regularly communicate with clients. Keeping a client informed about his or her case, keeping him or her abreast of changes, developing strategy with him or her, and keeping him or her involved in the progress of a case—including communicating settlement offers—is fundamental to the practice of law. Attorneys and legal assistants are bound by this ethical duty. Clients cannot make informed decisions about their cases if they do not know what is happening.

Rule 1.4 of the ABA *Model Rules of Professional Conduct* requires an attorney to reasonably consult with a client, to keep the client reasonably informed about the status of the legal matter, to promptly comply with reasonable requests for information from the client, and to explain matters to a client to the extent reasonably necessary to permit the client to make informed decisions about the matter.

Rule 1.4 specifically requires the attorney to reasonably consult with the client, to explain general strategy, and to keep the client reasonably informed regarding the status of the client's legal matter. The "reasonableness" of the situation will depend on the facts and circumstances of the particular case.

The comment to the rule states that: The guiding principle is that the lawyer should fulfill reasonable client expectations for information consistent with the duty to act in the client's best interests, and the client's overall requirements as to the character of representation.

Clients become extremely frustrated when they pay for legal services and the attorney or legal assistant refuses to take their calls, answer their letters, or otherwise communicate with them in any way.

The duty to communicate derives in part from the attorney's fiduciary duty of utmost good faith to the client. Figure 4-1 explains the specific duties of an attorney to communicate with clients as decided by case law.

> *The lawyer [must] promptly consult with and secure the client's consent prior to taking action unless prior discussions with the client have resolved what action the client wants the lawyer to take. For example, a lawyer who receives from opposing counsel an offer of settlement in a civil controversy or a proffered plea bargain in a criminal case must promptly inform the client of its substance unless the client has previously indicated that the proposal will be acceptable or unacceptable or has authorized the lawyer to accept or to reject the offer. See Rule 1.2(a). Comment to Model Rule 1.4*

Figure 4-1
Duties of an Attorney to Communicate with a Client

Client communication includes a duty of an attorney to

- Inform clients of the status of their case.
- Timely respond to a client's request for information.
- Inform clients promptly about important information.
- Not cover up a matter if the attorney failed to carry out the client's instructions.
- Notify clients if he or she is leaving a firm or quitting the practice of law.
- Notify clients if he or she is stopping work on a client's case.
- Explain the law and benefits and risks of alternative courses of action.
- Notify and communicate settlement offers to clients.

DUTY TO TIMELY RESPOND TO A CLIENT'S REQUEST FOR INFORMATION There is an absolute duty for an attorney to respond to reasonable requests for information. While this seems basic, many attorneys still do not return client phone calls, respond to client letters, respond to client e-mails, or show up for client appointments. There are thousands of state bar disciplinary opinions where attorneys have been reprimanded, suspended, and disbarred for failing to respond in a timely fashion to their clients.

DUTY TO INFORM CLIENTS PROMPTLY ABOUT IMPORTANT INFORMATION An attorney may not withhold important information that affects a legal matter without telling the client. For example, cases have held that an attorney has a duty to promptly tell a client that the client was named as a defendant in a civil action; an attorney cannot wait six months to tell an incarcerated defendant that the attorney had been appointed to represent the client; and an attorney had to tell a client that a case was set for docket and later dismissed for failure to prosecute.

DUTY TO NOT COVER UP A MATTER IF THE ATTORNEY FAILED TO CARRY OUT THE CLIENT'S INSTRUCTIONS If an attorney fails to carry out the instructions of a client by either neglect or design, the attorney has a duty to be up front and communicate this to the client. Many attorney discipline cases have been filed because an attorney agreed to file a claim and then did not, either due to negligence or because the attorney later changed his or her mind and then told the client the case was, in fact, filed. This type of behavior is also prohibited by Rule 1.4.

DUTY TO NOTIFY CLIENTS IF AN ATTORNEY IS LEAVING A FIRM OR QUITTING THE PRACTICE OF LAW An attorney has a duty to tell a client that he or she is leaving a firm and, therefore, representation of the client's case will be handled by someone else. The same holds true if the attorney is going to stop practicing law. The client needs to be made aware of this fact so that he or she can get his or her file returned and secure other counsel.

DUTY TO NOTIFY A CLIENT IF HE OR SHE IS STOPPING WORK ON A CLIENT'S CASE An attorney cannot cease working on a client matter without affirmatively telling the client, because doing so without the client's consent or knowledge could injure the client's legal interests. The withdrawal from a client matter should preferably be in writing, in the form of a letter to the client. If formal representation has been made in court, the attorney must file a motion to withdraw.

DUTY TO EXPLAIN THE LAW AND BENEFITS AND RISKS OF ALTERNATIVE COURSES OF ACTION An attorney has a duty to help the client make an informed decision about the client's matter. This may include explaining legal theories to the client, explaining the effects of contracts and other documents, advising a client on the consequences of accepting one alternative over another, and generally giving advice and counseling the client regarding the legal matter.

DUTY TO NOTIFY AND COMMUNICATE SETTLEMENT OFFERS TO CLIENTS   An attorney has a duty to notify a client of all settlement offers, including explaining the terms and conditions of the offer and the ramifications to the client. An attorney cannot ordinarily, without the prior direction of the client, unilaterally decline or accept a settlement offer.

> *I [as a legal assistant] am the one the clients often will speak to first, and I am the representative of the firm. It's a position of trust.*
>
> (2005, July/August). A look at corporate law. *Legal Assistant Today*, 88.

THE LEGAL ASSISTANT'S ROLE IN COMMUNICATING WITH CLIENTS   Legal assistants can play an active role in communicating with clients. Legal assistants are often more accessible to clients than attorneys and therefore may have many opportunities to work with clients and to keep them informed. This is admirable and encouraged as long as the attorney is actively involved with the case, is reviewing all documents prepared by the legal assistant, is the only party giving legal advice to the client, and meets with the client as needed.

CLIENT RELATIONSHIPS

A fundamental aspect of law office management is the commitment to provide quality legal service to clients. This is true whether you work in a private law firm or legal aid office with many clients, or in a corporation or government practice where you have only one client; service is the key. Providing quality legal services begins with a good working relationship with each client, and this relationship is not just for attorneys. Everyone in the office, including legal assistants, should be committed to this. Remember, the client always comes first; he or she is the one paying your salary in the end. Clients may not have the legal background to know whether or not they are receiving good legal representation. However, clients do know whether their phone calls are being returned, whether documents in their cases are poorly written and have typographical errors, whether deadlines are missed, or whether they are being treated respectfully. Merely providing good technical legal skills is not enough to please clients. Most clients are referred to attorneys and law offices by previous clients; if you provide poor service to existing clients, you will be depriving your firm of the best way to expand the practice.

What Clients Like	What Clients Dislike
Friendliness	Being talked down to
Competence	Arrogance
Promptness	Staff acting bored or uninterested
Being able to reach attorneys/staff on the first try	Impatience
Excellent follow-up	Rudeness
Not being billed for every two minute phone call	Calls and e-mails not returned
Attorneys/staff taking extra time to explain the legal process in layperson's terms	Incorrect billings
Listening and paying attention to what the client has to say	Being forgotten, treated as unimportant, or taken for granted
Demonstrating genuine interest in the client's problems and concerns year in and year out	Confidentiality breaches
Honesty	Errors
Good financial stewardship	Poor-quality work
Completing work on time	Multiple staff billing for the same event
	Waiting in the waiting room when they have an appointment and they are on time

Figure 4-2
What Clients Like and Dislike

Fostering Positive Client Relationships

Figure 4-2 shows a list of things that clients like and dislike about attorneys and law office staff. These likes and dislikes determine whether a client will come back for future business or refer others to the firm. Notice that the issue of winning or losing a case is not included in either list.

It is important to note that many of the items on the list are opinions of how the client perceives the legal professional.

- Does the client see you as friendly and willing to help, or inattentive and impersonal?
- Do you come across to the client as prompt and businesslike, or indifferent?
- Do you show common courtesy to the client, or do you come across as rude?
- Are you respectful of the client and what he or she is going through, or do you have a superior and condescending attitude?
- Do you at every possible opportunity let the client know what is going on with his or her case and establish a feeling of trust and cooperativeness, or is the client ignored?

Each of these areas is critical to the success of the client relationship. Fail in any of these areas, and the relationship is undermined. This section will provide you with some ideas about how to foster excellent client relationships (see Figure 4-3).

**Figure 4-3
Fostering Positive
Relationships with
Clients—"Clients
for Life"**

Description	Behavior
Know your client	• When dealing with the client, take into account his or her emotional/mental/physical state (consider how you would feel in the same circumstances), understand that many clients are anxious or nervous about seeing a legal professional and, based on this, respond and ask questions appropriately. • Establish basic trust in the relationship at every opportunity by listening to their needs, being honest, and being respectful. • Ask your client what his or her concerns are about the matter. • Ask your client what his or her business is about. • Do research on your own about the client's business and industry. • Ask how the client prefers to be communicated with (in person, e-mail, telephone, or voice mail). • Ask the client how often he or she want to be communicated with. • Ask how you can serve them better periodically.
Treat each client as if he or she is your only client	• When you meet with a client, only have that person's file on your desk. • Never take another call when meeting with a client, and let others know not to disturb you. • Never talk about how busy you are or about other cases to clients. • Particularly with new clients, it is important that the initial meeting go well and that law office staff are immediately available after a referral is made. • Particularly with new clients, be sure to mention whether the firm has handled similar cases in the past. Clients like to know that the firm is experienced regarding the subject matter of their case.
Send copies of all documents to clients	• Always send copies of documents to the client. This lets them know what you have been working on and keeps them informed. If the document is not particularly sensitive, attach it to an e-mail to the client; it's cheaper and faster.
Do not use legalese	• Talk to clients in layperson's terms and refrain from using jargon.
Return all phone calls and reply to e-mails and voice mails immediately	• Always return phone calls, e-mails and, voice mails immediately, no later than the end of the day.
Be courteous and professional	• Always be courteous, professional, and empathetic with clients. This is extremely important to most clients. • Dress professionally.
Respond to clients requests and keep promises	• Always respond to client requests in a timely manner; if you make a promise to get something to a client, make sure you get it done on time and contact the client to let him or her know the status.

Description	Behavior
Give periodic updates	• Be proactive and periodically give updates to a client on the status of his or her case, whether or not the client specifically asked for it.
Never share personal problems or complain to clients	• Avoid sharing personal problems with clients. Clients are there to receive a service. • Do not complain to clients at all, especially about how hard you are working on their case. They are paying the firm a significant fee.
Preserve client confidences	• Maintaining client confidentiality is critical to maintaining the foundation of trust in the relationship.
Survey clients	• Use formal client surveys to find out what clients think about your services.
Management must help promote good client relations	• Work with management to let them know how to better support positive client relationships.
Publish a client manual	• Publish a client manual to help clients understand what to expect from the law office and how the judicial system functions regarding their type of case.
Take conflicts of interests seriously and be ethical	• Ask yourself who the client is, if there is more than one person in your office. • Always do careful conflicts checks, disclose any issues whatsoever, and get any consents to conflicts in writing after full disclosure. • If a client sees you being unethical in any way, that client may assume that you are not ethical with him or her.
Do not procrastinate	• Do not put things off or delay communicating with clients, even when you do not have good news or when work has not been completed. Be honest and up front.

Figure 4-3
(Continued)

Know Your Client

Leading firms in any endeavor know the key to competitive advantage is to set your sights on being first to market with exceptional ideas and exceptional service offerings. They become obsessed with: "How can we serve clients in a way nobody else can?" "What potential clients are not being served adequately?" "What services can we offer that will make clients go 'wow'?" What can we do that will actually lead the market?"[4]

Knowing your client and your client's individual needs is extremely important. Each client has a unique set of needs, worries, and desires related to his or her legal matter. Firms with outstanding client relations discover what those specific needs are for each client, and then systematically deliver on each need.

Before you can understand a client and his or her needs, it is helpful to understand why a client comes to a legal professional. Like any other relationship, the client relationship is based on trust. Clients come to legal professionals because they need help. They are either in a crisis or trying to avoid a crisis, and this condition of need makes them feel vulnerable.[5] Whenever possible, take the client's emotional, mental, and physical state into consideration and empathize with him or her.

By showing the client that you understand and recognize his or her situation and concerns, you establish trust, which is the foundation of the relationship. Another way to establish trust is by being respectful and honest with the client at all times.

> *Simply listening is not enough, because clients want more than a legal solution. They want a solution to their unique needs. It's the total experience that counts. . . . Discover what they think of the way you treat them.*[6]

Once a relationship of trust is established with a client, it is important to know specifics about that individual, such as what his or her business is, what his or her concerns are about the legal matter, and what you can do to serve his or her needs.

Do not assume you know what the client needs or wants. You may or may not be right, but you will know for sure if you ask. Because communication is vitally important, ask the client how he or she wants to receive communication. Are office visits the most convenient? Is e-mail best? Does the client prefer telephone or voice mail? Again, the trick is to ask and then deliver services based on the client's needs.

> *The one thing that I always try to remember is that these clients pay my salary! It is important for them to believe that I am doing my job and that they can talk to me about their case and any questions they have. Throughout a case, I grow to care for my clients very much, and I consider the client relations portion of my job to be THE most important job I do every day.*
> —Andrea Blanscet, CLA

TREAT EACH CLIENT AS IF HE OR SHE IS YOUR ONLY CLIENT   Every client should be treated individually. Behave as if that client's case is the only thing you are working on and as if the case is your most important one. Everyone at the firm needs to put the client at ease. When you meet with a client, have only his or her file on your desk and give the client your undivided attention. Never take a call when meeting with a client, and let others know not to disturb you. This is a good idea not only because it shows the client that you are interested in his or her case, but because the confidentiality of your other clients needs to be maintained.

Never tell the client how busy you are or how many other cases you are working on; the client's case is the only one he or she is concerned about and the only one you should be talking to him or her about. If a client calls and asks if you are busy, say something such as "I'm never too busy to take a call from a good client" (even if you are swamped). If a client comes in for an appointment, never make him or her wait in the waiting room. A good law practice makes prompt, *personal* service a high priority. Take a personal interest in the client's affairs and be empathetic. It is always best to be personable with clients because this fosters good working relationships that will continue for years to come.

One law firm's client reported that he was sending additional business—both his own business and referrals—to other law firms in town. When asked why he wasn't sending it to his primary firm, he replied, "Because they're too busy already. The lawyers [and legal assistants] are always telling me how busy they are, and are slow in responding to my requests."[7]

SEND COPIES OF ALL DOCUMENTS TO CLIENTS   As a matter of practice, it should be the policy of the law office to always send copies of all letters, memos, pleadings, and documents to the client. In nearly all cases, the client will appreciate this, and it will increase his or her confidence, satisfaction, and trust; even though this might be just another case to you, this matter is of particular importance to the client. Although many people focus on the results of a case, the documents are a large piece of the product for which the client is paying. Even if the client does not understand everything sent, it still allows him or her to know what is happening in the case and how difficult the theories and complexities of the case are, and it lets the client know that you are actively working on the case. The cost of the copies can be charged to the client's account, so there is no real reason not to do it. Also, if the client has e-mail and the document isn't particularly sensitive, attach it to an e-mail and send it directly to the client. Clients are usually more willing to pay their attorney's fees when they have seen the work done on the case and may be frustrated if they do not know what is happening and then receive a bill.

DO NOT USE LEGALESE   Do not use legalese or legal jargon when talking with clients. Many clients do not understand legal jargon, and it is confusing and frustrating to them. Some clients may be too intimidated to ask what the terms mean. Try to explain legal concepts in words that a layperson will understand.

"They need to get explanations down to a level people can understand—I recently received an opinion letter from another law firm and was very impressed—it was succinct and easy to read."[8]

RETURN CLIENT PHONE CALLS IMMEDIATELY   It is essential that you return client phone calls immediately. If that is not possible, at least return the calls on the same day that they are made. It is not uncommon for clients to call legal assistants. Usually, legal assistants are easier to reach than attorneys, and legal assistants often work with clients quite closely, depending on the type of case. Because legal assistants typically are very busy and may be working on many projects at once, you will be inclined to put client calls off, but do not do this. Always return a client's call first and then finish the job at hand. If you do not reach the client on the first try, continue to try to reach the client rather than letting the client call back for you.

> *Believe it or not, one of the key reasons clients feel rejected is the misuse of the telephone. Clients feel that calls are excessively screened. To them, the telephone represents accessibility. [One satisfied client said:] "He always calls me back the same day. I know I'm not his biggest client, but he makes me feel like my problems are important too."[9]*

BE COURTEOUS, EMPATHETIC, AND PROFESSIONAL AT ALL TIMES   Some clients may be abusive at times. Do not take client comments personally. Never become impatient with a client, "snap" at a client, or act rudely. If you have a problem with a client treating you abusively, mention it to your supervising attorney or legal assistant manager and let him or her handle it. Act professionally in all situations.

Finally, never allow a secretary or receptionist to let a client stay on hold after calling for you. If you are on another call and cannot get to the client immediately, have the receptionist tell the client you will return the call as soon as you get off the phone, then follow up and call the client. If the client leaves a voice mail, return it as soon as possible.

> *When I talk to new paralegals about dealing with clients, I always tell them to practice common courtesy. Keep "please" and "thank you" active in your vocabulary, and use them frequently. Keep your word: when you tell a client or coworker you will do something, do it. Practice the art of being gracious, even to the most difficult client. Give clients the respect they deserve simply because they are the firm's clients. Treat others as you would like to be treated. This is good service. Good service and good manners never go out of style!*
>
> —Vanessa Beam, CLAS

RESPOND TO CLIENT REQUESTS IN A TIMELY FASHION AND KEEP YOUR PROMISES
It is not enough to simply return client phone calls. When clients request answers to questions, send letters, or need things from you, you must respond as quickly as possible. If you tell the client that you will have something to him or her by a particular time or date, keep your promise. If an emergency comes up and you cannot make the deadline, always contact the client and let him or her know and set a new deadline that you can meet.

GIVE CLIENTS PERIODIC STATUS REPORTS   Some cases can be sitting on appeal for months, waiting for a motion to be ruled on, or facing other things that make them lie in a dormant state. This will always frustrate clients, who would like quick remedies to their problems. On a weekly or not less than a monthly basis, review your cases, and, with the approval of your attorney, write or e-mail clients letting them know what is happening in their cases. E-mail and word processors can be configured to make this a very quick process by having form letters on file for different situations. If the case is waiting for some kind of action, you should still write the client and let him or her know that you are waiting and have not forgotten the case. If you do not review the case periodically, the case could very well sit for months with no contact with the client. Keeping in touch with the client never hurts; it reiterates that his or her business is important to you.

DO NOT SHARE PERSONAL OR OFFICE PROBLEMS WITH CLIENTS   Always keep your personal problems to yourself and never make comments that are derogatory about your supervising attorney, firm, or other staff members. Clients need to know that their legal matters are in good hands and that everything is under control. Also, never complain to a client regarding how hard you are working on their case. After all, that is what they are paying for.

PRESERVE CLIENT CONFIDENCES   Preserving client confidences is very important and cannot be overemphasized. Apart from the ethics question, you should keep in mind that if a release of client information gets back to the client, the relationship is most likely finished.

THE USE OF CLIENT SURVEYS   A client survey is a way to find out exactly what your clients think of your services (see Figure 4-4). Most client questionnaires are given at the conclusion of a case. Anytime you get information directly from a client, you should take it to heart. Most firms allow the client to remain anonymous in completing the questionnaire to ensure truthfulness, and it is usually short, not more than a page long, to make completion as easy as possible.

MANAGEMENT MUST HELP PROMOTE GOOD CLIENT RELATIONSHIPS   Management also has a duty to promote good client relationships. Figure 4-5 contains a sample client centered policy that would be found in a law office staff manual.

Figure 4-4
A Client
Questionnaire[10]

In order that we might provide efficient and skillful legal services to our clients at a cost that is not unreasonable, we are asking you to answer the questions listed below in the space provided. After doing so, please separate the top portion of this letter from the question section by tearing on the indicated line, and return the question section to us in the enclosed business reply envelope.

We are grateful for your time and effort involved in answering the questionnaire, and sincerely wish that your answers will help us obtain the results that we and our clients are striving for.

Sincerely,

1. Type of case: _____

2. Attorney or legal assistant: _____

3. Has any member of our firm represented you before?_____

   If so, how many months/years ago? _____

4. Why did you choose our firm to represent you?_____

5. Were your telephone calls or e-mails to our office returned within a reasonable time?

   _____

6. Were you treated courteously by the members of our staff?_____

   If not, please explain: _____

7. Did you ever wait in the waiting room for an unreasonable period of time before seeing the attorney or legal assistant you had an appointment with?_____

   If yes, the number of times: _____

8. Were you informed, at the beginning of the case, as to the basis of our charges for legal services?_____

9. Were you sufficiently informed as to the progress of your case by the assigned attorney or legal assistant? _____

10. In your opinion, was the fee charged reasonable?_____

    If no, why not? _____

11. Were you satisfied with the results obtained in your case?_____

    If no, why not? _____

12. Would you recommend our law firm to another?_____

    If yes, why? _____

    If no, why not? _____

13. Please rate the general quality of the services performed by our law firm. _____

    (Excellent, Very Good, Good, Fair, Poor) _____

14. Comments: _____

    _____

    _____

    _____

Part I: General Principles

Lawyers and staff shall endeavor to give priority to the following principles in their client relationships:

- Representation of a client is an interactive process.
- The lawyer and the entire staff must develop and consistently maintain the mindset that *it is all about the client.*
- Clients should be treated as people, not files.
- Responding to client contacts should be given priority.
- Every client contact by all staff should project genuine concern for the client's issue.

Part II: Telephone Communications

Communication with the client should be regular and consistent with the expectations established with the client during intake. Responses to client-initiated contacts should be prompt and meaningful.

- Client communication should meet the client's need and expectation.
- Clients should promptly receive information about significant events or changes.
- Communicating bad news should be a priority and should never be delayed.
- Client telephone calls should be returned within two hours, and if that is impossible, a staff member should return the call to explain the delay and find a way to get help if there is a need for immediate attention.
- Lawyers should return all calls on the same day, even if it means making a return call during evening hours.

Part III: Correspondence

Written communication with the client may include traditional correspondence, faxes, or e-mail messages.

- Clients should receive copies of documents and pleadings, along with a letter (should the enclosure need explanation).
- Clients should receive monthly status reports, unless some other arrangement has been made.
- E-mail may be used for brief messages but should not be used for confidential information or significant communication.

Part IV: Communications Through the Billing Process

The billing process is an excellent client communication tool.

- Time entries on itemized bills should avoid reciting mechanical functions and rather should be used to communicate substantive accomplishments and value provided.
- Monthly bills should be sent with a cover letter briefly summarizing the work performed and the work planned for the following month.

Part V: Managing Client Expectations

The client's expectations must be managed throughout the process.

- Any significant change in the course of a matter or a case plan must be shared with the client at the earliest possible time.
- The case plan and any fee estimate should be easily accessible and referred to regularly during the course of a matter.
- Lawyers and staff need to be familiar with the case plan and fee estimate, as everyone needs to cooperate in managing a case within the parameters of the client's expectations.

**Figure 4-5
Sample Client-
Centered Service
Policy[11]**

Figure 4-5
(Continued)

- Lawyers should refer to the fee estimate at the time of monthly billing.
- If the fee estimate cannot be met, the lawyer needs to adjust the way in which the matter is handled or contact the client to discuss adjusting the amount of the estimate.
- Contact a client in advance if a monthly bill is higher than the client expects, thereby being careful never to surprise a client with the amount of a bill.

Part VI: Recovery

If a client has a problem or becomes unhappy with some aspect of the service, the situation should be addressed as soon as possible so that the matter will not fester.

- If a client calls and leaves a message expressing unhappiness with some aspect of the service, the return of the phone call must have the highest priority.
- Staff members who are aware of a telephone message in which a client expresses unhappiness with some aspect of the service must get word of the call to the lawyer as soon as possible (and not simply leave the message on the lawyer's desk).
- Lawyers and staff should never delay returning a call to a client who has left a message expressing unhappiness with any aspect of the service.

PUBLISH A CLIENT MANUAL   Some law offices publish a manual for their clients, which explains what to expect from the law office, such as how attorney fees are calculated, how the attorney-client relationship works, what discovery is, how to prepare for a deposition, and what to expect at trial. This type of manual is very beneficial and will save the attorney and legal assistant from answering the same questions over and over for different clients.

TAKE CONFLICTS SERIOUSLY AND BE ETHICAL   Conflicts of interest must be taken seriously, and a careful conflicts check should be done before a case or client is accepted. If there are any possible conflicts found, these should be fully disclosed to the client and the client should consent in writing. It is also important to always act in an ethical manner to clients, *in everything you do*. If a client sees you being dishonest, the client will infer that you are dishonest to him or her as well.

DO NOT PROCRASTINATE   A law office is no place for people who procrastinate; procrastination always causes problems and never solves them. Handle client problems when they occur. Deliver bad news to clients or admit that a deadline was missed up front. That way, clients can at least respect you for being honest. Honesty is the best and only policy when it comes to dealing with clients. The whole attorney-client relationship is based on trust; if that fails, the attorney-client relationship will fail as well.

Resolving Client Dissatisfaction

Resolving client dissatisfaction is not an easy task and may not be up to the legal assistant to resolve at all. Client dissatisfaction can have many roots, including personality conflicts with the legal staff, disagreement on strategy, misunderstandings, lack of knowledge about the law or facts, or frustration with the legal system. Here are some ideas for how to resolve client dissatisfaction.

> *I have sincerely tried to respond to every negative person/situation I have encountered in my career with the "kill 'em with kindness" philosophy. It may not always soften them up, but it certainly keeps my conscience clear to know that I did not "stoop" to their level.*
>
> —Lenette Pinchback, CLA

LISTEN TO THE COMPLAINT; DO NOT INTERRUPT AND DO NOT ARGUE   When a client has a complaint, the first thing to do is to listen carefully and patiently. Listen with empathy and do not react. Avoid interrupting or arguing with the client; this is rude. In some instances, clients just want to vent about something they do not agree with, they see as unfair, or they believe was a mistake. The client may be fully satisfied simply by finding someone who will listen patiently and react in a courteous, professional manner. If the client is satisfied with this, thank him or her for the call, let him or her know you or the firm will try to correct this in the future, and then pass along the information to the appropriate parties who can prevent the problem from recurring.

> *I do not get involved with resolving client dissatisfaction and will leave it for the attorney to handle. In working with a difficult client, be careful about promising something that neither you nor the attorneys are capable of delivering. Be cordial to the difficult client, but do not be afraid to "punt" things to the attorney when necessary.*
>
> —Linda Rushton, CLA

> *There are some very simple phrases that clients appreciate: "I will do my best." "I understand." "I know this is difficult for you."*
>
> *One thing to remember is that, no matter what, some clients are not ever going to be happy and you cannot please everyone, but you should at least be able to honestly say you tried.*
>
> —Andrea Blanscet, CLA

EMPATHICALLY LISTEN   When speaking with a client regarding a complaint, it helps to acknowledge what he or she is saying and reaffirm that you are listening by saying "Yes" or "Hmmmm" or "I see." Responses like these show that you are actively listening.

DO NOT OVERSTEP YOUR BOUNDS OR PROMISE SOMETHING YOU CANNOT DELIVER   A client may try to extract a promise from you to do something that you do not have the authority to do. Do not let a client force you into doing something you are not comfortable with or that you do not have the authority to do. In those instances, say something like, "I will talk to my supervising attorney and get back to you as soon as possible, hopefully by X." Telling the client an exact time you will get back to him or her should alleviate fears that the complaint will be ignored.

TAKE NOTES   Always take careful notes so that you can recount exactly what the complaint is about, including the fine details. This will allow you to relay it to others for the purpose of resolving the matter.

FORWARD ALL COMPLAINTS TO YOUR SUPERVISING ATTORNEY AND BE HONEST   All complaints should be immediately referred to your supervising attorney. If a client is calling to complain about a mistake you made and you know it is a mistake, be honest, admit the mistake to your supervising attorney, generate possible solutions to the problem, and put procedures in place to keep it from happening again.

DO NOT IGNORE THE COMPLAINT   If you receive a client complaint, never procrastinate or ignore it. If a client believes he or she has been ignored or his or her comments summarily disregarded, he or she will only become more angry. Resolving the matter as quickly as possible is the best thing to do.

RECOGNIZE THAT SOME CLIENTS WILL ALWAYS COMPLAIN   Some clients are seemingly never happy and always have a complaint to make. Hopefully, the number of clients like this is very small, but nonetheless they do exist. Treat the client as considerately as you can and talk to your supervising attorney. In extreme cases, a firm may decide to simply terminate the relationship and move on.

WORK THROUGH PERSONALITY CONFLICTS   Some client complaints may be the result of personality conflicts. In most instances, you should work through personality conflicts; in severe instances, you may be able to request that another staff member handle the matter. This should be asked for as a last resort. You may have to handle the matter anyway, either because there is no one else to take over or there is no one else with your experience regarding that client or the legal/factual issues involved.

You may feel that the pace of technology creates unrealistic, and annoying, expectations. But try switching gears and start thinking of technology as a means of forging stronger and smoother connections with clients.

Law offices have spent millions of dollars to upgrade their technology. Not necessarily because they want to be current, but because their clients demand it.

Nance, R. J. (2004, October). Clients, technology, and you. *Law Practice*, 30.

Clients and Technology

Clients are demanding technology-based solutions. They demand access to their attorney and law office by e-mail; they want documents e-mailed to them immediately, instead of waiting for days before they arrive in the mail; they want law offices to use the same basic software programs they have, so they can access documents of all types, from word processing to spreadsheet to presentation files; and they want electronic access to documents so they can edit them in real time. They want their law offices to offer slick technological solutions from practice-based computer programs; they want everything from electronic discovery to the automated tracking of exhibits on a laptop for trial; they want online billing, so they can receive their bills immediately and in a format *they* want; they want electronic access to *their* files and information via extranets and other services that are available at all times; and they want their attorney's and legal assistant's mobile phone numbers so they can reach them when *they* have an emergency. It is important when working with a new client to understand exactly what the client's expectations for technology are and then meet those expectations. Clients mostly want these things because they result in direct access to their legal professionals; however, some clients demand these things, knowing that more technology means greater efficiency and lower hourly bills.

How to Lose Clients

Losing clients is easy (see Figure 4-6); keeping them for life is hard. Losing a client may result from missing an urgent phone call, making an inappropriate or unprofessional remark, losing an important document, giving legal advice that isn't well thought out, lacking trust, or making him or her think that you overbilled or that he or she was not treated ethically. There are many reasons why clients leave legal professionals and law offices; the goal is to keep this from happening. The legal professionals who retain their clients year in and year out keep their "eye on the ball" and on what is important to the client at all times.

Dealing with Difficult Clients

Not all clients are created equal. It was noted in Chapter 2 that successful attorneys and law practices are able to distinguish bad clients and cases from good ones.

Why Clients Leave Law Offices	Percent
Death	1%
Move	3%
Dislike the product	5%
Have a dispute that is not addressed or corrected	24%
Feel they were treated discourteously, indifferently, or simply were not given good service	67%

Figure 4-6
Why Do Clients Leave?[12]

Some clients may be extremely difficult to work with; some have completely unreasonable expectations about their case; some may have mental impairments; some may be vengeful; some may be violent; some may be dishonest; some may not be able to pay for legal services, and so on. It is up to the attorney to select what kind of clients and cases he or she will accept and work with. Once these decisions are made, it is up to the legal assistant to work with the clients to the best of his or her ability, even if the client proves difficult.

- **Stay calm and maintain professionalism** Always stay calm when working with a difficult client, no matter what the client does. Maintain a professional demeanor, and never react to a client's outburst with one of your own. If possible, ratchet down the dialogue and try to find common ground with the client. If a client becomes upset or abusive, which is very rare, immediately leave the area and inform the attorney. Some difficult clients are harder on staff than the attorney. It is important that you let the attorney know about the situation.
- **Document conversations** Protect yourself from difficult clients by carefully documenting your conversations with them—e-mail is a great tool for this. It never hurts to send the client an e-mail or letter confirming an important instruction, just to be sure that all parties are on the same page. Some case management programs provide a place in the program to document all conversations with clients. No matter what tool you use, always save it for future reference.
- **Be courteous, but maintain an arm's-length relationship** Always be courteous to clients, but consider treating a difficult client a little more at "arm's length." You do not need to be "chummy" or friends with clients in order to do your job. Be professional, be competent, and do not let your guard down. You also do not need to share personal information with clients, even if they ask for it. If a client asks for advice or wants to know how you would make a decision regarding something related to his or her case, do not provide an answer—these are decisions that the client must make.
- **Keep the attorney fully informed** It is important, when dealing with a difficult client, to always keep the attorney fully informed of all of your conversations or correspondence with the client. Copying or blind copying the attorney on e-mails to the client is an effective way to keep the attorney informed. Also, do not fail to let the attorney know if a client shows any unprofessional behavior toward you. It is the attorneys' job to prevent clients from abusing staff.

COMMUNICATION SKILLS

> *Basically, the whole [legal assistant] profession is communication, and many of the problems that arise are going to be in that area.*[13]

Possessing good communication skills is necessary in most professional jobs, but it is especially important in a law office. Legal assistants must communicate with clients, opposing counsel, supervising attorneys, office staff, court clerks, and witnesses on a daily basis regarding complex and important matters. Good communication skills also bear directly on the effectiveness of law office management. Communication is an important part of management because, without it, management could not plan, organize, control, or direct the business. Thus, having good communication skills bears directly on both legal services to clients and law office management.

Top [legal assistant] performers have naturally strong communication skills. They always keep clients, team members, staff, and supervising lawyers informed of their work progress. They understand how to communicate with different personality types by mentally sizing up the type of person they are dealing with and communicating accordingly. They actively listen to instruction and information communicated to them.[14]

General Communication

Professionals, such as legal assistants and attorneys, typically spend about 79 percent of each day communicating (see Figure 4-7). **Communication** is the transfer of a message from a sender to a receiver. Although communication can be quickly defined, it is more difficult to explain why there is so much poor communication in the world.

communication
The transfer of a message from a sender to a receiver.

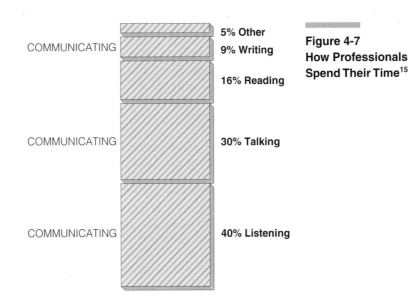

COMMUNICATING — 5% Other
COMMUNICATING — 9% Writing
16% Reading
COMMUNICATING — 30% Talking
COMMUNICATING — 40% Listening

**Figure 4-7
How Professionals
Spend Their Time**[15]

Figure 4-8
Communication
Diagram[16]

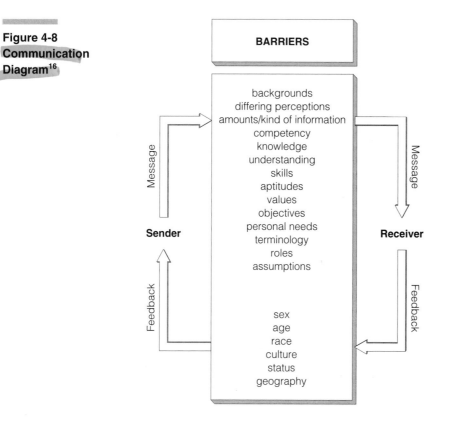

BARRIERS

Sender

Message

Feedback

backgrounds
differing perceptions
amounts/kind of information
competency
knowledge
understanding
skills
aptitudes
values
objectives
personal needs
terminology
roles
assumptions

sex
age
race
culture
status
geography

Receiver

Message

Feedback

communication barrier
Something that inhibits or prevents the receiver from obtaining the correct message.

noise
Any situation that interferes with or distorts the message being communicated.

feedback
Information sent in response to a message.

Figure 4-8 is a flow chart that shows how information is communicated. The abundance of communication barriers helps to explain why some messages are never properly received. A **communication barrier** inhibits or prevents the receiver from obtaining the correct message from the sender. These barriers include situations where the sender and receiver have different cultural backgrounds, perceptions, understandings, and ages. Noise is also a communication barrier; **noise** interferes with or distorts the message being communicated. A good example of noise is when one person is trying to listen to several senders at one time—the messages are distorted because the receiver cannot understand all of the messages at the same time.

There are many other communication barriers as well (see Figure 4-8). Effective communicators are able to overcome these communication barriers and make their point.

Feedback is an important part of effective communication. **Feedback** is information sent in response to the sender's message. There is no way for the sender to know whether his or her information has been properly received without feedback. Feedback allows the receiver to state his or her understanding of the message, and also allows the sender to evaluate the effectiveness of the message and to clarify misunderstood points. Feedback does not have to be verbal; it can be as simple as a puzzled look on the receiver's face.

Nonverbal Communication

Communication is much more than just speech. There are many nonverbal communicators, such as eye contact, facial expressions, posture, appearance, clothing, tone of voice, and gestures. All of these nonverbal means of communication have a hand in determining whether or not a message is properly received.

Improving Your Communication Skills

LISTEN   Listening is one of the most important features of communicating effectively, and although it sounds easy to do, often it is not. The average person forgets 50 percent of what was said to him or her within just a few minutes. We have all caught ourselves in the middle of conversations thinking about something unrelated to the conversation. We become "lazy listeners," only minimally listening. Figure 4-9 contains some excellent rules on listening. A common problem that attorneys and legal assistants are guilty of is that, instead of listening to what another person is saying, they formulate arguments and prepare for when they will speak. This effectively takes the listener out of good listening, and the listener may miss the total message.

Too often we listen with the ear of impatience, with the mind of a fixed idea. Sometimes our minds are so firmly fixed on formulating a response that we do not even hear what is being said.[17]

---

1. **STOP TALKING!**
   You cannot listen if you are talking.
2. **PUT THE TALKER AT EASE.**
   Help the person feel that he or she is free to talk.
3. **SHOW THE INDIVIDUAL THAT YOU WANT TO LISTEN.**
   Look and act interested. Do not read your e-mail while the person talks.
   Listen to understand, rather than to oppose.
4. **REMOVE DISTRACTIONS.**
   Do not doodle, tap, or shuffle papers. Will it be quieter if you shut the door?
5. **EMPATHIZE WITH THE PERSON.**
   Try to see the other's point of view.
6. **BE PATIENT.**
   Allot plenty of time. Do not interrupt. Don't start for the door or walk away.
7. **HOLD YOUR TEMPER.**
   An angry person gets the wrong meaning from words.
8. **GO EASY ON ARGUMENT AND CRITICISM.**
   This puts the person on the defensive. He or she may "clam up" or get angry. Do not argue: even if you win, you lose.
9. **ASK QUESTIONS.**
   This encourages the speaker and shows that you are listening. It also helps to develop points further.
10. **STOP TALKING!**
    This is first and last, because all other commandments depend on it. You cannot do a good listening job while you are talking. Nature gave people two ears but only one tongue, which is a gentle hint that a person should listen more than he or she talks.

**Figure 4-9
The 10
Commandments
of Good Listening**[18]

KEEP IT SIMPLE AND TO THE POINT   Most people understand more of a message when the sender uses short, direct sentences rather than long, complex ones. You can explain complex issues to others: just use words and phrases they will understand. Avoid jargon and legalese when dealing with clients. In the same vein, research has shown that short letters are read sooner than are long ones, and the reader actually remembers the message of the short letter more accurately.

CONSIDER YOUR NONVERBAL SIGNALS   Realize that when you are communicating with people, they look at you and your message as a total package. They are considering how you are dressed, if you are nervous, if you are fidgeting, if you have your hands in your pockets, and if you have confidence in yourself.

DO NOT BECOME EMOTIONAL   Try not to be emotional when communicating. Try to be objective and calm, without being cold and distant.

MAKE EYE CONTACT   Make eye contact with everyone you are talking to, since it conveys honesty and interest. Juries, for instance, often cite the lack of eye contact as a reason that they did not believe a witness.

BE AWARE OF YOUR BODY LANGUAGE   Crossed arms usually mean you are feeling defensive, scared, or cold about something; poor posture is sometimes interpreted as lazy or slothful. One kind of body language that is more important than anything else for setting a positive tone is a simple smile. Smiling relaxes both your audience and you.

BE PRECISE AND CLEAR   Always try to be as precise as possible when communicating with others. How often have you heard someone say, "Well, I thought you meant. . . ." Speak clearly and do not leave anything to the imagination. For example, if you tell a delivery person you need something filed at the courthouse, be sure you are precise and tell him or her whether you need it filed at the federal courthouse, the local courthouse, or the state courthouse. These subtle differences can be very important in a law office, so be absolutely clear when you communicate. Look for feedback. If someone has a puzzled look on his or her face, explain your message again or ask him or her to repeat it to you.

CONSIDER YOUR AUDIENCE   Always tailor your communication to the specific audience with which you are communicating. You can have the best message in the world, but if you are delivering it to someone who does not care about it, you have wasted your effort. If possible, find out what is important to your audience, what concerns it has, and then tailor everything you say to address these concerns.

CONSIDER THE TIMING AND CONTEXT   Timing is everything; a good communicator must know when to communicate his or her message. Be patient and wait until the time is right. Time your message so that noise and barriers are kept to a minimum. You may want to wait until the receiver is in a good mood or has just heard good news. Communication is an art; people will react to the same message in different ways depending on the timing. You must consider the context in which the communication is being made for your message to be effective. Is the receiver having a bad day? Where is the communication taking place: in a crowded hallway or in a private office? What type of relationship have you had with the receiver? Do you respect each other, dislike each other, or distrust each other?

Try to consider the other person's perception of your communication. Consider this: when you find yourself in a disagreement with someone, are you more likely to believe that *your behavior is motivated by context* (e.g., you had a bad day, you're tired, you're stressed out) while you believe that the *other person's behavior is motivated not by context, but by something personal* (e.g., spite, revenge, meanness, or unreasonableness)? This is a normal reaction. Consider the context and the environment in which the other person is viewing your communication; look at it from his or her point of view and be aware of your own biases. This will improve your ability to communicate with others.

AVOID NEGATIVES AND DO NOT BE JUDGMENTAL   Do not start with negative or judgmental comments such as "That probably will not work." This will only make your audience defensive. Try to be positive and explore the conversation in a positive light. If you do not think an idea will work, ask a question about why you think it might not work, such as "Well, have you considered what would happen if this occurred . . . ? Will your idea still be successful?" This allows the other person to consider your side but in a positive, constructive light.

ASK QUESTIONS   Never assume something based on unsupported evidence. It is very easy for people to misread or assume things about other people. Instead of assuming something incorrectly, ask questions and talk about it. This will allow you to verify whether or not your initial assumptions were accurate.

REPHRASE IDEAS   If you are not sure whether you truly understand what someone has told you, try rephrasing. **Rephrasing** is the technique of telling the sender your understanding of the conversation. It allows the sender to clarify information that might not have been understood clearly.

rephrasing
A technique used to improve communication by repeating back to a person your understanding of the conversation.

RECOGNIZE THE IMPORTANCE OF GOOD COMMUNICATION WITH THIRD PARTIES
A legal assistant deals with many types of people, including witnesses, court personnel, outside agencies, libraries, businesses, and other law offices. You must be professional at all times and have good relationships with these third parties, since they may provide information that will help you perform your job. When possible, cultivate these relationships.

Use Proper Telephone Techniques

Poor telephone techniques abound in many law offices. Here are some examples of what not to do.

- Office staff: "Law offices."
  Client: "May I speak to Mr. Smith?"
  Office staff: "Sure, just a sec."
- Office staff: "Law offices."
  Client: "May I speak to Mr. Smith?"
  Office staff: "He's yakking on the other line, you want to hold?"
- Office staff: "Law offices."
  Client: "May I speak to Mr. Smith?"
  Office staff: "He's not in. Why don't you call back this afternoon?"

Good telephone techniques are important in any legal organization. Most legal professionals spend a great deal of time on the phone and need courteous telephone skills.

ALWAYS COMMUNICATE IN A BUSINESSLIKE, PROFESSIONAL TONE   Because callers cannot see your body language and facial expressions on the phone, the words you say and the tone you use are very important. Always be calm and professional when talking on the phone. If you have a million things to do and you are flustered or might get short with the caller, then do not answer the phone. Call back when you are calm.

PUT THE CALLER AT EASE   Listen carefully and make appropriate responses that put the caller at ease whenever possible. You gain nothing by offering quick responses that may alienate the caller.

REFER TO THE CALLER BY NAME   When the caller tells you his or her name, call the person by that name: "Mr. Smith, I'll page her immediately." This puts the caller at ease and lets him or her know that you remember who he or she is. It also communicates personal service.

WHEN TAKING A MESSAGE, ALWAYS OBTAIN THE TELEPHONE NUMBER OF THE CALLER   Callers often will say that the person whom they are calling already has their number. Obtain a callback number from the caller anyway, just in case the number recently changed or has been lost, the caller has a new number, or just because it is more convenient for the person who will return the call.

WHEN TAKING A CALLER'S NAME OR PHONE NUMBER, ALWAYS REPEAT BACK THE INFORMATION   By repeating the information back to the caller, you confirm that you received the message correctly and that the name and number are accurate. Think how frustrated you get when someone takes a message and does not record the information accurately.

ALWAYS IDENTIFY YOURSELF AS A LEGAL ASSISTANT   If you are taking a call from a client, attorney, or a third party regarding a case, always identify yourself as a legal assistant early in the conversation.

WHEN TAKING A MESSAGE, GET A GENERAL "FEEL" FOR THE SUBJECT   It is important to get a general "feel" for what the caller needs when taking a message, because you might be able to handle the matter yourself. If you cannot, then do not ask for too much information, from clients in particular. Some clients do not like to give out details about their problems.

BE WARY OF MOBILE PHONES   Be careful that the conversation is not about sensitive client matters when speaking on a mobile phone. Although mobile phones are becoming more secure, it is still prudent to be careful.

WHEN TAKING A MESSAGE, EXPLAIN BRIEFLY WHY THE INDIVIDUAL CALLED IS NOT IN   Giving a short explanation as to why someone cannot take a call, such as "Susan is in court this morning," lets the caller know that the person is not ducking his or her call. Avoid saying that the person is "unavailable."

TRY TO ANSWER YOUR PHONE WHEN YOU ARE NOT WITH A CLIENT   In the era of e-mail and voice mail, sometimes clients want to talk to a person to discuss a matter. Try to answer your phone instead of letting it roll to voice mail whenever possible. Clients can become quite frustrated when they cannot reach someone on the phone, particularly when the client has an emergency.

The following is a client maxim to think about:

- I needed the help of a lawyer or legal assistant.
- I couldn't reach you.
- I reached a competing law office.
- I no longer need you.

DO NOT KEEP CALLERS ON HOLD EXCEPT FOR A VERY SHORT PERIOD OF TIME
Nothing is more frustrating to a caller than to be indefinitely put on hold. If you must place a caller on hold, do so for only a very short period of time. Continually update the caller as to the status of his or her call.

Leadership and Communication

Being a leader takes a special type of communication skill. Leadership was described in Chapter 1 as the act of motivating or causing others to perform and achieve objectives. Leaders give us direction, vision, and motivation. Leadership is an important part of any organization or department. Legal assistants need to take leadership roles, and there are opportunities for legal assistants who have leadership skills; for instance, legal assistants can be legal assistant managers or law office administrators. Legal assistant "leaders" can take on projects and cases that need innovation and have never been done before. Legal assistants with leadership characteristics are sought after and are important to growing law offices.

HOW DO I BECOME A LEADER?   Having determined that leadership qualities are essential for the legal assistant, the next question is: "How does one become a leader?" This has been a hotly debated issue over the years. Early leadership theories said that only exceptional people were capable of assuming the leadership role (i.e., you either were or were not born with it). But current research overwhelmingly shows that leaders are not born, they are made. The following are some suggestions on how to be a leader:

1. **Be an expert.** Effective leaders are experts in what they do. They know precisely what they are talking about. People around them have confidence in their abilities and rely upon their knowledge and judgment. They are inventive and ingenious and are able to plan, organize, and manage resources to solve problems. Before they give opinions, they do research and master the subject they are talking about. Leaders must be competent, make good decisions, and be able to evaluate situations and act accordingly.
2. **Be honest.** Effective leaders have a reputation for being extremely honest and forthright and for possessing a high degree of integrity. These are important qualities; subordinates must respect leaders and be motivated, inspired, and willing to follow their directives.
3. **Stay calm.** Good leaders stay cool and collected, even when they are "under fire." They have confidence in their own abilities and are not shaken by disagreement or challenge. Instead, they rise to the occasion.
4. **Trust and support those under you.** Good leaders choose effective and competent subordinates and then support them in their efforts. Subordinates know that they are trusted and that their abilities and skills are appreciated, and thus work even harder for the leader.
5. **Take risks and do not be afraid of failure.** Effective leaders take calculated risks. They focus on the positive and refuse to think about failure. Failures and mistakes are steps in the learning process and are to be expected. Leaders have the ability to make bold decisions and to stand by them when others are backpedaling.
6. **Encourage honest opinions from others.** Effective leaders encourage subordinates to be honest and to articulate their opinions, even if those opinions are in disagreement with the leader's. Debate sharpens the decision-making process so that all alternatives are considered and evaluated based on their merits. This is the only way situations can be properly evaluated. Leaders encourage others around them to cooperate and communicate with one another by listening to everyone's ideas and opinions.
7. **Set goals and visions.** Effective leaders set goals and have specific visions for the future. The goals and visions inspire and empower others to accomplish the goals and to work toward the common dream.
8. **Be respectful.** Good leaders respect, get along with, and care for other people. They foster meaningful personal and professional relationships with the people around them.

Communication is at the center of leadership. Leaders emerge when a new crisis arises or when a new challenge surfaces. Leaders are able to put together a solution, empower their subordinates to support it, reshape and retool their resources, and come up with a package that meets the new challenge and solves the problem.

Group Communication

Communicating in groups involves a whole different set of variables than communicating one on one. Legal assistants must routinely work with groups (including attorneys and legal assistants) on trials and similar projects, and with clients and attorneys on cases. Additionally, they serve on committees and associations. The following are some commonly known advantages and disadvantages of group work:

- Groups tend to make more accurate decisions than do individuals. As the adage says, "Two heads are better than one"; that is, there are more points of view to be heard and considered and a greater number of solutions offered and analyzed in a group.
- Once a group has arrived at a decision, there is an increase in the acceptance of the final choice because group members were involved in the process.
- Group members can communicate and explain the group's decision to others because they were included.
- Once a decision has been made by a group, implementation is easier because the group members were involved in the process and have a "stake in the action."
- Decisions by groups take up to 50 percent longer to make than do decisions by individuals.
- Group decisions are often compromises between different points of view rather than the most appropriate alternative.
- Group decisions can sometimes result in groupthink. **Groupthink** occurs when the desire for group cohesiveness and consensus becomes stronger than the desire for the best possible decision.
- Groups sometimes make more risky decisions than do individuals, especially when there is no one individual responsible for the consequences of the group decision.
- Groups are sometimes dominated by one or more individuals who rank higher in status within the organization.

groupthink
Term for when the desire for group cohesiveness and consensus becomes stronger than the desire for the best possible decision.

Communication in Interviewing Clients, Witnesses, and Third Parties

Interviewing clients, witnesses, and third parties is a specialized communication skill that you will need to possess. In many firms, interviews are conducted by experienced legal assistants or attorneys. However, new legal assistants sit in on interviews with an experienced legal assistant or attorney to learn good interviewing skills.

The initial client interview is very important, because it is usually the first real contact the client has with the firm. The purpose of the interview is to relax the client, to convince the client that he or she has come to the right firm, and to gather enough information to decide whether your firm and responsible attorney are interested in representing the client or at least finding out more about the case. The following are some suggestions for handling each part of the interview and what to do should you encounter difficulties. Figure 4-10 is an evaluation sheet to evaluate your interviewing skills. While Figure 4-10 is specifically geared toward a client interview, many of the same principles apply to all interviews.

PREPARE FOR THE INTERVIEW   One of the simplest things you can do to make sure an interview will go well is to prepare for it. Always try to get as much initial information as possible before the interview. Establish a checklist of questions you want to ask and specific information you want to gather. You must establish what the purpose or goal of the interview is, and then steer the interview toward the direction of the goal. For example, if you routinely interview clients regarding workers' compensation claims, there is certain information that you must have. Establish exactly what information you need and then draft a checklist and an agenda to ensure that you obtain the information.

Many law offices also have an intake form on which the client generally describes why he or she has come to the firm. All this information will help you to prepare for the interview. Whoever is setting up the interview should, in addition, always ask the client to bring in any documentation that may be relevant.

BREAK THE ICE   The beginning of any interview brings apprehension both for the interviewer and interviewee. Ways to break the ice include meeting the client in the waiting room, offering your hand for a handshake, accompanying the client back to your office, and talking to the client about the weather or other neutral topics. Always wear a smile and be warm and friendly. Another interesting way to break the ice is to ask the client or witness about his or her family. This allows you to gain some background information. Some people may think this is nosy; you may want to tell the person that the questions are not meant to embarrass him or her, but simply to understand who he or she is and to get the "big picture." You also may want to explain about the confidentiality of everything that he or she tells you.

ALWAYS INFORM THE PERSON YOU ARE INTERVIEWING OF YOUR STATUS AS A LEGAL ASSISTANT   Once the client is relaxed and is ready to talk about why he or she is there, indicate your status as a legal assistant. Do not make a prolonged speech, which may demonstrate your lack of confidence; simply state, "I am a legal assistant, and I work for Ms. Smith, who is an attorney here." You should also tell the person what you will be doing and what the attorney is going to do: "I will initially be talking to you about your case. I will take down the facts of your case and

Client Interviewing

1. Planning for client interviews
   a. In planning for client interviews generally, do I consider
      (1) the length of the typical first interview?
      (2) the best seating arrangement?
      (3) how to minimize interruptions?
      (4) discouraging the presence of third persons unless absolutely necessary?
      (5) my personal appearance?
      (6) what information I will give to the client?
   b. In planning for specific client interviews, do I
      (1) conduct an initial conflicts check?
      (2) conduct initial legal research or review?
      (3) note appropriate areas of factual inquiry?
      (4) consult checklists of general areas of inquiry?
      (5) identify which documents the client should bring to the interview?
      (6) consider giving the client a written questionnaire to complete and bring to the interview?
   c. Do I have readily available sources to consult in preparation for client interviews, such as
      (1) treatises?
      (2) texts?
      (3) form books?
      (4) sample checklists?
      (5) sample questionnaires?
2. Interviewing skills
   a. Do I seek to develop rapport with a client by
      (1) putting the client at ease?
      (2) adopting an attitude of friendliness, courtesy, and patience?
      (3) demonstrating interest without becoming overly emotional or involved?
      (4) maintaining a receptive, nonjudgmental attitude toward the client as a person?
      (5) encouraging and allowing the client to talk openly?
      (6) listening attentively to the client?
      (7) interrupting the client only when necessary?
      (8) using language understandable to the client?
      (9) using active listening responses?
      (10) offering support to the client?
      (11) recognizing communication blocks?
      (12) showing respect for the client and avoiding condescension?
      (13) encouraging client questions?
   b. Do I seek to maximize information gathering by
      (1) encouraging a complete factual narrative?
      (2) avoiding premature diagnosis of the client's problem?
      (3) focusing on topics likely to elicit relevant information?
      (4) identifying additional topics as the interview progresses?
      (5) sequencing questions from general to specific or vice versa?
      (6) avoiding undue influence on client responses?
      (7) using open-ended questions when appropriate?
      (8) using leading questions when appropriate?
      (9) making sure that the client understands my questions?
      (10) making sure that I understand the client's answers?

Figure 4-10
Client Interviewing:
Self-Evaluation[19]

Figure 4-10
(Continued)

> c. Do I periodically evaluate and attempt to improve my interviewing skills by
>   (1) reading current literature on interviewing skills?
>   (2) transcribing an interview, with the client's permission?
>   (3) reviewing the transcript?
>   (4) attending CLE programs designed to enhance interviewing skills?
> 3. Making a prompt, detailed, and accurate record
>   a. Do I have a reliable system for preserving information gained in the interview by
>   (1) taking notes during the interview?
>   (2) not disrupting communication (e.g., by maintaining eye contact)?
>   (3) making a detailed record immediately after the interview?
>   (4) including follow-up plans in this record?
>   (5) making this record sufficiently clear and detailed so that it could be reviewed or used by another lawyer?

then prepare a memo to the attorney about it. The attorney will then contact you to discuss it in more depth." Once you have done that, you are ready to begin the interview. Many people begin with an open-ended statement, such as, "Tell me why you are here. Start at the beginning."

LISTEN CAREFULLY   Listening carefully to the client's story is sometimes hard to do. The client may ramble, talk about events out of sequence, and talk about matters that may be irrelevant to the legal problem. However, refrain from leading the conversation, at least during the first part of the interview. Be patient and let the client tell the whole story his or her own way. Then go back and fill in the details by asking questions. Do not take too many notes during the first part of the interview. You should give the client your undivided attention and try to make eye contact. Clients need to be reassured that you are interested in their case. As you listen, determine whether the client's story makes sense and think of what facts the client may be leaving out.

COMMUNICATE SINCERITY   For any interview to be successful, you must communicate that you are sincerely interested in the client's problem. Characteristics such as dominance or defensiveness are counterproductive to establishing sincerity. One of the best ways you can communicate sincerity is to show you are really listening to what the person is saying by asking thoughtful questions. Avoid appearing as if you are "grilling" a client.

BE EMPATHETIC   Be empathetic with the client, letting him or her know that you feel for him or her and for the situation he or she is in. Empathy is distinguished from sympathy, which is feeling sorry for the individual. However, be sure to keep your objectivity. Sometimes the client may have to describe very personal, traumatic, or embarrassing information. In that case, you need to be extra sensitive and inform the client that everything said is confidential and is necessary so that you understand what happened.

ORGANIZE THE INFORMATION   Once you have listened to the client tell his or her story the first time through, you are ready to organize the information. A common way to organize the client's story is to build a chronology of events that starts at the beginning of the problem and works forward. This helps the client relive the facts in a particular order and may cause the client to remember more exact details. However, be aware that clients seldom remember things in exact order, so it usually takes several times through before your chronology is accurate.

ASK APPROPRIATE QUESTIONS   When you want to get detailed information about a particular event, remember to ask who, what, when, and where questions. Do not ask leading questions that might suggest a particular answer, such as, "You saw the traffic light as you were going through and it was green, right?" Ask your questions carefully. A better approach might be to say, "Describe the intersection before the accident."

In addition, avoid compound questions that ask the client to answer two or more questions; for example, "How many cars were in the intersection and when was the first time you saw the blue car?" Ask your questions one at a time.

DO NOT BE JUDGMENTAL   Never be judgmental toward a client. Saying things like "You really need to get a grip on yourself," "You are acting like a child," or "You can't mean that" is the opposite of being empathetic, which is what you ideally want to be. Avoid questions that begin with "Why did you . . . ?" This type of question might be viewed as judgmental and may put the client on the defensive.

NEVER SAY "YOU HAVE A GREAT CASE"   Be very careful about judging the client's case. Do not make any promises to the client and never tell the client what a great case he or she has, since this may be bordering on giving legal advice. At this stage you do not have enough information to make that determination. Lawsuits are usually too complex for this type of statement.

LEAVE FEE DISCUSSIONS TO THE ATTORNEY   Discussions regarding whether the firm is going to take the case and discussions about the amount of the fee should be left to the attorney.

CLOSE THE INTERVIEW APPROPRIATELY   Do not close the interview too quickly. Before you close, be sure to do the following:

- Get copies of all the documentation that the client brought.
- Instruct the client not to discuss the case with anyone else.
- Reassure the client by telling him or her exactly what your office will be doing and when it will be done. For example: "I will draft a memo to the attorney, our office will do some preliminary legal research, and this will be completed by Friday. Our office will call you Friday to set up an

appointment for early next week." Never tell the client that "the attorney will get back to you as soon as he can." Clients want to know exactly what is going to happen and when it is going to happen.

- Get the client's e-mail address.
- Review your checklist to make sure you have obtained all the information you need.
- Have the client sign any release or authorization you might need to get information, such as a medical release for the client's files from a doctor or hospital.
- List everything the client did *not* bring with him or her. Give a copy of the list to the client with a self-addressed return envelope.
- Thank the client for coming into the office, reassure the client that you will be in contact with him or her shortly, and instruct him or her that, if he or she remembers anything else that is important, to be sure to give you a call. Give the client your business card.

SUMMARY

Attorneys have an ethical duty to communicate with their clients, and legal assistants can play an active role in this process. This duty includes informing clients of the status of their case, responding to a client's request for information in a timely manner, explaining the law and benefits and risks of alternative courses of action, and notifying and communicating settlement offers, among other things.

Attorneys and legal assistants must also foster positive relationships with clients. This includes knowing your client, treating each client like he or she is your only client, sending copies of documents to clients, responding to client phone calls immediately, being courteous and professional to clients, giving clients periodic status reports, and preserving client confidences. When resolving client complaints, a legal assistant should listen to the client and forward complaints to the attorney.

Clients are also demanding the use of technology in how legal services are provided. This includes e-mail, attachments, extranets, electronic billing, and more. In dealing with difficult clients, a legal assistant should stay calm and maintain professionalism, document conversations with the client, be courteous but maintain an "arm's length" posture, and keep the attorney informed.

Legal assistant work is largely based on communication; communication is the transfer of a message from a sender to a receiver. Anytime you communicate, you must be prepared to work through communication barriers, such as noise, terminology differences, background differences, different competence levels, and many other factors. In enhancing communication, a person should consider the timing and context of the message, not be judgmental, use rephrasing, and ask questions.

Legal assistants must also work in group settings. Communicating in a group is different from communicating one on one with another person. Groups take longer to make decisions, tend to make better quality decisions, but can also fall into groupthink, where the desire for group cohesiveness and consensus becomes stronger than the desire for the best possible decision.

Legal assistants often must interview clients. Strategies for conducting a good client interview include preparing for the interview in advance, using an icebreaker to open the interview, clearly informing the client that you are a legal assistant, listening carefully, taking notes and organizing the information, asking appropriate questions, and closing the interview.

Helpful Web Sites

Organization	Description	Internet Address
Alabama State Bar—Law Office Management Assistance Program	Articles on a variety of law office management topics, including a manual on how to keep clients.	http://www.alabar.org/lomap/articles.cfm
American Bar Association (ABA)	Association for attorneys. The site has a large amount of information and publications relevant to individuals working in the legal profession.	http://www.abanet.org
ABA Law Practice Management	ABA site devoted to law practice management issues and concerns, including management publications, articles, and resources.	http://www.abanet.org/lpm
Legal Assistant Today	National magazine for legal assistants. The Web site has limited information but the magazine itself is full of useful articles, including ethical issues related to legal assistants.	http://www.legalassistanttoday.com
Maryland State Bar Association—Law Practice Management Assistance	The site has a wide variety of law office management topics, including using client surveys, tips for enhancing client relations, how to select clients, and much more.	http://www.msba.org/departments/loma/articles/index.htm
Mississippi State Bar Association	The site has a wide variety of law office management topics, including a handbook on client relations.	http://www.msbar.org/2_client_relations_handbook.php
National Association of Legal Assistants	National association for legal assistants. Contains many resources for legal assistants.	http://www.nala.org
National Federation of Paralegal Associations	National association for legal assistants. Contains many resources for legal assistants.	http://www.paralegals.org

Suggested Reading

1. Munneke, G. A., & Davis, A.E. (2003). *The essential form book—comprehensive management tools.* American Bar Association.

2. *Law Practice* magazine, published by the American Bar Association Law Practice Management Section [http://www.abanet.org/lpm].

3. *Legal Assistant Today* magazine, published by James Publishing [http://www.legalassistanttoday.com].
4. Foonberg, J. (2004). *How to start and build a law practice.* American Bar Association.
5. Foonberg, J. (1994). *How to get and keep good clients.* American Bar Association.
6. Ewalt, H. (2002). *Through the client's eyes.* American Bar Association.
7. Nelson, N. C. (1996). *Connecting with your client: Success through improved client communication techniques.* American Bar Association.

KEY TERMS

communication
communication barrier
feedback

groupthink
noise
rephrasing

TEST YOUR KNOWLEDGE

Test your knowledge of the chapter by answering these questions.

1. According to *Model Rule* 1.6, list at least four things an attorney must do regarding client communication.
2. True or false: if an attorney is leaving a firm, he or she does not have to contact the client if another attorney at the firm will be taking over the case.
3. True or false: an attorney must notify and communicate all settlement offers to a client.
4. Name three types of conduct that clients typically dislike.
5. Name five strategies for fostering positive relationships with clients.
6. True or false: technology has yet to play a large role in client relations.
7. What is the number one reason that clients leave law offices or attorneys and take their business elsewhere?
8. Name two strategies for dealing with difficult clients.
9. List four barriers to communication.
10. Name 5 of the 10 commandments of good listening.
11. When the desire for group cohesiveness becomes stronger than the desire for the best possible solution, it is called _____.

ON THE WEB EXERCISES

1. Go to the ABA Center for Professional Responsibility, find the *ABA Model Rules of Professional Conduct,* and read and print out Rule 1.4 Communication and the accompanying comment.

2. Using a general search engine, such as http://www.google.com or http://www.yahoo.com, search for state bar association sites (or go to state bar association sites listed in the Helpful Web Sites sections of Chapters 2, 3, and 4). Find three articles on issues related to client relations, print them out, and read them.

3. Using a general search engine, such as http://www.google.com or http://www.yahoo.com, search for sites related to improving communication skills. Review a number of sites and write a one-page paper summarizing the best article or information you found.

PROJECTS

1. Go to the Legal Information Institute Web site at http://straylight.law.cornell.edu/ethics/. Select "Listing by Topic" and research Rule 1.4. Write a paper that compares and contrasts three state bar association rules regarding client communication and include how each compares to *Model Rule 1.4.*

2. Using state bar association Web sites, find one of several client relation handbooks. Summarize the major points of in the handbook.

QUESTIONS AND EXERCISES

1. You are a legal assistant working for an attorney in a large law firm. A general counsel from one of the corporations you work with calls you and tells you that he had just read the legal arguments regarding a Motion for Summary judgment that the firm prepared and that you worked on. He tells you that the legal analysis is extremely weak. You can tell by his voice that he is unhappy. What do you do next?

2. You are a legal assistant for a sole practitioner. The attorney represents a client named Betty Johnson in a probate matter that has dragged on for years. Ms. Johnson calls to inquire about the status of her case. She says that she has not heard from the attorney in over a year, and that she has no idea what is going on in the case. You know that the attorney has long since quit working the case and has closed his file. The file takes up three file drawers in the file room. You tell the attorney about Ms. Johnson's call and he says not to worry about it. What is your analysis of the matter? What would you do next?

3. You are a legal assistant in a legal aid office. The executive director calls you into his office to let you know that he has received complaints from clients regarding legal assistants being less than courteous on the phone and in person. The executive director gives you one week to begin turning this situation around. He mentions on his way out the door that, in addition to a short-term solution, he wants a long-term solution to the problem. How would you proceed?

4. Over the years, you have become friends with one of your law office's best clients. The client likes you and believes in your ability as a competent

legal assistant. Recently, you have spent many hours, including evenings and weekends, working on the client's case. The client comes in for an appointment to see you about his case. The client notices that you look very tired and ragged. You tell the client how many hours you have been working on the case to let him know about the hard work that the law office is doing. The client responds by saying that he is going to the lead attorney on the case to demand that you be given an increase for all the extra time you have spent on the case. You are flattered that a client would think of your interest and you could certainly use the money. How would you handle this situation?

5. You are a legal assistant at a medium-size law office. The executive committee thinks that the law office needs to put more emphasis on client services. You are a respected part of the firm and the committee thinks you interact with clients exceptionally well. The committee has approved the development of a client manual that will be given to all its clients. The committee has chosen you to be in charge of developing the manual in the initial stages.

Your task is to prepare a client manual that will be presented to the executive committee within 30 days. In addition, once the committee approves the manual, you also will be in charge of implementing its use. The committee is giving you control over researching and developing the manual.

Assume you have never heard of or developed a client manual before. Assume you can choose to either accept the task or not accept it. Would you accept the assignment? Why or why not? How would you develop the client manual? Would you choose to

Kemp in October 1998 who assured her that the wage assignment documents had been sent to opposing counsel; he stated he would contact opposing counsel and advise the client of the status of the assignment. The client had no further contact with Milner after July 1998 and none with Kemp after October 1998. Milner did no further work on the case and did not file a motion to withdraw.

[1] [2] [3] Milner's failure to act on behalf of her client resulted in harm to the client: Aldridge was not able to obtain visitation while her children were with their father; she was forced to seek an alternative method to obtain a wage assignment; and her frustration and concern caused by Milner impacted her work performance. Milner did not refund any of the funds to the client. Milner's failure to return the client's phone calls and her failure to communicate with the client constituted a violation of Colo. RPC 1.4(a) (lawyer shall keep a client reasonably informed about the status of a matter and promptly comply with reasonable requests for information); her failure to notify the client of the change in hearing date, her *677 failure to file a motion concerning the client's visitation rights; and her failure to file a wage assignment on behalf of her client constitutes neglect in violation of Colo. RPC 1.3. Milner's paralegal, Kemp, misrepresented the status of the matter to the client. Milner failed to adequately supervise Kemp to assure that he did not make such misrepresentations. Her failure to do so constitutes a violation of Colo. RPC 5.3(b) (lawyer having direct supervisory authority over the nonlawyer shall make reasonable efforts to ensure that the person's conduct is compatible with the professional obligations of the lawyer).

Claim II: The Cordova Matter

On September 22, 1998, Darlene Cordova met with Kemp and Milner to determine whether to retain Milner in the client's divorce action. The client was advised that the initial consultation was free. Milner was not present for most of the meeting. Kemp told the client that she would be charged a fee of $75 per hour or a flat fee of $1,500 but he did not say which, and the client was not provided with a written fee agreement. The client paid $400. Milner billed the client

$100 per hour rather than the $75 per hour rate which the client had been quoted, and she charged for the initial consultation which she represented at the time of the meeting would be free of charge.

Milner met with the client to discuss service upon the client's husband. Milner stated that the husband would be served on October 12, 1998. The client received no response to her calls on October 12 and 13 to determine if service had been completed. Service was effected the following day. Milner met with the client on October 17, 1998 and stated that the petition for dissolution of marriage would be filed on October 20, 1998, and that the client would be contacted immediately thereafter. The petition was not filed on October 20, 1998; it was filed the following day. On October 26, 1998, the client went to Milner's office to retrieve her file. Kemp was abusive toward her and threatened to call the police.

[4] [5] Milner failed to adequately communicate the basis of her fee to the client before or within a reasonable time after commencing her representation in violation of Colo. RPC 1.5(b) (lawyer shall communicate the basis or rate of the fee within a reasonable time after commencing representation). The Amended Complaint charged a violation of Colo. RPC 1.4(a), which requires a lawyer to keep a client reasonably informed about the status of a matter and promptly comply with reasonable requests for information. The PDJ and Hearing Board cannot find by a clear and convincing standard that Milner violated Colo. RPC 1.4(a) in the Cordova matter. Milner and/or Kemp spoke with Cordova within a reasonable time on each occasion the client called. Accordingly, the alleged violation of Colo. RPC 1.4(a) in claim two of Case No. 99PDJ030 is dismissed. Milner failed to adequately supervise Kemp to ensure that Kemp's conduct was compatible with the professional obligations of a lawyer in violation of Colo. RPC 5.3(b) (failure to adequately supervise nonlawyer).

Claim III: The Wilhelm Matter

Milner met with Mr. Wilhelm and entered into an attorney-client relationship with him to collect monies owed pursuant to a promissory note. At the meeting, Milner obtained the original or a copy of the promissory

ANSWERS TO TEST YOUR KNOWLEDGE

1. 1) Reasonably consult with the client about the means by which the client's objectives are to be accomplished; 2) keep the client reasonably informed about the status of the matter; 3) promptly comply with reasonable requests for information; 4) explain a matter to the extent reasonably necessary to permit the client to make informed decisions regarding the representation.

2. False
3. True
4. Arrogance, rudeness, incorrect billings, calls/e-mails not returned, confidentiality breaches, errors, and poor-quality work.
5. See Figure 4-3.
6. False
7. They feel they were treated discourteously, indifferently, or were simply not given good service.
8. Stay calm and maintain professionalism, document conversations, be courteous but maintain an arm's-length relationship, and keep the attorney informed.
9. See Figure 4-8.
10. See Figure 4-9.
11. groupthink

CASE REVIEW

P.3d 670

Office of the Presiding Disciplinary Judge of the Supreme Court of Colorado.

The PEOPLE of the State Of Colorado, Complainant.

v.

Karen S. MILNER, Respondent.
Nos. 99PDJ030, 99PDJ093.

Aug. 7, 2001.

I. FINDINGS OF FACT AND CONCLUSIONS OF LAW

A. Case No. 99PDJ030

Claim I: The Aldridge Matter

On April 4, 1998, Milner [respondent] entered her appearance on behalf of Nancy Aldridge in a child support and visitation matter. Between April and June 1998, the client paid Milner fees and costs in the amount of $735. A hearing was scheduled regarding visitation issues and subsequently rescheduled. Milner failed to notify the client of the new hearing date. One week prior to the rescheduled hearing, Milner contacted the client and demanded that she pay fees in the amount of $385 or Milner threatened to withdraw. The client paid the fees. At the hearing, the client expressed concern to Milner about her visitation rights while her children were with their father for a six-week period. Milner assured her she would be allowed visitation. Subsequent to the hearing on July 16, 1998, the client left numerous messages for Milner but Milner did not return her calls. The client spoke to Milner's paralegal, Matthew Kemp ("Kemp"), who stated that a motion to clarify the issue of visitation would be filed with the court. Milner failed to file any such motion. Milner agreed to obtain a wage assignment from the client's ex-husband's employer and file it with the court. Subsequently the client, who was not receiving child support, attempted to contact Milner to determine whether the wage assignment had been submitted to the court. For approximately six weeks, Milner failed to respond. Finally, the client spoke with Kemp who promised that the papers would be filed. They were not. After numerous phone calls, the client contacted

Kemp in October 1998 who assured her that the wage assignment documents had been sent to opposing counsel; he stated he would contact opposing counsel and advise the client of the status of the assignment. The client had no further contact with Milner after July 1998 and none with Kemp after October 1998. Milner did no further work on the case and did not file a motion to withdraw.

[1] [2] [3] Milner's failure to act on behalf of her client resulted in harm to the client: Aldridge was not able to obtain visitation while her children were with their father; she was forced to seek an alternative method to obtain a wage assignment; and her frustration and concern caused by Milner impacted her work performance. Milner did not refund any of the funds to the client. Milner's failure to return the client's phone calls and her failure to communicate with the client constituted a violation of Colo. RPC 1.4(a) (lawyer shall keep a client reasonably informed about the status of a matter and promptly comply with reasonable requests for information); her failure to notify the client of the change in hearing date, her ***677*** failure to file a motion concerning the client's visitation rights; and her failure to file a wage assignment on behalf of her client constitutes neglect in violation of Colo. RPC 1.3. Milner's paralegal, Kemp, misrepresented the status of the matter to the client. Milner failed to adequately supervise Kemp to assure that he did not make such misrepresentations. Her failure to do so constitutes a violation of Colo. RPC 5.3(b) (lawyer having direct supervisory authority over the nonlawyer shall make reasonable efforts to ensure that the person's conduct is compatible with the professional obligations of the lawyer).

Claim II: The Cordova Matter

On September 22, 1998, Darlene Cordova met with Kemp and Milner to determine whether to retain Milner in the client's divorce action. The client was advised that the initial consultation was free. Milner was not present for most of the meeting. Kemp told the client that she would be charged a fee of $75 per hour or a flat fee of $1,500 but he did not say which, and the client was not provided with a written fee agreement. The client paid $400. Milner billed the client

$100 per hour rather than the $75 per hour rate which the client had been quoted, and she charged for the initial consultation which she represented at the time of the meeting would be free of charge.

Milner met with the client to discuss service upon the client's husband. Milner stated that the husband would be served on October 12, 1998. The client received no response to her calls on October 12 and 13 to determine if service had been completed. Service was effected the following day. Milner met with the client on October 17, 1998 and stated that the petition for dissolution of marriage would be filed on October 20, 1998, and that the client would be contacted immediately thereafter. The petition was not filed on October 20, 1998; it was filed the following day. On October 26, 1998, the client went to Milner's office to retrieve her file. Kemp was abusive toward her and threatened to call the police.

[4] [5] Milner failed to adequately communicate the basis of her fee to the client before or within a reasonable time after commencing her representation in violation of Colo. RPC 1.5(b) (lawyer shall communicate the basis or rate of the fee within a reasonable time after commencing representation). The Amended Complaint charged a violation of Colo. RPC 1.4(a), which requires a lawyer to keep a client reasonably informed about the status of a matter and promptly comply with reasonable requests for information. The PDJ and Hearing Board cannot find by a clear and convincing standard that Milner violated Colo. RPC 1.4(a) in the Cordova matter. Milner and/or Kemp spoke with Cordova within a reasonable time on each occasion the client called. Accordingly, the alleged violation of Colo. RPC 1.4(a) in claim two of Case No. 99PDJ030 is dismissed. Milner failed to adequately supervise Kemp to ensure that Kemp's conduct was compatible with the professional obligations of a lawyer in violation of Colo. RPC 5.3(b) (failure to adequately supervise nonlawyer).

Claim III: The Wilhelm Matter

Milner met with Mr. Wilhelm and entered into an attorney-client relationship with him to collect monies owed pursuant to a promissory note. At the meeting, Milner obtained the original or a copy of the promissory

PROJECTS

1. Go to the Legal Information Institute Web site at http://straylight.law.cornell.edu/ethics/. Select "Listing by Topic" and research Rule 1.4. Write a paper that compares and contrasts three state bar association rules regarding client communication and include how each compares to *Model Rule 1.4.*

2. Using state bar association Web sites, find one of several client relation handbooks. Summarize the major points of in the handbook.

QUESTIONS AND EXERCISES

1. You are a legal assistant working for an attorney in a large law firm. A general counsel from one of the corporations you work with calls you and tells you that he had just read the legal arguments regarding a Motion for Summary judgment that the firm prepared and that you worked on. He tells you that the legal analysis is extremely weak. You can tell by his voice that he is unhappy. What do you do next?

2. You are a legal assistant for a sole practitioner. The attorney represents a client named Betty Johnson in a probate matter that has dragged on for years. Ms. Johnson calls to inquire about the status of her case. She says that she has not heard from the attorney in over a year, and that she has no idea what is going on in the case. You know that the attorney has long since quit working the case and has closed his file. The file takes up three file drawers in the file room. You tell the attorney about Ms. Johnson's call and he says not to worry about it. What is your analysis of the matter? What would you do next?

3. You are a legal assistant in a legal aid office. The executive director calls you into his office to let you know that he has received complaints from clients regarding legal assistants being less than courteous on the phone and in person. The executive director gives you one week to begin turning this situation around. He mentions on his way out the door that, in addition to a short-term solution, he wants a long-term solution to the problem. How would you proceed?

4. Over the years, you have become friends with one of your law office's best clients. The client likes you and believes in your ability as a competent legal assistant. Recently, you have spent many hours, including evenings and weekends, working on the client's case. The client comes in for an appointment to see you about his case. The client notices that you look very tired and ragged. You tell the client how many hours you have been working on the case to let him know about the hard work that the law office is doing. The client responds by saying that he is going to the lead attorney on the case to demand that you be given an increase for all the extra time you have spent on the case. You are flattered that a client would think of your interest and you could certainly use the money. How would you handle this situation?

5. You are a legal assistant at a medium-size law office. The executive committee thinks that the law office needs to put more emphasis on client services. You are a respected part of the firm and the committee thinks you interact with clients exceptionally well. The committee has approved the development of a client manual that will be given to all its clients. The committee has chosen you to be in charge of developing the manual in the initial stages.

Your task is to prepare a client manual that will be presented to the executive committee within 30 days. In addition, once the committee approves the manual, you also will be in charge of implementing its use. The committee is giving you control over researching and developing the manual.

Assume you have never heard of or developed a client manual before. Assume you can choose to either accept the task or not accept it. Would you accept the assignment? Why or why not? How would you develop the client manual? Would you choose to use a work group or not? What sections or key points would you include in the manual? Give reasons for your answers.

6.   From an ethical perspective only, analyze what the benefits are to a law office that routinely sends copies of all documents to its clients.

7.   As a legal assistant in a busy office, you try your best to talk to clients when they call and to pass along information from the client to your supervising attorney, but sometimes you forget. On one such occasion, a client called you because she was unable to talk to the attorney. The client called with vital information that the attorney needed regarding an important aspect of the case. Unfortunately, you failed to pass the information along. Discuss from an ethics and malpractice standpoint the importance of communication skills.

8.   Think of someone you know who you think is a good leader. Write down why you think this person is a good leader and what outstanding qualities he or she has. How do the qualities listed compare with the information in the chapter? What leadership qualities do you have?

9.   Think about a group or committee that you have worked on. Write down the dynamics of how the group interacted. Who emerged as the leader, and why? Looking back, do you see any evidence of groupthink? Did the group members communicate with each other effectively? Was the group successful at accomplishing its purpose? Why or why not? Did you feel like an active member of the group? Why or why not? If you could have changed one thing about the group, what would it have been?

NOTES

1. *California Lawyer*, June 2000, p. 71. Reprinted with permission from *California Lawyer.*
2. *California Lawyer*, March 2000, p. 69. Reprinted with permission from *California Lawyer.*
3. Greene, R. (1992). *Making partner.* American Bar Association. Reprinted by permission.
4. American Bar Association. (2000). *Annotated model rules of professional conduct* (4th ed., p. 32)., citing *Sage Realty v. Proskauer Rose Goetz*, 666 N.Y.S.2d 985, 988 (App. Div. 1997). Reprinted by permission. Copies of the ABA *Model Code of Professional Responsibility,* 1999 edition, are available from Service Center, American Bar Association, 750 North Lake Shore Drive, Chicago, IL 60611-4497, 1-800-285-2221.
5. McKenna, P. J. (2000, January/February). Develop a 'first mover' advantage. *Law Practice Management.* Reprinted by permission.
6. Clawar, S. (1996). *You and your clients—a guide to client management skills for a more successful practice* (p. 3). American Bar Association. Reprinted by permission.
7. Zwicker, M. (2000, January/February). What can you glean from client feedback? *Law Practice Management*, 51. Reprinted by permission.
8. Schmidt, S. J. (1989). *What clients say* (p. 14). Burnsville, MN: Sally Schmidt Consulting, Inc.
9. Ibid., p. 19.
10. Adapted from American Bar Association. (1983). *The lawyer's handbook.* Reprinted by permission.
11. Greene, A. (2005). *The lawyer's guide to increasing revenue* (p. 140). American Bar Association.
12. Foonberg, J. (2004). *How to start and build a law practice* (p. 233). American Bar Association.
13. Ibid. pp. 19–20.
14. Gillis, E. (2003, May/June). Cream of the crop. *Legal Assistant Today*, 72.
15. Heller, D., & Hunt, J. M. (1988). *Practicing law and managing people* (p. 210). Butterworth. Courtesy of Heller, Hunt & Cunningham.
16. Ibid., p. 212. Courtesy of Heller, Hunt & Cunningham.
17. Mocine, M. H. (2000, July). The art of listening. *California Lawyer*, 23. Reprinted with permission from *California Lawyer.*
18. Davis, K. (1985). *Human behavior at work* (7th ed.). New York, NY: McGraw-Hill. Reprinted with permission of McGraw-Hill.
19. Copyright 1993 by the American Law Institute. Reprinted with the permission of the American Law Institute—American Bar Association Committee on Continuing Professional Education.

note. Subsequently, Milner did not take any action regarding the case. Despite the client's attempts to communicate with her and his requests that she return the promissory note to him, she failed to do so, and failed initially to provide it when the Office of Attorney Regulation Counsel ("OARC") requested it. Eventually, she provided OARC with a copy of the note.

[6] [7] Milner's failure to return the original or a copy of the client's promissory note upon the client's request constitutes a violation of Colo. RPC 1.15(b) (a lawyer shall promptly deliver to the client any funds or other property that the client is entitled to receive and render a full accounting regarding such property). Her failure to respond to the client's telephone calls and failure to communicate with him regarding the status of the matter constitutes a violation of Colo. RPC 1.4(a) (failure to communicate). Milner's failure to take any action on behalf of the client after agreeing to represent him ***678** constitutes neglect in violation of Colo. RPC 1.3 (lawyer shall act with reasonable diligence and promptness in representing a client and shall not neglect a legal matter entrusted to the lawyer).

Claim IV: The Chavez Matter

On March 31, 1998, Milner and Kemp met with Cherry Chavez regarding a divorce action. The client paid Milner $600 for fees and costs to represent her in the divorce. The client was told that if she and her husband could agree on settlement, Milner could complete all the paperwork. Kemp offered to assist the client and her husband as a mediator. The client and her husband met with Milner and Kemp again on April 11, 1998 to discuss their divorce, and agreed on all matters except child support. Milner stated that she would prepare a petition for dissolution of marriage and, in the meantime, the husband would consider the issue of child support. Thereafter, the client heard nothing from Milner, but was able to contact Kemp on several occasions, who indicated that the delay in preparing the petition for dissolution was caused by the client's husband's failure to cooperate. In fact, Kemp never attempted to speak with the client's husband. On June 22, 1998, a meeting was scheduled with the client and her husband to review

the petition for dissolution. When the client and her husband arrived, both Milner and Kemp were unavailable. Milner's secretary reviewed the documents and stated that they would be filed with the court within the next few days. The client thereafter attempted to contact Milner regarding the status of the case but received no response until late August, when Milner stated that the petition would be filed on or before September 1. Thereafter, Chavez again had difficulty contacting Milner, but spoke to Kemp. Kemp was abusive to Chavez and said he was not aware of the status of the case. On September 24, 1998, the client successfully contacted Milner who stated that the petition had been filed. The client contacted the court clerk's office in early October and was told that no petition had been filed. After the client contacted OARC, Milner filed the petition for dissolution on behalf of Chavez. Milner's failing to file the petition in a timely fashion delayed the divorce.

[8] [9] [10] Milner's failure to communicate with the client regarding the status of the case despite repeated attempts by the client constituted a violation of Colo. RPC 1.4(a) (failure to communicate). Milner's failure to timely file the petition constitutes neglect in violation of Colo. RPC 1.3 (neglect of a legal matter). Milner's statement to the client that she had filed the petition when in fact she had not was conduct involving misrepresentation when, at the time, she knew it had not been filed, was a violation of Colo. RPC 8.4(c) (conduct involving dishonesty, fraud, deceit, or misrepresentation).

[11] Kemp's knowing misrepresentation to Chavez that the delay in filing the divorce action was caused by the husband when it was not is conduct which would not be tolerated if undertaken by a lawyer. As a paralegal to Milner, it was Milner's responsibility to take reasonable efforts that his conduct was compatible with her professional responsibilities. She did not take such steps. Consequently, Milner failed to adequately supervise Kemp in violation of Colo. RPC 5.3(b) (failure to supervise a nonlawyer).

Claim V: The Fisher Matter

In April 1998, Jana Fisher retained Milner in connection with a divorce and to secure a temporary restraining order. In August 1998, Milner represented the client at a permanent orders hearing. The court ordered Milner to submit the permanent orders within 30 days of the hearing. Milner did not do so. The court issued an Order to Show Cause why Milner should not be sanctioned for failure to timely file the permanent orders. A hearing on the Order to Show Cause was set for November 24, 1998. Milner did not provide the client with a copy of the Show Cause Order. Milner filed the permanent orders on November 23, 1998, and the Show Cause Order was vacated. Thereafter, Fisher tried on several occasions to contact Milner because the permanent orders required her to refinance her house within 120 days. She needed a copy of the permanent orders to refinance the house. Unable to reach Milner, ***679** the client spoke with Kemp who told her to "stop calling and bitching." Milner did not provide the client with a copy of the permanent orders.

[12] [13] [14] [15] Milner's failure to timely submit an order to the court regarding the terms of the permanent orders violated <u>Colo. RPC 1.3</u> (neglect of a legal matter). Milner's failure to communicate with the client following the permanent orders hearing despite the client's repeated attempts to reach her constituted a violation of <u>Colo. RPC 1.4(a)</u> (failure to communicate). By failing to timely submit an order to the court regarding the terms of the permanent orders, Milner knowingly disobeyed obligations under the rules of a tribunal in violation of <u>Colo. RPC 3.4(c)</u> (knowingly disobeying an obligation under the rules of a tribunal), resulting in prejudice to the administration of justice in violation of <u>Colo. RPC 8.4(d)</u> (engaging in conduct prejudicial to the administration of justice). With regard to the alleged violation of <u>Colo. RPC 5.3(b)</u> (failure to adequately supervise a nonlawyer), that allegation is premised solely upon Kemp's outburst with Fisher to "stop calling and bitching." Although lacking in tact, not conducive to a harmonious attorney/client relationship and certainly below the level of professionalism to which the profession must aspire, the PDJ and Hearing Board do not conclude that a single impolite outburst toward a client constitutes conduct incompatible with the professional obligations of a lawyer. Accordingly, the charged violation of <u>Colo. RPC 5.3(b)</u> in claim five is dismissed.

Claim VI: The Abrahamson Matter

In April 1998, Norma Abrahamson retained Milner to assist her in recovering payment of a loan. The parties verbally agreed that Milner would be paid $250 out of the proceeds. Not having heard from Milner, Abrahamson contacted her in June to inquire into the status of the case. Milner admitted she had forgotten the matter, and would take action to proceed at that time. Despite several attempts, it was not until late August that the client was able to speak again with Milner, and Milner informed her that an injunction had been ordered. In October, the client attempted to speak with Milner and instead spoke with "Matthew" of Milner's office, who was unable to give her any information on the case. The client thereafter sent a letter to Milner inquiring about the status of the case. Between October 1998 and January 1999 the client called Milner on six occasions and Milner neither returned her calls nor responded to the letter.

[16] [17] Between April 1998 and June 1998, Milner "forgot" about the case and took no action on it. By agreeing to represent a client in a dispute and then failing to take those ministerial steps necessary to ensure that the matter is not "forgotten," Milner violated <u>Colo. RPC 1.3</u>. The facts reveal repeated failures to communicate with the client regarding the status of the case and therefore establish a violation of <u>Colo. RPC 1.4(a)</u> (failure to communicate). Milner is also charged with violating <u>Colo. RPC 1.16(d)</u> and <u>Colo. RPC 1.15(b)</u> based upon these facts. <u>Colo. RPC 1.16(d)</u> provides:

Upon termination of representation, a lawyer shall take steps to the extent reasonably practicable to protect a client's interests, such as giving reasonable notice to the client, allowing time for employment of other counsel, surrendering papers and property to which the client is entitled and refunding any advance payment of fee that has not been earned. The lawyer may retain papers relating to the client to the extent permitted by law.

The opening phrase of <u>Colo. RPC 1.16(d)</u> requires "[u]pon termination of representation. . . ." No evidence was presented that Milner's representation was terminated, nor is there an allegation of abandonment. Consequently, the PDJ and Hearing Board conclude that the charge under Colo. RPC 1.16(d) in claim six in Case No. 99PDJ030 was not established and is therefore dismissed. Colo. RPC 1.15 provides:

Safekeeping Property: Interest-Bearing Accounts to be Established for the Benefit of the Client or Third Persons or the Colorado Lawyer Trust Account Foundation: Notice of Overdrafts; Record Keeping. (b) Upon receiving funds or other property in which a client or third person has an ***680*** interest, a lawyer shall, promptly or otherwise as permitted by law or by agreement with the client, deliver to the client or third person any funds or other property that the client or third person is entitled to receive and, upon request by the client or third person, render a full accounting regarding such property.

[18] The People contend that Milner violated Colo. RPC 1.15(b) by virtue of her failure to return the promissory note and other documents to Abrahamson. There is no evidence, however, that the representation of the case was concluded, or the client had requested the return of documents. The only evidence presented was that Milner told Abrahamson that an injunction had been ordered. [FN1] Although it is possible to surmise that Milner did not undertake the requisite efforts necessary to obtain recovery on the note in light of the remaining facts in other claims of the Amended Complaint, surmise is not proof by clear and convincing evidence. Absent some evidence establishing a termination of the representation, the conclusion of the case, or a request by the client, the PDJ and Hearing Board cannot conclude that Milner violated Colo. RPC 1.15(b) by failing to return documents and the promissory note prior to the end of January 1999. Accordingly, the alleged violation of Colo. RPC 1.15(b) in claim six in Case No. 99PDJ030 is dismissed.

> FN1. Although the issuance of an injunction in a promissory note case seems curious, that statement by Milner suggests that a case was filed.

Claim VII: The Spargo Matter

In June 1998, Sherry Spargo retained Milner to represent her in a divorce. The client paid Milner a total of $800 in fees and $124 in costs. Thereafter, Spargo had minimal contact with Milner. Milner failed to notify the client of the permanent orders hearing date until a few days prior to the hearing. Pursuant to the permanent orders, Milner agreed to submit a wage assignment for child support to the employer of the client's husband and failed to do so. The client attempted to contact Milner regarding the wage assignment, but Milner did not return her phone calls. Milner filed the wage assignment after the client made a request for investigation with the OARC.

[19] [20] Milner's failure to communicate adequately with the client regarding the status of the matter and timely notify the client of the scheduled permanent orders hearing constitutes a violation of Colo. RPC 1.4(a) (failure to communicate). Milner's failure to timely notify the client of the permanent orders hearing, and her failure to file a wage assignment for child support until after the client had contacted OARC constitutes neglect of a legal matter in violation of Colo. RPC 1.3 (neglect).

Claim VIII: The Boroos Matter

June Hallinan died on September 18, 1998. In Hallinan's will, Mr. and Mrs. Boroos were named as Ms. Hallinan's sole beneficiaries and Milner was designated as the personal representative of the estate. On the date of death, Hallinan's trailer home was sold for $3,800. Hallinan also owned an automobile at the time of her death. Milner advised the beneficiaries that she had taken the automobile to her home for safekeeping. The beneficiaries discussed selling the vehicle to Milner, but did not finalize any agreement. Subsequently, they conducted a title search and learned that title to the car had been transferred to Milner's husband on October 20, 1998.

In December 1998, one of the beneficiaries met with Milner and requested a listing of the estate's assets. Milner failed to provide one. In January 1999, the beneficiaries met with Milner to discuss and close the estate. However, Milner had not prepared for the meeting nor did she provide to the beneficiaries a list of expenses and assets or any written statement concerning the amount of the final distribution under the estate. She did not show the beneficiaries any bills or bank statements and was not sure of the amounts she provided verbally. Milner scheduled a subsequent meeting in January. By letter, the beneficiaries requested a written statement summarizing the disposition of **681** assets of the estate. Milner did not respond to the letter. In January, the beneficiaries called Milner several times but Milner did not return their calls. On at least one occasion, the beneficiaries spoke to Kemp, who informed them that the estate was not completed because other claims were being filed against it. This statement was false; there were no other claims filed against the estate. In February 1999, the beneficiaries contacted the court and learned that the will of the deceased had not been filed. Thereafter, despite numerous requests by the beneficiaries, Milner failed to provide an accounting of the estate assets and failed to distribute the proceeds of the estate to its beneficiaries. The beneficiaries hired an attorney who wrote to Milner and requested information regarding the status of the estate and demanded the estate files. Milner neither responded nor provided the files to the beneficiaries' attorney. Thereafter, the beneficiaries obtained an order of court removing Milner as personal representative of the estate and appointing one of the beneficiaries as successor personal representative. The order directed Milner to provide all bank account records, all funds or property of the estate, records of Milner's law office trust account, the original will, the estate files, and records relating to the transfer of the vehicle. Milner did not provide the documents ordered by the court. The successor personal representative obtained the deceased's personal bank records and the estate's bank records himself. In April or May 1999, after the beneficiaries had made a request for investigation with the OARC, Milner made a distribution from the estate in the amount of $8,000, but did not provide any documentation or explanation for the $8,000. Milner eventually paid all but $1,071 owed to the beneficiaries.

[21] [22] [23] [24] Milner's actions resulted in harm to the beneficiaries resulting in an attempt to deprive them of their inheritance, causing them extreme stress and expenditure of time and research and requiring that they hire counsel. Milner's failure to promptly deliver to the beneficiaries of the estate funds or other property that the beneficiaries were entitled to receive and, upon request by the beneficiaries, render a full accounting with regard to such property constitutes a violation of Colo. RPC 1.15(b)

(lawyer shall promptly deliver to the client or third person any funds or other property the client or third person is entitled to receive and, upon request, render a full accounting). Milner retained property and funds belonging to the beneficiaries long beyond any period of time justifiable by virtue of her position as personal representative. Milner's conduct in acquiring the deceased's vehicle without finalizing a purchase agreement, transferring title of the vehicle to her husband and failing to disclose her actions in the face of requests to do so by the beneficiaries constitutes conduct involving dishonesty, fraud, deceit and misrepresentation in violation of Colo. RPC 8.4(c). The Amended Complaint charged Milner with a violation of Colo. RPC 8.4(h) (engaging in conduct that adversely reflects on the lawyer's fitness to practice law). Colo. RPC 8.4(h) requires proof that the lawyer engaged in conduct, the totality of which reflects that she lacked the personal or professional moral and/or ethical qualifications required of those authorized to practice law. Conduct involving violence, lack of honesty, violation of trust, serious interference with the administration of justice, criminal endeavors, or comparable misconduct is required to establish a violation of Colo. RPC 8.4(h). See People v. Cleland, No. GC98B118, slip op. at 9, 10 (Colo. PDJ September 17, 1999) 28 Colo. Law. 127, 128–129 (November 1999); People v. Theodore, 926 P.2d 1237, 1242–43 (Colo.1996) (holding that attorney's engaging in conduct involving dishonesty amounts to conduct that adversely reflects on his fitness to practice law). Viewing the totality of Milner's misconduct in the context of acting as personal representative of an estate as a serious violation of trust, the PDJ and Hearing Board find that such misconduct constitutes a violation of Colo. RPC 8.4(h).

[25] The remaining charge in this claim, [FN2] Colo. RPC 1.3 (a lawyer shall act with reasonable **682** diligence and promptness in representing a client) requires the existence of an attorney/client relationship. No evidence was presented to establish that Milner acted in any capacity other than as the personal representative of the estate. Such a capacity does not, in and of itself, create an attorney/client relationship. Consequently, the charged violation of Colo. RPC 1.3 in claim eight in Case No. 99PDJ030 is dismissed.

FN2. Upon the People's motion at the closing of the sanctions hearing, the alleged violation of Colo. RPC 1.4(a) in claim eight was dismissed with prejudice.

Claim IX: The Machina Matter

In November 1998, Anisa Machina hired Milner to represent her in a divorce proceeding. The client paid Milner an advance fee of $1,200. In January 1999, Kemp told the client that he had personally delivered papers to the client's husband and provided copies to him by certified mail. The client asked for proof of service on her husband and Kemp said he could not provide her with copies of the certified mail acceptance. The client made an appointment to meet with Milner and asked that she be provided with her husband's acceptance of certified mail. Milner stated that she would provide the client with receipt of the certified mail at the meeting. On January 30, 1999, the client met with Milner and again requested a copy of the receipt of certified mail. It was not provided to her. Milner said she would mail it to the client, and failed to do so. Thereafter, the client heard nothing more from Milner concerning the divorce proceeding.

Machina attempted to contact Milner on several occasions after January 30, 1999, to determine the status of her case and the date of the hearing. Milner did not return her calls. Finally, Machina successfully contacted Milner and told her she wished to terminate her services, and demanded a refund of a portion of the funds paid to Milner. Milner told Machina she could only refund $600 to $800 due to the service fees encountered in serving the husband in the dissolution case. Milner did not, however, refund the $600 to $800 as requested. Indeed, Milner made no refund to Machina until April 1999 after a request for investigation had been filed with the OARC.

[26] The client paid Milner $1,200 for her professional services regarding the client's divorce action. The client terminated Milner's services and requested a refund of a portion of the fees she had paid to Milner. Upon such a request it is the obligation of the attorney to promptly refund any unearned fees. Milner failed to do so. Milner delayed making any refund for approximately two months and did so only after a request for investigation had been filed.

Milner's failing to promptly provide a refund upon request by the client constituted a violation of Colo. RPC 1.15(b) (lawyer shall promptly deliver to the client any funds or other property that the client is entitled to receive). Milner's failure to return Machina's phone calls after January 30, 1999, constituted a failure to keep the client reasonably informed about the status of a matter and promptly comply with reasonable requests for information in violation of Colo. RPC 1.4(a).

B. Case No. 99PDJ093

Claim I: The Nelson Matter

In June 1998 Milner entered into an attorney/client relationship with Jannette Nelson who sought her assistance regarding the investigation into the death of her brother. The client paid Milner $2,000 and provided Milner with complete copies of the police file, medical reports, and the names and addresses of those who might have relevant information. Milner promised to investigate the death thoroughly, and told the client that she would schedule a meeting with the Denver District Attorney and the Denver Police Department. Milner and Kemp both assured the client that they would keep her informed of the status of the case.

A meeting was scheduled with the client, Milner and other individuals whom Milner had allegedly involved in the investigation. When the client went to the meeting, only Kemp was present, who told the client the meeting would have to be rescheduled. At the end of October 1998, Milner told the client that she had scheduled a meeting with the Denver Police Department and the Denver District Attorney for November 12, 1998, and that all the necessary work for the meeting had been done. Milner later admitted that she had never arranged such a meeting *683* with the Denver District Attorney and other parties. Milner promised to call the client but failed to call. When the client inquired about the scheduled meeting, she was told that none had been scheduled. Milner spoke to the client shortly thereafter and said that a report was being prepared regarding the case. From the second week of November 1998, to the third week of March 1999, the client repeatedly contacted Milner, who said that she was revising the report. Milner scheduled meetings with the client and later cancelled them. The client decided to terminate Milner and told Milner's secretary that she wanted to pick up her file. Milner then told the client that the report would be sent to her and to the Denver District Attorney by courier. The client did not hear from Milner again despite many attempts to reach her. Milner never sent a report to the client. The client requested by letter that Milner return the $2,000 in fees she had paid to her. Milner never responded to the client.

[27] [28] [29] [30] [31] Milner agreed to represent the client and investigate her brother's death and thereafter took no action on the case from June 1998 to March 1999. Her neglect of the client's matter constituted a violation of Colo. RPC 1.3. Milner's failure to keep appointments with the client, and failure to return the client's phone calls from June 1998 to March 1999, constituted a violation of Colo. RPC 1.4(a) (failure to communicate). Milner's taking $2,000 as payment for her professional services and failing to take any action from June 1998 through March 1999 on behalf of the client constituted the charging of an unreasonable fee in violation of Colo. RPC 1.5(a) (a lawyer's fee shall be reasonable). Milner's failure to return the file and the client's funds to the client upon request constituted a violation of Colo. RPC 1.15(b) (a lawyer shall promptly deliver to the client any funds or property that the client is entitled to receive). Milner's failure to take steps to the extent reasonably practicable to protect the client's interests upon termination, and failure to surrender papers and property to which the client was entitled including refunding any advance payment of fee that has not been earned constitutes a violation of Colo. RPC 1.16(d) (upon termination of representation, a lawyer shall take steps to protect a client's interests, including surrendering papers or property to which client is entitled).

[32] Milner's misrepresentations to the client that she had: sent a letter to a possible witness on the client's behalf; scheduled numerous meetings and drafted a report when she had not; as well as her failure to return the client's funds when she performed none of the professional services for which she was paid from June 1998 to March 1999 constituted dishonesty in violation of Colo. RPC 8.4(c).

Claim II: The Biggers Matter

In May 1999 Cindy Biggers went to Milner's law office seeking professional help with a bankruptcy and divorce. She met with Milner, Kemp, and a woman named "Patti." Milner stated that she would charge the client $1,000 to handle both her bankruptcy and her divorce. The client paid Milner $969. Milner stated that Kemp would be working on the client's matters. Milner prepared and filed a petition for dissolution of marriage, but took no further action in the divorce proceeding on behalf of the client. Milner took no action whatsoever in the bankruptcy matter.

[33] [34] Milner entered into an attorney/client relationship with the client and accepted $969 for both the divorce and bankruptcy proceeding. Taking into account the nature of professional services to be provided, neglect may justify a finding of abandonment under circumstances where an attorney neglects a client's matter and fails to communicate with the client. In both the divorce and the bankruptcy matter, Milner agreed to take action on behalf of the client. Having created the false expectation that she would do so, Milner completed minimal work in the divorce matter, took no action in the bankruptcy matter, and thereafter failed to communicate with the client. Milner's agreement to perform the services and her failure to do so taken together with her failure to communicate with the client established serious neglect, which justifies a finding of abandonment in violation of Colo. RPC 1.3 (neglect of a legal matter). Milner's failure to communicate *684 with the client despite the client's numerous attempts to contact Milner constituted a violation of Colo. RPC 1.4(a) (failure to communicate). By her continued retention of the client's funds, Milner converted the client's funds, in violation of Colo. RPC 8.4(c) (conduct involving dishonesty, fraud, deceit, or misrepresentation). See People v. Varallo, 913 P.2d 1, 12 (Colo.1996).

[35] [36] [37] [38] Milner's failure to perform any services with regard to the bankruptcy and failure to take action on behalf of the client in the divorce proceeding beyond the filing of the petition while retaining the $969 in client funds constituted the charging of an unreasonable fee in violation of Colo. RPC 1.5(a) (charging an unreasonable fee). The Complaint alleges a

violation of Colo. RPC 1.15(b) (upon receiving funds or other property in which a client or third person has an interest, a lawyer shall promptly deliver to the client any funds or other property that the client is entitled to receive and, upon request by the client, render a full accounting). By failing to perform the work requested by the client while retaining a portion of the client's funds which had not been earned, after effectively abandoning the client, Milner violated Colo. RPC 1.15(b). Milner's abandonment of the client effectively terminated the attorney/client relationship, triggering the provisions of Colo. RPC 1.16(d), requiring Milner to refund any advance payment of fees that had not been earned. Milner failed, upon termination, to take steps to the extent reasonably practicable to protect the client's interests, including failing to refund the advance payment of fee that had not been earned, in violation of Colo. RPC 1.16(d).

[39] The Complaint alleges that Milner violated Colo. RPC 5.5(b) (assisting a person who is not a member of the Colorado Bar in the performance of an activity that constitutes the unauthorized practice of law) by assisting Kemp in the unauthorized practice of law. There is no evidence that established Kemp engaged in the unauthorized practice of law with regard to the Biggers matter. Accordingly, the alleged violation of Colo. RPC 5.5(b) is dismissed.

Claim III: The Stephens Matter

[40] [41] Milner represented Gale Marie Stephens in a bankruptcy proceeding. United States Bankruptcy Judge Sidney B. Brooks dismissed the matter due to Milner's failure to cure deficiencies in the original filing despite an order to do so. Milner took no further action in the case following the court's dismissal. The client, through new counsel, filed a motion to reconsider the dismissal of Stephens' bankruptcy petition, which the court granted. Thereafter, on two separate occasions, the Court ordered Milner to attend a hearing on Milner's mismanagement of the case, the reasonableness of her fees, and whether sanctions should be entered against her. On both occasions, Milner failed to appear. Milner's failing to cure the deficiencies in the original bankruptcy filing constituted a failure to provide competent representation to the client in violation of Colo. RPC 1.1 (a lawyer shall provide competent repre-

sentation to a client). The failure to timely cure the filing deficiencies also constitutes neglect under Colo. RPC 1.3. Taking into account the nature of the professional services to be provided and the time frame within which those services were required, the level of neglect may justify a finding of abandonment under circumstances where an attorney neglects a client's matter and fails to communicate with the client. Under the circumstances in this case, the facts establish that Milner deserted, rejected, and/or relinquished her professional responsibilities owed to the client. *See People v. Carvell,* No. 99PDJ096 (Colo. PDJ September 11, 2000), 29 Colo. Law 136, 138 (November 2000), 2000 Colo. Discipl. LEXIS 26 (holding that to find abandonment rather than merely neglect, there must be proof that the attorney—during a given time period—was required to accomplish specific professional tasks for the client, failed to accomplish those tasks, and failed to communicate with the client). The level of neglect in the Stephens matter rises to the level of abandonment in violation of Colo. RPC 1.3.

[42] [43] Milner knowingly disobeyed an obligation under the rules of a tribunal on two separate occasions, constituting two separate violations of Colo. RPC 3.4(c) (knowingly ***685*** disobeying an obligation under the rules of a tribunal). Milner's conduct violated Colo. RPC 8.4(d) (conduct prejudicial to the administration of justice) by causing the bankruptcy court to dismiss and then reconsider the dismissal of the case, set and reset several hearings. Milner's conduct resulted in harm to the client and to the bankruptcy court: the client's wages were garnished resulting in an arrearage in her house payments, and the bankruptcy court expended unnecessary court time attempting to resolve the difficulties arising from Milner's misconduct.

Claim IV: The Venner Matter

[44] Milner represented Cobe and Sharon Venner who were debtors in a bankruptcy matter. The United States Trustee filed a motion questioning the reasonableness of the fees paid to Milner and questioning whether Milner was sharing fees with nonlawyers. The court ordered Milner to file an accounting for all fees and expenses charged in the case. Milner did not respond to the court's order. On three separate occasions, the

court issued an order requiring Milner to appear at hearings, and to show cause why sanctions should not be imposed and/or any monies she received be disgorged for her failure to properly provide representation to her clients. Milner did not appear.

Milner knowingly disobeyed an obligation under the rules of a tribunal by failing to provide an accounting when ordered to do so, and by failing to appear at court-ordered hearings in violation of <u>Colo. RPC 3.4(c)</u> (knowingly disobeying the rules of a tribunal). By causing the court to schedule additional hearings on its docket, Milner engaged in conduct prejudicial to the administration of justice in violation of <u>Colo. RPC 8.4(d)</u> (engaging in conduct prejudicial to the administration of justice). [FN3]

> FN3. Default was denied on the alleged violation of <u>Colo. RPC 1.1</u> and <u>Colo. RPC 1.3</u> in claim four in Case No. 99PDJ093, and the People moved to dismiss the charges, which were dismissed by the court on June 6, 2000.

Claim V: The Schmidt Matter

In July 1998, David Schmidt went to Milner's office and spoke with Kemp regarding Schmidt's divorce. Schmidt wanted custody of his two minor children. Kemp, Milner's paralegal, agreed that Milner would accept the case and took $420 from Schmidt. The client paid a total of $595 for Milner's representation. Kemp told Schmidt that Milner would be contacting him. Thereafter, Kemp called Schmidt and told him that Milner would meet with him on the morning of his court appearance date. When Schmidt met with her, Milner was completely unfamiliar with Schmidt's case. Schmidt explained to Milner that his wife was involved in drugs and mentally unstable, and that he wanted custody of the children. At the hearing scheduled that day, Milner arrived late. Moreover, Milner did not inform the court of Schmidt's intent to seek custody. The court ordered a subsequent hearing so that the wife could obtain counsel.

At the next hearing in August 1998, Milner again failed to inform the court of Schmidt's intent to seek custody of his children; on the contrary, she advised the court that the current visitation schedule was working for her client. Milner did not raise any concerns about the welfare of the children. A few days later, Schmidt learned that his estranged wife's boyfriend had beaten her and threatened Schmidt's children with bodily harm. The client called Milner and left a message and Kemp returned his call, stating that they could seek permanent orders in 8 to 12 months, that they could not seek temporary custody, and insisting that Schmidt not contact social services. At no time during the representation of Schmidt did Milner or Kemp inform Schmidt of the availability of court-ordered parenting programs. Schmidt was unable to learn from Milner where he could attend parenting class because Milner did not return his calls nor respond to his letters.

Schmidt wrote to Milner and terminated the representation, asking for the return of his file. Milner did not respond. Months later, on December 28, 1998, Schmidt left a message on Milner's voice mail stating that unless he heard back from her and she returned his file, he and his friends would picket outside her office. The next day he ***686** received a certified letter from Milner's office stating that she would no longer represent him based upon his threats to Milner and to his wife. The letter stated that the police had been notified. Schmidt had never made any threats concerning his wife. The next day, the client received another certified letter from Milner's office containing a court order dismissing his divorce. The client learned from the court that Milner had not taken proper action in his case.

Schmidt's estranged wife saw the letter from Milner's office claiming that he had threatened both his wife and Milner. She notified social services of the alleged threats and the department took action. Schmidt was served with a temporary restraining order preventing him from contacting his children or his ex-wife unless supervised. The statements in the letter regarding threats to his wife were not true.

Despite the client's prior requests, Milner did not return the file to him. The client hired successor counsel. Kemp told successor counsel that he had received information directly from Schmidt's ex-wife about the threats to her and to his children, and claimed that Kemp himself had heard Schmidt make threats regarding Schmidt's children and the ex-wife. None of Kemp's statements were true.

[45] [46] Milner's failure to be apprised of Schmidt's case prior to the hearing, her failure to arrive on time at the hearing, her failure to advocate her client's interests regarding child custody at the hearings, her failure to advise the client that he could seek temporary custody of his children, combined with her failure to advise the client regarding court-ordered parenting classes, constituted a failure to provide competent representation to the client in violation of Colo. RPC 1.1 (failure to provide competent representation) and neglect in violation of Colo. RPC 1.3 (neglect of a legal matter). Milner's failure to adequately communicate with the client despite his repeated efforts to discuss his case with her constituted a violation of Colo. RPC 1.4(a) (failure to communicate). Schmidt terminated Milner's representation, triggering the obligations of Colo. RPC 1.16(d), which required Milner to surrender papers and property to which the client was entitled. Milner failed to return Schmidt's file to him when requested and therefore violated Colo. RPC 1.16(d).

[47] The Complaint alleges a violation of Colo. RPC 5.5(b) (a lawyer shall not assist a person who is not a member of the Colorado bar in the performance of activity that constitute the unauthorized practice of law). Kemp met with the client for an initial interview without Milner's oversight and accepted legal representation of Schmidt. Kemp, also without supervision by Milner, advised Schmidt against seeking temporary custody of the client's children, and advised Schmidt against discussing the children's welfare with social services, all of which constitutes the unauthorized practice of law in violation of Colo. RPC 5.5(b).

[48] The Complaint alleges a violation of Colo. RPC 5.3(b), which provides "a lawyer having direct supervisory authority over the nonlawyer shall make reasonable efforts to ensure that the person's conduct is compatible with the professional obligations of the lawyer." Milner failed to adequately supervise Kemp in Kemp's initial meeting with Schmidt and in subsequent conversations with him; she failed to supervise Kemp when he falsely informed successor counsel that Schmidt had made threats regarding the client's wife and children. By failing to restrict Kemp's ability to act inappropriately with regard to Schmidt, Milner violated Colo. RPC 5.3(b).

II. ANALYSIS OF DISCIPLINE

These two disciplinary proceedings consist of 14 separate matters. In two matters, Milner violated Colo. RPC 1.1 by failing to provide competent legal advice to the client. In four matters, Milner violated Colo. RPC 1.15(b) by failing to deliver to the client or third person any funds or other property that the client or third person was entitled to receive, and upon request, provide a full accounting regarding such property. In three matters, Milner violated Colo. RPC 1.16(d) by taking reasonable steps to protect the client's interests upon termination. In 10 separate matters, Milner violated *687 Colo. RPC 1.3 by failing to act with reasonable diligence and promptness in representing the client, and by neglecting legal matters entrusted to her. In 11 separate matters, Milner violated Colo. RPC 1.4(a) by failing to keep her clients reasonably informed about the status of their matters and failed to promptly comply with reasonable requests for information. In two matters, Milner violated Colo. RPC 1.5(a) by charging an unreasonable fee. In one matter, Milner failed to comply with the requirements of Colo. RPC 1.5(b) requiring that she communicate the basis or rate of her fee in writing before or within a reasonable time after commencing the representation of the client. In three matters, Milner knowingly disobeyed an obligation under the rules of a tribunal. In four matters, Milner violated Colo. RPC 5.3(b) by acting as a lawyer having direct supervisory authority over a nonlawyer and failing to make reasonable efforts to ensure that the person's conduct is compatible with the professional obligations of the lawyer. In one matter, Milner violated Colo. RPC 5.5(b) by assisting a person who is not a member of the Colorado bar in the performance of an activity that constitutes the unauthorized practice of law. In four matters, Milner violated Colo. RPC 8.4(c) by engaging in conduct involving dishonesty, fraud, deceit, or misrepresentation. In three matters, Milner violated Colo. RPC 8.4(d) by engaging in conduct prejudicial to the administration of justice. In one matter, Milner violated Colo. RPC 8.4(h) by engaging in conduct that adversely reflects on the lawyer's fitness to practice law.

[49] [50] [51] [52] In the Biggers matter, Milner converted funds belonging to the client. Milner's retention

of Biggers' funds for an extended period of time, coupled with her lack of communication with the client, and her failure to account for or return the unearned funds for a significant period of time, constitutes willful and knowing conduct. Knowing conversion of clients' funds warrants disbarment. *See People v. Silvola*, 915 P.2d 1281, 1284 (Colo.1996) (finding that misconduct that occurred over an extended period of time must be deemed to be willful); *People v. Bradley*, 825 P.2d 475, 476–77 (Colo.1992) (lawyer's inaction over a period of two years deemed willful misconduct); *People v. Williams*, 824 P.2d 813, 814 (Colo.1992) (continued and chronic neglect over extended periods of time must be considered willful); *People v. Elliott*, 99PDJ059, slip op. at 8 (consolidated with 99PDJ086) (Colo. PDJ March 1, 2000), 29 Colo. Law. 112, 114, 115 (May 2000) (disbarring attorney for his accepting advance fees from two clients, performing some but not all of the services for which he was paid, retaining the fees for one year in one matter and two years in another matter, and abandoning the clients). Milner abandoned her clients in both the Biggers and Stephens matters. Abandonment of clients, absent significant mitigating circumstances, warrants disbarment. *See* ABA *Standards for Imposing Lawyer Sanctions* (1991 & Supp.1992) ("ABA *Standards*") 4.41(a)(providing that disbarment is generally appropriate when a lawyer abandons the practice and causes serious or potentially serious injury to a client). Disbarment is also the appropriate sanction for the extent of neglect and other rule violations demonstrated in these 14 separate client matters. *See* ABA *Standards* 4.41(c)(stating that disbarment is generally appropriate when a lawyer engages in a pattern of neglect with respect to client matters and causes serious or potentially serious injury to a client); *People v. Murray*, 887 P.2d 1016, 1021 (Colo.1994) (lawyer disbarred for knowingly failing to perform services for clients in 10 separate matters, constituting a pattern of neglect and causing potentially serious harm to clients); *People v. Dulaney*, 785 P.2d 1302, 1306 (Colo.1990) (lawyer disbarred for chronic neglect of client matters and use of deceit to cover the neglect).

The charges concerning Milner's failure to supervise Kemp, her paralegal, and her assisting him in the unauthorized practice of law are of particular concern and warrant a serious sanction. *See People v. Felker*, 770 P.2d 402, 406–407 (Colo.1989) (disbarring attorney for misrepresenting to a client that the legal assistant was a lawyer and permitting a nonlawyer to render legal advice to the client). Two prior Colorado disciplinary cases resulted in sanctions arising in part from an attorneys' failure to supervise the same paralegal, Matthew Kemp, and aiding ***688** him in the unauthorized practice of law. In *People v. Reynolds*, 933 P.2d 1295, 1305 (Colo.1997), the respondent attorney was suspended for three years and 30 days for 11 separate violations alleged in two complaints, with conditions upon reinstatement. As in this case, the respondent was found to have repeatedly neglected numerous client matters, engaged in dishonesty, misused client funds, and assisted a nonlawyer in the unauthorized practice of law. In *People v. Stewart*, 892 P.2d 875, 879 (Colo.1995), an attorney was suspended for three years with conditions placed upon reinstatement for making unauthorized charges to her law firm's credit card, aiding a nonlawyer in the unauthorized practice of law, and neglecting client matters after clients paid retainer fees to the nonlawyer assistant. The Supreme Court decided on the sanction of suspension rather than disbarment due to certain mitigating factors, including the fact that during the relevant time period, the respondent was suffering from depression and other physical and emotional problems.

The PDJ and Hearing Board find that Milner's misconduct, while similar to the misconduct in *Reynolds* and *Stewart*, is considerably worsened by her conduct before the United States Bankruptcy Court in the Venner and Stephens matter. Milner's failure to comply with the bankruptcy judge's orders that she appear, finally resulting in the issuance of a bench warrant for her arrest, demonstrates a flagrant disregard for the court system. Milner's conduct resulted in considerable waste of judicial resources and resulted in the Court making written findings in both matters that Milner's conduct on behalf of her clients was unprofessional, incomplete, and irresponsible, that she failed to disgorge fees despite being ordered to do so, and that she failed to pay sanctions ordered by the court. *See* the Commentary to ABA *Standards* 7.1 (providing that "[d]isbarment should be imposed in cases when the lawyer knowingly engages in conduct that violates a duty owed to the profession with the intent to benefit the lawyer or another, and which causes serious injury or potentially serious injury to a client, the public, or the legal system").

Milner's actions resulted in harm to her clients. Aldridge has been unable to modify visitation rights with her children. In the Chavez divorce, the rapport between the parties worsened as a result of Kemp's incorrectly blaming Milner's delay in the case on the unwillingness of the client's husband to cooperate. Chavez eventually represented herself in her divorce and was unable to obtain child support. In the Schmidt matter, Milner's and Kemp's actions resulted in Schmidt's divorce being dismissed for failure to prosecute, Schmidt's wife obtaining a temporary restraining order against him and his visitation rights were restricted. Nelson, who sought assistance investigating the death of her brother, was a particularly vulnerable client at the time she engaged Milner. The beneficiaries of the estate Milner was appointed to administer were required to obtain an attorney to appoint a successor personal representative and suffered considerable stress as a result of Milner's mishandling of the estate. In addition to the private harm, the public has been harmed by Milner's misconduct and her failure to supervise Kemp and provide assistance to him in the unauthorized practice of law. Such misconduct causes a heightened sense of public distrust in lawyers and their legal assistants.

[53] The PDJ and Hearing Board considered matters in mitigation and aggravation pursuant to ABA *Standards* 9.32 and 9.22 respectively. In mitigation, Milner has had no prior discipline, *see id.* at 9.32(a); however, the absence of prior discipline, standing alone, is insufficient to justify a sanction less than disbarment. *See People v. Steinman, 930 P.2d 596, 600 (Colo.1997)*. Milner was inexperienced at the time of the conduct in question, having been admitted to the bar of Colorado in 1992, *see id.* at 9.32(f), and she has demonstrated remorse for her actions, *see id.* at 9.32(l).

[54] Milner testified in mitigation that the facts giving rise to these proceedings were caused, at least in part, by Kemp. She stated that she was unaware of Kemp's unprofessional conduct with clients, and unaware of the number of cases Kemp had accepted on her behalf. However, Milner, as Kemp's employer and as the supervising lawyer, ***689** was accountable for his interactions with clients. Milner's lack of awareness regarding Kemp's activities cannot be considered a mitigating factor. It is incumbent upon the supervising lawyer to ensure that his or her paralegal adheres to the professional obligations of the lawyer. Ignorance of the paralegal's activities is no excuse. In aggravation, Milner acted with a selfish motive, *see id.* at 9.22(b); she demonstrated a patter of misconduct, *see id.* at 9.22(c); she committed multiple offenses, *see id.* at 9.22(d); she failed to cooperate in the disciplinary proceedings, *see id.* at 9.22(e); several of her clients were vulnerable, *see id.* at 9.22(h); and she exhibited indifference to making restitution, *see id.* at 9.22(j).

The People recommend a three-year suspension to disbarment in Case No. 99PDJ030, and disbarment in Case No. 99PDJ093. The PDJ and Hearing Board find that disbarment is the appropriate sanction considering Milner's chronic neglect in multiple client matters, knowing conversion of client funds, abandonment of two clients, multiple instances of failing to adequately supervise a nonlawyer, aiding another in the unauthorized practice of law, and complete disregard of court orders. The PDJ and Hearing Board further find that Milner must pay restitution to the parties set forth herein within one year of the date of this Order.

III. ORDER

It is therefore Ordered:

1. That KAREN S. MILNER, attorney registration number 21384 is DISBARRED from the practice of law effective 31 days from the date of this Order, and her name shall be stricken from the roll of attorneys licensed to practice law in this state;

2. Milner shall pay or make arrangements to pay the following amounts in restitution to the following clients within 12 (twelve) months of the date of this Order:

    A. Jannette Nelson $2,000;

    B. Cindy Biggers $484.50;

    C. David Schmidt $595; and

    D. Mr. and Mrs. Boroos $1,071.

3. As a condition of readmission, Milner must demonstrate that she has fully complied with Judge Brooks' Orders in the Stephens and Venner matters, paying $2,000 to Gale Marie Stephens, and paying $2,000 to Cobe and Sharon Venner.

4. Milner is ORDERED to pay the costs of these proceedings; the People shall submit a Statement of Costs within 15 (fifteen) days of the date of this Order. Respondent shall have 10 (ten) days thereafter to submit a response thereto.

Colo.O.P.D.J.,2001.

People v. Milner

35 P.3d 670

END OF DOCUMENT

EXERCISES

1. Of the 14 separate matters, how many included some kind of violation related to not communicating with a client adequately?

2. Were you surprised at the number and depth of the violations with which Milner was charged?

3. What role did Kemp play in Milner's office? What did Kemp specifically do wrong?

4. Is it fair that Milner was disbarred but nothing was done to Kemp?

PROLAW—CLIENT RELATIONSHIP MANAGEMENT

BASIC LESSONS

Number	Lesson Title	Concepts Covered
Lesson 1*	Introduction to ProLaw	Understanding the ProLaw interface
Lesson 2	Entering New Matters/Cases, Part 1	Entering a new client matter into ProLaw
Lesson 3	Entering New Matters/Cases, Part 2	Entering new client matters into ProLaw without step-by-step instruction
Lesson 4	Retrieving and Printing Client Event Reports	Searching and printing upcoming events or summaries of "what's going on in a case" for a client
Lesson 5	Case Management Notes	Entering case management notes

*Note: Lesson One—Introduction to ProLaw, is the same for every subject matter (conflicts of interest, client relationship management, time and billing, etc.). If you completed Lesson One in an earlier tutorial, you do not need to repeat it.

WELCOME TO JOHNSON AND SULLIVAN

Welcome to Johnson and Sullivan! We are an active and growing firm with four attorneys and two legal assistants. As you know, you have been hired as a legal assistant intern. We are very happy to have you on board; we can certainly use your help.

At Johnson and Sullivan we use computer systems extensively, so it is necessary that you have a basic understanding of our system. In this lesson you will focus on entering new cases or matters into ProLaw. You will learn how to retrieve and print client event reports and learn how to enter case management notes into the system. Delivering outstanding legal services to our clients is what our firm is about, and the computer skills you learn in this tutorial will help you do that. We know you want to begin using ProLaw immediately, so there is only a short "Getting Started" section that you should read before getting on the computer.

GETTING STARTED

Introduction

Throughout these exercises, information you need to type into the program will be designated in several different ways.

- Keys to be pressed on the keyboard will be designated in brackets, in all caps and bold type (e.g., press the **[ENTER]** key).
- Movements with the mouse will be designated in bold and italics (e.g., *point to File on the Menu Bar and click the mouse*).
- Words or letters that should be typed will be designated in bold and enlarged type (e.g., type **Training Program**).
- Information that is or should be displayed on your computer screen is shown in the following style: **Press ENTER to** continue.

Lesson 1: Introduction to ProLaw

In this lesson, you will load ProLaw and be introduced to the Contacts and Matters functions as an example of the basic interface of the program.

1. Load Windows. To load ProLaw, *click on the **Start** button, point with the mouse to **Programs** or **All Programs**, point to ProLaw Evaluation, and then point and click on **PROLAW**.*
2. When ProLaw is loaded the first time, you may see a window entitled Professional Information for User xx. The screen will ask you to enter your initials and name. At "Initials" type: **PD.** At "Full Name" type: **Pat Doe.** Then, *point and click on the green checkmark in the upper-right part of the window.*
3. You should now have the ProLaw window displayed, including the **Daily Docket** calendar for the current day on your screen.
4. *Point and click on the maximize icon at the top right of the **ProLaw** window* (it is just to the left of the red "X" and looks like two layered squares. If you point to an icon with your mouse for more than a second, the icon title will be displayed).
5. Notice that there is a column of icons on the left edge of the screen. These icons give you access to ProLaw's major functions; they include Contacts, Matters, Events, Files, Transactions, Journals, Ledger, and Reports.

6. Below is a table showing the purpose of each function in ProLaw.

ProLaw Icon/Function	Purpose
CONTACTS	Contains contact information for all clients, parties, attorneys, judges, etc. It is an electronic address book. Conflict of interest searches can also be performed using this function.
MATTERS	Contains detailed information about every case/client matter. This includes billing information, notes about the case, related contacts, related matters, and settlement information, among others.
EVENTS	Allows the user to run queries for a specific set of docket entries and print docket reports.
FILES	Allows the user to check files in and out and report on the location and status of physical file folders.
TRANSACTIONS	Allows the user to create time entries, run cost recovery imports, edit pre-bills, and produce statements.
JOURNALS	Allows the user to enter checks, cash receipts, reconcile accounts, and produce financial reports.
LEDGER	Allows the user to view client billing and payment history and view statement images and unbilled statements.
REPORTS	Allows the user to produce and print a wide variety of reports.

7. *Point and click with the mouse on* Contacts. The Contacts window is now displayed.

8. *Point and click with the mouse on* Quick find, located in the View section of the Shortcuts pane. *In the* Search for *field press the* **[BACKSPACE]** key. This will clear the field and search for all contacts in the database. Press the **[ENTER]** key.

9. Press the **[DOWN ARROW]** cursor key or *use the mouse* to scroll down through all of the contacts. Notice that the database is already populated with information.

10. *Scroll back until you find the entry for* Adam Schnieder, which is located near the bottom of the list. *Point and double-click on* Adam Schnieder.

11. Notice that the **Adam Schnieder—Contact** window is now displayed. You can now see the contact information for Adam Schnieder, including name, class (i.e., type of entry; in this case "client"), address, phone number, etc.

12. In the **Adam Schnieder—Contact** window, *point and click on the* Close *icon (the red "X" located in the upper-right corner of the window) to close this window.*

13. The "Contacts" window should now be displayed. *Point and click on "Recent"* (under "Shortcuts" "View"). Notice that only the entry for Adam Schnieder is listed. The Recent command contains a list of your most recently used contacts.

14. In the Contacts window, *point and click on the* Close *icon (the red "X" located in the upper right corner of the window) to close this window.*

15. You should now be back where you started at the **Daily Docket** screen.

16. *Point and click with the mouse on* **Matters.** The **Matters** window is now displayed.

17. *Point and click with the mouse on* Quick find, if it is not already displayed (located in the **View** section of the **Shortcuts** pane). In the **Search for** field, press the **[BACKSPACE]** key. This will clear the field and search for all matters in the database. Press the **[ENTER]** key.

18. In the Matters window, *point and click with the mouse on the* maximize *icon at the top right corner of the window* (located just to the left of the Close icon; it looks like two layered squares). This will allow you to see additional columns.

19. Press the **[DOWN ARROW]** cursor key or *use the mouse* to scroll down through all of the matters.

20. *Point and double-click with the mouse on the first entry* (Matter ID 1000-001—Maguire, Robert, Maguire—Chapter 7).

21. The **1000-001—Matter** window should now be displayed. Notice that there are a number of tabs in the window, including General, Notes, Billing, Related Contacts, and others. *Point and click on each of these tabs.* Then, close the **1000-01—Matter** window by *pointing and clicking on the* Close *icon.*

22. The **Matters** window should now be displayed. *Point and click on* **Recent** (located in the "View" section of the "Shortcuts" pane). Notice that only the "Maguire, Robert, Maguire—Chapter 7" matter is listed.

23. *In the* Matters *window, point and click on the* Close *icon to close this window.*

24. You should now be back where you started at the **Daily Docket** screen.

25. This concludes Lesson 1. To exit ProLaw, *point and click on the* Close *icon in the* ProLaw *window to close the program.* Alternatively, you may *point and click on* **File** *on the menu bar and then click on* **Exit.**

Lesson 2: Entering New Matters/Cases, Part 1

In this lesson, you will enter a new matter/case into ProLaw.

1. Load Windows. To load ProLaw, *click on the* Start *button, point with the mouse to* **Programs** *or* **All Programs,** *point to* **ProLaw Evaluation,** *and then point and click on* **PROLAW.**

2. You should now have the ProLaw window displayed, including the **Daily Docket** calendar for the current day on your screen.

3. *Point and click with the mouse on* Matters.

4. *Point and click with the mouse on* Quick find and press the **[BACKSPACE]** key until the Search for field is empty.

5. *Point and click with the mouse on the* Add item *icon on the toolbar at the top left of the window* (located just under **File** on the menu bar; it looks a file folder with a sun on it).

6. The **New Matter** window with an empty record should now be displayed. Your cursor should now be in the Desc. field. Note: The **Matter ID** field is automatically assigned by ProLaw, so you do not need to enter anything in this field. Also, the **Client Sort** field is automatically completed by ProLaw, so you need not enter anything in this field either.

7. In the **Desc.** (i.e., description) field, type **Kearns v. Pritchard** and then press the **[TAB]** key four times. Your cursor should now be in the **Full name** field.

8. In the **Full name** field, type **William Kearns** and then press the **[ENTER]** key. Before you can enter the full name of the client, he or she must be entered into ProLaw as a Contact.

9. The **Contacts List** window should now be displayed. "William Kearns" is entered in the **Search for** field. Notice that nothing has been returned in the **Quick find** pane. You must now add William Kearns as a contact.

10. *Point and click with the mouse on the* Add item *icon on the toolbar at the top left of the window* (located just under **File** on the menu bar; it looks a file folder with a sun on it).

11. The **New Contact** window should now be displayed. "William Kearns" should be entered in the Full Name field.

12. Press the **[TAB]** key two times. Your cursor should now be in the **Class** field.

13. With the cursor in the **Class** field, *point and click with the mouse on the down arrow of the drop-down box at the right edge of the field. Using the cursor keys or mouse, scroll down to* Client *and point and click on it.* Client should now be shown in the **Class** field.

14. *Press the* [TAB] *key.*

15. *Point and click with the mouse on the* General *tab.*

16. *Point and click in the blank field under the* General *tab.* This is where the mailing address goes.

17. Type **3332 53rd Street** and then press the **[ENTER]** key.

18. Type **Winter Park, FL 45063.**

19. You are now ready to enter a phone number for Mr. Kearns. Find the white box under Phone Number. *Point and click with the mouse on the* Add item *icon (a folder with a sun on it) to the right of* **Phone Number, Ext., Type, Main.** (Please note that there are three "Add" icons on the screen; select the one to the right of **Phone Number**). When you select the **Add item** icon, you are now allowed to type a phone number.

20. Type **676-862-7888** and then press the **[TAB]** key two times.

21. The cursor should now be in the **Type** field. *Point and click with the mouse on the down arrow of the drop-down box in the* Type *field. Point and click on the* Home *option* and then press the **[TAB]** key.

22. To enter the new contact, *point and click with the mouse on the icon that looks like a green checkmark in the upper-right corner of the* New Contact *window.*

23. The **New Matter** window should once again be displayed. Notice that Mr. Kearns' **Class, Phone,** and **Address** have all been entered.

24. *Point and click with the mouse on the down arrow of the drop-down box in the* Area of law *field* (this field is toward the bottom left of the **New Matter** window). *Point and click with the mouse on* **Litigation (General).**

25. *Point and click with the mouse on the down arrow of the drop-down box in the* Type *field. Point and click on* **Hourly Fee.** This tells ProLaw that the client will be billed on an hourly basis.

26. You are now ready to assign a paralegal to the case. *Point and click with the mouse on the* Add item *icon (a file folder with a sun on it) to the right of* **Assigned Type, Initials, Professional, Percent** *in the lower-right corner of the* New Matter *window.*

27. Your cursor should now be under Assigned Type. Choose **Paralegal** from the dropdown list and then press **[TAB].**

28. Your cursor should now be under Initials. *Point and click on the ellipses (three periods). In the* Professionals List *window, scroll down until you see* Pat Doe. *Point and click on* Pat Doe. *Then, point and click in the* Professional Type *column for Pat Doe. Choose* Paralegal *from the drop-down list.*

29. *Point and click with the mouse on the icon that looks like a green check-mark in the upper-right corner of the* Professionals list *window.* You should now be back at the **New Matter** window, and Pat Doe should be shown as the paralegal assigned to the case.

30. You are now ready to assign an attorney to the case. *Point and click with the mouse on the* Add item *icon (a folder with a sun on it) to the right of* **Assigned Type, Initials, Professional, and Percent** *in the lower-right corner of the* New Matter *window.*

31. Your cursor should now be under Assigned Type. *Choose* Billing *from the drop-down box* and then press **[TAB].**
    Your cursor should now be under Initials. *Point and click on the ellipses. In the* Professionals list *window, point and double-click on* Courtney C. Markham, Partner.

32. *In the* New Matter *window, point and click on the* **Notes** *tab.* In the blank field on the left, type **Mr. Kearns is a correctional officer at a maximum-security prison. Mr. Kearns was attacked and severely injured on the job. He is considering claims against his attackers and prison management for ineffective security and OSHA violations. His attackers were David Smith and Mark Melcher. The warden of the facility is Wayne Pritchard.** The notes field is where a variety of notes and comments can be made about a case, including a summary of the case. This notes field can hold up to 16 pages of information.

33. *Point and click on* **He** *for the* **Client Pronoun** *and* **They** *for the* **Opposing Pronoun.**

34. *Point and click on the* Billing *tab.* Notice that there are many options in ProLaw for how to customize billing for a client. The default values will work fine for this client.

35. *Point and click on the* Events *tab.* This is where a variety of events and docket entries can be entered. We will enter items in **Events** in future lessons.

36. *Point and click on the* Inquiry *tab.* Once billing and payments have begun, you can see an overall financial and billing summary of the case.

37. *Point and click on the* Litigation *tab.* This is where you can enter information about the case, including names of parties, the caption of the case, the court, the judge, and other information. Because the case is not filed, we will not enter anything yet.

38. *Point and click back on the* General *tab.*

39. You have now entered the basic information regarding a new matter. *Point and click on the green checkmark on the toolbar just under* **Help on the Menu Bar.**

40. *Point and click on the* Close *icon in the* **New Matter** *window.*

41. To confirm that the new matter has been saved, *point and click on* Quick find *if it is not already displayed.* Type **Kearns** in the Search for field. *In the* Search by *field, choose* Client Sort.

42. "Kearns, William" should now be displayed. *Double-click on the "Kearns, William" matter.* ProLaw retrieves the matter that you just entered.

43. *Click the* Close *icon in this window. Point and click on the* Close *icon in the* Matters *window.*

44. *Point and click with the mouse on* Contacts. In the **Search for** field, type **Kearns.** *Double-click with the mouse on the* **William Kearns** *contact that is displayed.*

45. *The* **William Kearns—Contact** *window should now be displayed. Point and click on the* Related Matters *tab.* Notice that the Kearns v. Pritchard case is now associated with Mr. Kearns' contact information.

46. This concludes Lesson 2. To exit ProLaw, *point and click on the* Close *icon in the* **ProLaw** *window to close the program.* Alternatively, you may *point and click on* **File** *on the menu bar and then click on* **Exit.**

Lesson 3: Entering New Matters/ Cases, Part 2

In this lesson, you will enter two new matters into ProLaw without step-by-step instruction.

1. Load Windows. To load ProLaw, *click on the* Start *button, point with the mouse to* **Programs** *or* **All Programs,** *point to* **ProLaw Evaluation,** *and then point and click on* **PROLAW.**

2. You should now have the ProLaw window displayed including the **Daily Docket** calendar for the current day on your screen.

3. *Point and click with the mouse on* Matters.

4. *Point and click with the mouse on* Quick Find *and press the* [**BACK-SPACE**] key *until the* Search for *field is empty.*

5. *Point and click with the mouse on the* Add item *icon on the toolbar at the top left of the window, just under* **File** *on the Menu bar.*

6. The "New Matter" window with an empty record should now be displayed. You are now ready to enter a new matter into ProLaw. Remember that you do not need to enter anything in the "Matter ID:" and "Client Sort" Fields, as ProLaw will enter these for you. Use the following information to create two additional matters. If you have problems, refer back

to Lesson 2. Also, if at any time you would like to quit the current new matter form you are working on and start over, you will need to point and click on the Delete Item icon (located just to the right of the Add item icon; it looks like a folder with a red X over it).

Matter 1:

Field	Data to Input
Desc.:	Long v. PBB Electronic Systems
Full name:	Tracy Long
Add Additional Client Contact (you will need to add a new contact):	Tracy Long
	18151 Mission Street
	Greensboro, NC 08113
	Phone: 617-343-4834
	Class: Client
	Salutation: Tracy
Area of Law:	Litigation (General)
Type:	Contingent
Assigned Type:	Billing
Initials:	Julie Moore
Notes (Under "Notes" Tab)	Products liability case where a sophisticated inhouse computer and electronics system started fire and burned down the client's house.
	Client Pronoun: He
	Opposing Pronoun: They

Matter 2:

Field	Data to Input
Desc.:	Mitchell Will/Trust Preparation
Full name:	David Mitchell
Add Additional Client Contact: (you will need to add a new contact)	David Mitchell
	43534 Clifton Lane
	Cleveland, OH 23343
	Phone: 886-947-4468
	Class: Client
	Salutation: Dave
Area of Law:	Estate Planning
Type:	Flat Fee
Assigned Type:	Billing
Initials	David Simon
Notes (Under "Notes" Tab)	Mr. Mitchell has sizeable assets and would like to run a number of estate planning scenarios and prepare a will and trust.
	Client Pronoun: He
	Opposing Pronoun: They

7. This concludes Lesson 3. To exit ProLaw, *point and click on the* Close *icon in the* **ProLaw** *window to close the program.* Alternatively, you may *point and click on* **File** *on the menu bar and then click on* **Exit.**

Lesson 4: Retrieving and Printing Client Event Reports

In this lesson, you will retrieve and print a client event report. Many law offices will periodically send to their clients a listing of past or upcoming events in their case. It is a way to keep the client informed about their case with minimal effort. Since this information is already contained in ProLaw, it is extremely easy to print out or e-mail the information to a client.

1. Load Windows. To load ProLaw, *click on the* Start *button, point with the mouse to* **Programs** *or* **All Programs,** *point to* **ProLaw Evaluation,** *and then point and click on* **PROLAW.**
2. You should now have the ProLaw window displayed, including the **Daily Docket** calendar for the current day on your screen.
3. *Point and click with the mouse on* Matters.
4. *Point and click with the mouse on* Quick find. In the **Search for** field, press the **[BACKSPACE]** key. This will clear the field and search for all contacts in the database. Press the **[ENTER]** key.
5. Press the **[DOWN ARROW]** cursor key or *use the mouse to scroll down through all of the contacts.* Notice that the database is already populated with information.
6. Find the matter of **Smith, Joseph, Incorporation, Matter ID 1002-001.** *Point and double-click on the record.*
7. The **1002-001 Matter** window should now be displayed. *Point and click on the* Events *tab.*
8. Notice that two events are listed; one for 1/5/2004: Engagement letter (Corporate) and another for 1/24/2005: New Incorporation.
9. *Point and click with the mouse on the* "+" (**plus sign**) *just to the left of* 1/24/2005: New Incorporation.
10. Notice that a number of additional subentries have been listed under 1/24/2005: New Incorporation.
11. Producing a report with this information is very easy. *Point and click with the mouse on* File *on the Menu Bar and then on* Print Reports.
12. The **Matters Reports** window should now be displayed. *Point and click with the mouse on the down arrow of the drop-down box under* Report Format; *scroll down and choose* Listing with Events.
13. *Point and click with the mouse on* Preview Report *in the Shortcuts pane.* The **Matters Listing with Events** report for the Smith, Joseph Incorporation matter should now be displayed.
14. There is no need to actually print the report, so *point and click with the mouse on the* Close *icon in the* **Listing with Events—Report** *window.*
15. *Point and click with the mouse on the* Close *icon in the* Matters Report *window.*

16. This concludes Lesson 4. To exit ProLaw, *point and click on the* Close *icon in the* **ProLaw** *window to close the program.* Alternatively, you may *point and click on* **File** *on the menu bar and then click on* **Exit.**

Lesson 5: Case Management Notes

In this lesson, you will learn to enter case management notes into ProLaw. This is very convenient for recording any notes in the case, such as client phone calls or opposing counsel phone calls. Case management notes allow you to document exactly what happened on the call. It also allows you or anyone else working on the case to see what has transpired in the case.

1. Load Windows. To load ProLaw, *click on the* Start *button, point with the mouse to* **Programs** *or* **All Programs,** *point to* **ProLaw Evaluation,** *and then point and click on* **PROLAW.**

2. You should now have the ProLaw window displayed, including the **Daily Docket** calendar for the current day on your screen.

3. *Point and click with the mouse on* Matters.

4. *Point and click with the mouse on* Quick find.

5. *In the* Search by *field, point and click on the down arrow of the drop-down box.* Notice that you can search by **Area of law, Client Sort, Matter Description, Matter ID,** and other options. *Point and click on* Client Sort.

6. In the **Search for** field, type **Hero** (for Hero Sandwich Company). Notice that the Matter ID 1008-001, Gerald v. The Hero Sandwich Company case is shown.

7. *Point and double-click with the mouse on the case.* **The 1008-001— Matter** window should now be displayed.

8. *Point and click with the mouse on the* Events *tab.*

9. Notice that there are five icons displayed under the tab names. *Hover your mouse over each icon to display its name.* The names of the icons are **In-clude dockets, Include completed dockets, Include documents, Include notes,** and **Include reminders.** These icons toggle each item off or on. If there is a black box around the icon, the icon is turned on. For example, the **Include completed dockets** is toggled on, so the event listing just below the icons shows the completed docket entry of 1/18/2004: New Litigation Matter Checklist.

10. *Point and click with the mouse on the* Include completed dockets *icon.* Notice that the **Include completed dockets** icon no longer has a black box around it and that the **1/18/2004: New Litigation Matter Checklist** is no longer shown.

11. *Point and click with the mouse back on the* Include completed dockets *icon,* and the **1/18/2004: New Litigation Matter Checklist** is again shown.

12. Notice that there are several more icons displayed on the right side of the window. *Hover the mouse on the icons displayed under tabs on the right side of the screen.* The names of the icons are **Add docket, Add document,** and **Add note.** This is where you can add these types of entries to the matter.

13. *Point and click with the mouse on the* Add note *icon.* A blank note has now been opened in the lower-right corner of the screen. The current date

and the initials for PD have been entered. The cursor should be in the **Type** field.

14. *Point and click with the mouse on the ellipses (three dots). Point and double-click with the mouse on* Telephone call notes.

15. Press the **[TAB]** key. Your cursor should now be in the field under **Notes**. In the **Notes** field, type **Call from John Linden, CEO, regarding his interrogatories. He asked if I remembered the name of the witness that had supposedly witnessed the slip and fall accident. I looked at the plaintiff's deposition and told him that on page 42 that plaintiff says it was "Sarah Johnson." He thanked me and hung up.**

16. *Point and click on the* Refresh Events *icon (it is yellow and looks like a wraparound arrow; it is the icon farthest to the right on the row of icons under the tabs).* Notice that the note has now been entered on the left side of the screen.

17. To add another note, *point and click with the mouse on the* Add note *icon.* Add the following notes:

Note 2:

Type:	Note to Input
E-mail	Opposing counsel e-mailed me today and asked if we would not mind giving her an additional five days to respond to our Motion to Quash. I spoke to Jim, the managing attorney, and he said that was fine.

Note 3:

Type:	Note to Input
Note	I spoke to Jim and the client about the possibility of running a criminal background check on the plaintiff to see if he had a record or had any convictions related to fraud or deceit. Both agreed this was a good avenue to proceed with.

Note 4:

Type:	Note to Input
Settlement Notes	Opposing counsel called and offered $10,500 to settle the case. Jim was in a deposition but during a break he told me to call the client and let him know what the offer was. I contacted the client and he said for Jim to make a counter offer of $5,000. Jim will make the counter offer tomorrow.

18. Notice that the date and note type have been entered to the left. *Point and click with the mouse on each note.* Notice that the full text of the note appears to the right.

19. Using case management notes like this, you can easily track exactly what is happening in a case. ProLaw also offers the user the option of sending the note as an e-mail to the client, supervising attorney, or other interested parties. Case management notes are an important aspect of client relationship management. They allow a user to quickly bring up exactly what has transpired in a case when a client calls.

20. This concludes Lesson 5. To exit ProLaw, *point and click on the* Close *icon in the* **ProLaw** *window to close the program.* Alternatively, you may *point and click on* **File** *on the menu bar and then click on* Exit.

This concludes the ProLaw Relationship Management Hands-on Exercises.

5

LEGAL FEES, TIMEKEEPING, AND BILLING

After you read this chapter, you should be able to:

- Differentiate between timekeeping and billing.
- Recognize major types of legal fee agreements.
- Know the difference between billable and non-billable time.
- Explain the concept of value billing.
- Discuss how the billing process works and what it entails.
- Differentiate between an earned and an unearned retainer.

When a Chicago-based law firm submitted its bill, the client company suspected something might have been wrong. Years later, an audit revealed that the invoice included nontechnical deposition summaries by paralegals, charged at four to five pages per hour. The usual rate, however, is 20 to 25 pages an hour. The paralegals were apparently working at 20 to 25 percent of the normal rate, so the client company was being billed four times what it should have been for that service.[1]

***

A federal grand jury indicted two men allegedly conspiring to defraud an insurance company by having tens of thousands of dollars in checks issued for expenses and legal services that were never provided. The defendants were a former litigation supervisor for the insurance company and a former partner in the law firm representing the company. The grand jury indicted them on 1 felony count of conspiracy, 3 felony counts of mail fraud, and 20 felony counts of wire fraud as a result of checks written over four years.

THE DIFFERENCE BETWEEN TIMEKEEPING AND BILLING

timekeeping
The process of tracking time for the purpose of billing clients.

In the legal environment, **timekeeping** is the process of tracking time for the purpose of billing clients. The obvious reason private attorneys and legal assistants keep track of their time is to bill clients. However, many corporate, government, and legal services/aid practices also keep time records for other reasons. Timekeeping can be used to manage and oversee what cases attorneys and legal assistants are working on and whether they are spending too much or too little time on certain cases; it can be used to evaluate the performance of attorneys and legal assistants and to help determine promotions and raises; and it also can be used to evaluate what types of cases are the most beneficial and profitable for the office.

billing
The process of issuing invoices for the purpose of collecting monies for legal services performed and being reimbursed for expenses.

Billing is the process of issuing invoices for the purpose of collecting monies for legal services performed and being reimbursed for expenses. The lifeblood of any organization depends on its ability to raise cash and be paid for the services it renders. In most cases, private law practices must be able to generate billings on at least a monthly basis to generate the cash they need to meet their expenses, such as rent, utilities, and salaries. Attorneys and legal assistants in corporate and government practices also need to know about billing to ensure that when they hire outside counsel (private law firms), the corporation or government gets the most for its money.

WHY DO LEGAL ASSISTANTS NEED TO KNOW TIMEKEEPING AND BILLING?

There are several reasons why legal assistants need to know about timekeeping and billing. In most private law practices, legal assistants are required to track their time so it can be charged to the case(s) on which they are working. Many law practices require legal assistants to bill a minimum number of hours a year. It is important to remember that private law firms are fundamentally businesses, and, like any business, their function is to make money, operate at a profit, and earn money for their owners. Therefore, the billing of time to a firm's clients is crucial to its operations and success as a business. A recent survey of legal assistants found that legal assistants were most often expected to bill between 26 and 40 hours a week (1,352 and 2,080 annually). Thus, it is necessary for legal assistants to understand how timekeeping and billing works. Legal assistants are sometimes discharged from their jobs because they fail to bill the required number of hours. The issue of tracking time and billing a minimum number of hours is very important in many offices.

In addition, legal assistants are sometimes put in charge of actually running the timekeeping and billing system, including managing the timekeeping process and generating bills. This usually occurs in smaller law offices. In those cases, it is important for legal assistants not only to know the process but also to know how to actually run and operate the system. Timekeeping and billing are important issues because the survival of law offices depends on their ability to track and bill time. However, before exploring the fundamentals of timekeeping and billing in depth, you first need a background in legal fee agreements, legal expenses, and trust accounts.

KINDS OF LEGAL FEE AGREEMENTS

Legal fees can be structured in many different ways. The kind of legal fee depends on the type of case or client matter, the specific circumstances of each particular client, and the law practice's preference toward certain types of fee agreements. Fee agreements can be hourly rate fees, contingency fees, flat fees, retainer fees, and others.

Hourly Rate Fees

An **hourly rate fee** is a fee for legal services that is billed to the client by the hour, at an agreed-upon rate. For example, suppose a client hires an attorney to draft a business contract. The client agrees to pay $250 for every hour the attorney spends drafting the contract and advising the client. If the attorney spent four hours working on the contract, the client would owe the attorney $1,000 ($250 × four hours equals $1,000).

One of the frustrations for clients regarding legal professionals billing by the hour is that a client has no idea what the total cost of the matter will be. Figure 5-1 contains a fee projection worksheet for a case in litigation. Using a tool like this at the beginning of a matter, a client can get an idea what the total cost will be.

hourly rate fee
A fee for legal services that is billed to the client by the hour at an agreed-upon rate.

**Figure 5-1
Fee Projection
Worksheet**

Source: Calloway, &
Robertson. (2002). Winning
alternatives to the billable hour
(p. 214). American Bar
Association

Johnson, Beck & Talyor Law Firm **Fee Projection Worksheet (Litigation)**			

Case: _____
Date: _____

	Partner	Associate	Paralegal
Billing Rate	$325	$225	$85

No.	Description	Partner Hours	Associate Hours	Paralegal Others
I.	Preliminary Work			
II.	Factual Investigation			
III.	Strategy Conference			
IV.	Initial Legal Research			
	Issue 1 _____			
	Issue 2 _____			
V.	Complaint/Answer/Counterclaim			
VI.	Motions (non discovery)			
	A. _____			
	B. _____			
VII.	Witness Interviews			
VIII.	Discovery			
	A. Drafting Interrogatories			
	B. Answering Interrogatories			
	C. Drafting Discover Requests			
	D. Reviewing Produced Documents & E-Discovery			
	E. Responding to Doc. Requests			
	F. Oppposing Party Depos			
	Party 1: _____			
	Witness 1: _____			
	G. Our Depos			
	Our Client: _____			
	Witness 2: _____			
	Witness 3: _____			
IX.	Discovery Motions			
X.	Additional Legal Research			
XI.	Motions (Substantive)			
	Motion 1: _____			
	Motion 2: _____			
XII.	Pretrial Memoranda/Conf			
XIII.	Settlement conference			
XIV.	Trial			
	Preparation Days _____			
	Trial Days _____			
XV.	Miscellaneous phone calls/strategy			
	Total Hours			
	TOTAL PROJECTED FEES			

Hourly rate agreements can be complicated. Law offices have several specific types of hourly rate contracts, including the following.

- Attorney or legal assistant hourly rate
- Client hourly rate
- Blended hourly rate fee
- Activity hourly rate

Some law practices use a combination of these to bill clients.

ATTORNEY OR LEGAL ASSISTANT HOURLY RATE   The **attorney** or **legal assistant hourly rate** is based on the attorney's or legal assistant's level of expertise and experience in a particular area; Figure 5-2 is an example of this type of contract. If a partner or shareholder worked on a case, his or her hourly rate charge might be considerably more than that of an associate or legal assistant's hourly rate charge. Partners typically can earn from $200 to $500 an hour. Legal assistants typically charge from $60 to $100 an hour. The difference in price is based on the expertise of the individual working on the case and on locally acceptable rates. In this type of fee agreement, it is possible for a client to be billed at several different rates in a given period if several attorneys or legal assistants work on a matter, because they all may have different rates.

attorney or **legal assistant hourly rate**
Fee based on the attorney's or legal assistant's level of expertise and experience in a particular area.

CLIENT HOURLY RATE   The **client hourly rate** method is based on one hourly charge for the client, regardless of which attorney works on the case and what he or she does on the case. For example, if an insurance company hired a law practice to represent it, the insurance company and the law practice might negotiate a client hourly charge of $225 for attorneys and $85 for legal assistants. This means that no matter which attorney or legal assistant works on the case, whether the attorney or legal assistant has one year's or twenty years' experience, and regardless of what the attorney or legal assistant does (e.g., making routine phone calls or appearing in court), the insurance company would be charged $225 an hour for attorney time or $85 an hour for legal assistant time.

client hourly rate
Fee based on one hourly charge for the client, regardless of which attorney works on the case and what he or she does on the case.

BLENDED HOURLY RATE FEE   A **blended hourly rate fee** is an hourly rate that is set taking into account the blend or mix of law office staff working on the matter. The "blend" includes the mix among associates, partners, and (sometimes) legal assistants working on the matter. Some states only allow the "blend" to include associates and partners, while other states allow legal assistants to be included. Billing is simpler, because there is one rate for all legal assistant and attorney time spent on the case. The bill is thus easier for the law office to produce and easier for the client to read. Some states will allow legal assistants to have their own "blend" and have one rate for all legal assistants, whether experienced or inexperienced.

blended hourly rate fee
An hourly rate that is set taking into account the blend or mix of attorneys working on the matter.

Figure 5-2   Attorney/Legal Assistant Hourly Rate Contract

HOURLY RATE CONTRACT FOR LEGAL SERVICES

This contract for legal services is entered into by and between H. Thomas Weber (hereinafter "Client") and Johnson, Beck & Taylor (hereinafter "Attorneys") on this _____ day of December, 200_. The following terms and conditions constitute the entirety of the agreement between Attorneys and Client and said agreement supersedes and is wholly separate and apart from any previous written or oral agreements.

1. Client hereby agrees to employ Attorneys and Attorneys hereby agree to represent Client in connection with a contract dispute in Jefferson County District Court of Clients claim against Westbridge Manufacturing.
2. Client agrees to pay a retainer fee of **$5,000.00,** which will be held in Attorney's trust account until earned.
3. Client agrees to pay associate attorneys at **$225** per hour, partners at **$200** per hour, legal assistants at **$80** per hour and senior legal assistants at **$100** per hour for legal services rendered regarding the matter in paragraph one. Attorneys are not hereby obligated to take an appeal from any judgment at the trial court level; if an occasion for an appeal arises, Attorneys and Client hereby expressly agree that employment for such an appeal must be arranged by a separate contract between Attorneys and Client.
4. Client agrees to reimburse Attorneys for all expenses incurred in connection with said matter; and Client agrees to advance all expenses requested by Attorneys during the duration of this contract. Client understands that he is ultimately responsible for the payment of all expenses incurred in connection with this matter.
5. Client understands that Attorneys will bill Client periodically (usually on a monthly or quarterly basis, depending on how quickly the case moves through the system) for copying costs at the rate of $.25 cents per copy, postage and handling costs, long-distance telephone costs, travel costs, and other costs, and that Client is obligated to make payments upon said billing for said fees and expenses described at paragraphs (2), (3), and (4) above, or otherwise satisfy said fees and expenses. Attorneys will also bill Client for all deposition costs incurred and Client is solely responsible for said deposition costs and Client will be required to advance the sum of $2,500 (or more as necessary) for trial costs (including subpoenas, travel costs, and preparation costs) once the case is set for trial.
6. Client understands and agrees that this litigation may take two to five years or longer to complete and that he will make himself available for Attorneys to confer with and generally to assist Attorneys in said matter. Client agrees he will not discuss the matter of his litigation with any unauthorized person at any time or in any way. Client understands and agrees that Attorneys may withdraw from representation of Client upon proper notice. Client further understands that he can apply for judicial review and approval of this fee agreement if he so desires.
7. Client agrees that associate counsel may be employed at the discretion of Attorneys and that any attorney so employed may be designated to appear on Client's behalf and undertake Client's representation in this matter and such representation shall be upon the same terms as set out herein. **Client understands that Attorneys cannot and do not guarantee any particular or certain relief and expressly state that they cannot promise or guarantee Client will receive any money damages or money settlement.**

The undersigned hereby voluntarily executes this agreement with a full understanding of same and without coercion or duress. All agreements contained herein are severable and in the event any of them shall be deemed to be invalid by any competent court, this contract shall be interpreted as if such invalid agreements or covenants were not contained herein. Client acknowledges receiving a fully executed copy of this contract.

_____   _____

Date

_____   _____

Date   JOHNSON, BECK & TAYLOR

NOTE: THIS IS ONLY AN EXAMPLE AND IS NOT INTENDED TO BE A FORM; CHECK WITH YOUR STATE BAR FOR A PROPER FORM.

ACTIVITY HOURLY RATE   An **activity hourly rate** is based on the different hourly rates, depending on what type of service or activity is actually performed. For example, offices using this approach might bill attorney time to clients as follows.

Court appearances	$300 per hour
Legal research by attorneys	$225 per hour
Drafting by attorneys	$200 per hour
Telephone calls by attorneys	$150 per hour
Legal research by legal assistants	$85 per hour
Drafting by legal assistants	$80 per hour

This is sliding-scale hourly fee based on the difficulty of an activity. Hourly rate agreements, no matter what the type, are the most common kind of fee agreement.

Contingency Fees

A **contingency fee** is a fee that is collected if the attorney successfully represents the client. The attorney is entitled to a certain percentage of the total amount of money awarded to the client. If the client's case is not won, and no money is recovered, the attorney collects no legal fees but is still entitled to be reimbursed for all expenses incurred (see Figure 5-3). Contingency fees are typically used in representing plaintiffs in personal injury cases, workers' compensation cases, employment cases, medical malpractice, and other types of cases in which monetary damages are generated. The individual who would like to bring the lawsuit usually has little or no money to pay legal fees up front. Contingency fees typically range from 20 to 50 percent.

For example, suppose a client hires an attorney to file a personal injury claim regarding an automobile accident the client was in. The client has no money but agrees to pay the attorney 20 percent of any money that is recovered (plus legal expenses) before the case is filed, 25 percent of any money that is recovered after the case is filed but before trial, and 33 percent of any money recovered during trial or after appeal. Suppose the claim is settled after the case is filed but before trial for $10,800. Suppose, also, that the legal expenses the attorney incurred were $800. Under most state laws, legal expenses are paid first and then the contingency fee is calculated. The attorney would deduct the expenses off the top and the remaining $10,000 would be divided according to the contingency fee agreement. Because the suit was settled after the case was filed but before the trial, the attorney would be entitled to receive 25 percent of any recovery. The attorney would be entitled to $2,500, and the client would be entitled to 75 percent, or $7,500 (see Figure 5-4).

Contingency fee agreements must be in writing. Figure 5-3 contains a sample contingency fee contract. Some states put a cap or a maximum percentage on what an attorney can collect in areas such as workers' compensation and medical malpractice claims; for example, some states prevent attorneys from receiving more than a 25 percent contingency in a workers' compensation case. Contingency fees, by their nature, are risky—if no money is recovered, the attorney receives no fee. However, even if no money is recovered, the client must still pay legal expenses such as filing fees and photocopying. Contingency fees and hourly fees also may be used together; some offices reduce their hourly fee and charge a contingency fee.

activity hourly rate
Fee based on the different hourly rates, depending on what type of service or activity is actually performed.

contingency fee
Fee collected if the attorney successfully represents the client.

Figure 5-3   Contingency Fee Contract

CONTINGENCY FEE CONTRACT FOR LEGAL SERVICES

Date:

Name: D.O.B.

Address: Phone:

1. I hereby employ **Johnson, Beck & Taylor** (hereinafter "attorneys") to perform legal services in connection with the following matter as described below:

   Personal injury claims arising out of an automobile accident which occurred January 12, 2005, on Interstate I-805.

2. I agree to pay a nonrefundable retainer fee of <u>$2,500</u> plus

3. I agree attorneys will receive <u>20%</u> of any recovery, if prior to filing suit.

   I agree attorneys will receive <u>25%</u> of any recovery, if prior to pretrial conference.

   I agree attorneys will receive <u>33%</u> of any recovery, if after first trial begins.

   I agree attorneys will receive <u>33%</u> of any recovery, if after appeal or second trial begins.

   Attorneys are not hereby obligated to take an appeal from any judgment at the trial court level; if an occasion for an appeal arises, attorneys and client hereby expressly agree that employment for such an appeal will be arranged by a separate contract between these parties. Further, I agree that attorneys will be entitled to the applicable above-mentioned percentage of recovery minus whatever a court may award, if I am a prevailing party and the court awards fees following my request therefor.

4. As to the expenses of litigation: I agree to reimburse attorneys for all expenses incurred in connection with said matter, and any expenses not fully paid as incurred may be deducted from my portion of any recovery. I agree to advance any and all expenses requested by attorneys during the duration of this contract. I agree to make an advance of expenses upon execution of this contract in the amount of <u>$1,500</u>. I understand that these litigation expenses do not pertain to the retainer fee or percentage of any recovery, and I am ultimately responsible for the payment of all litigation expenses.

5. I understand that attorneys will bill client periodically, and that client is obligated to make payments upon said billing for said fees and expenses described at paragraphs (2) and (4), or otherwise satisfy said fees and expenses.

6. I understand and agree that this litigation may take two to five years (or longer) to complete, and that I will make myself available for attorneys to confer with, and generally to assist attorneys in said matter. I will not discuss the matter of my litigation with an unauthorized person at any time in any way. I understand and agree that attorneys may withdraw from representation of client at any time upon proper notice.

7. I agree that associate counsel may be employed at the discretion of JOHNSON, BECK & TAYLOR, and that any attorney so employed may be designated to appear on my behalf and undertake my representation in this matter and such representation shall be upon the same terms as set out herein. Attorneys have not guaranteed, nor can they guarantee, any particular or certain relief.

The undersigned herewith executes this agreement with a full understanding of same, without coercion or duress, and understands the same to be the only agreement between the parties with regard to the above matter, and that if any other terms are to be added to this contract, the same will not be binding, unless and until they are reduced to writing and signed by all parties to this contract. I acknowledge receiving a fully executed copy of this contract. Further, the undersigned Client understands that said Client is entitled to apply for judicial review and approval of this fee agreement, if Client so desires.

———————   ————————————————————————————————————

Date

———————   ————————————————————————————————————

Date   JOHNSON, BECK & TAYLOR

NOTE: THIS IS ONLY AN EXAMPLE AND IS NOT INTENDED TO BE A FORM; CHECK YOUR STATE BAR FOR A PROPER FORM.

Written Contingency Fee Agreement Provisions

Attorney receives
- 20% of any money recovered (plus legal expenses) before case is filed.
- 25% of any money recovered (plus legal expenses) after case is filed, but before trial.
- 33% of any money recovered (plus legal expenses) during trial or after appeal.

Settlement

Case is settled for $10,800 after case is filed, but before trial.
Attorney has $800 worth of legal expenses.

Calculation of Contingency Fee

1. Legal expenses are paid first.

Settlement of	$10,800
Minus legal expenses	−800
Balance	$10,000

2. Contingency fee is calculated as follows:

Total recovery minus legal expenses	$10,000
Attorney's 25% Contingency Fee	
($10,000 × 25% = $2,500)	−2,500
TOTAL TO CLIENT	$7,500

3. Total fees and expenses to attorney

Reimbursement of legal expense	$800
Contingency fee	$2,500
TOTAL TO ATTORNEY	$3,300

**Figure 5-4
Contingency Fee
Example**

Flat Fee

A **flat fee** is a fee for legal services that is billed as a flat or fixed amount. Some offices have a set fee for handling certain types of matters, such as preparing a will or handling an uncontested divorce, a name change, or a bankruptcy (see Figure 5-5). For example, suppose a client agreed to pay an attorney a flat fee of $500 to prepare a will. No matter how many hours the attorney spends preparing the will, the fee is still $500. Flat fee agreements are usually used when a legal matter is simple, straightforward, and involves few risks.

Figure 5-6 shows a comparison of different methods of billing for drafting a routine or standard will. Flat rates will typically be the least expensive for the client in routine matters. In addition, flat rates and the blended methods are typically the easiest types of bills to both prepare and read.

flat fee
A fee for legal services that is billed as a flat or fixed amount.

Retainer Fees

The word "retainer" has several meanings in the legal environment. Generally, retainer fees are monies paid by the client at the beginning of a case or matter. However, there are many types of retainers. When an attorney or legal assistant uses the term "retainer," it could mean a retainer for general representation, a case retainer, a pure retainer, or a cash advance. In addition, all retainer fees are either earned or unearned.

Figure 5-5   Flat Fee Price List

⌐ PRICE LIST ⌐

Initial Consultation with Branch Lawyer..........$100.00

REAL ESTATE

Divorce - Uncontested................................1000.00
Domestic contracts and family litigation vary according to time involved.

REAL ESTATE

Purchase or Sale of House.........................1000.00
Each Mortgage—Additional..........................300.00
Each Discharge of Mortgage—Additional........200.00
Refinancing...700.00

WILLS & ESTATES

Basic Will...500.00
Estates, administrations, and estate litigation vary according to time involved

BUSINESS

Consultation..200.00
Incorporation...2000.00
We provide many other business services, including:
- *Commercial Leases*
- *Purchase and Sale of Businesses*
- *Trade Marks & Copyright*

ADDITIONAL SERVICES

Collection—demand letter............................200.00
Notarization (per signature)...........................20.00
Power of Attorney / Promissory Note...............50.00

⌐ PAYMENT POLICY ⌐

We require a retainer before commencing work on your behalf, which amount is paid into trust. We then draw checks on the retainer to pay out-of-pocket expenses made on your behalf and our fees.

We will advise you of completion of our services to you and ask you to come in and pick up the documentation involved and pay any balance owing at the same time.

In real estate transactions the balance must be paid prior to closing. In litigation and criminal matters, any outstanding account and the estimated fee for the appearance must be paid prior to the court appearance.

ETHICAL NOTE: Even if the firm has a price list, legal assistants should leave the matter of fees to the attorney.

---

earned retainer
Term for the money the law office or attorney has earned and is entitled to deposit in the office's or attorney's own bank account.

unearned retainer
Monies that are paid up front by the client as an advance against the attorney's future fees and expenses. Until the monies are actually earned by the attorney or law office, they belong to the client.

EARNED V. UNEARNED RETAINERS   There is a very important difference between an earned retainer and an unearned retainer. An **earned retainer** means that the law office or attorney has earned the money, is entitled to deposit it in the office's or attorney's own bank account, and can use it to pay the attorney's or law office's operating expenses, such as salaries, immediately upon deposit.

For example, suppose an attorney agrees to take a products liability case on a contingency fee basis, but requires that the client pay a nonrefundable (earned) retainer of $2,000. The attorney drafts a contract and both parties sign it; the contract clearly states that the $2,000 is nonrefundable. The earned, nonrefundable retainer is an incentive for the attorney to accept the case on a contingency basis. The attorney may deposit the $2,000 in his or her law office checking account and pay operating expenses out of it. This is an example of a case retainer, which is discussed in more detail later in this section.

An **unearned retainer** is money that is paid up front by the client as an advance against the attorney's future fees and expenses as a kind of down payment. Until the monies are actually earned by the attorney or law office, they belong to the client.

Figure 5-6   Comparison Legal Fees to Prepare a Will

Activities Provided:

1. Legal assistant interviews client (office conf.) regarding the law office drafting a will for client. Legal assistant gets background information including financial holdings, heirs, family tree, etc. . . . . 1.50 hours
2. Legal assistant drafts memo to associate attorney, itemizing the conference with client . . . . .25 hours
3. Associate attorney reads the legal assistant's memo and talks with client on the telephone . . . . .25 hours
4. Associate attorney conducts legal research and prepares a draft of the will that meets the expectations of the client . . . . .50 hours
5. Associate confers with senior partner regarding the will . . . . .50 hours
6. Client reviews will, holds office conf. with associate attorney, associate attorney discusses client's changes to the will, makes client's changes to the will, and the will is executed, witnessed, and notarized . . . . 1.0 hours

TOTAL HOURS . . . . 4.0 hours

- **CLIENT HOURLY RATE**

Assume attorneys agrees to charge the client to prepare the will for his/her time as follows:

- $225 an hour for all attorney's time
- $80 an hour for his/her legal assistant's time

TOTAL COST $646.25
(Legal asst. 1.75 hours × $80 = $140; Atty. 2.25 × $225 an hour = $506.25; $140 + $506.25 = $646.25)

- **ATTORNEY/LEGAL ASSISTANT HOURLY RATE**
- Assume the senior partner's normal hourly rate is $350.
- Assume the associate attorney's normal hourly rate is $250
- Assume the legal assistant's normal hourly rate is $80.

TOTAL COST $752.50
(Legal asst. 1.75 hours × $80 = $140; Assoc. atty. 1.75 × $250 an hour = $437.50; Sr. Partner .50 × $350 = $175; $140 + $437.5 + $175 = $752.50)

- **BLENDED (Attorneys and Legal Assistant) HOURLY RATE**
- Assume blended hourly rate for all attorney and legal assistant time is $175 an hour.

TOTAL COST $700 (4 hours × $175 = $700).

ACTIVITY HOURLY RATE

Assume:

- Legal assistant office conference rate is $70 an hour/Atty. is $200.
- Legal assistant time for drafting memo is $80 an hour/Atty. is $225.
- Attorney time for phone conferences is $150 an hour.
- Attorney time For drafting pleadings, will, legal research, and conferring with other partners is $225 an hour.

TOTAL COST $587.50
1.5 × $70 = $105; .25 × $80 = $20; .25 × $150 = $37.50; .50 × $225 = $112.5; .50 × $225 = $112.50, 1.0 × $200 = $200; Total $587.50

FLAT FEE RATE

Assume attorney and client agree on a flat rate of $500 to prepare the will.

TOTAL COST $500.00

CONTINGENCY RATE $0.00 (No monetary recovery—not applicable)

According to ethical rules, unearned retainers may not be deposited in the attorney's or law office's normal operating checking account; unearned retainers must be deposited into a separate trust account and can be transferred into the firm account as it is earned.

For example, suppose a business client wants to sue his or her insurance company for failing to pay a claim submitted by the business. The business signs a contract with the attorney to pay a (unearned) retainer of $10,000. The contract states that the $10,000 will be held in trust and paid to the attorney as the attorney incurs fees and properly bills the client. This is an example of a cash advance retainer, which is covered in more detail in the next section.

trust or escrow account
A separate bank account, apart from a law office's or attorney's operating checking account, where unearned client funds are deposited.

A **trust** or **escrow account** is a separate bank account, apart from a law office's or attorney's operating checking account, where unearned client funds are deposited. Client trust accounts are covered in detail in Chapter 6. As an attorney or law office begins to earn an unearned retainer by providing legal services to the client, the attorney can then bill the client and move the earned portion from the trust account to his or her own law office operating account.

The written contract should set out whether the retainer is earned or unearned. However, in some instances the contract may be vague on this point. Typically, when a contract refers to a "nonrefundable retainer," this means an earned retainer.

Additionally, flat fee rates, as discussed earlier, are said to be "nonrefundable" in many contracts, and thus are treated as earned. However, some state ethical rules regulate this area heavily and hold that all flat fees are a retainer, have been unearned, and must be placed in trust until they are earned. Whether a retainer is earned or unearned will depend on your state's ethical rules and on the written contract.

cash advance
Unearned monies that are the advance against the attorney's future fees and expenses.

CASH ADVANCE RETAINER   One type of retainer is a **cash advance,** unearned monies that act as an advance against the attorney's future fees and expenses. Until the cash advance is earned by the attorney, it actually belongs to the client. The cash advance is a typical type of unearned retainer.

Suppose a client wishes to hire an attorney to litigate a contract dispute. The attorney agrees to represent the client only if the client agrees to pay $200 an hour with a $2,500 cash advance against fees and expenses. The attorney must deposit the $2,500 in a trust account. If the attorney deposits the cash advance into his or her own account (whether it is the firm's account or the attorney's own personal account), the attorney has violated several ethical rules. As the attorney works on the case and bills the client for fees and expenses, the attorney will write him- or herself a check out of the trust account for the amount of the billing. The attorney must tell the client that he or she is withdrawing the money, and keep an accurate balance of how much the client has left in trust. If the attorney billed the client for $500, the attorney would write himself a check for $500 from the trust account, deposit the $500 in the attorney's or the firm's own bank account, and inform the client that there was a remaining balance of $2,000 in trust. If the case ended at this point, the client would be entitled to a refund of the remaining $2,000 in trust. Look closely at the payment policy in Figure 5-5; the firm described requires a cash advance before it will take any case.

RETAINER FOR GENERAL REPRESENTATION   Another type of retainer is a **retainer for general representation.** This type of retainer is typically used when a client such as a corporation or entity requires continuing legal services throughout the year. The client pays an amount, typically up front or on a prearranged schedule, to receive these ongoing services. For example, suppose a small school board would like to be able to contact an attorney at any time with general legal questions. The attorney and school board could enter into this type of agreement for a fee of $5,000 every six months; the school board could contact the attorney at any time and ask general questions; and the attorney would never receive more than the $5,000 for the six-month period. Retainers for general representation allow the client to negotiate and anticipate what his or her fee will be for the year. This type of agreement usually only covers general legal advice and would not include matters such as litigation (see Figure 5-7). Depending on the specific arrangements between the client and the attorney, and on the specific ethical rules in your state, many retainers for general representation are viewed as being earned because the client can call at any time and get legal advice. Retainers for general representation resemble a flat fee agreement. The difference is that, in a flat fee agreement, the attorney or law office is contracted to do specific work for a client, such as prepare a will or file a bankruptcy. In the case of a retainer for general representation, the attorney is agreeing to make him- or herself available to the client for all non-litigation needs.

retainer for general representation
Retainer typically used when a client such as a corporation or entity requires continuing legal services throughout the year.

Ms Gloria Smith, Chairperson
Unified School District
No. 453 School Board

    Subject: General Representation of the UDS No. 453 School Board

Dear Ms Smith:

Thank you for your letter informing us that the School Board would like to place our law firm on a general retainer of $_____ for the coming year. We will bill on a quarterly basis for the retainer plus any expenses incurred.

The retainer will include general advice concerning business operations, personnel questions, legislative initiative, and attendance at all board meetings. It will not cover litigated matters requiring appearances at boards or commissions, court, or state administrative agencies. Should any of the excluded services appear to be necessary, we shall be happy to discuss the cost of these services with you.

It is our hope that the knowledge that we are ready to serve you under the retainer will provide you with regular advice to avoid any serious problems or litigation. Please sign this letter and return it to us. If you have any questions, please feel free to give me a call.

Kindest Regards,

Sandra W. Johnson
JOHNSON, BECK & TAYLOR

Accepted for Unified School District No. 453 School Board by:

_____

Gloria Smith, Chairperson

Figure 5-7
Retainer for General Representation Agreement

case retainer
A fee that is billed at the beginning of a matter, is not refundable to the client, and is usually paid at the beginning of the case as an incentive for the office to take the case.

CASE RETAINER   Another type of retainer is a **case retainer,** which is a fee that is billed at the beginning of a matter, is not refundable to the client, and is usually paid to the office at the beginning of the case as an incentive for the office to take the case. As an example, say that a client comes to an attorney with a criminal matter. The attorney agrees to take on the case only if the client agrees to pay a case retainer of $2,000 up front plus $200 an hour for every hour worked on the case. The $2000 is paid to the attorney as an incentive to take the case and, thus, is earned. The $200 an hour is a client hourly basis charge. Because the case retainer is earned, the attorney can immediately deposit it in the office's own bank account.

A case involving a contingency fee presents another example of a case retainer. Suppose a client comes to an attorney to file a civil rights case. The attorney agrees to accept the case only if the client agrees to a 30 percent contingency fee and a nonrefundable or case retainer of $2,000. Again, the earned retainer is an incentive for the attorney to take the case and can be deposited in the attorney's or the office's own bank account.

pure retainer
A fee that obligates the office to be available to represent the client throughout the time period agreed upon.

PURE RETAINER   A rather rare type of retainer is a **pure retainer;** a pure retainer obligates the law office to be available to represent the client throughout the agreed-upon time period. The part that distinguishes a pure retainer from a retainer for general representation is that the office typically must agree to not represent any of the client's competitors or to undertake any type of adverse representation to the client.

Retainers for general representation, case retainers, and pure retainers are usually earned retainers; a cash advance is an unearned retainer. However, the language of the contract will determine whether amounts paid to attorneys up front are earned or unearned. The earned/unearned distinction is extremely important, and it is one reason all fee agreements should be in writing.

Court-Awarded Fees

Court-awarded fees are another type of fee agreement. In certain federal and state statutes, the prevailing party (i.e., the party that wins the case) is given the right to recover from the opposing side reasonable attorney's fees. The amount of the attorney's fees is decided by the court; thus, these are called **court-awarded fees.** Court-awarded fees are provided for in civil rights law, antitrust, civil racketeering, and in many other instances and statutes as well. The prevailing party must submit to the court detailed time records showing specifically how much time was spent on the case. If the prevailing law office did not keep such records, the court will not award fees. The purpose of court-awarded fees is to encourage potential plaintiffs in public interest issues to pursue legitimate claims while discouraging frivolous claims. For example, if an employee brought a sexual harassment suit against an employer and subsequently won the suit, the employee's attorneys would be entitled to receive reasonable attorney's fees from the defendant.

court-awarded fees
Fees given to the prevailing parties pursuant to certain federal and state statutes.

prepaid legal service
A plan that a person can purchase that entitles the person to receive legal services either free or at a greatly reduced rate.

Prepaid Legal Services

A prepaid legal service plan is another type of fee agreement. **Prepaid legal service** is a plan that a person can purchase, which entitles the person to receive legal services (as enumerated in the plan) either free or at a greatly reduced rate. In some cases, corporations or labor unions, for example, provide a prepaid legal service plan to their employees as a fringe benefit. For instance, if a person who is a member of a prepaid legal service plan needed a will drafted, that person would go to either an attorney employed by the prepaid plan—or a private attorney with whom the prepaid plan contracted—and get the will drafted free of charge or at a greatly reduced rate.

> *The billable hour has been the industry standard for accounting purposes within the legal profession for the past 50 years. Prior to that, the profession managed to function by relying on other arrangements, such as fee schedules set by bar associations, fixed fees, contingencies, and so forth. As a general rule, the larger a firm is, the more likely it is to rely on billable hours as the measure for charging clients and assessing lawyers' productivity.*[2]

VALUE BILLING

Recently, much has been written (in the legal press) about why private law practices should stop billing by the hour and use a different billing method instead. The arguments for the change from hourly billing include the following:

- The client never knows, during any stage of the work, how much the total legal fee will be.
- Clients sometimes avoid calling legal assistants and attorneys because they know they will be charged for the time, even if it is a simple phone call.
- Clients have trouble seeing the relationship between what is performed by the legal assistant or attorney and the enormous fees that can be generated.
- Hourly billing encourages lawyers and legal assistants to be inefficient (i.e., the longer it takes to perform a job, the more revenue they earn).
- Many law offices force attorneys and legal assistants to bill a quota number of hours a year, which puts a tremendous amount of pressure on the individual legal assistant and attorney.

> *Value billing works like the pricing method of your local mechanic. When a car needs work, you take it to a mechanic for an estimate. That estimate is a binding contract unless unforeseeable complications arise. To develop estimates, mechanics consult a shop manual that lists the approximate number of hours it takes to perform a given task. In an industry as client-driven as the legal profession, it's only a matter of time (no pun intended) before time billing gives way to value billing.*[3]

value billing
A type of fee agreement that is based not on the time spent to perform the work but on the basis of the perceived value of the services to the client.

So what is value billing? The **value billing** concept represents a type of fee agreement that is based not on the time required to perform the work but on the basis of the perceived value of the services to the client. Value billing typically provides that the attorney and client reach a consensus on the amount of fees to be charged. Because of increased competition in the legal environment and because of the power of the client as a buyer, clients are demanding that they have a say in how much they are going to pay for legal services, what type of service will be provided, and what the quality of the legal notice services will be for the price.

Notice, in the survey in Figure 5-8, that hourly billing accounted for 50 to 74 percent of all billings for 39 percent of the responding attorneys, and that hourly billings accounted for more than 50 percent of all billings for 67.3 percent of the responding attorneys. Also notice that value billing, while an interesting concept, is not widely used.

**Figure 5-8
Survey of Attorney
Billing Practices**

Source: American Bar Association. (2004). *2003 American Bar Association legal technology resource center survey report* (p. 38).

What percentage of your fees is based on hourly billing?

Percent of Total Fees That Are Hourly	Total Percent of Attorneys Responding
None	2.4%
1–24%	14.4%
25–49%	15.9%
50–74%	39%
75% or more	22.3%
Don't know/NA	6.0%
Total	100%

What percentage of your fees is based on contingent billing?

Percent of Total Fees That Are Contingent	Total Percent of Attorneys Responding
None	35.5%
1–24%	32.1%
25–49%	2.4%
50–74%	3.4%
75% or more	1.3%
Don't know/NA	25.3%
Total	100%

What percentage of your fees is based on fixed billing?

Percent of Total Fees That Are Fixed	Total Percent of Attorneys Responding
None	27.9%
1–24%	40.3%
25–49%	4.5%
50–74%	2.6%
75% or more	0.3%
Don't know/NA	24.4%
Total	100%

What percentage of your fees is based on value billing/other?

Figure 5-8
(Continued)

Percent of Total Fees That Are Value Billing/Other	Total Percent of Attorneys Responding
None	37.6%
1–24%	0.8%
25–49%	0.2%
50–74%	0.1%
75% or more	0.2%
Don't know/NA	61.1%
Total	100%

THE ETHICS OF TIMEKEEPING AND BILLING

There are more timekeeping- and billing-related ethical complaints filed against attorneys and law offices than all other types of complaints; thus, legal assistants should completely understand the ethics of timekeeping and billing. In years past, timekeeping and billing complaints were viewed simply as "misunderstandings" between the client and the law office. Recently, state bars have viewed timekeeping and billing disputes as having major ethical implications for attorneys; that is, such disputes were simply not misunderstandings, but law offices were sometimes flagrantly violating ethical rules regarding money issues.

Billing from the Corporate and Government Perspective

Corporate and governmental law practices sometimes hire outside counsel (private law offices). **Outside counsel** refers to when corporate and government law practices contract with private law offices (i.e., outside of the corporation or government practice) to help them with legal matters, such as litigation, specialized contracts, stock/bond offerings, and so forth. Thus, corporate and government law practices are purchasers of legal services and tend to look at billing from a different perspective.

Corporate and government law practices are concerned with limiting the costs of legal fees. Many corporate clients will state that they will not pay more than a certain amount—perhaps $200 an hour—for any attorney, regardless of experience. If the office wants to maintain the particular client, it will agree to the terms. Because corporations and governments have access to large sums of money and typically are good-paying clients, many offices will reduce their price to get and keep the business.

Corporate and government clients usually require very detailed bills to control costs and what is being done on the case; in some cases, corporations and governments use a competitive bidding process to select outside counsel. Thus, summary billings are usually not accepted. They also will typically limit the type and cost of expenses that are billed to them. For instance, some corporations require that

outside counsel
Term referring to when corporate and government law practices contract with law offices (i.e., outside of the corporation or government practice) to help them with legal matters, such as litigation, specialized contracts, stock/bond offerings, and so forth.

computerized legal research (Westlaw, LexisNexis, etc.), postage, fax costs, and similar expenses be borne by the office.

It is not uncommon for a corporate law practice to publish policies and guidelines covering exactly what outside counsel will charge, when it will charge, how payments will be made, how much and what type of legal expenses will be reimbursed, and so on. Figure 5-9 shows the top 10 reasons corporate law departments fail to pay private law offices.

Timekeeping and billing complaints by clients can lead not just to ethical complaints against attorneys, but may also turn into criminal fraud charges filed against attorneys and legal assistants.

Ethical Considerations Regarding Legal Fee Agreements

There are several important ethical considerations that need to be stressed about fee agreements. The first is that all fee agreements should be in writing, especially when a contingency fee is involved. Second, contingency fees should not be used in criminal or domestic-relation matters.

Fee Agreements Should be in Writing

It is highly recommended that, as a matter of course, all fee agreements be in writing. The days of a handshake cementing an agreement between an attorney and a client are long over. There is no substitute for reducing all fee agreements to writing. If the firm and the client have a dispute over fees, the document will clarify the understanding between the parties.

The ABA *Model Rules of Professional Conduct* at Rule 1.5(b) states that an attorney is responsible for communicating to a client the scope of the representation, and the basis and rate of the fee and expenses in the matter. The rule states that it is preferable for the communication to be in writing, but it is not required.

> *A fee agreement allows a lawyer and client to make clear from the inception of the legal representation the scope of that representation and the basis for the lawyer's compensation. A clearly drafted agreement, which is fully explained to the client at the time the representation begins, will minimize disagreement as the representation proceeds and assist in resolving any disputes that may arise when the representation ends.*[4]

Although the *Model Rules* states that the agreement "preferably" be in writing, nearly every authority on this subject, as well as most attorneys who have been in

Reason	Explanation
Legal services are below standard	The legal services provided were below standard or didn't meet the needs of the corporate client. Corporate law departments will typically attempt to negotiate down the fees. In these instances, the corporate law department staff must take the time to correct the problems, even though they paid to have it done correctly.
Too many attorneys and legal assistants working the case	When multiple timekeepers attend the same deposition or bill for the same work provided, the costs rise quickly. Many corporate law departments will try to set limits on the number of timekeepers working a case at one time. Also, if the attorneys or legal assistants who are working the case change, the client must pay for the new attorneys or legal assistants to get up to speed.
Billing lacks detail	Most law departments want to see detailed reports of how timekeepers spent their time and not just "for legal services provided."
Billing is incomplete	A bill doesn't include previous payments made or is otherwise incomplete.
Billing has numerical errors	The bill doesn't add up, or wrong billing rates are used.
Sticker shock	The corporate law department expects a bill for $5,000 and receives a bill for $25,000.
Attorneys and legal assistants conferencing with each other frequently	It is frustrating for a client to receive a bill where attorneys and legal assistants are frequently meeting to discuss strategy or otherwise, because this greatly increases the client's bill. This is particularly frustrating for the client when the bill does not say why the staff members working on the case were meeting.
Billing sent to the wrong person	Sending the bill to the wrong person can be frustrating in a large corporation. The bill can literally get lost inside the corporation unless the bill is sent to the correct person.
Billing every little thing	Clients strongly dislike being billed for every five-minute phone call, being billed for the time it takes to prepare the bill itself, or other items that—in the big picture—do not amount to much.
Being billed for another case	Occasionally, a client will be billed for time spent on another case. This undermines the whole billing process.
Billing is received late	Corporate clients become frustrated when they receive a bill for services that were delivered five months ago. Not only is the billing late, but it is difficult to remember that far back as to the details of the service.

Figure 5-9
Reasons Corporate Law Departments and Government Legal Departments Sometimes Refuse to Negotiate on Legal Bills

business for a while, will tell you that the agreement absolutely should be in writing to protect both the attorney and the client. Legal fee agreements should be in writing for the following reasons:

1. Clients file more ethical complaints against attorneys and law offices for fee disputes than for any other type of complaint.
2. The client and the attorney may (will) forget what the exact fee agreement was, unless it is reduced to writing.
3. In a factual dispute regarding a fee between a client and an attorney, the evidence is typically construed in the light most favorable to the client.

CONTINGENCY FEE AGREEMENT MUST BE IN WRITING   When a contingency fee is involved, most jurisdictions state that the agreement *shall* be in writing for the office to collect the fee. Rule 1.5(c) of the *Model Rules* states:

> . . . that contingency fee agreement shall be in writing and must be signed by the client. It also states that the agreement must state the percentages of the contingency arrangement, state what expenses the client is responsible for and how expenses are to be deducted, including whether such expenses are deducted before or after the contingency fee is calculated. The attorney must also provide a final written statement to the client at the end of the legal matter showing specifically what the recovery was, how it was arrived at, and how the monies were allocated.

Even the *Model Rules* makes a distinction between contingency agreements and other types of fee agreements, and requires that contingency agreements be in writing. It must be in writing because, in many cases, large sums of money are recovered, and the difference between 20 and 30 percent may be tens of thousands of dollars. Contingency agreements are risky for the attorney, and they simply must be reduced to writing so that the client and the attorney know what the proper percentage of fees should be. It also is important that the contingency agreement state, and the client understand, that even if there is no recovery in the case, the client must still pay for expenses.

NO CONTINGENCY FEES IN CRIMINAL AND DOMESTIC-RELATION PROCEEDINGS IN SOME JURISDICTIONS   Many jurisdictions prohibit contingency fees in criminal and domestic-relation proceedings as a matter of public policy. *Model Rule* 1.5(d) specifically states that an attorney shall not enter into a contingency fee arrangement regarding domestic relations or criminal matters. For example, suppose that an attorney agrees to represent a client in a criminal matter. The client agrees to pay the attorney $10,000 if the client is found innocent, but the attorney will receive nothing if the client is found guilty. This is an unethical contingency fee agreement; contingency fees in these types of cases appear to be against the public policy and should be prohibited.

Only a "Reasonable" Fee can be Collected

> *Billing a senior partner's rate for a lawyer to research discovery documents for several hours is a sure way to drive away clients. The work is essential, requiring someone with knowledge and savvy, but is more suited to a legal assistant who can ensure proficient performance while freeing the senior partner to address those tasks that only a senior partner can do—at a greater billing rate.*[5]

> *Today's clients are discriminating purchasers of legal services. Hourly rates and billing invoices are often challenged by long-standing clients.*[6]

No matter what the contract or legal fee agreement is with a client, it is important to keep in mind that attorneys and legal assistants can only receive a "reasonable" fee. Unfortunately, there is no absolute standard for determining reasonableness, except that reasonableness will be determined on a case-by-case basis. However, Rule 1.5 of the *Model Rules of Professional Conduct* gives a number of factors to be considered in determining reasonableness.

Model Rules 1.5, as well as cases on the subject, have provided a number of factors that must be considered when determining whether a fee is reasonable. These factors include the following:

- the amount of time and labor required
- the novelty or difficulty of the issues raised
- the skill required to perform the legal services
- the acceptance of the case and whether it would preclude the attorney from taking other cases
- the local "going rate" or fee customarily charged in the area for the services performed
- the end result of the case (how successful the representation was)
- the time limitations imposed by the client or by the circumstances
- the professional relationship with the client, including past dealings or history with the client
- the experience of the attorney
- the attorney's reputation and/or the ability of the lawyer (or lawyers) performing the services
- the type of fee agreement, including whether the fee was fixed or contingent

In one case, a court found that a fee of $22,500 pursuant to a written agreement for a real estate matter that involved little time for the attorney, and that was not unduly complex, was unreasonable. Figure 5-10 shows some additional examples of unreasonable fees.

- **Audit Questions Legal Assistant's 12-Hour Workdays**
  An audit of a paralegal's time found that for nearly a two-year period, the legal assistant worked (i.e., billed) an average of 12.45 hours each day, including Saturdays, Sundays, and holidays, without details to support the hours. During the nearly two-year period, the legal assistant took only one day off. The audit estimated that the paralegal overbilled by 2,220 hours, totaling $39,960.
- **Client Charged for Individual Attorneys Billing More Than the 24-Hour Day**
  A corporation recently received a monthly legal bill in excess of $300,000. The head of the corporate legal department was concerned. After hiring an outside audit firm to audit the billings, he discovered that:
  - Individual attorneys were billing in excess of the 24-hour day.
  - Attorneys were assigned to tasks that could have been provided by legal assistants at greatly reduced costs.
  - The client was billed by the firm for duplicate items.
  - Conferences were often attended by many attorneys who were not needed and whose time was charged to the client.
  - The client was billed for the same expert witness fees multiple times.
  - The firm charged the client for the time the firm spent working with an auditor to show them their overcharges.
- **Overbilling and Fraud by Elite Partners and Firms**
  In the winter of 1999, the *Georgetown Journal of Legal Ethics* published an exhaustive article on overbilling and fraud by 16 elite attorneys and/or law firms. Below are some quotes from the article.
  "In recent years, a disturbing number of well-respected lawyers in large, established firms have been caught stealing large amounts of money from their clients and their partners by padding, manipulating, and fabricating time sheets and expense vouchers. Some have gone to prison, been disbarred, and/or fired. . . . Billing fraud takes many different forms. Here are some examples:
  - Some lawyers are just sloppy about keeping time records.
  - Some systematically "pad" time sheets, or bill one client for work done for another.
  - Some create entirely fictitious time sheets.
  - Some record hours based on work done by other lawyers, paralegals, or secretaries, representing that they did the work. This may result in non-billable time being billed, or in work being billed at a rate higher than that of the person who actually did the work.
  - Some lawyers bill for time that their clients might not regard as legitimately billable— for schmoozing with other lawyers, chatting with clients about sports or families, doing administrative work that could be done by a nonlawyer, or for thinking about a case while mowing the lawn or watching television.
  The methods of expense fraud are equally diverse; the lawyers who engage in expense fraud may be stealing from their clients or their partners or both. . . . Billing fraud is far more difficult to detect than expense fraud, unless the lawyer is reckless enough to bill more than 24 hours per day. But regulation of this type of conduct is very difficult because no one except the lawyer really knows how much time was spent and how much was billed. . . .
  I undertook the research for this article because in recent years, I periodically noticed reports of cases of elite lawyers who had gone to jail, been disbarred, or been investigated for stealing by billing and expense fraud. . . . These 16 cases involve lawyers who came from privileged backgrounds, attended elite schools, and have:
  (a) been a managing partner, a member of the executive committee or a rainmaker at large, respected law firm or a spin-off from such a firm.

Figure 5-10
(Continued)

(b) been publicly accused of stealing over $100,000 from clients or from his or her law firm by fraudulent representations as to hours worked or expenses incurred.

(c) been jailed and/or disbarred for billing or expense fraud.

These lawyers engaged in patterns of fraud that went on for an average of five years. Their collective total proven or admitted theft is about $16 million. These highly educated successful lawyers were at the pinnacle of the profession.

Here are some specific examples:

Attorney
$3.1 million over a five-year period

- Attorney wrote fake time sheets, engaged in expense fraud, inflated hours, billed for work not done, billed for time of persons who did no work on matters billed, and engaged in "ad hoc value billing." One judge who reviewed the case described the methods as "almost fictional" and offered these examples: $98,700 billed for services never performed by David Levin; almost $500,000 for time attributed to legal assistants, medical experts, and law clerks, when the work billed for was, in fact, done by the firm's receptionist and secretaries, and $66,127.29 for legal and medical research that cost only $394.98.

- Attorneys' partners helped cover up the billing fraud after complaints were made. The partners and their wives spent part of a weekend at the firm producing fictitious time sheets to correspond with erroneous bills that had been sent to the client. The wives were enlisted so that time sheets would reflect the handwriting of several people.

- Attorney wrote over 100 checks on firm accounts for personal expenses, claiming they were payments to "expert witnesses" or other law-related work.

Attorney
$1.4 million over a five-year period

- Attorney intentionally overbilled the federal government and destroyed and concealed records to conceal his activities. As managing partner, he reviewed the time records of associates and partners in the firm. He forwarded them to the bookkeeper with written instructions directing the bookkeeper to increase the number of hours billed above the numbers recorded by the lawyers. When audited by FDIC, the attorney gathered the original time records and either concealed them or destroyed them, and directed the firm office manager to provide false information to the government.

Attorney
$1.1 million over a five-year period

- Attorney billed five firm clients (four corporations and one trade union) directly without firm authorization. He claimed to be taking vacation or doing client development during some periods when he was billing these clients. Attorney "had most of the payments mailed directly to his home, so that his secretary would not see them; he also forbade his secretary to open any of his mail . . . [He] spent many hours typing up facsimile legal bills to present to clients, himself, rather than having his secretary do them. And, of course, he kept all the records for the bills at his home." He "often shifted fees to expenses and vice versa, to make the bottom line agree with the billing totals he was submitting to his firm's accounting department." Attorney deceived his firm, sometimes with the knowledge and cooperation of clients. He also deceived clients, sometimes billing over 24 hours per day, or billing one expense to two clients. He billed $16,000 of personal expenses to one client.

Figure 5-10
(Continued)

Attorney
$500,000 over a five-year period
- While at the firm, attorney persuaded a French pharmaceutical client to hire a dummy consulting firm he had set up (which had no clients or employees) to arrange drug testing needed for FDA approval. The client paid nearly $1 million to the consulting firm; the attorney paid about half this amount into his checking account, his profit-sharing plan, or took it in cash.

Attorney
$225,000 over a four-year period
- Attorney charged personal expenses to the firm and to clients, including $27,000 for flowers for his children's weddings, and the cost of meals, floral displays for the office, plane tickets, and hotel accommodations for non-business-related family vacations. The attorney denied most of the charges, but admitted billing clients for airfare and hotel accommodations if he was working on a client's case during a particular vacation. He said his "clients have approved and ratified the specific expenses in question." Attorney also arranged for legal fees to be paid directly to him without firm approval.

Attorney
Over a four-year period (1991–1995)
- Attorney allegedly billed clients for hundreds of hours of work that he did not do; he continued to bill for legal work after he began to spend most of his time on investing that involved a $100 million Ponzi scheme.[7]

For many years, it was thought that overbilling and stealing from clients by attorneys was only done by sole practitioners and attorneys in small firms. Figure 5-10 shows that this is probably not true, and that these practices happen at all levels.

> *. . . A lawyer may not bill more than one client for the same hours worked by charging a client for the time it took to produce a document that the lawyer had already created for another client. The lawyer also is prohibited from charging clients for the same hours when the lawyer works on one client's matter while traveling for the benefit of the other client on a different matter.*

Source: American Bar Association. (2004). *The legal assistant's practical guide to professional responsibility* (2nd ed. p. 121). Reprinted by permission.

> *In John Grisham's modern classic,* The Firm, *Avery Tolar advises the young lawyer Mitchell McDeere on how to charge clients. He explains that the client should be charged for "every minute you spend even thinking about a case." It was this philosophy that got the Mafia's legal team into trouble. Unethical billing practices do not only exist in legal novels like* The Firm *but have been a pervasive problem in law firms across the country.*

> *Many critics blame a system that bills clients by the hour for the abuse, saying that it creates the pressure to overstate hours. "Time-based billing creates an inherent conflict of interest between the client's interest in the efficient disposition of its business and the attorney's interest in racking up hours."*
>
> *A Florida attorney was recently disbarred for five years for overcharging a client by more than $2 million. The defendant, James Dougherty, turned in padded bills for an insurance investigation that he conducted on behalf of London-based Lloyd's of London. The Court found that Dougherty overbilled by $300,000 for his own work, by $1.2 million for the work of his associates, and by over $1.2 million for expenses. The court held that "[f]ederal felony convictions for wire fraud by overbilling [the] client . . . warranted disbarment for five years."[8]*

Many State Bars' Rules Provide for Oversight/Arbitration on Fee Issues

One of the ways that state bar associations and courts have dealt with the abundance of fee disputes is to provide for immediate and informal review/arbitration of fee disputes. Many state ethical and court rules provide that clients have the right, at any time, to request that the judge in the case or an attorney representing the state bar review the reasonableness of the attorney's fees. The attorney is required to inform the client of this right in many states; in those states, the judge or attorney hearing the matter has the right to set the fee and determine what is reasonable under the particular facts and circumstances of the case.

Fraud and Criminal Charges

> *Intentionally overbilling clients for work not done is called "fraud." You can be criminally prosecuted by government officials and civilly prosecuted by your clients.*

Charging an unreasonable fee is no longer simply a matter of ethics. Recently, attorneys and legal assistants have been criminally charged with fraud for intentionally recording time and sending bills for legal services that were never provided. **Criminal fraud** is a false representation of a present or past fact made by the defendant, upon which the victim relies, resulting in the victim suffering damages.

Criminal charges for fraud are not filed against attorneys and legal assistants when there is simply a disagreement over what constitutes a reasonable fee. Criminal charges are filed when an attorney or legal assistant acts intentionally to defraud

criminal fraud
A false representation of a present or past fact made by a defendant.

clients. This usually happens when the attorney or legal assistant bills for time when he or she did not really work on the case, or in instances in which the office intentionally billed a grossly overstated hourly rate far above the market rate.

> *One of the most common temptations that can corrupt a paralegal's ethics is to inflate billable hours, since there is often immense pressure in law offices to bill high hours for job security and upward mobility. Such "creative billing" [or "padding"] is not humorous; it's both morally wrong and illegal.*[9]

Interestingly, many of the most recent criminal cases being brought are against well-respected large and small law offices specializing in insurance defense and corporate work. Some insurance companies and corporations, as a matter of course when a case has been concluded, hire an audit firm or independent attorney to go back and audit the firm's billing and files to be sure they were billed accurately. In some instances, these audits have concluded that intentional criminal fraud has occurred and have been referred to prosecutors where criminal charges have been filed. No matter what type of firm is involved, intentionally overstating bills can lead to very big problems. Figure 5-10 led to criminal prosecutions of the legal professionals involved.

Ethical Problems

There are several difficult ethical problems with no definite solutions regarding timekeeping and billing that need to be explored. The rule in answering ethical questions such as these is to use your common sense and notions of fairness and honesty.

BILLING MORE THAN ONE CLIENT FOR THE SAME TIME, OR "DOUBLE BILLING"
A situation happens from time to time in which a legal assistant or attorney has the opportunity to bill more than one client for the same time period. For instance, while you are monitoring the opposing side's inspection of your client's documents in case A, you are drafting discovery for case B. Another example: while traveling to attend an interview with a witness in case A, you work on case B.

If you were the client, would you think it fair for the attorney to charge full price for travel time related to your case while billing another case? A reasonable approach is to bill only the case on which you are actively working on, split the time between the cases, or bill the case you are actively working on at the regular hourly rate and bill the case you are inactively working on at a greatly reduced rate. Be fair and honest; your clients, as well as judges and others looking at the time, will respect you for it.

WHEN BILLING BY THE HOUR, IS THERE AN ETHICAL OBLIGATION TO BE EFFICIENT? DOES THE FIRM HAVE TO HAVE A FORM FILE IN LIEU OF RESEARCHING EACH DOCUMENT EACH TIME? MUST AN OFFICE USE A COMPUTER TO SAVE TIME?   These types of ethical questions are decided on a case-by-case basis. Billing by the hour rewards people who work slowly, since the more slowly they work, the more they are paid.

Common sense says that if you were the client, you would want your legal staff to be efficient and not to "milk" you for money. The real issue is whether the attorney or legal assistant acted so inefficiently and charged so much—when compared with what a similar attorney or legal assistant with similar qualifications would charge in the same community—that the fee is clearly unreasonable. When a judge rules on the reasonableness of fees, there is no doubt that he or she will consider what a reasonably efficient attorney or legal assistant in the same circumstances would have charged. Use your common sense and be honest and efficient, because someone in your office might have to justify your time and charges someday.

SHOULD YOU BILL FOR CLERICAL OR SECRETARIAL DUTIES?   Law offices cannot bill clients for clerical or secretarial tasks, because these tasks are viewed as overhead costs or are considered a normal part of doing business. An easy but unethical way to bill more hours is for a legal assistant to bill time to clients for clerical functions such as copying documents or filing material. Legal assistants clearly should not bill for these types of clerical tasks; legal assistants bill time for professional services, not for clerical functions.

This issue was addressed in the United States Supreme Court case of *Missouri v. Jenkins*, 491 U.S. 274, 109 S.Ct. 2463, 105 L.Ed. 2d 229 (1989). The Court found that when paralegals perform professional level work, these hours are recoverable as "attorneys fees," but services that are merely clerical or secretarial cannot be billed. The Court held

> It has frequently been recognized in the lower courts that paralegals are capable of carrying out many tasks, under the supervision of an attorney, that might otherwise be performed by a lawyer and billed at a higher rate. Such work might include, for example, factual investigation, including locating and interviewing witnesses; assistance with depositions, interrogatories, and document production; compilation of statistical and financial data; checking legal citations; and drafting correspondence. . . . Of course, purely clerical or secretarial tasks should not be billed at a paralegal rate, regardless of who performs them (p. 288).

If you are unsure about whether a task is clerical, ask your supervising attorney or record the time initially, point it out to the supervising attorney, and let him or her decide.

SHOULD YOU BILL FOR THE MISTAKES OF THE LAW OFFICE?   This is another tough problem. People make mistakes all the time. Clients generally feel that they should not have to pay for mistakes, since the reason they went to an attorney was to get an expert to handle their situation. This is a decision that should be left to every law office to decide, but generally the practice of billing for mistakes should be discouraged.

MUST A TASK BE ASSIGNED TO LESS EXPENSIVE SUPPORT STAFF WHEN POSSIBLE?
Common sense and efficiency will tell you that tasks should be delegated as low as possible. Clients should not have to pay for attorney time when the task could be completed by an experienced legal assistant. In addition, this practice is more profitable to the law office because higher-paid persons are free to do tasks for which they can bill clients at their normal rates.

Billing is important to the legal assistant because raises and bonuses may be reflected by the amount of time billed. Correctly bill no matter how much pressure there is about maintaining those high billable hours because at the end of the day, you will have to live with your conscience. Fortunately, I have never been placed in a position that I was asked to record time which I did not think was right. If I had that situation, I would obtain clarification for the reasoning because there could be a misunderstanding.

—Linda Rushton, CLA

LEGAL EXPENSES

In addition to recovering for legal fees, law practices are also entitled to recover from the client reasonable expenses incurred by the office in representing the client. For example, in Figure 5-11, the office needed to make copies of a motion to compel and mail them to opposing counsels. The cost of making the copies of the motion and mailing them out is directly related to the case, so the office is entitled to be reimbursed from the client for this expense. In most offices, it is important that the client is billed for the expense either through manual records, as in Figure 5-11, or some type of computerized or automated system. Such expenses typically include the costs of photocopying documents, postage, long-distance telephone calls, or travel expenses (see Figure 5-12).

The types of items to be charged back to clients are usually found in the law practice's staff manual. Figure 5-13 shows a sample policy.

The expenses alone can run into the tens of thousands of dollars in cases involving litigation. Therefore, the careful tracking of expenses is no trivial matter. Consider the revenues that would be generated if you billed copies at 25 cents and

Figure 5-11
Expense Slip

Johnson, Beck & Taylor
Expense Slip

Expense Type & Code

1 Photocopies	4 Filing Fees	7 Facsimile	10 Travel
2 Postage	5 Witness Fees	8 Lodging	11 Overnight Delivery
3 Long Distance	6 Westlaw/LesixNexis	9 Meals	12 Other _____

Court reporter fees (deposition transcripts)
Delivery charges (FedEx, etc.)
Expert witness fees
Facsimile costs
Filing fees
Long-distance phone calls
Photocopying
Postage
Travel expenses
Westlaw/LexisNexis
Witness fees

Figure 5-12
Expenses Typically
Billed to Clients

9.1   Legal Expenses/Disbursements

9.1.1   Client Costs

The Firm advances costs on behalf of clients in two ways

1. Through direct payment by issuance of a check to pay such costs as filing fees or services; e.g., secretary of state filing fees, court or county fees, witness fees, outside secretarial help, public notices, investigation and process services.
2. Through providing services or items such as document reproduction, word processing, telephone, messenger, postage, travel, and the like.

9.1.2   Forms and Instructions for Client Disbursements

The only way to obtain a check for a client disbursement is through the use of a Cost Card prepared as follows (see exhibit [#] at the end of this section):

- The Cost Card must be typed or printed legibly.
- Record lawyer [number/initials].
- Record client name and matter.
- Record file number.
- Record date charge incurred.
- Circle account number for coding classification.
- Enter amount.
- Obtain lawyer approval as detailed below.
- Send to _____.

All of the types of client disbursements are identified on the Cost Card. Cost Cards must be prepared concurrently with the transaction, except for the following:

1. *Document reproduction*
All requests for document reproduction from the Reproduction Center are made through a Reproduction Request Form, which must clearly identify the client name and matter, file number, and lawyer number. The Reproduction Center tabulates the number of copies run daily. This information is submitted to the Accounting Department for billing.

The separate satellite reproduction machines that are available for single-sheet copying are equipped with devices to record all copies made. The proper user identification, client, and matter number must be entered. The machine accumulates the information and recaps the charges monthly by matter for billing to the client.

2. *Database—LexisNexis or Westlaw*
Online research is also chargeable to the client. Accounting receives a monthly bill for database services that identifies the users, clients, and matters. _____ will prepare the necessary Cost Cards from these bills, which will be sent to the lawyer for approval.

Figure 5-13
Sample Legal
Expense Policy[10]

Source: Wert, R. C., & Hatoff, H. L. *Law office policy and procedures manual* (4th ed., p. 168). American Bar Association.

the office made 80,000 copies a year directly related to clients; this would be $20,000. Consider also the additional overhead an office would have if it did not bill clients for the copies.

As a legal assistant, you may be required to pay expenses for a case out of your own pocket from time to time. If this happens, be sure to ask for receipts. It also helps to know in advance what specific expenses the office will reimburse you for before they are incurred.

TIMEKEEPING

Timekeeping is the process of tracking what attorneys and legal assistants do with their time. Although this might seem like an incredibly easy task, it is not. Timekeeping is a necessary evil in most law practices. Keeping careful time records is important both for managerial reasons and for producing income.

From a managerial perspective, time records (a) provide the office with a way to monitor the progress of a case, who is working on the case, and/or who is responsible for the matter; (b) allow the office to determine which cases are the most profitable; and (c) allow office management to monitor the efficiencies of law practice staff.

From an income-producing perspective, time records (a) allow offices to bill their time to clients; and (b) allow the office to document its fees in probate matters and in cases where legal fees will be decided by a court.

Notice that managerial reasons could apply to any type of law practice, including corporate, government, or legal services/aid. It is also not uncommon for corporate, government, and legal services/aid practices to be given court-awarded attorneys fees from time to time.

time sheet or **time slip**
A record of detailed information about the legal services professionals provide to each client.

Figure 5-14 is an example of a manual time sheet. A **time sheet** or **time slip** is where legal professionals record detailed information about the legal services they provide to each client. Timekeeping entries must contain information such as the name of the case, the date the service was provided, and a description of the service.

Manual Timekeeping

There are many different types of manual timekeeping methods that can be purchased from most legal law office supply catalogs. Figure 5-13 is an example of a multiple-slip time sheet. The time slips are recorded chronologically and are completed by different billing people within the office for a variety of different cases. At some point, typically once a week, the time slips will be turned in to the billing department by everyone in the office. Each individual slip can be separated and has adhesive on the back. Each slip is separated and stuck to each client's time-slip page (see Figure 5-15); this provides a convenient method for tracking time for each client. All clients' time-slip pages can be stored in a three-ring notebook in alphabetical order by client name, or stored in each individual client's accounting file.

It is important to point out that time records do not automatically get charged to clients. The supervising attorney in the case typically reviews the time records turned in and determines whether they will be charged as is, or whether the time should be adjusted upward or downward. It should also be noted that it is common

Figure 5-14   Typical Manual Time Slip/Time Record Form

PC—Phone Conference	R—Review	Time Conversion
LR—Legal Research	OC—Office Conference	6 Minutes = .1 Hour 36 Minutes = .6 Hour
L—Letter	T—Travel	12 Minutes = .2 Hour 42 Minutes = .7 Hour
D—Dictation	CT—Court Hearing	15 Minutes = .25 Hour 45 Minutes = .75 Hour
		18 Minutes = .3 Hour 48 Minutes = .8 Hour
		24 Minutes = .4 Hour 54 Minutes = .9 Hour
		30 Minutes = .5 Hour 60 Minutes = 1.0 Hour

Date	Client/Case	File No.	Services Performed	Attorney	Time Hours & Tenths	
5-7-07	Smith v. United Sales	118294	Summarized 6 depositions; Client; Δ (Defendant) Helen; Δ Barney, Δ Rose; Witness Forrest & Johnson	BJP	6.	5
5-8-07	Marcel v. True Oil	118003	PC w/Client Re: Settlement offer; Discussions w/Attorney; Memo to file Re: offer	BJP	.	3
5-8-07	Johnson v. State	118118	PC w/Client's Mother, PC w/Client; LR Re: Bail; Memo to file; R correspondence	BJP	.	75
5-8-07	Potential claim of Watkins v. Leslie Grocery	Not Assigned Yet	OC w/Client; (New client); Reviewed facts; Received medical records Re; accident; Conf. w/atty	BJP	1.	50
5-8-07	Smith v. United Sales	118294	Computerized searches on depositions for attorney	BJP	.	75
5-8-07	Jay Tiller Bankruptcy	118319	PC w/Creditor, Bank One; Memo to file; Client; LJ to Client	BJP	.	3
5-8-07	Potential Claim of Watkins v. Leslie Grocery	—	LR Slip & Fall cases generally; Standard of care	BJP	1.	00
5-8-07	Marcel v. True Oil	118003	Conf. w/atty. & Client Re: Settlement; Drafted & prepared LJ to Δ's Re: Settlement offer	BJP	1.	10
5-8-07	Jay Tiller Bankruptcy	118319	Drafted Bankruptcy petition; OC w/Client; List of Debts; Fin. Stmt; Conf. w/atty	BJP	1.	00
5-8-07	Smith v. United Sales	118294	Drafted and prepared depo notice to Witness Spring	BJP	.	25
5-9-07	Seeley Real Estate Matter	118300	Ran amortization schedule to attach to 'Contract for Deed'	BJP	.	25

to have clients with more than one matter pending. Separate records need to be kept for each matter, and, typically, separate invoices are generated. Most manual time-keeping systems are being replaced with computerized methods, even in very small law firms.

Computerized Timekeeping

Nearly all timekeeping and billing computer programs can provide assistance in keeping track of time. In some programs, the user enters what case is being worked on and whether the time is billable or non-billable and then turns the "meter" on. The computer keeps track of the time until the user is completed with the project for that client. The computerized time slip is then stored in the program until a billing is generated. When a bill is generated, the computerized time slip is automatically calculated and included in the client's bill. Figure 5-16 is an example of a computer-ized time slip.

Billable v. Non-billable Time

One of the basics of timekeeping is the difference between billable and non-billable time. **Billable time** is actual time that a legal assistant or attorney spends working on a case and that is directly billed to a client's account. Any activity that an attorney or legal assistant performs to further a client's case, other than clerical functions, is usu-ally considered billable time, including interviewing witnesses, investigating a case, serving subpoenas, performing legal research, drafting, and so forth. **Non-billable time** is time that cannot be directly billed to a paying client. Nonetheless, it should still be tracked.

There are typically three types of non-billable time:

(a) general firm activities
(b) personal time
(c) pro bono work

General firm activities refer to time spent on personnel materials, planning, market-ing, client development, staff/committee meetings, library maintenance, and pro-fessional development. Personal time refers to taking breaks, cleaning and organiz-ing, and taking sick/vacation days. **Pro bono** work is legal services that are provided free of charge to a client who is not able to pay for the services. Pro bono may be required by your firm or by some state bars. Typically, pro bono cases are taken to generate goodwill in the community for the office or to provide a commu-nity service. Although handling pro bono cases is a morally proper thing to do, it is still counted as non-billable time.

Non-billable time is sometimes referred to as "overhead" or "office hours" be-cause the cost of non-billable time must be paid for by the office. **Overhead** refers to general administrative costs of doing business; they are incidental costs regarding the management and supervision of the business. Overhead includes costs such as rent, utilities, phones, office supplies, equipment, and salary costs for administra-tors who manage the business and others. Overhead costs are sometimes defined as any cost not directly associated with the production of goods or services.

billable time
Actual time that a legal assistant or attorney spends working on a case and that is directly billed to a client's account.

non-billable time
Time that cannot be directly billed to a paying client.

pro bono
Legal services that are provided free of charge to a client who is not able to pay for the services.

overhead
General administrative costs of doing business, including costs such as rent, utilities, phone, and salary costs for administrators.

Figure 5-15   Time Sheet Record for a Case

Time Records for Case Name: *Smith v. United Sales*   Case No: *118294*

5-7-07	Smith v. United Sales	118294	Summarized 6 depositions; Client; Δ (Defendant) Allen; Δ Barney, ΔRose; Witness Forest & Johnson	BJP	6.	5
5-8-07	Smith v. United Sales	118294	Computerized searches on depositions for attorney	BJP	.	75
5-8-07	Smith v. United Sales	118294	Drafted and prepared depo notice to Witness Spring	BJP	.	25

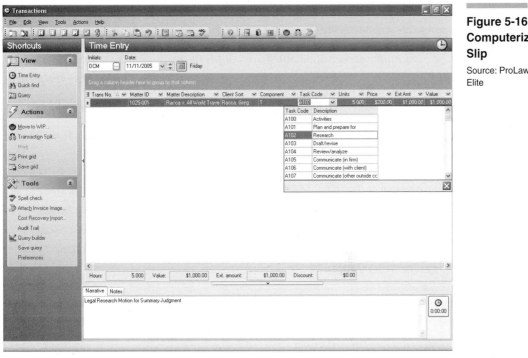

**Figure 5-16
Computerized Time
Slip**

Source: ProLaw, Thomson Elite

Figure 5-17
Billable Hours
Expected Per Week
for Legal Assistants

Billable Hours Per Week/(Annual Max)	Percent	Respondents
6–10 hours (520 hours)	1%	2
11–15 hours (780 hours)	1%	2
16–20 hours (1,040 hours)	4%	15
21–25 hours (1,300 hours)	9%	33
26–30 hours (1,560 hours)	31%	111
31–35 hours (1,820 hours)	31%	112
36–40 hours (2,080 hours)	17%	61
41–45 hours (2,340 hours)	1%	3
More than 45 hours	7%	25

Source: National Association of Legal Assistants, 2004 National Utilization and Compensation Survey Report, Table 3.2, Billable Hours Expected Per Week.

Timekeeping for Legal Assistants

Many law offices have a preoccupation with the billable hour concept and set billable hour quotas that legal assistants must meet (see Figure 5-17). The average number of annual billable hours for legal assistants ranges from 520 to more than 2,340; most legal assistants must bill between 1,400 and 1,800 hours annually. Historically, this was not the case. In the early 1960s, 1,300 billable hours was thought to be realistic. The minimum number of billable hours depends greatly on the location and size of the law office and on the types of cases it handles. When accepting a job, you should understand exactly what the expectation is regarding billable hours. There is obviously a big difference in the quality of life between billing 1,400 hours and 1,800.

—Then —

There are only approximately 1,300 fee-earning hours per year unless the lawyer works overtime. Many of the eight hours per day available for office work are consumed in personal, civic, bar, religious, and political activities, general office administration, and other . . . matters. Either five or six hours per day would be realistic, depending upon the habits of the individual lawyer. —ABA-1959[11]

— Now —

The overwhelming majority of law firms today have a minimum billable hour or target that they like for their legal assistants to achieve. [It's] anywhere from 1,400 to 1,800 billable hours a year, depending on the law firm. In the last couple of years, more and more firms have realized they have got to be more strict about billable minimums.[12]

Recording Time

There are several different ways to actually record or track your time. One method is to bill time in tenths of an hour, with .5 being a half-hour and 1.0 being an hour. Every six minutes is a tenth of the hour, so you would be billing on six-minute intervals. Billing in tenths works out as follows:

0–6 minutes = .1 hour	31–36 minutes = .6 hour
7–12 minutes = .2 hour	37–42 minutes = .7 hour
13–15 minutes = .25 hour	43–45 minutes = .75 hour
16–18 minutes = .3 hour	46–48 minutes = .8 hour
19–24 minutes = .4 hour	49–54 minutes = .9 hour
25–30 minutes = .5 hour	55–60 minutes = 1.0 hour

As an alternative, some offices will bill using a quarter of an hour as the basis, as follows:

0–15 minutes = .25 hour
16–30 minutes = .50 hour
31–45 minutes = .75 hour
46–60 minutes = 1.0 hour

PARALEGAL TRAPPED

A paralegal, on his way to an assignment on another floor, became trapped in an elevator just after getting on. Fellow employees gathered around the elevator door. The time-conscious paralegal called out from inside the elevator, "Is this billable or non-billable time?"[13]

Although the quarterly basis is easier to use, it is not as accurate as the tenth-of-an-hour system. Suppose you took a five-minute phone call from a client and your average billing rate is $70 an hour. Using the tenth of an hour system, the fee for the phone call would be $7 (.1 hour × $70 equals $7). However, using the quarterly system, the fee for the phone call would be $17.50, since .25 is the smallest interval (.25 × $70 equals $17.50), or more than twice as much.

It is important that you include as much detail as possible when completing your time records, that the language be clear and easily understood, and that the time record itself be legibly written. Clients are usually more willing to pay a bill when they know exactly what service was performed for them. For example, compare these general bill statements.

1. "Telephone conference—.50 hr. $35.00."
2. "Telephone conference with client on Plaintiff's Request for Production of Documents regarding whether or not client has copies of the draft contracts at issue—.50 hr. $35.00."

Which of these statements would you rather receive?

Many clients would prefer the latter, since they are able to see, and hopefully remember, exactly what specific services they received.

Timekeeping Practices

If the average legal assistant is required to bill between 1,400 and 1,800 hours a year, it is very important that he or she take the timekeeping function extremely seriously. The following are some suggestions to consider regarding keeping track of time.

Be very careful with your billing. Billing extra hours just to look good is foolish. Consider how much time it should take you to complete a task, and try to work within that time frame. If you are consistently a high biller because you spend an inordinate amount of time on projects, people will assume one of two things: (1) you don't know what you are doing, or (2) you are doing more than needed to accomplish the task. Remember that your client pays the bills. The most important consideration in being competitive is to provide the best service at the best price.[14]

- *Find out how many hours you must bill annually, monthly, and weekly up front, and track where you are in relationship to the quota*—One of the first things you should do when you start a new legal assistant job is to find out how many billable hours you must have. If the office requires that you bill 1,400 hours a year, budget this on a monthly and weekly basis, and keep track of where you are so that you will not have to try to make it all up at the end of the year.
- *Find out when time sheets are due*—Another thing you should do when starting a new position is to find out exactly what day time sheets are due so that you can submit them on time. Figure 5-18 contains a sample law office policy on time sheets.
- *Keep copies of your time sheets*—Always keep a copy of your time sheet or know how to access them electronically for your own file, in case the original is lost or misplaced. Having a record also allows you to go back and calculate your number of billable hours.
- *Record your time contemporaneously on a daily basis*—One of the biggest mistakes you can make is to not record your time as you go along during the day. If you wait until the end of the day to try to remember all the things you did, there is absolutely no way you will be able to accurately reconstruct everything. In the end, you will be the one suffering, doing work you did not get credit for. So be sure to keep a time sheet handy and fill it out as you go along.
- *Record your actual time spent; do not discount your time*—Do not discount your time because you think you should have been able to perform a job faster. If it took you four hours to finish an assignment and you worked the whole four hours, there is no reason to discount the time. *If the supervising attorneys think a discount is warranted, they can decide that, but it is not up to you to do*

9.2 Timekeeping Records

The Firm's income is generated, for the most part, through direct charges to clients for time spent on their behalf by the Firm's professional staff. Therefore, prompt and accurate completion of the time records is an important part of the billing process. Without accurate and complete information, the Firm is unable to prepare timely and accurate invoices for its clients. It is important to be precise because now legal auditors are analyzing lawyer's bills to make sure they are proper.

9.2.1 The Daily Time Sheet

All timekeepers shall record their daily time directly into the computerized billing system. All entries must follow specific guidelines to ensure that all entries are complete and correct. This will reduce the effort involved in correcting entries. The following guidelines must be followed in completing the Time Section of the Daily Time Sheet.

-1- MATTER: Enter the name of the matter (file) to which the time is to be charged.

-2- VERB CODE: Enter the appropriate verb code that begins the description of the service performed. When the entry is to be "no charge," a 400 verb code must be entered.

-3- ANNOTATION: Enter in this area the full text of the service performed or a description that, when added to the verb code, will complete the description of services performed. [The maximum number of characters to be used (spaces and special characters included) is _____.]

-4- CLIENT NO.: Required on all entries. Enter the number assigned to the client for whom the services are being performed.

-5- MATTER NO.: Required on all entries. Enter the number assigned to the matter for which the services are being performed.

-6- RATE: Required only on "no charge" and "special rate" entries.
    a. "No-Charge" Entry: The lawyer may want to show the client that services were performed but that no charge is being made to the client.
    b. "Special Rate" Entries: Certain services may be performed that require a special effort or expertise. These services may be billed at a higher rate than the normal hourly rate for regular services. Special rates are assigned to some lawyers. Enter the special rate code, when appropriate, as follows: _____.

-7- HRS. (HOURS): Required on all entries. Enter the number of whole (nonfractional) hours the service required.

-8- PARTIAL HOURS: Enter the portion of time less than one hour. An hour may be divided into .10-hour (six-minute) increments. Entries here must be in multiples of tenths of an hour, e.g., .20, .30, .40, etc. Generally, the minimum time entry charge is one-tenth (.10) hour.

-9- TOTAL: Enter the total number of hours accounted for on the Time Sheet. All timekeeping personnel must account for a minimum of eight hours for every workday. Time Records for weekdays falling on holidays, for days off for illness or vacation, or for days not spent on client services must be submitted and should show [7, 7.5, 8] hours. The only exception is for time records reflecting time spent on client services performed on weekends; these should have as few or as many hours accounted for as were actually spent on those services. The total must be accurate and is required on all time records.

-10- FIRM MATTERS: These matter numbers and their corresponding descriptions are to be used to account for time spent on activities other than client services and for Firm activities that are specifically required by the Firm's management. For further

Figure 5-18
Sample Time Sheet Policy

Source: Wert, R. C., & Hatoff, H. L. (2004). *Law office policy and procedures manual* (4th ed.). American Bar Association.

Figure 5-18
(Continued)

details regarding "chargeable" Firm activities, see exhibit [#] at the end of this section. Enter the appropriate matter number in the matter area of the time entry. These numbers must be used in conjunction with the Firm client number, _____. Enter this number in the client number area of the time entry.

When completed, the Time Sheet should be reviewed for any possible errors or omissions. The secretary will retain the original Time Sheet at her desk for future reference.

9.2.2 Submission of Time Records

All time records must be prepared and submitted on a "next day" basis.

The Accounting Department must have adequate time to properly process the input from the Time Records. This cannot be achieved if lawyers and legal assistants wait until the day before a payday or closing day to turn in their Time Sheets. No professionals will be entitled to receive their paychecks unless their Time Records are up to date and delivered to _____ through the second workday preceding the pay date. Periodic reports are circulated to the department heads and Firm management personnel indicating which individuals are late in submitting Time Records. Appropriate action may be taken to correct any deficiencies. Failure to adhere to these editing and time procedures is a serious matter and will be appropriately considered by the Firm's management in its annual evaluation of each professional.

Just starting out as a new legal assistant I had a very hard time remembering to complete time sheets. At the end of the day . . . or week . . . I would try to recall what I had done and then put it on the time sheet. I just couldn't remember. Things happen so fast in a law office that I didn't record half of what I actually did. It didn't take long before I was getting attention—all bad. The firm assumed I wasn't doing anything, even though I was. I learned right then, record your time as your go along in a day and as you move from one task to another. That is the only way to be accurate and the only way I stayed employed.

—Brent Roper

---

that. However, if you made a mistake or had a problem that you do not think the client should be billed for, tell your supervising attorney, and let him or her help you make the decision.

- *Be aware if billable hours are related to bonuses or merit increases*—Be aware of how billable hours are used. In some law offices, billable hours are used in distributing bonuses and merit increases and can be used in performance evaluations, so know up front how they will be used.
- *Be ethical*—Always be honest and ethical in the way you fill out your time sheets. Padding your time sheets is unethical and simply wrong. Eventually, wrongdoing regarding timekeeping, billing, or handling client funds will become apparent.

I worked closely with a paralegal who consistently had two or three more [billable] hours a day than I did, although we arrived around the same time and did similar work all day. We usually walked each other out at night (for safety reasons). I'd look at my time for a day: 10.5 hours; and she had 13. She didn't subtract for lunch or breaks. . . . An attorney called me in to ask about the discrepancy between her time and mine. . . . The lawyer talked to her. . . . Her time sheet was accurate after that.[15]

- *Be aware of things that keep you from billing time*—Be aware of things that keep you from having a productive day, such as:
  - People who lay their troubles at your feet or who are constantly taking your attention away from your work. An appropriate approach is to say, "I would really like to hear about it at lunch, but right now I am really busy."
  - Wasted time spent trying to track down other people or trying to find information you need.
  - Constant interruptions, including phone calls. If you really need to get something done, go someplace where you can get the work done, and tell others to hold your calls. However, check in every once in a while to return client phone calls. Clients should have their phone calls returned as soon as possible.

BILLING

To generate the necessary income to operate the firm, special attention must be paid to billing, the process of issuing bills for the purpose of collecting monies for legal services performed and for being reimbursed for expenses. Figure 5-19 shows primary practice areas for attorney's based on billing.

Billing For Legal Assistant Time and Profitability

Many law offices bill for legal assistant time as well as for attorney time. Clients often prefer this because the legal assistant hourly rates are much lower than attorney hourly rates. Figure 5-20 shows the average hourly rates for legal assistants in different regions of the country.

For example, assume an associate attorney and a legal assistant can both prepare discovery documents in a case and that the task will take seven hours. Assuming the legal assistant bills at $80 an hour and the associate bills at $175 an hour, the cost to the client if the legal assistant does the job is $560, and the cost if the associate drafts the discovery is $1,225. Thus, the client will have saved $665 by simply allowing the

Figure 5-19
Practice Areas Based on Billing

Source: American Bar Association. (2004). 2003 ABA legal technology resource center survey report, law office technology (p. 27).

What is (are) your primary practice area(s) based on billing?

	Total
Antitrust	1.5%
Banking and finance	5.4%
Bankruptcy	6.2%
Commercial	12.8%
Computer/technology/e-commerce law	1.1%
Construction	5.2%
Contracts	12.5%
Corporate	16.9%
Criminal	4.4%
Employment/labor	10.3%
Environmental	3.5%
Estates/trusts/wills	27.0%
Family law	10.3%
General practice (civil)	14.0%
Health law	3.3%
Immigration	1.0%
Insurance defense	7.4%
Intellectual property	5.4%
Litigation	29.3%
Medical malpractice	4.7%
Pension and benefits	1.4%
Personal injury	11.5%
Product liability	4.9%
Real estate	23.0%
Securities, mergers, and acquisitions	4.3%
Tax	8.8%
Worker's compensation	4.6%
Other	10.9%
Total	100%
Count	1,490

Figure 5-20
Average Legal Assistant Billing Rate by Region

Region	Legal Assistant 2004 Average Billing Rate
New England/Mideast	$93
Great Lakes	$95
Plain States	$77
Southeast	$91
Southwest	$89
Rocky Mountains	$79
Far West	$106

Source: National Association of Legal Assistants, 2004 National Utilization and Compensation Survey Report, Table 3.6, Billing Rates By Region.

legal assistant to do the job. The client would still have to pay for the attorney's time to review the legal assistant's discovery, but the cost would be minimal. This represents substantial savings to clients.

As mentioned earlier, the question of whether law offices can bill for legal assistant time was considered by the United States Court in *Missouri v. Jenkins*, 491 U.S. 274 (1989). In that case, the plaintiff was successful on several counts in a civil rights lawsuit and was attempting to recover attorney's fees from the defendant under a federal statute. The statutory language provided that the prevailing party could recover "reasonable attorney's fees" from the other party. The plaintiff argued for recovery for the time that legal assistants spent working on the case as well as for the time attorneys spent. The defendant argued that legal assistant time was not "attorney's fees." Alternatively, the defendants argued that if they did have to pay something for legal assistant time, they should only have to pay about $15 an hour, which represents the overhead costs to the office for a legal assistant.

The court found that legal assistants carry out many useful tasks under the direction of attorneys and that "reasonable attorney's fees" referred to the reasonable fee for work produced, whether by attorneys or legal assistants. The court also found that, under the federal statute, legal assistant time should not be compensated as overhead costs to the office but should be paid at the prevailing market rates in the area for legal assistant time. The court noted that the prevailing rate for legal assistants in that part of the country at that time was about $40 an hour and held that the office was entitled to receive that amount for legal assistant hours worked on the case. Thus, it is clear that offices can bill for legal assistant time if they choose to do so.

Leveraging and How Hourly Billing Rates Are Determined

Leveraging is an important concept in law office billing. **Leveraging** is the process of earning a profit from legal services that are provided by law office personnel (usually partners, associates, and legal assistants). Leveraging allows the office not only to recover the cost of an attorney or legal assistant's salary but also to pay overhead expenses and even make a profit on each such person. Thus, legal assistants are also a profit center for law firms. It is a win-win situation; clients pay lower fees for legal assistants over attorneys, and law firms still generate a profit on legal assistant time.

leveraging
The process of earning a profit from legal services that are provided by law office personnel (usually partners, associates, and legal assistants).

Functions of a Successful Billing System

An oft-forgotten aspect of any billing system is that the system must please the firm's customers or clients. A good billing system is determined by whether or not the firm's clients are satisfied with the billings and whether or not they are paying the bills that are sent to them. One quick way a firm can lose a good client is by mishandling the client's money in some way, by overbilling the client, or by giving the client the impression that her or his money is being used unjustly or unfairly. In addition, mishandling a client's money is a top reason that attorneys are disciplined. A good billing system, whether computerized or not, must do several things, including accurately tracking the client's account, providing regular billings, and providing clients with an itemization of the services performed.

ACCURATELY TRACK HOW MUCH A CLIENT HAS PAID THE FIRM   A successful billing system must be able to accurately track how much clients have paid the firm and whether the payments are made in cash, through a trust account, or otherwise. Although this may seem easy, often it is not. Consider how you feel when a creditor has either lost one of your payments or misapplied it in some manner. This is especially important for a law firm because, in many instances, large sums of money are involved. Payments can be lost, not entered into the system, or even applied to the wrong client. The firm must take great care with regard to what goes in and out of the billing system and ensure that the information is accurate.

SEND REGULAR BILLINGS   Nearly all clients like to receive timely billings. We all expect to receive regular billings for routine things, such as credit cards, utilities, and so forth. Likewise, most clients like to receive billings that are at least monthly. Imagine the frustration of a client who receives a quarterly billing that is four or five times more expensive than expected. Regular billings will alert the client to how he or she is being billed and how much needs to be budgeted. In addition, if a client sees timely bills that are more expensive than were planned for, he or she can tell the firm how to proceed so as to limit future bills before costs are incurred. This at least gives the client the option of cutting back on legal services instead of getting angry at the firm for not communicating the charges on a timely basis.

PROVIDE CLIENT BILLINGS THAT ARE FAIR AND RESPECTFUL   Billings that are fair and courteous are essential to a good billing system. If a client believes that the firm is overcharging for services or that the billings are curt and unprofessional, the client may simply not pay a bill or may hold payment. If you ever must speak to a client regarding a bill, always be courteous and respectful, and try to understand the situation from the client's point of view. If a dispute arises, simply take down the client's side of the story, relay the information to the attorney in charge of the matter, and let the attorney resolve the situation.

PROVIDE CLIENT BILLINGS THAT IDENTIFY WHAT SERVICES HAVE BEEN PROVIDED
When a client receives a billing, it is important that the client knows what services were received. Bills that simply say "For Services Rendered" are, for the most part, a thing of the past. Although the format of bills will depend on the client, it is recommended that you indicate exactly what service was performed, by whom, on what date, for how long, and for what charge. If a client can see exactly what the firm is doing and how hard the staff are working, the client may be more willing to pay the bill.

PROVIDE CLIENT BILLINGS THAT ARE CLEAR   Finally, billings should be clear and without legalese. They should be easy to read and should provide the information that a client wants to see. Payments on billings that are complicated and hard to read are often held up while a client tries to decipher a bill.

In short, a billing system should satisfy your customers so that they are willing to make payments on time.

Manual Billing Systems

Before legal billing software was widely available, billings were generated manually, using typewriters or word processors and time sheets. Law practices typically would store the time sheets in the accounting file of each case and then periodically send a statement. Although a few offices may still produce billings manually, manual systems have certain inherent limitations. Manual billings typically are slow and cumbersome, are prone to mathematical errors, and can take a great deal of overhead time to generate the bill. Thus, manual billings are sent out less frequently than most offices would like, which can cause cash-flow problems. In addition, management reports on manual systems are burdensome to produce. Computerized billing systems automatically produce management reports that show who is billing the most hours, which clients pay the best, and which types of cases generate the most money.

Computerized Billing Systems

Computerized billing systems solve many of the problems associated with manual systems. Generally, timekeepers still must record what they do with their time on a time slip or time sheet, or record the entry directly into the program. If the time slips are completed manually, then they must be entered into the legal billing software, usually on a daily or weekly basis. It is common for offices using computerized billing systems to produce monthly or even biweekly bills according to the wishes of the client. In addition to solving cash-flow problems, most legal billing software programs produce reports that can help the office make good management decisions (this is covered in more detail later in the chapter). Computerized timekeeping and billing also produces billings that are more accurate than manual methods because all mathematical computations are performed automatically by the computer. Because legal timekeeping and billing software prices have plunged several hundred dollars, nearly any office can afford these types of programs.

The Computerized Timekeeping and Billing Process

Timekeeping and billing software packages differ greatly from one another. However, the computerized timekeeping and billing process for most billing packages is as shown in Figure 5-21.

1. **The Client and the Attorney Reach an Agreement on Legal Fees** An attorney can bill for services in many different ways. At the outset of most cases, the client and the attorney reach an agreement regarding how much the

Figure 5-21   Computerized Timekeeping and Billing Cycle

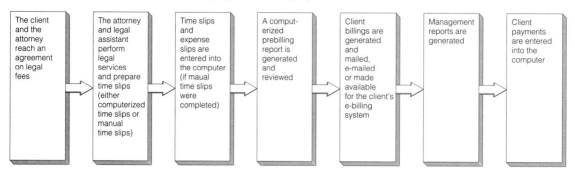

attorney will charge for her or his services. Preferably, the agreement is in writing in the form of a contract. After the legal fee has been agreed on, the new matter is set up in the computerized billing package by entering information, including the client's name and address, the type of case it is, and the type of legal fee that has been agreed upon.

2. **The Attorney and Legal Assistant Perform Legal Services and Prepare Time Slips** When attorneys or legal assistants perform work on a legal matter for a client, they fill out a time slip to track the exact services (either using a manual time slip form or entering the information directly into the computer). Many timekeeping and billing programs also support data entry from a handheld personal digital assistant (PDA).

3. **Time Slips and Expense Slips Are Entered into the Computer** If manual time slips are used, they must be entered into the computer. The information is typed into the computer in roughly the same format as it appears on the time slip. It is essential that the information be accurately entered into the computer. In addition, expense slips are also entered into the computer to track the expenses a firm incurs on behalf of a client.

4. **A Pre-billing Report Is Generated and Reviewed** After legal services have been performed and recorded in the time and billing software, the next step is for a pre-billing report to be generated. This is done before the final client bills are generated. A **pre-billing report** is a rough draft of billings that eventually will be sent to clients (see Figure 5-22). The pre-billing report is given to the attorney in charge of the case for review or to a billing committee to make sure the billing is accurate.

Attorneys may choose to discount bills for a variety of reasons, including thinking the task should have taken less time than it actually did. Discounts also are used for good customers, because of the client's hardship, for professional courtesy or for friends, or because the billing looks unreasonable. This can, however, be very frustrating to a legal assistant who has his or her time cut back. Typically, only the amount that is actually billed is counted against the target or minimum billable number of hours.

pre-billing report
A rough draft version of billings.

Figure 5-22
Prebilling Report

```
                    JOHNSON, BECK & TAYLOR
 8/12/07                Prebilling Report                    Page 1
 ---------------------------------------------------------------------
 Refrigeration, Inc.                       Corporate Matters
 Miscellaneous Corporate Matters           Monthly
 Case Number: Refrig-002                    Trust Balance: $2,825
 P.O. Box 10083                             Case Rate: $125
 500 East Fifth Street                      Case Attorney: MJB

 Los Angeles, CA 90014
 Phone: (213) 553-9342


                                      Previous Bill Owed $470.20


                      —Legal Fees—

 7/6/07   MJB   Telephone conference with
                Stevenson re: June minutes        .50 hr        $62.50

 7/7/07   MJB   Preparation of June minutes;
                prepared for review at next
                meeting of the board of directors  1.00 hr   $125.00 MJB

 7/9/07   MJB   Conference with Stevenson at home   .25 hr        none

                Total Legal Fees ............      1.75 hr   $187.50 MJB

                      —Costs Advanced—

 7/7/07   MJB   Photocopy documents; June 2005
                minutes (for board meeting)        $.25 ea
                                                  100 items      $25.00

                Total Costs Advanced ........                   $25.00



                      Continued on Page Two
```

5. **Client Billings Are Generated and Mailed** Formal client billings are generated by the computer (see Figure 5-23). Most timekeeping and billing software can produce many different billing formats. The computer automatically prints the bills, and they are subsequently mailed to the clients.
6. **Management Reports Are Generated** Most computerized timekeeping and billing programs have a wide variety of management reports available.

Figure 5-23
Final Client Billing

JOHNSON, BECK & TAYLOR
555 Flowers Street, Suite 200
Los Angeles, California 90038
(212) 585-2342

Mary Smith
Refrigeration, Inc.
P.O.Box 10083
500 East Fifth Street

Los Angeles, CA 90014

Billing Date: 08/15/07

Acct. Number: 4345AS3234
Previous Bal. in Trust
$2,825.00

RE: Refrigeration Miscellaneous Corporate Matters

DATE	PROFESSIONAL SERVICES	INDIV.	TIME	
7/6/07	Telephone conference with Stevenson re: June minutes	MJB	.50	$62.50
7/7/07	Preparation of June minutes: prepared for review at next meeting of the board of directors	MJB	1.00	$125.00
7/9/07	Conference with Stevenson at home	MJB	.25	$-0-
TOTAL FOR THE ABOVE SERVICES			1.75	**$187.50**

DATE	EXPENSES		
7/7/07	Photocopy documents; June minutes (for board meeting)		$25.00
TOTAL FOR ABOVE EXPENSES			**$25.00**
TOTAL BILLING			**$212.50**
CURRENT BALANCE IN TRUST			**$2,612.50**

Management reports are not used for billing clients; they are used to evaluate the effectiveness of a firm. For example, most programs generate a report that shows how much time is non-billable (i.e., not chargeable to clients). If a firm has a lot of non-billable time, it might indicate that the firm is not productive and is losing valuable time from its timekeepers.

Management reports can also be used to make management decisions, such as that particular types of cases are no longer profitable, the firm needs to raise hourly rates, or other types of decisions.

7. **Client Payments Are Entered into the Computer** Finally, payments made as a result of billings must be recorded or entered into the computer, giving clients proper credit for the payments.

Bill Formats

Generating bills is the most important aspect of any timekeeping and billing program. There is no uniform way that all law offices bill clients; the look and format of billings depend on the law office, its clients, the type of law it practices, and so forth. Thus, it is important that any timekeeping and billing system used, whether it is manual or computerized, be flexible in the number of client billing formats that are available. For example, some bill formats contain only general information about the services provided, while others show greater detail. In many computerized systems, the format of the bill is set up when the client's case is first entered into the system.

Historically, many offices did not itemize their billing, simply stating "For Services Rendered $XXX" on the bill. Although each client is different, most clients like to receive detailed billings of exactly what services are being provided. This allows the client to see what he or she is paying for. This also is beneficial to the office, since clients are more willing to pay the bill when they know what it is for. Producing detailed bills takes work. It requires timekeepers to make accurate, current time slips of what work they have provided. Although this seems enough, it is not. It is very hard to persuade timekeepers to write down each service they perform (e.g., 12/22/07, Telephone call to Larry Jones, witness, regarding statement given 10/10/07.........15 minutes). Yet, the whole point of billing is to be paid. So, if an office produces a bill that is not itemized and, therefore, the client does not pay it, nothing has been gained. Although itemized billings are sometimes inconvenient for the timekeeper and take longer to produce, the extra work has paid off if the bill is paid in the end.

Management Reports

Almost all timekeeping and billing software packages produce a wide variety of management reports (see Figure 5-24). **Management reports** are used to help management analyze whether the office is operating in an efficient and effective manner. Management reports can be used to track problems an office may be experiencing and to help devise ways to correct the problems. The following are explanations of some common management reports and how they are used by offices.

management reports
Reports used to help management analyze whether the office is operating in an efficient and effective manner.

**Figure 5-24
Timekeeping and
Billing Program—
Management Reports**

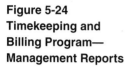

CASE/CLIENT LIST   Most billing packages allow the user to produce a case or client list. A list of all active cases an office has is very important in trying to effectively manage a large caseload. Most reports list not only the client names but also the appropriate account number (also called the "client identification number" by some programs). This is useful when trying to locate a client's identification number.

**aged accounts
receivable report**
A report showing all cases
that have outstanding
balances due and how
long these balances are
past due.

AGED ACCOUNTS RECEIVABLE REPORT   The **aged accounts receivable report** shows all cases that have outstanding balances due to the office and how long these balances are past due (see Figure 5-25). The report breaks down the current balances due and the balances that are 30, 60, and more than 90 days past due. Using this report, management can clearly see which clients are not paying and how old the balances are. This report also is helpful for following up on clients who are slow in paying their bills. Most programs allow the report to be run according to the type of case. Thus, management can see what types of cases (criminal, divorce, tax, etc.) have the most aged accounts. If one particular type of case has more than its share of aged accounts, it might be more profitable to stop taking that type. So, from a management perspective, this can be a very important report. It should be noted that aged account information should not appear on bills sent to clients. Bills that are more than 30 days old should simply say "past due."

Figure 5-25　Aged Accounts Receivable Report and Timekeeper Productivity Report

Courtesy of CompuLaw, Inc.

LAW OFFICES OF SMITH, SMITH AND JONES

5/ 1/07　　Aged Accounts Receivable　　　　　PAGE 1

Entire Alphabet　　　　　　　　　　　　　All Bill Types
All Attorneys　　　　　　　　　　　　　　All Case Types
Cycle: All Cycles (All Months)　　　　Ignore Cycle Due Date

Client/Matter	Balance	Current	30 Days	60 Days	Over 90
All Right Manufacturing C					
General Corporate Matt	127.50	None	127.50	None	None
Hinge Division - Paten	975.00	975.00	None	None	None
	1,102.50	975.00	127.50	None	None
Alta Loma Bookkeeping					
Purchase of Johnson Ch	800.00	175.00	175.00	450.00	None
Burton, Sarah					
Divorce	147.50	None	147.50	None	None
Protective order	440.00	None	None	440.00	None
	587.50	None	147.50	440.00	None
	1,500.00	1,500.00	None	None	None
	607.50	None	505.00	102.50	None
	427.75	427.75	None	None	None
	1,775.00	None	None	1,775.00	None
	500.00	None	None	500.00	None
	2,702.75	427.75	None	2,275.00	None
	175.00	175.00	None	None	None
	725.00	None	None	None	725.00
	112.50	None	None	None	112.50
	75.00	None	None	75.00	None
	912.50	None	None	75.00	837.50
	632.75	None	632.75	None	None
	7,500.00	7,500.00	None	None	None
	4,410.00	None	1,410.00	3,000.00	None
	475.00	475.00	None	None	None
	12,559.99	550.00	9,405.00	2,425.00	170.00
	330.00	330.00	None	None	None
	485.00	None	None	485.00	None
	34,770.50	12,107.75	12,402.75	9,252.50	1,007.50

LAW OFFICES OF SMITH, SMITH AND JONES

5/ 1/07　　Time/Productivity Analysis　　　PAGE 1

April 2007

		Fees	Hours
Arthur A. Alexander	Billed:	$8,852.50	77.75
	On Hold:	$100.00	1.00
Payments Rec'd $7,277.50	Non Chargeable:	$100.00	.75
Standard Rate: $75.00	Written Off:	$125.00	2.00
Realized Rate: $112.00	Administrative:	$125.00	1.00

• • • •

		Fees	Hours
Byron B. Brown	Billed:	$10,527.75	101.50
	On Hold:	None	None
Payments Rec'd $10,950.50	Non Chargeable:	None	None
Standard Rate: $95.00	Written Off:	None	None
Realized Rate: $93.00	Administrative:	None	None

• • • •

		Fees	Hours
Andrew B. Cabellero	Billed:	$12,750.00	101.00
	On Hold:	$1,250.00	10.00
Payments Rec'd $9,550.50	Non Chargeable:	$100.00	1.00
Standard Rate: $125.00	Written Off:	$250.00	2.20
Realized Rate: $125.00	Administrative:	$125.00	1.00

• • • •

Monthly Summary - All Attorneys Listed

		Fees	Hours
	Billed:	$31,130.25	280.25
Payments Rec'd	On Hold:	$1,350.00	11.00
This Month: $27,778.00	Non Chargeable:	$200.00	1.75
	Written Off:	$375.00	4.20
Realized Rate: $110.00	Administrative:	$250.00	2.00

TIMEKEEPER PRODUCTIVITY REPORT　The amount of billable and non-billable time being spent by each timekeeper is shown in the **timekeeper productivity report** (see Figure 5-25). This report can be used to identify which timekeepers are the most diligent in their work. For example, notice in Figure 5-25 that "Arthur A. Alexander" billed a total of only 77.75 hours for the month while the other staff billed more than 100 hours. Also, notice that "Byron B. Brown" produced the most billable hours and payments received by the office.

timekeeper productivity report
A report showing how much billable and non-billable time is being spent by each timekeeper.

**Figure 5-26
Case Type
Productivity Report**

Courtesy of CompuLaw, Inc.

		FENWICK, QUINT GERSON AND PECK			
7/31/07		Case Type Productivity			PAGE 1
Case Type	Hours Billable	Fees Billed	Fees Income	% Total Fee Inc	% Total Hours
		July 2007			
Bankruptcies	252.75	$26,450.00	$17,500.50	11.73	17.48
Civil Matters	32.50	$4,142.75	$3,655.75	2.45	2.24
Corporate Matters	125.75	$19,855.50	$12,500.25	8.38	8.70
Criminal Matters	22.00	$1,875.00	$2,250.00	1.51	1.52
Estate Planning	87.75	$9,475.00	$8,875.00	5.95	6.07
Family Law	52.25	$6,175.75	$5,495.75	3.68	3.61
General Business	108.70	$9,775.50	$8,975.50	5.95	7.52
General Practice	61.00	$6,552.75	$7,275.50	4.88	4.22
Litigation	225.00	$37,750.00	$44,550.75	29.87	15.56
Personal Injury	35.00	$4,500.00	$4,125.25	2.76	2.42
Probate Matters	0.00	0.00	0.00	0.00	0.00
Real Estate Matters	18.00	$2,150.00	$2,100.00	1.40	1.24
Taxation Matters	24.75	$2,650.00	$2,655.00	1.78	1.71
Other	9.00	$1,253.00	$1,253.50	.84	.62
Patents & Trademarks	36.50	$4,141.75	$4,155.50	2.78	2.52
International Law	44.00	$8,645.25	$3,440.00	2.31	3.04
Immigration Law	27.00	$3,150.00	$750.00	.50	1.86
Insurance Defense	111.50	$10,950.75	$7,555.25	5.06	7.71
Insurance Plaintiff	88.00	$8,125.00	$6,550.75	4.39	6.08
Consumer Law	6.75	$595.00	$500.00	.33	.46
Labor Unions	77.00	$5,845.00	$4,995.50	3.35	5.32
July Totals	1,445.20	$174,058.00	$149.161.00		

Finally, note the totals section, which shows that although the office billed 280.25 hours for a total of $31,130.25, the office received to date $27,778.00. Although the report in Figure 5-25 shows the results for only one month, most packages allow the productivity report to be run for a quarter or even a year.

case type productivity report
A report showing which types of cases (e.g., criminal, personal injury, bankruptcy, etc.) are the most profitable.

CASE TYPE PRODUCTIVITY REPORT   The **case type productivity report** shows which types of cases (criminal, personal injury, bankruptcy, etc.) are the most profitable (see Figure 5-26). For example, note in Figure 5-26 that the bankruptcy and litigation areas of the law office brought in $17,500.50 and $44,550.75, respectively, for the month of July, or 11.73 percent and 29.87 percent of the income earned. This report obviously shows which types of cases are the most profitable and which types are the least profitable. Management will use this type of report to decide which areas to concentrate on to become more profitable.

Instead of writing comments on paper bills, checking math manually, organizing comments into categories, and drafting a comment letter . . . a client can automate the process of bill review so that it can be done online by commenting electronically. A client can use e-billing software to flag potential problems, including checking the math, and to format the billing data for easier review. One client noted, "I'm spending 25 to 50 percent less time [using/viewing e-bills] on the review process, and doing a more complete review."[16]

Electronic Billing

Electronic billing is when law firms bill clients using electronic means, such as the Internet. Many large clients—such as Fortune 1000 and other businesses—are demanding that law firms bill them using electronic means. The Legal Electronic Data Exchange Standard specifies a uniform output for law firm time and billing systems to export to e-billing systems. Many of the e-billing vendors are application service providers (ASPs), third-party vendors that set up the e-billing part of the system, receive data from law firms, and operate the software over the Internet. Clients are able to see bills (from any law firm they use) in a standard format and then customize the reports to meet their particular needs. For large clients, electronic billing is a big enhancement over traditional paper billing.

electronic billing
When law firms bill clients using electronic means, such as the Internet.

SUMMARY

Timekeeping is the process of tracking time for the purpose of billing clients. Billing is the process of issuing invoices for the purpose of collecting monies for legal services performed and being reimbursed for expenses.

There are several different kinds of legal fee agreements. An hourly rate fee is a fee for legal services that is billed to the client by the hour at an agreed-upon rate. An attorney or legal assistant hourly rate is based on the attorney's or legal assistant's level of expertise and experience in a particular area. A client hourly rate is based on an hourly charge for that particular client; no matter what level of attorney (associate, partner, etc.) works on a case, the client is billed one rate. Likewise, no matter what level of legal assistant works on a case (entry level, senior level, etc.) the client is billed one rate. A blended hourly rate is an hourly rate that takes into account the blend or mix of office staff working on the matter. Depending on the state, a "blend" may include legal assistants. If a law office charges $175 for all staff (legal assistants, associates, senior partners, etc.), this would be a blend. An activity hourly rate means that different hourly rates are charged depending on the type of activity, e.g., $150 for

telephone calls, $200 for office conference and $250 for legal research and drafting.

A contingency fee is a fee that is collected if the attorney successfully represents a client. The attorney is entitled to a certain percentage of the money that is recovered. If the client's case is not won, and no money is recovered, the attorney collects no legal fees but is still entitled to recover expenses. Contingency fee agreements must be in writing. A flat fee is a fee for legal services that is billed as a flat or fixed amount, no matter how much time is actually spent on the matter.

An earned retainer means that the money has been earned and can be deposited in the law office's or attorney's operating bank account. An unearned retainer means that the money has not yet been earned and is placed in trust as an advance against the attorney's future fees and expenses. As the money is earned by the law office, the money is removed from the trust and placed in the law office's or attorney's operating account. A trust or escrow bank account is a separate bank account, apart from a law office's or attorney's operating checking account, where unearned client funds are deposited. A cash advance retainer is an unearned retainer.

A retainer for general representation is used when a client such as a corporation requires continuing legal services (not including litigation) throughout the year. The client pays a retainer and is entitled to the legal services without any additional fees. In many states, a retainer for general representation is an earned retainer, because the client can call at any time and receive legal services. A case retainer is a fee paid at the beginning of a matter, is nonrefundable, and is paid as an incentive for the attorney to take the case. Case retainers are earned retainers. A pure retainer obligates the office to be available to represent a client throughout a certain time period, and the firm agrees to not represent any of its competitors. A pure retainer is typically an earned retainer.

Court-awarded attorneys fees are given to prevailing parties pursuant to certain federal and state statutes. Value billing is a type of fee agreement that is based on the perceived value of the services to the client.

The *Model Rules* requires that the basis or rate of the fee and expenses for a matter be communicated to the client, preferably in writing, and that any fee charged be reasonable. Whether a fee is reasonable depends on a number of factors, including the time and labor required, the novelty and difficulty of the issues raised, the fee customarily charged, the results obtained, the nature and length of the professional relationship, and the experience and reputation of the attorney, among other things.

Attorneys and law offices can charge and be reimbursed for reasonable legal expenses. Billable time is time that a legal professional can directly bill to a client's account. Non-billable time cannot be billed to a client and includes pro bono work (services that are provided free of charge) and overheard costs such as general management, supervision, client development, and other activities. Legal assistants are allowed to bill for their time as long as the work is professional and not clerical in nature. Leveraging is the process of earning profit from legal services that are provided by legal assistants and attorneys.

A successful billing system, whether computerized or manual, accurately tracks how much clients have paid, can send out regular billings, and provides clients with fair, respectful, and detailed bills.

The computerized timekeeping and billing process includes a client and attorney reaching a fee agreement, legal services being provided, times and expense slips entered into the computer, a prebilling report generated, a final bill generated, management reports run, and client payment recorded. Most computerized time and billing systems can produce management reports, including case/client list, aged accounts receivable, timekeeper productivity, and case type productivity reports, among others. Electronic billing is when law offices bill clients using electronic means, such as the Internet.

HELPFUL WEB SITES

ORGANIZATION	DESCRIPTION	INTERNET ADDRESS
Alabama State Bar—Law Office Management Assistance Program	Articles on a variety of law office management topics, including billing-related articles and information.	http://www.alabar.org/lomap/articles.cfm
American Bar Association (ABA)	Association for attorneys. The site has a large amount of information and publications relevant to individuals working in the legal profession.	http://www.abanet.org

ORGANIZATION	DESCRIPTION	INTERNET ADDRESS
ABA Law Practice Today	ABA site devoted to law practice management issues, including timekeeping and billing issues.	http://www.abanet.org/lpm
ABA Legal Technology Resource Center	ABA site devoted to technology. Includes resources and articles.	http://www.abanet.org/tech/ltrc/home.html
Association of Legal Administrators	National association for legal administrators. Contains resources and information related to law office management and legal administration.	http://www.alanet.org
Georgia State Bar Association	Articles on a variety of law office management topics, including billing-related articles and information.	http://www.gabar.org
Law Office Computing magazine	Excellent magazine, but limited information online. The site has good links to manufacturers that offer law office software, including timekeeping and billing.	http://www.lawoffice computing.com
Law Technology News	Excellent periodical for legal technology issues. Good white papers on technology issues.	http://www.lawtechnews.com and http://www.law.com/jsp/ltn/whitepapers.jsp
Maryland State Bar Association—Law Practice Management Assistance	Articles on a variety of law office management topics, including billing-related articles and information.	http://www.msba.org/departments/loma/articles/index.htm
Mississippi State Bar Association	Articles on a variety of law office management topics, including billing-related articles and information.	http://www.msbar.org/2_client_relations_handbook.php
National Association of Legal Assistants	National association for legal assistants. Contains many resources for legal assistants.	http://www.nala.org
National Federation of Paralegal Associations	National association for legal assistants. Contains many resources for legal assistants.	http://www.paralegals.org
New Jersey State Bar Association—Law Office Management Articles	Articles on a variety of law office management topics, including billing-related articles and information.	http://www.njsba.com/law_office_manage/index.cfm?fuseaction=articles
New York State Bar Association	Articles on a variety of law office management topics, including billing-related articles and information.	http://www.nysba.org/Content/NavigationMenu/Attorney_Resources/Practice_Management/Practice_Management.htm
South Carolina Bar—Practice Management Section	Articles on a variety of law office management topics, including billing-related articles and information.	http://www.scbar.org/pmap/resources.asp

TIMEKEEPING AND BILLING SOFTWARE

ORGANIZATION	PRODUCT/SERVICE	INTERNET ADDRESS
ADC Legal Systems, Inc.	Perfect practice billing and accounting	http://www.adclegal.com
Alumni Group	PC LAW legal timekeeping and billing software	http://www.pclaw.com
DDI, Inc.	DDI time and billing	http://www.ddisoft.com
Elite Information Group	Timesolv/e-billing	http://www.elite.com
Journyx, Inc.	Journyx Timesheet/e-billing	http://www.journyx.com
Juris	Juris legal timekeeping and billing software	http://www.juris.com
Micro Craft, Inc.	Verdict time and billing	http://www.micro-craft.net
Omega Legal System	Omega billing and accounting	http://www.omegalegal.com
Peachtree Software, Inc.	Timeslips legal timekeeping and billing software	http://www.timeslips.com
ProLaw	ProLaw legal timekeeping and billing software	http://www.prolaw.com
RainMaker Software, Inc.	RainMaker Gold timekeeping and billing software	http://www.rainmakerlegal.com
Software Technology, Inc.	Tabs3 legal timekeeping and billing software	http://stilegal.com/

SUGGESTED READING

1. Abodeely, G. A., & Poll, E. (2005). *Collecting your fees: How to assure you get paid and be ethical at the same time.* American Bar Association.

2. Morgan, & Foonberg, J. (2003). *How to draft bills clients rush to pay* (2nd ed.). American Bar Association.

3. Foonberg, J. (2004). *How to start and build a law practice.* American Bar Association.

4. *Law Practice* magazine, published by the American Bar Association Law Practice Management Section [http://www.abanet.org/lpm].

5. *Legal Assistant Today* magazine, published by James Publishing [http://www.legalassistanttoday.com].

6. Munneke, G. A., & Davis, A. E. (2003). *The essential form book—comprehensive management tools.* American Bar Association.

7. Greene, A. G. (2005). *The lawyer's guide to increasing revenue.* American Bar Association.

8. American Bar Association. (2002). *Winning alternatives to the billable hour* (2nd ed.).

KEY TERMS

activity hourly rate
aged accounts receivable report
attorney or legal assistant hourly rate
billable time
billing
blended hourly rate fee
case retainer
case type productivity report
cash advance
client hourly rate
contingency fee
court-awarded fees
criminal fraud
earned retainer
electronic billing
flat fee
hourly rate fee

leveraging
management reports
non-billable time
outside counsel
overhead
pre-billing report
prepaid legal service
pro bono
pure retainer
retainer for general
   representation
timekeeper productivity report
timekeeping
time sheet or time slip
trust or escrow account
unearned retainer
value billing

TEST YOUR KNOWLEDGE

Test your knowledge of the chapter by answering these questions.

1. What is the difference between timekeeping and billing?
2. Name four types of hourly rates:
   _____, _____,
   _____, and _____.
3. When a lawyer takes a percentage of the recovery of the case, it is called a _____ fee.
4. True or false: it is strongly recommended that all fee arrangements be in writing.
5. True or false: a flat fee agreement must be in writing.
6. A retainer that can be deposited in the firm's or attorney's operating checking account is called an _____ retainer.
7. True or false: an account where unearned client monies are deposited is called a trust account.
8. A retainer for general representation is an _____ retainer.

9. A case retainer is an _____ retainer.
10. A cash advance retainer is an _____ retainer.
11. A plan that can be purchased that entitles the person to receive legal services either free or at a greatly reduced price is called _____.
12. A legal billing arrangement that is similar to the type used when you get your car fixed is called _____ billing.
13. For what activity do clients file the most ethical complaints against lawyers?
14. What must the attorney do at the end of a case where a contingency fee or agreement was used?
15. True or false: a contingency agreement can be used in all kinds of cases.
16. True or false: if a client signs a contract with an attorney and the fee turns out to be clearly excessive, it doesn't matter because a contract was signed and the contract prevails.

17. Name four of the eight factors that courts use to determine if a fee is unreasonable.
18. Define criminal fraud.
19. True or false: legal assistants can bill for time spent copying and other clerical duties.
20. Legal services that are provided free of charge are called _____ work.
21. True or false: legal assistants represent a profit center at most law firms (i.e., they bill more to clients than they are paid in salary and benefits).
22. What is e-billing?

ON THE WEB EXERCISES

1. Go to the ABA Center for Professional Responsibility at http://www.abanet.org/cpr/home.html, find the *ABA Model Rules of Professional Conduct*, and read and print out Rule 1.5 Fees and the comment.

2. Visit five state bar association Web sites and find three articles on legal timekeeping, billing, or legal fees. The following link will take you to a Web site that connects to all state bar sites: http://www.abanet.org/barserv/stlobar.html.

3. Go to the Georgia Bar Association Web site at http://www.gabar.org/programs/law_practice_management/forms/ and find a sample contingency fee agreement. Go to several other state bar association Web sites and try to find another sample contingency fee or hourly rate contract agreements.

4. Go to http://www.findlaw.com and print out and read the United States Supreme Court case of *Missouri v. Jenkins*, 491 U.S. 274 (1989). Try selecting "For Legal Professionals," scroll until you see "Cases and Codes," and then click on "Supreme Court" and "Supreme Court Opinions." You should then be able to enter the citation of the case—491 U.S. 274.

5. Visit the National Association of Legal Assistants Web site at http://www.nala.org and review the latest NALA National Utilization and Compensation Survey Report. Read and print out the section related to legal assistant billing rates. If you have difficulty finding it, try using the "Search" feature on the Web site. If you still have trouble finding it, go to http://www. google and search for the full title.

6. Go to the ABA Law Practice Management Section home page at http://www. abanet.org/lpm and find timekeeping, billing, fees, and finance-related articles.

PROJECTS

1. Using a general search engine, such as http://www.google.com or http://www.yahoo.com, search for legal value billing. Alternatively, go to a library or visit state bar association Web sites and write a detailed paper on value billing. Your paper should cover how it works and what are the positive and negatives of value billing.

2. Research and write a paper on computerized timekeeping and billing systems. Visit the American Bar Association Legal Technology Resource Center [http://www.abanet.org/tech/ltrc/home.html] and state bar association Web sites, as well as other legal technology sites, and review helpful articles and materials that you find. Next, go to the timekeeping and billing Web sites in the

Helpful Web Sites section of this chapter. Compare and contrast some of the different products that are available. Which one were you most impressed with, and why?

3. Using a law library, the Internet, and other resources, write an in-depth paper on the subject of legal billing. There are many, many resources available regarding the subject. Your paper should address why clients do not pay legal bills and what can be done to improve this. Your paper should include research from at least five different resources.

QUESTIONS AND EXERCISES

1. You are a new legal assistant and have worked for a medium-sized law office for three months. It has been a tremendous learning experience for you. It has taken time to learn how the office does business, its policies and procedures, what type of service you are expected to give to clients, and where resources are and how to use them (such as the office's computer systems, law library, copy machines, and form files). Although it has taken time for you to learn these things, you also have been productive and have received several compliments on the quality of your work.

One day, you read in the office's staff manual that all legal assistants are required to bill 1,500 hours annually or face possible discipline. You immediately contact your supervisor and ask whether, as a new legal assistant, you will be expected to bill this amount. Your supervisor responds, "Of course. You were told that when you were hired." You immediately begin gathering copies of your time sheets to compile your total. You also request that the billing department send you the total numbers of hours you have billed to date. When you get the report from billing, you panic; you have billed only 300 hours. You are 75 hours behind where you should be (1,500 divided by four [i.e., one-fourth of the way through the year] equals 375). What do you do now, and how could you have avoided this unfortunate situation?

2. On April 1, a billing goes out to John Myers, one of the clients whose cases you have been working on. Mr. Myers calls you a few days later and complains about the amount of time shown on the bill. He is extremely rude and discourteous.

Mr. Myers flatly states that he thinks he is being overbilled. How do you handle the phone call?

3. Your office is on the same side of the city as a major manufacturing plant. You notice that many of the plant's employees come to your office for routine legal services, such as wills, adoptions, and name changes. Although the office has been charging these clients on an hourly basis, you think that there might be alternatives. You talk to one of the partners, and she suggests that you look into the alternatives. Prepare a memorandum to the partner discussing billing options for this situation.

4. You are interviewing a new client. The client wants to hire your office to help negotiate the purchase of a small business. The seller has offered $20,000. The new client would be willing to pay this amount, although she thinks it is a bit high, but does not feel comfortable negotiating with the seller and would rather have an attorney involved in the deal for her protection. The new client is suspicious of legal assistants and attorneys and is especially concerned about how much her case will cost. You inform the client that the attorney will be the one who actually talks to her about the fee issue, but that typically this type of case is taken on an hourly basis and that the attorney will only be able to give her a very broad estimate of what the total matter will cost. The client states that this would be unacceptable to her because she does not have a lot of money to pay overpriced attorneys. The client also states that she would like this matter settled as soon as possible. You must prepare a memorandum to the attorney outlining the facts of the case. What type of fee arrangement would you suggest to the attorney? Please keep in mind the client's anxieties and her particular needs.

5. Recently, your office has found a niche in representing spouses collecting on past-due child support. In most cases, your clients have little money with which to pay you and are financially strapped, as they no longer have the income of their former spouses to support their children and have not received child support. In some cases, large amounts of money are owed, but finding the former spouses has proved difficult. Your supervising attorney decides that the best way to handle these types of cases is on a one-third contingency basis. Your supervising attorney asks for your comments. How do you respond?

6. You work for a firm with 17 attorneys. The firm has always done well financially, but recently it has begun to struggle. There is a great deal of pressure for you to meet your billing requirements of 1,800 hours, even if no one has work for you to do. The firm will not accept the answer, "No one is giving me any work." You are being encouraged to go to each attorney's office and drum something up. Discuss the ethical situation in which you are being placed and how you might handle it.

7. You and another legal assistant, Jonathan, were hired in a medium-sized law office approximately three months ago. You work very hard at your job, record your hours honestly, and always receive compliments on the quality of your work. However, your supervising attorney constantly compares you with Jonathan, who consistently bills more hours than you do. You suspect that Jonathan is padding his time. How do you handle the matter?

8. A client contacts your law office for representation regarding the routine sale of a piece of property. The client appears to be fairly wealthy. Your supervising attorney charges the client what amounts to be about double what the firm regularly charges. You know this because the office uses an internal fee schedule to help the attorneys set a proper

fee. Discuss the ethical considerations. How would you handle the situation?

9. You work in a relatively small law office. The office is having a cash-flow problem and has requested that staff members bill as much as they can and work on cases in which the firm may be able to solve some of its cash-flow problem. The office manager comes to you and tells you that a client on whose case you are working has several thousands of dollars in the trust account. Although not telling you directly, the office manager lets you know that she wants you to bill some hours to this client so the firm can get some of the money in the trust account. Discuss the ethical problems associated with this. Assume you bill the client when, in fact, no hours were worked on the case. What problems arise?

10. You just finished a hectic morning. Before you go to lunch, you fill out your timekeeping report for the day. Although you wanted to record your time earlier, you just could not get to it. Please record your time on a blank piece of paper or a spreadsheet; have columns set up for the date, client/case name, timekeeper, services rendered, billable or non-billable, and the amount of time spent on the matter (see Figure 5-11). For each activity listed, decide whether it is billable or not billable. Record your time, using tenths of hours. You should also fill out expense slips for items that should be charged back to clients. Record the expenses on a blank piece of paper and include date, client/case name, your name, type of expense, and cost. Please total the cost of each expense slip. The firm charges 25 cents each for copies and 50 cents per page to send a fax. Assume long-distance phone calls cost 25 cents a minute.

As best you can recall, this is how your day went:

8:00 A.M.–8:12 A.M.	Got a cup of coffee, talked to other law office staff members, reviewed your schedule/things to do for the day, and reviewed your e-mail inbox.

8:13 A.M.–8:25 A.M.	Talked to your supervising attorney (Jan Mitchell) about some research she needs done on the standards necessary to file a motion to dismiss in *Johnson v. Cuttingham Steel*. Ms. Mitchell also asked you to find a bankruptcy statute she needs for *Halvert v. Shawnee Saving & Loan*.	it in her box, and send it to her electronically.
		You get hold of a witness you have been trying to contact in *Menly v. Menly*. The call was long-distance. The call lasted 15 minutes, and the memo to the file documenting the call took 20 minutes.
		(8:51 A.M.–9:30 A.M.)
8:26 A.M.–8:37 A.M.	A legal assistant from another office calls to remind you that the legal assistant association you belong to is having a meeting at noon, and that you are running the meeting.	
		Ms. Mitchell asks you to contact the attorney in *Glass v. Huron* regarding a discovery question. You spend 10 minutes on hold. The call is long-distance but you get an answer to Ms. Mitchell's question.
		(9:31 A.M.–9:54 A.M.)
8:38 A.M.–8:40 A.M.	One of your least favorite clients, John Hamilton, calls to ask you when he is supposed to be at your office to prepare for his deposition tomorrow. You access the weekly schedule electronically and read him the information he needs.	
		One of the secretaries informs you that you must interview a new client, Richard Sherman. The person who was supposed to see Mr. Sherman got delayed. Mr. Sherman comes to your office regarding a simple adoption. However, in talking to Mr. Sherman, you find out that he also needs someone to incorporate a small business that he is getting ready to open. You gladly note that your office has a department that handles this type of matter. You take the basic information down regarding both matters. You tell the client that you will prepare a memo regarding these matters to the appropriate attorney and one of the office's
		(9:55 A.M.–10:45 A.M.)
8:41 A.M.–8:50 A.M.	You find the information you need re: the motion to dismiss in *Johnson v. Cuttingham Steel* in a motion in another case you helped prepare last month. The research is still current, so Ms. Mitchell will be pleased you found it so fast. You note that it took you two hours to research this issue when you did it the first time. You copy the material Ms. Mitchell needed (five pages), put	

	attorneys will contact him within two days to further discuss the matter. You also copy 10 pages of information that Mr. Sherman brought.
10:46 A.M.–10:54 A.M.	One of the secretaries asks you to cover her phone for her while she takes a quick break. Because the secretary always helps you when you ask for it, you gladly cover the phone for a few minutes. Ms. Mitchell asks you to send a fax in *Stewart v. Layhorn Glass*, so you use this time to send the six-page fax.
10:55 A.M.–12:00 P.M.	You were given the job of organizing some exhibits in *Ranking v. Siefkin* yesterday by Ms. Mitchell. You finally have some free time to organize the exhibits.
12:01 P.M.–1:00 P.M.	You attend the legal assistant association lunch.
1:01 P.M.–2:00 P.M.	You work on a pro bono criminal case that Ms. Mitchell is representing on appeal. In an effort to become familiar with the case, you read some of the transcripts from the trial.
2:01 P.M.–5:30 P.M.	Ms. Mitchell hands you a new case. Ms. Mitchell says that the office will be representing the defendant. She asks you to read the petition and client file, analyze the case, and draft interrogatories to send to the plaintiff. You spend the

rest of the day working on this case.

11. You have just been hired by a private law practice. You begin to get a little worried because your employers say you should "hold on" to your paycheck for an extra day to make sure it will clear the bank. You notice that many times staff members "forget" to fill out slips for charging expenses back to the clients, that bills are usually done on a quarterly basis, and that many expenses (such as copying) are included in the overhead of the office and not billed to the clients at all. Please identify what the problems are with the office and give a detailed answer on how you would go about addressing the problems.

12. You work for an insurance company. The head of the legal department asks you to begin drafting some billing guidelines for private law practices that represent your interests. The department currently reviews bills at varying hourly rates from firm to firm, and law offices are passing on to your office all types of expenses that they should not be including. Please draft a set of guidelines as requested.

13. Assume for this exercise that you can bill for all activities that relate to learning. Keep a detailed record of all your activities for one day, from when you wake up until you go to sleep. Record your time in tenths (i.e., in six-minute intervals). At the end of the day, calculate the amount due based on your time sheet.

14. Your law office recently began representing a client who had been defrauded in a security scam at a national brokerage firm. The client signed a 40 percent contingency contract. You know that the only thing your office has done on the case is to meet with the client several times, do some general research regarding the case, and prepare a demand letter to the brokerage firm setting out the facts of the case. The brokerage firm does not want bad publicity and has agreed to settle the claim for $1.2 million dollars. The client is going to accept the offer. Discuss the ethical implications. What should the law firm do?

NOTES

1. *Legal Assistant Today.* (1992, November/December), 25. Copyright 1992, James Publishing, Inc. Reprinted with permission from *Legal Assistant Today* magazine. For subscription information, call (714) 755-5450, or visit http://www.legalassistanttoday.com.

2. Pack, R. (2005). *The tyranny of the billable hour.* Washington, D.C. Bar Association.

3. Takacs, T. L., & Wagner, G. E. (2001, February/March). The time has come. *Law Office Computing,* 8.

4. American Bar Association. (2004). *The legal assistant's practical guide to professional responsibility* (2nd ed., p. 118). Reprinted by permission.

5. Bailey, K. C. (2000, August). All I really need to know I learned from a paralegal. *Facts and Findings,* 29. Reprinted with the permission of the National Association of Legal Assistants, http://www.nala.org, 1516S. Boston, # 200, Tulsa, OK 74119.

6. Conner, T. (2000, January). The challenges facing law firms. *Texas Bar Journal,* 22.

7. Lerman, L. (1999). Blue chip billing: Regulation of billing and expense fraud by lawyers. *Georgetown Journal of Legal Ethics* 12(2), 205. Reprinted with permission of the publisher, Georgetown University, and *Georgetown Journal of Legal Ethics,* copyright 1999.

8. Gharakhanian, A., & Krywy, Y. The Gunderson effect and billable mania: Trends in overbilling and the effect of new ages. *Georgetown Journal of Legal Ethics,* 14 1001.

9. Smith. (1991, January/February). AAFPE national conference highlights. *Legal Assistant Today,* 103. Copyright 1991, James Publishing, Inc. Reprinted with permission from *Legal Assistant Today* magazine. For subscription information, call (714) 755-5450, or visit http://www.legalassistanttoday.com.

10. Adapted from Altman, M. A. and Weil, R. I. (1986). *How to manage your law office* (pp. 4–6). Matthew Bender. Reprinted with the permission of Altman Weil Pensa Publications, Inc., copyright 1991 by Altman Weil Pensa Publication, Inc.

11. Special Committee on Economics of Law Practice of the American Bar Association, 1959. Reprinted by permission.

12. Mello, J. P., Jr. (1993, September/October). Paralegal billing trends. *Legal Assistant Today,* 127. Copyright 1993, James Publishing, Inc. Reprinted with permission from *Legal Assistant Today* magazine. For subscription information, call (714) 755-5450, or visit http://www.legalassistanttoday.com.

13. Statsky, W. (1992). *Introduction to paralegalism* (p. 826). St. Paul, MN: West Publishing Co., citing *A Lighter Note,* NALA Advance 15, Summer 1989.

14. Murray, T. I. (1998, May/June). The unwritten rules: Survival in a law firm. *Legal Assistant Today,* 13. Copyright 1998, James Publishing, Inc. Reprinted with permission from *Legal Assistant Today* magazine. For subscription information, call (714) 755-5450, or visit http://www.legalassistanttoday.com.

15. Milano, C. (1992, March/April). Hard choices: Dealing with ethical dilemmas on the job. *Legal Assistant Today,* 79. Copyright 1992, James Publishing, Inc. Reprinted with permission from *Legal Assistant Today* magazine. For subscription information, call (714) 755-5450, or visit http://www.legalassistanttoday.com.

16. Thomas, R. J. (2001, April). Electronic billing: What happens when you ditch the paper invoices?," *Law Practice Management,* 40.

ANSWERS TO TEST YOUR KNOWLEDGE

1. Timekeeping is tracking time, and billing is the process of issuing invoices to clients for the time tracked.
2. Attorney or legal assistant hourly rate, client hourly rate, blended hourly rate, and activity hourly rate.
3. Contingency
4. True
5. False
6. Earned
7. True
8. Earned
9. Earned
10. Unearned
11. Prepaid legal services
12. Value
13. Fees and billing
14. Provide a written statement of the outcome and show a remittance to the client and the method of its distribution.
15. False
16. False; an attorney can never collect a fee that is unreasonable.
17. (1) the time and labor required, the novelty and difficulty of the questions involved, and the skill requisite to perform the legal service properly;
   (2) the likelihood, if apparent to the client, that the acceptance of the particular employment will preclude other employment by the lawyer;
   (3) the fee customarily charged in the locality for similar legal services;
   (4) the amount involved and the results obtained;
   (5) the time limitations imposed by the client or by the circumstances;
   (6) the nature and length of the professional relationship with the client;
   (7) the experience, reputation, and ability of the lawyer or lawyers performing the services; and
   (8) whether the fee is fixed or contingent.
18. A false representation of a present or past fact.
19. False
20. Pro bono
21. True
22. When law firms bill clients using electronic means, such as the Internet.

CASE REVIEW

Eureste v. Commission for Lawyer Discipline

76 S.W.3d 184 (2002)
Court of Appeals of Texas,
Houston (14th Dist.).

Bernardo EURESTE, Appellant,
v.
COMMISSION FOR LAWYER DISCIPLINE, Appellee.
No. 14-01-00311-CV.
April 18, 2002.

OPINION

I. BACKGROUND

Eureste is an attorney licensed to practice law in Texas since 1990. During the relevant time period, his practice consisted almost entirely of representing claimants in workers' compensation matters. At the peak of his practice in 1996 and 1997, he had offices in 13 cities across Texas, over 60 employees, and approximately 1200 clients. The Texas Workers' Compensation Fund ("the Fund") [FN1] and Juan Granado, a former client, filed complaints against Eureste with the State Bar of Texas ("State Bar"). The basis of the Fund's complaint was Eureste's billing practices and resulting attorney's fees in workers' compensation cases. Granado's complaint arose from Eureste's allegedly deficient representation in a workers' compensation case. A brief overview of workers' compensation laws regarding attorney's fees is in order.

FN1. The Fund is a state-created entity that provides workers' compensation insurance and investigates cases of workers' compensation fraud in conjunction with the Texas Workers' Compensation Commission.

Texas Workers' Compensation Attorney's Fees

Section 408.221 of the Texas Labor Code governs the award of attorney's fees to the workers' compensation claimant's attorney. See Tex. Lab.Code Ann. § 408.221 (Vernon Supp.2002). Section 408.221 provides that the attorney's fees must be approved by the Texas Workers' Compensation Commission ("TWCC") or the court. Id. § 408.221(a). The fees are "based on the attorney's time and expenses according to written evidence presented to the commission or court." Id. § 408.221(b). The fees are paid from the claimant's recovery and may not exceed 25 percent of that recovery. Id. § 408.221(b), (i). The TWCC or the court shall consider the following factors in approving attorney's fees: (1) the time and labor required; (2) the novelty and difficulty of the questions involved; (3) the skill required to perform the legal services properly; (4) the fee customarily charged *189 in the locality for similar legal services; (5) the amount involved in the controversy; (6) the benefits to the claimant that the attorney is responsible for securing; and (7) the experience and ability of the attorney performing the services. Id. § 408.221(d). Section 408.221 requires that the TWCC provide guidelines for maximum attorney's fees for specific services in accordance with these provisions. See id. § 408.221(f).

The TWCC rules set forth additional requirements for the submission and approval of attorney's fees. The TWCC rules reiterate that any fee approved by the commission "shall be limited to 25 percent of each weekly income benefit payment to the employee, up to 25 percent of the total income benefits allowed, and shall also be based on the attorney's time and expenses." 28 Tex. Admin. Code § 152.1(c) (2001). To claim a fee, an attorney must submit Form TWCC 152 entitled "Application and Order for Attorney's Fees," with "time, hourly rate, and expenses itemized separately for the attorney and for any legal assistant." Id. § 152.3(a). On Form TWCC-152, the attorney must list the category of service rendered, the date of the service, the person who provided the service, the actions performed, the recipient of the action, and the hours requested. The TWCC has also established guidelines for the approval of attorney's fees that include a list of a maximum number of hours allowed per month for various legal services. See id. § 152.4(c). The TWCC automatically approves a fee for legal services without justification from the attorney if the number of hours for the services is within the guidelines. See id. § 152.3(b); Form TWCC-152. The guidelines also set the maximum hourly rate for an attorney at $150, and the maximum hourly rate for a legal assistant at $50. See 28 Tex. Admin. Code § 152.4(d). Once the fees are approved, the TWCC issues an order for payment. Id. § 152.3(b). The fees, up to the cap of 25 percent, are then deducted from the client's monthly income benefit checks and paid directly to the attorney. Id. § 152.1(c).

Eureste's Billing Practices

There was no dispute at trial regarding the method used by Eureste to submit attorney's fees to the TWCC. His office submitted a Form TWCC-152 for each client on a monthly basis. At the time of trial, Eureste had submitted approximately 200,000 TWCC-152 forms. Eureste did not account for actual time spent by him or his employees on the forms. Rather, he always reported he had personally worked a number of hours that, when multiplied by the statutory attorney rate of $150, resulted in a fee that was at least 25 percent of his clients' monthly income benefit. Eureste acknowledged that during the year and a half before August 1997, when the State Bar complaint arose, his policy was to bill the maximum allowed by the guidelines on every file. Some of the activities he billed for included opening the client's file and preparation and attendance at hearings. On most files, even though actual activities performed and time spent varied from client to client, he billed each client 2.5 hours per month (resulting in a fee of $375) for "file review" under the "Communications" category. This is the maximum time allowed for "Communications" under the TWCC guidelines. See 28 TEX. ADMIN. CODE § 152.4(c). His Form TWCC-152 submissions did not arouse any suspicion and were always automatically approved because they were always within the guidelines. At trial, Elliott Flood, an attorney and vice-president of special investigations for the Fund, referred to this practice as billing "beneath the radar."

*190 Eureste testified that on many of the cases, he was not spending the number of hours he billed every month. During the peak of his practice, he spent 80 percent of his time on administrative matters and 20 percent of his time on individual client's cases. Yet, he billed all time on the client's file under his name and at the attorney rate. He admitted that most of the attorney time he billed during the period before August 1997 was performed by nonattorneys or attorneys other than himself. Eureste estimated that only 25 percent of the work billed was performed by attorneys, while 75 percent of the work billed was performed by nonattorneys. [FN2] The nonattorney time was billed by Eureste at the higher attorney rate of $150. Eureste never billed legal assistant time at the legal assistant rate.

> FN2. Eureste's offices were staffed primarily by nonattorney caseworkers who conducted the "intake" of new clients, explained the workers' compensation system and attorney's fees procedures to clients, and "worked up" the clients' files.

At trial, Flood testified Eureste's case was unique because no other situation approached the number of hours that Eureste billed for each day on his Form TWCC-152s. Eureste's fees, approved by the TWCC from June 1, 1995, to May 31, 1996, totaled $2,330,376.32, while the next highest attorney's approved fees totaled $935,582.50. Flood testified Eureste billed an average of 80 to 90 hours per day. A summary of Eureste's TWCC attorney's fees orders from December 1, 1995, to November 30, 1996, reveals he billed as his own time more than 24 hours almost daily and on many days, Eureste billed more than 100 hours. Eureste did not dispute that he billed in excess of 24 hours per day of his own time. Rather, he testified it would have been too burdensome to base his billings on actual time. In support of that claim, he referred to a one-day test accounting in which he instructed his employees to account for every activity they performed during that one day and the time spent on the activity. [FN3] Ordinarily,

Eureste's employees input a description of the activities they performed on a case into the computer file for that case, but did not detail the time required to perform those activities. Based on the results of his one-day test, Eureste concluded it would be too onerous for him to submit bills based on actual time expended because that would require a larger number of entries per month.

> FN3. Eureste also performed another one-day test accounting, but the results were not entered into evidence.

Granado Complaint

On November 15, 1995, Granado fell from a tractor while on the job and injured both shoulders. On May 9, 1996, he retained Eureste's Amarillo office because he was experiencing difficulties advancing his workers' compensation claim. Granado signed a contract, which provided that Eureste would represent him in connection with his claim for workers' compensation benefits and that attorney's fees would be in an amount governed by the workers' compensation laws of Texas.

Before Granado retained Eureste, he had been classified as having a 10 percent Maximum Medical Improvement. Eureste's office successfully negotiated with the carrier and obtained a 20 percent Maximum Medical Improvement. This increase made Granado eligible for additional benefits. Furthermore, when Granado retained Eureste, the workers' compensation carrier had accepted his left shoulder injury as a compensable injury, but had refused to accept the right shoulder injury. An attorney from Eureste's office attended two Benefit *191 Review Conferences on Granado's behalf and secured an agreement establishing Granado's right shoulder injury as a compensable injury. Notwithstanding that agreement, the carrier denied payment for surgery to the right shoulder maintaining the surgery was not "reasonable and necessary." Granado testified that his physician, Dr. Brooker, repeatedly told him he could not treat his right shoulder because of the carrier's denials and that his lawyer would have to assist him further.

Eureste did not submit any letters or forms to obtain Medical Review for Granado regarding the denials of payment. *See* Tex. Lab.Code Ann. § 413.031 (Vernon Supp. 2002). He testified that he does not represent claimants during the Medical Review process because he cannot bill for that representation. Eureste maintained it is a doctor's responsibility to pursue Medical Review to obtain authorization for a particular treatment.

On April 8, 1997, Granado wrote a letter to Eureste expressing dissatisfaction with the handling of his case. Granado relayed his inability to work and the "agonizing pain" he experienced due to numerous delays and denials of benefits. He complained he had only met with a lawyer twice and that, despite numerous calls to Eureste's office, he still had received no treatment for his right shoulder. He implored Eureste to take immediate action on his case. Four months later, on August 29, 1997, Granado wrote another letter to Eureste complaining that his right shoulder still had not been treated, despite having had Eureste as his attorney for over a year. Granado stated he "called time after time and right now I've exhausted my income and my cabinets are bare."

Granado further testified that all he had received from Eureste during the time he needed surgery were charges for reviewing his file. Eureste billed at his hourly rate and under his name for the intake of Granado's file, although the intake was performed by nonattorney employees in the Amarillo office. He also billed at his rate and in his name for attending Granado's Benefit Review Conferences, although another attorney actually attended the conferences. As with his other clients, Eureste billed Granado's file two and a half hours for "file review" with a resulting fee of $375 per month from May of 1996 until November of 1997. Granado testified that although he rarely spoke with Eureste, he did speak to the ladies in his office for 15 to 20 minutes per month. Eureste admitted that neither he nor his staff had reviewed Granado's file for two and one-half hours every month. Eureste billed a total of $7,875 on Granado's file, of which he collected $5,753.38.

Shortly before Granado's benefits ran out in November 1997, he discovered that Eureste's Amarillo office was being closed. At that time, a staff person informed Granado that Eureste planned to withdraw as his attorney. On January 13, 1998, Eureste sent a letter to Granado withdrawing as his attorney. Eureste testified he withdrew because he was closing his Amarillo and Lubbock offices due to State Bar complaints. After Eureste withdrew, Granado continued on his own to pursue the treatment he needed. He requested a Medical Review hearing in Austin, drove from his home near Amarillo to the hearing, and appeared at the hearing opposite an attorney representing the insurance carrier. He was eventually successful in the Medical Review process and obtained approval for the surgery. He had the surgery in October of 1999, more than three years after he retained Eureste.

Trial Court Proceedings

After State Bar grievance panels conducted hearings and recommended discipline, ***192** Eureste exercised his right to trial de novo in district court. *See* Tex.R. Disciplinary P. 2.14, *reprinted in* Tex. Gov't Code Ann., tit. 2, subtit. G app. A 1 (Vernon 1998). The Commission for Lawyer Discipline ("CFLD") brought this attorney disciplinary action alleging violations of multiple provisions of the Texas Disciplinary Rules of Professional Conduct. The Supreme Court of Texas appointed Judge David Brabham of the 188th District Court of Gregg County to preside over Eureste's disciplinary action in the 152nd District Court of Harris County. *See* Tex.R. Disciplinary P. 3.02, 3.03; Tex. Gov't Code Ann. § 74.057 (Vernon 1998). After a bench trial, the trial court found Eureste had violated Texas Disciplinary Rules of Professional Conduct 1.01(b), 1.03(a), 1.03(b), 1.04(a), 1.15(d), 8.04(a)(1) and 8.04(a)(3). *See* Tex.R. Disciplinary Prof'l Conduct, *reprinted* in Tex. Gov't Code Ann. tit. 2, subtit. G app. A (Vernon 1998). The trial court then imposed sanctions that included a two-year active suspension and a one-year probated suspension. The court also ordered Eureste to pay restitution in the amount of $3,000 to Granado, and to reimburse the CFLD's attorney's fees in the amount of $18,310.

Sufficiency of the Evidence Issues

Eureste challenges the legal and factual sufficiency of the evidence to support the trial court's conclusions regarding his violations of the Texas Disciplinary Rules of Professional Conduct.

1. Standard of Review

[5] [6] In reviewing a challenge to the legal sufficiency of the evidence, a reviewing court must consider only the evidence and reasonable inferences therefrom, which, when viewed in the most favorable light, support the findings of the fact finder. *Southwestern Bell Mobile Sys., Inc. v. Franco*, 971 S.W.2d 52, 54 (Tex.1998); *Foye v. Montes*, 9 S.W.3d 436, 438 (Tex.App.-Houston [14th Dist.] 1999, pet. denied). We must disregard all evidence and inferences which are contrary to the findings. *Franco*, 971 S.W.2d at 54; *Foye*, 9 S.W.3d at 438. If the evidence is legally ***195** sufficient when viewed in this light, then we may not reverse the trial court's judgment. *Franco*, 971 S.W.2d 52, 54; *Harris County Dist. Attorney's Office v. M.G.G.*, 866 S.W.2d 796, 797–98 (Tex.App.-Houston [14th Dist.] 1993, no writ).

[7] [8] When reviewing a challenge to the factual sufficiency of the evidence, we examine the entire record, considering both the evidence in favor of, and contrary to, the challenged finding. *Plas-Tex, Inc. v. U.S. Steel Corp.*, 772 S.W.2d 442, 445 (Tex.1989); *Mayes v. Stewart*, 11 S.W.3d 440, 450 (Tex.App.-Houston [14th Dist.] 2000, pet. denied). We shall set aside the verdict only if it is so contrary to the overwhelming weight of the evidence as to be clearly wrong and unjust. *Ortiz v. Jones*, 917 S.W.2d 770, 772 (Tex.1996); *Mayes*, 11 S.W.3d at 450–51. The trier of fact is the sole judge of the weight and credibility of the witnesses' testimony. *Mayes*, 11 S.W.3d at 450–51; *Knox v. Taylor*, 992 S.W.2d 40, 50 (Tex.App.-Houston [14th Dist.] 1999, no pet.). The appellate court may not substitute its own judgment for that of the trier of fact, even if a different answer could be reached on the evidence. *Knox*, 992 S.W.2d at 50; *Mayes*, 11 S.W.3d at 450. The amount of evidence necessary to affirm a judgment is far less than that necessary to reverse a judgment. *Mayes*, 11 S.W.3d at 450–51; *Knox*, 992 S.W.2d at 50.

2. Eureste's Fees

In his second issue, Eureste challenges the trial court's conclusions regarding his billing practices and resulting fees. Specifically, the trial court found Eureste violated Texas Disciplinary Rules of Professional Conduct 1.04(a) and 8.04(3).

a. Rule 1.04(a)—Illegal or Unconscionable Fees

Texas Disciplinary Rule of Professional Conduct 1.04(a) provides that a lawyer shall not enter into an arrangement for, charge, or collect an illegal or unconscionable fee. Tex.R. Disciplinary P. 1.04(a). Eureste contends there was no evidence at trial that his fees were illegal because they were not prohibited by statute. In support, he argues that "time and labor required" is only one of several factors enumerated by the Labor Code that the TWCC must consider in approving attorney's fees. He further argues the Labor Code does not specify that fees must be billed in a certain manner. We disagree.

[9] Although Section 408.221 of the Labor Code does list certain factors to be considered in approving a fee, only one of which is the time and labor required, Section 408.221 clearly requires that the fees be based on the attorney's actual time. *See* Tex. Lab.Code Ann. § 408.221(b). The TWCC rules also require that fees be based on actual time. 28 Tex. Admin. Code § 152.1(c).

[10] Eureste further contends his fees were not illegal because only the TWCC rules require that time be itemized separately for attorneys and legal assistants, and this requirement is not included in the more general provisions of the Labor Code. This contention is without merit. Eureste apparently maintains that because the Labor Code mentions only attorneys, and not legal assistants, it does not prohibit him from billing legal assistant's time at the attorney's rate. Although legal assistants are not specifically mentioned by Section 408.221 of the Labor Code, nothing in Section 408.221 of the Labor Code authorizes Eureste to submit legal assistant time as attorney time. *See* Tex. Lab.Code Ann. 408.221. Furthermore, the Labor Code should be read together with the TWCC rules. *See* 28 Tex. Admin. Code 152.4(a) (providing that guidelines outlined in Rule 152.4 shall be considered by TWCC along with factors and maximum ***196** fee limitations set forth in Section 408.221 of Labor Code). The Labor Code provides that fees must be approved by the TWCC,

and allows the TWCC to promulgate guidelines for maximum attorney's fees for specific services. *See* Tex. Lab.Code Ann. 408.221(a), (f). The TWCC rules are more specific than, but do not conflict with, Section 408.211 of the Labor Code. The TWCC rules address legal assistants, and allow their time to be billed, but separately and at a different rate than attorney time. *See* 28 Tex. Admin. Code § 52.3(a). Additionally, the instructions accompanying Form TWCC-152 could not be more direct in requiring itemization of each individual's actual time. *See* Form TWCC-152.

[11] Eureste acknowledged he submitted fees that were not based on actual time expended in many cases. He also testified he charged legal assistant time at the higher attorney rate and billed other attorneys' time as his own. Although Eureste urges on appeal that his fees were not prohibited by law, he, in effect, has admitted to submitting fees prohibited by law. The practical effect of his billing method was that his fees would equal 25 percent of the client's recovery irrespective of actual time spent on the case. Twenty-five percent is the maximum an attorney may bill, not an amount that should be billed regardless of actual time expended. Eureste's billing practices clearly controverted the mandated time based billing system. *See* Tex. Lab.Code Ann. § 408.221; 28 Tex. Admin. Code § 152.1.

[12] Eureste also challenges the court's finding that his fees were unconscionable. Rule 1.04 of the Texas Disciplinary Rules of Professional Conduct provides that a fee is unconscionable if a competent lawyer could not form a reasonable belief that the fee is reasonable. Tex. Disciplinary R. Prof'l Conduct 1.04(a). Rule 1.04(b) lists certain factors that *may* be considered in determining the reasonableness of a fee, *but not to the exclusion of other relevant factors. Id.* Eureste complains the trial court focused almost exclusively on his billing practices, which are not an enumerated factor for determining reasonableness under Rule 1.04, when it should have focused on the fees themselves. The gist of Eureste's argument is that if the trial court had focused on the actual fees instead of his billing practices, the court would have concluded his fees were reasonable. This argument is based on Eureste's contention that the amounts he billed were less than he would have billed had he completed the Form TWCC 152s differently and submitted all billable hours by person and by rate.

The evidence does not support Eureste's contention that his fees were reasonable because he would have billed more had he billed actual activities performed. The only evidence offered by Eureste in support of this contention was Eureste's very general testimony. Although some of Eureste's TWCC fee orders were entered into evidence, there were no corresponding client files in the record showing the work justified the fee award in every case. [FN8] Eureste's logic results in grossly disproportionate billing for those clients who had very little work done on their files. Because the factors enumerated in Rule 1.04(a) are not exclusive, the trial court could consider all relevant evidence, including evidence regarding Eureste's billing ***197*** practices, to determine whether the resulting fees were reasonable. One of the enumerated factors in determining reasonableness under Rule 1.04 is the amount involved and the results obtained. *See* Tex. Disciplinary R. Prof'l Conduct 1.04(b)(4). If a client who had very little work performed on her file is billed the same as every other client, the amount of that fee cannot be considered reasonable in relation to the work performed.

> FN8. The record contains an exhibit prepared by Eureste showing that the total amount of his actual fees billed in July of 1997 was less than the fees would have been if all employees had billed 40 hours per week at the rates set forth in the TWCC rules. However, this report relates to his total billings and not his billings for each client. Moreover, the report only covered one month.

On the other hand, there was evidence that Eureste billed more than he would have billed by using the prescribed method. In fact, the computer file for one particular client reflects that Eureste continued to bill two and one-half hours for file review every month for almost a year after the client's death although the only activity during that entire period consisted of three telephone calls to the decedent's mother. Additionally, Flood calculated that Eureste would have billed approximately $900,000 instead of approximately $2,300,000 during the period from June 1, 1995, to May 31, 1996, had he billed actual time for each file. Assuming that 50 percent of the billings were collected, which is the usual percentage based on Flood's experience, Eureste earned approximately $700,000 above and beyond a reasonable fee.

Moreover, Eureste's argument that his fees were reasonable because they conformed with the TWCC fee guidelines is without merit. Flood testified that the presumption that a fee is reasonable if it does not exceed the guidelines is a rebuttable presumption based on actual time spent by the attorney. Clearly, the guidelines are just that: guidelines. They are the maximum amount that the TWCC will automatically approve for various activities, not the maximum amount an attorney may bill regardless of actual time expended. *See* 28 TEX. ADMIN. CODE § 152.3(b), 152.4(b).

The record reflects it was possible for Eureste to accurately account for his and his employees' time, but it would have cut into his profits to do so because of the size of his practice. He candidly admitted he could not ask an employee to whom he paid $7–8 per hour to keep track of time in the manner prescribed by the TWCC rules. However, Flood testified all other law firms keep track of actual time and that he also kept track of actual time when he represented workers' compensation claimants. Eureste was aware that numerous law firms, including large law firms, bill attorney time at $150 per hour and use elaborate computer accounting programs to keep track of time. Nevertheless, he chose to employ a system whereby he billed every one of his clients (including Granado) $375 per month regardless of the amount of work actually performed. The result was that he billed and collected payment for legal services that were not rendered. That his excessive fees came directly out of his clients' benefit checks is particularly disturbing. Comment 8 to Rule 1.04 states that overreaching by a lawyer, particularly of a client who is unusually susceptible to overreaching, may indicate that a fee is unconscionable. Tex. Disciplinary R. Prof'l Conduct 1.04 cmt. 8. Comment 8 further explains that a fee arrangement with an uneducated or unsophisticated individual having no prior experience in such matters should be more carefully scrutinized for overreaching. *Id.* According to Flood, many of Eureste's clients did not speak English, were not educated, could not read or write, and were not sophisticated. Yet, many of them were penalized as a result of Eureste's billing practices. Accordingly, we hold the evidence is legally and factually sufficient to support the finding that Eureste charged illegal and unconscionable fees. The trial court did *198 not err in concluding that Eureste violated Rule 1.04(a).

b. Rule 8.04(a)(3)—Conduct Involving Dishonesty, Fraud, Deceit, or Misrepresentation

[13] Rule 8.04(a)(3) of the Texas Disciplinary Rules of Professional Conduct provides that a lawyer shall not engage in conduct involving dishonesty, fraud, deceit, or misrepresentation. Tex. Disciplinary R. Prof'l Conduct 8.04(a)(3). Fraud is defined under the rules as conduct having a purpose to deceive and not merely negligent misrepresentation or failure to apprise another of relevant information. Tex. Disciplinary R. Prof'l Conduct terminology. Eureste contends he did not commit fraud because there is no evidence he intended to deceive the TWCC, the Fund, or his clients as to the legal representation provided. However, he ignores the fact that fraud is not the only conduct prohibited by Rule 8.04(a)(3). Any conduct involving dishonesty, deceit, or misrepresentation is also prohibited by Rule 8.04(a)(3). *See* Tex. Disciplinary R. Prof'l Conduct 8.04(a)(3).

Eureste testified he approved the placement of his facsimile signature on each Form TWCC-152 generated by his office. He understood that by approving the placement of his signature on the forms, he was certifying that "every statement, numerical figure, and calculation contained herein is within my personal knowledge and is true and correct, that it represents services, charges, and expenses provided by me or my legal assistant under my supervision." The record, however, demonstrates that in many instances, Eureste's forms contained false information. Eureste's testimony reflects that he was aware of the requirement that the fees be itemized for attorneys and legal assistants and that they be based on actual time. Notwithstanding his knowledge of those requirements, he made a conscious decision to submit false information and disregard the requirement. Most significantly, he submitted the bills in such a manner that the inaccuracies would not be detected. The trial court could infer an intent to deceive from Eureste consistently billing "beneath the radar." Thus, the record supports the conclusion that his conduct constituted fraud, in addition to dishonesty, deceit, and misrepresentation.

Eureste next contends his representations, even if false, were immaterial because no one was misled since he did not submit fees that were greater than they would have been had he properly completed the forms. However, Rule 8.04(a)(3) does not contain a requirement that the representations be material to constitute a violation. See Tex. Disciplinary R. Prof'l Conduct 8.04(a)(3). Eureste cites *Curtis v. Commission for Lawyer Discipline*, 20 S.W.3d 227, 234 (Tex.App.-Houston [14th Dist.] 2000, no pet.) as holding that a misrepresentation under Rule 8.04(a)(3) must be material and have been knowingly made by the attorney with the goal of misleading the party to whom the representation was made. In *Curtis*, the court found that a lawyer had violated Rule 7.02(a)(1), which prohibits a lawyer from making a material representation about his qualifications or services. *Id.* Although the *Curtis* court also considered a separate Rule 8.04(a)(3) violation, it did not establish a requirement of materiality for a Rule 8.04(a)(3) violation. *See id.* Nevertheless, the record reveals that Eureste's fraud was material because as previously discussed, it resulted in some clients being billed for work that was not performed. Some clients were misled because their contracts provided they would be billed in accordance with the workers' compensation laws, but the falsified forms ensured they were not billed in accordance with the workers' compensation *199 laws. The TWCC was misled because the fees were billed in such a manner that the falsifications would not be detected.

We find the evidence is both legally and factually sufficient to show that Eureste engaged in conduct involving dishonesty, fraud, deceit, or misrepresentation. The trial court did not err in finding that Eureste violated Rule 8.04(a)(3).

3. Issues Regarding Representation of Granado

In his third issue, Eureste challenges the trial court's conclusions regarding his representation of Juan Granado. Specifically, the trial court found Eureste violated Texas Disciplinary Rules of Professional Conduct 1.01(b), 1.03(a) and (b) and 1.15(d).

a. Rule 1.01(b)—Adequacy of Representation

[14] Rule 1.01(b) prohibits a lawyer from neglecting a legal matter entrusted to the lawyer or frequently failing to carry out completely the obligations that the lawyer owes to a client. Tex. Disciplinary R. Prof'l Conduct 1.01(b). As used in the rule, "neglect" means inattentiveness involving a conscious disregard for the responsibilities owed to a client. Tex. Disciplinary R. Prof'l Conduct 1.01(c). Comment 6 to Rule 1.01 explains that having accepted employment, a lawyer should act with competence, commitment, and dedication to the interest of the client and with zeal in advocacy upon the client's behalf. Tex. Disciplinary R. Prof'l Conduct 1.01 cmt. 6. Granado's complaints against Eureste center on Eureste's failure to assist Granado in obtaining surgery on his right shoulder. In essence, Eureste argues he adequately represented Granado because there was nothing more for him to do when he withdrew. Eureste's contract with Granado provided that Eureste would represent Granado in connection with his "claim for workers' compensation benefits." Eureste contends the contract did not impose a duty to represent Granado in pursuing the surgery through Medical Review because Medical Review is not a benefit but a forum for resolving medical disputes after benefits have attached.

[15] There are four types of benefits available to injured workers under the Texas Workers' Compensation Act: medical, income, death, and burial. *Continental Cas. Insur. Co. v. Functional Restoration Assocs.*, 19 S.W.3d 393, 396 (Tex.2000). Medical Review is the "dispute resolution procedure for certain types of medical benefits disputes." *Id.* Eureste's contract did not specify that Eureste's representation would be limited or would not encompass Medical Review.

[16] The record reflects that the statements and actions of Eureste and his staff led Granado to believe Eureste felt an obligation to assist him in obtaining the right shoulder surgery. The contractual relationship between an attorney and client, whereby the attorney agrees to render professional services for the client, may be express or implied from the parties' conduct. *Byrd v. Woodruff*, 891 S.W.2d 689, 700 (Tex.App.-Dallas 1994, writ denied). Although Eureste contends he repeatedly informed Granado that he could not represent him in Medical Review, the record contains evidence that neither Eureste nor his staff replied to Granado's requests for assistance with a statement that they could not assist him further. Instead, during the time Granado inquired about the surgery, Eureste told him to "be patient" because these matters "take time." The notes in Granado's file reflect that on November 4, 1997, Granado called Eureste's office and inquired if his shoulder was going to be treated. A staff ***200** person responded that she would talk to the attorney and "find out what we can do." Eureste admitted that one could conclude from Granado's August 29, 1997, letter requesting Eureste's assistance that Granado thought Eureste had a duty to help him get his operation. Moreover, Eureste provided conflicting testimony regarding the extent of his duties. At trial, he denied he had a duty to represent claimants in Medical Review. However, he previously testified by deposition that "[m]aybe we have a duty, even though we cannot be compensating [sic] to continue to represent people at that level."

Finally, Eureste's contention that he had no duty to further assist Granado in obtaining surgery is controverted by his own withdrawal letter. Eureste wrote, "[p]lease attempt to seek the services of another attorney to represent you in your case. While having an attorney to represent you in workers' compensation claims in Texas is not required, I am convinced that legal representation in these matters is important." At that time, obtaining surgery to the right shoulder was the only benefit left to obtain in Granado's case. The letter acknowledges there was further work for an attorney to perform on Granado's case.

Therefore, the record contains sufficient evidence from which the trial court could conclude Eureste did not take appropriate steps to obtain Medical Review for Granado or otherwise assist him through that process.

We hold the evidence is both legally and factually sufficient to show neglect and failure to completely carry out Eureste's obligations to Granado. The trial court did not err in finding that Eureste violated Rule 1.01(b).

b. **Rules 1.03(a) and (b)—Communications with Granado**

[17] Rule 1.03(a) requires a lawyer to keep a client reasonably informed about the status of a matter and promptly comply with reasonable requests for information. Tex. Disciplinary R. Prof'l Conduct 1.03(a). Rule 1.03(b) requires a lawyer to explain a matter to the extent reasonably necessary to permit the client to make informed decisions regarding the representation. Tex. Disciplinary R. Prof'l Conduct 1.03(b). Comment 2 to Rule 1.03 illustrates that it is not the quantity, but the quality and content of the communications that shows compliance with Rule 1.03. *See* Tex. Disciplinary R. Prof'l Conduct 1.03 cmt. 2. According to Comment 2, the guiding principle is that the lawyer should reasonably fulfill client expectations for information consistent with the duty to act in the client's best interests and the client's overall requirements as to the character of representation. *Id.*

As Eureste notes, the record shows numerous telephone conversations between Granado and Eureste's office. Eureste contends the only evidence of inadequate communication with Granado was Granado's testimony that he did not believe Eureste communicated with him enough. However, Granado assailed the quality as well as the quantity of Eureste's communication with him. It is clear from Granado's testimony that his expectations were not met. Granado testified that when he tried to call Eureste at his office, he was told Eureste was not there or was unavailable. Then, the staff in the Amarillo office became angry at Granado and told him: "You are supposed to come to us before you talk to him." However, the staff never explained to Granado what they were doing to help him. Instead, Granado testified the staff told him: "You are just going to have to talk to Mr. Eureste. He is your lawyer." According to Granado, Eureste called him about four times, but Eureste ***201** never told Granado what he was doing to help him obtain the operation. Most importantly, the communications between Granado and Eureste or his office led Granado to believe Eureste had an obligation to help him obtain the surgery. Granado was clearly left with the expectation that Eureste would help him obtain the surgery.

We find the evidence is both legally and factually sufficient to show Eureste failed to keep Granado reasonably informed. The trial court did not err in finding that Eureste violated Rule 1.03(a) and Rule 1.03(b).

c. Rule 1.15(b)—Withdrawal from Representation

[18] Rule 1.15(d) provides that upon termination of representation, a lawyer shall take steps to the extent reasonably practicable to protect a client's interests, such as giving reasonable notice to the client, allowing time for employment of other counsel, surrendering papers and property to which the client is entitled, and refunding any advance payments of unearned fees. Tex. Disciplinary R. Prof'l Conduct 1.15(d). Eureste contends his withdrawal complied with the requirements of Rule 1.15 in that he gave reasonable notice both verbally and in writing, allowed time for employment of other counsel, and returned Granado's file. He also contends that because Granado did not ask for the return of any unearned fees, he was in full compliance with Rule 1.15. We disagree with Eureste's contention that he complied with Rule 1.5.

There is evidence from which the trial court could reasonably infer that Eureste abruptly withdrew when there were no more benefits from which to extract attorney's fees. Eureste's withdrawal corresponded with the time that Granado's benefits ran out. Granado testified he did not even know the Amarillo office was being closed until he called the office and was informed he had reached the Houston office instead. He was also not informed that Eureste planned to withdraw until he was informed by a staff person that "Bernardo Eureste is going to drop you."

We find the evidence is legally and factually sufficient to show that Eureste failed to take reasonable steps to protect Granado's interests when Eureste withdrew. The trial court did not err in finding that Eureste violated Rule 1.15(b).

d. Rule 8.04(a)(1)—General Violations

[19] [20] In his fourth issue, Eureste challenges the legal and factual sufficiency of the evidence supporting the trial court's finding that he violated Rule 8.04(a)(1). Rule 8.04(a)(1) is a general rule that prohibits a lawyer from violating, or knowingly assisting, inducing, or acting through another to violate the Texas Disciplinary Rules of Professional Conduct. Tex. Disciplinary R. Prof'l Conduct 8.04(a)(1). All that is necessary to establish a violation of Rule 8.04(a)(1) is a violation of another rule. *See id.* We conclude that because the evidence is legally and factually sufficient to support the trial court's finding that Eureste violated Rules 1.01(b)(1), 1.01(b)(2), 1.03(a), 1.03(b), 1.04(a), 1.15(d) and 8.04(a)(3), the evidence is legally and factually sufficient to support the trial court's finding that Eureste violated Rule 8.04(a)(1).

C. Sanctions

[21] [22] [23] [24] Eureste contends in his fifth and final issue that the trial court abused its discretion when it ordered the sanction of suspension. Sanctions for professional misconduct may include disbarment, resignation in lieu of disbarment, indefinite disability suspension, suspension for a certain term, probation of suspension, interim suspension, ***202** public reprimand, and private reprimand. Tex.R. Disciplinary P. 1.06(T). A trial court has broad discretion to determine the consequences of professional misconduct. *Love v. State Bar of Texas*, 982 S.W.2d 939, 944 (Tex.App.-Houston [1st Dist.] 1998, no pet.); *State Bar of Texas v. Kilpatrick*, 874 S.W.2d 656, 659 (Tex.1994); *Curtis*, 20 S.W.3d at 234–35. However, the judgment of a trial court in a disciplinary proceeding may be so light or heavy as to amount to an abuse of discretion. *Love*, 982 S.W.2d at 944; *Kilpatrick*, 874 S.W.2d at 659. An appellate court should only reverse the trial court's decision if an abuse of discretion is shown. *Love*, 982 S.W.2d at 944. A court abuses its discretion only when it acts in an unreasonable and arbitrary manner, or when it

acts without reference to any guiding principles. _Furr's Supermarkets, Inc. v. Bethune_, 53 S.W.3d 375, 379 (Tex.2001); _Love_, 982 S.W.2d at 944. The court must consider the following factors in determining the appropriate sanction: (1) the nature and degree of the professional misconduct for which the respondent is being sanctioned; (2) the seriousness of and circumstances surrounding the professional misconduct; (3) the loss or damage to clients; (4) the damage to the profession; (5) the assurance that those who seek legal services in the future will be insulated from the type of professional misconduct found; (6) the profit to the attorney; (7) the avoidance of repetition; (8) the deterrent effect on others; (9) the maintenance of respect for the legal profession; (10) the conduct of the respondent during the course of the Committee action; (11) the trial of the case; and (12) other relevant evidence concerning the respondent's personal and professional background. Tex.R. Disciplinary P. 3.10; _Kilpatrick_, 874 S.W.2d at 659; _Curtis_, 20 S.W.3d at 235.

We find that in imposing the sanctions, the trial court did not act in an unreasonable and arbitrary manner or without reference to any guiding principles. To the contrary, the record shows the trial court considered the relevant factors outlined in Texas Rule of Disciplinary Procedure 3.10. In particular, the trial court found: (1) Eureste's actions were of a serious nature and degree; (2) the loss to Eureste's clients from their workers' compensation benefits was great; (3) the legal profession had been badly damaged by Eureste's conduct; (4) it is important to insulate future workers' compensation claimants and other clients from the risk of Eureste's billing practices; (5) Eureste profited greatly from his fraudulent billing scheme; and (6) other attorneys should be deterred from similar actions regarding their billing practices.

Eureste argues the sanction of suspension is unduly harsh because he has assisted many clients and his streamlined office procedures may have maximized client benefits. Eureste cites cases in which attorneys who committed allegedly more egregious conduct than Eureste received lighter sentences. However, the trial court had broad discretion in balancing the evidence in this case and applying it in terms of the statutory factors. [FN9] Considering the range of sanctions available to the court, the conduct at issue, and the trial ***203** court's reasoning, we conclude the trial court did not abuse its broad discretion in imposing the sanction of suspension upon Eureste.

> FN9. The trial court, in fact, specifically found Eureste genuinely believed his method of practicing was a means and manner to help people although he did so in the wrong way and that Eureste was cooperative during the disciplinary process. However pure Eureste's intentions may have been, the result of his conduct was that he greatly profited at the expense of his clients whose workers' compensation checks were reduced by his illegal and unconscionable fees. One of his clients, Granado, suffered personally from Eureste's lack of adequate representation, while Eureste overbilled and profited from his case.

EXERCISES

1. How did the attorney manipulate the TWCC rules regarding not having to justify bills?

2. When the attorney overbilled the TWCC, who was the real loser?

3. Did you feel the attorney's internal policy of billing the maximum amount possible complied with the TWCC's rules of billing actual time spent?

4. Were you surprised that this billing "beneath the radar" scheme was so effective?

5. Did the attorney commit fraud?

6. What did you think of the attorney's practice of billing legal assistant time as attorney time?

7. What was the attorney's rationale for billing more than 24 hours in a day for himself? Was it credible?

8. Do you suppose that for a very small part of the $2.3 million the attorney billed in one year, he could have secured computers and a state-of-the-art timekeeping and billing system that could have tracked actual time spent?

9. Did the attorney earn the hours he billed for in the Granado case?

10. Did you find it unconscionable that the attorney billed 2.5 hours a month for almost a year after a client had died?

11. What did you think of the trial court's decision to give the attorney a two-year active suspension, a one-year probated suspension, and restitution in the amount of $3,000 to Granado, and to reimburse the CFLD's attorney's fees of $18,310? Did you agree with their reasoning? How much money did the investigator find that the attorney received beyond what was a reasonable fee?

CASE REVIEW

Committee for Public Counsel Services v. Lookner, 47 Mass.App.Ct. 833, 716 N.E. 2d 690 (1999).

(Cite as: 47 Mass.App.Ct. 833, 716 N.E.2d 690)

Appeals Court of Massachusetts, Suffolk.

COMMITTEE FOR PUBIC COUNSEL SERVICES

v.

Norman S. LOOKNER.

No, 97-P-2138.

Argued April 8, 1999.

Decided Sept. 29, 1999.

Mary Murphy-Hensley, Boston, Assistant Attorney General, for the plaintiff.

Present: LAURENCE, SMITH, & SPINA, JJ.

LAURENCE, J.

Norman S. Lookner is an attorney licensed to practice in the Commonwealth. As part of his practice, he was certified to, and did, accept paid assignments from the Committee for Public Counsel Services (committee) (see G.L. c. 211D) to represent indigent clients in cases involving custody of children, delinquency charges, and termination of parental rights.

In early 1995, he was the subject of an audit by the committee, which investigated his billing practices (see G.L. c. 211D, § 12).

A committee auditor found that Lookner had over-billed the committee $18,445 in fiscal year 1994 by billing at least .25 hours for each task, such as a short telephone call, as opposed to billing the actual time worked in a given day rounded off to the nearest quarter of an hour. In addition, Lookner's time sheets did not record the actual amount of time spent on bill-able*834 tasks or explain the nature of the work performed. Lookner had billed the committee 2,327 hours over 364 days of the fiscal year and was paid $79,022.63 for fiscal year 1994 services. The auditor recommended to the committee's executive committee that Lookner repay $18,445 in overbillings within 24 months.

Lookner appealed the auditor's recommendation and requested a hearing. On November 1, 1995, pursuant to the procedures set forth in Section E of the committee's Manual for Counsel Assigned Through the Committee for Public Counsel Services—Policies and Procedures (June 1995) (manual), a hearing officer conducted a hearing at which Lookner was represented by an attorney. The manual, which is binding upon all "[a]ttorneys who accept **692 assignments of cases through the Committee," expressly provides that "[t]he action of the Executive Committee Hearing Officer shall be final." On February 28, 1996, the hearing officer issued his findings and final decision, concurring with the auditor's findings but reducing the overbilled amount to $11,130, payable within 12 months on terms to be mutually agreed upon by Lookner's attorney and the committee's audit staff.

After a hearing on the committee's motion to dismiss the complaint on August 16, 1996, a judge of the Superior Court ruled that the time for seeking relief under G.L. c. 249, §4, had expired but that Lookner's count for declaratory relief had been timely asserted. After a further hearing, on December 19, 1996, a second Superior Court judge allowed the committee's motion to dismiss, not only on the ground that it was untimely, [FN1] but also because Lookner's claim for declaratory relief could not be maintained against the judiciary department (see G.L. c. 231A, § 2), of which the committee is a part. We conclude that the dismissal of Lookner's certiorari count was correct on this record. [FN2]

EXERCISES

1.   Do you think Mr. Lookner expected the Committee for Public Counsel Services to conduct an audit of his billings?

2.   Do you think a court would take into account the types of clients Lookner would be representing and the fact that the Committee is a nonprofit/governmental entity?

3.   What do you think of the auditor's conclusion that the Committee had been overbilled by Lookner's rounding tasks to .25 hours instead of billing for the actual time incurred?

4.   What if Lookner had argued that in some instances he billed .25 when the service was actually .30 or .35, that he actually rounded down, and that it "all came out in the wash" and was, in fact, reasonably fair? Is this argument compelling to you?

5.   Lookner failed to keep detailed records of exactly what he did on cases, but did record the amount of time he spent. Why was this not enough to please the auditors? What other fact concerned the auditors and led them to question even the amount of time that he recorded?

6.   Did Lookner's billing practices violate the *Model Rules?* Why?

CASE REVIEW

In the Matter of Lloyd Clareman, 219 A.D.2d 195 (640 N.Y.S.2d 84) (1996).

640 N.Y.S.2d 84
(Cite as: 219 A.D.2d 195,
640 N.Y.S.2d 84)

Supreme Court, Appellate Division, First Department, New York.

In the Matter of Lloyd CLAREMAN, Esq. (admitted as Lloyd Samuel Clareman), an attorney and counselor-at-law:

Departmental Disciplinary Committee for the First Judicial Department,

Petitioner,

Lloyd Clareman, Esq., Respondent.

April 4, 1996.

Raymond Vallejo, of counsel (Hal R. Lieberman, attorney), for petitioner.

Frank H. Wright, of counsel (Wright & Manning, attorneys), for respondent.

Before SULLIVAN, J.P., and MILONAS, ROSENBERGER, KUPFERMAN and NARDELLI, JJ.

PER CURIAM.

Respondent was admitted to the practice of law in the State *196 of New York by the First Judicial Department, as Lloyd Samuel Clareman, on April 11, 1977. At all times relevant to these proceedings, he has maintained an office within the First Department.

After his second year of law school, the respondent was a summer associate at the now defunct law firm of Webster & Sheffield, where he met one of the firm's star litigation partners, Harvey Myerson. After completing the bar exam, he returned to the firm as an associate, working almost exclusively on litigation matters for Myerson. The Hearing Panel classified the relationship between Myerson and the associates of the firm as one of domineering manipulation. It found that Myerson virtually controlled the lives of the respondent and the other young associates at the firm by convincing them that their careers depended upon how he felt and what he said about them.

In 1983, while at Webster & Sheffield, the respondent became concerned about the legitimacy of a disbursement requested by Myerson on a matter over which the respondent had primary day-to-day responsibility. The request was for $70,000 in outside counsel fees for an attorney with whom the respondent was not familiar. Despite the risks to his career, the respondent brought the suspicious request to the attention of the managing partner of the firm. Although it later came to light that the requested disbursement was a fraud which the firm had agreed to ignore, the respondent incurred the wrath of Myerson for his actions, his mentor accusing the respondent of a rash act of betrayal.

Shortly after this incident, Myerson left Webster & Sheffield to become a partner at Finley, Kumble, Wagner, Heine, Underberg, Manley, Myerson & Casey. The respondent joined him in the move, and also became a partner at this firm. When this firm collapsed in 1987 and filed for bankruptcy, the respondent lost over $150,000.

In early 1988, Myerson formed Myerson & Kuhn, where the respondent became a litigation partner, while also serving on the executive committee, which was dominated and controlled by Myerson. The respondent was also the attorney in charge of most of the litigation conducted on behalf of one of Myerson's major clients, Shearson Lehman Hutton. In April 1988, Myerson confided to respondent that Shearson had agreed to pay the firm a flat fee of up to $800,000 per month to handle its litigation. Under Myerson's direction and assurance of propriety, the respondent and another attorney, Mark Segall, were to *197 prepare monthly statements for Shearson, reflecting charges of at least $800,000, even when the actual monthly fees were considerably less. During the period from April 1988 through January 1989, respondent assisted in preparing statements reflecting about $1.2 million worth of excess time, a major portion of the $2 million Shearson was defrauded under this overruling scheme. When the respondent expressed misgivings to Myerson about the billing practices, Myerson screamed at him: "You are just to do it. I am instructing you to do it." The respondent was subjected to numerous tirades from Myerson each time he was resistant to Myerson's orders. Ultimately, the firm went under, and again respondent paid all his debts. His full cooperation with government investigators, including testimony before the grand jury and in court, led to successful prosecution of Myerson (see, Matter of Myerson, 182 A.D.2d 242, 588 N.Y.S.2d 142; In re Myerson, 206 A.D.2d 299, 615 N.Y.S.2d 271) and others. The assistant United States attorney assigned to the Myerson investigation noted that the respondent **86 was the government's best cooperating witness. Meanwhile, adverse publicity surrounding the investigation made it difficult for the respondent to find work.

There are substantial mitigating factors in this case, including respondent's subordinate level of participation in the overbilling scheme, from which he received no personal financial benefit; his early, truthful, and complete cooperation; his immediate acknowledgement of wrongdoing and sincere expression of remorse; the significant adverse personal and professional consequences he has suffered as a result of his affiliation with Myerson; his hard-fought attempt to obtain restitution for Shearson; and his otherwise clean record and good moral character. Viewing the misconduct in light of these mitigating factors, the Hearing Panel recommended a public censure.

Respondent is guilty of engaging in misconduct involving dishonesty, fraud, deceit, or misrepresentation (Code of Professional Responsibility DR 1-102[A][4] [22 NYCRR 1200.3]), which adversely reflects on his fitness to practice law (DR 1-102[A][8]). In Matter of Segall, 218 A.D.2d 331, 638 N.Y.S.2d 444, this court sanctioned another attorney to a public censure for violation of the same disciplinary rules based upon the identical acts of misconduct at issue here. The same considerations which guided our decision in Segall lead us to conclude that a public censure is also appropriate here. In fact, we find the mitigating factors in the respondent's case to be even more compelling than those present in Segall. Accordingly, the motion to *198 confirm the Hearing Panel's report and recommendation is granted, and respondent is publicly censured for his misconduct.

Respondent is publicly censured.

All concur.

END OF DOCUMENT

EXERCISES

1. Clareman admitted to helping Myerson defraud their clients of more than a million dollars of the clients' money. Why was Clareman not disbarred?

2. What did Clareman do correctly concerning this matter, and at what cost?

3. What *Model Rules* regarding fees did Clareman violate?

PROLAW—TIMEKEEPING AND BILLING

TRAINING MANUAL OUTLINE

Number	Lesson Title	Concepts Covered
Lesson 1*	Introduction to ProLaw	Understanding the ProLaw interface
Lesson 2	Entering Time Sheets	Making time entries into ProLaw
Lesson 3	Using the Timer Feature and Entering Expense Slips	Making expense entries into ProLaw and using the timer feature to automatically track and record time
Lesson 4	Producing Pre-bills, Final Bills, and Reports	Producing pre-bill reports, final bills, and other timekeeping and billing reports

*Note: Lesson 1—Introduction to ProLaw, is the same for every subject matter (conflicts of interest, client relationship management, time and billing, etc.). If you completed Lesson 1 in an earlier tutorial, you do not need to repeat it.

WELCOME TO JOHNSON AND SULLIVAN

Welcome to Johnson and Sullivan! We are an active and growing firm with four attorneys and two legal assistants. As you know, you have been hired as a legal assistant intern. We are very happy to have you on board; we can certainly use your help.

At Johnson and Sullivan we put an emphasis on providing quality legal services to our clients. We bill our clients on a regular basis for these quality services, typically on a monthly basis, depending on the needs of our client. We strive to make sure our billings are timely and without errors. Because billings and fee disputes are some of the most common types of ethical complaints filed against lawyers, we require that all staff members understand the billing process. In addition, we want our staff members to have many job skills and to be flexible enough to enter their own time entries into the computer. All staff members are required to have at least minimal training in our billing system. We have developed this training manual to help you learn our system.

We currently use ProLaw, which is a comprehensive, legal-specific program that has many functions, including timekeeping and billing. One of the reasons we chose ProLaw was because it is very powerful and customizable. Please note that during this training exercise you will be entering information for Pat Doe, paralegal. We know you want to begin using ProLaw immediately, so there is only a short "Getting Started" section that you should read before you get on the computer.

GETTING STARTED

Introduction

Throughout these exercises, information you need to type into the program will be designated in several different ways.

- Keys to be pressed on the keyboard will be designated in brackets, in all caps and bold type (e.g., press the [ENTER] key).
- Movements with the mouse will be designated in bold and italics (e.g., *point to File on the menu bar and click the mouse*).
- Words or letters that should be typed will be designated in bold and enlarged (e.g., type **Training Program**).
- Information that is or should be displayed on your computer screen is shown in the following style: **Press ENTER to continue.**

Lesson 1: Introduction to ProLaw

In this lesson, you will load ProLaw and be introduced to the Contacts and Matters functions as an example of the basic interface of the program.

1. Load Windows. To load ProLaw, *click on the* **Start** *button, point with the mouse to* **Programs** *or* **All Programs**, *point to* **ProLaw Evaluation**, *and then point and click on* **PROLAW.**
2. When ProLaw is loaded the first time, you may see a window entitled **Professional Information for User xx.** The screen will ask you to enter your initials and name. At "Initials" type: **PD.** At "Full Name" type: **Pat Doe.** Then, *point and click on the green checkmark in the upper-right part of the window.*
3. You should now have the **ProLaw** window displayed, including the **Daily Docket** calendar for the current day on your screen.
4. *Point and click on the maximize icon at the type right of the* **ProLaw** *window* (it is just to the left of the red "X" and looks like two layered squares. If you point to an icon with your mouse for more than a second, the icon title will be displayed.)
5. Notice that there is a column of icons on the left edge of the screen. These icons give you access to ProLaw's major functions; they include Contacts, Matters, Events, Files, Transactions, Journals, Ledger, and Reports.
6. The table on next page is showing the purpose of each function in ProLaw.
7. *Point and click with the mouse on* Contacts. The **Contacts** window is now displayed.
8. *Point and click with the mouse on* Quick find, located in the View section of the Shortcuts pane. *In the* Search for *field press the* [BACKSPACE] key. This will clear the field and search for all contacts in the database. Press the [ENTER] key.

ProLaw Icon/Function	Purpose
CONTACTS	Contains contact information for all clients, parties, attorneys, judges, etc. It is an electronic address book. Conflict of interest searches can also be performed using this function.
MATTERS	Contains detailed information about every case/client matter. This includes billing information, notes about the case, related contacts, related matters, and settlement information, among others.
EVENTS	Allows the user to run queries for a specific set of docket entries and print docket reports.
FILES	Allows the user to check files in and out and report on the location and status of physical file folders.
TRANSACTIONS	Allows the user to create time entries, run cost recovery imports, edit pre-bills, and produce statements.
JOURNALS	Allows the user to enter checks, cash receipts, reconcile accounts, and produce financial reports.
LEDGER	Allows the user to view client billing and payment history and view statement images and unbilled statements.
REPORTS	Allows the user to produce and print a wide variety of reports.

9. Press the **[DOWN ARROW]** cursor key or *use the mouse* to scroll down through all of the contacts. Notice that the database is already populated with information.

10. *Scroll back until you find the entry for* Adam Schnieder, which is located near the bottom of the list. *Point and double-click on* Adam Schnieder.

11. Notice that the **Adam Schnieder—Contact** window is now displayed. You can now see the contact information for Adam Schnieder including name, class (i.e., type of entry; in this case, "client"), address, phone number, etc.

12. In the Adam Schnieder—Contact window, *point and click on the* Close *icon (the red "X" located in the upper-right corner of the window) to close this window.*

13. The "Contacts" window should now be displayed. *Point and click on "Recent"* (under "Shortcuts" "View"). Notice that only the entry for Adam Schnieder is listed. The Recent command contains a list of your most recently used contacts.

14. In the Contacts window, *point and click on the* Close *icon (the red "X" located in the upper-right corner of the window) to close this window.*

15. You should now be back where you started at the **Daily Docket** screen.

16. *Point and click with the mouse on* **Matters.** The **Matters** window is now displayed.

17. *Point and click with the mouse on* Quick find if it is not already displayed (located in the **View** section of the **Shortcuts** pane). In the **Search for** field, press the **[BACKSPACE]** key. This will clear the field and search for all matters in the database. Press the **[ENTER]** key.

18. In the **Matters** window, *point and click with the mouse on the* maximize *icon at the top right corner of the window* (located just to the left of the Close icon; it looks like two layered squares). This will allow you to see additional columns.

19. Press the **[DOWN ARROW]** cursor key or *use the mouse* to scroll down through all of the matters.

20. *Point and double-click with the mouse on the first entry* (**Matter ID 1000-001—Maguire, Robert, Maguire—Chapter** 7).

21. The **1000-001—Matter** window should now be displayed. Notice that there are a number of tabs in the window, including **General, Notes, Billing, Related Contacts,** and others. *Point and click on each of these tabs.* Then, close the **1000-01—Matter** window by *pointing and clicking on the* Close *icon.*

22. The **Matters** window should now be displayed. *Point and click on* **Recent** (located in the "View" section of the "Shortcuts" pane). Notice that only the "Maguire, Robert—Maguire—Chapter 7" matter is listed.

23. *In the* Matters *window, point and click on the* Close *icon to close this window.*

24. You should now be back where you started at the **Daily Docket** screen.

25. This concludes Lesson 1. To exit ProLaw, *point and click on the* Close *icon in the* **ProLaw** *window to close the program.* Alternatively, you may *point and click on* **File** *on the menu bar and then click on* **Exit.**

Lesson 2: Entering Time Sheets

In this lesson, you will enter a new matter/case into ProLaw.

1. Load Windows. To load ProLaw, *click on the* Start *button, point with the mouse to* **Programs** *or* **All Programs,** *point to* **ProLaw Evaluation,** *and then point and click on* **PROLAW.**

2. You should now have the **ProLaw** window displayed, including the **Daily Docket** calendar for the current day on your screen.

3. *Point and click with the mouse on* Transactions. This is where you record time spent on matters for tracking and billing purposes. The **Transactions** window should now be displayed

4. In ProLaw, transactions go through three stages: Batch, Work In Progress (WIP), and Billed. You will enter your time into the Batch stage. You will then move the entry to WIP. An entry must be in WIP before it will appear on a pre-bill or statement. After WIP, the entry is moved to the Billed stage. Once the entry is at the Billed stage, the entry cannot be edited without un-billing the statement first.

5. The heading **Time Entry** should be displayed in the main part of the window to the right. If it is not, *point and click with the mouse on* Time Entry *in the* View *section of the* Shortcuts *pane.*

6. *Point and click with the mouse on the* Add *item icon on the toolbar at the top left of the window, just under* **File** *on the menu bar.*

7. *Point and click on the* maximize *icon in the top right of the* Transactions *window (it looks like two layered squares).*

8. Notice that **PD** is shown in the **Initials** field and the current date is shown in the **Date** field. *Point and click on the ellipses (three periods) under* Initials.

9. Press the **[BACKSPACE]** key in the **Search for** field in the **Professionals List** window.

10. *Point and double-click on the entry for* **Daniel Martinez (DCM).**

11. Your cursor should now be in the "Trans No" field. This field will be automatically completed by ProLaw, so you can skip it for now.

12. Press the **[TAB]** key to go the **Matter ID** field.

13. *At the* Matter ID *field, point and click on the ellipses.*

14. The **Matters List** window is now displayed. *In the* Matters List *window, point and click on* Quick find. *In the* Search by *field, point and click on the down arrow of the drop-down box and select* **Client Sort.** In the **Search for** field, type **Hero. Matter ID 1008-001, Gerald v. The Hero Sandwich Company** should now be displayed. *Double-click on this entry.*

15. 1008-001 should now be entered in the **Matter ID** field, **Gerald v. the Hero Sandwich Company** should be entered in the **Matter Description** field, and **Hero Sandwich Company** should be entered in the **Client Sort** field. Press the **[TAB]** key three times. Your cursor should now be in the **Component** field.

16. *In the* Component *field, point and click on the ellipses.*

17. The **Components List** window should now be displayed. The **Component** field is used to identify the transaction type, such as time, expert witness, fax, and photocopies. *Scroll down and point and double-click on the* Time *entry.*

18. Press the **[TAB]** key to go to the **Task Code** field. The **Task Code** field further defines the type of entry you are making. *Point and click on the ellipses. Point and click on the* **Research** *entry.*

19. Press the **[TAB]** key to go to the **Units** field. The **Units** field is where you enter the hours or minutes for the entry. Type: **2.0** (i.e., 2 hours).

20. Press the **[TAB]** key to go to the **Price** field. Notice that the **Price, Ext Amt,** and **Value** fields have all been automatically completed by ProLaw.

21. *Point and click in the* Narrative *field at the bottom left of the screen.* The narrative field is where you describe how the time was spent. These comments will appear on the statement.

22. **Type Legal research, "Motion to Compel," regarding plaintiff's refusal to fully complete interrogatories.**

23. *Point and click on the* Save record *icon on the toolbar (green checkmark at the top of the screen, just under* Actions *on the menu bar).*

24. *Enter the following additional entries under the same date for Daniel Martinez for Gerald v. The Hero Sandwich Shop. Remember to add a new entry point and click on the* Add Item *icon on the toolbar at the top left of the window, just under* File *on the menu bar.* Notice that when you click on the **Add item** icon, ProLaw assumes you want to make an additional entry for the Gerald v. The Hero Sandwich shop case. Just press **[TAB]** to go to the **Component** field.

Entries for DCM—Daniel Martinez—Gerald v. The Hero Sandwich Shop

Component	Task Code	Units	Narrative
T-Time	A101—Plan and prepare for	2	Prep for deposition of defendant
T-Time	A103—Draft/revise	.50	Letter to counsel re: interrogatories
T-Time	A106—Communicate (with client)	5	Meet with client regarding his deposition
T-Time	A104—Review/analyze	.50	Letter from counsel
T-Time	A105—Communicate (in firm)	1	Strategy meeting with partner re: defendant's deposition

25. To make sure that the entries are in the system, *point and click on* Quick find.

26. *Point and click on the* Stage *field and then choose* Batch *from the drop-down list.*

27. *Point and click in the* Search for *field and press the* **[ENTER]** *key.* Notice that all of the entries that you just made are displayed.

28. *Point and click on* Move to WIP *under* Actions *on the left side of the screen.* When the **Confirm** dialog box appears, click **Yes** to move the transactions to WIP.

29. *Point and click on the* Stage *field and then choose* WIP *from the drop-down list.*

30. There are a number of other entries in the WIP stage. *Scroll to the bottom of the list* and notice that all of the entries you just made in the Hero case are displayed.

31. This concludes Lesson 2. To exit ProLaw, *point and click on the* Close *icon in the* **ProLaw** *window to close the program.* Alternatively, you may *point and click on* **File** *on the menu bar and then click on* **Exit.**

Lesson 3: Using the Timer Feature and Entering Expense Slips

In this lesson, you will learn how to use the timer feature and enter expense slips into ProLaw.

1. Load Windows. To load ProLaw, *click on the* Start *button, point with the mouse to* **Programs** *or* **All Programs,** *point to* **ProLaw Evaluation,** *and then point and click on* **PROLAW.**

2. You should now have the **ProLaw** window displayed, including the **Daily Docket** calendar for the current day on your screen.

3. *Point and click with the mouse on* Transactions.

4. *Point and click on* Time Entry *in the* View *section of the* Shortcuts *pane.*

5. Notice that **DCM** (Daniel Martinez) is shown in the **Initials** field and the current date is shown in the **Date** field. If the current date is not shown, edit the date to show the current date.

6. *Point and click with the mouse on the* Add item *icon on the toolbar at the top left of the window, just under* File *on the menu bar.*

7. Your cursor should now be in the **Trans No** field. This field will be automatically completed by ProLaw, so you can skip it for now.

8. Press the **[TAB]** key to go the **Matter ID** field.

9. *At the* Matter ID *field, point and click on the ellipses.*

10. The **Matters List** window is now displayed. *In the* Matters List *window, point and click on* Quick find. *In the* Search by *field, point and click on the down arrow of the drop-down box and select* **Client Sort**. In the **Search for** field, type **Hero. Matter ID 1008-001, Gerald v. The Hero Sandwich Company** should now be displayed. *Double-click on this entry.*

11. 1008-001 should now be entered in the **Matter ID** field, **Gerald v. the Hero Sandwich Company** should be entered in the **Matter Description** field, and **Hero Sandwich Company** should be entered in the **Client Sort** field.

12. The Timer feature can be used to track the time you spend on each matter. For example, if you receive a telephone call from a client, you can turn the timer feature on and it will automatically track the amount of time you spend on the phone until you turn it off.

13. *Point and click on the* Timer *icon in the lower-right part of the screen (it looks like a clock, with* **0:00:00** *under it). Alternatively, you can point and click on* Tools *on the menu bar and then on* Start/Stop Timer.

14. Notice that the clock starts to count up. Wait for a minute or two and then *point and click on the* Timer *feature again.* Notice that ProLaw stopped the clock and automatically made an entry into the **Units** field.

15. In the **Component** field, type **T** for Time. In the "Task Code." *scroll down and click on* **E105—Telephone.**

16. In the **Narrative** field, type **Telephone call with Client regarding witness fees.**

17. *Point and click with the mouse on the* Spell check *icon on the toolbar (it has the letters* **ABC** *and a checkmark).* Correct any misspellings in the narrative.

18. *Point and click on the* Save Record *icon (green checkmark) on the toolbar at the top of the screen (just under* Actions *on the menu bar).*

19. You are now ready to enter some client expenses in the Gerald v. The Hero Sandwich Company case. *Point and click with the mouse on the* Add item *icon on the toolbar at the top left of the window, just under* File *on the menu bar.*

20. *In the* Component *field, select the entry for* **Copies— Photocopies.**

21. *In the* Task Code, *select the entry for* **E101—Copying**.

22. In the **Units** field, type **150** and press the **[ENTER]** key. Notice that ProLaw has a default entry of .25 cents for copies in the **Price** field. Also notice that when you entered 150 in the **Units** field, ProLaw calculated the **Ext Amt** field for you at $37.50.

23. In the **Narrative** field, notice that ProLaw entered Photocopies. In the **Photocopies** field, type **of Motion for Summary Judgment** after "Photocopies."

24. *Point and click on the* Save Record *icon (green checkmark) on the toolbar at the top of the screen (just under* Actions *on the menu bar).*

25. *Enter the following additional expense entries:*

Expense Entries for DCM—Daniel Martinez—Gerald v. The Hero Sandwich Shop

Component	Test Code	Units	Narrative
Copies	E101—Copying	50	Photocopies of PreTrial Questionnaire
Postage	E108—Postage	2	Letter to counsel re: interrogatories
Postage	E108—Postage	1	Letter to Client
LD (long distance charges)	E105—Telephone	1 Unit; $5 Price	Long distance charges for call to expert witness

26. *Point and click on the* Save Record *icon on the toolbar at the top of the screen (just under* Actions *on the menu bar).*

27. *Move all of these entries to WIP by pointing and clicking on* Move to WIP *under* Actions.

28. To make sure that the entries are in the system, *point and click on* Quick find.

29. *Point and click on the drop-down box of the* Stage *field and choose* **WIP.**

30. *Point and click on the drop-down box of the* Type *field and choose* **(all).** This will retrieve all fees and expenses. Notice that all of the entries that you just made are displayed.

31. This concludes Lesson 3. To exit ProLaw, *point and click on the* Close *icon in the* **ProLaw** *window to close the program.* Alternatively, you may *point and click on* **File** *on the menu bar and then click on* **Exit.**

Lesson 4: Producing Pre-bills, Final Bills, and Reports

In this lesson, you will print a pre-bill, a final bill, and some additional reports.

1. Load Windows. To load ProLaw, *click on the* Start *button, point with the mouse to* **Programs** *or* **All Programs,** *point to* **ProLaw Evaluation,** *and then point and click on* **PROLAW.**

2. You should now have the **ProLaw** window displayed, including the **Daily Docket** calendar for the current day on your screen.

3. *Point and click with the mouse on* **Transactions.**

4. *Point and click with the mouse on* Quick find *in the* View *section of the* Shortcuts *pane.*

5. Before proceeding, make sure the **Search by** field has **Client Sort** entered, the **Stage** field has **WIP,** and the **Type** field has **(all)** selected. If these options are not selected, choose the correct option from the drop-down list.

6. *Point and click with the mouse in the* Search for *field* and press the **[BACKSPACE]** key. Type **Hero.**

7. Notice that all of your entries are now displayed.

8. *Point and click on* Print Pre-bills/Statements *in the* Actions *section of the* Shortcuts *pane.*

9. **The Pre-bills/Statements** window should now be displayed; under **Matters List,** the Hero Sandwich Company matter should be shown. (If not, *click the* Add item *icon on the far right side of the window.* In the **Client Sort** field, type **Hero.** Press **[TAB].** The **Matters List** window should open on the screen. *Double-click the Hero Sandwich Company entry.* The Hero Sandwich Company matter should be shown.)

10. Make sure the **Closing date** and the **Statement date** are set for the current date (the closing/statement date must be past the date you entered for the transactions; otherwise, they will not show up in the pre-bill report). Also, make sure the **Matter activity** shows **WIP or A/R** and **Pre-bills** is selected under **Type.**

11. *Point and double-click with the mouse on the* Start query *icon on the right side of the* Pre-bills/Statements *window (it looks like a file folder with a magnifying glass on it).* Notice that the case is shown in the bottom portion of the screen with amounts in the **Fees** and **Soft Costs** columns.

12. *Point and double-click with the mouse on the* Preview statements *icon on the toolbar (it looks like a piece of paper with a magnifying glass) in the* Pre-bills/Statements *window.*

13. *Scroll down and view the pre-bill. Point and click with the mouse on the up arrow at the top of the window to go to the second page of the bill.* If you would like to print the pre-bill, *point and click with the mouse on the* Printer *icon on the toolbar in the* Pre-bill Preview 1008-001 *window.*

14. *Point and click with the mouse on the green checkmark to close the window.*

15. Printing final bills (which ProLaw refers to as "Statements") is the same as printing pre-bills. The only difference is that you would select **Statements** instead of selecting **Pre-bills** as the **Type** in the **Pre-bills/Statements** window.

16. *Point and click the mouse on the green checkmark to close the* Pre-bills/Statements *window.*

17. *Point and click on the* Close *icon in the* Transactions *window.*

18. *Point and click on* Reports *in the* ProLaw *window.*

19. Notice, to the left under **Management Reports,** that there are a number of standard billing-related reports.

20. *Scroll down and point and click on the* WIP Aging *report under* Management Report. Notice the heading on the top right portion of the screen says **WIP Aging.**

C. *Ranges*—A range is a group of cells. Cell ranges can be created by *dragging the mouse* or holding the **[SHIFT]** key on and using the arrow (cursor) keys.

D. *Format*—Cells can be formatted, including changing the font style, font size, shading, border, cell type (currency, percentage, etc.), alignment, and more by *selecting* Format *from the menu bar and then clicking on cells*, or by *right-clicking* (for right-handed mouse users) *on the cell and then selecting* Format Cells.

E. *Editing a Cell*—You can edit a cell by *double-clicking with the mouse on the cell* or by *clicking once with the mouse on the cell and then pointing and clicking with the mouse on the formula bar.* (The formula bar is directly under the toolbar and just to the right of the = (equals) sign or "fx" sign.) The formula bar shows the current contents of the selected cell, and it allows you to edit the cell contents. You can also edit the contents of a cell by *pointing and clicking with the mouse on the cell* and then pressing the **[F2]** key.

F. *Column Width*—You can change the width of a column by *pointing at the column letters* (at the top of the screen) *and moving the cursor to the edge of the column.* The cursor then changes to double-headed vertical arrows. Simply *drag the mouse to the right to increase the column width or to the left to decrease the column width.* You can change the height of a row by *pointing and dragging the mouse on the row numbers.* You can also change the width of a column by going to the column you want to change and selecting **Format** from the menu bar, then **Column**, and then **Width.** You can change the height of a row by going to the row you want to change and selecting **Format** from the menu bar, then **Row**, and then **Height.**

G. *Insert*—You can insert one row or column by selecting **Insert** from the menu bar, and then Column or Row. You can also insert a number of rows or columns by *dragging the mouse over the number of rows or columns you want to add and selecting* Insert *from the menu bar, and then either* Column *or* Row. Finally, you can *right-click with the mouse and select* Insert *from the menu.*

H. *Erase/Delete*—You can erase data by *dragging the mouse over the area* and then pressing the **[DELETE]** key. You can delete whole columns or rows by *pointing with the mouse on a column or row, selecting* Edit *from the menu bar, and then* Delete, and following the menus. You can also delete whole columns or rows by *pointing with the mouse on the column or row, right-clicking with the mouse, and selecting* Delete.

I. *Quit*—To quit Excel, *point and click with the mouse on* File *and then* Exit.

J. *Copy*—To copy data, *click on the cell and then select the* Autofill *command,* which is the small black box at the bottom right corner of every cell. Then *drag the mouse to where the data should be placed.* You can also copy data by *selecting the cell, right-clicking the mouse and selecting* Copy, *moving the cursor to the location where the information should be copied,* and

MICROSOFT EXCEL (ALL VERSIONS)

BASIC LESSONS

Number	Lesson Title
Lesson 1	Creating a Client Settlement Worksheet
Lesson 2	Creating a Fee Projection Worksheet

GETTING STARTED

Overview

Microsoft Excel is a powerful spreadsheet program that allows you to create formulas, "what-if" scenarios, graphs, and much more.

Introduction

Throughout these lessons and exercises, information you need to operate the program will be designated in several different ways:

- Keys to be pressed on the keyboard will be designated in brackets, in all caps and bold type (e.g., press the **[ENTER]** key).
- Movements with the mouse will be designated in bold and italics (e.g., *point to File on the menu bar and click the mouse*).
- Words or letters that should be typed will be designated in bold and enlarged (e.g., type **Training Program**).
- Information that is or should be displayed on your computer screen is shown in the following style: **Press ENTER to continue.**

OVERVIEW OF EXCEL

I. Worksheet

    A. *Menu/commands—Click on the toolbar or the menu bar* to access menus and/or to execute commands.

    B. *Entering Data*—To enter data, type the text or number, and press the **[ENTER]** key or one of the arrow (cursor) keys.

C. *Ranges*—A range is a group of cells. Cell ranges can be created by ***dragging the mouse*** or holding the **[SHIFT]** key on and using the arrow (cursor) keys.

D. *Format*—Cells can be formatted, including changing the font style, font size, shading, border, cell type (currency, percentage, etc.), alignment, and more by ***selecting*** Format ***from the menu bar and then clicking on cells***, or by ***right-clicking*** (for right-handed mouse users) ***on the cell and then selecting*** Format Cells.

E. *Editing a Cell*—You can edit a cell by ***double-clicking with the mouse on the cell*** or by ***clicking once with the mouse on the cell and then pointing and clicking with the mouse on the formula bar.*** (The formula bar is directly under the toolbar and just to the right of the = (equals) sign or "fx" sign.) The formula bar shows the current contents of the selected cell, and it allows you to edit the cell contents. You can also edit the contents of a cell by ***pointing and clicking with the mouse on the cell*** and then pressing the **[F2]** key.

F. *Column Width*—You can change the width of a column by ***pointing at the column letters*** (at the top of the screen) ***and moving the cursor to the edge of the column.*** The cursor then changes to double-headed vertical arrows. Simply ***drag the mouse to the right to increase the column width or to the left to decrease the column width.*** You can change the height of a row by ***pointing and dragging the mouse on the row numbers.*** You can also change the width of a column by going to the column you want to change and selecting **Format** from the menu bar, then **Column,** and then **Width.** You can change the height of a row by going to the row you want to change and selecting **Format** from the menu bar, then **Row,** and then **Height.**

G. *Insert*—You can insert one row or column by selecting **Insert** from the menu bar, and then Column or Row. You can also insert a number of rows or columns by ***dragging the mouse over the number of rows or columns you want to add and selecting*** Insert ***from the menu bar, and then either*** Column *or* Row. Finally, you can ***right-click with the mouse and select*** Insert ***from the menu.***

H. *Erase/Delete*—You can erase data by ***dragging the mouse over the area*** and then pressing the **[DELETE]** key. You can delete whole columns or rows by ***pointing with the mouse on a column or row, selecting*** Edit ***from the menu bar, and then*** Delete, and following the menus. You can also delete whole columns or rows by ***pointing with the mouse on the column or row, right-clicking with the mouse, and selecting*** Delete.

I. *Quit*—To quit Excel, ***point and click with the mouse on*** File ***and then*** Exit.

J. *Copy*—To copy data, ***click on the cell and then select the*** Autofill ***command,*** which is the small black box at the bottom right corner of every cell. Then ***drag the mouse to where the data should be placed.*** You can also copy data by ***selecting the cell, right-clicking the mouse and selecting*** Copy, ***moving the cursor to the location where the information should be copied,*** and

4. *Point and click with the mouse on* Quick find *in the* View *section of the* Shortcuts *pane.*

5. Before proceeding, make sure the **Search by** field has **Client Sort** entered, the **Stage** field has **WIP,** and the **Type** field has **(all)** selected. If these options are not selected, choose the correct option from the drop-down list.

6. *Point and click with the mouse in the* Search for *field and press the* **[BACKSPACE]** key. Type **Hero.**

7. Notice that all of your entries are now displayed.

8. *Point and click on* Print Pre-bills/Statements *in the* Actions *section of the* Shortcuts *pane.*

9. **The Pre-bills/Statements** window should now be displayed; under **Matters List,** the Hero Sandwich Company matter should be shown. (If not, *click the* Add item *icon on the far right side of the window.* In the **Client Sort** field, type **Hero.** Press **[TAB].** The **Matters List** window should open on the screen. *Double-click the Hero Sandwich Company entry.* The Hero Sandwich Company matter should be shown.)

10. Make sure the **Closing date** and the **Statement date** are set for the current date (the closing/statement date must be past the date you entered for the transactions; otherwise, they will not show up in the pre-bill report). Also, make sure the **Matter activity** shows **WIP or A/R** and **Pre-bills** is selected under **Type.**

11. *Point and double-click with the mouse on the* Start query *icon on the right side of the* Pre-bills/Statements *window (it looks like a file folder with a magnifying glass on it).* Notice that the case is shown in the bottom portion of the screen with amounts in the **Fees** and **Soft Costs** columns.

12. *Point and double-click with the mouse on the* Preview statements *icon on the toolbar (it looks like a piece of paper with a magnifying glass) in the* Pre-bills/Statements *window.*

13. *Scroll down and view the pre-bill. Point and click with the mouse on the up arrow at the top of the window to go to the second page of the bill.* If you would like to print the pre-bill, *point and click with the mouse on the* Printer *icon on the toolbar in the* Pre-bill Preview 1008-001 *window.*

14. *Point and click with the mouse on the green checkmark to close the window.*

15. Printing final bills (which ProLaw refers to as "Statements") is the same as printing pre-bills. The only difference is that you would select **Statements** instead of selecting **Pre-bills** as the **Type** in the **Pre-bills/Statements** window.

16. *Point and click the mouse on the green checkmark to close the* Pre-bills/Statements *window.*

17. *Point and click on the* Close *icon in the* Transactions *window.*

18. *Point and click on* Reports *in the* ProLaw *window.*

19. Notice, to the left under **Management Reports,** that there are a number of standard billing-related reports.

20. *Scroll down and point and click on the* WIP Aging *report under* Management Report. Notice the heading on the top right portion of the screen says **WIP Aging.**

21. *Point and click with the mouse on the* Preview report *icon on the toolbar.*
22. A balance should be showing for the Hero Sandwich Company case. We did not actually print the statements, so that is why there is a balance still showing in the **Work In Progress** stage. Had we printed that statement (final bill), it would have cleared the amount in the **Work In Progress** stage.
23. *Close the* Listing—Report *window.*
24. *Point and click with the mouse on the* Missing Time *report.* The report shows days where no time was recorded for each professional. This is a great tool for ensuring that all time has been appropriately recorded. *Point and click with the mouse on the* Preview report *icon on the toolbar.*
25. *Close the* Listing—Report *window.*
26. *Point and click with the mouse on the* A/R Aging Listing *report.* The report shows what has been currently billed for each case and which amounts are 30, 60, and 90 days overdue.
27. *Close the* Listing—Report *window.*
28. This concludes Lesson 4. To exit ProLaw, *point and click on the* Close *icon in the* **ProLaw** *window to close the program.* Alternatively, you may *point and click on* **File** *on the menu bar and then click on* **Exit**.

This concludes the ProLaw Timekeeping and Billing Hands-on Exercises.

pressing the **[ENTER]** key. Data can also be copied by *clicking with the mouse on the information to be copied and selecting* Edit *from the menu bar and* Copy. Then go to the location where the information should be copied and select **Edit** from the menu bar and then **Paste.**

K. *Move*—Move data by *clicking on the cell, right-clicking the mouse, selecting* Cut, *moving the cursor to the location where the information should be inserted,* and pressing the **[ENTER]** key. Data can also be moved by *clicking with the mouse on the information to be moved, selecting* Edit *from the menu bar and* Cut, *going to the location where the information should be copied, and selecting* Edit *from the menu bar and then* Paste.

L. *Saving and Opening Files*—Save a file by *pointing with the mouse on* File *and then* Save, and typing the file name. You can also save a file by *clicking on the* Save *icon* (a floppy disk) on the toolbar. Open a file that was previously saved by *pointing with the mouse on* File *and then* Open and typing the name of the file to be opened.

M. *Print*—You can print a file by *pointing and clicking with the mouse on the* Printer *icon* on the toolbar or by *selecting* File *from the menu bar and then* Print *and* OK.

II. Numbers and Formulas

A. *Numbers*—To enter a number in a cell, simply type the number and press the **[ENTER]** key or an arrow (cursor) key.

B. *Adding Cells (Addition)*—You can add the contents of two or more cells by three different methods:
1. To add the contents of two or more cells,
   a. Go to the cell location where the total should be placed.
   b. *Point and click with the mouse on the* AutoSum *icon* on the toolbar, which looks a little like an E. (*Note:* To see the name of an icon, point at the icon for a second, and the name of the icon will be displayed.)
   c. Excel guesses at what cells you want to add. Press **[ENTER]** if the correct range is entered or edit the range by pressing the **[SHIFT]** key and moving the arrow cursor keys until the correct cell address is displayed. Then press **[ENTER]**.
2. To add the contents of two cells,
   a. Go to the cell location where the total should be placed.
   b. Press =.
   c. Enter the first cell address (or point to it with the cursor).
   d. Press +.
   e. Enter the second cell address (or point to it with the cursor).
   f. Press the **[ENTER]** key. (For example, to add the values of C4 and C5, the formula would read =C4+C5.)
3. To add the contents of two cells,
   a. Go to the cell location where the total should be placed.
   b. Type =**SUM(.**

         c. Enter the first cell address (or point to it with the cursor).
         d. Press the period (.).
         e. Enter the second cell address (or point to it with the cursor).
         f. Press the closing parenthesis ()).
         g. Press the **[ENTER]** key. (For example, to add the values of C4 and C5, the formula would read =SUM(C4:C5).)

C. *Subtracting Cells*—To subtract one cell from another,
    1. Go to the cell location where the total should be placed.
    2. Press =.
    3. Enter the first cell address (or point to it with the cursor).
    4. Press −.
    5. Enter the second cell address (or point to it with the cursor).
    6. Press the **[ENTER]** key. (For example, to subtract the value of C4 from the value of C5, the formula would read =C5−C4.)

D. *Multiplying Cells*—To multiply two cells,
    1. Go to the cell location where the total should be placed.
    2. Press =.
    3. Enter the first cell address (or point to it with the cursor).
    4. Press the *([SHIFT]-[8]).
    5. Enter the second cell address (or point to it with the cursor).
    6. Press the **[ENTER]** key. (For example, to multiply the value in C4 times the value in C5, the formula would read =C5*C4.)

E. *Dividing Cells*—To divide two cells,
    1. Go to the cell location where the total should be placed.
    2. Press =.
    3. Enter the first cell address (or point to it with the cursor).
    4. Press the front slash (/).
    5. Enter the second cell address (or point to it with the cursor).
    6. Press the **[ENTER]** key. (For example, to divide the value in C4 by the value in C5, the formula would read =C4/C5.)

BEFORE STARTING LESSON 1—SETTING THE TOOL AND MENU BAR

Before starting Lesson 1, complete the exercise below to adjust the toolbar and menu bar so that they are consistent with the instructions in the lessons.

    1. Load Windows. Then, *double-click on the* Excel *icon on the desktop* to load Excel for Windows. Alternatively, *click on the "Start" button, point with the mouse to "Programs" or "All Programs," and then click on the* Microsoft Excel *icon. Or click on the "Start" button, point with the mouse to "Programs" or "All Programs," point to* Microsoft Office, *then click on the* Microsoft Office Excel 2003 *icon.*

2. A blank workbook should be open. If you are not in a blank workbook, *click on "File" on the menu bar, then click on "New," and then click or double-click (depending on the Excel version you are using) on "Blank workbook."*

3. *Click on "View" in the menu bar and then point with the mouse to "Toolbars."*

4. Only the "Standard" and "Formatting" toolbars should be checked. If the "Standard" and "Formatting" toolbars are not checked, then click on them to select them (the checkmark indicates they have been selected). If another toolbar has been selected (marked with a checkmark—such as the "Chart" toolbar or other option), click on it to remove it from toolbar. Please note that you can only make changes to the toolbar one at a time, so it may take you a few steps to only have "Standard" and "Formatting" selected, or your computer may already be set for this and you may not have to make any changes. If you do not have to make changes, just push the **[ESC]** key twice to exit out of the "View" menu.

5. We also want to a) make sure that the full menus are displayed when you select an item from the menu (Excel normally will only show the most recent/commonly used selections) and b) that the toolbar is shown on two rows, so that you can see all of the options.

6. *Click on "View" in the menu bar, point with the mouse to "Toolbars," and then click on "Customize."*

7. *Click on the "Options" tab. Then, under "Personalized Menus and Toolbars" make sure that checkmarks are next to "Show Standard and Formatting toolbars on two rows" and "Always show full menus."* Note: if, under "Personalized Menus and Toolbars," it says "Standard and Formatting Toolbars share one row," do not check the box (the toolbars are already on two rows). Also, if "Menus Show recently used commands first" is displayed, do not check the box (full menus will already be displayed). *Click on "Close."*

Please note that depending on the version of Excel you are using, the toolbars, icons, and menus may look slightly different than the figures, but the differences should be minor. You are now ready to begin Lesson 1.

Lesson 1: Creating a Client Settlement Worksheet

This lesson shows you how to build the spreadsheet in Figure 1—Excel Tutorial Spreadsheet. Keep in mind that if you make a mistake at any time during this lesson, you can simply press **[CTRL]-[Z]** to undo what you have done.

1. Load Windows. Then, *double-click on the* Excel *icon on the desktop to* load Excel for Windows. Alternatively, *click on the "Start" button, point with the mouse to "Programs" or "All Programs," and then click on the* Microsoft Excel *icon. Or click on the "Start" button, point with the mouse to "Programs" or "All Programs," point to* Microsoft Office, *then click on the* Microsoft Office Excel 2003 *icon.*

Figure 1
Excel Tutorial Spreadsheet

Screen shot reprinted by permission of Microsoft Corporation

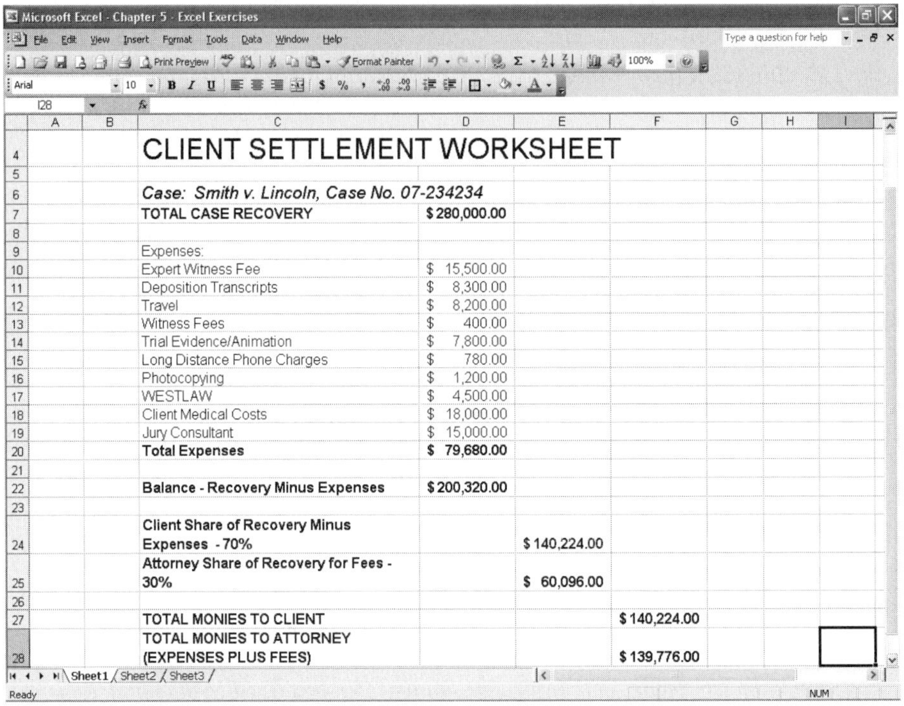

CLIENT SETTLEMENT WORKSHEET			
Case: Smith v. Lincoln, Case No. 07-234234			
TOTAL CASE RECOVERY	**$ 280,000.00**		
Expenses:			
Expert Witness Fee	$ 15,500.00		
Deposition Transcripts	$ 8,300.00		
Travel	$ 8,200.00		
Witness Fees	$ 400.00		
Trial Evidence/Animation	$ 7,800.00		
Long Distance Phone Charges	$ 780.00		
Photocopying	$ 1,200.00		
WESTLAW	$ 4,500.00		
Client Medical Costs	$ 18,000.00		
Jury Consultant	$ 15,000.00		
Total Expenses	**$ 79,680.00**		
Balance - Recovery Minus Expenses	**$ 200,320.00**		
Client Share of Recovery Minus Expenses - 70%		**$ 140,224.00**	
Attorney Share of Recovery for Fees - 30%		**$ 60,096.00**	
TOTAL MONIES TO CLIENT			**$ 140,224.00**
TOTAL MONIES TO ATTORNEY (EXPENSES PLUS FEES)			**$ 139,776.00**

2. A blank workbook should be open. If you are not in a blank workbook, *click on "File" on the menu bar and click on "New," and then click or double-click (depending on the Excel version you are using) on "Blank workbook."*
3. Notice that the cell pointer is at cell A1 and the current cell indicator (also called the name box by Excel) shows A1. The name box is just under the toolbar in the upper-left comer of the screen. Also notice that you can move the cell pointer around the worksheet by either using the cursor keys or by pointing with the mouse and clicking the left mouse button once.
4. Go to cell C4 by *pointing with the mouse on cell C4 and pressing the left mouse button once.* The name box should now show cell C4.
5. You will now increase the width of column C. *Point and click with the mouse on "Format" on the menu bar. Then, point to "Column" and point and click on "Width."* Enter **45** at the "Column Width" prompt and then *point and click on "OK."* Notice that the width of column C was expanded to the right.
6. *At cell C4 type:* **CLIENT SETTLEMENT WORKSHEET** *and press the* **[ENTER]** *key.*
7. *Point and click with the mouse back on cell C4, then point and click with the mouse on the "Font Size" icon on the toolbar. type* **24**, *and then press the* **[ENTER]** *key* (or alternatively, you can select the down arrow key next to the "Font Size" icon and select 24 from the list). *Note:* the "Font Size" icon is on the upper left of the screen on the toolbar and typically will have a

number displayed, such as 10. If you point to an icon on the toolbar and leave it there for about one second, the name of the icon will displayed. The text in cell C4 should now be displayed in 24-point type.

8. *Point and click with the mouse on cell C6 and type:* **Case: Smith v. Lincoln, Case No. 07-234234** *and press the* [**ENTER**] *key.*

9. *Point and click with the mouse back on cell C6, point and click with the mouse on the "Font Size" icon on the toolbar, type* **14**, *and then press the* [**ENTER**] *key.* The text should now be displayed in 14-point type.

10. *Point and click with the mouse back on cell C6, and then point and click with the mouse on the "Italics" icon on the toolbar.* The "Italics" icon looks like an italicized capital "*I*" on the toolbar (about two icons over from the "Font Size" icon). The text should now be displayed in 14-point italicized type.

11. You will now select an area in the worksheet and make it all 12-point type. *Point and click on cell C7 with the mouse, drag the mouse (i.e., hold the left mouse button down) to cell F28, and then release the mouse button.* The area from C7 to F28 should now be highlighted. *Point and click with the mouse back on the "Font Size" icon on the toolbar, type* **12**, *and then press the* [**ENTER**] *key.*

12. *Point and click with the mouse on cell C7 and type:* **Case: TOTAL CASE RECOVERY** *and press the* [**ENTER**] *key.*

13. *Point and click with the mouse back on cell C7 and then point and click with the mouse on the "Bold" icon on the toolbar.* The "Bold" icon on the toolbar looks like a bold capital "B" just to the right of the "Font Size" icon.

14. You will now increase the width of columns D, E, and F. *Point to cell D7 with the mouse, drag the mouse to cell F7, and then let go of the mouse button.* Cells D7, E7, and F7 should now be highlighted. *Point and click with the mouse on "Format" on the menu bar. Then, point to "Column" and point and click on "Width."* Enter **15** at the "Column Width" prompt and then *point and click on "OK."* Notice that the width of columns D, E, and F were expanded.

15. *Point and click with the mouse on cell D7 and type:* **280000** *and press the* [**ENTER**] *key.* Do not press the dollar sign or a comma.

16. You will now change the formal of cells D7 through F28 to currency. *Point and click on cell D7 with the mouse, drag the mouse (i.e., hold the left mouse button down) to cell F28, and then release the mouse button.* The area from D7 to F28 should now be highlighted. *Point and click with the mouse on the "Currency Style" icon on the toolbar.* The "Currency Style" icon is near the middle of the toolbar, and it looks like a dollar sign ("$"). Cell D7 should now be displayed as $280,000.00.

17. *Point and click with the mouse on cell D7, and then point and click on the "Bold" icon on the toolbar.*

18. You should now be able to enter information. Enter the following information into the cells indicated:

    —**Expenses:** in C9

    —**Expert Witness Fee** in C10

—**Deposition Transcripts** in C11

—**Travel** in C12

—**Witness Fee** in C13

—**Trial Evidence/Animation** in C14

—**Long Distance Phone Charges** in C15

—**Photocopying** in C16

—**Westlaw** in C17

—**Client Medical Costs** in C18

—**Jury Consultant** in C19

—**TOTAL EXPENSES** in C20 (bold)

—**Balance—Recovery Minus Expenses** in C22 (bold)

—**Client Share of Recovery Minus Expenses—70%** in C24 (bold)

—**Attorney Share of Recovery for Fees—30%** in C25 (bold)

—**TOTAL MONIES TO CLIENT** in C27 (bold)

—**TOTAL MONIES TO ATTORNEY (EXPENSES PLUS FEES)** in C28 (bold)

19. Notice that some of the longer text may flow into the next cell. We will wrap the text to fix this. *Point and click on cell C24 with the mouse, drag the mouse to cell C28, and then let go of the mouse button.* Cells C24 to C28 should now be highlighted. *Point and click with the mouse on "Format" on the menu bar.* Then, *point and click on "Cells," point and click on the "Alignment" tab, click in the box next to "Wrap Text," and then click on "OK."* The text should now be wrapped so it fits within the cell.

20. Enter the following information into the cells indicated:

—**15500** in D10

—**8300** in D11

—**8200** in D12

—**400** in D13

—**7800** in D14

—**780** in D15

—**1200** in D16

—**4500** in D17

—**18000** in D18

—**15000** in D19

21. You are now ready to enter formulas into the worksheet. *Point and click with the mouse on cell D20.* Type: =**SUM** and then *point and click on D10.* Next, type *(period) to anchor the range.* Then, *point and click on D19, press the:) (close right parenthesis), and press the* [**ENTER**] *key.* The completed

formula should read: =SUM(D10:D19). *Note:* You can select cell D20 to see the formula in the formula bar at the top of the screen. The correct amount of $79,680.00 should be displayed in cell D20. *Point and click with the mouse on cell D20* and then *point and click on the "Bold" icon on the toolbar.*

22. *Point and click with the mouse on cell D22.* Type: **= D7-D20** and then press the **[ENTER]** *key. Point and click with the mouse on cell D22 and then point and click on the "Bold" icon on the toolbar.* The formula subtracts D20 (Total Expenses) from D7 (Total Case Recovery). The correct answer of $200,320.00 should be displayed.

23. *Point and click with the mouse on cell E24.* Type: **= D22*.70** and then press the **[ENTER]** *key. Point and click with the mouse on cell E24 and then point and click on the "Bold" icon on the toolbar.* The formula calculates the client's share of the recovery (which is 70% after expenses are paid). The correct answer of $140,224.00 should be displayed.

24. *Point and click with the mouse on cell E25.* Type: **= D22*.30** and then press the **[ENTER]** *key. Point and click with the mouse on cell E25 and then point and click on the "Bold" icon on the toolbar.* The formula calculates the attorney's share of the recovery for fees (which is 30% after expenses are paid). The correct answer of $60,096.00 should be displayed.

25. *Point and click with the mouse on cell F27.* Type:**+E24** and then press the **[ENTER]** *key. Point and click with the mouse on cell E24 and then point and click on the "Bold" icon on the toolbar.* Since the client receives no monies other than 70% of the recovery after expenses, this is the total amount the client gets. The correct answer of $140,224.00 should be displayed.

26. *Point and click with the mouse on cell F28.* Type: **+D20+E25** and then press the **[ENTER]** *key. Point and click with the mouse on cell F28 and then point and click on the "Bold" icon on the toolbar.* This formula adds the total amount of expenses for which the attorney must pay, together with the attorney's contingency fee of 30%, and adds them together for the total amount of the settlement the attorney will receive. The correct answer of $139,776.00 should be displayed.

27. You will next print out your spreadsheet on one page. *Point and click on "File" on the menu bar and then on "Page Setup."* On the "Page" tab, *click on "Fit to"* (it should default to one page). Then, *click on "OK."* This will compress everything in the print area to one page.

28. *Point and click with the mouse on the "Print" icon on the toolbar.* The "Print" icon looks like a picture of a printer. It is on the standard toolbar, toward the left. The worksheet should print out on one page.

29. To save the document, *point and click on "File" from the menu bar*, and then *click on "Save As."* Then type **settlement** next to "File Name." *Select "Save" to save the workbook to the default directory.*

30. *Click on "File" on the menu bar and then on "Close"* to close the document; to exit Excel, *click on "File" from the menu bar, and then click on "Exit."*

This concludes Lesson 1.

**Figure 2
Excel Tutorial
Spreadsheet**

Screen shot reprinted by
permission of Microsoft
Corporation

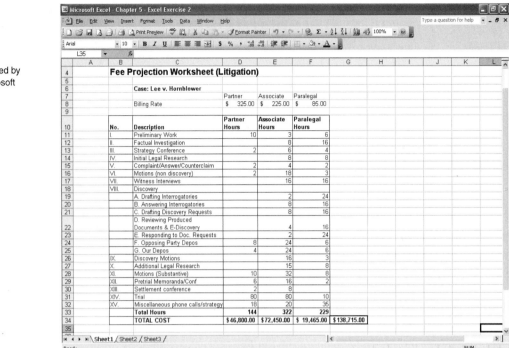

Lesson 2: Creating a Fee Projection Worksheet

This lesson shows you how to build the fee projection worksheet shown in Figure 2—Excel Tutorial Spreadsheet. This lesson assumes you have successfully completed Lesson 1. Keep in mind that if at any time you make a mistake in this lesson, you can simply press **[CTRL]-[Z]** to undo what you have done.

1. Load Windows. Then, *double-click on the* Excel *icon on the desktop to load* Excel for Windows. Alternatively, *click on the "Start" button, point with the mouse to "Programs" or "All Programs," and then click on the* Microsoft Excel *icon*. Or *click on the "Start" button, point with the mouse to "Programs" or "All Programs," point to* Microsoft Office, *then click on the* Microsoft Office Excel 2003 *icon.*

2. A blank workbook should be open. If you are not in a blank workbook, *click on "File" on the menu bar, click on "New," and then click or double-click (depending on the Excel version you are using) on "Blank workbook."*

3. Enter the data in Figure 2—Excel Tutorial Spreadsheet from cells B4 through F33. Below is some additional clarification regarding these entries.

   —Cell B4—**Fee Projection Worksheet (Litigation)** is 14-point bold type.

   —The width of column C will need to be changed to 30 if you use 10-point type.

   —The following cells will need to have their cell formats changed so that the text wraps: C22, D10 to F10.

—Cells D8, E8, F8, D34, E34, F34, and G34 will need to have their formats changed to currency style.

4. The following formulas should be entered:

— **= SUM(D11:D32)** in cell D33

— **= SUM(E11:E32)** in cell E33

— **= SUM(F11:F32)** in cell F33

— **= D33*D8** in cell D34

— **= E33*E8** in cell E34

— **= F33*F8** in cell F34

— **= SUM(D34:F34)** in cell G34

5. The following cells should be bold: C6, B10 to F10, C33 to F33, and C34 to G34.

6. You will next put a border around each square. *Point to cell B10 with the mouse, click and drag the mouse to cell F34, and then let go of the mouse button. Point and click with the mouse on the down arrow next to the "Borders" icon on the toolbar*; it looks like a square with four smaller squares in it. Remember, you can point your mouse to any icon on the toolbar for about one second and the name will be displayed. After selecting the down arrow, you will be given a number of choices; *click on the "All Borders" option,* the one that has a border around each of the four smaller squares (it appears on the bottom row of choices, the second selection from the left).

7. To put a heavy border around cell G34, *point and click with the mouse on cell G34, point and click with the mouse on the down arrow next to the "Borders" icon on the toolbar, and select "Thick Box Border" (the icon in the lower-right corner).*

8. You will next print out your spreadsheet on one page. *Point and click on "File" on the menu bar and then on "Page Setup." On the "Page" tab, click on "Fit to"* (it should default to one page). *Then, click on "OK."* This will compress everything in the print area to one page.

9. *Point and click with the mouse on the "Print" icon on the toolbar.* The "Print" icon looks like a picture of a printer. It is on the toolbar, toward the left. The worksheet should print out on one page.

10. To save the document, *point and click on "File" from the menu bar, and then click on "Save As."* Then, type **Fee Project Worksheet** next to "File Name." *Select "Save" to save the letter to the default directory.*

11. *Click on "File" on the menu bar and then on "Close"* to close the document. To exit Excel, *click on "File" from the menu bar, and then click on "Exit."*

This concludes Lesson 2 and the Excel tutorials for this chapter.

For additional resources, visit our Web site at www.westlegalstudies.com

6

CLIENT TRUST FUNDS AND LAW OFFICE ACCOUNTING

Chapter Objectives

After you read this chapter, you should be able to:

- Understand the purpose and importance of trust/escrow accounts.
- Discuss the ethics rules regarding safeguarding client funds.
- Explain the budgeting process.
- Identify strategies for maintaining strong financial internal controls.

An attorney represented a married couple in mediation and settled the case for $107,500. The money was to be held in trust for the clients. The attorney was to disburse $16,651 to the wife, $18,920 to an insurance company, and $71,928 to a second insurance company. The $107,500 was deposited into the attorney's trust account. After one month, the attorney wrote $42,789 in checks against the client trust account. One check was used to obtain a cashier's check for $17,439, paid to a Jaguar dealer. After five months, the balance in the client trust account was $494. The attorney failed to pay the second insurance company the funds it was supposed to receive. The second insurance company sent repeated letters to the attorney for payment. The attorney told the insurance company that he was waiting to disburse the funds until the clients had signed releases. The insurance company later sued the attorney. The attorney wrote the insurance company and told them that the had sent the funds to settle the case, but that the settlement check had been returned by the post office marked "refused." The insurance company denied refusing the check. A court issued a judgment in favor of the insurance company for $88,466, which included $10,000 in punitive damages and costs. The attorney was also disbarred for failing to maintain client funds in trust, misappropriation, failure to competently perform legal services, and engaging in acts of moral turpitude.[1]

WHY LEGAL ASSISTANTS NEED A BASIC UNDERSTANDING OF LAW OFFICE ACCOUNTING

Legal assistants need to have a basic understanding of law office accounting for several reasons. One reason is that legal assistants either directly or indirectly work with trust/escrow accounts on a regular basis and thus need to have an understanding of what they are and how they work. Another reason is that financial decisions drive the law office. It is important to understand how and why a law office operates and to know some basic accounting concepts. In smaller law offices, legal assistants may actually have some bookkeeping or accounting responsibilities. Finally, legal assistants will help prepare office or department budgets in some firms; thus, it is important to have at least a basic knowledge of how to prepare a budget.

CLIENT FUNDS—TRUST/ESCROW ACCOUNTS

A trust account, sometimes called an "escrow account" or "client account," is an important part of how law practices manage money. A trust or escrow account is a bank account, separate from a law office's or attorney's business or operating

Figure 6-1   Operating and Trust Checks

Law Office Operating Account

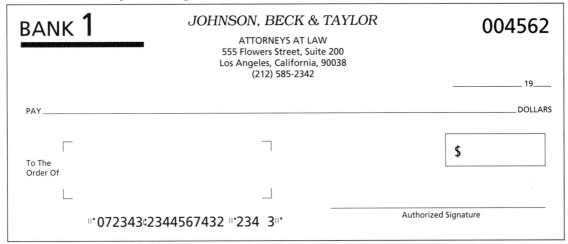

Law Office Trust Account

checking account, where unearned client funds are deposited. Nearly all private law practices have at least two checking accounts, one account from which normal business deposits and expenses are paid and a separate trust account, typically a checking account as opposed to a savings account, where only client funds are kept (see Figure 6-1). Checks used with the trust/escrow account will carry the title of "Trust Account," "Client Trust Account," or "Escrow Account." Deposit slips also will have this designation, and a separate bank statement will be received for the trust account.

It is important to manage a client's trust account accurately. This goes back to gaining and keeping the trust and respect of the client. The monies in the trust account belong to the client, so there must be a high level of responsibility owed to the client to manage those funds correctly.
—Linda Rushton, CLA

No Commingling of Client and Law Office Funds

Ethical rules prohibit the commingling of client funds and law office funds in the same account. This rule cannot be overemphasized, and there is virtually no flexibility regarding it.

Examples of How a Trust Account Is Used

There are times when clients will pay a cash advance or an unearned retainer to an office to apply against future fees and expenses. Until the office has actually earned these monies, it must keep these funds in the trust account. The reason is simple: if client funds are commingled in the same bank account with general law practice funds, creditors could seize these funds to repay debts of the law practice.

settlement
A mutual agreement to resolve a dispute on specified terms.

The cash advance is just one way that the trust account is used. Trust accounts also are used in other ways, such as for distributing settlement checks. A **settlement** occurs when both parties in a dispute mutually agree to resolve the dispute on specified terms, such as for one party to pay to the other party a certain sum of money.

For example, suppose that an attorney represented a client in a personal injury case and the matter was settled out of court for $10,000. Suppose that the defendant issued a $10,000 check made payable to both the attorney and the client, and that the attorney was entitled to $2,000 and the client to $8,000. The proper way to dispose of the monies would be for both the attorney and the client to endorse the settlement check. Then, the attorney would deposit the $10,000 settlement check in the trust account and subsequently write an $8,000 check from the trust account to the client and a $2,000 check from the trust account to the law office.

Ethics and Trust Accounts

Most courts treat misappropriation of client funds as an ethical violation warranting [attorney] disbarment. Even inadvertent breaches frequently result in discipline by regulatory authorities. The rules offer protection for clients by imposing three obligations: the lawyer must segregate funds and property of clients, keep careful and correct financial records, and make timely notification to clients of the receipt of funds on their behalf.[2]

Trust Funds and Office Operating Funds Cannot Be Commingled

Every state bar's ethical rules prohibit the commingling of client and law office funds. *Model Rule* 1.15 provides that an attorney must hold the property of a client (such as unearned monies) in a separate account from the attorney's own operating account. An attorney must also maintain complete and accurate records regarding the client's property or monies, and such records must be maintained for five years after termination of the representation. According to the rule, the only time an attorney can deposit the attorney's own money in the trust account is to pay for bank service charges on the trust account. An attorney can only withdraw monies from the trust account as they are earned or actual expenses incurred. An attorney also has an ethical duty under the rule to promptly deliver to a client monies that are owed to the client and to render to the client a full accounting of the monies in the matter.

It is permissible to use one trust account for all client funds as long as there is sufficient record-keeping to know how much each client has in the trust account. Law practices do not have to have separate trust accounts for every client. In fact, many law offices have only one trust account for all client monies. Larger offices may choose to have several trust accounts to help organize and control the large numbers of cases they have.

For example, suppose Attorney A has 25 clients who have monies deposited in one trust account, and each client has differing amounts. This is perfectly acceptable, as long as Attorney A knows—and has records to prove—exactly how much each client has in the trust account and maintains a running ledger to show what money was taken out check by check and deposited for each client (see Figure 6-2). This is why good record-keeping regarding trust accounts is crucial. Law offices must know to the penny how much each client has in the trust account so that when it comes time to give the money back to the client, the money will be there. Most state bars require that the bank statement for the trust account be reconciled every month, showing exactly which clients have what amounts in the trust account. A failure of the law office to keep detailed records could result in a finding by the state bar that the attorney is subject to disciplinary action.

TRUST ACCOUNTS CANNOT BE USED TO PAY LAW OFFICE OR PERSONAL EXPENSES Ethical rules also prohibit attorneys from using trust funds to pay for general office expenses. For example, if an attorney had client money in the trust account but did not have enough money in law office checking account to cover his rent, the attorney would be absolutely prohibited from writing the rent check on the trust account.

Sometimes attorneys will say that they are simply "borrowing" money from the trust fund and will pay it back. This, too, is a violation of the ethical rules, even if the money is in fact repaid to the trust account within the same day. Client funds simply cannot be used in any way for the personal use of the law office or attorney.

Under Rule 1.15(d), once the client is entitled to receive monies held in trust, the attorney must deliver the monies promptly. For example, if a client's case is concluded and the client still has money left in trust from a cash advance, the attorney has a duty to promptly return the funds.

Figure 6-2   Trust Account Ledgers

Johnson Law Firm
Trust Account Checkbook Register

Check No.	Date	Payee or Deposit Source	Check Amount	Deposit Amount	Balance
	01/01/07	Balance from Previous Month			$10,000.00
	01/02/07	Roger Smith v. Cunningham Steel		$2,000.00	$12,000.00
	01/16/07	Barbara Jackson Tax Matter		$2,000.00	$14,000.00
2001	01/23/07	Dist Ct. – Filing Fee – Smith v. Steel	$100.00		$13,900.00
2002	01/23/07	Process Server Inc.– Smith v. Steel	$200.00		$13,700.00
2003	01/23/07	Court Reporting Inc.– Smith v. Steel	$700.00		$13,000.00
2004	01/24/07	Johnson Law Firm – Fees – Jackson Tax	$500.00		$12,500.00
2005	01/25/07	Koehn & Koehn CPAs – Jackson Tax	$500.00		$12,000.00
2006	01/31/07	Johnson Law Firm – Fees – Smith v. Steel	$500.00		$11,500.00

Trust Account Client Subsidiary Ledger Page
Roger Smith v. Cunningham Steel
Case No. 00-2342

Check No.	Date	Description of Transaction	Funds Paid	Funds Received	Balance
	01/02/07	Cash Advance Retainer		$2,000.00	$2,000.00
2001	01/23/07	Filing Fee	$100.00		$1,900.00
2002	01/23/07	Service of Process	$200.00		$1,700.00
2003	01/23/07	Court Reporter Fees	$700.00		$1,000.00
2006	01/31/07	Attorney's Fees	$500.00		$500.00

Trust Account Client Summary Ledger Page
Balance as of 1/31/07

Client	Balance as of 1/31/07
Roger Smith	$500.00
Barbara Jackson	$1,000.00
John Shoemaker	$5,000.00
Paul Page	$5,000.00
TOTAL BALANCE IN TRUST ACCOUNT	$11,500.00

Commingling of Client Funds
Is a Common Problem

The commingling of client funds with attorney or law office funds is not a trivial or uncommon matter (see Figure 6-3). Hundreds of attorneys are disbarred or suspended from practice every year for commingling client funds. In nearly every issue of every state's bar association journal, one can read about an attorney being disciplined for commingling client monies. Funds that *must* be held in a client trust account include:

- client funds
- third-party funds
- funds that belong partly to a client and partly to an attorney (such as settlement funds)
- retainers for legal services that are unearned and that are the client's property until they are earned

Funds that *cannot* be held in a client trust account include:

- personal funds of the attorney or staff
- business funds of the law firm
- investment funds of the law firm
- earned fee payments that have become the property of the attorney or law firm

State disciplinary authorities have taken notice of the problem of attorneys commingling client and business funds and attorneys stealing from their clients. Many jurisdictions now have rules in place that require a bank or financial institution to contact the state disciplinary authorities when any attorney trust account has checks returned as insufficient. When this happens, state disciplinary authorities conduct an audit of the law firm's trust account. In addition, many state disciplinary authorities conduct random audits of attorney trust accounts in an effort to prevent these problems from occurring. Commingling of client funds is a common problem that nearly always results in harsh discipline being levied against the attorney.

BONDING FOR PEOPLE HANDLING FUNDS   Law offices should routinely buy a dishonesty bond from an insurance company to cover all employees handling client or law office funds. If an employee covered by an employee dishonesty bond were to steal client or law office funds, the insurance company would cover the loss up to the amount of the bond. Bonding is a prudent way to protect funds.

TRUST ACCOUNT MANAGEMENT   Figure 6-4 shows a list of practices and strategies for proper trust account management. Careful and accurate record-keeping is crucial to properly maintaining a trust account. There are many computerized trust account programs available that allow even sole practitioners to inexpensively

Figure 6-3   Commingling and Misappropriation of Client Trust Funds

Anthony Bernard Gulley[3]
An attorney represented a client regarding the client's former employer. The case involved a claim for back pay for a four-year period. The client also retained him in a contested divorce. The case regarding the client's former employer settled for $105,000. The attorney distributed approximately $15,000 to opposing counsel in the divorce case but did not disburse any funds to the complainant until 10 months later, at which time he forwarded $2,000 to the client. The attorney failed to account for the balance of the funds, did not keep the client informed about the settlement funds, and refused to respond to the client's request for information about the funds. The attorney was disbarred and ordered to pay $38,000 in restitution to the client.

Christina M. Arnall[4]
An attorney represented a three-generation extended family regarding an elevator incident at a hotel. The case was settled for $20,000. A total of $11,221 was placed in trust for the benefit of the attorney's clients. The attorney failed to disburse any of the funds to the clients. The balance in the trust account eventually fell to negative $333. The clients hired new counsel and the attorney stipulated a judgment of $30,000. The attorney agreed to pay the money to the clients at a rate of $500 per month. The attorney made four payments and then quit. The attorney was suspended for two years and placed on probation for three years (and until she makes restitution).

Melanie Lorraine Jones[5]
Attorney commingled personal funds with client funds by failing to remove the attorney's fees from the trust account in a timely manner. The

attorney wrote 52 checks against the trust account for personal and non-client purposes. At a later time, the attorney wrote 16 checks against the trust account when there were insufficient funds to cover them. The attorney was suspended for six months and placed on probation.

In re Cavuto[6]
Attorney had practiced law for 33 years. The attorney settled a personal injury claim for a client for $36,000. The settlement proceeds were deposited in the attorney's trust account. The attorney was to pay himself a fee of $12,000, the client's health care providers a fee of $12,727, and the rest to the client. Within a month of depositing the funds in this trust account, the attorney paid himself 22 checks from the trust account, for a total of $26,259. The attorney never paid the medical expenses. The client did not discover that the medical expenses had not been paid until more than five years later when the doctor refused to treat the client because the client's bill had not been paid. The client complained to the disciplinary authorities and an audit was done. The audit showed that the attorney had very few trust account matters and that the attorney did not keep a trust account receipts journal, a disbursement journal, or client record cards. The attorney did not reconcile his trust account. The attorney tracked his trust account through the running balance on the check stubs. The attorney said that he kept fees in his trust account to keep them from the attorney's spouse, since the spouse had authority to sign checks on the attorney's business account. The attorney said that he had tried to review the file after the client complained, but that the file had been mistakenly purged

by his spouse. The attorney then asked the client to bring in the client's records. Still, the attorney could not remember whether the medical providers had been paid. The attorney told the client that he did not have the money to pay the bills at that time, but that he would pay them from another settlement that he was handling for the client. The attorney never paid the medical providers. The attorney suffered from diabetes, depression, fatigue, forgetfulness, and memory loss. The New Jersey Supreme Court found that the attorney knowingly misappropriated client funds and disbarred the attorney. At the time of the disbarment, the actions of the attorney were 13 years old.

Committee on Professional Ethics and Conduct of the Iowa State Bar Association v. Minette[7]
Attorney was client's financial advisor. Client was the recipient of a $40 million trust funded through 842,120 shares of stock. Attorney was authorized to write checks on client's bank account and to approve the sale of stock from the trust when greater funds were needed to pay client's expenses. Attorney paid himself $9,000 from client's account to settle a professional negligence claim against him and paid himself a $2,500-per-month retainer. When the complaint was received, attorney had misappropriated about $88,000 in client funds. Attorney had no written fee agreement to establish any of these payments. Attorney was disbarred.

Unpublished California Case'[8]
Attorney entered into an arrangement with a nonlawyer in which the nonlawyer offered to provide the overhead to operate a law office

Figure 6-3   *(Continued)*

(including legal work) and to provide the expenses for start-up costs. The nonlawyer also agreed to pay the attorney a monthly draw of $500 plus expenses. The attorney agreed to do legal work in the office for one day a week. After one year, the attorney's salary increased to $3,000 a month and his hours increased to three days a week. The nonlawyer and the attorney both had signature authority on the office checking account. The attorney gave the nonlawyer a power of attorney authorizing him to sign for the attorney. For the first two years, the office did not have a client trust account. Client settlement funds were all deposited in an operating account under the nonlawyer's control. After the state bar requested copy of the law office's trust account records, the attorney opened a trust account and made the nonlawyer a signatory to it. Non-client funds were commingled in the trust account on three occasions. The nonlawyer embezzled $120,000 from client settlements. The attorney received a six-month suspension and was placed on three years of probation.

In re petition for Disciplinary Action Against Erickson[9]
A bank notified the state bar that an attorney's trust account was overdrawn. The state bar found that the attorney's trust account records were incomplete; that client subsidiary ledgers for several clients had not been timely established; and that, on occasion, the trust account had contained both client and personal funds, because the attorney had not promptly withdrawn earned fees. In three instances where there were no client funds in the trust account, only earned fees, respondent wrote checks on the account for filing fees, thus using the trust account as a personal business account. Attorney was suspended for 60 days.

In the Matter of Discipline of Tidball[10]
Attorney practiced law for more than 20 years. Attorney fell on hard times and was being pressed by creditors. To avoid their garnishment attempts, he placed his personal funds in his trust account. Deposits and withdrawals were made with such randomness that it was impossible to tell with exactness which transactions were of a personal nature and which involved a specific client. He failed to keep contemporaneous ledgers or other records regarding the trust account. In one case, the attorney received some $62,000 for settlement of a case. Of that, $40,000 never went into this trust account at all. Attorney received a three-year suspension.

1. Have a trust account and use it for all client monies.
2. Only a managing partner should sign on the account.
3. Follow the Interest On Lawyers Trust Account (IOLTA) Rules for your state.
4. Notify the client in writing, at least on a monthly basis, regarding all deposits and withdrawals from the client's account balance.
5. Unearned fees and unexpended costs belong in the trust account until earned or spent.
6. Do not commingle or put attorney/law firm funds in the trust account.
7. Reconcile the trust account monthly and maintain a written record of the reconciliation.
8. Review individual client balances monthly and do not delay giving clients their money.
9. Maintain written, detailed records justifying every deposit and every withdrawal in the trust account, including a detailed journal of all transactions and a client ledger.
10. Retain trust records even after the matter is closed according to state rules.

▨▨▨▨▨▨▨▨

Figure 6-4
10 Rules of Good Trust Account Management

Source: Adapted from Foonberg, J. (2004). *How to start and build a law practice* (p. 576). American Bar Association.

automate the tracking of a trust account. It is recommended that clients be notified in writing at least monthly regarding all activities in the trust account that affect their case. It is also recommended that the trust account be carefully reconciled every month and a document kept that verifies it. State disciplinary administrators routinely ask for attorney trust account reconciliation reports to prove that an attorney or office has such an account and that it is being properly used and maintained. Records should be kept regarding every deposit and withdrawal, including receipts, statements, and so forth, so that each transaction can be verified. *Model Rule* 1.15(a) requires that client trust account records be maintained for a minimum of five years after termination of the client matter, so it is important that records are carefully maintained even after a client's case is concluded.

Interest on Lawyers' Trust Account (IOLTA)
An interest-bearing account set up specifically to hold trust funds. The interest that accrues on an IOLTA account is given to a state bar foundation or other nonprofit legal organization for the good of the public.

INTEREST ON LAWYERS' TRUST ACCOUNT (IOLTA)   An **Interest on Lawyers' Trust Account (IOLTA)** account is an interest-bearing account set up specifically to hold trust funds. The interest that accrues on an IOLTA account is given by the financial institution to a state bar foundation or other nonprofit legal organization for the good of the public, such as funding for legal services/aid offices. The exact way that IOLTA programs operate differs from state to state, but most states provide that IOLTA accounts can only be used for client funds that are a nominal amount or that are expected to be held for only a short time. If a large amount of client funds are involved, or if an amount is to be held for a long period, then the attorney should open a separate interest-bearing account for that specific client and the interest should be given to the client. In 2003, the United States Supreme Court upheld the use of IOLTA accounts in *Brown v. Legal Foundation of Washington*, 538 U.S. 216, 123 S.Ct. 1406 (2003).

BUDGETING

Budgeting in any kind of law office is a good tool to control expenses and make a profit. Firms that develop and use budgets recognize that the budgeting process allows them to project and manipulate the profitability they want to achieve.

budget
A projected plan of income and expenses for a set period of time, usually a year.

A **budget** is a projected plan of income and expenses for a set period of time, usually a year. Budgets allow firms to plan for the future, to anticipate problems, needs, and goals for the firm, and to allocate and manage resources. A budget also is a management tool used to keep revenues and expenses moving toward the profit goal. Figure 6-5 shows an example of a typical law office budget. Notice that the budgeting process involves careful development of planned operating expenses, professional and administrative staff sizes, professional and administrative salaries, desired income, and planned capital expenditures for items such as computers, copiers, and furniture.

It is not uncommon for legal assistants to prepare budgets for their department, their office, or, in small firms, for the whole practice.

Budgeting and Planning

Budgeting and planning go hand in hand; a budget is just a specific type of plan. For example, if a firm's long-term strategic and marketing plans call for $30,000 of marketing expenditures, the budget needs to reflect that amount.

Step 1—Income Budget	Hours	Rate	Total
R. Johnson, Partner	1750	$350	$612,500
C. Beck, Partner	1750	$350	$612,500
J. Taylor, Partner	1750	$400	$700,000
J. B. Rile, Associate	2100	$250	$525,000
H. Smith, Associate	2100	$250	$525,000
L. Niquist, Associate	2100	$250	$525,000
C. Sullivan, Legal Assistant	1700	$90	$153,000
B. Jones, Legal Assistant	1700	$80	$136,000
Other Income			$150,000
SUBTOTAL (Total Billing)			$3,939,000
Time-to-Billing Percentage (actually billed)			95%
TOTAL TO BE BILLED			$3,742,050
Realization Rate			90%
TOTAL GROSS INCOME			**$3,367,845**

**Figure 6-5
Law Firm Budget—
Master Budget**

Step 2—Staffing Plan/Salaries	Expense
EXPENSE BUDGET—SALARY EXPENSES & BONUS	
J. B. Rile, Associate	$140,000
H. Smith, Associate	$120,000
L. Niquist, Associate	$120,000
C. Sullivan, Legal Assistant	$62,500
B. Jones, Legal Assistant	$52,500
M. Lee, Legal Administrator	$85,000
J. Myers, Computer/Network Specialist	$70,000
J. Thomas, Secretary	$47,500
J. Lucas, Secretary	$42,000
C. Glass, Secretary	$40,000
T. Munn, Secretary/File Clerk	$37,500
B. Davis, Bookkeeper/Clerk	$37,500
R. Hunt, Receptionist	$35,000
TOTAL SALARY EXPENSE	**$889,500**

Step 3—Other Expenses	Expense
Accounting Professional Services	$10,000
Amortization of Leasehold Improvements	$7,500
Association/Membership Dues	$7,500
Client Billings/Write-offs	$75,000
Continuing Legal Education	$15,000
Copying Costs (not billed to clients)	$45,000
Depreciation	$50,000
Employee Benefits and Taxes	$225,000
Entertainment	$20,000
Equipment Purchase/Computers/Network	$85,000
Equipment Rental	$8,500
Forms, Stationary, Paper	$7,500
Insurance (P/C, Malpractice, etc.)	$125,000

Figure 6-5
(Continued)

Step 3—Other Expenses	Expense
Housekeeping/Cleaning Services	$7,500
Marketing	$30,000
Office Supplies	$25,000
Other Taxes	$10,000
Postage	$14,000
Reference Materials/Library/Westlaw	$40,000
Rent Expense	$200,000
Repairs/Maintenance	$35,000
Telephone/Internet/Communication/Mobile	$50,000
Travel (not billed)	$45,000
Utilities	$100,000
TOTAL OTHER EXPENSES	**$1,237,500**
TOTAL ALL EXPENSES	**$2,127,000**

Step 4—Determine Acceptable Profit Goal	
NET INCOME TO BE DISTRIBUTED TO PARTNERS	**$1,240,845**

Steps in the Budget Process

income budget
Estimate of how many partners, associates, legal assistants, and others will bill for their time, what the appropriate rates of hourly charge should be, and the number of billable hours each timekeeper will be responsible for billing.

Step 1. Income budget One of the first steps in developing a firm-wide budget is to draft an income budget (see Figure 6-5). An **income budget** estimates how many partners, associates, legal assistants, and others will bill for their time, what the appropriate rates of hourly charge should be, and the number of billable hours each timekeeper will be responsible for billing.

When preparing an income budget, you should estimate as close to possible what the actual amount will be. However, if you are unsure of something, it is usually recommended that you be conservative in estimating the income budget; if you overestimate income and then rely on the overestimate in the expense budget and spend it, and income is actually lower than expected, you have a net loss. However, if you underestimate income and then the actual income is above the level (and expenses stay the same as budgeted), the firm makes a larger profit than was estimated and there is no harm done. One way to minimize this problem is to use a "time-to-billing" percentage. The **time-to-billing percentage** adjusts downward the actual amount that will be billed to clients, taking into account the fact that timekeepers are not always able to bill at their optimum levels due to vacations, sickness, and other unforeseeable events. Notice in Figure 6-5 that the firm used a time-to-billing of 95 percent, thus reducing its billing estimate by 5 percent. The time-to-billing percentage for most firms ranges from 85 to 100 percent. The purpose of the time-to-billing percentage is to build into the budget the fact that the firm may not bill all the hours it would like to.

time-to-billing percentage
System of adjusting downward the actual amount that will be billed to clients during the budget process, taking into account the fact that timekeepers are not always able to bill at their optimum levels.

Reasons that timekeepers may not bill their required number of hours include the following.

- Extended medical leave of timekeepers
- Too few clients

- Procrastination or other bad work habits
- Disorganization or inefficiencies in case management
- Failure to consistently report all billable hours
- Extensive use of the timekeeper on pro bono or other non-billable tasks
- Marketing effects not as effective as planned

In some instances, legal assistants' and attorneys' actual hours end up being greater than the budgeted hours. The firm makes an even larger profit than expected when this happens, as long as expenses remain as budgeted.

Realization is also an important concept in budgeting income. **Realization** is what a firm actually receives in income as opposed to the amount it bills. In Figure 6-5, the firm anticipates that it will actually receive or collect 90 percent of what it bills. Some firms strive for a 95 percent rate, while others are comfortable with a rate as low as 80 percent.

Notice in Figure 6-5 that the firm usually sets the hourly rates for the year at this point. Setting rates in the income budget can be difficult. If a firm sets the rate too high, clients may take their business to a competing firm, but if rates are too low, it could mean a loss of revenue. It also is quite difficult to try to project income if the firm has many contingency fee arrangements. One way to do it is to look at gross income figures for contingency fees for the past several years to help in estimating future contingencies.

Step 2. Staffing plan A staffing plan should also be established early in the budgeting process. A **staffing plan** estimates how many employees will be hired or funded by the firm, what positions or capacities they will serve, what positions will need to be added, what positions will be deleted, and how much compensation each employee will receive. One of the largest expenses of any professional service is salary costs. Thus, it is important that the firm determine whether positions will be added or cut, or whether existing staff members will receive cost-of-living adjustments or merit increases. A staffing plan also goes hand in hand with preparing the income budget.

Step 3. Estimating overhead expenses Firms also must accurately estimate their general operating or overhead expenses. This can be fairly tricky because, in many cases, the estimates are covering a period that ends a minimum of a year in advance. For example, if a person is preparing a budget in November 2007, and the budget covers the period of January 2008 to December 2008, the person will not know until 14 months later whether the estimates were accurate. The time problem makes budgeting difficult; if insurance rates go up unexpectedly, if marketing costs rise significantly, or if large equipment breaks down unexpectedly, your budget will be greatly affected. When discussing the income budget, it was noted that the preparer should be conservative in estimating income. However, when you get to the expense budget, the opposite is true. As always, you should try to be as accurate as possible in estimating expenses. However, if you question the validity of an item, you should be liberal in estimating the expense. This allows the firm to forecast unforeseeable events that might otherwise leave the budget short.

Step 4. Profit margin The last step is to calculate income and expenses so that the firm budgets the targeted profit margin it needs. That is, if after the draft budget the firm is not happy with the profit margin, the preparer can manipulate and make

realization
Amount a firm actually receives in income as opposed to the amount it bills.

staffing plan
Estimate of how many employees will be hired or funded by the firm, what positions or capacities they will serve in, what positions will need to be added, what old positions will be deleted, and how much compensation each employee will receive.

changes in the budget—such as adding additional profit-making positions or cutting expenses further—to reach the desired goal. The following are some additional suggestions about budgets:

- **Communicate the budget to everyone involved.** For a budget to be effective, everyone in the firm should be aware of it, and there should be a consensus reached by the firm's management on major issues such as desired profits and equipment purchases. For instance, if even one timekeeper fails to charge the number of estimated hours, it can completely throw the budget off. Thus, it is very important that management stress the importance of the budget and communicate it effectively.
- **Track budgets year-round and consult them regularly.** For budgets to be useful, they must be taken out of the desk drawer. That is, if a firm wants to purchase a piece of computer equipment, it is important that the budget be consulted to see if the purchase was planned or if there is room in the budget to allow for it.
- **Track the progress of the budget on a monthly basis.** As suggested before, budgets are of little value if they are not updated and used throughout the year. One way to use the budget year-round is to compare "budget" v. "actual." This allows the firm to know whether it is staying in line with its budget or if it needs to make midyear adjustments.
- **Always document your budget.** Always document budgets well, making notes and narrative statements in the budget itself. It is common to make assumptions when formulating a budget, and, unless the preparer notes why the assumption was made, he or she may forget its purpose. It also helps in preparing the budget for next year.
- **Use zero-based budgets.** Although it is common for organizations to start the budgeting process for a new year by using the actual figures from the previous year and adding 4 or 5 percent, this is not an effective way of controlling costs and managing the firm. By using a **zero-based budgeting system,** everyone in the organization must justify and explain his or her budget figures in depth without using last year's figures as justification. In short, each year's budget is taken on its own merit.

zero-based budgeting system
Procedure that forces everyone in the organization to justify and explain his or her budget figures in depth without using prior years' figures as justification.

COLLECTION/INCOME

It is better not doing the work [not taking a case] and not getting paid than doing the work and not getting paid.[11]

Collecting monies that have been billed to clients is an important financial aspect of any law office; this is particularly true in small law offices but can cause problems in large ones as well. Collection and income are closely tied to each other. Most newcomers to the legal field quickly find out that it is easy to bill but much more difficult to actually get paid for legal services rendered. Billing large amounts of time and not getting paid is a direct path to bankruptcy for any law office. The first step in collecting a high percentage of billings is for the attorney to carefully select and weed out what clients' cases he or she will accept in the first place. Attorneys must do a good job of weeding out cases that will not be profitable; there is no substitute for this. Another strategy that many law offices take is to get monies up front using deposits in the form of earned and unearned retainers.

The client who can't or won't pay cash up-front is usually the same client who can't or won't pay cash during the case or at the end of the case . . .

Abraham Lincoln is reputed to have said, "The lawyer should always get some part of this fee in advance from the client. In this way, the client knows he has a lawyer and the lawyer knows he has a client." Before doing a significant amount of work for a new client, the lawyer should always obtain part, if not all, of the fee in advance.[12]

Other strategies law offices use for collecting fees billed include sending regular monthly billings and withdrawing from cases as soon as possible once it is determined the client will not pay. This is sometimes difficult to do since ethical rules put limits on when attorneys can withdraw from cases. *Model Rule* 1.16 provides that an attorney may withdraw from representing a client when:

- the withdrawal can be done without negatively affecting the interests of the client.
- the attorney believes that the client's conduct is criminal or fraudulent, or that the client has used the attorney's services to commit a crime or fraud.
- the client persists in a course of conduct with which the lawyer fundamentally disagrees.
- the client has not completed an obligation to the attorney regarding the attorney's services.
- the representation of the client is causing an unreasonable financial burden on the attorney.
- the client is unreasonably difficult to work with.
- other good cause.

In most courts, an attorney must ask for permission to withdraw from the matter. If a court denies an attorney's request to withdraw, the attorney must ordinarily continue to represent the client. For example, if an attorney requests to withdraw from a complex criminal case right before trial, the interests of the client could be affected negatively and a court might reasonably deny the attorney's request to withdraw. If an attorney is permitted to withdraw from a case, the attorney must act prudently to protect the client's interests, such as giving the client reasonable notice, providing the client with his or her file, and refunding unused monies for fees or expenses.

Another strategy to collect on billings is for the attorney to actually sue the client for the fee. This is usually a method of last resort, as no attorney wants to be put in the situation of suing his or her own client; in some instances, however, this is the only option.

INTERNAL CONTROLS

internal control
Procedures that an organization establishes to set up checks and balances so that no individual in the organization has exclusive control over any part of the accounting system.

Law offices of every type—private, corporate, government, and legal aid—must establish good internal control procedures. **Internal control** refers to procedures that an organization establishes to set up checks and balances so that no one individual in the organization has exclusive control over any part of the accounting system. Internal controls discussions are usually saved for accounting professionals. However, embezzlement by law practice personnel has become a major issue (see Figure 6-6) and is quite prevalent. If embezzlement occurs in an organization, it signals that its internal controls are weak and ineffective.

Internal controls must be established in both large and small firms. Interestingly enough, small law offices need internal controls more than large firms do. Why? Because fewer people handle the finances in a small office, and there are typically fewer written and strict procedures. Thus, the opportunity to embezzle tends to be greater in a smaller office. Therefore, it is absolutely critical in a small law office to have exceptionally good internal controls. The downside of internal controls is that it takes time to do them right and they can slow down the financial process (e.g., by requiring a partner to sign all checks instead of having a bookkeeper sign them). This is particularly true in small firms, but it is the only way to ensure that embezzlement and fraud do not take place.

What type of internal control procedures could limit the possibility of embezzlement? There are several.

- **Never allow a bookkeeper or person preparing checks to sign checks or to sign on the account.** Never let the individual who writes the checks sign on the account. In addition, never let any one person record the checks in the checkbook (or equivalent), prepare the checks, obtain signature(s) on the checks, and mail the checks. Embezzlement is more likely to happen in that case. A partner or ranking member of the firm should sign all checks, if possible. An alternative is to require two signatures on all checks.
- **Have careful, unannounced, routine examination of the books.** A partner or other ranking member of the law office with no direct accounting responsibilities should carefully look over the books on a weekly basis. A partner also should account for all monies on a regular basis (once every week or two weeks) by reviewing bank statements and canceled checks for the authenticity of the signatures, reviewing the reconciliation register, ensuring that check numbers out of sequence are not being cashed, and looking through cash disbursement records carefully. These procedures must be done for both the office business account and the trust account.
- **All documents must routinely be read and examined—no exceptions.** Never sign or let someone else sign checks, correspondence, or other important documents without carefully reading the material. It is very easy

Figure 6-6   Embezzlement Is Common in Law Practices

LEGAL ASSISTANT SENTENCED TO FOUR YEARS IN PRISON[13]

A legal assistant with five years of experience stole more than $102,000 by forging the names of attorneys he worked for on settlement checks that should have been deposited into the attorneys' trust account. The legal assistant passed himself off as a lawyer to the attorneys he was working for and kept the monies from 10 personal injury settlements. The legal assistant began the scheme by only taking the attorney's portion of the settlement check and quickly graduated to taking all of the monies in several settlements. The legal assistant was sentenced to four years in a state prison and restitution.

LEGAL ASSISTANT ALLEGEDLY LAUNDERS INSURANCE REBATE CHECKS[14]

A legal assistant allegedly stole approximately $724,000 from an insurance company over a two-month period. The legal assistant allegedly conspired with another person to issue 34 fraudulent rebate checks to policyholders. The legal assistant allegedly laundered the checks through a number of different accounts. The insurance company realized that something was wrong and started an investigation, but not before nearly three-quarters of a million dollars was gone. The legal assistant was charged with 5 counts of money laundering, 14 counts of embezzlement, and conspiracy and forgery charges.

FORMER PARALEGAL SENTENCED IN EMBEZZLEMENT CASE[15]

A former paralegal was sentenced to two months of home detention and one year of probation for having embezzled $8,000 in funds belonging to a bankruptcy debtor while employed as a paralegal at an East Coast law firm. The paralegal faced a maximum penalty of five years' imprisonment and a $250,000 fine. The paralegal was custodian of the bankruptcy debtor's account and was responsible for preparing checks for the bankruptcy trustee. The embezzlement was discovered a few months after the paralegal left the firm while he was working at another firm. "We discovered certain irregularities during a routine inventory of accounts and turned the information over to the proper authorities," said one of the firm's directors. The case was investigated by the FBI. At the time of sentencing, the paralegal informed the U.S. attorney's office that he was no longer working at the new firm and that he voluntarily withdrew from law school entirely.

BOOKKEEPER ALLEGEDLY EMBEZZLES $2 MILLION OVER 15-YEAR PERIOD[16]

A Boston personal injury attorney alleges that his bookkeeper of 15 years stole $2 million from him. The bookkeeper had complete authority over the office's finances. She was able to write and sign checks for unlimited amounts of money without

the attorney's approval. The attorney felt confident about the bookkeeper. Then one day, he discovered that some checks were missing and that there were inaccuracies in the case settlement and disbursement records. One of the bookkeeper's schemes was to write partial settlement checks between $3,000 and $6,000. She would then endorse these in clients' names, take them to the bank, and cash them as a "favor" to the clients. But she kept the money. Among other things, the bookkeeper converted $30,000, which she used to make a down payment on a condominium in the Caribbean.

$400,000 EMBEZZLED FROM LEGAL AID ORGANIZATION[17]

A neighborhood legal service's history of 25 years of service was overshadowed by the shocking revelation that the program executive director confessed that he was a compulsive gambler and had diverted nearly $400,000 in program funds to feed his addiction. Apparently the executive director forged board member signatures to documents that enabled him to open a false corporate account, giving a post office box as the program address. He was able to intercept and deposit program checks into the phony account and later withdraw such funds by using his own signature. The embezzlement took place over a two-and-a-half-year time span before it was discovered.

to hand documents to people and ask for their signature immediately. Do not do this, and do not let someone else do it. Everyone involved should always check all the supporting documentation of a check.

- **All checks should be stored in a locked cabinet.** All checks should be kept under lock and key at all times when not in use, and access for writing checks should be given to as few people as possible.

- **Never let the person signing the checks reconcile the account.** The person writing or signing the checks should not be allowed to reconcile the bank account or even open the monthly bank statement. If the person who is preparing and signing the checks is allowed to reconcile the account, that person will be able to write him- or herself a check, sign it, and destroy the check when it comes in the bank statement. This might tempt even a basically honest person. Oversight is the key. Never let anyone have the opportunity to embezzle; set up good procedures and follow them.

- **Use check request forms.** Check request forms also are used to bolster internal control procedures. If, for instance, an employee or attorney needed a check for a client expense or for an expense charged to the firm, the person would be required to complete a form similar to the one shown in Figure 6-7. Small law offices should also use check requests whenever possible.

- **Establish guidelines for how the mail should be opened.** The mail should be opened by someone with no accounting duties, such as a receptionist, secretary, or mailing clerk. When a check is received, the person opening the mail should be instructed to immediately endorse the check on the back with "FOR DEPOSIT ONLY" in ink or with a stamp. If the bookkeeper or someone in accounting opens the mail, there is absolutely nothing to stop that person from taking the check and cashing it. This would be easy to do, because the firm would have no record of it.

- **Use non-accounting personnel to help with internal controls.** An additional internal control would be for the receptionist, secretary, or another person to prepare the bank deposits, because he or she would be separated from the accounting department and would not have recorded the cash receipts in the accounts receivable system. In this way, all cash receipts and bank deposits are independently verified by someone completely outside the accounting department who has no access to accounting records.

  A very common way embezzlement occurs is through refund checks. For example, it is not uncommon for firms to receive large refund checks from insurance companies and other vendors. If a person in the accounting department opens the mail, he or she could endorse the check and deposit it into his or her own account with little possibility of someone finding out about it. Why? Because the original invoice would be shown as paid on the firm's books, and no one else would know that a refund had ever been received.

- **Require two signatures on checks over $10,000.** Checks over a certain dollar amount might also require a signature by a second individual (i.e., two signatures on the check). This is another example of an internal control; it would limit large checks from going out of the firm with the authority of only one individual.

- **Stamp invoices "CANCELED."** Once a check has been paid, the invoice should be stamped "CANCELED," so that no one could intentionally resubmit the same invoice for payment.

- **Have an audit done once a year or hire a CPA to help you set up internal controls.** A yearly audit by an accounting firm can help find embezzlement, and strengthen and monitor internal control procedures. If your firm cannot justify the cost of an audit, hire a CPA to help you set up good internal controls and have him or her come in once a year to review them.

Figure 6-7   Check Request Form

JOHNSON, BECK & TAYLOR
ATTORNEYS AT LAW
555 Flowers Street, Suite 200
Los Angeles, California, 90038
(212) 585-2342

CHECK REQUEST FORM

Client Name and File Number: _____

Date of Request: _____

Request Made By: _____

Bank Account: General Business Account   Trust Account   (Circle One)

Amount of Check: $ _____

Check Should Be Made Payable To: _____

Address of Payee: _____

Detailed Description: _____

_____

_____

_____

Accounting Use Only

Account No./Code: _____

Approved by: _____   Date: _____

ORGANIZATION	DESCRIPTION	INTERNET ADDRESS
ABA Model Rules for Trust Account Overdraft Notification	Rules for trust account overdraft notification.	http://www.abanet.org/cpr/clientpro/opreface.html
Association of Legal Administrators	National association for legal administrators. Contains resources and information related to law office management and legal administration.	http://www.alanet.org
Georgia State Bar Association	Articles on a variety of law office management topics, including finance-related articles and information.	http://www.gabar.org
Law Office Computing magazine	Excellent magazine, but limited information online. The site has good links to manufacturers that offer law office software, including trust and accounting software.	http://www.lawoffice-computing.com
Law Technology News	Excellent periodical for legal technology issues. Good white papers on technology issues.	http://www.lawtechnews.com and http://www.law.com/jsp/ltn/whitepapers.jsp
Maryland State Bar Association— Law Practice Management Assistance	Articles on a variety of law office management topics, including finance-related articles and information.	http://www.msba.org/departments/loma/articles/index.htm
Minnesota Lawyers Professional Responsibility Board	Articles on a variety of law office topics, including excellent articles on trust funds, fees, and finance-related topics.	http://www.courts.state.mn.us/lprb/subjectindex.htm and http://www.courts.state.mn.us/lprb/index.asp?content=menutrust
Mississippi State Bar Association	Articles on a variety of law office management topics, including finance-related articles and information.	http://www.msbar.org/2_client_relations_handbook.php
National Association of Legal Assistants	National association for legal assistants. Contains many resources for legal assistants.	http://www.nala.org
National Federation of Paralegal Associations	National association for legal assistants. Contains many resources for legal assistants.	http://www.paralegals.org
New Jersey State Bar Association—Law Office Management Articles	Articles on a variety of law office management topics, including finance-related articles and information.	http://www.njsba.com/law_office_manage/index.cfm?fuseaction=articles
New York State Bar Association	Articles on a variety of law office management topics, including finance-related articles and information.	http://www.nysba.org/Content/NavigationMenu/Attorney_Resources/Practice_Management/Practice_Management.htm
South Carolina Bar—Practice Management Section	Articles on a variety of law office management topics, including finance-related articles and information.	http://www.scbar.org/pmap/resources.asp

SUMMARY

Ethical rules require that client funds not be commingled with law office operating funds, meaning that a law office must have a trust or escrow account. A trust accounting is a bank account, separate from a law office's or attorney's operating checking account, where unearned client funds are deposited, such as unearned retainers or the proceeds of a settlement. Attorneys have an ethical responsibility to safeguard client property. Attorneys and law offices must carefully track all clients' funds in a client trust account. This includes having trust account ledgers for all transactions in the account, including ledgers for each individual client. In addition, the only time an attorney can have his or her own funds in the client trust fund is to pay for bank services charges. IOLTA is an acronym meaning Interest on Lawyers' Trust Account; an IOLTA account is an interest-bearing bank account set up specifically to hold client trust funds. The interest that accrues on an IOLTA account is given by the financial institution to a designated state bar foundation or other nonprofit legal organization (in accordance with state rules) for the good of the public.

A budget is a projected plan of income and expenses for a set period of time, usually a year. Most budgets consist of an income budget, staffing plan, general overhead expenses, and an estimated profit.

Collecting monies after they have been billed is an important issue for all law offices. Strategies for collecting monies that are due to an attorney or law office include carefully selecting and accepting cases; obtaining monies in the way of deposits/ retainers up front, before legal work on a case has started; withdrawing from cases where a client will not pay (if allowed); and suing clients as a last resort if they do not pay.

Law offices must safeguard their assets by implementing internal control procedures, which establish checks and balances so that no one individual in the firm has exclusive control over any accounting system. It is generally unethical for an attorney to share a fee with a nonlawyer.

HELPFUL WEB SITES

ORGANIZATION	DESCRIPTION	INTERNET ADDRESS
Alabama State Bar—Law Office Management Assistance Program	Articles on a variety of law office management topics, including finance-related articles and information. The site has a comprehensive manual on trust funds.	http://www.alabar.org/lomap/articles.cfm
American Bar Association (ABA)	Association for attorneys. The site has a large amount of information and publications relevant to individuals working in the legal profession.	http://www.abanet.org
ABA Law Practice Management Section	ABA site devoted to law practice management issues and including financial issues.	http://www.abanet.org/lpm
ABA Legal Technology Resource Center	ABA site devoted to technology. Includes resources and articles.	http://www.abanet.org/tech/ltrc/home.html
ABA Model Rule for Auditing Lawyer Trust Accounts	Rules for auditing lawyer trust accounts.	http://www.abanet.org/cpr/clientpro/apreface.html
ABA Model Rule on Financial Recordkeeping	Rules for maintaining and tracking client funds.	http://www.abanet.org/cpr/clientpro/fpreface.html

ORGANIZATION	DESCRIPTION	INTERNET ADDRESS
ABA Model Rules for Trust Account Overdraft Notification	Rules for trust account overdraft notification.	http://www.abanet.org/ cpr/clientpro/opreface.html
Association of Legal Administrators	National association for legal administrators. Contains resources and information related to law office management and legal administration.	http://www.alanet.org
Georgia State Bar Association	Articles on a variety of law office management topics, including finance-related articles and information.	http://www.gabar.org
Law Office Computing magazine	Excellent magazine, but limited information online. The site has good links to manufacturers that offer law office software, including trust and accounting software.	http://www.lawoffice-computing.com
Law Technology News	Excellent periodical for legal technology issues. Good white papers on technology issues.	http://www.lawtechnews.com and http://www.law.com/jsp/ ltn/whitepapers.jsp
Maryland State Bar Association— Law Practice Management Assistance	Articles on a variety of law office management topics, including finance-related articles and information.	http://www.msba.org/ departments/loma/articles/ index.htm
Minnesota Lawyers Professional Responsibility Board	Articles on a variety of law office topics, including excellent articles on trust funds, fees, and finance-related topics.	http://www.courts. state.mn.us/lprb/ subjectindex.htm and http:// www.courts.state.mn.us/lprb/ index.asp?content=menutrust
Mississippi State Bar Association	Articles on a variety of law office management topics, including finance-related articles and information.	http://www.msbar.org/ 2_client_relations_ handbook.php
National Association of Legal Assistants	National association for legal assistants. Contains many resources for legal assistants.	http://www.nala.org
National Federation of Paralegal Associations	National association for legal assistants. Contains many resources for legal assistants.	http://www.paralegals.org
New Jersey State Bar Association—Law Office Management Articles	Articles on a variety of law office management topics, including finance-related articles and information.	http://www.njsba.com/ law_office_manage/ index.cfm?fuseaction=articles
New York State Bar Association	Articles on a variety of law office management topics, including finance-related articles and information.	http://www.nysba.org/Content/ NavigationMenu/ Attorney_Resources/ Practice_Management/ Practice_Management.htm
South Carolina Bar—Practice Management Section	Articles on a variety of law office management topics, including finance-related articles and information.	http://www.scbar.org/ pmap/resources.asp

Figure 6-7   Check Request Form

JOHNSON, BECK & TAYLOR
ATTORNEYS AT LAW
555 Flowers Street, Suite 200
Los Angeles, California, 90038
(212) 585-2342

CHECK REQUEST FORM

Client Name and File Number: _____

Date of Request: _____

Request Made By: _____

Bank Account: General Business Account   Trust Account   (Circle One)

Amount of Check: $ _____

Check Should Be Made Payable To: _____

Address of Payee: _____

Detailed Description: _____

_____

_____

_____

Accounting Use Only

Account No./Code: _____

Approved by: _____   Date: _____

LAWYERS AND NONLAWYERS CANNOT SHARE FEES

Attorneys are generally barred from directly sharing their legal fees with a nonlawyer, such as a legal assistant; in fact, Rule 5.4 of the ABA *Model Rules of Professional Conduct* prevents a lawyer from sharing legal fees with a nonlawyer. The sharing of a fee between a lawyer and a nonlawyer could interfere with the lawyer's professional judgment and lead to the nonlawyer being concerned only with profits and not the best interests of his or her clients. Regarding legal assistants, this typically arises when a legal assistant refers a person to an attorney for representation. The attorney is prohibited from sharing the representation fee with the legal assistant or paying the legal assistant specifically for the referral. Figure 6-8 presents an example of lawyers sharing fees with nonlawyers.

**Figure 6-8
Lawyers Cannot
Share Fees with
Nonlawyers**

Source: (2000, June). *California Lawyer*, 73. Reprinted by permission of *California Lawyer*.

Charles Harold Kavalaris, State Bar # 46853, San Jose (December 15). Kavalaris, 56, was suspended for one year and placed on four years of probation for splitting fees with nonattorneys, commingling, writing checks against a client trust account when there were insufficient funds in the account, engaging in acts of moral turpitude, and practicing law while suspended.

Kavalaris and his law partner had an agreement with a nonlawyer, an officer of the local Teamsters Union, to refer personal injury cases to the law firm. For 6 years Kavalaris and his partner paid the Teamsters' officer approximately $130,000 in referral fees. The money represented 10 percent of the attorneys' fees the law firm realized from the cases. Kavalaris and his partner also paid $150,000 to other nonlawyers in exchange for case referrals.

A federal investigator was appointed by a federal judge to look into Teamsters Union activities. The investigator conducted the deposition of the Teamsters' officer that Kavalaris had paid for case referrals. A Teamsters' officer was eventually indicted for perjury for giving false testimony during his deposition. The Teamsters' officer pleaded guilty and was sentenced to prison. The state bar learned about Kavalaris when a state bar attorney read a newspaper article about the Teamsters' officer's guilty plea and that Kavalaris had been named as a participant in a kickback scheme.

In a second matter, Kavalaris wrote two checks against his client trust account totaling $4,770. There were insufficient funds in the account to cover the amount of the checks. He also commingled funds by depositing $1,000 in personal funds into the client trust account.

In a third matter, Kavalaris was suspended for failure to pass the professional responsibility exam. During the time of his suspension, he represented clients at two arbitrations, made a court appearance, and settled a case.

In aggravation, Kavalaris had a prior record of discipline. He was previously placed on two years of probation for failure to communicate, improper withdrawal, failure to pay court-imposed sanctions, failure to report court-ordered sanctions to the state bar, and failure to comply with the laws of California. He was also suspended for 60 days for failure to comply in a timely fashion with conditions to the previous probation. In mitigation, Kavalaris admitted to being an alcoholic. He has remained sober for three years and attends meetings several times a week of Alcoholics Anonymous and the Other Bar. Kavalaris cooperated with the state bar during its investigation of the kickback scheme, and he and his partner admitted their role in the kickbacks.

FINANCIAL AND TRUST ACCOUNTING SOFTWARE

ORGANIZATION	PRODUCT/SERVICE	INTERNET ADDRESS
Abacus Data Systems	Full-featured legal accounting software.	http://www.abacuslaw.com/products/goldfeatures.html
Alumni Group	Full-featured legal accounting software.	http://www.pclaw.com
DDI, Inc.	Full-featured legal accounting software.	http://www.ddisoft.com
Elite Information Group	Variety of financial and trust accounting products.	http://www.elite.com
Juris	Full-featured legal accounting software.	http://www.juris.com
Micro Craft, Inc.	Full-featured legal accounting software.	http://www.micro-craft.net
Omega Legal Systems, Inc.	Full-featured legal accounting software.	http://www.omegalegal.com
Software Technology, Inc.	Tabs3 full-featured legal accounting software.	http://stilegal.com/

SUGGESTED READING

1. Foonberg, J. G. (1996). *Lawyer trust accounts.* American Bar Association.

2. American Bar Association. (1995). *ABA model rules for client protection: Model rule on financial record keeping* (preface).

3. American Bar Association. (1995). *ABA model rules for client protection: Model rules for trust account overdraft notification.*

4. American Bar Association. (1995). *ABA model rules for client protection: model rule for random audit of lawyer trust accounts.*

5. Poll. E. (2002). *Collecting your fee: Getting paid from intake to invoice.* American Bar Association.

6. Iezzi, J. (2003). *Results-oriented financial management.* American Bar Association.

7. Munneke, G., & Davis, A. (2003). *The essential form book: Comprehensive management tools for lawyers.* American Bar Association.

8. Poll, E. (2002). *The business of law* (2nd ed.). American Bar Association.

9. Greene, A. (2005). *The lawyer's guide to increasing revenue: Unlocking the profit potential in your firm.* American Bar Association.

KEY TERMS

budget
income budget
Interest on Lawyers' Trust
    Account (IOLTA)
internal control

realization
settlement
staffing plan
time-to-billing percentage
zero-based budgeting system

Test Your Knowledge

1. Another name for a trust account is

    _____.

2. True or false: it is okay to put an attorney's operating funds in the client trust account.

3. True or false: an attorney can put his or her own monies in the client trust account to cover bank service charges.

4. True or false: an attorney cannot commingle multiple client funds into one trust account.

5. True or false: it is alright for an attorney to borrow monies from the client trust account as long as it is paid back within one banking day.

6. What two things should an attorney do regarding a client trust account on at least a monthly basis?

7. According to the *Model Rules,* an attorney must maintain client trust fund records for at least ____ years after a client's case is concluded.

8. True or false: with an IOLTA, the interest monies are paid to the client.

9. There are usually two restrictions on the kinds of client funds that can go into an IOLTA account. Only _____ and _____ can go into an IOLTA account.

10. Name two strategies for collecting on client accounts.

11. _____ refers to procedures to set up checks and balances so no one individual has exclusive control of any part of an accounting system.

On the Web Exercises

1. Go to the ABA Center for Professional Responsibility at http://www.abanet.org/cpr/home .html, find the *ABA Model Rules of Professional Conduct,* and read and print out Rule 1.15 Safekeeping Property and the Comment.

2. Visit five state bar association Web sites and find three articles on trust accounting, legal financial management, legal budgeting, law office profitability, or accounting for client funds. The following link will take you to a Web site that connects to all state bar sites: http://www.abanet.org/barserv/stlobar.html.

3. Using a general search engine, such as http://www.google.com or http://www.yahoo.com,

or state bar association Web sites, find a model chart of accounts for a law office.

4. Using a general search engine, such as http://www.google.com or http://www.yahoo.com, find a minimum of three sites (they do not need to be law-related) that discuss what internal controls are and why they are important. Print out your results.

5. Using a general search engine, such as http://www.google.com or http://www.yahoo.com, find a minimum of three accounting or trust accounting programs (not listed in the Helpful Web Sites section of this chapter) that can be used in a law office.

Projects

1. Using a general search engine, such as http://www.google.com or http://www.yahoo.com, search for trust accounting procedures. Alternatively, go to a library or visit state bar association Web sites, such as the Alabama State Bar Association [http://www.alabar.org], and write a detailed paper on ethical trust account practices.

2. Research the issue of IOLTA accounts. Go to http://www.findlaw.com and print out and read the United States Supreme Court case of *Brown v. Legal Foundation of Washington,* 538 U.S. 216, 123 S.Ct. 1406 (2003). Try selecting "For Legal Professionals," scroll until you see "Cases and Codes," and then click on "Supreme Court" and "Supreme Court Opinions."

You should then be able to enter the site of the case—538 U.S. 216. Why is the issue of IOLTA so controversial? What did the plaintiffs argue in the case? How did the Court decide? Why was there a descent in the case?

3. Research and write a paper on computerized financial management and trust accounting systems. Visit the American Bar Association Technology Resource Center [http://www.abanet.org/tech/ltrc/home.html] and state bar association Web sites, as well as other legal technology sites, and review helpful articles and materials you find. Also go to the financial and trust accounting software Web sites listed in the Helpful Web Sites section of this chapter. Compare and contrast some of the different products that are available. Which one were you most impressed with, and why?

4. Using a general search engine, such as http://www.google.com or http://www.yahoo.com, search for law office profitability. Alternatively, go to a library or visit state bar association Web sites and write a detailed paper on how law offices can be profitable. Your paper should cover such topics as how to increase revenue, control expenses, increase collections, and related topics.

5. Using a law library, state bar journal magazine, Westlaw/LexisNexis, or the Internet, write a paper that summarizes a minimum of three attorney discipline cases regarding the misuse of client funds, client trust accounts, or related topics. Be sure to include an analysis of the case, what the court found, what ethical rules were at issue, what rules were violated, what discipline was imposed, and why.

ANSWERS TO TEST YOUR KNOWLEDGE

1. Escrow account
2. False
3. True
4. False
5. False
6. Reconcile it (and maintain a written record of same) and send a written account to every client with funds in the client trust account, letting him or her know of all deposits and withdrawals for the month.
7. Five
8. False
9. Nominal amounts; funds which will be held a short time
10. Careful selection of client cases; obtaining money upfront; sending monthly statements; withdrawing from cases where the client does not pay; suing the client
11. Internal controls

QUESTIONS AND EXERCISES

1. You are a legal assistant in a five-attorney legal services/aid practice. The office manager, who writes all the checks for the organization, will not be back for several hours. Your supervising attorney asks you to get the checkbook out of the office manager's desk and issue a check that she needs right now. You fill in the manual check stub and type the check. Because the office manager is not there to sign the check, you hand the check to your supervising attorney to sign with several other papers. The attorney quickly signs her name while looking at the other documents. On your way to your office, the receptionist asks you to drop off the office manager's mail in his office. You notice that one of the envelopes appears to be a check from the local bar association that makes contributions to the practice as a community service. You also notice that another of the envelopes appears to be a bank statement and returned checks for the previous month. The office manager uses the returned checks and bank statement to reconcile the bank account. You place all the items on the office manager's desk as requested. Do you see any potential problems? Would it matter if the office manager had been there for 20 years, was extremely trustworthy, and refused to even take a vacation in that it might take him away from work? What recommendations would you make?

2.   Your office represented a business client in litigation. During the litigation, the client made several cash advances. The matter has been concluded for approximately two months and the client has a balance in the trust account of about $20,000. The client has requested that the money be returned, but the supervising attorney has not gotten around to it yet. How do you analyze the situation, and what would you do?

3.   You have just been given the assignment to begin work on incorporating a new business. At the first meeting with the client, the client hands you a check for $5,000 and states that although no work has been performed on the case, this was the agreement that the client and your supervising attorney worked out last week on the telephone. Later, you hand the check to the supervising attorney. The attorney says to just deposit it in the office's account. What problems do you see, what would you do, and why?

4.   As a legal assistant in a sole practitioner's office, you sometimes become "burned out" and tired. The attorney you work for is very appreciative of your hard work and would like to give you incentives when possible to keep you motivated. The attorney mentions that she will pay you a bonus equal to 10 percent of any new client retainers you are responsible for bringing in. How does this sound to you? Analyze this arrangement from an ethics perspective.

5.   You are a legal assistant in a relatively small office. One day, one of the partners in the office instructs you to transfer $5,000 from the trust account into the office's general account. You ask him what case is involved. The partner says "There is no case name, but it doesn't concern you." What would you do? Explain your answer.

6.   At 8:00 A.M. on a Monday morning, your supervising attorney rushes into your office. She states that at 10:00 A.M. she has a meeting with one of the firm's administrators to go over her draft version of the proposed budget for her satellite office. Although the office is relatively small, she must submit a budget that will produce a reasonable profit for the firm. Unfortunately, she has a meeting with a client and a court appearance to go to before the 10:00 A.M. meeting. She hands you a list of her notes and asks you to please come through for her on this one. You reluctantly agree, but then remember that your bonus at the end of the year will depend on how profitable your office is. Suddenly, you feel better about the assignment.

Below are the attorney's notes.

- Rent is $5,000 a month, but halfway through the year the lease calls for a 5 percent increase.
- The legal assistants will bill at $80 an hour and must work a minimum of 1,750 hours. You think that they will do this, since they will not be eligible to receive a bonus unless they work this amount.
- Utilities are included in the lease agreement, so do not worry about these.
- Associates will bill at $225 an hour. You figure that they will bill no less than 1,900 hours because if they do not, they will not look good for a partnership position.
- From past history, the firm has determined that its time-to-billing percentage is 98 percent and the realization rate is 92 percent.
- Telephone cost is expected to be $4,000 a month.
- Staffing is as follows:
  Two legal assistants
  Four secretaries
  Three associates

Last year, legal assistants were paid, on average, $50,000; secretaries, $40,000; and associates, $90,000. Budget a 3.5 percent cost-of-living adjustment and a 2.5 percent merit increase.

- Fringe benefits and taxes are figured at 25 percent of the total of the salaries.

- Office supplies and stationery expenses will be about $20,000.
- The office must purchase four computers. Your best estimate is that they will cost about $3,000 each when all costs are included (installation, cabling, software, printers, network hardware, training, maintenance contract, etc.).
- All other items, such as malpractice/general liability insurance and professional services, will be prorated to your office by the accounting office. You do not need to worry about this now.

What profit or loss is the office budgeted for?

7. You are a legal assistant manager in a small- to medium-sized firm. The firm administrator asks you to prepare a proposed income budget for your department of six legal assistants. You are not required to do an expense budget, as this is handled by the administrators and the accounting department. From years past, you know that you must sit down with each of the legal assistants and discuss billable hours, hourly rates, and so forth. You don't relish this much, because the firm has consistently pressed for more and more billable hours. Thus, this topic can be somewhat touchy for you as a manager. Below is the information you obtained to help you. Also, note that time-to-billing percentage is figured at 95 percent, and the realization rate is also 95 percent.

Legal assistant #1 typically works for one of the firm's general litigators. Because of her extensive background in this area, her hourly charge is about $90. However, during trial and trial preparation, her hourly charge is usually about $100. She figures that about 40 percent of her time will be spent either in trial or preparing for trial. About 10 percent of her time is spent traveling to and from trials, finding witnesses, and so on. Her travel time is billed at $60 an hour. She is a very hard worker, and although she billed 1,900 last year, she is requesting that her billable hours be lowered to 1,800. You tentatively agree.

Legal assistant #2 has recently been given a new assignment: to work almost exclusively on insurance defense cases. His typical hourly billing rate was $85. However, you know that the insurance company he will primarily be working for will only pay a maximum of $75 an hour for legal assistant time. In addition, the insurance company is extremely picky about its invoices and absolutely refuses to pay for anything even remotely close to secretarial functions. The legal assistant states he thinks that 1,750 is a reasonable number of billable hours, considering his present salary. You figure that, based on your experience, the insurance company will either reasonably or unreasonably question about 40 hours that he bills. You reduce your estimate by this amount just to be safe.

Legal assistant #3 handles workers' compensation cases. Unfortunately, these cases are almost all taken on a contingency basis. The firm typically recovers 25 percent of these types of cases. You estimate that the firm will receive about $600,000 in revenues from this gross part of its practice. You also note that about one-third of this is usually allocated to the work of the legal assistant.

Legal assistant #4 works mainly in the probate area. She typically receives about $70 per hour for her work. You note that although she billed more than 2,000 hours last year, she did not take any vacation and took very little time off. Your conversation reveals that she is going to take three weeks off for an extensive vacation and that she may need to take an additional week off for medical reasons.

Legal assistant #5 is new to the firm. From your past experience, you do not want to burn him out by putting too many billable hours on him at first. You also recognize that he will have many non-billable hours during the first several months due to staff training and general unfamiliarity with the firm. You budget him for 1,600 hours. He will be a rover, working for many different people, and thus his hourly billing rate is hard to estimate, but you budget $70.00 an hour.

Finally, legal assistant #6: yourself. You have many administrative responsibilities. You would like to set a good example, so you budget yourself at 1,400 hours. You bill at $90 per hour. You are responsible for coordinating the efforts of the legal assistants under you, for handling personnel-related issues, and many other duties. You also remember that you are to take a greater role in marketing this year and that approximately 160 hours of your time will be non-billable while you handle this function.

8. Your managing attorney has asked you to compute the current Balance in Trust for the Singer case for both fees and expenses. She asks you to track each of them separately. Here is what you find in the file:

- January 1, initial deposit/retainer against future fees (unearned) of $20,000 paid by client
- January 1, initial deposit/retainer against future expenses (unearned) of $10,000 paid by client
- February 1, client billed for $3,500 in fees and the same amount paid out of the client trust fund to the attorney
- February 1, client billed for $2,000 in expenses and the same amount paid out of the client trust fund to the attorney
- February 15, check from the client trust fund for filing fees of $100
- February 21, check from the client trust fund for $200 for service of process
- March 1, client billed for $5,500 in fees and the same amount paid out of the client trust fund to the attorney

- April 1, client billed for $10,000 in fees and the same amount paid out of the client trust fund to the attorney
- April 17, check from the client trust fund for court reporting charges of $6,000

9. A case settles in the amount of $120,000 for your client. The money has been deposited into the firm's client trust account. Your managing attorney has asked you to calculate the amount owed to all of parties. Below are the facts.

- Your firm is to pay medical expenses of your client out of the settlement of $10,000.
- Your firm has incurred $12,000 in legal expenses.
- Your firm billed hourly on the case in the amount of $40,000 but your managing attorney agreed to reduce the fee to $35,000.
- The client owes the firm $10,000 on another case and has agreed in writing to pay the firm that fee from this settlement.

NOTES

1. *California Lawyer*, (2000, April), 77.
2. American Bar Association. (1998). *The legal assistant's practical guide to professional responsibility* (p. 92). Reprinted by permission.
3. *Texas Bar Journal*, (2005, July), 644.
4. *California Lawyer*, (2000, July), 79.
5. *California Lawyer*, (2000, May), 79.
6. New Jersey Supreme Court, D-122, July 30, 1999.
7. 499 N.W. 2d 303 (la. 1993)
8. *California Lawyer*, (1993, September), 76.
9. 1993 WL 408187 (Minn.).
10. 503 N.W.2d 850 (SD. 1993).
11. Foonberg, J. (2004). *How to start and build a law practice* (p. 283). American Bar Association.
12. Ibid.
13. N. J. paralegal jailed for theft. (2004, January/February). *Legal Assistant Today*, 24.
14. A "clean" getaway . . . almost. (1999, May/June). *Legal Assistant Today*, 19.
15. *Legal Assistant Today*, (1992, July/August), 27.
16. Stealing your practice blind: Embezzlement in the law office. (1987, August). *ABA Journal* 73, 78.
17. Hellman, L. (1992, October). Overcoming the shock of embezzlement. *Los Angeles Lawyer*,

CASE REVIEW

386 Md. 341, 872 A.2d 693
**ATTORNEY GRIEVANCE
COMMISSION**

v.

Charles J. ZUCKERMAN.
April 13, 2005.

349 The Attorney Grievance Commission of Maryland, petitioner, by Bar Counsel, acting pursuant to <u>Maryland Rule 16-751</u>, filed a Petition For Disciplinary or Remedial Action against Charles Zuckerman, respondent. The case was referred to this court, Pursuant to <u>Rules 16-752(a)</u>, for hearing pursuant to <u>Rule 16-757(c)</u>. The petition charged that the respondent violated <u>Maryland Rule of Professional Conduct 5.3</u>, Responsibilities regarding nonlawyer assistants, 1.3, Diligence, 1.4, Communication, 1.15, Safekeeping Property, and Md. Bus. Occ. & Prof.Code Ann. § <u>10-304</u> by failing to deposit trust money in a trust account and <u>§ 10-306</u> by regularly advancing payments to clients, by failing to pay clients, medical providers, and himself funds due to them from personal injury settlements, by failing to notify clients and medical providers that he was holding funds due to them, by having a negative balance in his trust account on March 16, 2000, and by making duplicate payments to himself. Petitioner further alleged that Respondent's conduct was prejudicial to the administration of justice in violation of <u>Rule 8.4(d)</u>. Having reviewed and considered the evidence presented at trial on October 27, 2004, the following findings of fact and conclusions of law have been made.

I. Rule 5.3(a) and (b) (Responsibilities Regarding Nonlawyer Assistants).

A. Findings of Fact

The respondent has been a member of the Maryland Bar since June 20, 1974. He served for about five and a half years as an Assistant State's Attorney in Baltimore City and as an Assistant Attorney General assigned to the Public Service Commission for about a year and a half. For the last 22 years the respondent has conducted a private law office in Baltimore City. His cases consisted of a high volume of small personal injury cases (settlements averaging under $10,000) and few family law and criminal law cases as well. He has no history of any disciplinary ***350*** sanction or involvement prior to the occurrence which gave rise to the instant case.

On or about May 7, 2002, respondent hired Shannon Becker as a paralegal. Ms. Becker had previously worked in his employ for six (6) months in 1999 answering the telephone and performing other clerical duties. She left respondent's employ to take what she considered a better job. Karen Kinsely, Ms. Becker's aunt, was respondent's office manager for three years prior to her retirement. While working for the respondent in that capacity, Ms. Kinsely had check-signing authority. In May of 2002, Ms. Becker was rehired by the respondent who requested her job back. She was then 23 or 24 years old. Ms. Kinsely had left the employ of the respondent in Ms. Becker's absence. Ms. Becker was to do generally what she had done before, but was also to handle what her aunt had formerly done, which was to handle the accident settlements after a case was settled. This required Ms. Becker to meet with clients, go over the settlement sheet, and disburse their money.

Within one or two days of her hiring, he delegated to her the authority to write checks on his trust account so that he could "concentrate on trying cases." ****699*** He did so because of the constant need for someone to always be available to sign checks in connection with financial aspects of accident cases whenever such checks were needed. Though he personally had signed each check in the beginning, he later found he could not continue to regularly be available for that purpose, since he did the office's trial work, and it seemed much more efficient to delegate authority to do so to an employee, as he had delegated it to Ms. Kinsely and occasionally other office managers. One of the tasks assigned to Ms. Becker was to go through a group of old files to see if any money was owed to medical providers and, if so, to distribute it, some monies having accumulated during the period of Ms. Kinsely's tenure as office manager. Prior to the discovery of Ms. Becker's defalcations, respondent used a manual system, in which a separate escrow sheet was kept in each *351 case file on which all trust account transactions were entered. Respondent currently maintains a computerized system controlling his trust account which satisfies the Bar Counsel's office.

In early May, 2002, Ms. Becker devised a scheme to steal the money in the respondent's trust account. She did so by filling out check stubs made payable to appropriate payees for what appeared to be proper amounts, but the corresponding checks were made out for considerably larger amounts made payable to friends of Ms. Becker's, who cashed the checks and turned over the proceeds to her.

The statement for the respondent's trust account arrived in his office on or about June 15, 2002. A comparison of the check stubs with the bank statement and investigation into the missing return checks from the statement would have revealed Ms. Becker's theft. However, respondent delegated that task to Stacy Kohler, another of his employees who never reported back to him concerning the assigned task. As a result, Ms. Becker continued to steal from respondent's trust account until mid-July, when an anonymous telephone call informed him that Ms. Becker was stealing from him. Upon this information becoming known to him, respondent examined the June bank statement, and detected her theft. He immediately began an intense examination of his trust account, which resulted in his discovery that Ms. Becker had been stealing from the trust account. On or about July 15, 2002, respondent contacted the police and took out criminal charges against Ms. Becker. Respondent cooperated fully with police and prosecuting authorities in connection with the charges brought against Ms. Becker, who plead

guilty. She was ordered to pay restitution of approximately $137,000 and sentenced to ten (10) years incarceration with all but three years suspended.

B. Conclusion of Law: Respondent Violated Rule 5.3(a) and (b).

Maryland Rule of Professional Conduct 5.3(a) provides that "a partner in a law firm shall make reasonable efforts *352 to ensure that the firm has in effect measures giving reasonable assurance that the person's conduct is compatible with the professional obligations of the lawyer." Rule 5.3(b) provides that "a lawyer having direct supervisory authority over the nonlawyer shall make reasonable efforts to ensure that the person's conduct is compatible with the professional obligations of the lawyer.

The evidence presented shows that respondent's conduct violated both 5.3(a) and (b). Respondent did not have in place reasonable measures to ensure that his trust account had on deposit all **700 of the funds for clients for whom he was holding money. While respondent gave one of his employees, Stacy Kohler, the task of balancing the checkbook for May 2002, he made no effort to ensure that she accomplished her task. Had the employee reported to respondent after having balanced the checkbook as requested, the theft of Ms. Becker would not have occurred for another month. Further, the act of giving a new employee with no history of reliability was, by itself, a failure to make reasonable efforts to ensure that the firm had in effect measures giving reasonable assurance that the conduct would be compatible with the professional obligations of the lawyer.

It is also directly inferable from the fact that there was a negative balance in the trust account that the employee Kohler, given the task of balancing the checkbook, was not properly instructed on how to do so. As will be discussed below, funds were regularly advanced to clients and, in one instance, on May 16, 2000, the trust account had a negative balance of which respondent was never made aware. Therefore it is apparent that respondent did not instruct his employees of the proper management of the trust account and inform himself of the status of his employees' efforts to monitor the funds in the account. Had he done so, Ms. Becker's theft would have been discovered on or about June 15, 2002 instead of July 15, 2002, when respondent received the anonymous phone call.

*353 II. Rule 1.15(a) and Md. Bus. Occ. & Prof. Code Ann. § 10-306 (Safekeeping Property and Misuse of Trust Money)

A. Findings of Fact

Ms. Becker's theft prompted the respondent to direct another employee, Rhonda Elkins, to review his records. Since then, Ms. Elkins has spent at least two days per workweek on tasks connected with the instant case. The subsequent investigation revealed that between October 2002 and August 2004, the respondent had sixty-two (62) clients that had negative balances at some point or another. A subsequent investigation by John DeBone, a paralegal for the Attorney Grievance Commission, who examined respondent's trust account statements, deposit slips, and deposited items, shows that a total of 109 client's of the respondent had negative balances between 1998 and 2002.

The analysis also showed that respondent advanced a total of $311,898.11 to his personal injury clients with checks drawn on his trust account before the funds belonging to those clients were deposited in his trust account. On March 16, 2000, respondent's trust account had a negative balance of $363.13. Mr. DeBone testified that after March 16, 2000, respondent disbursed $21,997.96 on behalf of thirty-four (34) clients, whose funds were supposed to have been on deposit in respondent's trust account at the time the account had a negative balance. Respondent spent the funds belonging to these clients on other matters and did not preserve the funds for his clients.

In addition, respondent charged a duplicate fee in connection with the representation of Linwood Smith. On April 23, 1999, respondent deposited $5,500 in his trust account, representing the amount of the settlement. On April 27, 1999, he removed $1,833 from his trust account as a fee in the case and an additional $30 for expenses. On May 10, 1999, respondent again removed $1,833 from the account as a fee and **701 another $30 for expenses. As a result

of his charging duplicate fees, he invaded the funds of *354 other clients when he removed his fees from his trust account.

B. Conclusion of Law: Respondent Violated Rule 1.15(a) and Md. Bus. Occ. & Prof.Code Ann. § 10-306.

The conduct described above violates Rule 1.15(a), which provides in part that "a lawyer shall hold the property of clients or third persons that is in the lawyer's possession in connection with a representation separate from the lawyer's own property. The funds shall be kept in a separate account maintained pursuant to Title 16, Chapter 600 of the Maryland Rules." His conduct also violates BOP § 10-306, which provides that "a lawyer may not use the trust money for any purpose other than the purpose for which the trust money is entrusted to the lawyer."

Respondent violated the Rule and the Code by writing checks drawn on his trust account to clients who had no funds on deposit in his trust account. In doing so, respondent was giving these clients funds belonging to other clients and thereby failing to keep funds belonging to the other clients in a separate account. In other words, he was giving funds belonging to one client to another. This is a misuse of the money he was holding in trust, which was given to him for the purpose of paying the obligations of the clients to whom the settlement checks were written.

The facts recited above show that this practice was routine in the respondent's office. Time after time, checks were written to clients from respondent's trust account before their settlement checks had been deposited. For example, in the cases of Frances Hubbard and Sally Smith, there was a 13-day gap between the writing of the check and the deposit of the funds. In the case of a loan to Brittingham, it was a 27-day gap. In the case of McKinley Richardson, it was five months.

It is further evident from respondent's testimony that he did not view this practice as a matter of concern, even though on one occasion it produced an overdraft. His testimony concerning the overdraft was to the effect that it *355 was not a matter of great import because the account balance was up to several thousand dollars the same day of the overdraft. It is inferable that respondent's view of the matter was that as long as there were funds available to cover the checks that were coming in on any one day, the advancing of funds to individual clients was not a matter of concern. As the Court made clear in *Attorney Grievance Commission v. Glenn,* 341 Md. 448, 671 A.2d 463, 474, an attorney's trust account must have funds in it to cover the outstanding obligations of the account. Respondent failed to do this and thereby violated Rule 1.15(a) and BOP § 10-306.

III. Rules 1.1, 1.3, 1.4, 1.15(b) (Competence; Diligence; Communication; Failure to Notify or Deliver the Funds of Medical Providers and Others).

A. Findings of Fact

Respondent routinely held money from personal injury settlements for the purpose of paying medical providers. He did not pay the providers promptly after the settlements because he wanted to resolve PIP issues before disbursing the funds to the medical providers. He directed his office employees to put the **702 files which had undisbursed funds aside, to be reviewed periodically. When respondent hired Ms. Becker, money had accumulated in the account for a period of over three years. When respondent reported Ms. Becker's theft to the Attorney Grievance Commission, he believed that she had stolen approximately $115,000. On October 7, 2002, respondent wrote to the Commission that the amount taken was approximately $144,000. From October 2002 until August 2004, respondent's paralegal, Ms. Elkins, worked approximately two days per week trying to identify the owners of the stolen funds.

In his deposition in answer to a question about his notification of the medical providers in the case of Elmer Green, respondent testified that the provider would know it had an outstanding bill and that he was handling the case *356 and that nobody was complaining. Respondent did not know if he had notified the medical providers in Mr. Green's case or not. Respondent received a deposited settlement check on February 28, 2001 and did not pay Medical Service Center nor did he pay Mount

Vernon Pharmacy until December 17 and 18, 2002, almost twenty-two (22) months later. Respondent testified that "a lot of times" his office would tell medical providers that they were holding money pending the resolution of PIP issues. Respondent did not know if he had any letters notifying medical providers that he was holding funds belonging to them, nor did he identify any medical providers whom he had told were due money he was holding in trust. Respondent's paralegal did not find any letters to medical providers to the effect that he was holding funds in trust. Respondent did not notify the medical providers to whom he refunded money that he was holding money for them before he mailed them their checks. Respondent began refunding money to clients in December 2002 and continued refunding money to clients through August 2004. Respondent did not notify the clients to whom he mailed the checks that he was holding money for them at any time before he mailed them their checks.

B. Conclusion of Law: Respondent Violated Rules 1.1, 1.3, 1.4, 1.15(b) (Competence; Diligence; Communication; Failure to Notify or Deliver the Funds of Medical Providers and Others)

Rule 1.15 (b) states:

Upon receiving funds or other property in which a client or third person has an interest, a lawyer shall promptly notify the client or the third person except as stated in this Rule or otherwise permitted by law or by agreement with the client, a lawyer shall promptly deliver to the client or the third person any funds or other property that the client or third person is entitled to receive and, upon request by the client or the third person shall promptly render a full accounting regarding such property.

*357 It is clear from the evidence that respondent for a period of years maintained in his account substantial money belonging to both clients and third parties, namely, his client's medical providers, and did not notify those individuals that he was holding money for them or promptly deliver it to them.

It was respondent's frequent practice not to disburse all funds when the case was settled but to wait to see if the client's personal injury protection insurance (PIP) paid any of the medical bills. He would put these files aside and periodically review the files to see if PIP had paid the bills. There is no documentary **703 evidence that he told anyone, either clients or medical providers, that he was holding the funds due them. Moreover, he has not identified any client or medical provider whom he advised about the funds he was holding. When Ms. Becker stole the money from his trust account, it took him more than two years to identify some of the owners of the funds and the amounts they were due.

It is clear, therefore, that respondent was far behind in closing out his files. An examination of Petitioner's Exhibit 6 from his deposition, the computer run from Ms Elkin's work dated August 18, 2004, shows that he was paying off medical providers and clients several years after the cases were settled. For example, respondent received the money from Jamel Charmichael's settlement on October 27, 1999 and respondent paid Mr. Charmichael's medical bills on June 26, 2003. Clearly he did not promptly deliver to the clients or medical providers the funds they were due. It is also inferable that he let these matters sit as he handled new cases and did not advise anyone that he held their funds. It is apparent that prior to Ms. Becker's theft of the funds that there had been no activity in these files for several years. If they had been reviewed more frequently and promptly, they would have been closed out with payments made to providers.

In *AGC v. Stolarz*, 379 Md. 387, 842 A.2d 42 (2004), the Court of Appeals held that an attorney who failed to pay off *358 a client's debt from personal injury settlement funds in violation of a written assignment in favor of the lender and who failed to notify the lender of his receipt of the settlement check violated Rule 1.15(b) even though he had made an innocent mistake and did not personally profit from the mistake. In this case, respondent made a practice of violating both the prompt notification and prompt delivery requirements of the Rule. Respondent had paid a client or a medical provider in 155 client files as a result of his file review after Ms. Becker's theft. This means that, at the time of the theft, respondent had 155 cases in which he had not promptly disbursed funds to either clients or medical providers in violation of Rule 1.15(b).

Respondent's failure to pay clients and medical providers promptly is also a violation of Rules 1.1 (Competence), 1.3 Diligence, and 1.4(a) (Communication). Respondent's repeated failures to pay medical providers and clients for periods of years demonstrates a lack of organization and competence to complete all the tasks necessary to protect his clients' interests, namely, payment of all medical bills and the disbursement of all amounts due the client. Respondent's failure to pursue the payment of the medical bills and the disbursement of client funds for a period of years clearly demonstrates a lack of reasonable diligence. Respondent's failure to advise his clients that he had not paid their medical bills or was holding funds for them violates the requirement of Rule 1.4(a) that he keep a client reasonably informed about the status of the client's matter.

IV. Rules 1.15(a) and 16-607 (Commingling Funds)

A. Findings of Fact

In the case of Kristina Mason and Tyrell Wilson, respondent received a $500 settlement check on May 3, 1999 and did not remove his $200 fee until February 1, 2004. In the case of Monica Flight, respondent received a settlement check of $3,629 on February 28, **704 2001 and did not pay himself a fee of $1,175 plus expenses of $25 until *359 February 11, 2004. Petitioner's Exhibit 8. In the case of Alfred Fincher, respondent received a settlement check on May 7, 2001 and did not take his fee until June 22, 2004. Petitioner's Exhibit 8.

B. Conclusion of Law: Respondent Violated Rules 1.15(a) and BOP § 16-607.

By failing to remove funds promptly from his trust account, respondent violated both the requirement of Rule 1.15(a) that a client's property be kept separate from the lawyer's property and the requirement of BOP § 16-607(b)(2) that attorney's funds be withdrawn promptly when the attorney becomes entitled to them. In some cases the respondent did not remove his fee from the account for years after it was earned. This failure is a violation of the Rules.

V. Rule 1.15 and BOP § 10-304 (Failure to Deposit Trust Money)

A. Findings of Fact

Respondent represented individuals in divorce, criminal, and bankruptcy cases. In those cases, he charged flat fees, some of which were paid in advance, at least in part. Petitioner's Exhibit 8. Respondent deposited these fees in his operating account up until 2003. Petitioner's Exhibit 8, pages 81–84. Respondent's clients would sometimes pay him the balance on or shortly before the day of trial. Petitioner's Exhibit 7, page 21. Those payments were also deposited in his operating account. Respondent now deposits any advance fee payments in his trust account.

Respondent's testimony and his answers to interrogatories show that he never deposited advance payments of flat fees in his trust account. This conclusion is also inferable from the fact that no advance payments were stolen by Ms. Becker, even though he handled criminal and divorce cases as well as personal injury. As he stated in his answers to interrogatories, respondent would collect the full fee a few *360 days before the trial and not deposit it in his trust account, even though he had not completed the case.

B. Conclusion of Law: Respondent Violated Rule 1.15 and BOP § 10-304

The full flat fee is not earned until all the work associated with the fee is completed. Therefore, the deposit of an advance fee payment in the lawyer's operating account is a violation of the requirement of Rule 1.15 that the lawyer keep the client's property separate from his own and the requirement of BOP § 10-304 that a lawyer deposit trust money, which would include an advance fee payment, in a trust account. *AGC v. McLaughlin, 372* Md. 467, 813 A.2d 1145 (2002); *ACG v. Blum,* 373 Md. 275, 818 A.2d 219 (2003).

VI. Violation of Rule 8.4 (Conduct Prejudicial to the Administration of Justice)

A. Findings of Fact and Conclusion of Law

Respondent's repeated failures to pay either clients or medical providers as he was required to do was conduct prejudicial to the administration of justice.

The respondent's inactions both prevented the appropriate resolution of the client's matter and subjected his clients to potential collection actions by their medical providers. His failure to preserve client funds also endangered payment to his clients of funds belonging **705 to them. For these reasons, respondent's conduct was prejudicial to the administration of justice.

CONCLUSION

There are several mitigating factors in this case that must be acknowledged. In addition to the usual stresses encountered in conducting his law practice, for several years immediately prior to the occurrence of Ms. Becker's defalcations the respondent was affected by significant additional stresses. These included the dissolution of his marriage, *361 the illness, imminency, and occurrence of the death of his former wife from cancer, which left respondent with the sole responsibility to care for his preteen son. Respondent also continues to suffer from the consequences of injuries he had sustained in an automobile collision many years ago, including recurring surgical procedures. When it came to his attention, Ms. Becker's theft added considerably to respondent's already ample burden of stress. Despite all such stress factors, respondent continued to exert his best efforts in conducting his law practice. Respondent has been under voluntary psychological counseling in an effort to mitigate the effects of stresses to which he has been and to which he is still exposed, and states that he has made significant progress.

Respondent, who appears to have sustained the greatest (and the only) monetary loss as a result of events here involved, did not improperly misappropriate any monies for himself from the trust account or in any other way profit or benefit from Ms. Becker's defalcations. Immediately upon becoming aware of Ms. Becker's theft, respondent closed his then existing trust account and at once opened a new trust account, in the same bank, to which he properly transferred the remaining proceeds of the former account. At Bar Counsel's request, respondent has from time to time produced thousands of pages of documents and records pertaining to both his former and new trust account. Those records included bank statements containing entries upon entries pertaining to deposits and withdrawals from the trust accounts, from which Bar Counsel's office gleaned and stated in their Petition for Remedial Action that respondent's trust account had a negative balance on May 26, 2000.

The negative balance did not appear in the statement for May 26, 2000. The existence of the negative balance was repeated several times in papers filed in this case or in discovery material furnished by petitioner until Bar Counsel's office informed respondent's counsel shortly before trial that the date so alleged was wrong and should have been May 16, 2000. This Court permitted the petitioner to ***362** amend the date in the petition to May 16, 2000 at the evidentiary hearing.

While checks pertaining to settled clients' cases were on some occasions not deposited in respondent's trust account prior to issuance of checks to the clients involved for their respective shares of the proceeds of the settlements, such payments to clients were never made prior to settlement of the case, receipt and execution of all settlement documents, and receipt of the settlement funds. Such payments were not advanced payments. Any funds to pay medical providers being held in respondent's trust account at the time of Bar Counsel's investigation of his trust accounts were held for good reasons, although for too long a period of time.

Interested medical providers were fully aware when cases were settled. ****706** Such providers, in order to keep themselves informed in that regard, frequently telephoned respondent's office and were kept informed of the status of the cases in which they were interested. Moreover, no medical provider complained to respondent about any lack of notice that respondent failed to give. Any duplicate payments and failure by respondent to remove earned fees promptly from his trust account were unintentional oversights which were promptly addressed when brought to the respondent's attention. Respondent never made any loans to clients while litigation was pending or contemplated. Moreover, at the evidentiary hearing, petitioner withdrew its charges

regarding any alleged loans. Respondent has expended many hours, much effort, and considerable funds rectifying the consequences of his employee's defalcations and has taken substantial steps, including installing an accounting system recommended by Bar Counsel, to maintain his trust account.

Despite the mitigating factors described above, there still exist several Rule violations. The evidence shows that respondent was deficient in the management of his trust account for a period of several years. He regularly failed to promptly pay medical providers and paid clients and others with funds belonging to others. Both practices are violations of Rule 1.15, which would have been avoided had respondent ***363** closed the files when settlement occurred. Had he done this, the funds would not have been available for Ms. Becker to steal. Furthermore, the giving of check-writing authority to an unproven, nonlawyer employee within is further evidence of respondent's lax attitude toward his trust account. This attitude is underscored by his lack of interest in the reconciliation of the May account, which, had it been properly performed, would have uncovered Ms. Becker's theft sooner.

Petitioner takes no exceptions to the hearing judge's findings of fact and conclusions of law and recommends indefinite suspension with the right to reapply after two years. On February 3, 2005, Mr. Zuckerman filed several exceptions to the hearing judge's findings.

STANDARD OF REVIEW

[1] [2] [3] [4] In proceedings involving attorney discipline, this Court has original and complete jurisdiction. *Attorney Grievance Comm'n v. James,* 385 Md. 637, 654, 870 A.2d 229, 239 (2005); *Attorney Grievance Comm'n v. O'Toole,* 379 Md. 595, 604, 843 A.2d 50, 55 (2004). Clear and convincing evidence must support the hearing judge's findings. *Attorney Grievance Comm'n v. Gore,* 380 Md. 455, 468, 845 A.2d 1204, 1211 (2004). As a result, we review the record independently but generally accept the hearing judge's findings of fact unless they are clearly erroneous. *Attorney Grievance Comm'n v. Potter,* 380 Md. 128, 151, 844 A.2d 367, 380-381

(2004). Any conclusions of law made by the hearing judge, such as whether provisions of the MRPC were violated, are subject to our *de novo* review. _Attorney Grievance Comm'n v. McLaughlin_, 372 Md. 467, 493, 813 A.2d 1145, 1160 (2002).

DISCUSSION

A. Zuckerman's Exceptions Regarding the Findings of Fact.

We have reviewed the record and conclude that Judge Prevas's findings of fact are supported by clear and convincing evidence.

***364** Zuckerman takes exception to several factual findings, each of which we will address and overrule.

****707** *Exception 1:* Respondent excepts to the following findings of fact by the hearing judge: "In May of 2002, Ms. Becker was rehired by the respondent who requested her job back." Since so much of that sentence . . . may be susceptible to being interpreted . . . that the respondent requested that Ms. Becker, a former employee whose subsequent defalcations gave rise to the instant attorney grievance proceeding, return to his employment, a factual conclusion that is diametrically opposed by the record, which clearly establishes that the course of events which led to Ms. Becker's rehiring was initiated by her written request to have her job back and not by any action on respondent's part.

The trial judge's factual findings do not directly state or impliedly suggest that Mr. Zuckerman sought to rehire Ms. Becker on his own accord without any prompting by Ms. Becker. The findings clearly establish that in May of 2002, Ms. Becker asked to be rehired and that Mr. Zuckerman did rehire her.

This exception is denied.

Exception 2: Respondent excepts to so much of the hearing judge's quoted writing as apparently concludes that the additional interval of theft by Ms. Becker was the "result" of delay in examination of the June 2002 bank statement. While the relatively brief additional window of time involved may have afforded Ms. Becker further opportunity to

steal, her theft certainly was neither caused by or resulted from that circumstance, but was occasioned by Ms. Becker's criminal activity and intent. . . .

The trial judge's factual findings do not indicate that Ms. Becker's theft was *caused* by Mr. Zuckerman's failure to timely review the June 2002 bank statement. Rather, Ms. Becker's acts went undetected for a longer period because Mr. Zuckerman did not timely review the June 2002 bank statement, ***365** which would have revealed the theft. Indeed, Judge Prevas found:

The statement for the respondent's trust account arrived in his office on or about June 15, 2002. A comparison of the check stubs with the bank statement and investigation into the missing return checks from the statement would have revealed Ms. Becker's theft. However, respondent delegated that task to Stacy Kohler, another of his employees, who never reported back to him concerning the assigned task. As a result, Ms. Becker continued to steal from respondent's trust account until mid-July, when an anonymous telephone call informed him that Ms. Becker was stealing from him. Upon this information becoming known to him, respondent examined the June bank statement, and detected her theft. He immediately began an intense examination of his trust account, which resulted in his discovery that Ms. Becker had been stealing from the trust account.

Mr. Zuckerman was responsible for oversight of his trust account, which he abrogated. In his exceptions, Mr. Zuckerman, in fact, admits that "the relatively brief additional window of time involved may have afforded Ms. Becker the further opportunity to steal." Thus, this exception is denied.

Exception 3: Mr. Zuckerman alleges that the hearing judge's factual findings were that there were 109 instances in which clients had negative balances in his trust account. He argues that the record does not show by clear and convincing evidence that any such ****708** negative balances existed on his account.

[5] First of all, Judge Prevas did not find that there were 109 times where the trust account had a negative balance. Rather, Judge Prevas explicitly found

that "A subsequent investigation by John Debone, a paralegal for the Attorney Grievance Commission, who examined respondent's trust account statements, deposit slips, and deposited items, shows that a total of 109 clients of the respondent had negative balances between 1998 and 2002."

366 The bank statements, admitted in evidence as exhibit 10, indicate that on 109 occasions Mr. Zuckerman paid out more money on behalf of the client than he had on deposit in his trust account for that client, which is also corroborated by the testimony of Ms. Elkins, a paralegal hired by Mr. Zuckerman to review the trust account statements. An analysis of the trust account statements and the corresponding client ledgers, admitted in evidence as exhibit 6, shows that the total amount paid to Mr. Zuckerman's clients in this manner was $311,898.11. We, therefore, conclude that the hearing judge's factual findings are supported by clear and convincing evidence and overrule this exception.

Exception 4: Respondent vigorously excepts to the judge's characterization . . . "that [Zuckerman] *advanced* a total of $311,898.13 to his personal injury clients with checks drawn on his trust account before the funds belonging to those clients were deposited in his trust account."

Exception 6: Respondent excepts, for the same reasons heretofore stated, to any other instances where the hearing judge in the Findings makes a factual finding that an improper advance had occurred or that respondent did not properly safeguard his clients' funds or other assets, or was not concerned with doing so or otherwise acted improperly with respect to his trust account.

By his own admission, Mr. Zuckerman "readily acknowledges that [he paid clients with funds belonging to others] on occasions, but only where the case involved had been settled, the settlement funds received, appropriate releases executed and delivered, and the client involved having been furnished a proper and fully explained settlement sheet." He disputes that in so doing, he advanced "the money to clients from other clients' funds" because of his entitlement theory. Judge Prevas's finding of fact that

Mr. Zuckerman "advanced" the money to those clients whose funds were not on deposit is supported by clear and convincing evidence because the clients' funds were only available from deposited funds of other clients, so that the funds paid were "on credit" from the funds of others or "advances." *See* WEBSTER'S NEW COLLEGE DICTIONARY *341* 17 (1999) (defining "advances" as "[t]he supplying of funds or goods on credit"). Thus, we overrule both exceptions.

Exception 5: Respondent excepts to the following findings of fact by the hearing judge: "On March 16, 2000, [Mr. Zuckerman's] trust account had a negative balance of $363.13." The hearing judge then refers to testimony of Mr. Debone, [AGC's investigator], as to the subsequent transactions involving the trust account and concludes that . . . "'[Mr. Zuckerman] spent funds belonging to these clients on other matters and did not preserve the funds for his clients.'"

As to the factual finding that the trust account had a negative balance, Mr. Zuckerman argues that the Petitioner initially alleged that the negative balance occurred on May 16, 2000, instead of March 16, **709** 2000, which "misled or at least misdirected [him]" in preparation of his defense, because he had a ready response with respect to the date so long relied upon by Petitioner (on which no overdraft or other "negative balance" [was] disclosed on the pertinent bank statement), only to have that comfortable cushion pulled out from under him by Petitioner's shifting its ground at or shortly before the hearing below.

This exception is disingenuous to the extent that Mr. Zuckerman in argument before this Court and the hearing court below, "acknowledge[d] that a '-363.13' figure appear[ed] on the bank statement for the date to which Petitioner formally shifted at the hearing below. . . ." The record indicates that in its Petition for Disciplinary or Remedial Action, Bar Counsel alleged that a negative balance of Mr. Zuckerman's trust account occurred on May 16, 2000. At the hearing, Judge Prevas allowed Bar Counsel to amend its petition to state the correct date of March 16, 2000, over Mr. Zuckerman's objection. Regardless of the date,

Mr. Zuckerman admits that there was a negative balance on his trust account, and bank statements were admitted in evidence as Exhibit 13 during the hearing establishing the date on which the negative balance occurred.

*368 This exception is denied.

Mr. Zuckerman's last factual exception relates to Judge Prevas's "Conclusion" section addressing the mitigating factors in this case. To that end, Mr. Zuckerman argues that the hearing judge's findings of mitigating factors "militate strongly against any conclusion that clear and convincing evidence was produced to establish petitioner's allegations and charges."

[6] We note that the facts tending to show mitigation are used to determine the severity of the sanction and not whether the evidence adduced has established a violation of the Rules by clear and convincing evidence. *See Attorney Grievance Comm'n v. Glenn, 341 Md. 448, 484, 671 A.2d 463, 480 (1996)*. As a result, mitigation factors are not weighed in the balance of whether clear and convincing evidence was adduced to prove the allegations. This exception is denied.

B. Exceptions to Conclusions of Law

Neither petitioner nor respondent takes any specific exception to the Conclusions of Law rendered by Judge Prevas; however, respondent asks this Court to find that he did not violate the Rules on the basis of his Exceptions to the Findings of Fact. Because we already have denied his exceptions, we need not address this issue further.

Judge Prevas found violations of MRPC 1.1, 1.3, 1.4, 1.15(a) and (b), 5.3(a) and (b), 8.4, and Maryland Rule 16-607, and Sections 10-304 and 10-306 of the Business Occupations and Professions Article.

1. MRPC 1.1, 1.3, 1.4, 1.15(b)

[7] The hearing judge concluded that Mr. Zuckerman's mishandling of the funds in his trust account violated MRPC 1.1, 1.3, 1.4 and 1.15(b). With respect to Rule 1.1 requiring competent representation to a client, Mr. Zuckerman routinely failed to pay clients after settlement for periods of years due to a lack of established procedures to properly maintain his trust account. Once a case settled, Mr. Zuckerman held the *369 client's settlement money to pay the medical providers, but would not pay them immediately because he wanted to resolve PIP issues before disbursing the funds. He directed his office employees to set aside the files with undisbursed funds and to review those files periodically. At the time that Mr. Zuckerman hired Ms. Becker some settlement monies owed to **710 clients had accumulated in the trust account for longer than three years. In addition, he failed to advise his clients that he was holding their funds and had not paid their medical bills. We have previously held that a respondent's failure to promptly deliver money to a client and to pay third parties demonstrates incompetence in violation of the Rules. *Attorney Grievance Comm'n v. Morehead, 306 Md. 808, 821, 511 A.2d 520, 527 (1986)*. Thus, we conclude that Mr. Zuckerman's conduct constitutes a violation of Rule 1.1.

[8] Mr. Zuckerman's failure to pay medical bills in a timely manner and to disburse client funds also demonstrates a lack of reasonable diligence in violation of Rule 1.3 and a failure to keep his clients reasonably informed about the status of their cases in violation of Rule 1.4. In essence, Mr. Zuckerman's inability to properly maintain adequate records of the deposits and disbursements of his trust account provides clear and convincing evidence that he violated Rules 1.3 and 1.4. *See Attorney Grievance Comm'n v. Gallagher, 371 Md. 673, 710, 810 A.2d 996, 1018 (2002)*.

[9] Likewise, Mr. Zuckerman's failure to inform the medical providers and his clients of funds due to them constituted a violation of MRPC 1.15(b), which states:

Upon receiving funds or other property in which a client or third person has an interest, a lawyer shall promptly notify the client or third person. Except as stated in this Rule or otherwise permitted by law or by agreement with the client, a lawyer shall promptly deliver to the client or third person any funds or other property that the client or third person is entitled to receive and, upon request by the client or third person, shall promptly render a full accounting regarding such property.

***370** We have previously held that an attorney who fails to notify the lender of his receipt of a settlement check and does not pay a client's debts from settlement funds violates Rule 1.15(b). *See Attorney Grievance Comm'n v. Stolarz, 379 Md. 387, 399, 400, 842 A.2d 42, 49 (2004).*

The evidence adduced at the hearing revealed that Mr. Zuckerman had not properly disbursed funds to either clients or medical providers in 15 cases. He routinely would not pay the medical providers and clients until several years after the cases were settled. Obviously, he did not deliver the settlement funds when they were due. Moreover, Mr. Zuckerman testified that he did not know whether he had paid all of the outstanding medical provider's bills or if he had sent out any letters notifying medical providers and clients that he was holding funds belonging to them. Although Mr. Zuckerman alleges that he did not purposefully act to violate this Rule, this argument is of no consequence because this Court has explained on several occasions that "an unintentional violation of [Rule 1.15] . . . is still a violation of the attorney's affirmative duties imposed by the rule." *See Stolarz, 379 Md. at 399, 842 A.2d at 49; Attorney Grievance Comm'n v. Sheridan, 357 Md. 1, 20, 741 A.2d 1143, 1154 (1999)* (quoting *Glenn, 341 Md. at 472, 671 A.2d at 475); Attorney Grievance Comm'n v. Adams, 349 Md. 86, 96–97, 706 A.2d 1080, 1085 (1998).*

2. MRPC 1.15(a), Maryland Rule 16-607, and Md.Code §§ 10-304 and 10-306 of the Business Occupations and Professions Article.

[10] The hearing judge found violations of MRPC 1.15(a) and Maryland Rule 16-607(b)(2) because Mr. Zuckerman failed to remove his earned fees promptly from ***711** the trust account, thereby commingling his client's funds with his own. MRPC 1.15(a) states:

A lawyer shall hold property of clients or third persons that is in a lawyer's possession in connection with a representation separate from the lawyer's own property. Funds shall be kept in a separate account maintained pursuant to Title 16, Chapter 600 of the Maryland Rules. ***371** Other property shall be identified as such and appropriately safeguarded. Complete records of such account funds and of other property shall be kept by the lawyer and shall be preserved for a period of five years after termination of the representation. Rule 16-607(b)(2) states:

An attorney or law firm may deposit into an attorney trust account funds belonging in part to a client and in part presently or potentially to the attorney or law firm. The portion belonging to the attorney or law firm shall be withdrawn promptly when the attorney or law firm becomes entitled to the funds, but any portion disputed by the client shall remain in the account until the dispute is resolved.

On several occasions, Mr. Zuckerman deposited settlement money belonging to clients into his trust account but failed to promptly remove his fee from the trust account for years after it was earned. For example, Mr. Zuckerman received a $500 settlement check on May 3, 1999 and did not remove his fee until February 11, 2004. Likewise, in the year 2001, Mr. Zuckerman deposited money into his trust account from settlement checks, but did not take his fees until one year later. In failing to remove his earned fees promptly from the trust account, Mr. Zuckerman violated both Rule 1.15(a) that a client's property be kept separate from the lawyer's property and Section 16-607(b)(2) of the Business and Professions Article requiring an attorney promptly to withdraw fees once they are earned. *See Attorney Grievance Comm'n v. Sliffman, 330 Md. 515, 526, 625 A.2d 314, 319 (1993)* (holding that a failure to timely transfer earned fees from an attorney trust account involves an impermissible commingling of funds).

[11] The hearing judge also found that Mr. Zuckerman violated Section 10-304 of the Business Occupations and Professions Article because he deposited advance fee payments from his clients into his operating account rather than his trust account, although the fees had not yet been earned. We have previously held that funds given to an attorney in ***372** anticipation of future services qualify as "trust

money" under Section 10-301 of the Business Occupations and Professions Article, *see Attorney Grievance Comm'n v. Blum*, 373 Md. 275, 298, 818 A.2d 219, 233 (2003); *McLaughlin*, 372 Md. at 504, 813 A.2d at 1167, which is defined as "a deposit, payment, or other money that a person entrusts to a lawyer to hold for the benefit of a client or a beneficial owner." According to Section 10-304 of the Business Occupations and Professions Article, an attorney "expeditiously shall deposit trust money into an attorney trust account." Furthermore, Section 10-306 of the Business Occupations and Professions Article provides that "[a] lawyer may not use trust money for any purpose other than the purpose for which the trust money is entrusted to the lawyer."

The evidence adduced at the hearing established that Mr. Zuckerman often represented clients in divorce, criminal, and bankruptcy matters. He admitted to this Court, and the hearing court below, that in those cases he would charge clients a flat fee, which was paid in advance of the **712 services rendered, usually on or shortly before the day of trial, and then deposit it into Mr. Zuckerman's operating account. As such, he would deposit the funds into his operating account as if he already had earned them rather than properly placing the funds into his trust account in contravention of the purpose for which they were entrusted. Thus, we agree with the hearing judge's conclusions that such practices violate Sections 10-304 and 10-306 of the Business Occupations and Professions Article, as well as, MRPC 1.15(a). *See Blum*, 373 Md. at 298, 818 A.2d at 233; *McLaughlin*, 372 Md. at 503–04, 813 A.2d at 1166–70.

Zuckerman also committed violations of 1.15(a) and Section 10-306 of the Business Occupations and Professions Article when he disbursed funds to his clients from his trust account before their settlement checks had been deposited into the trust account, thereby providing funds belonging to one client to another. The record establishes that this was a routine practice in Zuckerman's office and on occasion months would lapse before the settlement checks for the clients would be *373 deposited into the trust account. According to Zuckerman's testimony, he

would write the checks so long as there were funds available in the trust account without regard to which client's funds were in the account to cover the checks. We have held that such a failure to maintain the integrity of client funds violates Section 10-306. *See Glenn*, 341 Md. at 481–82, 671 A.2d at 479–80.

3. MRPC 5.3(a) and (b)

[12] The hearing judge found that Mr. Zuckerman had violated MRPC 5.3(a) and (b) because he did not have reasonable measures in place to ensure that his trust account had all of the funds on deposit for clients to whom he was holding money. Rule 5.3, "Responsibilities Regarding Nonlawyer Assistants," provides in relevant part:

With respect to a nonlawyer employed or retained by or associated with a lawyer

(a) a partner in the law firm shall make reasonable efforts to ensure that the firm has in effect measures giving reasonable assurance that the person's conduct is compatible with the professional obligations of the lawyer;

(b) a lawyer having direct supervisory authority over the nonlawyer shall make reasonable efforts to ensure that the person's conduct is compatible with the professional obligations of the lawyer. . . .

Respondent delegated the task of balancing the trust account to one of his employees, Stacy Kohler, and her job was to reconcile the bank statements against the check stubs for the trust account. Respondent testified that Stacy Kohler "had not finished [balancing the trust account] because she was doing other things," and that the bank statements usually would come in within two weeks of the date that appeared on them, but that sometimes a month or two would pass without the statements being reviewed. He further admitted that checks were written on funds that had not been deposited in the bank and on March 16, 2000, the trust account had a negative balance of which he was unaware.

*374 We concur with the hearing judge that "respondent did not instruct his employees of the proper management of the trust account and inform himself of the status of his employees' efforts to monitor the funds in the account." Such a failure to oversee his employees' tasks constitutes a violation of MRPC 5.3(a) and (b) because Mr. Zuckerman did not make reasonable efforts to ensure that his employees' conduct complied ****713** with his own professional obligations. We have held that "had the respondent exercised a reasonable degree of supervision over [his employee], he might have detected [the employee's] error before any ethical proscriptions had been violated" under Rule 5.3. _Glenn_, 341 Md. at 481, 671 A.2d at 479 (quoting _Attorney Grievance Comm'n v. Dacy_, 313 Md. 1, 5, 542 A.2d 841, 843 [1988]).

4. MRPC 8.4(d)

[13] Judge Prevas found that "Respondent's repeated failure to pay either clients or medical providers as he was required to do was conduct prejudicial to the administration of justice" in violation of MRPC 8.4(d). We have found violations of Rule 8.4(d) when the lawyer misappropriated client funds or misused his or her trust account. _See Attorney Grievance Comm'n v. Brown_, 380 Md. 661, 846 A.2d 428 (2004) (misappropriation of client funds); _Attorney Grievance Comm'n v. Gallagher_, 371 Md. 673, 810 A.2d 996 (2002) (misappropriation of client funds); _Attorney Grievance Comm'n v. Santos_, 370 Md. 77, 803 A.2d 505 (2002) (commingling client funds into operating account); _Attorney Grievance Comm'n v. Powell_, 369 Md. 462, 800 A.2d 782 (2002) (misuse of attorney trust account); _Attorney Grievance Comm'n v. McCoy_, 369 Md. 226, 798 A.2d 1132 (2002) (commingling of client funds); _Attorney Grievance Comm'n v. Snyder_, 368 Md. 242, 793 A.2d 515 (2002) (misuse of trust account); _Attorney Grievance Comm'n v. Hollis_, 347 Md. 547, 702 A.2d 223 (1997) (misappropriation of client funds).

In this case, Mr. Zuckerman misused his trust account, commingled client funds in his operating account, and commingled client funds in the trust account. We agree with the ***375** hearing judge that such actions constitute conduct that was prejudicial to the administration of justice in violation of Rule 8.4(d).

SANCTIONS

[14] As we recently stated in _Attorney Grievance Comm'n of Maryland v. Goodman_, 381 Md. 480, 850 A.2d 1157 (2004), the appropriate sanction for a violation of the MRPC depends on the facts and circumstances of each case, including consideration of any mitigating factors. _Id._ at 496, 850 A.2d at 1167; _Attorney Grievance Comm'n v. Awuah_, 374 Md. 505, 526, 823 A.2d 651, 663 (2003); _Attorney Grievance Comm'n v. McClain_, 373 Md. 196, 211, 817 A.2d 218, 227 (2003). Primarily, we seek "to protect the public, to deter other lawyers from engaging in violations of the Maryland Rules of Professional Conduct, and to maintain the integrity of the legal profession." _Awuah II_, 374 Md. at 526, 823 A.2d at 663 (quoting _Blum_, 373 Md. at 303, 818 A.2d at 236). To achieve the goal of protecting the public, we impose a sanction that is "commensurate with the nature and gravity of the violations and the intent with which they were committed." _Id._ To assist us in determining what would be appropriate, we have reviewed the ABA Standards for Imposing Lawyer Sanctions.

Along with our own cases as precedent in determining the appropriate sanction, it is helpful for us to refer to the ABA Standards. These standards create an organizational framework that calls for a consideration of four questions: (1) What is the nature of the ethical duty violated; (2) What was the lawyer's mental state; (3) What was the extent of the actual or potential injury caused by the lawyer's misconduct; (4) Are there any aggravating or mitigating circumstances?

Glenn, 341 Md. at 484, 671 A.2d at 480 (citing Standard 3.0 of the ABA Standards ****714** for Imposing Lawyer Sanctions, _reprinted in Selected Statutes, Rules and Standards on the Legal Profession_ 301 [1987]).

*376 [15] [16] Petitioner has recommended that we impose an indefinite suspension with the right to apply for reinstatement no earlier than two years, while Mr. Zuckerman advocates that he should receive a reprimand. We have held that the sanction for misappropriation of client funds is disbarment absent compelling extenuating circumstances justifying a lesser sanction, _see James_, 385 Md. at 665–66,

870 A.2d at 246; *Attorney Grievance v. Sperling,* 380 Md. 180, 191–92, 844 A.2d 397, 404 (2004); *Attorney Grievance Comm'n v. Smith,* 376 Md. 202, 237, 829 A.2d 567, 588 (2003); *Attorney Grievance Comm'n v. Spery,* 371 Md. 560, 568, 810 A.2d 487, 491–92 (2002); *Attorney Grievance Comm'n v. Vanderlinde,* 364 Md. 376, 410, 773 A.2d 463, 483 (2001); however, "[w]here there is no finding of intentional misappropriation . . . and where the misconduct did not result in financial loss to any of the respondent's clients, an indefinite suspension ordinarily is the appropriate sanction." *Sperling,* 380 Md. at 191–92, 844 A.2d at 404 (quoting *Attorney Grievance Comm'n v. DiCicco,* 369 Md. 662, 687, 802 A.2d 1014, 1028 [2002]); *see also Attorney Grievance Comm'n v. Seiden,* 373 Md. 409, 424–25, 818 A.2d 1108, 1117 (2003); *Attorney Grievance Comm'n v. Jeter,* 365 Md. 279, 293, 778 A.2d 390, 398 (2001); *Awuah I,* 346 Md. at 435–36, 697 A.2d at 454. In this regard we have stated, "Although ignorance does not excuse a violation of disciplinary rules, a finding with respect to the intent with which a violation was committed is relevant on the issue of the appropriate sanction. This is consistent with the purpose of a disciplinary proceeding. . . ." *Spery,* 371 Md. at 568, 810 A.2d at 491–92 quoting *Attorney Grievance Comm'n v. Awuah,* 346 Md. 420, 435, 697 A.2d 446, 454 (1997).

[17] We have not previously addressed the appropriate sanction where there was a misappropriation of trust account funds based upon the lawyer's ineffectual accounting procedures and theft of funds by an employee. This Court has issued sanctions ranging from a reprimand to an indefinite suspension with a right to reapply after 90 days when the lawyer's conduct did not amount to an intentional misappropriation. *See Sperling,* 380 Md. at 193, 844 A.2d at 405 (imposing **377* an indefinite suspension with the right to reapply after ninety days for violations of MRPC 1.15, 8.4 and Maryland Code, Section 10-306 of the Business Occupations and Professions Article where the attorney created an unintentional shortfall in his trust account, none of the clients suffered as a result, but the attorney had a prior disciplinary record

and acted with significant delay in bringing the trust account into balance); *Stolarz,* 379 Md. at 405, 842 A.2d at 52–53 (holding that attorney's unintentional failure to notify the creditor bank of his client's receipt of the settlement funds did not warrant imposition of discipline, but rather a dismissal and a warning); *Seiden,* 373 Md. at 425, 818 A.2d at 1117 (imposing a 30-day suspension with the right to reapply for violations of MRPC 1.1, 1.15(a), 8.4(a), and 8.4(d) because the attorney improperly obtained his fee from his escrow account after depositing settlement funds, but was remorseful, had no previous disciplinary action against him, and the conduct resulted from representing a difficult client); *McClain,* 373 Md. at 212, 817 A.2d at 229 (imposing a 30-day suspension for violations of MRPC 1.15 and Maryland Code, Section 16-606 of the Business Occupations and Professions Article where the attorney negligently failed to designate his escrow account as an attorney trust account and failed to hold a bidder's deposit from a foreclosure sale, ****715** but there was an absence of intentional misconduct, he took a course in escrow account management, and had no prior disciplinary record); *Attorney Grievance Comm'n v. Culver,* 371 Md. 265, 284, 808 A.2d 1251, 1262 (2002) (imposing a 30-day suspension for violations of MRPC 1.5(c) and Maryland Rule 16-607(b)(2) where the attorney failed to reduce a contingency fee modification to writing and unintentionally commingled funds when he attempted to resolve a fee dispute with clients instead of disbursing his portion of the settlement proceeds to himself); *DiCicco,* 369 Md. at 688, 802 A.2d at 1028 (imposing an indefinite suspension with the right to reapply after 90 days for violations of MRPC 1.15(a) and (c), and 8.4 where the attorney negligently administered his trust account, but there was an absence of fraudulent intent, the attorney had no previous ***378** disciplinary problems and the clients suffered no financial loss); *Adams,* 349 Md. at 98–99, 706 A.2d at 1086 (imposing a 30-day suspension for violations of MRPC 1.15 and Maryland Rule 16-604 where the lawyer improperly used client funds to pay the client's tax obligations prior to depositing the funds into a trust account, but the conduct was unintentional, he had no prior disciplinary history, and the monies subsequently were paid to the Comptroller).

Several courts from other jurisdictions addressing specific instances of misappropriation of funds due to poor administration of trust funds and theft by an employee have imposed sanctions varying from 30-day to six-month suspensions. See _In the Matter Marshall_, 331 S.C. 514, 498 S.E.2d 869, 882 (1998) (imposing a six-month suspension for violations resulting from the attorney's delegation of the office's financial affairs to office manager with no supervision, which contributed to manager's embezzlement of client trust fund); _Office of Disciplinary Counsel v. Ball_, 67 Ohio St.3d 401, 618 N.E.2d 159, 162 (1993) (imposing a six-month suspension for attorney's failure to supervise secretary who misappropriated client funds over a 10-year period); _Louisiana State Bar Association v. Keys_, 567 So.2d 588, 593 (La.1990) (imposing a 30-day suspension for lawyer's negligent supervision of client funds where the lawyer's secretary misappropriated the funds); _In the Matter of Scanlan_, 144 Ariz. 334, 697 P.2d 1084, 1087–88 (1985) (imposing a 90-day suspension on attorney for failing to exercise minimal care over client trust accounts, and negligently allowing employee to embezzle trust account funds); _In re Privette_, 92 N.M. 32, 582 P.2d 804, 805–06 (1978) (imposing a 5-month suspension with provision for a 12-month probationary period for attorney's negligent handling of client trust funds and failure to supervise employee who embezzled client funds).

[18] In fashioning a sanction, we are mindful of the fact that mitigating factors should be considered, including

[A]bsence of a prior disciplinary record; absence of a dishonest or selfish motive; personal or emotional problems; *379 timely good faith efforts to make restitution or to rectify consequences of misconduct; full and free disclosure to disciplinary board or cooperative attitude toward proceedings; inexperience in the practice of law; character or reputation; physical or mental disability or impairment; delay in disciplinary proceedings; interim

rehabilitation; imposition of other penalties or sanctions; remorse; and finally, remoteness of prior offenses.

Glenn, 341 Md. at 488–89, 671 A.2d at 483. Judge Prevas found several of those to be compelling in the present case.

716 Mr. Zuckerman has been a member of the Bar of this State since 1974 and has no prior disciplinary record. Once he learned of the theft of the trust account, he notified Bar Counsel immediately and fully cooperated during the investigation by providing full disclosure of his bank statements and records pertaining to his trust account. Moreover, there is no evidence that Mr. Zuckerman acted with an intent to steal money, nor did he benefit personally from the misappropriation of the funds. When he became aware of Ms. Becker's theft, Mr. Zuckerman closed the then existing trust account and transferred the remaining funds to a new account. He also repaid the stolen monies, and none of his clients suffered any financial loss as a result of the theft. In addition, the hearing judge found that Mr. Zuckerman had significant stresses during the time when the theft occurred, namely that he had been recently divorced, his former wife had died, leaving him with the sole responsibility of caring for his preteen son, and that he had been suffering from injuries due to a car accident. Mr. Zuckerman also voluntarily participated in psychological counseling and had implemented a computerized accounting system to maintain his trust account to Bar Counsel's satisfaction.

These mitigating factors lead us to believe that an appropriate sanction would be an indefinite suspension with the right to reapply after 30 days. See _Seiden_, 373 Md. at 425, 818 A.2d at 1117; _Culver_, 371 Md. at 284, 808 A.2d at 1262.

*380 IT IS SO ORDERED; RESPONDENT SHALL PAY ALL COSTS AS TAXED BY THE CLERK OF THIS COURT, INCLUDING COSTS OF ALL TRANSCRIPTS, PURSUANT TO MARYLAND RULE 16-715(C), FOR WHICH SUM JUDGMENT IS ENTERED IN FAVOR OF THE ATTORNEY GRIEVANCE COMMISSION.

HARRELL, J., dissents.

I dissent because I do not believe the sanction imposed in the Majority opinion is commensurate with our treatment of past cases involving misconduct most analogous to that present in this case. In short, the Majority's minimum "sit-out time" for the Respondent is too short in duration.

As a foundational point of reference, it bears repeating that "[t]he purpose of these proceedings is not to punish the lawyer, but any sanction imposed should deter other lawyers from engaging in similar misconduct." *Attorney Grievance Comm'n v. Stolarz*, 379 Md. 387, 402, 842 A.2d 42, 50 (2004) (citing *Attorney Grievance Comm'n v. Mooney*, 359 Md. 56, 96, 753 A.2d 17, 38 [2000]). We protect the public by preventing future attorney misconduct only when the sanctions imposed "are commensurate with the nature and gravity of the violations and the intent with which they were committed." *Id.* (citing *Attorney Grievance Comm'n v. Awuah*, 346 Md. 420, 435, 697 A.2d 446, 454 [1997]).

The determination of what sanction is commensurate is made often (but not exclusively) by contrasting and comparing the case at hand with prior cases of varying degrees of similarity. My review of more recent attorney grievance cases sharing similar characteristics to the present one indicates that a more stringent sanction is more appropriate than is imposed by the Majority opinion, both to deter generally other lawyers from similar misconduct and to deter specifically an individual lawyer from future transgressions. *Attorney Grievance Comm'n v. DiCicco*, 369 Md. 662, 686, 802 A.2d 1014, 1027 (2002) (quoting *Attorney Grievance Comm'n v. Garfield*, 369 Md. 85, 98, 797 A.2d 757, 764 (2002) [citations omitted]).

****717** ***381** In *Attorney Grievance Comm'n v. Sperling*, 380 Md. 180, 844 A.2d 397 (2004), we ordered an indefinite suspension with a right to reapply no sooner than 90 days. In *Sperling*, a $42,415.91 shortfall in the attorney's trust account was discovered. We held that Sperling violated Maryland Rules of Professional Conduct (MRPC) 1.15 (Safeguarding property) and 8.4(a) (Misconduct), and § 10-306 of the Business Occupations and Professions Article, Md.Code (1989, 2000 Repl.Vol.), due to his failure to reconcile his trust account. No client complaints instigated the investigation. The misappropriation was deemed unintentional. There was no evidence of any theft of funds by anyone, no evidence of client loss from the shortfall of funds, and no additional errors were discovered after the initial shortfall. *Id.* at 185, 844 A.2d at 400.

Although we took into consideration as mitigation in *Sperling* that the misappropriation was unintentional, the attorney's remorse, and his cooperation with Bar Counsel (to correct the shortfall and accounting problems in his practice), we noted that the shortfall was "quite serious" because it was "in particular one so large." *Id.* at 192, 844 A.2d at 404. In assessing Sperling's sanction, we acknowledged Bar Counsel's warning that Sperling's failure to manage his attorney trust account for several years exposed his clients to risk over that lengthy period. In addition, Bar Counsel argued that the length of time—from May 2002 to January 2003—between when Sperling became aware of the shortfall and when he corrected the balance supported a sanction of indefinite suspension, with a right to reapply no sooner than six months. In settling instead on a 90-day minimum sit-out period, we also rejected Sperling's request for a reprimand, in part because, in a similar set of circumstances, an attorney without a prior disciplinary history in another case received an indefinite suspension with a right to reapply no sooner than 90 days. *Id.* at 192–93, 844 A.2d at 405 (citing *Attorney Grievance Comm'n v. Dicicco*, 369 Md. 662, 802 A.2d 1014 [2002]).

We suspended DiCicco for numerous violations of MRPC 1.15(a) and 8.4(a) after he repeatedly used his attorney escrow ***382** account for his personal interests. [FN1] *Attorney Grievance Comm'n v. Dicicco*, 369 Md. 662, 675–76, 802 A.2d 1014, 1027 (2002). The hearing judge in *DiCicco* noted that there were at least 11 instances of misconduct involving different clients (unexplained low and negative balances from 1997 to 1999) and disbursement checks from DiCicco's attorney trust account that appeared to be unrelated to any of his clients' matters. *Id.* at 670–71, 802 A.2d at 1018–19. In ordering his indefinite suspension with a right to seek reinstatement no sooner than 90 days, we considered several mitigating factors. Among them was a lack of evidence that any client suffered a financial loss from DiCicco's misconduct, which misconduct lacked any fraudulent intent. _Id. at 688, 802 A.2d at 1028._ We noted that DiCicco had no record of prior disciplinary problems in his then 38-year membership in the Maryland Bar. _Id._

> FN1. We also concluded that he violated MRPC 1.15(c) with regard to one client.

At the lesser end of the sanction spectrum from _Sperling_ and _DiCicco_ is _Attorney Grievance Comm'n v. Adams,_ 349 Md. 86, 706 A.2d 1080 (1998). In _Adams,_ we reviewed an attorney's misconduct regarding his attorney operating account and involving but a single client. We ordered an indefinite suspension with a right to reapply no sooner than 30 days. Adams represented his client before the Comptroller of the Treasury in negotiating an **_718_** outstanding tax delinquency. _Id. at 91, 706 A.2d at 1082._ After settling on a $2,000 payment to the Comptroller, Adams drafted a check from his attorney operating account to pay this amount. This check was returned for insufficient funds because Adams' client had not given him $2,000 to pay the Comptroller and the attorney's operating account had a negative balance at the time the check was drafted. Adams subsequently received funds from the client, albeit in an amount insufficient to pay fully the negotiated tax bill. Adams deposited these funds into his operating account and supplemented them with money from sources unrelated to the particular client's representation. **_383_** We held that Adams' conduct violated MRPC 1.15(a) and Maryland Rule 16-604.

In arriving at the appropriate sanction, we observed that Adams' handling of the client's money was "sloppy and negligent," but unintentional. _Id. at 98, 706 A.2d at 1086._ We credited as mitigating factors Adams' lack of a prior disciplinary record and that the funds provided by the client ultimately were received by the Comptroller. [FN2]

> FN2. Adams forwarded the $1,900.00 received from the client to the Comptroller by a cashier's

check four months and one day after the negotiated settlement occurred. Adams received the client's funds one week after negotiating the tax delinquency settlement.

Even further along the sanction spectrum is _Attorney Grievance Comm'n v. Stolarz,_ 379 Md. 387, 842 A.2d 42 (2004). In _Stolarz,_ we held that an attorney, with no history of past disciplinary infractions before this Bar for 23 years, negligently violated MRPC 1.15(b) when he failed to pay one creditor of a client $300 out of the client's settlement proceeds. [FN3] _Id. at 391–94, 842 A.2d at 44–45._ We observed that Stolarz's unintentional negligence (failing to note the assignment in the client's file when he disbursed the settlement proceeds; moreover, the client failed to draw his attention to the missing payment) may be better disposed of, upon remand, by termination of the investigation with a warning to respondent, thereby deterring future, repeated transgressions. _Id. at 405, 842 A.2d at 50._ We noted that Stolarz made only one mistake (of a relatively small amount) with one client that impacted only one assignee of that client. Stolarz ultimately paid the client's assignee from his own funds and expressed remorse for his error. _Id._

> FN3. Stolarz's client had assigned $300 of any personal injury settlement proceeds as collateral for a loan.

Against this backdrop, I turn to the appropriate sanction in this case. Zuckerman was first alerted to the gravity of his employee's misappropriation of funds in July of 2002 when he received an anonymous tip. His part-time investigation into the extent of the damage began in October 2002, but was not **_384_** completed until August 2004. The investigation revealed impacts affecting 60 clients. His response to his own unfortunate accounting practices and the theft was considerably slower than Sperling, who took "only" nine months to assess and correct the discrepancy there. Bar Counsel's independent investigation in Zuckerman's case uncovered _109 clients_ with negative balances between 1998 and 2002—indicating the widespread scope of the accounting problems from Zuckerman's irresponsible business practices. Many of these clients' accountings had negative balances _before_

Ms. Becker defrauded Zuckerman in May 2002. Arguably, if it were not for Ms. Becker's theft, Zuckerman would have been unaware of these negative client balances in his attorney trust account and would have continued his improvident conduct indefinitely.

719 The sum total of funds at risk throughout this period was $311,898.11, based on checks drawn on his trust account to clients before funds belonging to those clients were deposited in his trust account. This recipe for disaster reached its nadir on 16 March 2000 when he disbursed $21,997.96 on behalf of 34 clients, at a time when he had a negative account balance of $363.13. Zuckerman readily admitted that he issued client checks on an "entitlement" basis, rather than waiting for the settlement proceeds to be deposited and completion of the appropriate waivers and accounting statements. Although he periodically did no more than "rob Peter to pay Paul," sometimes for short periods, [FN4] he routinely advanced money rightfully belonging to other clients to satisfy different clients he felt were "entitled" to their money. Zuckerman's attempts at justifying this ongoing violation of the Maryland Rules of Professional Conduct regarding the safekeeping of client property are unavailing.

> FN4. Judge Prevas noted that Zuckerman's routine practice of loaning money from existing client accounts to pay "entitled" clients had resulted in loans ranging from 13 days to five months in duration.

Zuckerman, as a matter of routine practice, also did not distribute funds in timely fashion to third-party medical providers and thereby violated MRPC 1.15(b). He claims as *385* his defense that he did not pay these providers because he was waiting for personal injury protection insurance coverage issues "to resolve." This routine practice left at least $144,000 in limbo over a period of at least three years. [FN5] In order to correct this situation, it took Zuckerman until December 2004 to pay the medical providers their money. [FN6]

> FN5. Ms. Becker stole approximately this amount from his attorney trust account.

> FN6. Zuckerman also violated MRPC 1.1 (Competence), 1.3 (Diligence), 1.4 (Communication),

5.3(a) & (b) (Responsibilities regarding non-lawyer assistants), and 8.4 (Misconduct). In addition, Zuckerman violated Maryland Rule 16-607 and §§ 10-304 and 10-306 of the Business Occupations and Professions Article. Md.Code (2000, 2004 Repl.Vol.).

By comparison, in *DiCicco* we sanctioned the attorney for negligent transgressions that impacted perhaps *11* clients, without a conclusive holding as to the amount of funds in question, by imposing an indefinite suspension with a right to reapply no sooner than 90 days. Sperling received the identical sanction, notwithstanding the lack of a specific holding as to the number of clients whose funds were misappropriated negligently, where his attorney escrow account had a *$42,415.91* shortfall. In the present case, Zuckerman's unethical accounting practices impacted at least *155 clients and third parties* and endangered *$311,898.11 of client trust money* and *at least $144,000 owed to third parties*. Unlike *Stolarz* and *Adams,* where the unintentional transgressions involved only one client and in much smaller amounts ($300 and $2,000, respectively), Zuckerman's unintentional (negligent) misappropriations were of greater impact and scope. [FN7]

> FN7. Other cases relied on by the Majority in support of an indefinite suspension with a right to reapply no sooner than 30 days are, upon close examination, not comparable to the facts in this case. They reflect instead a single client benchmark and involved ethical violations of lesser magnitude than those committed by Zuckerman. *Attorney Grievance Comm'n v. Seiden,* 373 Md. 409, 818 A.2d 1108 (2003) (violation of MRPC 1.1 (Competence), 1.15 (Safekeeping property), 8.4(a) & (d) (Misconduct) involved a single client where the attorney deducted a legal fee of $4,400 from estate funds without a Fee Petition to the Orphans Court or consent of the personal representative of the estate); *Attorney Grievance Comm'n v. Culver,* 371 Md. 265, 283–84, 808 A.2d 1251, 1262 (2002) (violation of MRPC 1.5(c) (Fees) and Maryland Rule 16-607(b)(2) involving a single incident with one client and a fee paid to the attorney of $8,714.50).

Lastly, I consider the mitigating factors. Like DiCicco, Zuckerman has no history of ****720** prior disciplinary proceedings. Yet, having an unblemished record is not a salve that cures all ***386** ills. It may have greater weight where the transgressions are minor in scope, apparently impact one client or only a few clients, and the misconduct may be characterized fairly as an isolated incident in a long career. See Stolarz, Adams, supra. When the misconduct of an attorney impacts potentially hundreds of clients and third parties and significant sums of money, a lesser sanction, even though the attorney has a "spotless" disciplinary record, hardly seems commensurate as a general deterrent against similar conduct by other attorneys. Dicicco, 369 Md. at 686, 802 A.2d at 1028. If a sanction is to protect generally the public from future, similar transgressions by lawyers, it must encourage all lawyers, not just those who have prior disciplinary records, to account responsibly for their client trust accounts. An indefinite suspension with a right to reapply no sooner than 90 days is the more appropriate sanction in the present case.

Questions

1. How did the internal controls in Zuckerman's offices break down, and why?
2. Did it seem unfair that Zuckerman ended up being responsible for Becker's criminal activity when he did not intend to violate the rules and did not profit in anyway from Becker's stealing?
3. Why did the court make so much out of Zuckerman fronting $311,898 to his personal injury clients and the fact that the trust account had a negative balance at times?
4. Why did it take Zuckerman's paralegal two days per week from October 2002 until August 2004 to identify the owners of the money that Becker stole?
5. What was the basis of the dissenting opinion?

CASE REVIEW

Iowa Supreme Court Board of Professional Ethics and Conduct v. Sunleaf, 588 N.W.2d 126 (1999).

588 N.W.2d 126
(Cite as: 588 N.W.2d 126)

Supreme Court of Iowa.

IOWA SUPREME COURT BOARD OF PROFESSIONAL ETHICS AND CONDUCT,

Complainant,

Roger W. SUNLEAF, Respondent.

No. 98-1644.

Jan. 21, 1999.

Mark McCormick of Belin Lamson McCormick Zumbach Flynn, a P.C., Des Moines, and Roger W. Sunleaf, Montezuma, pro se, for respondent.

Considered by HARRIS, P.J., and CARTER, NEUMAN, SNELL, and TERNUS, JJ.

HARRIS, Justice.

In myriad lawyer disciplinary cases we have noted the axiom that we give respectful consideration to the sanction recommended by the grievance commission, but must reserve to ourselves the ultimate responsibility in the matter. A corollary to the axiom is that the commission's recommendation weighs most heavily in cases where the appropriate discipline is most difficult to assess. The misconduct in the present case lies at the precise boundary between suspension and public reprimand. Under the circumstances we impose the public reprimand recommended by the commission.

[1] Roger W. Sunleaf, the respondent attorney, was admitted to practice in 1963 and has concentrated on probate and personal injury cases. Our ethics board was alerted to this matter by a letter from

Sunleaf's former secretary, accusing him of commingling his own funds with his clients' trust accounts. Although Sunleaf vigorously denied the charge in a letter he sent in response to an inquiry by the board, the commingling was established as true by an audit directed by our client security and disciplinary commission. Sunleaf used his trust account for the deposit of earned fees and for the payment of both personal and business expenses. He did so in order to hide funds from the federal internal revenue service which had levied on his business account for two unpaid payroll tax obligations. The commingling violated DR 9-102(A) of the Iowa *127 code of professional responsibility for lawyers.

[2] Sunleaf compounded the commingling by his letter to the board denying it, and also by certifying there was no commingling of funds on his 1997 combined statement and questionnaire to our client security and attorney disciplinary commission, a clear violation of DR 1-102(A)(4) of the Iowa code of professional responsibility for lawyers.

[3] The commission was on track in discounting the factors Sunleaf suggested in palliation for his misconduct: a personal health crisis, pressing financial problems, and a bout with alcoholism. We regularly see this trio lurking in the background of lawyer disciplinary cases, and routinely explain that, although our sympathy is frequently aroused, protection of the public interest prevents us from being swayed by them. In Committee on Professional Ethics & Conduct v. Cook, 409 N.W.2d 469, 470 (Iowa 1987), we put it this way:

Nearly every lawyer involved in these cases could cite personal problems as the cause of the professional downfall. But life in general is a series of problems and it is the fundamental purpose of our profession to face and solve them. Our profession certainly cannot excuse misconduct on the basis of personal problems.

[4] The commission was also correct in refusing to give consideration to the motive of Sunleaf's former secretary in alerting the board to Sunleaf's misconduct. In re Boyer, 231 Iowa 597, 600, 1 N.W.2d 707, 709 (1942), we said a complainant's motives were not a bar to disbarment. We now prefer to say that a complainant's motives are irrelevant in lawyer disciplinary cases.

The commission was prompted to its recommendation after becoming convinced this episode is an aberration, wholly out of plumb with Sunleaf's many years of practice, which appear to have been honorable. His reputation for honesty was established by lawyers of unquestioned ability and discernment. Sunleaf has come to terms with his alcoholism. The audit uncovered no evidence of misappropriation of client funds. We accordingly accede to the commission's recommendation.

Roger W. Sunleaf is hereby publicly reprimanded for the misconduct hereinbefore described.

ATTORNEY REPRIMANDED.

END OF DOCUMENT

EXERCISES

1. How did substance abuse and the attorney's reputation play a part in the case?

2. Why was the court not concerned about the ill motives of the attorney's former secretary? Why did the court not dismiss these allegations of the former secretary as simply "sour grapes"?

3. The attorney's clients did not seem to be harmed by any of the attorney's activity. That is, the attorney was never even accused of misappropriating client funds. So what harm was done?

CASE REVIEW

In the Matter of James A. Cleland, 2p.3d 700 (2000).

2 p.3D 700
2000 CJ C.A.R. 2672
(Cite as: 2 P.3d 700)

Supreme Court of Colorado, En Banc.

In the Matter of James A. CLELAND, Attorney—Respondent.

No. 99SA89.

May 22, 2000.

*****700** John S. Gleason, Attorney Regulation Counsel, James C. Coyle, Assistant Regulation Counsel, Denver, Colorado, Attorneys for Complainant.

No Appearance By or on Behalf of Attorney—Respondent.

PER CURIAM.

The respondent in this attorney regulation case, James A. Cleland, admitted that he knowingly misappropriated funds belonging to his clients. We have consistently held that disbarment is the appropriate sanction for this type of misconduct, unless significant extenuating circumstances are present. No such circumstances exist in this case. Nevertheless, a hearing panel of our former grievance committee [FN1] accepted the findings and recommendation of a hearing board that Cleland should be suspended for three years, rather than disbarred. The complainant filed exceptions to the findings and recommendation, contending that Cleland should be disbarred. On review, we determine that certain of the board's findings are clearly erroneous, and we disagree with some of its legal conclusions. On the other hand, we agree with the complainant that disbarment is the only appropriate sanction in this case. Accordingly, we reject the panel's and board's recommendations and we order that Cleland be disbarred, effective immediately.

FN1. By order of the Supreme Court dated June 30, 1998, effective January 1, 1999, the grievance committee was superseded by the reorganization of the attorney regulation system. The same order provided: "All attorney discipline cases in which trial has occurred prior to January 1, 1999 before a Hearing Board . . . shall be reviewed by the applicable Hearing Panel at a final meeting to be held in 1999. . . ." Order re Reorganization of the Attorney Regulation System (Colo. June 30, 1998), reprinted in 12 C.R.S. at 605 (1999). This case was tried on April 29, 1998, and was reviewed by the hearing panel on February 20, 1999.

I.

James A. Cleland was first licensed to practice law in Colorado in 1989.

2 P.3d 700

(Cite as: 2 P.3d 700, *700)

[FN2] The amended complaint contained six counts. Count I charged Cleland with commingling his personal funds with a client's funds, knowingly mishandling contested funds, and knowingly misappropriating funds belonging to the client. Count II alleged that Cleland *****701** knowingly misappropriated $5000 of his client's funds to reimburse a third party for an earnest money deposit that Cleland was supposed to have held in trust. Count III of the complaint charged that Cleland consistently mismanaged his trust account from September 1995 to February 1996. Count IV alleged that Cleland unilaterally charged his client interest on past-due attorney's fees, without the client's authorization. In Count V, the complainant asserted that Cleland had failed to file a collection matter for a client; that he failed to keep the client reasonably informed about the status of the matter; and that he misrepresented that he had settled the case when in fact he had not. Finally, Count VI charged Cleland with making misrepresentations to one of the complainant's investigators and a paralegal during the investigation of Count V. [FN3]

FN2. In an unrelated attorney regulation matter heard after the hearing panel acted in this case, the presiding disciplinary judge and hearing board suspended Cleland for two years, effective October 18, 1999. See In re Cleland, No. GC98B118, slip op. at 14 (Colo. PDJ Sept. 17, 1999).

FN3. The hearing board found that the charges in Count VI had not been proven by clear and convincing evidence. The complainant did not except to this finding; we therefore dismiss Count VI and do not discuss it further.

The evidence before the hearing board consisted of the testimony of the complainant's and respondent's witnesses (including Cleland himself), documents, and a stipulation of facts contained in the trial management order the parties submitted. As the facts are sometimes complex, we address each count of the complaint separately, together with the hearing board's findings and conclusions pertaining to that count.

A. Count I—The Kasnoff Funds

Cleland represented George M. Kasnoff Jr. and his various business entities. In 1994, however, Cleland and Kasnoff had a disagreement over the attorney's fees Kasnoff owed Cleland. One of the business entities involved was Kas-Don Enterprises, Inc., which was owned by Kasnoff and Don Shank. Kasnoff and Shank decided to dissolve Kas-Don in the summer of 1995; Shank agreed to buy out Kasnoff s interest in the real estate the corporation owned. Cleland was to prepare the documents that were necessary to transfer the property and to terminate Kas-Don. This was completed in August 1995 and the corporation was dissolved.

Because he was on his honeymoon in Europe on the closing date, Kasnoff made arrangements for Cleland to deposit the net proceeds from the closing into Cleland's trust account. The parties agreed that once the funds were in the trust account, they would be disbursed for certain business expenses. In addition, Kasnoff authorized Cleland to pay himself $5,000 for past attorney's fees. Cleland was to deposit the balance of the funds in Kasnoff's bride's bank account.

On August 16, 1995, Cleland deposited proceeds from the closing in the amount of $16,576.56 into

his trust account. With his client's permission, Cleland paid certain business expenses that Kasnoff owed with funds from the trust account. On August 17, 1995, Cleland asked Kasnoff to pay attorney's fees over and above the $5,000 that Kasnoff had agreed to pay. Kasnoff did not authorize any additional sums to be taken out. Nevertheless, Cleland paid himself an additional $4,581.94 for legal services, including $600 for fees that had not yet been earned. Cleland deposited these unauthorized funds into his operating account and used them for his own purposes. When Kasnoff called from Europe on August 16, Cleland told him that he had deposited the balance of the funds (including the $4,581.94 he had paid himself without permission) into Kasnoff's wife's bank account. This was untrue.

The hearing board found that Kasnoff frequently paid the attorney's fees he owed Cleland slowly. Cleland also reasonably believed that Kasnoff was in financial difficulties. The exact amount of attorney's fees that Kasnoff owed was in dispute even at the hearing (although after these disciplinary proceedings were underway, Cleland returned the clearly unearned $600 in fees through his lawyer). The hearing board also found that at the time he paid himself the unauthorized funds, Cleland was under considerable financial and personal pressure, and that he was clinically depressed.

The board concluded that Cleland's conduct violated Colo. RPC 1.15(a) (failing to keep the client's property—in this case, the $4,581.94—separate from the lawyer's own ***702** property), and 1.15(c) (failing to hold separate any property that the lawyer and another—in this case, the client—both claim an interest in). The board found, however, that the complainant did not prove by clear and convincing evidence that Cleland violated Colo. RPC 8.4(c) (engaging in conduct involving dishonesty, fraud, deceit, or misrepresentation). The complainant did not specifically complain about this finding in his opening brief, and we find it unnecessary to address it.

B. Count II—The Clearly Colorado Matter

On June 19, 1995, about two months before Kas-Don was dissolved, Clearly Colorado, L.L.C. entered into a contract with Kasnoff to purchase the latter's one-half interest in Kas-Don real estate. The contract provided that Clearly Colorado would pay a $5,000 earnest money deposit, and that this would be held in Cleland's trust account. After receiving the $5,000, Cleland used the trust funds for his own use. This was not authorized. [FN4] The real estate transaction fell through and Clearly Colorado demanded the return of its $5,000 deposit. Because he had already diverted the trust funds, however, the balance in Cleland's trust account on August 3, 1995 was only $66.40. Nevertheless, on August 15, 1995, Cleland wrote a $5,000 check drawn on his trust account as a refund to Clearly Colorado. This $5,000 was paid from the proceeds of the Kas-Don transaction referred to in Count I above.

> FN4. It is unclear why Cleland was not charged with initially misappropriating this $5,000 from his trust account.

The board concluded that Cleland knowingly misappropriated client funds to reimburse Clearly Colorado in violation of Colo. RPC 8.4(c) (engaging in conduct involving dishonesty, fraud, deceit, or misrepresentation).

C. Count III—Commingling and Misappropriation

Count II details numerous transactions that Cleland engaged in with respect to client funds and his trust account. For our purposes here, it is sufficient to note that Cleland admitted to commingling his own funds with those belonging to his clients in his trust account and that he knowingly misappropriated client funds without the authorization or knowledge of the clients affected. [FN5]

> FN5. The board did find that client funds belonging to Donna Nazario were transferred to Cleland's operating account by mistake, and thus did not constitute commingling or misappropriation.

In particular, the hearing board found that Cleland: (1) knowingly misappropriated $1376.95 of client funds from his trust account to repay another client; (2) commingled personal funds with client funds in his trust account on numerous occasions between November 1995 and August 1996; and (3) disbursed trust account funds belonging to various clients to other clients, without the authorization or knowledge

of the clients affected. The board thus concluded that Cleland's conduct violated Colo. RPC 8.4(c).

D. Count IV—Kasnoff Interest

Without his client's consent or agreement, Cleland charged interest on Kasnoff's past-due accounts. The board found that this practice violated Colo. RPC 1.5(a) (charging an unreasonable fee), and 8.4(c) (conduct involving dishonesty).

E. Count V—Robin Caspari

Robin Caspari hired Cleland to prosecute a landlord-tenant dispute, and gave him $91 to file suit against two tenants for past-due rent. The hearing board concluded that Cleland failed to keep Caspari reasonably informed about the status of the matter, in violation of Colo. RPC 1.4(a). In addition, Cleland told the client, falsely, that he had filed an action against one of the tenants, when he had not; that hearings had been set and orders had been entered in the case, when in fact there was no case; and that he had settled the matter with one of the clients for $600, which he then paid to the client. The $600 was actually from Cleland's personal funds. This conduct violated Colo. RPC 1.3 (neglecting a legal matter), and 8.4(c) (engaging in dishonest conduct).

*703 II.

[1] The hearing panel approved the hearing board's recommendation that Cleland be suspended for three years, with conditions. The complainant filed exceptions, claiming that certain of the board's factual and legal conclusions were erroneous, and that the appropriate disciplinary sanction was disbarment. The key to the appropriate discipline is also the most serious misconduct here—the knowing misappropriation of client funds in Counts II and III.

[2] As we have said numerous times before, disbarment is the presumed sanction when a lawyer knowingly misappropriates funds belonging to a client or a third person. "When a lawyer knowingly converts client funds, disbarment is 'virtually automatic,' at least in the absence of significant factors in mitigation." People v. Young, 864 P.2d 563, 564 (Colo. 1993) (knowing misappropriation of clients' funds warrants disbarment even absent prior disciplinary history and despite cooperation and making restitution); see also

In re Thompson, 991 P.2d 820, 823 (Colo. 1999) (disbarring lawyer who knowingly misappropriated law firm funds); People v. Varallo, 913 P.2d 1, 12 (Colo. 1996) (disbarring lawyer who knowingly misappropriated client funds); People v. Ogborn, 887 P.2d 21, 23 (Colo. 1994) (misappropriating client funds warrants disbarment even in absence of prior discipline and presence of personal and emotional problems); People v. Robbins, 869 P.2d 517, 518 (Colo. 1994) (converting client trust funds warrants disbarment even if funds are restored before clients learn they are missing but not before the conversion is discovered by the lawyer's law firm).

[3] Consistent with our approach, the ABA Standards for Imposing Lawyer Sanctions (1991 & Supp. 1992) provides that, in the absence of mitigating circumstances, "[d]isbarment is generally appropriate when a lawyer knowingly converts client property and causes injury or potential injury to a client." Id. at 4.11. Neither this standard nor our cases require serious injury before disbarment is appropriate. On the other hand, "[s]uspension is generally appropriate when a lawyer knows or should know that he is dealing improperly with client property and causes injury or potential injury to a client." Id. at 4.12.

The hearing board found that the following aggravating and mitigating factors were present. In aggravation, Cleland has prior discipline in the form of a letter of admonition for neglecting a legal matter, see id. at 9.22(a); and multiple offenses are present, see id. at 9.22(d). The board also determined that there was a pattern of misconduct, see id. at 9.22(c), but only with respect to Cleland's "continuing recklessness and gross negligence in management of his trust account from approximately mid-1995 to mid-August 1996."

According to the board, mitigating factors included the absence of a dishonest motive or intention on Cleland's part, see id. at 9.32(b); Cleland admitted that he committed some of the misconduct and otherwise cooperated in the proceedings, see id. at 9.32(e), Cleland was relatively inexperienced in the practice of law, see id. at 9.32(f); and he has expressed remorse, see id. at 9.32(1). Additional mitigating factors found were the presence of personal financial and emotional problems, see id. at 9.32(c); and a timely good faith effort to rectify the consequences of at least part of his misconduct, see id, at 9.32(d). The board noted that Cleland was diagnosed with a depressive disorder that impaired his judgment, concentration, and thinking. The conclusion that Cleland tried to rectify some of the consequences of his misconduct stems from the board's belief that he offered to arbitrate the fee dispute with Kasnoff before he was aware that he was under investigation.

While acknowledging our statement in Varallo, 913 P.2d at 12, that disbarment is the presumed sanction when knowing misappropriation is shown, the board declined to apply what it deemed such a "bright-line" rule to the facts in this case. In particular, the hearing board cited three cases that we decided after Varallo that it believed contradicted a literal reading of the case: People v. Zimmermann, 922 P.2d 325 (Colo. 1996); People v. Reynolds, 933 P.2d 1295 (Colo. 1997); and People v. Schaefer, 938 P.2d 147 *704 (Colo. 1997). However, these cases did not modify Varallo's "bright-line" rule. [FN6]

> FN6. The virtue of a bright-line rule like this one is not that it is easy to apply, although it is. Rather, such a rule strives to eliminate the disparate treatment of lawyers who have committed serious misconduct, when the unequal treatment may otherwise be based on invidious and irrelevant factors.

We decided Zimmermann three months after Varallo. The respondent in Zimmermann, John Delos Zimmermann, seriously mismanaged the funds in his trust account. He commingled funds that should have been placed in his trust account with funds that should have been deposited in his operating account; he improperly used clients' funds to pay his personal or business expenses; and refunded unearned attorney's fees to clients from funds advanced by different clients. See 922 P.2d at 326–29. We suspended Zimmermann for one year and one day. See id. at 330. Zimmermann's misconduct is similar to that charged in Count III of the complaint in this case, with one important exception. That exception serves to distinguish Zimmermann from this case, however, in the same way that we distinguished Zimmermann from Varallo. We stated that:

> The single most important factor in determining the appropriate level of discipline in this case is whether [Zimmermann's] misappropriation of client funds was knowing, in which case disbarment is

the presumed sanction, People v. Varallo, 913 P.2d 1, 12 (Colo. 1996), or whether it was reckless, or merely negligent, suggesting that a period of suspension is adequate. People v. Dickinson, 903 P.2d 1132, 1138 (Colo. 1995).

Zimmermann, 922 P.2d at 329 [emphasis added]. However, the hearing board specifically found that Zimmermann's mental state when he was mismanaging his trust account was one of recklessness. See id. We noted that although the evidence before the board would have supported a finding that Zimmermann's conduct was knowing, rather than reckless, the board's conclusion found support in the record and we would not overturn it. See id. at 329 n. 1. Zimmermann therefore stands for the same proposition as Varallo—the lawyer's actual mental state is the most significant factor for determining the proper discipline. Because the board found that Zimmermann's mental state when he mismanaged his trust and operating accounts was reckless, not knowing, Dickinson (suspension) governed the result, not Varallo (disbarment).

We suspended the respondent in People v. Reynolds, 933 P.2d 1295 (Colo. 1997), for three years. John Kerz Reynolds engaged in an extensive pattern of "neglect of client matters, misrepresentations to clients, dishonesty, misuse of client funds, and assisting a nonlawyer in the unauthorized practice of law." Id. at 1305. He also failed to account for, or return, unearned advance fees he received from various clients. See id. at 1296–1301. The case did not involve the knowing misappropriation of client funds, however. Reynolds was not charged with misappropriation, nor did the hearing board in that case make any findings on the issue. Reynolds is therefore distinguishable.

Finally, in People v. Schaefer, 938 P.2d 147 (Colo. 1997), we suspended Richard A. Schaefer for two years. Citing Zimmermann and Varallo, we concluded that "[t]he hearing board's determination that [Schaefer's] mishandling of his client's funds was negligent rather than intentional is not clearly erroneous and we will not overturn it." id. at 150. Schaefer is thus completely consistent with Varallo.

The present case cannot be distinguished from Varallo. In two separate counts, Cleland admitted, and the hearing board found, that he knowingly misappropriated client funds. The board erred when it did not just accept Cleland's admissions and its own initial findings, and then go on to determine whether the factors in mitigation were weighty enough to justify a sanction less than disbarment. Because there is no evidence in the record that supports the conclusion that Cleland's mental state was merely reckless or negligent, that finding is clearly erroneous, and we reject it.

Having determined that disbarment is the presumed sanction in this case, we must now independently review the record with an eye *705 toward the factors in mitigation. The hearing board first found that Cleland did not have a dishonest motive or intention when he committed the misconduct. As the complainant points out, this is directly contrary to the stipulation and a large part of the evidence. The hearing board specifically concluded that Cleland engaged in conduct involving dishonesty, fraud, deceit, or misrepresentation in Counts II (knowing misappropriation of client funds), III (knowing misappropriation of client funds), IV (unilaterally charging unauthorized interest), and V (misrepresenting the status of a case and that it had settled), in violation of Colo. RPC 8.4(c). The fact that Cleland may not have had a dishonest motive in every single instance of misconduct does not demonstrate that the mitigating factor exists. We reject this as a mitigating factor.

Next, the board found that Cleland's admissions of misconduct and his cooperative attitude in the proceedings were mitigating factors. See ABA Standards, supra, at 9.32(e). We agree that these constitute bona fide mitigating circumstances, but we accord them little ultimate weight, given Cleland's failure to appear and participate in this court, and his noncooperation and default in the proceedings before the PDJ for the misconduct (similar to that in this case because it involved mismanagement of trust funds) that earned him a two-year suspension. The reason we consider mitigating factors at all is so we may gauge the level of danger that an attorney poses to the public and, ideally, to arrive at a disciplinary sanction that adequately balances the seriousness of the danger against the gravity of the misconduct.

Although Cleland's cooperation before the hearing board warrants some consideration, we are troubled by his later noncooperation, and feel that this does not bode well for Cleland's future as a lawyer.

The board also considered Cleland's relative inexperience in the practice of law as a mitigating factor. It is such a factor; but inexperience does not go far in our view to excuse or to mitigate dishonesty, misrepresentation, or misappropriation. Little experience in the practice of law is necessary to appreciate such actual wrongdoing. On the other hand, Cleland's expressions of remorse are mitigating, as the board found. See id. at 9.32(1).

The hearing board also considered that the personal, financial, and emotional problems that Cleland was experiencing were mitigating. See id. at 9.32(c). Specifically, the board noted that Cleland had been diagnosed with a depressive disorder that impaired his judgment, concentration, and thinking. However, we deem it worthy of note that, despite the advice of the psychiatrist who testified for him, Cleland had not sought treatment for the disorder. Moreover, we reject the proposition that Cleland's financial difficulties mitigate his misappropriation of client funds in any way. Finally, the board found that by offering to arbitrate the fee dispute with Kasnoff, Cleland made some effort to rectify the consequences of at least part of his misconduct. See id. at 9.32(d). Despite the fact that Cleland's clients may not have suffered significant actual damages, as the hearing board found (a point that is debatable given the record in this case), the potential for injury was nevertheless substantial.

Taking all of the above factors into consideration, we conclude that they are not significant enough to call for any result other than disbarment. However, two members of the court disagree and would approve the recommendation to suspend Cleland for three years. Accordingly, we reject the board's and panel's recommendation, and we order that Cleland be disbarred.

III.

We hereby order that James A. Cleland be disbarred, effective immediately. Should Cleland ever seek readmission to practice law pursuant to C.R.C.P. 251.29, he must first demonstrate that he has complied with the following conditions:

(1) Cleland must pay George M. Kasnoff Jr. any amount awarded in Kasnoff's favor in the fee arbitration proceedings between Cleland and Kasnoff;

(2) Cleland must pay the costs incurred in this proceeding in the amount of $2,188.73, to the Attorney Regulation ***706** Committee, 600 Seventeenth Street, Suite 200 South, Denver, Colorado 80202.

END OF DOCUMENT

EXERCISES

1. Why did the court disagree with the board's findings that the attorney should only be suspended for three years and instead find that the attorney should be disbarred?

2. Why do you think the attorney requested disbarment?

3. How did the attorney "consistently mismanage" his trust account?

4. In the Kasnoff matter (Count I), why could the attorney not place the $600 of unearned fees in his operating account?

5. How did the attorney complicate matters by writing a check in *The Clearly Colorado Matter* (Count II) for $5,000 when there was only $66.40 in the account at the time? Apparently, the check cashed because another deposit was made. Where did this money come from?

6. In the Robin Caspari matter (Count V), what was wrong with the attorney's taking the $600 from his own personal account, as a client actually received a benefit and no client was harmed?

7. When considering mitigation, was the court persuaded by the fact that the attorney had been diagnosed with a depressive disorder that impaired his judgment, concentration, and thinking? Why or why not?

PROLAW—CLIENT TRUST FUNDS

TRAINING MANUAL OUTLINE

Number	Lesson Title	Concepts Covered
Lesson 1	Introduction to ProLaw	Understanding the ProLaw interface
Lesson 2	Entering Trust Deposits	Details on generating trust deposits
Lesson 3	Enter Trust Checks	Details on generating trust checks
Lesson 4	Printing Trust Reports	Printing a trust report including a balance of trust monies for each case

WELCOME TO JOHNSON AND SULLIVAN

Welcome to Johnson and Sullivan! We are an active and growing firm with four attorneys and two legal assistants. As you know, you have been hired as a legal assistant intern. We are very happy to have you on board; we can certainly use your help.

At Johnson and Sullivan, keeping detailed and accurate records of client trust monies is a priority. In this tutorial, you will learn how easy it is to track client trust funds in ProLaw. ProLaw does all of the work for you. If you have completed Lesson 1 in a prior tutorial, please go directly to Lesson 2.

GETTING STARTED

Introduction

Throughout these exercises, information you need to type into the program will be designated in several different ways.

- Keys to be pressed on the keyboard will be designated in brackets, in all caps and bold type (e.g., press the [ENTER] key).
- Movements with the mouse will be designated in bold and italics (e.g., *point to File on the menu bar and click the mouse*).
- Words or letters that should be typed will be designated in bold and enlarged (e.g., type **Training Program**).
- Information that is or should be displayed on your computer screen is shown in the following style: **Press ENTER to continue.**

Lesson 1: Introduction to ProLaw

In this lesson, you will load ProLaw and be introduced to the Contacts and Matters functions as an example of the basic interface of the program.

1. Load Windows. To load ProLaw, *click on the* Start *button, point with the mouse to* **Programs** *or* **All Programs,** *point to* **ProLaw Evaluation,** *and then point and click on* **PROLAW.**

2. When ProLaw is loaded the first time, you may see a window entitled **Professional Information for User xx.** The screen will ask you to enter your initials and name. At "Initials" type: **PD.** At "Full Name" type: **Pat Doe.** Then, *point and click on the green checkmark in the upper-right part of the window.*

3. You should now have the **ProLaw** window displayed, including the **Daily Docket** calendar for the current day on your screen.

4. *Point and click on the maximize icon at the top right of the* **ProLaw** *window* (it is just to the left of the red "X" and looks like two layered squares. If you point to an icon with your mouse for more than a second, the icon title will be displayed).

5. Notice that there is a column of icons on the left edge of the screen. These icons give you access to ProLaw's major functions; they include Contacts, Matters, Events, Files, Transactions, Journals, Ledger and Reports.

6. Below is a table showing the purpose of each function in ProLaw.

Prolaw Icon/Function	Purpose
CONTACTS	Contains contact information for all clients, parties, attorneys, judges, etc. It is an electronic address book. Conflict of interest searches can also be performed using This function.
MATTERS	Contains detailed information about every case/client matter. This includes billing information, notes about the case, related contacts, related matters, and settlement information, among others.
EVENTS	Allows the user to run queries for a specific set of docket entries and print docket reports.
FILES	Allows the user to check files in and out and report on the location and status of physical file folders.
TRANSACTIONS	Allows the user to create time entries, run cost recovery imports, edit pre-bills, and produce statements.
JOURNALS	Allows the user to enter checks, cash receipts, reconcile accounts, and produce financial reports.
LEDGER	Allows the user to view client billing and payment history and view statement images and unbilled statements.
REPORTS	Allows the user to produce and print a wide variety of reports.

7. *Point and click with the mouse on* Contacts. The **Contacts** window is now displayed.

8. *Point and click with the mouse on* Quick find, located in the **View** section of the **Shortcuts** pane. *In the* Search for *field press the* **[BACKSPACE]** key.

This will clear the field and search for all contacts in the database. Press the **[ENTER]** key.

9. Press the **[DOWN ARROW]** cursor key or *use the mouse* to scroll down through all of the contacts. Notice that the database is already populated with information.

10. *Scroll back until you find the entry for* **Adam Schnieder,** which is located near the bottom of the list. *Point and double-click on* **Adam Schnieder.**

11. Notice that the **Adam Schnieder—Contact** window is now displayed. You can now see the contact information for Adam Schnieder including name, class (i.e. type of entry; in this case, "client"), address, phone number, etc.

12. In the **Adam Schnieder—Contact** window, *point and click on the* Close *icon (the red "X" located in the upper-right corner of the window) to close this window.*

13. The "Contacts" window should now be displayed. *Point and click on "Recent"* (under "Shortcuts" "View"). Notice that only the entry for Adam Schnieder is listed. The **Recent** command contains a list of your most recently used contacts.

14. In the **Contacts** window, *point and click on the* Close *icon (the red "X" located in the upper-right corner of the window) to close this window.*

15. You should now be back where you started at the **Daily Docket** screen.

16. *Point and click with the mouse on* Matters. The **Matters** window is now displayed.

17. *Point and click with the mouse on* Quick find if it is not already displayed (located in the **View** section of the **Shortcuts** pane). In the **Search for** field, press the **[BACKSPACE]** key. This will clear the field and search for all matters in the database. Press the **[ENTER]** key.

18. In the **Matters** window, *point and click with the mouse on the* maximize *icon at the top right corner of the window* (located just to the left of the **Close** icon; it looks like two layered squares). This will allow you to see additional columns.

19. Press the **[DOWN ARROW]** cursor key or *use the mouse* to scroll down through all of the matters.

20. *Point and double-click with the mouse on the first entry* (**Matter ID 1000-001—Maguire, Robert, Maguire—Chapter 7**).

21. The **1000-001—Matter** window should now be displayed. Notice that there are a number of tabs in the window, including **General, Notes, Billing, Related Contacts,** and others. *Point and click on each of these tabs.* Then, close the **1000-01—Matter** window by *pointing and clicking on the* Close *icon.*

22. The **Matters** window should now be displayed. *Point and click on* Recent (located in the "View" section of the "Shortcuts" pane). Notice that only the "Maguire, Robert—Maguire—Chapter 7" matter is listed.

23. *In the* Matters *window, point and click on the* Close *icon to close this window.*

24. You should now be back where you started at the **Daily Docket** screen.

25. This concludes Lesson 1. To exit ProLaw, *point and click on* Close *icon in the* **ProLaw** *window to close the program.* Alternatively, you may *point and click on* **File** *on the menu bar and then click on* **Exit.**

Lesson 2: Entering Trust Deposits

In this lesson, you will enter several trust deposits. You will use the current month and date for all transactions.

1. Load Windows. To load ProLaw, *click on the* Start *button, point with the mouse to* **Programs** *or* **All Programs,** *point to* **ProLaw Evaluation,** *and then point and click on* **PROLAW.**
2. You should now have the **ProLaw** window displayed, including the **Daily Docket** calendar for the current day on your screen.
3. *Point and click with the mouse on* Journals.
4. *Point and click with the mouse on* Quick find. *Then, point and click on the ellipses (three dots) in the* Account No. *field.*
5. In the **Search for** field, press the **[BACKSPACE]** key. *Point and double-click on* **Account No. 10100 Trust Account Checking.**
6. *Point and click on the ellipses in the* Matter ID *field. Point and click with the mouse on* Quick find. In the **Search for** field, press the **[BACKSPACE]** key. *Point and double-click on* **Matter ID 1005-001, Brakes R US, Holster v. Brakes R Us.**
7. *In the* Journals *window, point and click on* Type; *point and click on the down arrow of the drop-down box and choose* Deposits.
8. Notice at the bottom of the screen, the **Matter Balance** field shows a balance of $3,436.80.
9. *Point and click with the mouse on the* Add item *icon on the toolbar at the top left of the window, just under* File *on the menu bar.*
10. *Point and click with the mouse in the* Debit *field and type* **10000.**
11. Use the **[TAB]** key to proceed to the **Memo** field, and type **Pre-pay fees.**
12. *Point and click on the* Save record *icon (green checkmark) on the toolbar.* Notice in the **Matter Balance** field at the bottom of the screen that the balance is now $13,436.80.
13. *Enter the additional deposits for Matter ID, 1005-001, the Holster v. Brakes R Us case.* You can press the **[TAB]** key to cycle through the fields, and ProLaw will automatically add another line where you can enter additional deposits.

Deposit	Memo
$2500	Witness fees
$5000	Travel expenses to take Depo of expert
$1500	Prepay expenses
$2500	Transcript fees

14. *After you have entered the deposits, point and click on the* Save record *icon (green checkmark) on the toolbar to save and enter the deposits.* Notice that the new **Matter Balance** in the lower right of the screen shows $24,936.80.

15. This concludes Lesson 2. To exit ProLaw, *point and click on the* Close *icon in the* **ProLaw** *window to close the program.* Alternatively, you may *point and click on* **File** *on the menu bar and then click on* **Exit.**

Lesson 3: Entering Trust Checks

In this lesson, you will enter several trust checks. You will use the current month and date for all transactions.

1. Load Windows. To load ProLaw, *click on the* Start *button, point with the mouse to* **Programs** *or* **All Programs,** *point to* **ProLaw Evaluation,** *and then point and click on* **PROLAW.**

2. You should now have the **ProLaw** window displayed, including the **Daily Docket** calendar for the current day on your screen.

3. *Point and click with the mouse on* Journals.

4. ProLaw brings up the most recent account you were working on, so you should see the deposits you entered for the **Brakes R US case, Matter ID 1005-001, Account No. 10100, Trust Account Checking.**

5. *Point and click with the mouse on the* Type *field. Point and click on the down arrow of the drop-down box, and point and click on* Checks.

6. Notice at the bottom of the screen that the "Matter Balance" field shows a balance of $24,936.80.

7. *Point and click with the mouse on the* Add item *icon on the toolbar at the top left of the window, just under* File *on the menu bar).*

8. *Point and click with the mouse in the* Credit *field,* and type **500,** and press the **[TAB]** key to go to the **Payee Company** field.

9. *Point and click with the mouse on the ellipses in the* Payee Company *field.*

10. *Point and click on* Quick find *in the* Contacts List *window.* Press the **[BACKSPACE]** key. *Point and double-click on* Advanced Court Reporting.

11. Use the **[TAB]** key to proceed to the **Memo** field and type **Deposition of Plaintiff.**

12. *Point and click on the* Save record *icon (green checkmark) on the toolbar.* Notice in the **Matter Balance** field at the bottom of the screen that the balance is now $24,436.80.

13. Enter the additional checks for **Matter ID, 1005-001, the Holster v. Brakes R Us** case below. You can press the **[TAB]** key to cycle through the fields, and ProLaw will automatically add another line where you can enter additional checks.

Check	Payee Company	Memo
$150	Clerk of Courts, State of New Mexico	Court fee
$100	U.S. Post Office	Shipping
$750	American Reporting	Deposition of defendant
$2500	Universal Investigation Services	Investigation re: damages

14. *After you have entered the checks, point and click on the* Save record *icon on the toolbar to save and enter the checks.* Notice that the new **Matter Balance** in the lower right of the screen shows $20,936.80.

15. *Point and click with the mouse on the* Print Checks *icon on the toolbar. Note:* there are two icons that look like a printer on the toolbar. The **Print Checks** icon is the fifth icon from the right; it looks like a printer with a dollar sign ($) on it. Remember, you can hover your mouse over an icon to see its name.

16. The **Print Checks** window should be displayed. Notice that there are six checks entered, including a check to Simon & Moore for $15,945; this represents a trust check to the firm for payments on fees and expenses. *Note:* "Simon & Moore" is the name of the firm used by the evaluation version of ProLaw.

17. *Point and click with the mouse on the* Print preview *icon on the toolbar.*

18. *Press the up arrow on the toolbar (to the right of* Page) *to go to page 2. Scroll down or maximize the window to see the check and stub. Scroll through all the checks.*

19. *Point and click with the mouse on the green checkmark in the* Check Preview *window to close the window.*

20. *Point and click with the mouse on the green checkmark in the* Printing Checks *window to close the window.*

21. This concludes Lesson 3. To exit ProLaw, *point and click on the* Close *icon in the* **ProLaw** *window to close the program.* Alternatively, you may *point and click on* **File** *on the menu bar and then click on* **Exit.**

Lesson 4: Printing Trust Reports

In this lesson, you will print a trust report that includes the trust balances for each matter. You will use the current month and date for all transactions.

1. Load Windows. To load ProLaw, *click on the* Start *button, point with the mouse to* **Programs** *or* **All Programs,** *point to* **ProLaw Evaluation,** *and then point and click on* **PROLAW.**

2. You should now have the **ProLaw** window displayed, including the **Daily Docket** calendar for the current day on your screen.

3. *Point and click with the mouse on* Reports.

4. *Point and click with the mouse on the* Matter Trust Balances *under* Management Reports.

5. *Point and click on the* Preview report *on the toolbar. Scroll through the report.* Notice **Matter ID 1005-001,** the **Brakes R Us** case. All of the entries you made should appear. A few additional entries also appear (these were done as a part of the demonstration version of the software).

6. Notice that all of the cases show an ending balance, so it is easy to see exactly which clients have money in the trust account.

7. This concludes Lesson 4. To exit ProLaw, *point and click on the* Close *icon in the* **ProLaw** *window to close the program.* Alternatively, you may *point and click on* **File** *on the menu bar and then click on* **Exit.**

This concludes the Client Trust Funds Hands-On Exercises.

Hands-On Exercises

MICROSOFT EXCEL (ALL VERSIONS)

LESSONS

Number	Lesson Title
Lesson 1	Building a Simple Budget Spreadsheet—Part 1
Lesson 2	Building a Simple Budget Spreadsheet—Part 2
Lesson 3	Building a Complex Budget Spreadsheet
Lesson 4	Client Trust Account— Checkbook Register
Lesson 5	Client Trust Account— Client Registers
Lesson 6	Client Trust Account— Client Summary Ledger

GETTING STARTED

Overview

Microsoft Excel is a powerful spreadsheet program that allows you to create formulas, "what-if" scenarios, graphs, and much more.

Introduction

Throughout these lessons and exercises, information you need to operate the program will be designated in several different ways:

- Keys to be pressed on the keyboard will be designated in brackets, in all caps and bold type (e.g., press the **[ENTER]** key).
- Movements with the mouse will be designated in bold and italics (e.g., *point to File on the menu bar and click the mouse*).
- Words or letters that should be typed will be designated in bold and enlarged (e.g., type **Training Program**).
- Information that is or should be displayed on your computer screen is shown in the following style: **Press ENTER to continue.**

OVERVIEW OF EXCEL

I. Worksheet

A. *Menu/commands*—***Click on the toolbar or the menu bar*** to access menus and/or to execute commands.

B. *Entering Data*—To enter data, type the text or number, and press the **[ENTER]** key or one of the arrow (cursor) keys.

C. *Ranges*—A range is a group of cells. Cell ranges can be created by ***dragging the mouse*** or holding the **[SHIFT]** key on and using the arrow (cursor) keys.

D. *Format*—Cells can be formatted, including changing the font style, font size, shading, border, cell type (currency, percentage, etc.), alignment, and others by ***selecting*** Format ***from the menu bar and then clicking on cells,*** or by ***right-clicking*** (for right-handed mouse users) ***on the cell and then selecting*** Format Cells.

E. *Editing a Cell*—You can edit a cell by ***double-clicking with the mouse on the cell*** or by ***clicking once with the mouse on the cell and then pointing and clicking with the mouse on the formula bar.*** (The formula bar is directly under the toolbar and just to the right of the = (equals) sign or "fx" sign.) The formula bar shows the current contents of the selected cell, and it allows you to edit the cell contents. You can also edit the contents of a cell by ***pointing and clicking with the mouse on the cell*** and then pressing the **[F2]** key.

F. *Column Width*—You can change the width of a column by ***pointing at the column letters*** (at the top of the screen) ***and moving the cursor to the edge of the column.*** The cursor then changes to double-headed vertical arrows.

Simply *drag the mouse to the right to increase the column width or to the left to decrease the column width.* You can change the height of a row by *pointing and dragging the mouse on the row numbers.* You can also change the width of a column by going to the column you want to change and selecting **Format** from the menu bar, then **Column,** and then **Width.** You can change the height of a row by going to the row you want to change and selecting **Format** from the menu bar, then **Row,** and then **Height.**

G. *Insert*—You can insert one row or column by selecting **Insert** from the menu bar and then **Column** or **Row.** You can also insert a number of rows or columns by *dragging the mouse over the number of rows or columns you want to add and selecting* Insert *from the menu bar, and then either* Column *or* Row. Finally, you can *right-click with the mouse and select* Insert *from the menu.*

H. *Erase/Delete*—You can erase data by *dragging the mouse over the area* and then pressing the **[DELETE]** key. You can delete whole columns or rows by *pointing with the mouse on a column or row, selecting* Edit *from the menu bar, and then* Delete, and following the menus. You can also delete whole columns or rows by *pointing with the mouse on the column or row and then right-clicking with the mouse and selecting* Delete.

I. *Quit*—To quit Excel, *point and click with the mouse on* File *and then* Exit.

J. *Copy*—To copy data, *click on the cell and then select the* Autofill *command,* which is the small black box at the bottom right corner of every cell. Then *drag the mouse to where the data should be placed.* You can also copy data by *selecting the cell, right-clicking the mouse and selecting* Copy, *moving the cursor to the location where the information should be copied,* and pressing the **[ENTER]** key. Data can also be copied by *clicking with the mouse on the information to be copied and selecting* Edit *from the menu bar and* Copy. Then go to the location where the information should be copied and select **Edit** from the menu bar and then **Paste.**

K. *Move*—Move data by *clicking on the cell, right-clicking the mouse, selecting* Cut, *moving the cursor to the location where the information should be inserted,* and pressing the **[ENTER]** key. Data can also be moved by *clicking with the mouse on the information to be moved, selecting* Edit *from the menu bar and* Cut, *going to the location where the information should be copied, and selecting* Edit *from the menu bar and then* Paste.

L. *Saving and Opening Files*—Save a file by *pointing with the mouse on* File *and then* Save, and typing the file name. You can also save a file by *clicking on the* Save *icon* (a floppy disk) on the toolbar. Open a file that was previously saved by *pointing with the mouse on* File *and then* Open and typing the name of the file to be opened.

M. *Print*—You can print a file by *pointing and clicking with the mouse on the* Printer *icon* on the toolbar or by *selecting* File *from the menu bar and then* Print *and* OK.

II. Numbers and Formulas

A. *Numbers*—To enter a number in a cell, simply type the number and press the **[ENTER]** key or an arrow (cursor) key.

B. *Adding Cells* (*Addition*)—You can add the contents of two or more cells by three different methods:

   1. To add the contents of two or more cells,
      a. Go to the cell location where the total should be placed.
      b. ***Point and click with the mouse on the*** AutoSum ***icon*** on the toolbar, which looks a little like an E. (*Note:* to see the name of an icon, point at the icon for a second and the name of the icon will be displayed.)
      c. Excel guesses at what cells you want to add. Press **[ENTER]** if the correct range is entered or edit the range by pressing the **[SHIFT]** key and moving the arrow cursor keys until the correct cell address is displayed. Then press **[ENTER]**.

   2. To add the contents of two cells,
      a. Go to the cell location where the total should be placed.
      b. Press =.
      c. Enter the first cell address (or point to it with the cursor).
      d. Press +.
      e. Enter the second cell address (or point to it with the cursor).
      f. Press the **[ENTER]** key. (For example, to add the values of C4 and C5, the formula would read =C4+C5.)

   3. To add the contents of two cells,
      a. Go to the cell location where the total should be placed.
      b. Type =**SUM(.**
      c. Enter the first cell address (or point to it with the cursor).
      d. Press the period (.).
      e. Enter the second cell address (or point to it with the cursor).
      f. Press the closing parenthesis ()).
      g. Press the **[ENTER]** key. (For example, to add the values of C4 and C5, the formula would read =SUM(C4:C5).)

C. *Subtracting Cells*—To subtract one cell from another,
   1. Go to the cell location where the total should be placed.
   2. Press =.
   3. Enter the first cell address (or point to it with the cursor).
   4. Press –.
   5. Enter the second cell address (or point to it with the cursor).
   6. Press the **[ENTER]** key. (For example, to subtract the value of C4 from the value of C5, the formula would read =C5–C4.)

D. *Multiplying Cells*—To multiply two cells,
   1. Go to the cell location where the total should be placed.
   2. Press =.
   3. Enter the first cell address (or point to it with the cursor).
   4. Press the *([SHIFT]-[8]).
   5. Enter the second cell address (or point to it with the cursor).

6. Press the **[ENTER]** key. (For example, to multiply the value in C4 times the value in C5, the formula would read =C5*C4.)

E. *Dividing Cells*—To divide two cells,
   1. Go to the cell location where the total should be placed.
   2. Press =.
   3. Enter the first cell address (or point to it with the cursor).
   4. Press the front slash (/).
   5. Enter the second cell address (or point to it with the cursor).
   6. Press the **[ENTER]** key. (For example, to divide the value in C4 by the value in C5, the formula would read =C4/C5.)

Before Starting Lesson 1—Setting the Tool and Menu Bar

Before starting Lesson 1, complete the exercise below to adjust the toolbar and menu bar so that they are consistent with the instructions in the lessons.

1. Load Windows. Then, *double-click on the* Excel *icon on the desktop to* load Excel for Windows. Alternatively, *click on the "Start" button, point with the mouse to "Programs" or "All Programs," and then click on the* Microsoft Excel *icon. Or click on the "Start" button, point with the mouse to "Programs" or "All Programs," point to* Microsoft Office, *then click on the* Microsoft Office Excel 2003 *icon.*
2. A blank workbook should be open. If you are not in a blank workbook, *click on "File" on the menu bar, click on "New," and then click or double-click (depending on the Excel version you are using) on "Blank workbook."*
3. *Click on "View" in the menu bar and then point with the mouse to "Toolbars."*
4. Only the "Standard" and "Formatting" toolbars should be checked. If the "Standard" and "Formatting" toolbars are not checked, then click on them to select them (the checkmark indicates they have been selected). If another toolbar has been selected (marked with a check mark—such as the "Chart" toolbar or other option), then click on it to remove it from the toolbar. Please note that you can only make changes to the toolbar one at a time, so it may take you a few steps to only have "Standard" and "Formatting" selected—or, your computer may already be set for this and you may not have to make any changes. If you do not have to make changes, just push the **[ESC]** key twice to exit out of the "View" menu.
5. We also want to a) make sure that the full menus are displayed when you select an item from the menu (Excel normally will only show the most recent/commonly used selections) and b) that the toolbar is shown on two rows so that you can see all of the options.
6. *Click on "View" in the menu bar, point with the mouse to "Toolbars," and then click on "Customize."*
7. *Click on the "Options" tab. Then, under "Personalized Menus and Toolbars," make sure that checkmarks are next to "Show Standard and Formatting toolbars on two rows" and "Always show full menus."* Note: if under "Personalized Menus and Toolbars" it says "Standard and Formatting Toolbars

share one row," do not check the box (the toolbars are already on two rows). Also, if "Menus Show recently used commands first" is displayed, do not check the box (full menus will already be displayed). *Click on "Close."*

Please note that depending on the version of Excel you are using, the toolbars, icons, and menus may look slightly different than the figures, but the differences should be minor. You are now ready to begin Lesson 1.

Lesson 1: Building a Budget Spreadsheet—Part 1

This lesson shows you how to build the spreadsheet in Figure 1—Excel Tutorial Budget Spreadsheet. It explains how to move the cell pointer; enter text, values, and formulas; change the format of cells; copy formulas; and print and save a spreadsheet. Keep in mind that if at any time you make a mistake in this lesson, you may press **[CTRL]-[Z]** to undo what you have done.

1. Load Windows. Then, *double-click on the* Excel icon *on the desktop* to load Excel for Windows. Alternatively, *click on the "Start" button, point with the mouse to "Programs" or "All Programs," and then click on the* Microsoft Excel *icon. Or click on the "Start" button, point with the mouse to "Programs" or "All Programs," point to* Microsoft Office, *then click on the* Microsoft Office Excel 2003 *icon.*

2. Notice that the cell pointer is at cell A1 and the current cell indicator (also called the name box by Excel) shows A1. The name box is just under the

Figure 1
Excel Tutorial Budget Spreadsheet

Screen shot reprinted by permission from Microsoft Corporation.

	A	B	C	D
3			BUDGET	
4		Item	Jan.	Jan.
5			Budget	Actual
6		EXPENSES		
7		Utilities	$1,000.00	$900.00
8		Equipment Rental	$500.00	$600.00
9		Rent	$1,500.00	$1,500.00
10		Marketing	$200.00	$200.00
11		Salaries	$15,000.00	$14,750.00
12		Office Supplies	$750.00	$875.00
13		TOTAL EXPENSES	$18,950.00	$18,825.00
14				
15		INCOME		
16		Fees	$22,000.00	$23,500.00
17		Retainers	$5,000.00	$4,000.00
18		TOTAL INCOME	$27,000.00	$27,500.00
19				
20		PROFIT/LOSS	$8,050.00	$8,675.00

toolbar all the way to the left. Also notice that you can move the cell pointer around the spreadsheet using the cursor keys. Go back to cell A1 by pressing the **[CTRL]-[HOME]** keys.

3. Go to cell C3 by pressing **[RIGHT ARROW]**, **[RIGHT ARROW]**, and then pressing **[DOWN ARROW]**, **[DOWN ARROW]**.

4. You will now enter the title of the spreadsheet in cell C3. Type **BUDGET** and then press the **[ENTER]** key.

5. Notice that the cell pointer is now at cell C4.

6. Press the **[UP ARROW]** to go back to cell C3. Notice that **BUDGET** is left aligned. To center **BUDGET** in the column, *point and click with the mouse on the* Center *icon on the toolbar.* It is the icon with several lines on it that appear centered. (If you place the mouse cursor over icons on the toolbar for a second, the name of the icon will be displayed.) Alternatively, you can *select* Format *from the menu bar, then* Cells, Alignment, *and then* Center *in the* Horizontal *field. Then click on* OK.

7. You should now be able to enter information. First, move the cell pointer to where the cell should go, then type the data, and finally, enter the data by pressing the **[ENTER]** key or one of the arrow (cursor) keys. Enter the remaining row labels as follows:

   Item in B4
   EXPENSES in B6
   Utilities in B7
   Equipment Rental in B8
   Rent in B9
   Marketing in B10
   Salaries in B11
   Office Supplies in B12
   TOTAL EXPENSES in B13
   INCOME in B15
   Fees in B16
   Retainers in B17
   TOTAL INCOME in B18
   PROFIT/LOSS in B20

8. Notice in Column B that some of the data (such as **EXPENSES** and **Equipment Rental**) actually extend into Column C. To correct this, you must increase the column width for column B. *Point with the mouse at the column letter B at the top of the screen. Move the cursor to the right edge of the column.* The cursor should then change to a double-headed vertical arrow. *Drag the mouse to the right until the column width is 18.* Alternatively, you can change the cell width by *placing the cell pointer anywhere in Column B, pointing and clicking on* Format *from the menu bar, and then* Column *and* Width, *typing* 18, *and then clicking on* OK.

9. Notice that all of the data now fits in the columns. Enter the following:

   Jan. in C4
   Budget in C5
   Jan. in D4
   Actual in D5

10. *Go to cell C4 and drag the mouse over to cell D5* (so that all of the column headings are highlighted), *then click with the mouse on the* Center *icon and the* Bold *icon on the toolbar.*

11. You are now ready to enter values into your spreadsheet.

12. *Move the cell pointer to cell C7.* Enter **1000** (do not place a dollar sign or commas; these will be added later). Press the **[ENTER]** key to enter the value.

13. Enter the following:

    500 in C8
    1500 in C9
    200 in C10
    15000 in C11
    750 in C12
    22000 in C16
    5000 in C17
    900 in D7
    600 in D8
    1500 in D9
    200 in D10
    14750 in D11
    875 in D12
    23500 in D16
    4000 in D17

14. The values you entered do not have dollar signs or the appropriate commas (i.e., a currency format). You will now learn how to format a range of cells for a particular format (such as the currency format).

15. *Go to cell C7 and drag the mouse over to cell D20. Click with the mouse on* Format *from the menu bar, and then on* Cells. *From the* Number *tab, point and click on* Currency *and then on* OK. Notice that the cell format has now been changed. *Click on any cell to get rid of the cell range.*

16. *Go to cell B13, drag the mouse over to cell D13, and click with the mouse on the* Bold *icon on the toolbar.* This will make the **TOTAL EXPENSES** row appear in bold.

17. *Go to cell B18, drag the mouse over to cell D18, and click with the mouse on the* Bold *icon on the toolbar.* This will make the **TOTAL INCOME** row appear in bold.

18. *Go to cell B20, drag the mouse over to cell D20, and click with the mouse on the* Bold *icon on the toolbar.* This will make the **PROFIT/LOSS** row appear in bold.

19. Your spreadsheet is nearly complete; all you need to add are the six formulas.

20. *Go to cell C13.*

21. Type **=SUM**(and press **[UP ARROW]** six times until the cell pointer is at cell C7. Press the . (period) to anchor the range.

22. Press the **[DOWN ARROW]** five times, press the) (close parenthesis), and then the **[ENTER]** key.
23. Go back to cell C13 and look at the formula in the formula bar. The formula should read =SUM(C7: C12*). The total should read $18,950.* Note that you also could have typed the formula (=C7+C8+C9+C10+C11+12).
24. Enter the following formulas:

    =SUM(D7:D12) in D13
    =SUM(C16:C17) in C18
    =SUM(D16:D17) in D18

25. We now need to enter formulas for the **PROFIT/LOSS** columns. Enter the following formula:

    =C18-C13 in C20 (The total should read $8,050.)

26. *Go to cell C20 and point and click on the* AutoFill *command* (it is the small black square at the bottom right of the cell). *Drag it one column to the right and release the mouse button.* Notice that the formula has been copied. The total should be $8,675. Alternatively, you could have *gone to cell C20, pointed and clicked on* Edit *and* Copy *from the menu bar, moved your cursor to cell D20,* and pressed the **[ENTER]** key.
27. The spreadsheet is now complete.
28. To save the spreadsheet, *point and click on* File *and then* Save *from the menu bar and type* **Budget1.** *Click on* Save.
29. If you would like to print the spreadsheet, *point and click on the printer icon on the toolbar.*

This concludes Lesson 1.
To exit Excel, *click with your mouse on File from the menu bar and then point and click on Exit.*
To go to Lesson 2, stay at the current screen.

Lesson 2: Building a Budget Spreadsheet—Part 2

This lesson assumes that you have completed Lesson 1, have saved the spreadsheet in the lesson, and are generally familiar with the concepts covered in that lesson. Lesson 2 gives you more experience in copying formulas, formatting cells, and working with ranges of cells. It also shows you how to insert a row of data (see Figure 2—Excel Tutorial Expanded Budget Spreadsheet). If you did not exit Excel after Lesson 1, skip numbers 1 and 2 below and go directly to number 3.

1. Load Windows. Then, *double-click on the* Excel *icon on desktop* to load Excel for Windows. Alternatively, *click on the "Start" button, point with the mouse to "Programs" or "All Programs," and then click on the* Microsoft Excel *icon. Or click on the "Start" button, point with the mouse to "Programs" or "All Programs," point to* Microsoft Office, *then click on the* Microsoft Office Excel 2003 *icon.*

**Figure 2
Excel Tutorial
Expanded Budget
Spreadsheet**

Screen shot reprinted by
permission from Microsoft
Corporation.

	Item	BUDGET				
		Jan.	Jan.	Jan.	Percent	
		Budget	Actual	Difference	Of Budget	
	EXPENSES					
	Utilities	$1,000.00	$900.00	$100.00	90.00%	
	Equipment Rental	$500.00	$600.00	-$100.00	120.00%	
	Insurance	$500.00	$450.00	$50.00	90.00%	
	Rent	$1,500.00	$1,500.00	$0.00	100.00%	
	Marketing	$200.00	$200.00	$0.00	100.00%	
	Salaries	$15,000.00	$14,750.00	$250.00	98.33%	
	Office Supplies	$750.00	$875.00	-$125.00	116.67%	
	TOTAL EXPENSES	$19,450.00	$19,275.00	$175.00	99.10%	
	INCOME					
	Fees	$22,000.00	$23,500.00	$1,500.00	106.82%	
	Retainers	$5,000.00	$4,000.00	-$1,000.00	80.00%	
	TOTAL INCOME	$27,000.00	$27,500.00	$500.00	101.85%	
	PROFIT/LOSS	$7,550.00	$8,225.00	$675.00	108.94%	

2. To retrieve the spreadsheet in Lesson 1, *point and click on* File *from the menu bar and then on* Open. *Then point and click on your file and click on* Open.

3. You will be entering the information shown in Figure 2—Excel Tutorial Expanded Budget Spreadsheet.

4. Notice in Figure 2—Excel Tutorial Expanded Budget Spreadsheet that a line for insurance appears in row B9. You will insert this row first.

5. *Go to cell B9, right-click on the mouse* (for right-handed mouse users), *point and click on* Insert *and* Entire Row, *and then click on* OK. A new row has been added. You could also have *clicked on* Insert *front the menu bar and then on* Row.

6. Enter the following:

   Insurance in B9
   500 in C9
   450 in D9

7. Notice that when the new values for insurance were entered, all of the formulas were updated. Since you inserted the additional rows in the middle of the column, the formulas recognized the new numbers and automatically recalculated to reflect them. Be extremely careful when inserting new rows and columns into spreadsheets that have existing formulas. In some cases, the new number will not be reflected in the totals, such as when

rows or columns are inserted at the beginning of the range that a formula calculates. It is always prudent to go back to each existing formula, examine the formula range, and make sure the new values are included in the formula range.

8. Change the column width in Column E to 12 by *pointing and clicking on the column letter E,* at the top of the screen. *Move your cursor to the right edge of the column.* Your cursor should then change to a double-headed vertical arrow. *Drag the mouse to the right until the column width is 12.* Alternatively, change the cell width by *placing the cell pointer anywhere in column E, pointing and clicking on* Format *and* Column *from the menu bar and then* Width, *and typing* **12.** *Click on* OK.

9. Enter the following:

   Jan. in E4
   Difference in E5
   Percent in F4
   Of Budget in F5

10. *Go to cell E4 and drag the mouse over to cell F5* (so that the additional column headings are highlighted). *Click with the mouse on the* Center *icon and then the* Bold *icon on the toolbar.*

11. *Go to cell E14 and drag the mouse over to cell F14. Then click with the mouse on the* Bold *icon on the toolbar.*

12. *Go to cell E19 and drag the mouse over to cell F19. Then click with the mouse on the* Bold *icon on the toolbar.*

13. *Go to cell E21 and drag the mouse over to cell F21. Then click with the mouse on the* Bold *icon on the toolbar.*

14. You are now ready to change the cell formatting for column E to currency and column F to percent. *Go to cell E7 and drag the mouse down to cell E21. Click with the mouse on* Format *from the menu bar and then on* Cells. *From the* Number *tab, point and click on* Currency *and then on* OK. *Click on any cell to get rid of the cell range.*

15. *Go to cell F7 and drag the mouse down to cell F21. Click with the mouse on* Format *from the menu bar and then on* Cells. *From the* Number *tab, point and click on* Percentage *and then on* OK. *Click on any cell to get rid of the cell range.*

16. All that is left to do is to enter the formulas for the two new columns. The entries in the **Jan. Difference** column subtract the budgeted amount from the actual amount for each expense item. A positive amount in this column means that the office was under budget on that item. A negative balance means that the office was over budget on that line item. The **Percent of Budget** column divides that actual amount by the budgeted amount. This shows the percentage of the budgeted money that was actually spent for each item.

17. You will first build one formula in the **Jan. Difference** column and then copy it. Go to cell E7, enter **=C7-D7,** and press the **[ENTER]** key.

18. Using the **AutoFill** command or the **Copy** command, copy this formula down through cell E14.

19. Go to cell E17, enter **=D17-C17**, and press the **[ENTER]** key.
20. Using the **AutoFill** command, copy this formula down through cell E21. Delete the formula in cell E20 *by clicking on cell E20* and pressing the **[DELETE]** key.
21. You will now build on the formula in the **Percent of Budget** column and copy it. Go to cell F7, enter **=D7/C7**, and press the **[ENTER]** key.
22. Using the **AutoFill** command, copy this formula down through cell F21. Delete the formula in cells F15, F16, and F20 by *clicking on the cell* and then pressing the **[DELETE]** key.
23. The spreadsheet has now been built. We will now build a bar chart that shows our budgeted expenses compared to our actual expenses.
24. *Click with the mouse on cell B7 and then drag the mouse down and over to cell D14.*
25. *Click on the* Chart Wizard *icon on the toolbar* (it looks like a multicolored column chart/vertical bar chart). Alternatively, you could *select* Insert *from the menu bar and then* Chart. The **Chart Wizard—Step 1 of 4—Chart Type** window is displayed. This is where you select the type of chart you want.
26. *Click on* Bar *from the Chart Type list.*
27. *Click on Next.* The **Chart Wizard—Step 2 of 4—Chart Source Data** window is now displayed. This is where you define where the data range will come from for the chart. The data range is correct.
28. *Click on the* Series *tab in the* Chart Wizard—Step 2 of 4—Chart Source Data *window.*
29. Under **Series,** Series 1 is highlighted in blue. *Click in the white box next to* Name *and type* Budget.
30. Then, under **Series** click on Series 2. *Click in the white box next to* Name *and type* Actual.
31. Then, *click on* Next. The **Chart Wizard—Step 3 of 4—Chart Options** window is now displayed.
32. The **Titles** tab should be displayed. In the **Chart Title** box type **January Expenses—Actual v. Budget.** In the **Category (X)** axis: type **Expense Item.** In the **Category (Y)** axis type **Dollars.** The default values for the other tabs are fine, so *click on* Next.
33. The **Chart Wizard—Step 4 of 4—Chart Location** window should now be displayed. The **As** object in Sheet 1 option should be selected. *Click on* Finish.
34. The chart is now superimposed over the top of your spreadsheet.
35. *Click in the lower left portion in the chart (in a white space) and then drag the chart over to column H*—so the upper left portion of the chart starts at cell H2.
36. *Now, click on the box in the lower-right corner of the chart* (the cursor will turn to a double-headed arrow and will say Chart Area). *Drag the box down and to the right* (see Figure 3—Excel Tutorial Bar Chart)—this will expand the chart proportionately and make it larger. Stop expanding the chart when you get it over to the O column and down to the 21 row. You may have to use the scroll bars to get to the lower-right corner of the chart.

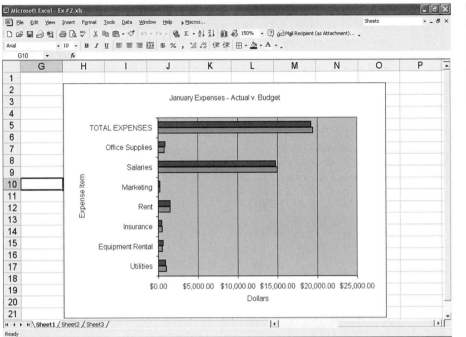

Figure 3
Excel Tutorial
Bar Chart

Screen shot reprinted by permission from Microsoft Corporation.

37. *Right-click anywhere in the lower-left portion of the chart (in a white space). Then, select* Format Chart Area. *Click on 8 under* Font Size. *Then, click on* OK.

38. *Click on the chart and then click on the* Printer *icon on the toolbar to print the chart.*

39. To print the spreadsheet *click out of the chart and onto one of the cells in the spreadsheet.* Press **[CTRL]-[HOME]** to go to cell A1.

40. *Click on cell B3 and then drag the mouse to cell F21.*

41. *Click on* File, Print *and under* Print What, *click on* Selection. This will print only the portion of the spreadsheet that is highlighted.

42. You will next print the spreadsheet and the chart on one page. *Click on cell B3 and then drag the mouse until both the spreadsheet and the chart are highlighted* (roughly cell B3 to cell O21).

43. *Click on* File *and then on* Page Setup. *On the* Page *tab click on* Fit to (it should default to one page). *Then, click on* OK. This will compress everything in the print area to one page.

44. *Click on* File, Print *and under* Print What, *click on* Selection.

45. To save the document *click on* File *from the menu bar, and then click on* Save As. Then, type **Budget 2** next to File Name. *Select* Save *to save the letter to the default directory.* To save the letter to a floppy disk, *click on the down arrow icon next to* Save In, *select drive A, and then click on* Save.

46. *Click on* File *on the menu bar and then on* Close to close the document, or *click on File from the Menu Bar, and then click on Exit* to exit Excel.

This concludes Lesson 2.

Lesson 3: Building a Complex Budget Spreadsheet

This lesson shows you how to build the spreadsheet in Figures 4 and 5—Excel Tutorial More Complex Budget. This is the same spreadsheet as in Figure 6-5 earlier in the chapter. Keep in mind that if at any time you make a mistake in this lesson, you can simply press **[CTRL]-[Z]** to undo what you have done.

1. Load Windows. Then, *double-click on the* Excel *icon on the desktop* to load Excel for Windows. Alternatively, *click on the "Start" button, point with the mouse to "Programs" or "All Programs," and then click on the* Microsoft Excel *icon. Or click on the "Start" button, point with the mouse to "Programs" or "All Programs," point to* Microsoft Office, *then click on the* Microsoft Office Excel 2003 *icon.*
2. A blank workbook should be open. If you are not in a blank workbook, *click on "File" on the menu bar, click on "New," and then click or double-click (depending on the Excel version you are using) on "Blank workbook."*

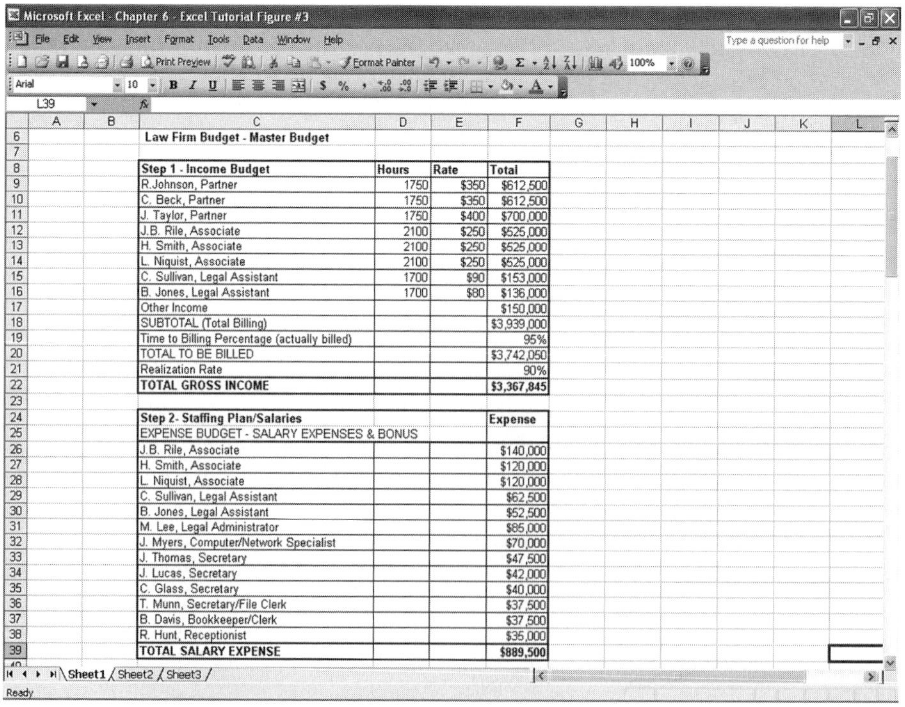

	C	D	E	F
6	**Law Firm Budget - Master Budget**			
7				
8	**Step 1 - Income Budget**	**Hours**	**Rate**	**Total**
9	R.Johnson, Partner	1750	$350	$612,500
10	C. Beck, Partner	1750	$350	$612,500
11	J. Taylor, Partner	1750	$400	$700,000
12	J.B. Rile, Associate	2100	$250	$525,000
13	H. Smith, Associate	2100	$250	$525,000
14	L. Niquist, Associate	2100	$250	$525,000
15	C. Sullivan, Legal Assistant	1700	$90	$153,000
16	B. Jones, Legal Assistant	1700	$80	$136,000
17	Other Income			$150,000
18	SUBTOTAL (Total Billing)			$3,939,000
19	Time to Billing Percentage (actually billed)			95%
20	TOTAL TO BE BILLED			$3,742,050
21	Realization Rate			90%
22	**TOTAL GROSS INCOME**			**$3,367,845**
23				
24	**Step 2- Staffing Plan/Salaries**			**Expense**
25	EXPENSE BUDGET - SALARY EXPENSES & BONUS			
26	J.B. Rile, Associate			$140,000
27	H. Smith, Associate			$120,000
28	L. Niquist, Associate			$120,000
29	C. Sullivan, Legal Assistant			$62,500
30	B. Jones, Legal Assistant			$52,500
31	M. Lee, Legal Administrator			$85,000
32	J. Myers, Computer/Network Specialist			$70,000
33	J. Thomas, Secretary			$47,500
34	J. Lucas, Secretary			$42,000
35	C. Glass, Secretary			$40,000
36	T. Munn, Secretary/File Clerk			$37,500
37	B. Davis, Bookkeeper/Clerk			$37,500
38	R. Hunt, Receptionist			$35,000
39	**TOTAL SALARY EXPENSE**			**$889,500**

Figure 4
Excel Tutorial More Complex Budget Part 1

**Figure 5
Excel Tutorial More
Complex Budget
Part 2**

	A	B	C	D	E	F	G	H	I	J	K	L
38			R. Hunt, Receptionist			$35,000						
39			**TOTAL SALARY EXPENSE**			**$889,500**						
40												
41			**Step 3 - Other Expenses**			**Expense**						
42			Accounting Professional Services			$10,000						
43			Amoritzation of Leavehold Improvements			$7,500						
44			Association/Membership Dues			$7,500						
45			Client Billings Write-offs			$75,000						
46			Continuing Legal Education			$15,000						
47			Copying Costs (not billed to clients)			$45,000						
48			Depreciation			$50,000						
49			Employee Benefits and Taxes			$225,000						
50			Entertainment			$20,000						
51			Equipment purchase/computers/network			$65,000						
52			Equipment Rental			$8,500						
53			Forms, Stationary, Paper			$7,500						
54			Insurance (P/C, Malpractice, etc.)			$125,000						
55			Housekeeping/Cleaning Services			$7,500						
56			Marketing			$30,000						
57			Office Supplies			$25,000						
58			Other taxes			$10,000						
59			Postage			$14,000						
60			Reference materials/library/WESTLAW			$40,000						
61			Rent Expense			$200,000						
62			Repairs/Maintenance			$35,000						
63			Telephone/Internet/Communication/Mobile			$50,000						
64			Travel (not billed)			$45,000						
65			Utilities			$100,000						
66			**TOTAL OTHER EXPENSES**			**$1,237,500**						
67			**TOTAL ALL EXPENSES**			**$2,127,000**						
68												
69			**Step 4 - Determine Acceptable Profit Goal**									
70												
71			**NET INCOME TO BE DISTRIBUTED TO PARTNERS**			$1,240,845						

3. Enter the data in Figure 4—Excel Tutorial More Complex Budget from cells C6 through E39 and use the same formatting as in the figure. Below is some additional clarification about making these entries.

   — The width of column C will need to be changed to approximately 38 if you use 10-point type.

4. The following formula should be entered:

   =D9*E9 in cell F9

   Use the AutoFill *command or the* Copy *command to copy the formula from F9 to cells F10 through F16.*

5. Enter: **150000** in cell F17.
6. Add cells F9 through F17 in cell F18 (e.g., =SUM(F9:F17).
7. Enter: **.95** in cell F19 and change the cell format to percent by *pointing and clicking on the* Percent *style on the toolbar (it looks like a percent sign).*
8. Enter: **.90** in cell F21 and change the cell format to percent.
9. The following formula should be entered:

   =F19*F18 in cell F20
   =F21*F20 in cell F22

10. Enter the values in cells F26 to F38.

11. Add cells F26 to F38 in cell F39.
12. Add any formatting changes that you have not made yet. Your spreadsheet should generally look like the spreadsheet in Figure 4—Excel Tutorial More Complex Budget.
13. Look at Figure 5—Excel Tutorial More Complex Budget and enter the text and values in cells C41 through F65.
14. Enter the text in cells C66 to C71.
15. The following formulas should be entered:

    =SUM(F42:F65) in cell F66
    =F66+F39 in cell F67
    =F22-F67 in cell F71

16. Add any formatting changes that you have not made yet. The second part of your spreadsheet should generally look like the spreadsheet in Figure 5—Excel Tutorial More Complex Budget.
17. You will next print out your spreadsheet on one page. *Point and click on "File" on the menu bar and then on "Page Setup." On the "Page" tab, click on "Fit to"* (it should default to one page). *Then, click on "OK."* This will compress everything in the print area to one page.
18. *Using the mouse, point and click on cell C6. Drag the mouse to cell F71. Point and click with the mouse on "File" on the menu bar, click on "Print," point and click on "Selection" under "Print What," and then point and click on "OK."*
19. To save the document *point and click on "File" from the menu bar, and then click on "Save As."* Then, type **Complex Budget Spreadsheet** next to "File Name." *Select "Save" to save the letter to the default directory.*
20. *Click on "File" on the menu bar and then on "Close"* to close the document; to exit Excel, *click on "File" from the Menu Bar, and then click on "Exit."*

This concludes Lesson 3.

Lesson 4: Client Trust Account—Checkbook Register

This lesson assumes that you have completed the previous three lessons and have a basic understanding of Excel. In this advanced lesson, you will learn how to build the spreadsheet in Figure 6—Excel Tutorial Client Trust Account. After you have built the spreadsheet template, you will decide what information is entered into the spreadsheet based on facts that are given to you. Keep in mind that if at any time you make a mistake in this lesson, you can simply press [**CTRL**]-[**Z**] to undo what you have done.

1. Load Windows. Then, *double-click on the* Excel *icon on the desktop* to load Excel for Windows. Alternatively, *click on the "Start" button, point with the mouse to "Programs" or "All Programs," and then click on the* Microsoft Excel *icon. Or click on the "Start" button, point with the mouse*

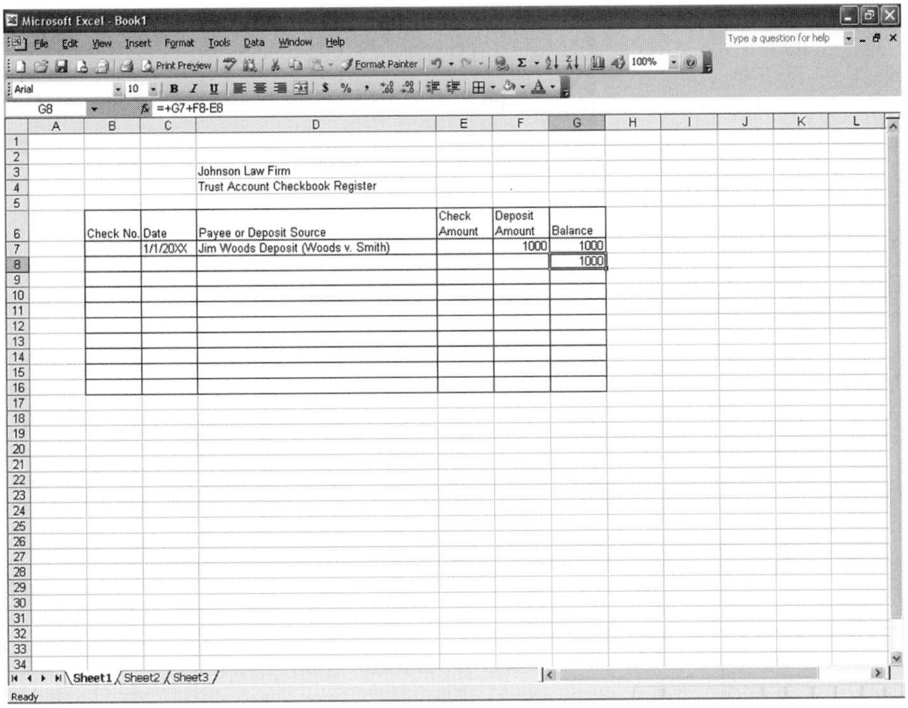

Figure 6
Excel Tutorial Client
Trust Account
Part 1

to *"Programs" or "All Programs," point to* Microsoft Office, *then click on the* Microsoft Office Excel 2003 *icon.*

2. A blank workbook should be open. If you are not in a blank workbook, *click on "File" on the menu bar, click on "New," and then click or double-click (depending on the Excel version you are using) on "Blank workbook."*

3. To start building the spreadsheet in Figure 6—Excel Tutorial Client Trust Account, increase the width of Column D to 38 characters ("Format," "Column," "Width").

4. *Point and click with the mouse on cell C7 and drag the mouse to cell C90.* Since this is a date column, you need to change the format of the column to hold a date. With cells C7 through C90 still highlighted, *point and click with the mouse on "Format" on the menu bar, then on "Cells," click on "Date" under the "Number" tab, and then click on "OK."*

5. Change the format for cells E7 to G90 to currency by selecting the area (dragging the mouse over the area) and then *point and click with the mouse on "Format" on the menu bar, then on "Cells," click on "Currency" under the "Number" tab, change the "Decimal places" to 0, and then click on "OK."*

6. Looking at Figure 6—Excel Tutorial Client Trust Account, enter the data in Columns B, C, and D.

7. Enter the column headings in E6, F6, and G6. You will need to wrap the text down in cells E6 and B6 ("Format," "Cells," "Alignment," "Wrap to Text").

8. Enter the value: **1000** in cell F7.

9. The following formula should be entered:

   =F7-E7 in cell G7

   =G7+F8-E8 in cell G8

   -Use the AutoFill *command or the* Copy *command to copy the formula from cell G8 to cell G16.*

10. You have now built the template of the spreadsheet and you are ready to enter information into it. Using the spreadsheet, enter information into the Checkbook Register (see below). For each entry, you will need to input the check number (if it is a check), who is the payee or deposit source, the case name and what it is for (e.g., Clerk of the Court (Woods v. Smith) File Fee), and place the amount in either the check amount or deposit amount column. The spreadsheet will automatically calculate the balance in the checking account.

11. The Johnson Law Firm opened the trust account on January 1 with a balance of zero in the account. Please record the following transactions in the spreadsheet:

    a. January 1, deposit for $1,000 from Jim Woods regarding Woods v. Smith.

    b. January 4, check number 1001 in the amount of $50 to Clerk of the Court in Woods v. Smith for a filing fee.

    c. January 5, check number 1002 in the amount of $250 to AAA Process Serving in Woods v. Smith for serving process.

    d. January 8, deposit for $1,000 from Metro National for incorporation work.

    e. January 10, check number 1003 in the amount of $200 to the Secretary of State for the incorporation fee in the Metro National matter.

    f. January 14, check number 1004 in the amount of $500 to Johnson Law Firm for attorneys' fees incurred in Metro National incorporation matter.

    g. January 18, check number 1005 in the amount of $700 to Dr. Jones in Woods v. Smith for an expert witness fee.

    h. January 20, deposit from Jim Woods (Woods v. Smith) of $1,000.

    i. January 23, check number 1006 in the amount of $100 to Copy Center, regarding copying charges for Metro National incorporation.

    j. January 27, check number 1007 in the amount of $500 to Johnson Law Firm for attorneys' fees incurred in Woods v. Smith.

12. After entering all of the transactions, the balance in the trust account should be $700.

13. If you would like to add borders around each cell, highlight the area by dragging the mouse, **point and click on the "Borders" icon on the toolbar, and click on "All Borders."**

14. You will next print out your spreadsheet on one page. *Point and click on "File" on the menu bar and then on "Page Setup." On the "Page" tab, click on "Fit to"* (it should default to one page). *Then, click on "OK."* This will compress everything in the print area to one page.

15. *Using the mouse, point and click on cell C3. Drag the mouse to cell G16. Point and click with the mouse on "File" on the menu bar, click on "Print," point and click on "Selection" under "Print What," and then point and click on "OK."*

16. To save the document *point and click on "File" from the menu bar, and then click on "Save As."* Then type **Trust Account Spreadsheet** next to "File Name." *Select "Save" to save the letter to the default directory.*

17. *Click on "File" on the menu bar and then on "Close"* to close the document. To exit Excel, *click on "File" from the menu bar, and then click on "Exit."*

This concludes Lesson 4.

Lesson 5: Client Trust Account—Client Registers

This lesson assumes that you have completed Lesson 4 and have a basic understanding of Excel. In this advanced lesson, you will learn how to build the spreadsheet in Figure 7—Excel Tutorial Client Trust Account. You will be building subsidiary ledgers for each client (see Figure 6-2 earlier in the chapter). After you have built the spreadsheet template, you will copy information from Lesson 4 into them. Keep in mind that if at any time you make a mistake in this lesson, you can simply press [**CTRL**]-[**Z**] to undo what you have done.

1. Load Windows. Then, *double-click on the* Excel *icon on the desktop to* load Excel for Windows. Alternatively, *click on the "Start" button, point with the mouse to "Programs" or "All Programs," and then click on* the Microsoft Excel *icon. Or click on the "Start" button, point with the mouse to "Programs" or "All Programs," point to* Microsoft Office, *then click on the* Microsoft Office Excel 2003 *icon.*

2. To open the previously saved "Trust Account Spreadsheet" (from Lesson 4), *point and click on "File" from the menu bar, and then click on "Open." Point and click on* **Trust Account Spreadsheet** *next to "File Name" and then point and click on* Open.

3. Look at Figure 7—Excel Tutorial Client Trust Account and enter the data in rows 19, 20, 29, and 30. Use the "Wrap Text" feature for cells E20, F20, E30, and F30.

4. Draw the borders for the subsidiary ledgers for Jim Woods and Metro National.

5. The following formulas should be entered:

   =**F21-E21** in cell G21
   =**G21+F22-E22** in cell G22

Figure 7
Excel Tutorial
Client Trust Account
Part 2

Microsoft Excel - Chapter 6 - Excel Tutorial Figure #5

	Check No.	Date	Payee or Deposit Source	Check Amount	Deposit Amount	Balance
			Trust Account Checkbook Register			
7		1/1/20XX	Jim Woods Deposit (Woods v. Smith)		$1,000	$1,000
8						$1,000
9						$1,000
10						$1,000
11						$1,000
12						$1,000
13						$1,000
14						$1,000
15						$1,000
16						$1,000

Jim Woods (Woods v. Smith), Subsidiary Ledger

	Check No.	Date	Description of Transaction	Funds Paid	Funds Received	Balance
21		1/1/20XX	Jim Woods Deposit (Woods v. Smith)		$1,000	$1,000
22						$1,000
23						$1,000
24						$1,000
25						$1,000
26						$1,000

Metro National Incorporation Work, Subsidiary Ledger

	Check No.	Date	Description of Transaction	Funds Paid	Funds Received	Balance
31						$0
32						$0
33						$0
34						$0

Sheet1 / Sheet2 / Sheet3

Use the AutoFill *command or the* Copy *command to copy the formula in cell G22 to cells G23 through G26.*
=F31-E31 *in cell G31*
=G31+F32-E32 *in cell G32*
Use the AutoFill *command or the* Copy *command to copy the formula from cell G22 to cells G33 and G34.*

6. With the subsidiary ledgers now built, you are ready to enter the data that applies to each client in his or her respective ledger. (You will not even have to retype the data!)

7. *Point and click on cell C21. Then, type* = (an equals sign), *point and click on cell C7, and press the* [ENTER] *key.* Notice that the contents of C7 now appear in cell C21.

8. *Point and click on cell D21. Then, type* = (an equals sign), *point and click on cell D7, and press the* [ENTER] *key.* Notice that the contents of D7 now appear in cell D21.

9. *Point and click on cell F21. Then, type* = (an equals sign), *point and click on cell F7, and press the* [ENTER] *key.* Notice that the contents of F7 now appear in cell F21.

10. Using this method, copy all of the transitions from the Trust Account—Checkbook Register down to the appropriate subsidiary ledger for each client. When you are finished, the balance of the Jim Woods ledger should be $500 and the balance for Metro National should be $200.

11. Print out the Trust Account Checkbook Register and both subsidiary ledgers on one page.

12. To save the document, *point and click on "File" from the menu bar, and then click on "Save."*

13. *Click on "File" on the menu bar and then on "Close"* to close the document. To exit Excel, *click on "File" from the menu bar, and then click on "Exit."*

This concludes Lesson 5.

Lesson 6: Client Trust Account—Client Summary Ledger

This lesson assumes that you have completed Lessons 4 and 5 and have a basic understanding of Excel. In this advanced lesson, you will learn how to build the spreadsheet (Client Summary Ledger) in Figure 8—Excel Tutorial. You will be putting the balance of the client subsidiary ledgers into a client summary ledger report (see Figure 6-2 earlier in the chapter). Keep in mind that if at any time you make a mistake in this lesson, you can simply press [**CTRL**]-[**Z**] to undo what you have done.

						$1,000	
						$1,000	
						$1,000	
						$1,000	

Jim Woods (Woods v. Smith), Subsidiary Ledger

Check No.	Date	Description of Transaction	Funds Paid	Funds Received	Balance
	1/1/20XX	Jim Woods Deposit (Woods v. Smith)		$1,000	$1,000
					$1,000
					$1,000
					$1,000
					$1,000
					$1,000

Metro National Incorporation Work, Subsidiary Ledger

Check No.	Date	Description of Transaction	Funds Paid	Funds Received	Balance
					$0
					$0
					$0
					$0

Johnson Law Firm - Trust Account Client Summary Ledger Page
Balance as of 1/31

Client	Balance as of 1/31
Woods v. Smith	$500
Metro National Incorporate	$200
TOTAL BALANCE IN TRUST ACCOUNT	**$700**

For additional resources, visit our Web site at www.westlegalstudies.com

Calendaring, Docket Control, and Case Management

After you read this chapter, you should be able to:

- Explain how to make docketing entries.
- Discuss how to calculate court deadlines.
- Explain why a poor docket system is harmful to a law office.
- Differentiate between manual and computerized docket systems.
- Explain how a poor docket control system leads to ethical and malpractice claims.

A client sued his former attorney (and the attorney's partners) for legal malpractice for failing to timely file a medical malpractice claim. In October the client met with a Michigan attorney regarding a claim against a hospital for medical malpractice. After the initial meetings, the client made repeated telephone calls and sent letters to the attorney. However, the attorney never responded to the client's communications. Eighteen months later, the attorney finally responded. The client received a letter from the attorney.

My sincere apologies for the delay in responding to your earlier communications; however, we have been making a thorough inquiry into the facts of your alleged complaints. We have not been able to find an expert to make the appropriate causal relationship to support our theories of possible malpractice. Accordingly, we are not going to be proceeding on your claim and will close our file.

Within two weeks, the client sought the advice of another attorney and filed a legal malpractice claim against the first attorney. A jury awarded the client $150,000 in damages against the attorney for allowing the statute of limitations on the medical malpractice claim to lapse.[1]

CALENDARING, DOCKET CONTROL, AND CASE MANAGEMENT DEFINITIONS

The practice of law is filled with appointments, deadlines, hearings, and other commitments for every case that is handled; considering that a single legal professional can have a caseload between 20 and 100 cases at any one time, just staying organized and on top of what needs to get done is a big job. It is extremely important that these dates be carefully tracked for ethical, customer service, and general business reasons. Most, but not all, legal organizations track these deadlines by computer. This chapter introduces calendaring, docket control, and case management. These terms are somewhat confusing and are often used interchangeably.

calendaring
A generic term used to describe the function of recording appointments for any type of business.

Calendaring is typically a generic term used to describe the recording of appointments for any type of business. For example, an accounting or engineering firm might use a generic calendaring or scheduling form that comes with an office suite of software programs to track appointments.

docket control
A law-office-specific term that refers to entering, organizing, and controlling all the appointments, deadlines, and due dates for a legal organization.

Docket control is typically a law-office-specific term that refers to entering, organizing, and controlling all the appointments, deadlines, and due dates for a legal organization. There are many legal-specific software programs and manual systems that perform docket control functions for law offices, corporate law departments, and government law departments.

Case management is also a legal-specific term, but it always means more than just tracking appointments and schedules. The breadth of features in current case management programs seems to grow every day. Some of the features found in case management programs include docket control (scheduling/appointments), things to do, contact information database (name, address, e-mail, phone, fax, etc.) by case (parties, cocounsel, opposing counsel, judges, etc.), case notes, document assembly, document tracking/management, integrated billing, e-mail, and more. All information is centered around and tied to cases in case management programs. This is very helpful for legal organizations that view and organize most of their data according to the case to which it is tied. This is a different approach than general calendaring/personal information managers or docket control.

As the legal software market has matured, more and more manufacturers have entered the market. In addition, nearly all of the current legal products available in this market have gotten significantly more sophisticated at meeting the needs of attorneys, legal assistants, and legal organizations.

A final term sometimes used to describe docket control is *tickler,* because it "tickles" the memory for upcoming events.

> *As a paralegal, how can you accommodate each client individually, while still effectively handling the many demands competing for your time? How can you better organize your work to prevent rush jobs? How can you promptly take care of the little things to keep a case or file moving forward—and still keep the client and yourself content? One of the best ways to achieve your goals is to invest your time and energy in a tickler [docket control] system.[2]*

In many law offices, legal assistants operate the docket control system for the whole office, while in others, legal assistants only use the system to manage and track cases. Although the calendaring and docketing subject may seem trivial at first, the examples of dire consequences resulting from docketing system failures at the beginning of this chapter should indicate the grave nature and importance of this subject. Thus, it is critical for the legal assistant to know how to use docket control so that important deadlines are tracked and kept.

APPOINTMENTS

A legal professional will have many appointments during the course of a case or legal matter: meetings with clients and cocounsel, witness interviews, interoffice meetings, and so forth. Keeping appointments is very important. Law offices that must constantly reschedule appointments with clients may find their clients going to other attorneys who provide better service. The concept of rescheduling appointments or legal deadlines is often called getting a **continuance** (e.g., the deposition was continued because the witness was sick).

case management
A legal term that usually refers to functions such as docket control, things to do, contact information by case, case notes, document assembly, document tracking by case, integrated billing, and e-mail.

continuance
Rescheduling an appointment or court date.

DEADLINES AND REMINDERS

The practice of law is filled with deadlines at practically every stage of a legal matter. One of the most important types of deadlines is a statute of limitations. A **statute of limitations** is a statute or law that sets a limit on the length of time a party has to file a suit. For instance, some states impose a five-year statute of limitations on lawsuits alleging a breach of a written contract. That is, if a lawsuit is brought or filed more than five years after a contract is breached or broken, the lawsuit is barred by the statute, and a court will dismiss the action. The purpose of a statute of limitations is to force parties to bring lawsuits in a timely fashion so that evidence is not destroyed, before witnesses leave the area, and so forth. If an attorney allows a statute of limitations to run or expire without filing a case, he or she may be liable for legal malpractice.

There also are many deadlines that are set after a case has been filed. In some courts, the judge and the attorneys on both sides sit down and schedule a list of deadlines that the case must follow. The schedule may look something like the one shown in Figure 7-1. These deadlines must be adhered to and tracked; an attorney who does not adhere to the deadlines may be penalized or cause the case to be dismissed. Some courts are very reluctant to continue deadlines once they have been set.

Because attorneys and legal assistants are busy, usually working on many cases, the law office must have a system of tracking upcoming deadlines. This is done not only by calendaring the deadline itself but also by creating reminder notices in the calendar so that a deadline does not catch a person by surprise. These reminders are called warnings. For example, regarding the January 30 motion to dismiss in Figure 7-1, the attorney or legal assistant may want to be reminded 30, 15, and 5 days before the deadline. Therefore, reminder notices would be made on January 1, January 15, and January 25, in addition to the deadline itself being recorded on January 30. It is common for an attorney or legal assistant to request from one to four reminders for each deadline. If reminders are not entered in the docket system,

statute of limitations
A statute or law that sets a limit on the length of time a party has to file a suit. If a case is filed after the statute of limitations, the claim is barred and is dismissed as a matter of law.

Figure 7-1
A Typical Case Schedule

Deadline Item	Deadline Date
All Motions to Dismiss must be filed by:	Jan. 30
Responses to Motions to Dismiss must be filed by:	Mar. 1
Discovery (depositions, interrogatories, request for production) to be completed by:	Dec. 20
Summary Judgment Motions to be filed by:	Feb. 1
Responses to Summary Judgment Motions to be filed by:	Mar. 1
Pretrial order to be filed by:	June 1
Settlement Conferences to be completed by:	June 30
Pretrial Motions to be completed and decided by:	July 15
Trial to start no later than:	Sept. 1

it may make it hard to meet the deadline. Thus, logging reminder notices of upcoming events is crucial to the effective practice of law.

Some deadlines are automatically set by the rules of procedure that are in effect in any given court. Rules of procedure are court rules that govern and tell parties what procedures they must follow when bringing and litigating cases. For instance, in some courts, the rules of procedure hold that after a final decision in a case has been rendered, all parties have 30 days to file an appeal.

For a law office that practices in the tax area, April 15, the date that federal income tax returns are due, is an example of an automatic or procedural deadline that must be tracked. Thus, this automatic or procedural deadline must be tracked by the office's docket system, and appropriate reminders must be made so that returns are not filed late and penalties assessed.

Docket control is not just a "secretarial" function. The importance of working closely with the secretarial staff in calendaring and docketing matters cannot be stressed enough. In litigation firms, one of the legal assistant's primary responsibilities is tracking deadlines relating to timeliness of pleadings, discovery requests, interrogatories and answers, mediation statements, pretrial requirements, timely notification, and service regarding discovery and trial subpoenas. All deadlines, dates, and appointments should be maintained on one central calendar (preferably computerized) for each attorney. This calendar should be accessible by the attorney, the secretary, and the legal assistant. All three should be cognizant of all deadlines, depositions, appointments, meetings, and hearings. All three should review upcoming deadlines and docket (tickler) notes on a daily basis.

—Lenette Pinchback, CLA

HEARINGS AND COURT DATES

Hearings and court dates are formal proceedings before a court. It is extremely important that these dates be carefully tracked. Most courts have little tolerance for attorneys who fail to show up for court. In some instances, the attorney can be fined or disciplined for missing court dates.

In larger cases, especially when the case is being litigated in court, there may be hundreds of entries in the docket system. Figure 7-2 includes a list of common docket entries, including both substantive and law office management-related entries.

**Figure 7-2
Common Docket
Control Entries**

- Expiration dates for statutes of limitations
- Judgment renewal dates
- Employee-benefit annual filings
- Renewal dates for copyrights, trademarks, and patents
- Renewal dates for leases and licenses
- Renewal dates for insurance coverage
- Trial court appearance dates
- Due dates for trial court briefs
- Due dates on various pleadings: answers; depositions; replies to interrogatories and requests for admissions; various motions and notices, etc.
- Due dates in probate proceedings, such as inventory and appraisal dates
- Appearances in bankruptcy proceedings
- Action dates in commercial law matters
- Due dates in corporate or security matters
- Closing dates for real estate transactions
- Due dates for appellate briefs and arguments
- Tax return due dates
- Due dates in estate matters, such as tax return dates, valuation dates, and hearing dates
- Dates of stockholder meetings
- Dates of board of directors meetings
- Review dates for wills
- Review dates for buy and sell valuations of business interests
- Review dates for trusts
- Renewal dates for leases on offices
- Renewal dates for attorney licenses
- Expiration dates on notary certificates
- Renewal dates for malpractice and other insurance
- Personal property tax return dates
- Dates for partner (and other recurring and nonrecurring) meetings
- Review dates for billings and accounts receivable
- Review dates for work-in-process
- Review dates for evaluation of associates and staff
- Review dates for raises and bonuses
- Due dates for quarterly payroll withholding reports

RECEIVING DOCUMENTS, FOLLOWING COURT RULES, AND CALCULATING DEADLINES

Receiving documents that need to be calendared, calculating deadlines, and following the local court rules are important aspects of docket control.

Receiving Documents

When documents arrive in the mail, e-mail, or otherwise, response dates and other deadlines should be immediately and systematically entered into the law office's docket system. This includes pleadings, motions, discovery documents, and other documents that require responses within a certain time period.

Suppose that your office received interrogatories (written questions that your client must complete and send back) in the mail for one of your clients. Also, suppose that in the particular court where the suit is filed, interrogatory responses must be answered within 30 calendar days of the date they are received. When the interrogatories are received by the mail department (or whoever opens the mail), the documents with calendar entries should be routed immediately to someone who has the responsibility to record the deadlines in the docket control system. If there is confusion as to whose responsibility it is to enter the calendar item, or confusion as to when the documents should be calendared (i.e., there is no systematic system), there is an excellent chance that the calendar dates will not be entered into the docket system. If that happens, it is virtually guaranteed that deadlines, response dates, and so forth will be missed and ethical problems will follow.

Know the Local Court Rules

It is imperative to know the local court rules for each court in which your office has cases. Even courts in the same state can have vastly different rules, depending on the internal operating procedures of each court.

Calculating Deadlines

Calculating deadlines depends on the local rules. However, the following are some of the different ways that deadlines can be calculated, and some problems that may arise in making calculations.

CALENDAR DAYS V. WORKDAYS Some courts make a distinction between calendar days and workdays. For example, if a court rule says that a party responding to a motion has 15 days from the file date to file a response, you need to know if the 15 days refers to all days (i.e., calendar days) or only to workdays.

When calculating deadlines, **calendar days** typically mean literal days, counting all days including weekends and holidays. For example, if a motion is filed on the 1st and you have 15 calendar days to respond, the response must be filed by the 16th. When you count days, you count from one day to the next; for example, the 1st to the 2nd is one day, the 2nd to the 3rd is two days, and so on. So, you actually start your count on the day *after* you receive the motion. When using the calendar-day method, a deadline may fall on a Saturday or Sunday; in many courts, the due date would simply be the Monday following the Saturday or Sunday. If the deadline falls on a holiday, the deadline is typically the next day the court is open for business.

When calculating deadlines, **workdays** typically refer to only those days when the court is open. Because courts usually are not open on holidays and weekends, these days are omitted from the calculation. For example, if a motion is filed on the 1st and you have 15 workdays to respond, and assuming the 1st is a Monday (with no holidays in between), the response would be due on the 22nd (see Figure 7-3).

calendar days
System for calculating deadlines that counts all days including weekends and holidays.

workdays
System for calculating deadlines that refers to only days when the court is open.

Figure 7-3   Calendar for Calculating Calendar Days and Workdays Example

Monday	Tuesday	Wednesday	Thursday	Friday	Saturday	Sunday
1 Motion filed	**2**	**3**	**4**	**5**	**6**	**7**
8	**9**	**10**	**11**	**12**	**13**	**14**
15	**16** Response Due if 15 Calendar Days	**17**	**18**	**19**	**20**	**21**
22 Response Due if 15 Work Days						

Sample Event:	Number of days:	Due Date:
Motion filed on 1st	15 Calendar Days	Tuesday, 16th
Motion filed on 1st	15 Work Days	Monday, 22nd

You need to know whether the court rules are figured on calendar days or workdays because there is a big difference between the two.

File Date v. Document Receipt Date

Court rules will typically state when deadlines are. Deadlines can be calculated either on the date the person actually receives the document or on the date when the document is stamped "FILED" at the clerk's office.

FILE DATE   A typical court rule may state, for a civil action, that a party has 30 days from when the judgment is "FILED" to file an appeal. Assume the court files a judgment on the 1st and that the party receives the judgment on the 3rd; the deadline is calculated from the file date, and if there were 30 days in the month, the appeal would have to be filed by the 1st of the next month.

DOCUMENT RECEIPT DATE Discovery document deadlines typically are calculated by receipt date. For example, a court rule may state that a party has 30 days to answer interrogatories. This is usually calculated from when the document is actually received by the law office needing to respond. So, if the document was mailed on the 1st and actually received on the 3rd, then the party has until the 4th of the next month to send responses to the opposing side. Thus, it can be very important for the law office to establish when a document was received. Law offices should routinely stamp all documents that come into the office with a received stamp that shows the date the document was received (e.g., "RECEIVED 10/1/2007").

In addition, when a party prepares a court document in a case there typically is a **"Certificate of Service"** at the very end of the document. The purpose of the "Certificate of Service" is to certify and establish when the document was placed in the mail. The "Certificate of Service" must also be signed. This way, the clerk of the court and the involved parties know when a document was placed in the mail.

A **"Bates stamp"** is sometimes used to number every page of a document. A "Bates stamp" stamps a document with a sequential number and then automatically advances to the next number. In this way, it is possible to establish the order of every page in a document, particularly large documents such as those that have been produced for evidence.

Certificate of Service
A statement at the end of a court document that certifies or establishes when a document was placed in the mail.

Bates stamp
Stamps a document with a sequential number and then automatically advances to the next number.

Due Date—File Date v. Mail Date

When reading court rules, it is important to know whether documents can be mailed in or if they must actually be "FILED" within the specified deadline. For example, assume you receive a document on the 1st and the court rule says you have 20 days to respond; the response would be due on the 21st. In some courts, it is acceptable to put the response in the mail on the 21st. That is, you do not actually have to get the document stamped "FILED" on the 21st. Some courts automatically give you three days' mail time before they say the document is late. Different courts have different rules; again, be sure you know if due dates are calculated on file dates or mail dates. This distinction becomes more important in rural areas.

ETHICAL AND MALPRACTICE CONSIDERATIONS

The ramifications of missing deadlines and otherwise failing to track the progress of cases can be severe. In fact, there are two types of negative outcomes that can result from case neglect: an ethical proceeding against the attorney and a legal malpractice claim filed against the attorney or firm. An attorney who neglects a case can be disciplined by a state ethics board. Such discipline in an ethics case may include reprimand, suspension, or even disbarment. In a legal malpractice case, the attorney involved is sued for damages for providing substandard legal work. These types of cases are not remote or obscure. There are thousands of legal ethics and malpractice proceedings filed throughout the country every year alleging case neglect.

Ethical Considerations

Studies of attorney disciplinary opinions have found that the number one and two reasons that clients file disciplinary proceedings and that courts discipline attorneys are (1) attorneys failing to communicate with their clients and (2) attorneys neglecting or not pursuing client cases diligently. Both of these problems are easily preventable when attorneys and legal assistants use good docket control systems and effective time management.

The ABA *Model Rules of Professional Conduct* gives direct guidance on these issues. The *Model Rules* states that attorneys should be competent in the area in which they are practicing and that they are reasonably prepared to represent the client. The *Model Rules* states that the attorney must act with reasonable diligence and promptness when representing a client, and, finally, that an attorney must keep the client reasonably informed about what is going on in the representation of the client. While these ethical rules have been discussed in previous chapters, it is important to include them again in the context of docket control because it is through docket control and organization that a legal professional complies with these rules. Each of these areas is explored in detail.

COMPETENCE AND ADEQUATE PREPARATION   The *Model Rules* holds that an attorney must be competent to represent the client; that is, he or she should reasonably know the area of law in which the client needs representation and, assuming the attorney does know the area of law, he or she should take the preparation time needed to become familiar with the case in order to represent the client adequately.

Model Rule 1.1 states that an attorney must provide competent representation to a client, including reasonable preparation necessary to perform the legal work. The purpose of this rule is to ensure that an attorney does not undertake a matter in which he or she is not competent and to ensure that the attorney has had adequate preparation. The amount of "adequate preparation" depends on what type of legal matter the client has. Major litigation, for example, will require far more preparation time than the amount of time it takes to prepare a will. Attorneys should not undertake to represent a client if, for some reason, they cannot do it with the skill and preparation time necessary. Legal professionals use docket control systems to plan adequate preparation time for cases.

> *At one point in time, because we were so busy—we were in the process of bringing on another person for clerical support—we missed a deadline for filing [a] response to requests for admissions. . . . We did file a motion to approve an extension of time in order to file [a response], and we were granted that . . . but had that not been the case, the admission would have been deemed admissible or admitted and that could have really hindered the defense of the case. That was a horror story I about had a nervous breakdown over. . . . You never want that. Your heart drops to the floor.*[3]

DILIGENCE *Model Rule* 1.3 requires that an attorney act with a reasonable degree of diligence and promptness in pursuing a client's case. Rule 1.3 specifically requires an attorney to act with commitment and dedication when representing a client and to avoid procrastination. Further insight is contained in the comment to the rule:

> A client's interests can be adversely affected by the passage of time or the change of conditions; in extreme instances, as when a lawyer overlooks a statute of limitations, the client's legal position may be destroyed. Even when the client's interests are not affected in substance, however, unreasonable delay can cause a client needless anxiety and undermine confidence in the lawyer's trustworthiness.[4]

The comment to this rule also notes that the attorney should carry through to conclusion all legal matters undertaken for a client unless the relationship is properly and clearly terminated. If doubt exists about whether an attorney-client relationship exists, the attorney should clarify the situation "in writing so that the client will not mistakenly suppose the attorney is looking after the client's affairs when the lawyer has ceased to do so." The purpose of this rule is to ensure that attorneys put forth reasonable effort and diligence to represent a client. Attorneys cannot adequately represent the interests of clients if they ignore the case, if they are lazy and do not work on the case, or if they do not have the systems in place to manage deadlines, appointments, and things to be done.

COMMUNICATION WITH CLIENTS An attorney also must communicate regularly with the client. *Model Rule* 1.4 requires an attorney to reasonably consult with a client, to keep the client reasonably informed about the status of the legal matter, to promptly comply with reasonable requests for information from the client, and to explain matters to a client to the extent reasonably necessary to permit the client to make informed decisions about the matter.

This rule specifically requires the attorney to keep in reasonable contact with the client, to explain general strategy, and to keep the client reasonably informed regarding the status of the client's legal matter. The "reasonableness" of the situation will depend on the facts and circumstances of the particular case. The comment to the rule states:

> The guiding principle is that the lawyer should fulfill reasonable client expectations for information consistent with the duty to act in the client's best interests, and the client's overall requirements as to the character of representation.[5]

Figure 7-4 shows only a few examples of attorneys and legal assistants failing to follow up on client cases. A basic element of due diligence to a client requires an attorney to meet deadlines and limitation periods and appear at requisite legal proceedings. Many of these failures could have been avoided by a good docket control system and attorneys' and legal professionals' willingness to plan, organize, and simply get the work done. There is little excuse for poor organization and poor docket control in the modern law office. Firms today have access to an unlimited supply of outstanding computerized docket control systems and case management programs made specifically for law firms, and an even greater supply of generic calendaring software that comes with most computers. With all these systems and technology, however, failure to properly perform work on time is a major reason that attorneys are disciplined in this country.

**Figure 7-4
Cases Regarding
Lack of Diligence**

Legal Assistant's Heavy Caseload Not an Excuse for Failing to Respond Timely to a Motion to Dismiss—Case Dismissed   An attorney filed an employment action for a client against the client's former employer one day after the statute of limitation. The defendant company moved to dismiss the complaint in August. No response was filed and in February of the following year the Court granted the motion and dismissed the client's case. In October of that year, more than a year after the Motion to Dismiss was originally filed, the plaintiff's attorney filed a Motion to Set Aside Judgment of Dismissal on the grounds that his legal assistant had a heavy caseload and failed to respond to the motion to dismiss. The Court denied the motion and upheld the dismissal. The Court noted that the neglect of the legal assistant was not a reason to set aside the judgment and that even if a response had been filed, the case was filed outside of the statute of limitations and most likely would have been dismissed anyway. *Deo-Agbasi v. Parthenon Group,* 2005 WL 1953407 (D. Mass.).

Paralegal Scheduling Clerk Fails to Properly Docket Three Court Appearances for Attorney   An attorney's paralegal neglected to properly docket three court appearances for an attorney. As a result of this, the "answer" that was filed by the attorney for the client was stricken and the Court entered default judgment against the attorney's client. The attorney appealed the default judgment. The appellate court found that when the trial court granted the default judgment, it served to punish the innocent client for the paralegal's neglect. The appellate court reversed and allowed the attorney to file the answer. *Hu v. Fang,* 104 Cal.App 4th 61, 127 Cal.Rptr. 2d 756 (2002).

Attorney Files Suit for Special Education Student and Then Loses Interest
An attorney accepted $4,000 to file a suit on behalf of a mother and her daughter, a special education student, so the daughter could be placed in a public school. The attorney then took no action in the case, never sent the client a detailed accounting, and refused to communicate with the client. Three and a half years later, the client received a letter from the attorney stating that in light of his "other business projects," he did not anticipate practicing law any longer. When the client requested the return of the $4,000 in legal fees and her file, the attorney denied both requests. The attorney received a one-year suspension followed by a six-month period of supervised probation. *In Re Dunn,* 2002 WL 31488272 (L.A.).

Attorney Fails to Record Deed—Costs Client $1.3 Million Dollars   At attorney was hired by a client to provide legal representation regarding the sale of the client's lease. The attorney did not timely execute the deed of trust in the lease matter and did not secure or record the deed, resulting in the loss of $1.3 million. The attorney accepted a six-month suspension. *Texas Bar Journal,* March 2000, p. 298.

Attorney Failed to Tell Convicted Client He Needed Five Extensions of Time to File an Appeal and Failed to Communicate with Client about the Appeal at All—Attorney Disbarred   An attorney filed an appeal of a criminal conviction for first-degree theft for a client. The attorney filed the brief, but only after the court granted him five extensions of time. The attorney never communicated with the client, never advised the client of the five extensions, never discussed or reviewed the brief with the client, never told the client that the brief was filed or gave him a copy, never told the client about the oral arguments, never told the client about the court's decision to affirm the conviction, and never gave the client a copy of the decision. The attorney was disbarred. *Conduct of Bourcier,* 325 Or. 429, 939 P.2d 604 (1997).

CONFLICT OF INTEREST

Attorneys must take steps to prevent conflict of interest problems. A conflict of interest occurs when an attorney or legal assistant has competing personal or professional interest with a client's case that would preclude him or her from acting impartially toward the client. Before an attorney or law firm accepts a case, he or she should perform a thorough conflict of interest search. Many attorneys and law firms use computerized software to perform such a conflict search. Many case management programs allow attorneys to perform a conflict of interest search on current clients, past clients, law office contacts, adverse clients, counsel, and much more. A thorough conflict search using computerized software is an effective way of avoiding conflict of interest problems.

Legal Malpractice Considerations

[A] client sued his former attorney(s) alleging that they neglected his case by, among other things: not taking the depositions of the defendants, not taking depositions of related witnesses, and failing to secure expert witness testimony, which all led to the dismissal of the client's case. The client also testified that when he questioned the attorney about when the depositions would be taken, the attorney responded "all in due time." The client was awarded a judgment of $700,000 against his former attorneys.[6]

In addition to the ethical considerations of neglecting a client's legal matter, the client may also have a legal malpractice claim against the attorney for negligence. The general theory in a **legal malpractice** claim is that the attorney breached an ordinary standard of care applicable to a reasonable attorney under those circumstances. In a legal malpractice case, both the plaintiff and defendant must rely on attorneys who are expert witnesses to testify that the defendant either did or did not act like a reasonable attorney would in the same situation.

Figure 7-5 shows some common deadlines that, when missed, may lead to malpractice claims. In fact, many malpractice insurers will refuse to write malpractice insurance for a law office that does not have an effective docket control system.

legal malpractice
A claim that an attorney breached an ordinary standard of care that a reasonable attorney would have adhered to in that same circumstance.

Carefully tracking . . . deadlines can be the difference between diligence and malpractice. This is certainly an area where a paralegal can have a profound effect—good or bad—on the fortunes of the firm. In the law office, responsibility for the calendar often falls to a legal assistant. If you are alert and careful with the calendar, you will please your employers, and be in a position to solicit interesting work and expanded opportunities in the office.[7]

1. Expiration of the statute of limitations
2. Failure to appear or plead, resulting in a default judgment
3. Dismissal of a lawsuit for lack of prosecution
4. Failure to file tax returns or other documents within the time required
5. Failure to file pleadings or to comply with an order within the time required
6. Failure to answer interrogatories within the time required
7. Failure to give timely notice when such notice is a precondition to a recovery of damages
8. Failure to communicate with clients
9. Not knowing what to do next (i.e., the attorney not being competent in an area)

In recent years, the number of legal malpractice claims that have been filed has gone up dramatically. In some cases, the amount of damages can be substantial. Some insurance companies that offer legal malpractice coverage actually meet with staff members who are in charge of docket control to ensure that a docket control system is being used. Thus, attorneys and law offices have two powerful reasons to maintain a quality docket system.

MANUAL DOCKET CONTROL SYSTEMS

There are many types of manual docketing systems, including a simple calendar, a card system, and others. Manual docketing systems work best for fairly small law offices. As a law office grows, manual systems become more difficult to manage.

CALENDAR   Small law offices may use simple computer calendar programs or a page-a-day calendaring system. Many calendars provide a section to record "things to do" or reminders, in addition to providing a place to schedule appointments.

As cases or legal matters are opened, deadlines and reminders (i.e., "ticklers") are entered into the calender. Notices from courts, attorneys, and so forth also are entered. In addition to the due dates or appointment date being entered, reminders also must be manually entered into the calendar. This process of manually entering due dates and reminders can be very time consuming; for instance, if a deadline with two reminders was entered, the whole entry would have to be manually entered a total of three times in three places.

In some offices, each attorney and legal assistant maintains his or her own separate calendar. The issue with this approach is that often the attorneys and legal assistants fail to coordinate their schedules and calendars. This can be a serious problem.

Finally, if attorneys wanted a short list of things to be done, appointments, or critical deadlines for a day, week, or month, it would have to be compiled and entered into a word processor by a staff member.

CARD SYSTEM   A card system (sometimes called a "tickler card system") uses index cards or their equivalent to track deadlines and things to be done. A manual card or form is used for each deadline or task to be completed and includes client name, action to be performed, client number, reminder date, and due date. Cards can be color-coded to indicate different types of deadlines. In most cases, the card or slip of paper is kept in duplicate or triplicate; copies are used as reminders and filed before the actual due date. An index-card holder or expanding file folder with dividers for each month and each day must be maintained to file each card. When the date on a card tickler is reached, the card is pulled and given to the appropriate person to perform the task, or a list of the deadlines and things to do is made.

An individual must check the card system every day in order for it to work properly. However, if a slip is lost or misfiled, the system breaks down. Although computerized systems may occasionally break down as well, manual systems are far more likely to be error prone than their computerized counterparts. In addition, like the manual calendar, any daily, weekly, or monthly report must be typed by hand.

Manual calendaring systems also lack the ability to track information by case. For example, if a client asked to see all the upcoming events for his or her case, a staff person would have to go through the calendar and manually put together a list. Depending on the case, there could be many entries. Again, this is a time-consuming process.

Another problem with a manual calendaring system is that successive calendars must be purchased every year (e.g., one for 2006, one for 2007, one for 2008, and so on). It is also difficult to schedule dates far in the future—five years down the road for a statute of limitations entry, for instance—because you will need the appropriate calendar.

Manual calendaring systems are prone to error and time consuming to administer. Because the process is slow and tedious, it encourages users to make as few docket entries as possible. Further, manual systems simply do not have the flexibility and reporting capabilities that computerized versions can deliver.

An effective [docket control/tickler] system weaves the fabric of a case together, propelling each element of a case toward its conclusion. . . . Maintaining a tickler [docket control] system, keeping it updated, and making total use of it would be very beneficial to your performance as a paralegal.[8]

TYPES OF COMPUTERIZED DOCKET CONTROL SYSTEMS

There are a variety of computer programs that can be used to schedule and track events for a legal organization. These include generic calendaring/personal information manager programs and case management programs. Most of these programs can be purchased for stand-alone computers or for local area networks. Networked systems, whether generic or legal specific, have the principal advantage of allowing individual users throughout an organization to see and have access to the calendars of other users in the office.

Generic Calendaring and Personal Information Manager Programs

Generic calendaring programs computerize the functions of a paper desk calendar. Since they are generic and can be used by any type of business, they lack many features that are helpful to a legal organization. These types of programs are usually very inexpensive and typically manage only the calendar, things to do, contacts, and e-mail functions.

personal information manager (PIM)
Consolidates a number of different tasks into one computer program. Most PIMs include calendaring, things to do, a contact database that tracks names and addresses of people, note taking, and other tasks as well.

    A generic **personal information manager (PIM)** program consolidates a number of different tasks into one computer program. Most PIMs include calendaring, things to do, a contact database that tracks names and addresses of people, note taking, e-mail, and other tasks as well. Microsoft Outlook is a type of PIM that can come bundled with Microsoft's Office Suite of programs. Outlook is an extremely powerful program. As the generic calendaring and scheduling software market has matured, most new programs are PIMs. PIMs are very popular and convenient to use since they allow a user to organize a number of related tasks into one easy-to-use interface. Generic PIMs are not specifically suited to the needs of legal professionals but they still have many useful features, and some legal organizations use them. For example, for consistency purposes a corporate law department might use a product like Microsoft Outlook, which can be implemented throughout the corporation, instead of a legal-specific program that only its department can use.

OVERVIEW OF COMPUTERIZED LEGAL CASE MANAGEMENT AND DOCKET CONTROL

Most case management programs offer a variety of features, including the following.

Monthly, Daily, and Weekly Calendar Views

Almost all case management programs have some type of monthly display, which allows the user to get an overview of his or her schedule. In addition to monthly and daily views, most programs allow users to see a weekly view of their schedules as well (see Figure 7-6).

Event Entry Screen

A typical event entry screen is shown in Figure 7-7; this is where new entries are entered into the case management program. These can include deadlines, things to be

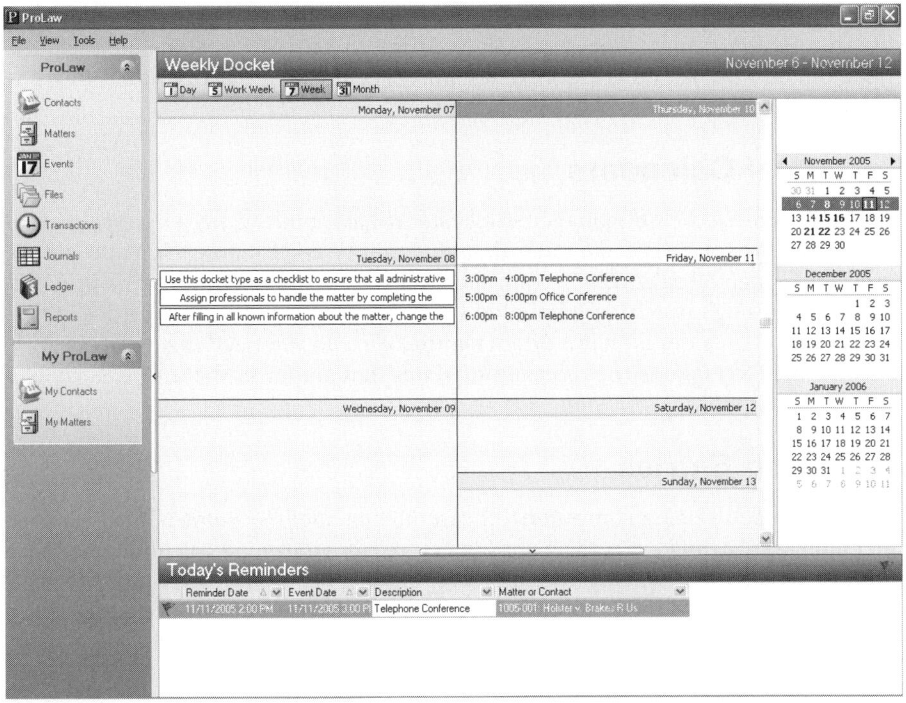

Figure 7-6
Case Management
Program Weekly
Calendar
Source: ProLaw

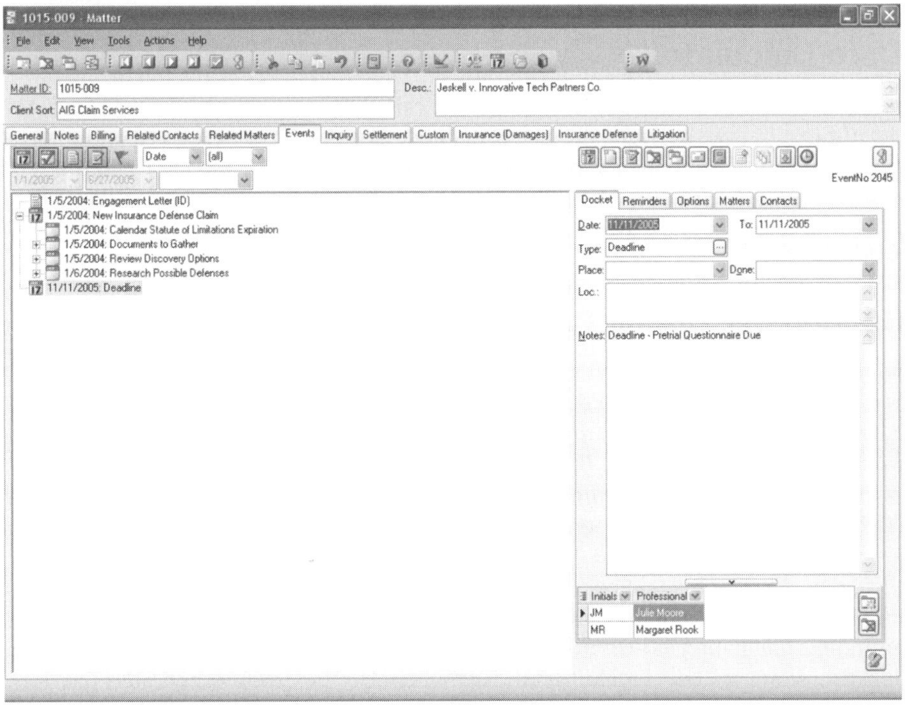

Figure 7-7
Event Entry Screen
Source: ProLaw

done, or appointments. The data entry process for most programs is easy and straightforward. Information that is entered into most entry screens includes the client, matter number, description, date, time, type of entry, place, who the event is for, notes, reminders, and other information.

Perpetual Calendars

Most computerized case management systems have built-in perpetual calendars that allow a person to see and enter data that will be used many years into the future. Unlike manual calendars, a computerized system does not have to be updated annually (although purchasing updated versions of the software may be desirable). The perpetual calendar is an important feature of a computerized system, since it allows the user to make entries concerning dates that are far in the future, such as a statute of limitations.

Recurring Entries

recurring entry
A calendar entry that recurs.

One advantage of using computerized case management systems is that the user can automatically make recurring entries. A **recurring entry** is a calendar entry that typically recurs daily, weekly, monthly, or annually. For instance, if an office has a staff meeting every Monday morning, the entry could be entered once as a weekly recurring appointment, since most computerized case management systems can make recurring docket entries daily, weekly, monthly, quarterly, and annually. Thus, an entry that would have had to be entered 52 times in a year in a manual system would have to be entered only once in a computerized docket control program.

Date Calculator

Some case management systems have a date calculator that automatically calculates the number of days between dates. For instance, suppose you have 20 calendar days from a specific date to file a motion (see Figure 7-8). The date calculator feature will automatically calculate the deadline. This is useful when you have deadlines that take into account only workdays (i.e., do not count Saturdays, Sundays, and holidays).

Scheduling Conflict Alert

Some case management systems automatically alert the user to possible conflicts. For instance, if a user mistakenly tries to schedule two appointments for the same date and time, nearly all computerized docket systems will automatically alert the user to the possible conflict. If the user knows of the conflict, most systems can be overridden and both appointments entered anyway. Some systems have a "lock-out" feature that prevents users from scheduling more than one appointment for a given time period.

Some systems even allow the user to enter such information as the individual's regular office hours and days of the week that are usually taken off. If, for instance, an individual's office hours are from 7:00 A.M. to 4:00 P.M. and an entry is made for 4:30 P.M., some systems will automatically recognize the problem and alert the user.

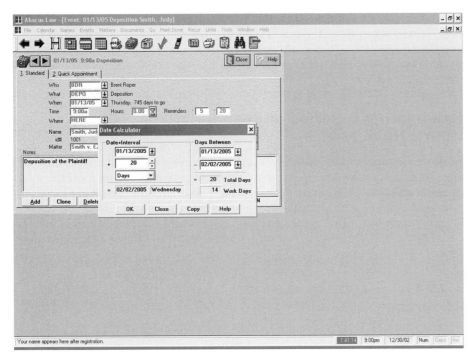

Figure 7-8
Date Calculator
Function

Screen shot reprinted by permission of Abacus Data Systems.

Scheduling Multiple Parties

Scheduling free time for an interoffice meeting can sometimes be difficult, since all parties must have an open block of time. Many case management systems that operate on a local area network can automatically bring up dates and times that a group of people have free, thus making scheduling meetings easy.

A computerized case management system also allows other individuals working on a case to see what docketing entries have been made and to find out what is going on in the case. This eases the process of multiple people working on the same case.

Centralized and Decentralized Systems

Most case management systems work well in either a centralized or decentralized system. In a centralized system, one person (like a secretary) can make time entries for many individuals; this is beneficial because only one individual is responsible for making the docketing entries. A decentralized system, where the attorney or legal assistant enters his or her own deadlines into the docket program, also works well for some offices.

Automatic Reminders

Most computerized case management systems allow the user to make one entry into the system that also contains the reminder dates. For instance, when an appointment or deadline is entered into the computer, the system automatically asks the user when he or she wants to be reminded of it. If a reminder date is entered, the computerized method automatically makes reminder entries. This is a great timesaving feature over manual systems where every reminder must be entered individually.

Calendaring a Series of Events from a Rule

Some case management programs allow a user to enter one event that, in turn, automatically triggers a list of subsequent calendaring events based on court rules. For instance, in Figure 7-9, a complaint is filed. Sixty days after the complaint is filed, according to court rules the complaint must have been served. Therefore, the docketing program automatically enters a deadline to serve the complaint 60 days after the complaint is filed. This kind of feature is very powerful and can be a real time-saver. Many case management programs allow the user to program his or her own court rules into the program or to add on purchased court rule setups.

Reporting

Most computerized systems allow the user to generate a variety of reports that manual systems cannot produce, including daily, weekly, or monthly schedules and

Figure 7-9
Calendaring a Series of Events from a Rule

Source: ProLaw

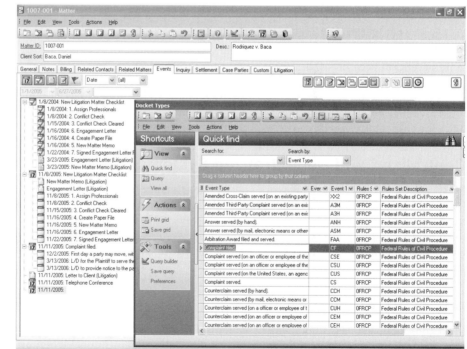

things-to-do entries for one person or a group of people. Most systems can also search and sort the entries in a variety of different formats.

DAILY CALENDAR REPORTS   This is an in-depth listing of a timekeeper's or office's daily schedule. The daily report is sometimes called a "daysheet." Many attorneys and legal assistants will use this report every day for an accurate listing of the day's events.

DAILY CALENDAR REPORT FOR A WEEK   This is similar to the daily calendar report except that the report shows docket entries for the entire week. Again, legal assistants and attorneys may want this report at the beginning of the week to get a "snapshot" of what their schedule looks like, so they can plan accordingly.

PER CASE DOCKET REPORT   Most computerized case management systems allow the user to generate a docket report by case—that is, a report showing all the docketing dates for any one case (see Figure 7-10). This report can be very helpful in trying to determine how to proceed with certain cases. Figure 7-10 provides a listing of all entries for the case *Bolin v. McPherson.* This is particularly helpful when scheduling other events for the same case and also to give to clients. Keeping clients informed about their cases is very important when it comes to client satisfaction and when it is time for the client to pay the legal bill. A client who is consulted often and kept aware of the progress of the case is more likely to pay the bill and generally will be more satisfied than a client who is not notified about a case's progress. Again, this report is very beneficial to clients who want to know what is going on in a case, and also to recently assigned attorneys or legal assistants who would like to see what has happened and where the case is headed.

Figure 7-10   Docket Report for a Case

Brent Roper
Schedule for Bolin v. McPherson
Case Number: 1237

Day	When	Time	Last, First	What	Who	Note
Fri	09/28/07	8:30a	Bolin, L.	DISCOVER	AMS	Discovery Deadline
Tue	10/02/07	9:00a	Bolin, L.	HEARING	AMS	Hearing on Pending Motions
Thu	11/01/07	9:00a	Bolin, L.	C-STATUS	AMS	Status Conference
Thu	11/15/07	1:00p	Bolin, L.	PRETRIAL	AMS	Pretrial Conference
Thu	11/29/07	10:00a	Bolin, L.	C-SETTLE	AMS	Settlement Conference
Thu	12/06/07	8:00a	Bolin, L.	TR PR	AMS	Trial Preparation
Fri	12/07/07	8:00a	Bolin, L.	TRIAL	AMS	TRIAL

Number of Events: 7

PAST DUE REPORT   The past due report prints a listing of all docket entries that are past due (i.e., the deadline or due date has passed) or that have not been marked "Done." The past due report is a safeguard against forgetting or not completing items.

FREE TIME REPORT   The free time report shows the times that one timekeeper or several timekeepers have unscheduled or open. This is useful when adding scheduling items or when setting up a conference of three or four individuals. Attorneys and legal assistants who have a lot of appointments and court dates also can use this report so they can see when free time is available for scheduling other matters.

Searching

Most computerized case management systems allow the user to search for entries. For instance, if a client calls and wants to know the date of her deposition, the user could enter the client's name into the computer and the system would retrieve the entry showing the deposition date.

ADVANCED CASE MANAGEMENT FEATURES

Up to this point, the case management program features we have covered have for the most part been confined to docket control. Now some advanced case management features will be covered as well.

Case Contacts

Case contacts allow the user to enter people into a contact database (which tracks phone, address, e-mail, etc.), just as in a PIM. The difference is that once they are entered in the database, the person(s) can be linked to a case or cases. So, if a user wanted to see or print a list of cocounsel or opposing counsel on a case, it could be easily done. Also, if the case management system is networked, the legal organization could have one master contact database (linked to cases) for the whole organization. Thus, there would be no duplication in multiple places throughout the legal organization.

Synchronizing with PIMs/PDAs

Most case management systems will synchronize calendars with PIMs (such as Outlook) and personal digital assistants (PDAs). Thus, if a corporate law department wanted to use a case management system, but the rest of the corporation was using Outlook, the two could be set up to share information or synchronize so that all of the entries in the case management program would not have to be entered by hand in Outlook.

Case Diary/Notes

Most case management systems provide a place to maintain a case diary or notes for the file. This allows legal professionals a central place to place their notes, record summaries of phone calls, and much more. A large benefit to case management programs is not only that the information can be stored electronically but that any users in a networked environment can immediately access and use the information at a touch of the button, without having to pull the hard-copy file. Thus, a good case management system is also a communication enhancement tool (see Figure 7-11).

> *The case diary is a key component in a case management system. The attorney and paralegal will use this function more than any other feature because it becomes the center for case information and communications. Your attorney no longer has to search a file for details about the last conversation you had with the client. No more searching through endless computer directories for the last letter sent to opposing counsel. It's all tied together in the case management systems.*[9]

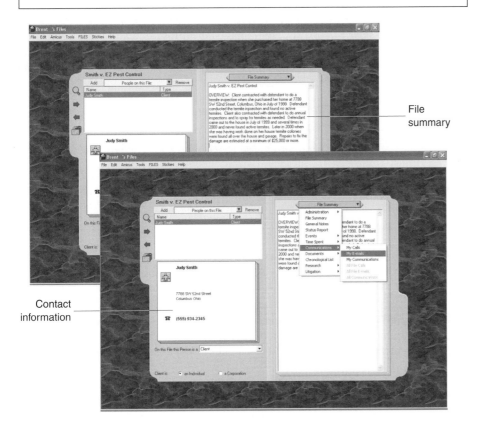

File summary

Contact information

Figure 7-11
Case Diary/Notes
Gavel & Gown Software, Inc.

Document Assembly/Generation

As indicated previously, case management programs store a great deal of information about a case, parties, attorneys, case-related information, case numbers, and much more. Most case management programs can merge that information into a merge document (see Figure 7-12). So, a legal professional can automatically generate standard letters, forms, pleadings, and reports right from the case management system without having to reenter any additional data. Most case management systems also work with Word and Word Perfect, so they can merge documents into these programs as well. Also, when a case user creates a document in the case management system, in many instances it will automatically note this—including the date—in the case diary/notes. A user simply has to indicate what file the document needs to be merged with, and then the user is given a list of documents to choose from, including file reports, letters, memos, and others. Users are, of course, allowed to create their own forms as well.

Other Features

LEGAL RESEARCH LIBRARY   Some case management programs give the user a place to store electronic legal research, or allow the user to access functions within Westlaw and/or other electronic research tools.

CONFLICT OF INTEREST   Most case management programs allow the user to do conflict of interest searches. Since the database tracks clients, parties, counsel, and much more case-related information, the conflict search can be very comprehensive.

> *For me, an e-mail . . . [interface] is an essential part of a case management package. The less places I have to look for something, the better. I use . . . [my case management program] to track incoming and outgoing e-mail and associate it with particular projects [cases] and clients. The process is extremely easy: open the e-mail message, select your project or client from a pull-down menu, and save.*[10]

E-MAIL INTERFACE   Many programs now include an e-mail interface that allows users to link e-mails with cases. This is extremely important given the heavy use of e-mails in communicating with clients and handling client matters.

DOCUMENT MANAGEMENT   Many case management programs can now associate documents with cases. A link can be made between a document/file and a case in a case management program. This allows legal professionals to index and manage case documents from the program.

TIME AND BILLING/ACCOUNTING INTERFACE   Many programs share information with timekeeping and billing programs and, in some instances, accounting programs as well.

Figure 7-12   Document Assembly/Generation

CASE MANAGEMENT DATABASE

Client Name:	First National Bank
Contact Person–First Name:	Sam
Contact Person–Last Name:	Johnson
Client Address:	P.O. Box 1000
Client City:	Philadelphia
Client State:	Pennsylvania
Client Zip:	98934
Client Phone:	943/233-9983
Case Number:	2006-9353
Court:	Philadelphia Superior Court—District 13, Philadelphia, Pennsylvania
Debtor Name:	Philip Jones
Debtor Address:	3242 Wilson Ave. SW
Debtor City:	Philadelphia
Debtor State:	Pennsylvania
Debtor Zip:	98984
Amount Owed to Client:	$25,234
Type of Debt:	Mortgage
Type of Asset:	House at 3242 Wilson Ave SW, Philadelphia, Pennsylvania

Merge function

DOCUMENT TEMPLATE 1—"Complaint"

In the {Court}

{Client name}

Plaintiff

Case No. {Case Number}

{Debtor Name}
{Debtor Address}
{Debtor City}{Debtor State}{Debtor Zip}

Defendant.

COMPLAINT

Comes now the plaintiff, {Client Name}, and states that the defendant, {Debtor Name}, is indebted to the plaintiff in the amount of {Amount Owed to Client} on a {Type of Debt} regarding a {Type of Asset}. Attached to this complaint as Appendix "A" is a fully executed copy of the mortgage above referenced.

MERGED DOCUMENT—"Complaint"

In the Philadelphia Superior Court – District 13, Philadelphia, Pennsylvania

First National Bank

Plaintiff

Case No. 2006-9353

Philip Jones
3242 Wilson Ave. SW
Philadelphia, Pennsylvania 98984

Defendant.

COMPLAINT

Comes now the plaintiff, First National Bank, and states that the defendant, Philip Jones, is indebted to the plaintiff in the amount of $25,234 on a mortgage regarding a house at 3242 Wilson Ave SW, Philadelphia, Pennsylvania. Attached to this complaint as Appendix "A" is a fully executed copy of the mortgage above referenced.

The Docket Cycle

The docket cycle refers to how information is entered into a case management program. There are three primary ways that information can flow into and out of such a program: a centralized method, decentralized method, and combined method.

Centralized Docket Control Cycle

In a centralized docket control cycle, one person typically is responsible for entering all docket entries into the docket program. This is usually a secretary or, in some cases, a legal assistant. In this type of system, step one would be for a user to manually complete a docket slip (see Figure 7-13). In the second step, the secretary enters the event into the docket control program. The third step is for reports to be generated, and the last step is for entries to be marked "done."

Decentralized Docket Control Cycle

In a decentralized docket control cycle, the user enters docket information directly into the computer, controlling her or his own docket. In this type of system, the first step would be for the user to enter a docket entry into the case management program. Second, the user views or prints reports as necessary, and third, the user marks entries "done." The advantage of this system is that the user has ultimate control over his or her own docket; the disadvantage is that the user is doing the data entry instead of a clerk or secretary.

Combined Docket Control Cycle

In a combined docket control cycle, a user can decide whether to enter information into the program or have a clerk or secretary do it. Some docket control programs allow

Figure 7-13 Sample Docket Slip

JOHNSON, BECK & TAYLOR **DOCKET SLIP**

Client/Case Matter: *Smith v. United Sales* File No.: *118294*

Event: *Pre-Trial Hearing*

Date of Event: *10/1/2007* Time of Event: *10:00 AM – 1:00 PM*

Place of Event: *U.S. Ct. House, Div. 8*

To Be Handled By: *MJB* Reminder Dates: *9/15/2007*

Priority: (1) 2 3 4 5 (Circle one, Top Priority is 1).

Slip Completed By: *BRR* Date Slip Completed: *8/15/2007*

Notes: *Meet Client at 9:45 at Ct. House*

Docket Clerk Use Only

Date Entered in Docket: *8/17/2007*

Entered By: *JCC*

multiple people to enter data into a user's schedule. For example, some networked docket programs allow both an attorney and his or her secretary to enter information into the attorney's schedule. Both have full access to the attorney's calendar.

In this type of system, the first step would be for either the user or a third party to enter a docket entry into the case management program. Second, either the user or the third party views or prints reports as necessary, and third, either the user or third party marks entries "done." In some ways, this is the best of both worlds, since the user still has control over his or her calendar but can delegate the data entry to someone else.

SUMMARY

The practice of law is filled with appointments, deadlines, hearings, and other commitments for every case that is handled. It is extremely important that these dates be carefully tracked for ethical, customer service, and general business reasons. Calendaring is a generic term used to describe the function of recording appointments for any business. Docket control is a law-office-specific term that refers to entering, organizing, and controlling all of the appointments, deadlines, and due dates for a legal organization. Case management is a legal-specific term that usually refers to computer programs that not only have docket control but a number of other features, including contact management, document assembly, case notes, document management, and much more.

Ethical issues related to docket control include the duty to competently and adequately prepare for a client's matter, diligently and promptly serve clients, communicate with clients in a timely manner, and to avoid conflicts of interest.

Manual docket control systems include basic calendars and card systems. Computerized systems include generic calendaring and personal information management programs (such as Microsoft Outlook), and docket control/case management programs. Case management programs include a plethora of advanced and powerful features.

HELPFUL WEB SITES

ORGANIZATION	DESCRIPTION	INTERNET ADDRESS
American Bar Association (ABA)	Association for attorneys. The site has a large amount of information and publications relevant to individuals working in the legal profession.	http://www.abanet.org
ABA Law Practice Management Section	ABA site devoted to law practice management issues, including docket control and case management.	http://www.abanet.org/lpm
ABA Legal Technology Resource Center	ABA site devoted to technology. Includes resources and articles.	http://www.abanet.org/tech/ltrc/home.html
Law Office Computing magazine	Excellent magazine, but limited information online. The site has good links to manufacturers that offer law office software, including docket control and case management.	http://www.lawoffice-computing.com
Law Technology News	Excellent periodical for legal technology issues. Good white papers on technology issues.	http://www.lawtechnews.com and http://www.law.com/jsp/ltn/whitepapers.jsp

Docket Control and Case Management Software

ORGANIZATION	PRODUCT/SERVICE	INTERNET ADDRESS
Abacus Data Systems	AbacusLaw (legal PIM/case management)	http://www.abacuslaw.com
Bridgeway Software	Law Quest (case management for corporate law departments)	http://www.bridge-way.com
Chesapeake Interlink, Ltd.	Needles (legal PIM/case management)	http://www.needleslaw.com
CompuLaw	CompuLaw (case management)	http://www.compulaw.com
RainMaker Software, Inc.	RainMaker Practice Management (legal PIM/case management)	http://www.rainmakerlegal.com
LexisNexis	Time Matters (legal PIM/case management)	http://www.timematters.com
De Novo Systems, Inc.	Trial De Novo (legal PIM/case management)	http://www.denovosys.com
Thomson Elite	ProLaw and LawManager	http://www.eliteis.com
Gavel & Gown Software	Amicus Attorney (legal PIM/case management)	http://www.amicusattorney.com
KeyPoint	Case-In-Point (case management for criminal defense attorneys)	http://www.key-point.com
Lawex Corp.	TrialWorks (legal case management)	http://www.trialworks.com
Legal Files Software	Legal Files (legal PIM/case management)	http://www.legalfiles.com
LegalEdge Software	Case management for criminal defense attorneys, prosecutors, and general law offices	http://www.legaledge.com
ADC Legal Systems, Inc.	Perfect Practice (case management)	http://www.perfectpractice.com
Software Technology, Inc.	PracticeMaster (case management)	http://www.tabs3.com
Client Profiles, Inc.	Client Profiles (case management)	http://www.clientprofiles.com

SUGGESTED READING

1. *Law Practice* magazine, published by the American Bar Association Law Practice Management Section [http://www.abanet.org/lpm].

2. *Legal Assistant Today* magazine, published by James Publishing [http://www.legalassistanttoday.com].

3. *Law Technology News* periodical [http://www.lawtechnologynews.com].

4. Munneke, G. A., & Davis, A. E. (2003). *The essential form book—comprehensive management tools.* American Bar Association.

5. *Law Office Computing* magazine, published by James Publishing [http://www.lawofficecomputing.com].

KEY TERMS

Bates stamp
calendar days
calendaring
case management
Certificate of Service
continuance

docket control
legal malpractice
personal information manager
recurring entry
statute of limitations
workdays

TEST YOUR KNOWLEDGE

1. What is a legal-specific term for entering, organizing, and controlling appointments, deadlines, and due dates?
2. A legal term that usually refers to docket control and other functions, including things to do, contacting information, case notes, and document assembly is _____.
3. When calculating deadlines, what two ways are there to count days?
4. A statement at the end of a court document that certifies or establishes when a document was sent is called a _____.
5. Two major types of manual docket control systems are _____ and _____.
6. A generic computer program that consolidates a number of different functions including calendaring, things to do, contact, and e-mail is called _____.
7. Name two features usually found in case management software.

ON THE WEB EXERCISES

1. Go to the ABA Center for Professional Responsibility at http://www.abanet.org/cpr/home.html, find the ABA *Model Rules of Professional Conduct,* and read and print out the Comments to Rules 1.1, 1.3, 1.4, and 1.7.

2. Visit several bar association Web sites (including the Georgia Bar Association) and find three articles on case management, docket control, or a related subject. The following link will take you to a Web site that connects to all state bar sites: http://www.abanet.org/barserv/stlobar.html.

3. Visit the American Bar Association Technology Resource Center at http://www.abanet.org/tech/ltrc/home.html and review any materials they have on case management software programs.

PROJECTS

1. Research and write a paper on computerized case management and docket control systems. Go to the docket control and case management Web sites listed in the Web Links section of this chapter. Obtain demonstration copies of the programs, if you can. Compare and contrast at least two of the different products that are available. Which one were you most impressed with, and why?

2. Using a law library, state bar journal magazine, Westlaw/LexisNexis, or the Internet, write a paper that summarizes a minimum of three attorney discipline cases regarding the failure to complete work on time. Be sure to include an analysis of the case, the court's findings, the ethical rules that were at issue, the rules that were violated, and what discipline was imposed.

◻

Answers to Test Your Knowledge

1. Docket control
2. Case management
3. Calendar days and workdays
4. Certificate of Service
5. Calendars; card system
6. Personal information manager

7. Perpetual calendar, date calculator, recurring entries, scheduling conflict alert, scheduling multiple parties, automatic reminders, calendaring a series of events from a court rule, case contacts, synchronizing with

PIMs/PDAs, case diary/notes, document assembly/generation, legal research library, conflict of interest searches, e-mail interface, document management, and time and billing/accounting interface.

◻

Questions and Exercises

1. Your law office currently uses a manual docket system. It works fairly well because the office is small. However, several clients have requested a detailed listing of what is going on in their cases and what is coming up in the future. It takes a staff member quite a while to compile this information. Even though the office's manual system is working, should the office consider a change? What benefits would be realized? Please note that the office is driven by quality and productivity.

2. As a legal assistant in a legal services/aid practice, you notice that one of the attorneys in the office filed a case on behalf of an indigent client. The defendant's attorney has attempted on three separate occasions to take the client's deposition. However, the attorney asked for and received continuances on each occasion. The client's health is deteriorating and the client has anxiety over the deposition. The client's deposition is set for tomorrow, but the attorney tells you that something has "come up" and to please call the defendant's counsel, the court reporter, and the client, and get it continued. Although you have covered for the attorney on multiple occasions, you know that the client really wants to talk to the attorney and not to you, and that the client would like to finish the deposition as soon as possible. Please respond to the attorney's request.

3. From time to time, you see new clients who come into the office. On this occasion, you interview a client who has a potential workers' compensation claim. After the client has left, you note that in a month the statute of limitations on the claim will expire. After discussing the case with your supervising attorney, the attorney says that he does not believe that the client has a viable case. The attorney tells you to not waste any more time on the matter and that you should simply call the client and tell her that the office will not be representing her. As you pick up the phone, you hesitate and then put the phone down. You go back into the attorney's office. What would you tell your supervising attorney?

4. You and your supervising attorney are overworked. You have two days to prepare for a trial that you really need 8 to 10 days to adequately prepare for. Your supervising attorney says, "It's okay, we'll just do the best we can." Discuss this situation from an ethical perspective.

5. One of the five attorneys you work for is taking on a new case. Unfortunately, the attorney has never handled a case like this before. This is particularly troubling to you, because you doubt whether either the attorney or you has the time or inclination to do the necessary research to properly handle the case. Address any concerns you might have to the attorney. Try to be diplomatic. Give the attorney options that will address your concerns but will still allow the attorney to work on the case in some capacity.

6. Calculate the following due dates.

   a. Motion for Summary Judgment filed 8/1/08; response due 17 days from file date. Court rules use calendar days in this case.

   b. Motion to Compel filed Monday 3/5/08, response due 10 days from file date. Court rules use workdays only in this case. Assume there is one weekend.

   c. Request for Admissions is received 6/1/08, response is due 25 days from receipt. Court rules use calendar days in this case. Response must be mailed by what date?

   d. Request for Publication of Documents is received 12/10/08; response is due within seven days. Court rules use workdays only in this case. Assume there is one weekend and two holidays.

7. Set up and maintain a docket of class assignments for a semester. Use index cards to represent each assignment and file them in chronological order, or use a computerized calendaring program. For quizzes and assignments, give yourself one three-day reminder before the assignment or quiz is due, in addition to recording the quiz or assignment itself. For exams or lengthy papers, give yourself three reminders—a 10-day reminder, a 5-day reminder, and a 3-day reminder before it is due—in addition to docketing the deadline itself.

8. Read the disciplinary report section of your state bar association journal or magazine and prepare a short memorandum on several cases related to diligence and/or docket control.

NOTES

1. Gore v. Rains & Block, 189 Mich. App. 729, 473 N.W.2d 813 (1991).
2. Ruff, K. (1999, September/October). Time out—incorporation of a tickler system will help you best utilize your time, energy, and resources. *Legal Assistant Today*, 70.
3. Ruff, K. (1999, September/October). Time out—incorporation of a tickler system will help you best utilize your time, energy, and resources. *Legal Assistant Today*, 70.
4. Reprinted by permission. Copies of the ABA *Model Code of Professional Responsibility*, 1999 edition, are available from Service Center, American Bar Association, 750 North Lake Shore Drive, Chicago, IL 60611-4497, 1-800-285-2221.
5. Reprinted by permission. Copies of the ABA *Model Code of Professional Responsibility*, 2004 edition, are available from Service Center, American Bar Association, 750 North Lake Shore Drive, Chicago, IL 60611-4497, 1-800-285-2221.
6. Mayol v. Summers, 223 Ill. App. 3d 794, 585 N.E.2d 1176 (1992).
7. Heath, J. (2003, January/February). Calendar madness. *Legal Assistant Today*, 84.
8. Ruff, K. (1999, September/October). Time out—incorporation of a tickler system will help you best utilize your time, energy, and resources. *Legal Assistant Today*, 72.
9. Adkins, A. A., III. (May/June). Case management might be exactly what your firm needs. *Legal Assistant Today*, 49.
10. Grierson, K. (2001, August/September). The verdict is unanimous. *Law Office Computing*, 12.

CASE REVIEW

74 P.3d 566

**The PEOPLE of The State of
Colorado, Complainant,**

v.

Matthew S. SMITH, Respondent.

Aug. 13, 2003.

OPINION AND ORDER IMPOSING SANCTIONS

SANCTION IMPOSED: NINE MONTH SUSPENSION

A trial in this matter was held on February 27 and 28, 2003, before a Hearing Board consisting of the Presiding Disciplinary Judge, Roger L. Keithley and two Hearing Board Members, Robert A. Millman and Marilyn L. Robertson, both members of the bar. Kim E. Ikeler, Assistant Attorney Regulation Counsel, represented the People of the State of Colorado (the "People"). Gary D. Fielder represented respondent Matthew S. Smith ("Smith"), who was also present.

At the trial, the People's exhibits 1 through 4 and 6 through 37, and Smith's exhibit A, were admitted into evidence. Jennifer Reynolds, Roy Reynolds, Jr., Jeanette Ross, and Matthew Smith testified on behalf of the People. Smith testified on his own behalf. The Hearing Board considered the testimony of the witnesses and the exhibits admitted into evidence, the Joint Stipulation of Facts submitted by the parties, and made the following findings of fact which were established by clear and convincing evidence.

I. FINDINGS OF FACT

Matthew S. Smith has taken and subscribed the oath of admission, was admitted to the bar of the Supreme Court on May 13, 1993, and is registered upon the official records of the Court, attorney registration number 22681. He is subject to the jurisdiction of this court pursuant to C.R.C.P. 251.1(b).

During the relevant time period from 1999 to 2001, Smith was a sole practitioner. He handled a large-volume practice with approximately half of the

practice devoted to domestic law. Jeanette Ross ("Ross") worked as Smith's legal assistant from 1996 to 2001. During the period of her employment, Smith put measures in place to assure that all communications, oral and written, were brought to his attention. Ross was required to receive, open, and sort mail and record telephone messages. Ross would review incoming mail and place matters requiring prompt attention on Smith's desk with the client file. Less critical communication was placed in sorted stacks for Smith's review. Smith would then review his mail or telephone messages and instruct Ross what action to take on a given case. It was Smith's practice to review all court orders. Smith did not utilize computer software to track deadlines in cases. Smith and Ross did, however, manually record dates on two calendars. In addition, Smith allowed Ross to prepare form pleadings, prepare and send correspondence, docket court appearances, communicate with clients by phone, and handle settings with the court. Smith periodically reviewed case files to determine if cases were properly advancing.

Smith did not give Ross permission to sign his name to pleadings. Ross was permitted to write checks on Smith's operating account and utilize his signature stamp on operating account checks without prior authorization from Smith. Ross testified that she signed Smith's name to routine pleadings. Ross's testimony that Smith permitted her to sign his name to pleadings was not credible.

Roy and Jennifer Reynolds were married in 1995. In late 1998, Roy Reynolds, Jr. ("Reynolds") retained Smith to represent him in an uncontested divorce and paid him $800. Reynolds's address and phone numbers were noted on the client intake sheet. [FN1]

> FN1. The Reynolds file disappeared when a new management company took over Smith's office. On January 27, 1999, Smith filed Reynolds's Petition for Dissolution of Marriage together with a Summons for Dissolution of

Marriage or Legal Separation and Temporary Injunction in Arapahoe County District Court, Case No. 99DR0234. On the same day, the court issued a form order entitled "Domestic Case Management and Delay Reduction Order" requiring that Smith take specified actions by a date certain. The order required Smith *569 to provide a copy to Mrs. Reynolds. Although Smith did not see the order, he was fully aware of the routine procedure in uncontested divorces and knew what deadlines were imposed by the court as a matter of course. Smith did not set a Temporary Orders Hearing or engage in the pre-hearing conference as required by the court's order. Smith knew that Mrs. Reynolds was pregnant and he felt it necessary to wait for the birth of the child before requesting that the court enter child support orders. Smith did not file a plan for alternative dispute resolution by the stated deadline due to his unconfirmed belief that Reynolds desired to forestall the divorce.

Thereafter, Mrs. Reynolds, who resided in Kansas, signed a Waiver and Acceptance of Service and Affidavit with Respect to Financial Affairs prepared by Smith, and returned both documents to Smith's office. Mrs. Reynolds did not obtain counsel at that time.

Between January and May, Smith and Reynolds were in communication. In May 1999, Smith drafted a Settlement Agreement and gave it to Reynolds to review. Reynolds took the Separation Agreement prepared by Smith to Kansas for Mrs. Reynolds to sign, and she signed it on June 16, 1999, had it notarized, and gave it back to Reynolds. Reynolds gave it back to Ross shortly thereafter. Reynolds failed to sign it. Smith was unaware that Reynolds had returned the Separation Agreement to his office.

On May 20, 1999, Ross filed a Notice to Set regarding a hearing on Permanent Orders. Ross affixed Smith's signature to the Notice to Set. Thereafter, she neglected to call the court at the appointed time to set the hearing.

On June 7, 1999, the court issued a form Status Order notifying the parties that the Reynolds case would be dismissed unless Smith took certain specific actions. Smith did not see the Status Order, did not take any of the actions the court directed him to take, and did not provide a copy of the Order to the parties. Smith believed that the case was proceeding on course and that he was waiting for a return of the signed Separation Agreement by the parties.

Ross, in an effort to cover her failure to follow through on the Notice to Set, filed another Notice to Set on June 10, 1999. Smith signed the notice but did not confirm with Ross that she set the hearing. A hearing was not set.

Ross attempted to contact Reynolds but was unable to do so. Smith told Ross to send a letter to Reynolds and advise him that the case may be dismissed if the Separation Agreement was not filed. Smith believed Ross did so, but did not check the file to confirm that she had. Ross did not send a letter to Reynolds.

During July and August 1999, Reynolds attempted to contact Smith several times but was able to only speak to Ross. The calls were not routed to Smith, and Smith was not advised that Reynolds was attempting to reach him.

On August 11, 1999, the court dismissed the case on the grounds that the parties had not complied with the court's June 7, 1999 Status Order and required Smith to provide a copy of the order to the parties. Smith did not see the order and therefore did not comply with it. Smith continued to believe that Reynolds had lost interest in pursuing the divorce.

In October, Ross contacted the court to set the matter for a Permanent Orders hearing. It was at this point that she discovered the case had been dismissed. She determined to conceal this fact from Smith. On October 25, 1999, without Smith's knowledge or approval, Ross filed a Notice to Set Uncontested Permanent Orders, an Affidavit With Respect to Financial Affairs and the Separation Agreement, both of which Mrs. Reynolds had signed on June 16, 1999. Ross hoped that the court would reopen the case. Nothing further occurred in Case No. 99DR0234.

In November 1999, Reynolds tried to reconcile with his wife, and she declined.

In early 2000, due to the lack of communication with Smith, Reynolds came to Smith's office to inquire about the status of his case. Reynolds never spoke directly with Smith; rather, he believed at the time that Ross was his lawyer. Reynolds confronted Ross with the court order dismissing the case in August *570 1999, which he first saw when he reviewed the court file at the courthouse. Ross told Reynolds the court had lost the paperwork and it would be necessary to file a new case. Ross did not tell Smith about Reynolds's visit to the office.

On March 6, 2000, without Smith's knowledge or approval, Ross commenced a new action on behalf of Reynolds by filing a Summons for Dissolution of Marriage and Temporary Injunction in Arapahoe County District Court under Case No. 00DR0782. Ross affixed Smith's signature to the documents. Ross falsely notarized a Waiver and Acceptance of Service and affixed Mrs. Reynolds's signature without her knowledge or authority.

The next day, without informing Smith, Ross sent a letter to Reynolds enclosing financial affidavits, a Separation Agreement, and Child Support Worksheets. After receiving these documents, Reynolds came to the office and was angry with Ross. Ross did not inform Smith that Reynolds had visited the office. Smith believed the case was closed because Reynolds had not signed the Separation Agreement. Smith had no communication with Reynolds in 2000.

On March 20, 2000, Ross filed a Petition for Dissolution of Marriage and affixed Smith's name to the pleading.

In July 2000, Mrs. Reynolds believed the divorce had been finalized. She contacted Smith's office and spoke to Ross numerous times and to Smith once, asking for a copy of the decree. Ross informed her she would inquire into the status of the case and get back to her. Later Ross told Mrs. Reynolds she was not sure why there was no decree and that there was some confusion in Smith's office. After receiving a call from Mrs. Reynolds's father, Smith asked Ross about the status of the case. Ross said that Reynolds came in to sign the Separation Agreement and that they were waiting to receive a decree from the court. Smith then told Mrs. Reynolds that he was waiting for a decree from the court and that he would get back to her. Smith did not get back to Mrs. Reynolds.

On July 15, 2000, Ross drafted a second Separation Agreement. She affixed the signatures of Smith as counsel for Reynolds, Mrs. Reynolds, and the attorney's name who shared Smith's office as counsel for Mrs. Reynolds. Ross notarized the signatures stating that she witnessed the signatures in Adams County, even though Mrs. Reynolds continued to reside in Kansas. Ross filed it with the court. Neither Smith, Mrs. Reynolds, nor the attorney who was purportedly signing as counsel for Mrs. Reynolds knew that Ross had affixed their signatures to the document. Ross knew at the time that Smith would not condone her drafting the Separation Agreement and affixing signatures to it.

In August 2000, Ross filed an Affidavit for Decree Without Appearance of Parties with the court. She affixed the signatures of Smith and the attorney who shared Smith's office as counsel for Mrs. Reynolds without their knowledge or approval. Ross knew the court would rely on the document as containing valid signatures and knew at the time she filed the document that she was making a false statement to the court.

Finally, in the spring on 2001, Mrs. Reynolds hired an attorney in Kansas to commence a new divorce proceeding at a cost of $1,500. On April 3, 2001, Ross sent a letter to Mrs. Reynolds's attorney in Kansas stating that the dissolution of marriage action in Arapahoe County had not been dismissed. She wrote the letter on behalf of Smith and affixed his signature to the letter without his knowledge. On the same date, she notified the clerk of the district court in Shawnee County, Topeka, Kansas that the matter had not been dismissed, and again affixed Smith's name to the letter without his knowledge.

On April 12, 2001, a Decree of Dissolution of Marriage issued from Arapahoe District Court in Case No. 00DR0782. The Magistrate entered the Decree unaware that it had been presented by Ross with falsified signatures of the attorneys and parties.

Shortly thereafter, the divorce proceeding in Kansas was completed and Mrs. Reynolds obtained a decree.

Smith acknowledged that he was responsible for Ross's actions, but also believed that ***571** his actions were based on his belief that Reynolds had decided not to go forward with the divorce. Smith also believed that were it not for Ross's actions as an "intervening cause," he would have been aware of the court's orders and of Reynolds's communication with Ross.

Both parties suffered harm as a result of the delay in obtaining the divorce: Mrs. Reynolds applied for but could not obtain financial aid because she was required to include Mr. Reynolds's income on her application, and she paid additional attorneys' fees to resolve the divorce. Mr. Reynolds was required to resolve child support issues in another jurisdiction. Both parties suffered personal inconvenience and stress for over one and one-half years.

Smith refunded the $800 Reynolds paid to him. [FN2]

> FN2. The second divorce action filed by Ross was eventually dismissed upon Smith's motion.

II. CONCLUSIONS OF LAW

The Complaint filed in this matter alleges that Smith's conduct violated Colo. RPC 1.3 (an attorney shall act with reasonable diligence and promptness in representing a client) in claim one; Colo. RPC 1.4(a) (an attorney shall keep a client reasonably informed about the status of a matter and promptly comply with reasonable requests for information) and Colo. RPC 1.4(b) (an attorney shall explain a matter to the extent reasonably necessary to permit the client to make informed decisions regarding the representation) in claim two; Colo. RPC 5.3(a) (a partner in a law firm shall make reasonable efforts to ensure that the firm has in effect measures giving reasonable assurance that the person's conduct is compatible with the professional obligations of the lawyer) and Colo. RPC 5.3(b) (a lawyer having direct supervisory authority over the nonlawyer shall make reasonable efforts to ensure that the person's conduct is compatible with the professional obligations of the lawyer) in claim three, and Colo. RPC 1.16(d) (upon

termination an attorney take steps to the extent reasonably practicable to protect a client's interests) in claim four.

Colo. RPC 5.3 provides:

With respect to a nonlawyer employed or retained by or associated with a lawyer:

> (a) a partner in a law firm shall make reasonable efforts to ensure that the firm has in effect measures giving reasonable assurance that the person's conduct is compatible with the professional obligations of a lawyer;

> (b) a lawyer having direct supervisory authority over the nonlawyer shall make reasonable efforts to ensure that the person's conduct is compatible with the professional obligations of the lawyer. . . .

[1] Smith entered into an attorney/client relationship with Reynolds, thereby forming an obligation to perform the agreed-upon professional services, including obtaining a divorce for Reynolds through the entry of permanent orders. By agreeing to perform the requested services, Smith inherently agreed that he would perform the services in accordance with the Colorado Rules of Professional Conduct. The Complaint alleges that Smith did not have measures in place which would give reasonable assurance that Ross's conduct was compatible with the obligations of a lawyer. [FN3] The evidence presented, however, revealed that Smith did have measures in place to reasonably assure that all communications with his office were promptly brought to his attention and that Ross would conduct herself in such a manner as was compatible with his professional responsibilities. Ross didn't follow those measures. Since such measures were in place, the charged violation of Colo. RPC 5.3(a) is dismissed.

> FN3. It is not clear that the provisions of Colo. RPC 5.3(a), referring only to partners in law firms, is applicable to a lawyer practicing as a solo practitioner. That issue, however, was not argued before the Hearing Board and is not decided here. For purposes of this decision we assume, without deciding, that Colo. RPC 5.3(a) applies to a solo practitioner.

[2] The charged violation of Colo. RPC 5.3(b) requires a different consideration. Colo. RPC 5.3(b) focuses upon whether the attorney having direct supervisory authority over a nonlawyer adequately supervises that *572 individual. Smith had direct supervisory authority over Ross in this case. He delegated substantial responsibility to her and failed to review her work. Indeed, although the client file was in his office for the entire period of time the events were unfolding, he did not review that file to determine if Ross was, in fact, attending to the case as she described to him. Smith's failure to adequately supervise Ross allowed her to conceal the court's orders requiring that Smith take specific action on Reynolds's behalf, including setting a temporary orders hearing, engaging in alternative dispute resolution or informing the court that none was necessary, calendaring all deadlines set by the court, confirming that Smith's office was in contact with the client, and confirming the correct status of the case. A simple examination of the Reynolds file would have disclosed Ross's activities and alerted Smith of the problems developing in the case.

[3] Smith's failure to adequately supervise Ross resulted in her engaging in the unauthorized practice of law. Smith's acting as Ross's direct supervisor but failing to fulfill his professional obligations with regard to that supervision violated Colo. RPC 5.3(b). Allowing a nonlawyer assistant to engage in the unauthorized practice of law by failing to supervise the nonlawyer is grounds for discipline. People v. Reynolds, 933 P.2d 1295, 1298-99 (Colo. 1997); People v. Stewart, 892 P.2d 875, 877–78 (Colo. 1995).

Smith argues that but for Ross's failing to advise him of Reynolds's attempts to contact him, her failing to provide him with the court's orders, and her failing to advise him that the case had been dismissed, he would not have neglected the client's case. Smith's argument is without merit.

Other jurisdictions have examined this issue. The Restatement (Third) of Law Governing Law. § 11 (2003) concerning a lawyer's duty of supervision, provides:

Supervision is a general responsibility of a principal (see Restatement Second, Agency § 503, Comment

f, & id. §§ 507 & 510). A . . . lawyer with authority to direct the activities of another lawyer or nonlawyer employee of the firm is such a principal. Appropriate exercise of responsibility over those carrying out the tasks of law practice is particularly important given the duties of lawyers to protect the interests of clients and in view of the privileged powers conferred on lawyers by law. The supervisory duty, in effect, requires that such additional experience and skill be deployed in reasonably diligent fashion.

Lack of awareness of misconduct by another person, either lawyer or nonlawyer, under a lawyer's supervision does not excuse a violation of this Section. To ensure that supervised persons comply with professional standards, a supervisory lawyer is required to take reasonable measures, given the level and extent of responsibility that the lawyer possesses. Those measures, such as an informal program of instructing or monitoring another person, must often assume the likelihood that a particular lawyer or nonlawyer employee may not yet have received adequate preparation for carrying out that person's own responsibilities.

In State ex rel. Oklahoma Bar Ass'n v. Braswell, 663 P.2d 1228, 1231–32 (Okla. 1983) the attorney raised the same argument as Smith, intimating that losing track of the client's case may have been occasioned by the inaction or neglect of his law clerk. The Oklahoma Supreme Court stated "[w]hile delegation of a task entrusted to a lawyer is not improper, it is the lawyer who must maintain a direct relationship with his client, supervise the work that is delegated, and exercise complete, though indirect, professional control over the work product. . . . [t]he work of lay personnel is done by them as agents of the lawyer employing them. The lawyer must supervise that work and stand responsible for its product." See, e.g., In re Morin, 319 Or. 547, 878 P.2d 393, 401 (1994) (lawyer responsible for unauthorized practice of law by paralegal where, following lawyer's initial warning to paralegal, lawyer took no further steps to enforce instruction or to test employee's ability to identify inappropriate activities); In re Bonanno, 208 A.D.2d 1117, 617 N.Y.S.2d 584 (N.Y.App.Div.1994) (attorney reprimanded respondent for his conduct in the supervision of a nonattorney employee and in the management *573 of his law office in violation of the rules of professional conduct of New Jersey prohibiting gross neglect, aiding the unauthorized practice of law, and failure to supervise adequately a nonattorney employee); _Florida Bar v. Rogowski, 399 So.2d 1390, 1391 (Fla. 1981)_ (noting that an attorney's nonlawyer personnel are agents of the attorney and attorney is responsible for seeing that the agents' actions do not violate the Code of Professional Responsibility); _State v. Barrett, 207 Kan. 178, 483 P.2d 1106, 1110 (1971)_ (noting that the work done by secretaries and other laypersons is done as agents of the lawyer employing them and the lawyer must supervise their work and be responsible for their work product or the lack thereof).

[4] After initially pursuing the Reynolds matter and drafting a separation agreement, Smith lost contact with Reynolds and failed to inform himself of the status of the case. He failed to comply with the court's January 27, 1999 and June 7, 1999 orders. Even if, as Smith asserts, he did not see the court orders and therefore could not comply with them, he was fully aware of the procedures and deadlines set forth by the court in a divorce proceeding. Smith failed to make every effort to locate the client and acquire his signature on the Separation Agreement, and failed to take adequate measures to confirm the status of the case. Instead, he relied on Ross to oversee the file. Smith's failing to take the required steps to resolve the Reynolds matter constitutes neglect in violation of Colo. RPC 1.3.

[5] [6] Although Smith's conduct clearly constitutes neglect, it does not, however, rise to the level of abandonment. To find abandonment rather than mere neglect, the evidence must objectively indicate that counsel deserted, rejected, and/or relinquished his professional responsibilities. In the present case, although Smith should have taken measures to locate Reynolds, Ross did not inform Smith that Reynolds had come to the office inquiring about the status of the case. Smith continued to believe that Reynolds had lost interest in pursuing the divorce. Ross fostered Smith's lack of awareness of Reynolds's numerous attempts to contact him. He did not, therefore, desert, reject, or relinquish his

professional responsibilities. Smith's actions did not terminate the attorney-client relationship with Reynolds and the provisions set forth in Colo. RPC 1.16(d) were not triggered. Accordingly, claim four alleging a violation of Colo. RPC 1.16(d) is dismissed.

[7] Initially, for approximately the first four months of representation, Smith stayed in adequate contact with Reynolds and kept him informed of the case status. Thereafter, however, for a period of a year and a half, Smith violated Colo. RPC 1.4(a) by failing to keep Reynolds reasonably informed about the status of the divorce proceeding. Smith violated Colo. RPC 1.4(b) by failing to explain the procedural status of the case to Reynolds to the extent reasonably necessary to permit the client to make informed decisions. His failure to inform himself of the status of the case does not abrogate his responsibility to keep the client reasonably informed.

Smith's conduct regarding the Reynolds matter resulted in injury to Reynolds: his divorce matter was dismissed, both parties suffered considerable distress not knowing whether they were divorced over a considerable period of time, and Reynolds must suffer the inconvenience of pursuing his legal rights in another jurisdiction.

III. IMPOSITION OF SANCTION

[8] The ABA _Standards for Imposing Lawyer Sanctions_ (1991 & Supp.1992) ("ABA _Standards_") are the guiding authority for electing the appropriate sanction to impose for lawyer misconduct. ABA _Standard_ 4.42(b) provides that suspension is generally appropriate when "a lawyer engages in a pattern of neglect and causes injury or potential injury to a client." Because Smith's continuing failure to properly supervise Ross in the Reynolds case covered a period of nearly 27 months, his conduct established a pattern of neglect. A six-month suspension is consistent with other disciplinary measures ordered by the Supreme Court. _See People v. Williams, 824 P.2d 813, 815 (Colo. 1992)_ (attorney suspended for six months for continued and chronic neglect of three separate legal matters with requirement *574 of reinstatement); _People v. Barber, 799 P.2d 936, 941 (Colo.1990)_ (attorney suspended for six months for

handling legal matter without adequate preparation, neglect of legal matter, failure to seek lawful objectives of client and gross negligence); *People v. Larson*, 716 P.2d 1093 (Colo. 1986) (neglect of entrusted legal matter and failure to carry out contract of employment warrants six-month suspension); *People v. Bugg*, 200 Colo. 512, 616 P.2d 133 (1980) (failure to process estate, to file action, and to communicate with clients, when considered with the mitigating factor of personal problems, warrants six-month suspension).

Factors in aggravation and mitigation were considered pursuant to ABA *Standards* 9.22 and 9.32, respectively. In mitigation, Smith does not have a prior disciplinary record, *see id* at 9.32(a); he did not have a dishonest or selfish motive, *see id.* at 9.32(b); Smith made a timely, good-faith effort to make restitution by returning to Reynolds his retainer, and endeavored to assist in rectifying the filing of multiple divorce cases, *see id* at 9.32(d), and Smith has made a full and free disclosure and has demonstrated a cooperative attitude toward the disciplinary proceedings, *see id.* at 9.32(f). In aggravation, Smith declined to acknowledge the wrongful nature of his conduct. He testified that he did not believe he did anything wrong in the matter. *See id.* 9.22(g). Moreover, the length of time involved in his neglect of the Reynolds case and the supervision of Ross established a pattern of misconduct. *See id.* 9.22(c).

[9] In this case, Smith's lack of recognition of his wrongdoing in combination with the substantial damage imposed upon the administration of justice by the filing and processing of an unauthorized dissolution of marriage proceeding, as well as the injury suffered by his client arising from his neglect and failure to supervise a nonlawyer employee, suggests that a period of suspension greater than six months is required. The Hearing Board finds that a nine-month suspension is appropriate under both Colorado law and the ABA *Standards*.

IV. ORDER

It is therefore ORDERED:

1. MATTHEW S. SMITH, attorney regulation number 22681, is suspended from the practice of law for a period of nine months, effective 31 days from the date of this Order.

2. Pursuant to C.R.C.P. 251.32, Smith shall pay the costs in conjunction with this matter. Complainant shall file a Statement of Costs within fifteen (15) days of the date of this Order; Smith shall have ten (10) days thereafter to file a Response.

Questions

1. What parameters did the attorney (Smith) put on the legal assistant (Ross) to make sure she was properly supervised?
2. What did the attorney (Smith) do that was improper?
3. What did the legal assistant (Ross) do that was improper?
4. What did the court find?
5. Do you agree with the Court and the imposition of the nine-month suspension?

CASE REVIEW

In the Matter of Riva, 157 N.J. 34, 722 A.2d 933 (N.J. 1999).

722 A.2d 933
(Cite as: 157 N.J. 34, 722 A.2d 933)

Supreme Court of New Jersey.

In the Matter of Robert E. RIVA, an Attorney at Law.

Argued Sept. 28, 1998.

Decided Feb. 5, 1999.

**934 *35 Lee A. Gronikowski, Deputy Ethics Counsel, argued the cause on behalf of the Office of Attorney Ethics.

Robert E. Riva, argued the cause pro se.

PER CURIAM.

This attorney discipline matter arises from a Report and Recommendation of the Disciplinary Review Board (DRB) that respondent be publicly reprimanded. Three members of the DRB concluded that a public reprimand would be insufficient discipline and recommended a three-month suspension. The majority recommendation is based on findings of the District VB Ethics ***36** Committee (DEC), concurred in by the DRB, that respondent had been guilty of gross neglect, a violation of RPC 1.1(a), and a lack of diligence, a violation of RPC 1.3. The misconduct involved the failure to file a timely answer to a complaint against his clients and his subsequent failure to act with necessary diligence to vacate a default entered on the complaint. Respondent also failed to communicate with his clients in a timely manner and misrepresented the status of the matter.

Respondent does not deny the essential facts but asserts that the conduct resulted from a misunderstanding that his adversary had withdrawn the complaint and his failure to have received notice of the proposed default judgment. Respondent contends that the Court should not follow the DRB's recommendation that he be publicly reprimanded.

Based on our independent review of the record, we find clear and convincing evidence that respondent engaged in conduct proscribed by RPC 1.1(a) and RPC 1.3, and that a public reprimand is warranted.

**9351

The matter involves respondent's representation of Robert Palceski and his wife, Janet, who owned a company against which a former employee threatened to file an employment-practices claim. The disgruntled employee had hired an attorney in 1992. Respondent told that attorney that if the employee sued, the employer would file a counterclaim based on alleged financial improprieties engaged in by the employee. That attorney did not file an action. The employee hired a new attorney.

In January 1993, the new attorney served a summons and complaint on the employer. The employer retained respondent again. After some modification of the documents, respondent obtained a stipulation to extend the time for filing an answer to the complaint.

*37 Respondent never filed the stipulation or the answer and counterclaim. Although he testified that his conversation with the employee's attorney led him to believe that she would voluntarily dismiss the matter, the adversary testified that she had never made such a statement because her client was "adamant" about pursuing the claim. Meanwhile, respondent had told the Palceskis that he had filed the answering papers and that, because he had heard nothing further from opposing counsel, the case would just "go away."

The employee's attorney said that she called respondent several times and left a number of messages on his answering machine between March and May 1993 to determine whether respondent intended to file an answer to the complaint. She eventually learned by calling the court that respondent had never filed an answer on behalf of his client.

In May 1993, the employee's attorney obtained an order entering default. Her transmittal letter to the court and an affidavit of service prepared by her secretary indicated that the request for entry of default and a copy of the proposed default order had been sent to respondent by regular mail. Respondent denied receiving them.

The court entered a default judgment against the employer for $1.7 million in September 1993. A court officer seized the trucks, tools, and bank accounts of the employer. A constable sought to seize the personal cars and other assets of the Palceskis.

Robert Palceski telephoned respondent while the constable was at his home. Respondent assured him that he would go to court the next day to have their assets returned to them. He went to the Palceskis' home that evening to obtain copies of the papers served on them to prepare an emergent motion to vacate the default and assured them that he was working on the motion. The Palceskis asked for a copy of the motion, but respondent "put them off." It was only when Robert Palceski threatened to drive to respondent's office to pick up a copy of the motion that respondent agreed to fax him a copy. The faxed copy consisted of ***38** 14 blank pages. When later asked about the blank pages, respondent stated that he might have put the pages in the machine backwards or improperly transmitted the document.

When respondent went to court two days later, he was only able to obtain the release of the Palceskis' trucks and tools. (Respondent contends that the default judgment improperly included a business entity not named in the original complaint.) Although respondent filed a later motion to vacate the default in full, the trial court held that respondent's papers were deficient and that additional information was needed to set forth a meritorious defense to the claim.

From September through December 1993, respondent told the Palceskis on a number of occasions that he was consulting with other attorneys and conducting research on their defense. By the time that the court considered the motion again in December, the Palceskis had retained a new attorney. It was several weeks before respondent turned over the file.

The only papers in the file were the motion to vacate the default with its accompanying inadequate certification, a cover letter to the employee's attorney with the draft stipulation extending the time to answer, and the draft answer and counterclaim. Only the motion to vacate had been filed with the ****936** court. The Palceskis later settled the lawsuit of the employee by a payment of $11,500.

In his testimony before the DEC, respondent acknowledged that although he knew that a stipulation of dismissal was necessary to have resolved the litigation once the complaint had been filed, he never obtained one. He believed that he had resolved the problem with the employee's attorneys.

The DRB agreed with the DEC that respondent's conduct displayed gross neglect and a lack of diligence from the time that he failed to file a timely answer to the complaint through his failure to act with necessary haste to vacate the default.

The dissenting members stressed respondent's continuous misrepresentations to his clients about the status of the matter both ***39** before and after the entry of the default, and the great financial and emotional injury suffered by the clients, who had relied on respondent's false assurances that their interests were being protected. The experience was a "nightmare" for respondent's clients, who were threatened with bankruptcy and the loss of their personal assets. In the dissenters' view,

> this is precisely the sort of attorney who contributes to the lamentable state of disrepute in which the attorney population has fallen, and who is responsible for the public's loss of trust in the legal profession. In order to assure the public that such conduct will never be tolerated, we believe that a period of suspension must be imposed. We would suspend this respondent for three months.

II

We have attempted to establish over a long period of years predictable standards for the imposition of discipline in cases of attorney misconduct. On one end of the spectrum are the cases in which disbarment of an attorney will be "almost invariable." In re Wilson,

81 N.J. 451, 453, 409 A.2d 1153 (1979) (misappropriating client funds).

Crimes of dishonesty touch upon a central trait of character that members of the bar must possess. In re Di Biasi, 102 N.J. 152, 506 A.2d 719 (1986). Such crimes are defined as a "serious crime" pursuant to Rule 1:20-13b(2). We have repeatedly held that "when a crime of dishonesty touches upon the administration of justice," id. at 155, 506 A.2d 719, the offense "is deserving of severe sanctions and would ordinarily require disbarment." In re Verdiramo, 96 N.J. 183, 186, 475 A.2d 45 (1984); In re Edson, 108 N.J. 464, 530 A.2d 1246 (1987) (counseling client to commit perjury and lying to prosecutor). Such conduct "poisons the well of justice." In re Pajerowski, 156 N.J. 509, 721 A.2d 992 (1998) (quoting In re Verdiramo, supra, 96 N.J. at 185, 475 A.2d 45). Serious crimes not touching on the administration of justice often warrant the same penalty of disbarment. In re Lunetta, 118 N.J. 443, 572 A.2d 586 (1989) (conspiring to receive and sell stolen securities); In re Mallon, 118 N.J. 663, 573 A.2d 921 (1990) (conspiring to commit tax fraud).

*40 Nevertheless, "even in proceedings involving 'serious crimes,' mitigating factors may justify imposition of sanctions less severe than disbarment or extended suspension." Compare In re Imbriani, 149 N.J. 521, 533, 694 A.2d 1030 (1997) (disbarment for engaging in numerous acts of misconduct that involved substantial amounts of money) with In re Litwin, 104 N.J. 362, 517 A.2d 378 (1986) (five-year suspension for arson); In re Kushner, 101 N.J. 397, 502 A.2d 32 (1986) (three-year suspension for false certification); In re Labendz, 95 N.J. 273, 471 A.2d 21 (1984) (one-year suspension for instigating fraudulent representations to federally insured lender for purposes of obtaining a mortgage, despite excellent reputation, unblemished record, and lack of personal gain); and In re Silverman, 80 N.J. 489, 404 A.2d 301 (1979) (18-month suspension for filing false answer with the bankruptcy court to retain custody of certain assets).

Other crimes of dishonesty not touching upon the administration of justice nonetheless demonstrate an absence of character that ordinarily warrants extended periods of suspension.

[1] Crimes that subvert the public policy and good order of the State will ordinarily warrant a period of suspension. In re Kinnear, ****937** 105 N.J. 391, 522 A.2d 414 (1987) (one-year suspension for criminal drug use); In re Herman, 108 N.J. 66, 527 A.2d 868 (1987) (three-year suspension for criminal sexual contact).

[2] Material misrepresentations of fact in sworn affidavits will warrant a long period of suspension. In re Lunn, 118 N.J. 163, 570 A.2d 940 (1990) (three years). Even misrepresenting a reason for an overlooked court appearance may result in a suspension. In re Johnson, 102 N.J. 504, 509 A.2d 171 (1986) (three months).

[3] Charges of client neglect "are serious and can have a detrimental impact on the confidence the public should have in the [b]ar of this state." In re O'Gorman, 99 N.J. 482, 492, 493 A.2d 1233 (1985) (citation omitted). When such ethical infractions demonstrate a pattern of neglect and of misrepresentation to clients, a period of suspension is warranted. In re Cullen, 112 ***41** N.J. 13, 20, 547 A.2d 697 (1988); In re O'Gorman, supra, 99 N.J. at 492, 493 A.2d 1233; In re Getchius, 88 N.J. 269, 276, 440 A.2d 1341 (1982).

We have noted, however, in such cases that "the picture presented is not that of an isolated instance of aberrant behavior unlikely to be repeated. [The attorney's] conduct over a period of years has exhibited a 'pattern of negligence or neglect in the handling of matters.' "In re Getchius, supra, 88 N.J. at 276, 440 A.2d 1341 (quoting In re Fusciello, 81 N.J. 307, 310, 406 A.2d 1316 [1979]). The Cullen case involved two instances of neglect; O'Gorman involved four instances of neglect after being suspended for five prior similar complaints; and Getchius involved six instances of neglect. Other cases of suspension for client neglect and misrepresentation include In re Terner, 120 N.J. 706, 577 A.2d 511 (1990) (three-year suspension for pattern of neglect for failure to communicate with 13 clients despite potential mitigating factor of drug addiction, which respondent denied); In re Stein, 97 N.J. 550, 483 A.2d 109 (1984) (six-month suspension for "pattern of neglect" in handling three matters coupled with self-dealing in another matter); In re Goldstaub, 90 N.J. 1, 446 A.2d

1192 (1982) (one-year suspension for pattern of neglect involving three civil cases and one criminal case combined with long history of ethical complaints). In light of respondent's unblemished record for almost two decades, he does not fall within the end of the spectrum that warrants suspension.

III

[4] [5] [6] [7] "[T]he principal reason for discipline is to preserve the confidence of the public in the integrity and trustworthiness of lawyers in general," In re Kushner, supra, 101 N.J. at 400, 502 A.2d 32 (quoting In re Wilson, supra, 81 N.J. at 456, 409 A.2d 1153). In making disciplinary decisions, we must consider the interests of the public as well as of the bar and the individual involved. Ibid. "The severity of discipline to be imposed must comport with the seriousness of the ethical infractions in light of ***42** all the relevant circumstances." In re Nigohosian, 88 N.J. 308, 315, 442 A.2d 1007 (1982). For that reason, we consider factors in mitigation of the seriousness of the offense. In re Hughes, 90 N.J. 32, 36, 446 A.2d 1208 (1982).

Although respondent's conduct was inexcusable in that he had compounded his initial neglect in not filing an answer with his later neglect and misrepresentation concerning his efforts to vacate the default judgment, the ethical misconduct is related to one client transaction. The closest analogous case, In re Kantor, 118 N.J. 434, 435, 572 A.2d 196 (1990), also involved a single failure to file an appellate brief and to represent truthfully the status of the appeal, but the one-year suspension reflected that it was conduct "viewed in combination with a prior ethics infraction and lack of mitigating factors." Generally, in the absence of conduct evidencing a disregard for the ethics system, cases involving a similar mixture of ethics infractions have resulted in a reprimand. See, e.g., In re Onorevole, 144 N.J. 477, 677 A.2d 210 (1996) (reprimand for gross neglect, lack of diligence, failure to communicate, failure to cooperate with disciplinary authorities and misrepresentation; attorney misrepresented to client that he had filed a complaint and that court was backlogged in filing complaints, when in fact attorney had not filed the complaint at all); In re ****938** Horton, 132 N.J. 266,

624 A.2d 1367 (1993) (reprimand for lack of diligence, failure to communicate, failure to provide sufficient information to allow client to make informed decisions and misrepresentation; attorney allowed an appeal to be procedurally dismissed, based on his belief that he could not win appeal, first allowing his client to believe that appeal was pending and then attempting to mislead client into believing that appeal was dismissed on merits).

[8] [9] "We ordinarily place great weight on the recommendation of the Disciplinary Review Board." In re Kushner, supra, 101 N.J. at 403, 502 A.2d 32; see also In re Vaughn, 123 N.J. 576, 589 A.2d 610 (1991) (adopting DRB's recommendation to reprimand publicly attorney who had failed to keep client informed, ***43** displayed pattern of neglect, and had failed to reply to DEC investigation). We greatly respect, as well, the views of the dissenting members of the DRB but believe that predictability and uniformity in the imposition of ethical decisions call for a public reprimand in these circumstances. We do not find that respondent's misconduct demonstrates dishonesty, deceit, or contempt for law, but rather an aberrational neglect of his responsibilities as an attorney. Respondent will suffer the reproach of his peers for the suffering inflicted on his client. Finally, we cannot overlook the fact that the default judgment of $1.7 million was entered (perhaps against the wrong parties) in a case that settled for $11,500.

For all of these reasons, we conclude that the appropriate discipline is a public reprimand.

Respondent shall reimburse the Disciplinary Oversight Committee for appropriate administrative costs, including the costs of transcripts.

For reprimand—Chief Justice PORITZ and Justices HANDLER, POLLOCK, O'HERN, GARIBALDI, STEIN, and COLEMAN—7.

Opposed—None

ORDER

It is ORDERED that ROBERT E. RIVA of SHORT HILLS, who was admitted to the bar of this State in 1979, is reprimanded; and it is further

ORDERED that the entire record of this matter be made a permanent part of respondent's file as an attorney at law of this State; and it is further

ORDERED that respondent reimburse the Disciplinary Oversight Committee for appropriate administrative costs incurred in the prosecution of this matter.

END OF DOCUMENT

EXERCISES

1. List each of the attorney's actions in this case that amounted to a lack of diligence, incompetence, or failure to communicate with his client.

2. Discuss how you might have felt if you had been the attorney's client in this matter.

3. Why did the New Jersey Supreme Court only reprimand the attorney?

4. Alter reading the case, did you tend to agree with the New Jersey Supreme Court that ordered the attorney be reprimanded or with the Disciplinary Review Board that recommended a three-month suspension of the attorney? Explain your answer.

Hands-On Exercises

ProLaw—Docket Control

TRAINING MANUAL OUTLINE

Number	Lesson Title	Concepts Covered
Lesson 1	Introduction to ProLaw	Understanding the ProLaw interface
Lesson 2	Making Docket Entries	Entering docket entries in ProLaw
Lesson 3	Docketing by Rules and Searching and Retrieving Docket Entries	Making a docket entry with rules, and searching and retrieving docket entries

WELCOME TO JOHNSON AND SULLIVAN

Welcome to Johnson and Sullivan! We are an active and growing firm with four attorneys and two legal assistants. As you know, you have been hired as a legal assistant intern. We are very happy to have you on board; we can certainly use your help.

At Johnson and Sullivan, we take pride in carefully docketing and tracking all appointments and deadlines so that we meet and exceed our duty to our clients with respect to providing outstanding legal services. In this tutorial, you will learn how to use our computer system's docketing functions. We use ProLaw, a sophisticated legal-specific program. ProLaw has many features related to docket control. It is important that you have a basic understanding of these features since most of our staff enter and track their own deadlines, appointments, and things to do. If you have completed Lesson 1 in a prior tutorial, please skip it and go directly to Lesson 2.

GETTING STARTED

Introduction

Throughout these exercises, information you need to type into the program will be designated in several different ways.

- Keys to be pressed on the keyboard will be designated in brackets, in all caps and bold type (e.g., press the **[ENTER]** key).
- Movements with the mouse will be designated in bold and italics (e.g., *point to File on the menu bar and click the mouse*).
- Words or letters that should be typed will be designated in bold and enlarged type (e.g., type **Training Program**).

Information that is or should be displayed on your computer screen is shown in the following style: **Press ENTER to continue.**

Lesson 1: Introduction to ProLaw

In this lesson, you will load ProLaw and be introduced to the Contacts and Matters functions as an example of the basic interface of the program.

1. Load Windows. To load ProLaw, *click on the* Start *button, point with the mouse to* **Programs** *or* **All Programs,** *point to* **ProLaw Evaluation,** *and then point and click on* **PROLAW.**
2. When ProLaw is loaded the first time, you may see a window entitled **Professional Information for User xx.** The screen will ask you to enter your initials and name. At "Initials" type: **PD.** At "Full Name" type: **Pat Doe.** Then, *point and click on the green checkmark in the upper-right part of the window.*
3. You should now have the **ProLaw** window displayed, including the **Daily Docket** calendar for the current day on your screen.
4. *Point and click on the maximize icon at the top right of the* **ProLaw** *window* (it is just to the left of the red "X" and looks like two layered squares. If you point to an icon with your mouse for more than a second, the icon title will be displayed).
5. Notice that there is a column of icons on the left edge of the screen. These icons give you access to ProLaw's major functions; they include Contacts, Matters, Events, Files, Transactions, Journals, Ledgers, and Reports.
6. Below is a table showing the purpose of each function in ProLaw.

ProLaw Icon/Function	Purpose
CONTACTS	Contains contact information for all clients, parties, attorneys, judges, etc. It is an electronic address book. Conflict of interest searches can also be performed using this function.
MATTERS	Contains detailed information about every case/client matter. This includes billing information, notes about the case, related contacts, related matters, and settlement information, among others.
EVENTS	Allows the user to run queries for a specific set of docket entries and print docket reports.
FILES	Allows the user to check files in and out and report on the location and status of physical file folders.
TRANSACTIONS	Allows the user to create time entries, run cost recovery imports, edit pre-bills, and produce statements.
JOURNALS	Allows the user to enter checks, cash receipts, reconcile accounts, and produce financial reports.
LEDGER	Allows the user to view client billing and payment history, statement images, and unbilled statements.
REPORTS	Allows the user to produce and print a wide variety of reports.

7. *Point and click with the mouse on* Contacts. The **Contacts** window is now displayed.

8. *Point and click with the mouse on* Quick find, located in the **View** section of the **Shortcuts** pane. *In the* Search for *field press the* **[BACKSPACE]** key. This will clear the field and search for all contacts in the database. Press the **[ENTER]** key.

9. Press the **[DOWN ARROW]** cursor key or *use the mouse* to scroll down through all of the contacts. Notice that the database is already populated with information.

10. *Scroll back until you find the entry for* Adam Schnieder, which is located near the bottom of the list. *Point and double-click on* Adam Schnieder.

11. Notice that the **Adam Schnieder—Contact** window is now displayed. You can now see the contact information for Adam Schnieder, including name, class (i.e., type of entry; in this case, "client"), address, phone number, etc.

12. In the **Adam Schnieder—Contact** window, *point and click on the* Close *icon (the red "X" located in the upper-right corner of the window) to close this window.*

13. The "Contacts" window should now be displayed. *Point and click on "Recent"* (under "Shortcuts" "View"). Notice that only the entry for Adam Schnieder is listed. The **Recent** command contains a list of your most recently used contacts.

14. In the **Contacts** window, *point and click on the* Close *icon (the red "X" located in the upper-right corner of the window) to close this window.*

15. You should now be back where you started at the **Daily Docket** screen.

16. *Point and click with the mouse on* Matters. The **Matters** window is now displayed.

17. *Point and click with the mouse on* Quick find, if it is not already displayed (located in the **View** section of the **Shortcuts** pane). In the **Search for** field, press the **[BACKSPACE]** key. This will clear the field and search for all matters in the database. Press the **[ENTER]** key.

18. In the **Matters** window, *point and click with the mouse on the* maximize *icon at the top right corner of the window* (located just to the left of the **Close** icon; it looks like two layered squares layered). This will allow you to see additional columns.

19. Press the **[DOWN ARROW]** cursor key or *use the mouse* to scroll down through all of the matters.

20. *Point and double-click with the mouse on the first entry* (**Matter ID 1000-001—Maguire, Robert, Maguire—Chapter** 7).

21. The **1000-001—Matter** window should now be displayed. Notice that there are a number of tabs in the window, including **General, Notes, Billing, Related Contacts**, and others. *Point and click on each of these tabs.* Then, close the **1000-01—Matter** window by *pointing and clicking on the* Close *icon.*

22. The **Matters** window should now be displayed. *Point and click on* Recent (located in the "View" section of the "Shortcuts" pane). Notice that only the "Maguire, Robert—Maguire—Chapter 7" matter is listed.

23. *In the* Matters *window, point and click on the* Close *icon to close this window.*

24. You should now be back where you started at the **Daily Docket** screen.
25. This concludes Lesson 1. To exit ProLaw, *point and click on the* Close *icon in the* **ProLaw** *window to close the program.* Alternatively, you may *point and click on* **File** *on the menu bar and then click on* **Exit**.

Lesson 2: Making Docket Entries

In this lesson, you will enter several docket entries. You will use the current month and date for all transactions.

1. Load Windows. To load ProLaw, *click on the* Start *button, point with the mouse to* **Programs** *or* **All Programs**, *point to* **ProLaw Evaluation**, *and then point and click on* **PROLAW**.
2. You should now have the **ProLaw** window displayed, including the **Daily Docket** calendar for the current day on your screen.
3. *Point and click with the mouse on* Matters.
4. *Point and click with the mouse on* Quick find.
5. *Point and click with the mouse in the* Search by *field, point and click with the mouse on the down arrow of the drop-down box, and then select* Client sort.
6. In the **Search for** field, press the **[BACKSPACE]** key and then **[RETURN]**.
7. *Point and double-click on* **Matter ID 1005-001, Brakes R Us, Holster v. Brakes R Us**.
8. *In the* **1005-001—Matter** *window, point and click on the* Events *tab*.
9. Notice under the **General** tab that there are five icons. *Hover your mouse point over each icon to display the name of each one.* The names of the icons are **Include dockets, Include completed dockets, Include documents, Include notes,** and **Include reminders.** These icons toggle each item off or on. If there is a black box around the icon, the feature is turned on. For example, the **Include completed dockets** is toggled on, so the event listing just below the icons shows the completed docket entry of **1/5/2004: New litigation Matter Checklist**.
10. *Point and click with the mouse on the* Include completed dockets *icon.* Notice that the **Include completed dockets** icon no longer has a black box around it and that the **1/5/2004: New Litigation Matter Checklist** event is no longer shown.
11. *Point and click with the mouse back on the* Include completed dockets *icon* and the **1/5/2004: New Litigation Matter Checklist** is again shown.
12. Notice that there are several more icons displayed on the right side of the window. *Hover the mouse on the icons displayed under tabs on the right side of the screen.* The names of the icons are **Add docket, Add document,** and **Add note.** This is where you can add these types of entries to the matter.
13. *Point and click with the mouse on the* Add docket **icon.** A blank docket entry has now been opened in the lower-right corner of the window. The current date is in the **Date** field.
14. *Point and click with the mouse on the down arrow of the drop-down box in the* Date *field.* Notice that a calendar and a clock appear.

15. *Point and click with the mouse on the up arrow next to* **12:00** AM *under the clock. Continue clicking on the up arrow until it says* **03:00** PM. *Point and click on* OK *just under the clock.*

16. Notice that an appointment for the current date at 3:00 PM. has been added.

17. *Point and click on the down arrow of the drop-down box in the* To *field.*

18. *Point and click with the mouse on the up arrow next to* **03:00** PM. *under the clock until it says* **04:00** PM. This is the ending time of the appointment. *Point and click on* OK *under the clock.*

19. *In the* Type *field, point and click on the ellipses (three dots).* You can enter as many event types as you like; for now, just *point and double-click with the mouse on* Telephone Conference.

20. In the **Loc.** field ("location"), type **David's Office.**

21. *Point and click with the mouse on* Melissa Conrad *on the bottom portion of the window (near the middle), and then point and click with the mouse on the* Delete *icon on the bottom right edge of the window.* The entry for **Melissa Conrad** (the default person assigned to this case) is now gone.

22. *Point and click with the mouse on the* Add *icon on the bottom right edge of the window.*

23. *Point and click on the ellipses in the* Initials *field and then scroll down and double-click on* Pat Doe.

24. *Point and click with the mouse on the* Reminders *tab just to the right of the* Docket *tab.* A default entry of one day before the event is shown. *Point and click on the down arrow of the drop-down box of the* Frequency *tab; select* **hour(s)** *from the list.* This will now give you a reminder one hour before the event. In ProLaw, you can add as many reminders as you need.

25. *Point and click on the green checkmark on the toolbar to save the docket entry.*

26. *Add the following docket entries:*

Additional Entry 1—for the current date for the Holster v. Brakes R Us case

Field	Data to Enter
Date/Time	Current Date, 5:00 PM
Type:	Office Conference (*you will need to enter this. Click on the ellipses, click on the* Add item *icon, enter* Office Conference *in the* Description, *then click the green checkmark on the right side of the screen*)
Loc:	David's Office
Notes:	Office Conference with Client re: Trial
Initials/Professional	DJS (David Simon) and PD (Pat Doe)
Reminders	Current Day, Unit: 2, Frequency: Hours

Additional Entry 2—for the current date for the Holster v. Brakes R Us case

Field	Data to Enter
Date/Time	Current Date, 6:00 PM
To:	Current Date, 8:00 PM
Type:	Office Conference
Loc:	Conference Room
Notes:	Trial Preparation
Initials/Professional	DJS (David Simon) and PD (Pat Doe)
Reminders	Current Day; Unit: 2, Frequency: Hours

Additional Entry 3—for the current date for the Holster v. Brakes R Us case

Field	Data to Enter
Date/Time	One week from the current date (don't enter a time)
To	(leave blank)
Type:	Deadline—Motion Due *(You will need to enter this. Click on the ellipses, click on* Add item, *type* Deadline—Motion Due *in the* Description, *and then click on the green checkmark on the right edge of the screen).*
Loc:	(leave blank)
Notes:	Deadline—Motion Due—Motion for Summary Judgment
Initials/Professional	DJS (David Simon) and PD (Pat Doe)
Reminders	*Don't enter a date in the* Reminder Date *field.* Instead press the [TAB] key to go to the Units field, and type 4. *Then go to the* Frequency *field and select* Day(s). ProLaw will then automatically enter the date for you. Add additional reminder dates for two and three days before.

27. *Note:* it may take a few minutes for the entries to appear on your **Daily Docket** in the **ProLaw** window.
28. This concludes Lesson 2. To exit ProLaw, *point and click on the* Close *icon in the* **ProLaw** *window to close the program.* Alternatively, you may *point and click on* **File** *on the menu bar and then click on* **Exit**.

Lesson 3: Docketing by Rules and Searching and Retrieving Docket Entries

In this lesson, you will enter several trust deposits. You will use the current month and date for all transactions.

1. Load Windows. To load ProLaw, *click on the* Start *button, point with the mouse to* **Programs** *or* **All Programs**, *point to* **ProLaw Evaluation**, *and then point and click on* **PROLAW**.

2. You should now have the **ProLaw** window displayed, including the **Daily Docket** calendar for the current day on your screen.

3. *Point and click with the mouse on* Matters.

4. *Point and click with the mouse on* Quick find.

5. *Point and click with the mouse on the drop-down box of the* Search by *field and choose* Client sort.

6. In the **Search for** field, press the **[BACKSPACE]** key and then **[ENTER]**.

7. *Point and double-click on* **Matter ID 1007-001, Baca, Daniel, Rodriquez v. Baca.**

8. *In the* **1007-001—Matter** *window, point and click on the* Events *tab if it is not already displayed.*

9. *Point and click with the mouse on* Trial Date *and then on the* Delete *icon (the icon below the list of tabs; it looks like a folder with a red X through it). The* Confirm *dialog box will appear, asking* **Delete this event and its children?** *Point and click on* Yes.

10. *Point and click with the mouse on the* Add docket *icon.* A blank docket entry has now been opened in the lower-right corner of the window. The current date is in the **Date** field.

11. *In the* Type *field, point and click on the ellipses (three dots).* Notice that there are many entries to choose from. This is because this case was set up using the **Federal Rules of Civil Procedure** rule set. Using a rule set like this, the user is allowed to standardize many docket entries.

12. *Point and double-click with the mouse on* Complaint filed. Notice that under **Complaint filed** there are additional entries (these are called "children" because they are tied to the main entry, called the "parent" entry).

13. *Point and click on the* Save record *icon in the toolbar.*

14. *In the* **1007-001—Matter** *window, point and click on the* Close *icon.*

15. *In the* Matters *window, point and click on the* Close *icon.*

16. *In the* ProLaw *window, point and double-click with the mouse on* Events.

17. *In the* Events *window, point and click with the mouse on* Quick find. *Make sure* Matters Events **is** *selected and* PD *(Pat Doe) is selected under* Initials.

18. *In the* Time frame *field, choose* Today *from the drop-down list.*

19. In the **Search for** field, press the **[ENTER]** key. Notice that all of the entries for the current date are displayed. You can point and click on any of the returned records to see the detail.

20. *Point and click on the* Calendar *on the toolbar (the second icon from the right; it looks like a monthly calendar).* Notice that your entries on displayed on a calendar. This feature of ProLaw allows you to print a wide variety of docket reports based on your needs.

21. *In the* Calendar *window, point and click on the* Close *icon. Close any other windows you have opened until you are at the* **ProLaw** *window with the* **Daily Docket** *displayed.*

22. Notice that the entries you made for the current date are displayed. Also, notice that at the bottom of the screen there is a listing of **Today's Reminders;** this is where your reminders will appear.

23. *Point and double-click with the mouse on any of the appointments on your* **Daily Docket.** Notice that the matter and docket entry was retrieved. These features allow you to manage and access your docket. *Point and click on the* Close *icon in the matter you just opened.*

24. This concludes Lesson 3. *Point and click on the* Close *icon in the ProLaw window to exit ProLaw.*

This concludes the ProLaw Docket Control Hands-on Exercises.

For additional resources, visit our Web site at www.westlegalstudies.com

Legal Marketing

Chapter Objectives

After you read this chapter, you should be able to:

- Explain what marketing is.

- Differentiate between advertising and marketing.

- Discuss different marketing options that are available to most law offices.

- Identify ethical problems that may arise in carrying out a marketing plan.

- Explain what cross-selling is and why it is important in law offices.

- Discuss what the purpose of a marketing plan is.

LEGAL MARKETING

legal marketing
The process of educating consumers on the legal and business activities a firm uses to deliver quality and ethical legal services.

Legal marketing is the process of educating consumers on the legal and business activities a firm uses to deliver quality and ethical legal services. Thirty years ago, law office marketing was virtually nonexistent. It was not until the landmark Supreme Court case of *Bates v. State Bar of Arizona*, 433 U.S. 350 (1977), that this began to change. In *Bates*, two young attorneys placed an ad in the *Arizona Republic* that stated: "Do you need a lawyer? Legal services at very reasonable fees." In response, the Arizona State Bar Association took disciplinary action against the attorneys. The U.S. Supreme Court held that a ban on attorney advertising was a violation of the First Amendment right to commercial free speech and that it was a restraint of trade. Today, attorney advertising is a given. With more than one million attorneys practicing law, the "Why should we market our practice?" question has long been forgotten. The increased competitiveness of the legal field has forced law practices to promote themselves or face the reality of getting left behind by losing business to more aggressive firms. In addition, law offices not only compete against other law offices, they also compete against accounting firms when it comes to handling some types of tax matters, real estate companies regarding real estate transactions, and other types of organizations as well. The only question truly left for a law office is *how* to market itself.

> *Many lawyers strongly believe that advertising undermines the dignity of the legal profession. Others argue that it not only allows law firms to operate as businesses but also provides an important consumer benefit.*
>
> *A legal assistant can play an important role in marketing the law firm's services and assuring that the firm's marketing activities are conducted in an ethical manner.*[1]

Why Is Marketing Important to Legal Assistants?

Marketing is the job of everyone who works in a private law office. Your job depends on the firm's ability to find and serve additional clients. Therefore, the legal assistant has a vested interest in the marketing function. Your friends, family members, acquaintances, social groups, and fellow legal assistants are worthy of your marketing effort. Make sure people know the name of the organization you work for, network with other professionals, and be prepared to talk to others about what your law office does. By marketing your firm, you will establish that you have an interest in and loyalty to the firm, and you also will be building some degree of job security. Law offices cannot do business without new clientele. In addition, many marketing-savvy law firms now require legal assistants to participate in marketing efforts. After all, as an employee a legal assistant has a vested interest in the survival of the law firm.

> *Although my position is in no way a "marketing" position, I find that I inadvertently do a lot of marketing for my firm by virtue of my involvement with my local legal assistant organization. Also, I was recently interviewed by a statewide legal publication regarding an upcoming article about legal assistants. My name, position, and employer were included in the article. These types of things always reflect positively on the firm or organization for which you are employed.*
>
> —Lenette Pinchback, CLA

Marketing Goals

There is a misconception that advertising and marketing are the same thing; they are not. Advertising is simply getting your name out to the public. Marketing, on the other hand, includes advertising, but is much more: marketing encompasses providing quality services to clients, gaining insight and feedback into client needs, having a good reputation in the community, and exercising good public relations. Law office marketing has focused objectives and goals.

- Educate clients and potential clients regarding the firm's array of services.
- Educate clients and potential clients as to the particular expertise of the firm in certain areas.
- Create goodwill and interest in the firm.
- Create positive name recognition for the firm.
- Create an image of honesty, ethics, and sincere interest in clients.
- Publicize the firm's accomplishments to the profession and community.
- Educate clients on changes in the law, thus creating client confidence in the firm.
- Improve the firm's competitive position in the marketplace.
- Obtain referrals from other attorneys.
- Maintain communication with existing clients.
- Increase client loyalty and retention.
- Increase staff morale and reinforce the firm's self-image.
- Obtain referrals from clients.
- Obtain repeat business from existing clients.

Basic Restrictions on Marketing

There are several restrictions on law office marketing. These restrictions involve ethical obligations and are discussed in depth at the end of this chapter, but the most fundamental restriction is that, no matter what the marketing entails, it must not be false or misleading.

> *If a legal assistant is asked to input, proofread, or review marketing materials, he or she should take extra care that there is nothing false or misleading contained therein.*[2]

THE LEGAL MARKETING PLAN

marketing plan
It specifies a target audience the firm is trying to reach, the exact goals that the marketing program is to accomplish, and establishes a detailed strategy of how the goals will be achieved.

A law firm must have a marketing plan before it can begin marketing. A **marketing plan** specifies a target audience the firm is trying to reach, the exact goals that the marketing program is to accomplish, and establishes a detailed strategy of how the goals will be achieved. In specifying the target audience, it is important that the law office understand exactly who their clients are (see Figure 2-3 in Chapter 2 regarding practice management and strategic planning). Many law offices, even relatively small offices, hire marketing consultants, advertising agencies, and marketing managers who are responsible for the firm's marketing efforts (see Figure 8-1). Figure 8-2 provides a sample job description for a marketing director. Due to the increased competition in the legal industry and the continual need for an influx of clients, marketing—as a part of a firm's overall management responsibility—simply cannot be ignored. A recent article found that corporations typically spend from 10 to 15 percent of revenues on marketing, and a recent legal survey found that law offices spend an average of 1.7% of revenues on marketing. Figure 8-3 shows how much law firms are spending on marketing per lawyer and as a percent of revenue.

Figure 8-1
Legal Marketing Staff and Consultants[3]

Does your firm currently employ individuals in the following in-house roles?

Description	Percent
Professional marketing staff	50%
Client service staff	24%
Professional sales staff	6%
Business development coach	6%

Do you currently have an ongoing relationship with any of the following?

Description	Percent
Legal marketing/business development	70%
Legal management consultant who advises on marketing	35%
Advertising agency	44%
Public relations counsel	62%
Personal coach	43%

MARKETING DIRECTOR[4]

Job Description

Position Reports to: Marketing committee

RESPONSIBILITIES

Overall Responsibility: Position is responsible for developing a marketing plan and coordinating all activities that relate to the plan and the overall attainment of marketing objectives.

PRIMARY RESPONSIBILITIES

Internal data depository and market research

Collect, prepare, and maintain firm data

Marketing information systems

Design or supervise the preparation of mailing lists and client and referral-source databases. Set up systems to develop and keep current marketing databases and follow-up activities, and retrieve information upon request by lawyers, staff, or clients.

Press relations

Draft press releases and coordinate the process to achieve approval and distribution. Work with news media. Place articles written by lawyers and pitch places for individual lawyers on target publications' editorial boards. If the firm retains public relations counsel, serve as liaison for above activities. Maintain a clippings file and circulate articles on the firm or its professionals internally and externally.

Public relations

Plan and coordinate receptions, seminars, and alumni programs. Organize community-related activities and opportunities to raise firm's visibility and name recognition.

Internal communications

Create awareness of marketing activities with written and oral vehicles. Circulate articles. Facilitate communications between professionals in various practice areas and offices.

Publications and promotional materials

Develop, edit, or supervise outside preparation of brochures, newsletters, and other promotional publications. Prepare directory listings and announcement cards. Place professional advertisements.

Client relations

Develop or supervise client surveys.

Training

Provide or arrange for marketing training for partners and staff.

Proposals and presentations

Assist in preparing written proposals and in-person presentations for new business. Keep a reference file of proposals. Help lawyers rehearse sales presentations.

Budget

Supervise and track a marketing budget and expenditures.

Figure 8-2
Marketing Director
Job Description

Figure 8-2
(Continued)

QUALIFICATIONS

Knowledge of

- Law office environment
- Marketing techniques and principles

Ability to

- Coordinate multiple functions
- Communicate with and motivate professionals

EXPERIENCE

Marketing manager in a law or other professional services firm

EDUCATION

College or course work in marketing, writing, commercial art, or related fields

Figure 8-3
How Much Law Firms
Spend on Marketing
Annually[5]

No. of Lawyers	Marketing Dollars Spent per Lawyer Annually	Percent of Firm Revenue
Under 9	$6,260	2.0%
9–20	$5,866	1.8%
21–40	$6,200	1.9%
41–75	$6,336	1.8%
76–150	$6,682	1.7%
150+	$6,635	1.5%

Even a small firm with nine attorneys may be spending as much as $56,000 on marketing efforts, according to Figure 8-3. Therefore, marketing must be done in an effective manner, and it is important that money not be wasted on efforts that are not effective for a firm. A well-thought-out marketing plan will help ensure that money, time, and efforts are not wasted. A law firm's marketing plan should include the following:

- Overall goals of the marketing program
- Strategies and activities that will be necessary to achieve the goals (including who, what, when, how, and in what order the activities will be implemented)
- Estimated cost of the marketing program
- Estimated profit the successful marketing program would bring in

The marketing plan and the strategic business plan are related documents. To develop an effective marketing plan, consider the steps presented in Figure 8-4. A key component of the marketing plan is to conduct research. The drafter needs relevant information in order to write a good marketing plan, such as what the target group actually wants in the way of legal services; this is a departure from the usual method, which is to provide a target group with what you have to offer. Research in

1. **Develop a Strategic Plan for the Firm**—The firm must decide what will define it, including how it will practice law, what it will practice, what business the firm is in, what market segments it will specialize in, who its competitors are, what areas are the most profitable, who its clients are, what the clients' needs are, and in what direction the firm is headed. All of these items fundamentally have a direct bearing on the marketing program.

2. **Define the Target Market the Marketing Plan Will be Aimed At and Determine the Goals of the Marketing Program**—The firm should define its clients by geographic area, gender, age, education, occupation, financial status, and marital status, among other classifications. The firm should determine where it can expect to find such people and consider the best methods to make them aware of the firm's services. The firm must also decide upon the exact purpose of the marketing plan. Is it to expand the firm's expertise into additional areas? Is it to expand into different types of clients? Is it to expand into a new geographic area?

   Types of Client Markets:
   - Government—international, federal, state, local
   - Business organizations—publicly owned, privately owned, nonprofit institutions, small businesses, large businesses
   - Labor organizations
   - Individuals—middle class, wealthy, disadvantaged

   Legal Specialty Markets
   - Administrative Law
   - Admiralty Law
   - Antitrust Law
   - Banking Law
   - Bankruptcy Law
   - Civil Rights Law
   - Collections Law
   - Communications Law
   - Contract Law
   - Corporate Law
   - Criminal Law
   - Employee Benefit Law
   - Employment Law
   - Entertainment Law
   - Environmental Law
   - Estates, Trusts, and Probate
   - Ethics and Professional Responsibility
   - Family Law
   - Government Contract Law
   - Immigration Law
   - Insurance Law
   - International Law
   - Intellectual Property Law
   - Labor Law
   - Landlord and Tenant Law
   - Litigation
   - Mergers and Acquisitions
   - Military Law
   - Municipal Finance Law
   - Oil and Gas Law
   - Real Estate Law
   - Social Security Law
   - Tax Law
   - Tort Law
   - Tribal Law
   - Water Law
   - Workers' Compensation Law

3. **Research the Market**—Once you have determined your goals and target group, you still need to learn more about the target group itself. You need to know their wants, needs, who they are, where they are, and how you can serve them.

   Researching the Market
   - Study your own marketing successes/failures.
   - Study the marketing efforts of your competitors.
   - Survey your target group (talk to them, know their needs).
   - Use in-house surveys to survey your own clients (what do they need/want?).
   - Talk to consultants.
   - If it is a specific group, read their trade journals and find out what issues are important to them.

4. **Strategize What Problems the Firm Will Likely Face During Implementation and Develop Solutions**—Now that you know your goals and you have conducted some

**Figure 8-4
Developing the
Marketing Plan**[6]

Figure 8-4
(Continued)

market research, what problems will impede the firm from reaching those goals? Anticipate the problems and devise solutions to them. Think about contingency plans in case
something goes wrong.

5. **Develop Specific Strategies and an Action Plan for Meeting the Goals**—In this stage,
you must set specific strategies for achieving the goal. How are you going to get there?
What marketing techniques will best convey your message and reach the target group?
What pricing will you use? A plan or timeline should be developed stating exactly when
each step of each strategy or marketing technique is to be accomplished, and who is
going to accomplish it. All of the strategies should be coordinated and complement one
another.

6. **Develop a Marketing Budget and Analyze Resources**—Now you must determine if the
firm's resources are large enough to carry out the specific marketing plan you laid out in
the previous step. Enough resources must be available to carry out the plan. If the firm
does not have the resources to carry out the plan, the plan may need to be scaled back.

the way of studying competitors, interviewing clients, surveying clients, talking to
experts, and really finding out what makes the target group "tick" forms the foundation of a good marketing plan. Another important part of the marketing plan is to
develop specific strategies for reaching the target audience in the most effective
way. There are innumerable ways to reach a target audience, but finding the most
effective way that will actually bring clients to the law firm takes thought, skill, and
experience. Developing a marketing budget and funding an adequate marketing
campaign are also integral parts of the plan.

> _Sadly, although many [firms] would not admit it, they practice a haphazard_
> _approach to marketing. They proceed without direction, wasting valuable_
> _funds with an unfocused plan. These costly mistakes cause many . . . to_
> _question the value of marketing as a component in their firm's budget._[7]

Typical Law Practice Marketing Options and Strategies

The strategies and options that a law firm can use to market their services are many
and varied. Figure 8-5 shows a number of strategies and marketing alternatives that
are available, some of which are described in more detail in this section. One of the
most important things an office can do is to actually _track_ what marketing techniques
are the most successful and then concentrate resources and funds on these methods.
When a new client comes into the office, the New Client Questionnaire form should
include a question regarding specifically how the client heard about the law firm,
and statistics/reports should be maintained to show what sources are the most effective. Future marketing efforts should be based on the results of these reports.

- **Quality legal services**—There's that word again: _quality_. Before a firm can
  market its services, it must have something of quality to market! Keep in
  mind that it is always easier to sell a quality product that people want to buy

- Internet site
- E-mail newsletter
- Online yellow pages
- Keyword searching advertising on search engine sites
- Firm brochures and resume
- Hard-copy newsletter
- Promotional materials (folders, pencils, etc., with law office logo)
- Business cards/letterhead/announcement cards
- Subject area information brochures (e.g., tax, auto accidents, etc.)
- Public relations
  - belonging to boards, associations, and community groups
  - speaking at public functions
  - writing articles on legal subjects for the local newspaper
  - issuing press releases
  - handling publicized pro bono cases
  - volunteering in "law day" activities
  - volunteering staff time to help with fundraisers for community groups
  - running for public office
- Firm open house
- Public advertising
  - yellow page ads
  - newspaper ads
  - newspaper inserts
  - television ads
  - radio ads
- Client seminars
- Direct mail (not allowable in some states)
- Mining other legal professionals
  - Obtaining referrals
  - Joining legal associations
  - Networking with other legal professionals
- Mining friends, associates, and social contacts regarding the legal services offered
  - Making a call or contact list, including a mailing list
  - Contacting them monthly or quarterly
  - Breakfast, lunch, or dinner engagements regarding their needs and your services
- Mining existing clients
  - Contacting current and past clients monthly
  - Cross-selling
  - Breakfast, lunch, or dinner engagements regarding their needs and your services
  - Personal notes of congratulations for accomplishments
  - Holiday cards
  - Thank-you notes for referrals
  - Reading trade journals regarding a client's business

Figure 8-5
Marketing Strategies and Options

than to sell a product you want to sell. Earlier in this book, it was explained how important existing clients are for bringing repeat business back to the firm and for making referrals to others. This is why quality is so important. Everything a firm does affects quality and, therefore, its marketing effort. Remember: it's easier to satisfy and keep a client for life by continually meeting and exceeding his or her expectations than it is to have to continually find new clients who stay for a while and then go to a competitor.

An employee who treats clients rudely, a docket control system that does not work, or billing practices that make clients upset in the end are all quality problems. Law office management must ensure quality; marketing and quality are parts of the same equation.

> *There is no substitute for the quality of the work of the lawyers [and parale-*
> *gals]. No marketing ploy, no firm brochure, no slick public relations program*
> *will cover for the poor work of an attorney [or paralegal].*[8]

- **Firm Internet site**—Operating a firm Internet site is a standard marketing practice for many law firms. A recent survey found that two-thirds of all law firms had an Internet site, and this number is growing. Solo practitioners have generally been the slowest to move to the Internet. A definite advantage of a firm Web site is that, unlike the office itself, it stays open 24 hours a day, 7 days a week, to local, national, and international customers and clients. A Web site is a particularly good idea for a legal organization with a specialized practice; a firm with a unique niche or specialized practice can reach potential clients anywhere in the world. Many organizations have found the marketing potential of a Web site to be enormous. In addition, because it operates all the time, it is cost effective when compared to other types of marketing alternatives.

  Depending on the information on the Web site, the organization can also provide timely information to current and potential clients. Many legal organizations offer information in their specialty area that would be useful to their clients. Thus, a Web site can provide a service to an organization's clients that hopefully will create goodwill toward the firm. Most experts say that "content is king." It is extremely important that the content of the law firm's Web site be strong, fresh, and changed often. A Web site can also be used for recruiting employees, such as legal assistants and other staff. Figure 8-6 presents a list of features that can help establish a top-notch law firm Web site.

> *We want to be THE online source for information on U.S. immigration law. We*
> *have worked for five years to develop a Web site that includes nearly 2,000*
> *original articles on immigration law, 100-plus government forms . . . a high-*
> *traffic discussion board on immigration law, an advocacy center with informa-*
> *tion and links to dozens of immigration-related bills pending in Congress . . .*
> *and a good deal more. We also distribute an e-mail newsletter that is typi-*
> *cally 50-plus pages of the latest news and analysis in our field. By develop-*
> *ing strong content, we have been able to develop a regular and substantial*
> *readership. The site has had more than 13 million hits to date and the*
> *newsletter is e-mailed to 21,000 subscribers every month. . . . It is the engine*
> *that has helped our firm grow from a solo practice to one of the nation's*
> *largest immigration law firms in just five years.*[9]

Tip	Explanation
List success stories	If the firm has been successful in a matter, tell the story on the Web site. Change the stories on a regular basis. You should not promise the same results, but you can tell the story.
Focus on the client	The whole site should be geared to the client. It should be user friendly and meet the needs of the client. It should clearly spell out in layperson's terms what services are available, including resources regarding the subject matters of the areas practiced. It's really about the client, not about the law firm.
List existing clients	Clients like to know that the firm has represented others "like them"; references help.
Demonstrate the firm's experience	Experience counts. Most clients want to know that the firm is an expert in the subject matter of the case they are bringing to the firm.
Keep content up to date	Out-of-date content gives the client no reason to come back to the site. Keep it updated and current at all times.
Include a search function	Clients want to be able to quickly find what they need; a search function on the site greatly helps in this process.
Make it printer friendly	The site should be printer friendly so that clients can print out information as needed.

Figure 8-6
Tips for a Strong Law Firm Internet Web Site

While firm Internet sites are allowed, there is at least one case where an attorney violated a state's ethical rules by misusing e-mail. In *In re Canter*, Term. Sup. Ct., Nos. 95-831-O-H, etc. (6/5/97), the Tennessee Supreme Court found that an attorney who sent an e-mail advertisement message to thousands of Internet groups and lists (called "spamming") had violated the state's ethical rules. The message did not comply with state rules that required noting that the message was an advertisement, and a copy was not filed with the Board of Professional Responsibility as required.

- **Firm brochure/resume**—A firm brochure is typically a pamphlet that informs the general public about the nature of the firm (see Figure 8-7). In many ways, it is like a resume—some even call it a firm resume. Firm brochures often contain the following types of information:

  (a) History of the firm
  (b) Ideology or philosophy of the firm
  (c) Services offered by the firm (e.g., the types of law it practices, specific departments, etc.)
  (d) The firm's fee or billing policies
  (e) Description of the firm's attorneys (background, items of interest, awards, degrees, etc.)
  (f) Description of the firm's support staff

A Word About Our Firm

We are a general practice law firm, established in 1972 with four attorneys. We can handle almost every type of legal work that you, your family or your business may require. We take great pride in our team of lawyers, legal assistants, legal secretaries, and staff members. Each lawyer, legal assistant and legal secretary is an expert in one or more fields. This expertise allows us to provide superior legal services in a number of fields of law (See our "Legal Services" section). We hope you will meet our well-qualified team and allow them to work together for your benefit.

APPOINTMENTS: We prefer to work by appointment. Agreeing on the date and hour to get together allows both of us to make better use of our time. It is more efficient for us and more economical for you if we meet at our office. If due to illness or disability you are unable to come to our office, we can make arrangements to meet in the most convenient place for you. Our office is open from 8:30 to 5:00 Monday through Friday for appointments. If an unusual situation requires, an appointment can be arranged for other days and times. If you are confronted with a legal emergency, you won't need any appointment. Just give us a call!

Selecting a Lawyer

We will help you select the right member of the firm to handle your work. Contact any of our lawyers that you know, or call the office number and speak to the receptionist. When you explain the type of legal matter that concerns you, you will be referred to someone in our firm who is well-qualified for that type of work. We will introduce you, at your convenience, to the lawyer we believe will be able to handle your legal need most effectively (See the bibliographical profiles in the "Our Lawyers" section). If you consider one of our lawyers to be your lawyer, continue to do so and feel free to consult with him at any time. We are here to serve you!

Attorney-Client

between th
however, y
obligated t
other.

Your w
ever learn

We wil
as we go al
sometimes
send out o
heard or d
important

Our Work

When you retain our firm, there should be a clear understanding between us about the extent of the work we are authorized to do. We will discuss the types of legal remedies or legal work required by the situation and the estimated time and legal expense involved. It is a good time to be practical. If, as the work progresses, there are unexpected developments which result in a longer time period or greater expense than anticipated, we will tell you when we recognize this.

an hourly
cases, such
fee basis, v
amount of
arrangemen
firm. In sc
fee. In ler
matters, th

DISBURSEMENTS: The work we do for you may require us to make disbursem
Sometimes the estimated disbursements are payable in advance. Sometimes they are
RETAINERS: In many cases, our office policy requires an advance payment, kno
payments are deposited in our trust account and are paid to us periodically as your wor

Our Lawyers

Edward R. Parker (Ned), born Richmond, Virginia, June 19, 1929; admitted to bar, 1952, Virginia. Preparatory education, University of Virginia (B.A., 1951); legal education, University of Virginia (LL.B., 1952). Adjunct Assistant Professor, T.C. Williams School of Law, University of Richmond 1973-1979. Legal Specialities: Estate Planning, Administration of Decedent's Estate, Business Law and Taxation.

Henry R. Pollard, IV (Harry), born Richmond, Virginia, August 5, 1943; admitted to bar 1967, Virginia. Preparatory education, Hampden-Sydney College (B.S., 1964); legal education, University of Richmond (LL.B., 1967). Legal Specialities: Litigation, Business Law, Commercial Real Estate, Securities Law.

William N. Pollard, born Richmond Virginia, April 4, 1945; admitted to bar 1971, Virginia. Preparatory education, Hampden-Sydney College (B.S., 1967); legal education, University of Virginia (J.D., 1971). Legal Specialities: Real Estate, Business Planning and Corporate Law, Litigation, Estate Planning, Administration of Decedent's Estates, Family Law.

T. Lee
1949;
educat
legal ed
1974).
Corpor
istratio
Comm

Barry
1955;
educat
educat
Legal S
Planni

Micha
Decen
ginia.
(B.A.,
T.C.W
(J.D., 1
ruptcy

Legal Services

BUSINESS AND CORPORATE: Partnerships, incorporation of businesses, advising individuals, partnerships and corporations, business contracts.

PERSONAL INJURY CLAIMS: Investigation and evaluation of claims for injuries resulting from accidents, bringing lawsuits and conduct of trials to enforce claims.

GENERAL TRIAL WORK: Bringing or defending lawsuits in a variety of legal disputes, including bankruptcy.

WORKERS' COMPENSATION: The representation of persons injured on their jobs.

WILLS AND TRUSTS: The preparation of wills, and of revocable and irrevocable trusts.

ESTATE PLANNING: The preparation of a plan for the transfer of your assets prior to or upon your death to carry out your wishes in a cost efficient manner.

ESTATE ADMINISTRATION: Serving as executor or representing the executor or family of the deceased person in settling an estate.

TAX AND FINANCIAL PLANNING: Planning the shape of business and personal transactions for minimum tax impact, representation before Federal and State tax authorities, answering tax questions.

REAL ESTATE TRANSACTIONS: The sale or purchase of real estate, mortgage transactions, leases, contracts, title searches and title insurance.

INVESTMENT MANAGMENT: Offering investment counceling on your investment portfolio through your trust or directly.

FAMILY LAW: Adoptions; appointment of guardians, and conservators; separation agreements; divorces; annulments; and legal separations.

Our Locations

We are easily accessible to you. Richmond: Take the Staples Mill Road West Exit off Interstate 64 and we are at 5511 Staples Mill Road between Southside and Northside Avenues. Tidewater: In Norfolk, travel east on Northampton Boulevard (Route 13) from its intersection with Interstate 64 to the northeast corner of Diamond Springs Road and Northampton Boulevard.

Parker, Pollard & Brown, P.C.
Attorneys at Law

5511 Staples Mill Road
Richmond, Virginia 23228
(804) 262-4042

1300 Diamond Springs Road
Northampton Executive Center
Virginia Beach, Virginia 23455
(804) 460-5050

Parker, Pollard & Brown, P.C.
Attorneys at Law

5511 Staples Mill Road
Richmond, Virginia 23228
(804) 262-4042

1300 Diamond Springs Road
Northampton Executive Center
Virginia Beach, Virginia 23455
(804) 460-5050

www.parkerpollard

Figure 8-7
Small Law Firm Brochure

Printed with permission of Parker, Pollard, and Brown, P.C.

(g) Address, phone number, Web site address

(h) Whether the firm has a newsletter or other types of client services

(i) Notable firm accomplishments

(j) Important clients the firm has represented (must have client's permission)

Figure 8-7 is a firm brochure for a smaller law office. In some cases, this may be the only brochure the law office has. Larger firms typically take a different marketing approach; instead of having one brochure that markets the whole firm, they may have separate brochures for each department or brochures that target specific industries. Figure 8-8 is an example of a large law firm's brochure that markets its legal health care department to the health care industry.

- **Firm newsletters and e-mail newsletters**—Firm newsletters and e-mail newsletters are a popular way of maintaining contact with clients and generating goodwill. Firm newsletters can be on a single topic, such as real estate, or on a potpourri of topics. Some firms focus on a different legal issue in each issue: family law, real estate, tax, and so on. It is important that the firm knows and understands who its clients are and what type of information would be beneficial to them. Newsletters are also used to inform clients of legislative changes, whether local, state, or national. Newsletters can be produced in-house, by ad agencies, or by purchasing ready-made legal newsletters. With a ready-made newsletter, all the law office has to do is add its logo, firm name, and address. E-mail newsletters are popular because they are relatively low cost and can be distributed immediately.
- **Informational brochures**—These are brochures aimed at informing clients about a specific topic, such as "Why You Need a Will," "What to Do in Case of an Auto Accident," "How to Set Up Your Own Business," or "How to Protect Your Ideas through Copyrights, Trademarks, and Patents." They are informational pieces that are used to inform clients about legal problems, and many firms publish them on their firm's Web site.
- **Public relations**—Generating goodwill and a positive public image is a long-standing, successful way that firms have marketed themselves. Legal assistants and attorneys can promote themselves and their firms as members of social groups, churches, committees, nonprofit boards, and associations.

  Speaking at public and association meetings is another way to attract interest and goodwill; other methods of generating and maintaining good public relations include handling pro bono cases and issuing press releases when a firm wins a case or achieves other notable accomplishments.
- **Firm open house**—Some firms hold annual open houses, where clients and visitors can come to the firm and socialize with attorneys and staff members outside the normal pressures of coming to the office with legal problems.
- **Business cards, letterhead, and announcement cards**—Announcement cards are used quite frequently by law offices. An announcement card is usually a postcard that a firm sends to other firms to publicize a change, such as when new attorneys have been added or firms have merged. Business cards and letterhead are also a frequent way firms promote themselves and their staff.

Health Representation – Skills and Experience

Reed Smith's Health Care Group works to solve its clients' problems. Our representation begins by listening to you — the client. Systematically, our lawyers will analyze complex problems, advise you on various courses of action and, when necessary, advocate on your behalf to achieve a prompt and reasonable solution.

Legislative and Regulatory: Legislative representation for health care clients includes drafting and advocacy on proposed and enacted health care legislation. We have successfully challenged major regulatory actions through negotiations with federal agencies, including HCFA, OMB, the FTC, and others, and we regularly advise clients on a host of regulatory compliance issues. The firm assists clients throughout the legislative and regulatory process by drafting comments, testimony and legislative amendments, as well as presenting clients' positions directly to Members of Congress, Administration officials, and key regulatory personnel. A number of our attorneys previously served in high-level positions with both Republican and Democratic administrations, as well as in agency and various congressional positions.

Legal Fees

The particular backgrounds of our health attorneys make it possible for our clients to obtain comprehensive, targeted legal advice at competitive prices. Moreover, we believe that our wide range of specialties saves our clients money, if by using our services they have access to a coordinated team, and can thus avoid the need to consult specialists at a number of firms. Our health group is often retained by other law firms on specific projects requiring a high degree of technical advice, such as reimbursement, fraud and abuse, biotechnology, and the like. We are happy to provide more detailed information on our fee structure and billing procedures.

Future

Reed Smith attorneys welcome the opportunity to talk with you about your company, business, or organization. We would like to hear how the changing health care environment affects you, and discuss how Reed Smith can bring thoughtful, innovative, and responsive solutions to your health care problems. The lawyers in the Reed Smith Health Care Group are listed on the card at the end of this brochure. Please feel free to call any of them to discuss your particular needs.

Legal

Solutions

for the

Health Care Industry

REED SMITH

Figure 8-8   Large Law Firm—Specific Industry Brochure

- **Public advertising—yellow pages, newspaper, television, and radio ads**—Public advertisements are another popular form of marketing. They come in all sizes, shapes, and price ranges, and may appear in local yellow pages, newspapers, and television and radio stations.
- **Firm seminars**—Some firms hold seminars aimed at educating their clients or the general public (prospective clients) on legal issues. These seminars may be held on any legal topic that is of interest to clients. Businesses might be interested in the legal issues of hiring, firing, and evaluating employees and employee benefits, and individual clients might be interested in tax planning, trusts and estates, and other issues. Client seminars are usually held for the purpose of creating client loyalty and should be conducted by an attorney.
- **Direct mail pieces**—Some firms send out direct mail pieces aimed at a specific audience. Usually, the pieces are unsolicited; that is, they are sent out to people without being requested. For example, if your firm primarily handles real estate matters, you might send out a letter to all real estate businesses. Note, however, that direct mail is very controversial, especially when the mailing is targeted to a specific group. Ethical rules in some states strictly prohibit targeted mailing under the theory that it is direct solicitation. Attorneys are specifically prohibited from directly soliciting clients.
- **Involvement in legal associations**—Attorneys and legal assistants can also market themselves by being active in local, state, and national bar and legal assistant associations. Many firms that involve themselves in these types of organizations gain the respect and goodwill of others and may gain referrals from another firm that may not have the expertise to handle a particular type of case.
- **Sending information to clients that you know will be of interest to them**—Whenever you come across information that you think will interest clients, bring it to the attention of your supervising attorney and have the attorney send it to them. For example, if you come across a newspaper article that concerns their business or new laws that might affect them, clip it out and have the attorney send it. Or, if you come across a case in which they might be interested in, get your attorney's approval and send it to them with a note (but do not bill them for it!). Clients appreciate a law office that takes a personal interest in them.
- **Marketing your services to existing clients**—A firm's current clients are among its biggest assets. Firms not only want to market to new clients but also need to keep the business of their current clients. Thus, firms will typically spend a great deal of time cultivating their existing clients using techniques described earlier, such as newsletters and client seminars. Firms also have other techniques for marketing to existing clients.

  (a) **Cross-selling**—**Cross-selling** refers to selling additional services to existing clients. For instance, suppose a law office represented XYZ business in a tax matter, but XYZ used another firm to handle its personnel disputes. If possible, the law office would like to cross-sell XYZ to use its firm for both the tax matter and the personnel matters.

cross-selling
Selling additional services to existing clients.

> *A satisfied client will produce more clients and generate more business for you than any other single source. There are two ways in which existing clients can generate business:*
>
> *1. **They can bring in new clients.** A satisfied client is your most likely and probable source of new clients. Clients who have been well served have all of the zeal of missionaries. They will recommend many clients to you over the years.*
>
> *2. **They can bring you their own repeat business.** As a general rule, clients want more attention, not less. . . . The lawyer [or law firm] that stays in close touch with clients will get a telephone call from the client ("Before I sign this lease, I want you to look at it"), which will not happen if the lawyer [or law firm] is inaccessible to the client.*[10]

(b) **Client questionnaires**—Many firms send out client questionnaires at the end of a legal matter to see how the client felt about the services that were provided. In addition to being a quality-control device, this is also a marketing technique because it is aimed at correcting problems that the client might have had.

(c) **Keeping the firm's name in front of the client**—What happens if a client's case is completely finished and the client has no other business for the firm at the time? Should the firm forget about the client? No, most firms continue to keep in contact with the client with newsletters, seminars, letters, and holiday cards. Firms want clients to feel wanted and to be reminded that the firm is there to serve them.

(d) **Developing client relationships**—With whom would you rather do business: friends or strangers? Friends are the unquestionable answer, because you trust and feel comfortable with them. This is the kind of relationship that firms want to promote.

(e) **Thanking clients for referring others to you**—Always send a thank-you letter to clients (or other attorneys) for making referrals to the office.

The Role of the Rainmaker

rainmaking
Bringing in new clients to a law office.

Rainmaking refers to the ability to bring in new clients to a law office. Sometimes law offices bring attorneys into the firm for the sole purpose of being "rainmakers." Some rainmakers are well connected politically or have inroads into certain industries. Rainmakers use their influence and skills to bring new clients into the firm. However, a recent survey of successful rainmakers found, without exception, that helping their clients achieve their business goals and dreams was what made them a good rainmaker. One rainmaker summed it up: "I like to think that I have a special relationship with my clients. My legal antennae are always sensitive to any issues which may affect them. . . . It gives them comfort to know we're here. They can sleep because the 'national guard' is awake." Many private law offices use rainmakers in their marketing schemes.

Marketing—An Ethics Perspective

Although ethical limitations on marketing have eased up over the past 20 years, there are still many pitfalls that can occur from an ethical perspective, including making false or misleading statements in an advertisement, failing to comply with general requirements about advertisements, directly soliciting a client, or putting forth an attorney as a specialist.

FALSE OR MISLEADING STATEMENTS   *Model Rule* 7.1 states that attorneys are not allowed to make false or misleading statements in any kind of marketing or advertising piece. Rule 7.1 of the ABA *Model Rules of Professional Conduct* states:

> This is a fairly straightforward rule. Attorneys cannot promote themselves using advertisements that are less than completely truthful. The Comment to the rule specifically addresses advertisements that talk about the lawyer's achievements. The comment states:
>
> > *An advertisement that truthfully reports a lawyer's achievements on behalf of clients or former clients may be misleading if presented so as to lead a reasonable person to form an unjustified expectation that the same results could be obtained for other clients in similar matters without reference to the specific factual and legal circumstances of each client's case.*

Thus, when an advertisement discusses a past victory it must be careful to not create an expectation that the attorney can always achieve the same result, since cases depend on the specifics of each circumstance. Figure 8-9 provides several examples of false or misleading advertisements.

ADVERTISING IN GENERAL   Rule 7.2 of the *Model Rules* states some general guidelines that apply to all types of advertising, including that an attorney may advertise his or her legal services in the public media or through written, recorded, or electronic communication. The rule generally prohibits an attorney from paying a person who recommends a client to him or her. The rule also provides that any communication shall include the name and address of at least one lawyer or law firm responsible for its content, so that the authorities will know who to contact if there is an ethical violation. This rule broadly allows lawyers to advertise using virtually any method.

NO DIRECT SOLICITATION OR "AMBULANCE CHASING"   Rule 7.3 of the ABA *Model Rules* restricts attorneys from directly soliciting persons they do not know either in person, by live telephone, or by real-time electronic means. The rule does not apply if the attorney is soliciting another lawyer, if the person is a family member or close personal friend, or if the person has had a prior professional relationship with the lawyer. In addition, the rule provides that an advertisement must include the words

**Figure 8-9
Examples of False
or Misleading
Advertisements**

Advertisement	Ethical Analysis
"On personal injury and worker's compensation cases, there are no attorney's fees unless we win for you."	Most lawyers will charge clients for the costs of bringing the claim, whether or not they are successful. Since people do not generally distinguish between *fees* and *costs,* it could be misleading to omit information in an advertisement stating that the clients are responsible for costs.[1]
"Our firm recently won a $10,000,000 award—we can do the same for you."	This would create an unjustified expectation and would imply that the next case would have a similar result, even though every case is different.[2]
"We do it well." "Quickly becoming recognized as a premier personal injury law firm." "We are the best and smartest firm in the city."	Generally, the use of unsupportable, absolute terms are prohibited. It is also false or misleading for lawyers to compare their services to those of other lawyers unless that comparison can be factually substantiated.[3]
"We are specialists in personal injury and litigation." "Specializing in medical malpractice."	Violates Rule 7.4 that prohibits attorneys from claiming they are specialists unless it is an area in which some particular certification is required.[4]

[1]American Bar Association. (2004). *The legal assistant's practical guide to professional responsibility* (2nd ed., p. 110). Reprinted by permission.
[2]Ibid.
[3]Ibid.
[4]American Bar Association. (2004). *Model rules of professional conduct* (4th ed., p. 534). Reprinted by permission.

"advertising material" so that the public clearly understands the nature of the communication.

Direct, in-person telephone contact with individuals that the lawyer does not know is prohibited because of the possibility of undue influence, intimidation, or overreaching when a skilled attorney contacts a layperson. However, prerecorded communications may be acceptable, as the attorney is not "live." This rule also squarely prohibits attorneys from making harassing communication or bothering persons who do not want to be solicited.

A distinction is made in the rule between directly soliciting persons that are known by the attorney, such as family members or past clients, and soliciting unknown individuals. Attorneys and staff may solicit individuals they know. This is quite common, and there is nothing unethical about mentioning to friends and relatives that your law office handles certain types of cases and could help them if the need ever arose. What is prohibited is directly soliciting absolute strangers in person. Written solicitation, such as newsletters, brochures, and—in many jurisdictions—targeted mail, is allowed.

ADVERTISING FIELDS OF PRACTICE AND SPECIALIZATION   *Model Rule* 7.4 generally prohibits attorneys from presenting themselves as specialists. Attorneys are allowed to communicate that they practice in a particular field of law, but a lawyer generally cannot state that he or she is certified as a specialist in a particular field unless the attorney has been certified as a specialist by an organization approved by a state authority or the American Bar Association. The word "specialist" has a secondary meaning, implying formal recognition (this rule would not apply in states that provide procedures for certification in particular areas). There are a few stated exceptions in the rule related to patent and admiralty law.

Each state has specific ethical rules about lawyer advertising, so whoever performs the marketing needs to be familiar with the rules of your state. One way to avoid ethical problems is to show advertising to the disciplinary administrator for the state before it is run and ask his or her opinion on the matter.

SUMMARY

Legal marketing is the process of educating consumers on the legal and business activities a firm uses to deliver quality and ethical legal services. Advertising entails getting your name out to the public, while marketing encompasses much more. A marketing plan specifies a target audience, sets goals for the marketing program, and establishes detailed strategies for achieving the goals. Marketing strategies and options for law offices include a law firm Internet site, brochure/resume, e-mail newsletters, public relation activities, public advertising, law firm seminars, and much more. "Rainmaking" refers to the ability to bring in new clients to the office. Ethical regulations related to marketing include not providing false or misleading information in advertising, not directly soliciting clients, and not allowing an attorney to present him- or herself to the public as a specialist without some kind of certification from an accredited organization.

HELPFUL WEB SITES

ORGANIZATION	DESCRIPTION	INTERNET ADDRESS
American Bar Association (ABA)	Association for attorneys. The site has a large amount of information and publications relevant to individuals working in the legal profession.	http://www.abanet.org
ABA Information on Professionalism and Ethics in Lawyer Advertising and Marketing	ABA site devoted to ethics related to attorney marketing.	http://www.abanet.org/cpr/clt-dev/home.html
ABA Law Practice Today	ABA site devoted to law practice management issues, including coverage of legal marketing.	http://www.abanet.org/lpm
Legal Marketing Association	Nonprofit association for legal marketing professionals.	http://www.legalmarketing.org

ORGANIZATION	DESCRIPTION	INTERNET ADDRESS
FindLaw's Lawyer Marketing page	Web site with articles and information on legal marketing.	http://marketing.lp.findlaw.com/index.html
New Jersey Bar Association	Web site with many articles and information on legal marketing.	http://www.njsba.com/law_office_manage/index.cfm?fuseaction=articles
Lawmarketing.com	Legal marketing portal, including articles and information on legal marketing.	http://www.lawmarketing.com
Legalmarketingblog.com	Legal marketing blog, including articles and information related to legal marketing.	http://www.legalmarketingblog.com/

SUGGESTED READING

1. Rose, J. (2005). *How to capture and keep clients: Marketing strategies for lawyers*. American Bar Association.
2. Foonberg, J. (1994). *How to get and keep good clients* (2nd ed.). American Bar Association.
3. *Law Practice* magazine, published by the American Bar Association Law Practice Management Section [http://www.abanet.org/lpm].
4. Hornsby, W. (2000). *Marketing and legal ethics*. American Bar Association.
5. American Bar Association. (2004). *Marketing success stories: Conversations with leading lawyers* (2nd ed.).
6. American Bar Association. (1996). *Successful client newsletters: The complete guide to creating powerful newsletters*.
7. Munneke, G. A., & Davis, A. E. (2003). *The essential form book—comprehensive management tools*. American Bar Association.
8. American Bar Association. (2002). *The lawyer's guide to marketing on the Internet* (2nd ed.). American Bar Association.
9. Durhan, J., & McMurray, D. (2004). *The lawyer's guide to marketing your practice*. American Bar Association.
10. Snyder, T. C. (2003). *Women rainmakers' best marketing tips*. American Bar Association.

KEY TERMS

cross-selling
legal marketing

marketing plan
rainmaking

TEST YOUR KNOWLEDGE

1. Why is the case of *Bates v. State Bar of Arizona* important?
2. True or false: according to the text, marketing is the exclusive duty of attorneys.
3. What is the difference between marketing and advertising?
4. True or false: it is easier to sell a quality product that people want to buy than to sell a product you want to sell.
5. Before a law firm begins to market, it is essential that it have a _____.
6. What should an effective marketing plan contain?
7. Name two ways to obtain research for a marketing plan.
8. One of the most important things a law office can do is to actually _____ what marketing techniques are the most successful and then

concentrate resources and funds on those methods.

9. When it comes to law firm Web sites, _____ is king.

10. Name five ways a law office can market its services.

11. _____ is the ability to bring in new clients to a law firm.

12. No matter what type or kind of advertisement/marketing, any public advertising communication by a lawyer cannot be found to be either _____ or _____.

13. True or false: a law firm ad can guarantee future results based on a recent victory of the firm.

14. True or false: according to the *Model Rules*, a lawyer may advertise services via written, recorded, or electronic communication, including public media.

15. Any ad or marketing piece an attorney or law firm publishes *must* have two things somewhere in the ad; what are they?

16. True or false: an attorney may personally solicit legal business from family and people with whom the attorney has had a close personal or prior professional relationship.

ON THE WEB EXERCISES

1. Go to the ABA's Information on Professionalism and Ethics in Lawyer Advertising and Marketing home page at http://www.abanet.org/cpr/clt-dev/home.html and read two ethics opinions related to lawyer advertising/marketing.

2. Using a general search engine, such as http://www.google.com or http://www.yahoo.com, or the ABA's Web site on Information on Professionalism and Ethics in Lawyer Advertising and Marketing, find and print out a copy of *The Handbook on Lawyer Advertising and Solicitation,* published by the Florida Bar Association.

3. The state bar of Texas requires that some marketing material be reviewed by the bar before it is published. Find the advertising review rules and read any "Frequently Asked Questions" document they may have. Try starting at the ABA's Information

on Professionalism and Ethics in Lawyer Advertising and Marketing home page at http://www.abanet.org/cpr/clt-dev/home.html.

4. Go to the ABA Center for Professional Responsibility [http://www.abanet.org/cpr/home.html], find the *ABA Model Rules of Professional Conduct,* and read and print out the comments to Rules 7.1, 7.2, 7.3, and 7.4.

5. Visit several bar association Web sites and find a minimum of five articles on legal marketing. The following link will take you to a Web site that connects to all state bar sites: http://www.abanet.org/barserv/stlobar.html.

6. Visit the American Bar Association Law Practice Management section [http://www.abanet.org/lpm/home.shtml] and review any materials they have on legal marketing.

PROJECTS

1. Go to the ABA's Information on Professionalism and Ethics in Lawyer Advertising and Marketing home page at http://www.abanet.org/cpr/clt-dev/home.html. Review the "Cases on Lawyer Advertising" section and summarize three cases. Include the facts and an analysis of each case, what the

court found, what the ruling was, and whether or not you agree with it.

2. Research and write a paper on any subject related to legal marketing. There are many resources available online or in most law libraries. Select a specific topic on legal marketing that interests you or cover the topic from a broad perspective. Your paper should cite at least five different resources.

3. Preparation of a marketing plan—Several attorneys you currently work with are considering starting their own practice in your area. The practice will have five attorneys and other staff as needed. They would like to have three practice groups. The attorneys trust your business judgment and would like you to develop a detailed marketing plan for the first year of their practice. The attorneys agree that you cannot spend more than $20,000 for this first year. Your plan should be well thought out and be specific to your area. You will need to do research, get actual prices for what your marketing plan will cost, and attach examples or give narrative explanations of what the marketing will entail (e.g., if you will decide to have a TV commercial, you will need to develop a script; if you decide to have an Internet site, you will need to attach an example, etc.).

Your plan should cover the following topics:

A. Practice Groups
- What practice areas do you recommend in your area, and why?
- Consider whether why you think the new firm will be able to get into this market.
- What firms are currently in the market (i.e., who will your competitors be)?
- What services will the practice groups provide?
- How will the services differ from services currently provided by existing firms?
- Who will be the targeted clients (be very specific)?
- How profitable are these areas?
- How will existing firms react to your firm getting into the market?
- How will you compete with existing firms (on quality, price, better location, etc.)?

B. Marketing Options
- What marketing options will you use, and why (be specific)? List the timing of your marketing options (e.g., 1st month = mailing announcing firm, 2nd month = newspaper advertising, etc.).
- How long will each marketing option last?
- How will your marketing options reach your targeted clients?
- How many people will your marketing options reach (you can obtain some of this information from the vendors you would use—newspaper subscription numbers, TV and radio ratings figures, etc.)?
- Attach examples or explanations, including the content of your marketing options.

C. Budget
- Get bids and/or estimates of how much your marketing plan will cost, and include a detailed cost projection.

D. New Client Business Projections
- Based on your marketing plan, how many new clients do you project you can bring into the firm?

4. Using the Internet, find three law firm Web sites. Try to find one Web site that is truly outstanding, another that is representative of an average site, and another one that is very simple and basic. From a client's perspective, compare and contrast the Web sites in terms of graphics/visual appeal, content, ease of use, depth of information about the firm and legal areas it specializes in, information about the attorneys, and so on. What are the things that you liked about the outstanding site and the things you didn't like about the simple and average site?

QUESTIONS AND EXERCISES

1. You and your supervising attorney have just spent 16 weeks in a complicated products liability case regarding vaccine immunization shots for children. Your firm's client contracted the disease from the immunization shot. Your firm received the largest verdict in history for this type of case. Given the success of this case, the firm would like to handle more of these types of cases. When you get back to the office, you are shown a draft of an advertisement that is going to run in newspapers across the country, which reads:

"MILLER AND HASTINGS Law office SPECIALIZES IN PHARMACEUTICAL CASES! Recently,

our firm won a $100 million judgment against the manufacturer of a drug company for producing an unsafe drug. We can win for you too—please call us if you would like us to represent your interests."

Your supervising attorney asks you for your comment. How do you respond?

2. Your client from number 1 above is absolutely ecstatic about the verdict in the immunization case. She learns of your intentions and volunteers to appear in a television ad to do a testimonial about the verdict and the great services the firm provided. What do you think about this?

3. You work in a solo practitioner's office and she is considering a number of different marketing strategies. One is a high client turnover strategy that includes a high profile, big television campaign that would presumably generate a lot of new clients. What are your concerns?

4. As a legal assistant for a small but respected firm, you know that the firm wishes to expand and move into more lucrative legal areas. You believe that environmental issues, such as toxic waste, would be a very good area for the firm to expand into and would also be a good fit, based on work the firm has done in the past. However, you know that you need to review the matter a little closer regarding the feasibility of this. Specifically delineate what you would do to research this (be creative), and then develop a draft plan of how you might present this to your managing attorney.

5. Your law office is considering placing a yellow-pages ad. You are to research the issue by looking in the yellow pages under "attorneys." You are to pick out two yellow-pages ads that you like. Consider what it is that you like about the ads and what their messages are. Do the same with television ads. Which attorney ads are the best, and why?

NOTES

1. American Bar Association. (2004). *The legal assistant's practice guide to professional responsibility* (2nd ed., p. 107). Reprinted by permission.
2. Ibid., p. 111. Reprinted by permission.
3. Solo and small firm marketing pulse 2005. (2005, March). *Law Practice*, 44.
4. Munneke, G. A., & Davis, A. E. (2003). *The essential form book—comprehensive management tools* (Vol. II). American Bar Association.
5. Solo and Small Firm Marketing Hurdle. (2005, March). *Law Practice*, p. 33, citing 2004 Altman Weil Survey of Law Firm Economics.
6. Adapted from Anderson, A. G. (1986). *Marketing your practice* (p. 64). American Bar Association.
Reprinted by permission of the American Bar Association.
7. Stewart, L. M., & Gonyea, P. J. (1992, June). Marketing for the small law firm. *New Hampshire Bar Journal*, 389. Reprinted with the permission of the *New Hampshire Bar Journal*.
8. Wahl, D. C. (1992, Spring). Managing for quality. *The LAMA Manager*, 8. Reprinted with the permission of the Legal Assistant Management Association.
9. White, J. M. (1999, July/August). Trend setters—pioneers in the new world of law practice. *Law Practice Management*, 55. Reprinted by permission.
10. Foonberg, J. G. (2004). *How to start and build a law practice*. American Bar Association.

ANSWERS TO TEST YOUR KNOWLEDGE

1. It was the United States Supreme Court case that allowed attorneys to publicly advertise under the First Amendment right to commercial free speech.
2. False; most experts on law firm advertising encourage support staff to get involved in marketing efforts.
3. Advertising is simply getting one's name out in the public

domain, while marketing includes much more, such as providing quality legal services to clients, understanding clients' needs, fostering a good reputation in the community, and building good public relations, among other things.

4. True
5. Marketing plan
6. The overall goals of the marketing program; strategies and activities that will be necessary to obtain the goals (including who, what, when, how, and in what order the activities will be implemented); the estimated cost of the marketing program; and the estimated profit the successful marketing program would bring in.
7. Study competitors, interview clients, survey clients, and talk to experts on marketing.
8. Track or study
9. Content
10. Web site, newsletters, brochures, public relations, open house, business cards, public advertising, firm seminars, direct mail, joining associations and community groups, sending information to clients, cross-selling, developing client relationships, thanking clients for referrals, and many others.
11. Rainmaking
12. False; misleading
13. False; this would create an unjustified expectation that the same result could be obtained for other clients without reference to the specific factual and legal circumstances of each client's case.
14. True
15. The name/address of at least one lawyer or law firm responsible for its content, and it must contain the words "Advertising Material."
16. True

CASE REVIEW

—*Doe v. Condon, 2000 WL 718448 (S.C.)*

2000 WL 718448
(Cite as: 2000 WL 718448 (S.C.))

Only the Westlaw citation is currently available.

NOTICE: THIS OPINION HAS NOT BEEN RELEASED FOR PUBLICATION IN THE PERMANENT LAW REPORTS. UNTIL RELEASED, IT IS SUBJECT TO REVISION OR WITHDRAWAL.

Supreme Court of South Carolina.

John DOE, Alias, Petitioner,

v.

Charles M. CONDON, Attorney General for the State of South Carolina,

Respondent.

No. 25138.

Submitted May 23, 2000.

Decided June 5, 2000.

Assistant Attorney General Jennifer A. Deitrick, of Columbia, for respondent.

Disciplinary Counsel Henry B. Richardson, Jr., of Columbia, for amicus curiae Office of Disciplinary Counsel.

IN THE ORIGINAL JURISDICTION

PER CURIAM.

*1 Petitioner sought to have the Court accept this matter in its original jurisdiction to determine whether certain tasks performed by a nonattorney employee in a law firm constitute the unauthorized practice of law. Specifically, petitioner asks (1) whether it is the unauthorized practice of law for a paralegal employed by an attorney to conduct informational seminars for the general public on wills and trusts without the attorney being present; (2) whether it is the unauthorized practice of law for a paralegal employed by an attorney to meet with clients privately at the attorney's office, answer general questions about wills and trusts, and gather basic information from clients; and (3) whether a paralegal can receive compensation from the paralegal's law firm/employer through a profit-sharing arrangement based upon the volume and type of cases the paralegal handles. The Office of the Attorney General filed a return opposing the petition for original jurisdiction.

The Court invoked its original jurisdiction to determine whether the paralegal's activities constituted the unauthorized practice of law, and, pursuant to S.C.Code Ann. § 14-3-340 (1976), John W. Kittredge was appointed as referee to make findings of fact and conclusions of law concerning this matter. A hearing was held and the referee issued proposed findings and recommendations.

[1] [2] We adopt the referee's findings and recommendations attached to this opinion and hold that a nonlawyer employee conducting unsupervised legal presentations for the public and answering legal questions for the public or for clients of the attorney/employer engages in the unauthorized practice of law. See State v. Despain, 319 S.C. 317, 460 S.E.2d 576 (1995). We further hold that a proposed fee arrangement which compensates nonlawyer employees based upon the number and volume of cases the nonlawyer employee handles for an attorney violates the ethical rules against fee splitting with nonlawyer employees. Rule 5.4 of the Rules of Professional Conduct, Rule 407, SCACR.

PROPOSED FINDINGS AND RECOMMENDATIONS OF THE REFEREE

This is a declaratory judgment action in the Supreme Court's original jurisdiction. The Court referred this matter to me as Referee. Petitioner, a paralegal, has submitted a generalized list of tasks he wishes to perform and has inquired whether performing them constitutes the unauthorized practice of law. Petitioner also seeks a determination of the propriety of his proposed fee-splitting arrangement with his attorney-employer. Despite my repeated offers for an evidentiary hearing, neither party requested a hearing. The record before me is sufficient to address and resolve whether the activities in question constitute the unauthorized practice of law.

I find that a paralegal conducting unsupervised legal presentations for the public and answering legal questions from the audience engages in the unauthorized practice of law. Further, I find that a paralegal meeting individually with clients to answer estate-planning questions engages in the unauthorized practice of law. Finally, I find the proposed fee arrangement is improper and violates the ethical prohibition against fee splitting.

BACKGROUND

*2 Petitioner submitted the following questions to the Court:

(1) Is it the unauthorized practice of law for a paralegal employed by an attorney to conduct educational seminars for the general public, to disseminate general information about wills and trusts, including specifically a fair and balanced emphasis on living trusts, including answering general questions, without the attorney being present at the seminar as long as the seminar is sponsored by the attorney's law firm and the attorney has reviewed and approved the format, materials, and presentation to be made for content, truthfulness, and fairness?

(2) Is it the unauthorized practice of law for a paralegal employed by an attorney to meet with clients privately in the law office for the purpose of answering general questions about wills, trusts, including specifically living trusts, and estate planning in general, and to gather basic information from said clients for such purposes as long as it is done under the attorney's direction, and the clients have a follow-up interview and meeting with the attorney who would have primary responsibility for legal decisions?

(3) Can a paralegal receive compensation from the law firm he is employed by, through a profit-sharing arrangement, which would be based upon the volume and type of cases the paralegal handled?

DISCUSSION

To protect the public from unsound legal advice and incompetent representation, South Carolina, like other jurisdictions, limits the practice of law to licensed attorneys. S.C.Code Ann. § 40-5-310 (1976). While case law provides general guidelines as to what constitutes the practice of law, courts are hesitant to define its exact boundaries. Thus, the analysis in 'practice of law' cases is necessarily fact-driven. The Supreme Court has specifically avoided addressing hypothetical situations, preferring instead to determine what constitutes the unauthorized practice of law on a case-by-case basis. In Re Unauthorized Practice of Law Rules Proposed by the South Carolina Bar, 309 S.C. 304, 422 S.E.2d 123 (S.C.1992). I find that Petitioner's proposed actions constitute the unauthorized practice of law and that the proposed fee agreement violates the ethical prohibition against fee splitting.

Our Supreme Court has set forth a succinct standard of the proper role of paralegals:

> The activities of a paralegal do not constitute the practice of law as long as they are limited to work of a preparatory nature, such as legal research, investigation, or the composition of legal documents, which enable the licensed attorney-employer to carry a given matter to a conclusion through his own examination, approval or additional effort. Matter of Easler, 275 S.C. 400, 272 S.E.2d 32, 33 (S.C. 1980).

While the important support function of paralegals has increased through the years, the Easler guidelines stand the test of time. As envisioned in Easler, the paralegal plays a supporting role to the supervising attorney. Here, the roles are reversed. The attorney would support the paralegal. Petitioner would play the lead role, with no meaningful attorney supervision and the attorney's presence and involvement only surfaces on the back end. Meaningful attorney supervision must be present throughout the process. The line between what is and what is not permissible conduct by a nonattorney is oftentimes "unclear" and is a potential trap for the unsuspecting client. State v. Buyers Service Co., Inc., 292 S.C. 426, 357 S.E.2d 15, 17 (S.C.1987). The conduct of the paralegal contemplated here clearly crosses the line into the unauthorized practice of law. It is well settled that a paralegal may not give legal advice, consult, offer legal explanations, or make legal recommendations. State v. Despain, 319 S.C. 317, 460 S.E.2d 576 (S.C.1995).

A. Educational Seminars

*3 Petitioner intends to conduct unsupervised "wills and trusts" seminars for the public, "emphasizing" living trusts during the course of his presentation. Petitioner also plans to answer estate-planning questions from the audience. I find Petitioner's proposed conduct constitutes the unauthorized practice of law.

I find, as other courts have, that the very structure of such "educational" legal seminars suggests that the presenter will actually be giving legal advice on legal matters. See, In Re Mid-America Living Trust Assoc. Inc., 927 S.W.2d 855 (Mo.banc 1996); People v. Volk, 805 P.2d 1116 (Colo. 1991); Oregon State Bar v. John H. Miller & Co. 235 Or. 341, 385 P.2d 181 (Or. 1963). At the very least. Petitioner will implicitly advise participants that they require estate-planning services. Whether a will or trust is appropriate in any given situation is a function of legal judgment. To be sure, advising a potential client on his or her need for a living trust (or other particular estate-planning instrument or device) fits squarely within the practice of law. These matters cry out for the exercise of professional judgment by a licensed attorney. Thus, in conducting these informational seminars, Petitioner would engage in the unauthorized practice of law as a nonattorney offering legal advice.

Petitioner plans to answer "general" questions during his presentation. I have reviewed the Estate-Planning Summary submitted by Petitioner and his attorney-employer. This summary sets forth the subject matter to be covered by the paralegal. Petitioner would present information on, among other things, revocable trusts, irrevocable living trusts, credit shelter trusts, qualified terminable interest property trusts, charitable remainder trusts, qualified personal residence trusts, grantor retained annuity trusts, grantor retained unitrusts, and charitable lead trusts. It is difficult to imagine such specific estate-planning devices eliciting "general" questions or a scenario in which the exercise of legal judgment would not be involved. It is, after all, a legal seminar, apparently for the purpose of soliciting business.

[FN1] To suggest that some "plan" would anticipate all possible questions with predetermined nonlegal responses is specious. And so complex is this area of law that many states, including South Carolina, have established stringent standards for an attorney to receive the designation of "specialist" in Estate Planning and Probate Law. SCACR, Part IV, Appendices D and E. This is the practice of law.

> FN1. While this marketing method may raise ethical implications for the attorney involved, the issue before me is whether the activities of the paralegal constitute the unauthorized practice of law. See Rule 7.3, Rules of Professional Conduct, 407 SCACR; Matter of Morris, 270 S.C. 308, 241 S.E.2d 911 (1978) (lawyer improperly solicited employment); Matter of Craven, 267 S.C. 33, 225 S.E.2d 861 (1976) (an attorney's knowledge that his employee is engaged in solicitation of professional employment for attorney constitutes professional misconduct); Matter of Crosby, 256 S.C. 325, 182 S.E.2d 289 (1971) (attorney improperly solicited business). Thus, not only does Petitioner's solicitation of legal clients raise possible ethical concerns for his sponsoring attorney, Petitioner's involvement clearly constitutes the unauthorized practice of law.

I fully recognize the prevailing popularity of 'financial planners' and others "jump[ing] on the estate planning bandwagon." (Estate-Planning Summary submitted by Petitioner's attorney-employer, p. 1). This trend in no way affects the decision before the Court. This paralegal would not be presenting the estate-planning seminar as a financial planner. This seminar would be conspicuously sponsored by the paralegal's attorney-employer. The attorney's law firm is prominently displayed in the brochure submitted, e.g., name, address, telephone number, and "Firm Profile." In promoting the law firm and representing to the public the 'legal' nature of the seminar, neither the paralegal nor his attorney-employer can escape the prohibition against the unauthorized practice of law.

B. Initial Client Interview

*4 Petitioner intends to gather client information and answer general estate-planning questions during his proposed "initial client interviews." While Petitioner may properly compile client information, Petitioner may not answer estate-planning questions. See Matter of Easler, supra. Petitioner's answering legal questions would constitute the unauthorized practice of law for the reasons stated above. While the law firm in which Petitioner is employed plans to direct clients to an attorney for "follow-up" consultations, a paralegal may not give legal advice in any event. Moreover, permissible preparatory tasks must be performed while under the attorney's supervision. The proposed after-the-fact attorney review comes too late.

C. Compensation

Petitioner's law firm intends to compensate him based upon the volume and types of cases he "handles." A paralegal, of course, may not "handle" any case. [FN2] This fee arrangement directly violates Rule 5.4 of the Rules of Professional Conduct, SCACR 407. [FN3] This limitation serves to "discourage the unauthorized practice of law by laypersons and to prevent a nonlawyer from acquiring a vested pecuniary interest in an attorney's disposition of a case that could possibly take preeminence over a client's best interest." Matter of Anonymous Member of the S.C.Bar, 295 S.C. 25, 26, 367 S.E.2d 17, 18 (S.C. 1998). This compensation proposal arrangement coupled with Petitioner's desire to market the law firm's services via the educational seminars and meet individually with clients creates a situation ripe for abuse. Indeed, the proposal by Petitioner presents the very evil Rule 5.4 was designed to avoid. Accordingly, I find Petitioner's proposed compensation plan violates both the letter and the spirit of Rule 5.4 prohibiting fee splitting with nonattorneys.

> FN2. The suggestion that Petitioner and the law firm intend for him to "handle" cases speaks volumes about the anticipated role of Petitioner, far beyond the permissible tasks performed by paralegals.

> FN3. Nonlawyer employees may certainly participate "in a compensation or retirement plan, even though the plan is based in whole or in part on a profit sharing arrangement." Rule 5.4(a)(3), Rules of Professional Conduct, SCACR 407.

RECOMMENDATIONS

1. Offering legal presentations for the general public constitutes the practice of law.

2. Answering estate-planning questions in the context of legal seminars or in private client interviews constitutes the practice of law.

3. Fee-sharing arrangements with nonattorneys based on volume and cases "handled" by a paralegal violates Rule 5.4, Rules of Professional Conduct, SCACR 407.

RESPECTFULLY SUBMITTED.

END OF DOCUMENT

Copr. © West 2000. No Claim to Orig. U.S. Govt. Works.

EXERCISES

1. Why was the court not persuaded by the legal assistant's argument that, because an attorney had reviewed and approved all of the information in the public seminar, there should not be a problem regarding the unauthorized practice of law?

2. The legal assistant seemed to argue that, in reality, he or she would be performing a good deed by educating the public on topics such as wills, trusts, and living trusts. Why was the court not persuaded by this argument?

3. If an attorney had been at the seminar, and the legal assistant and attorney had jointly conducted the seminar, would the court have arrived at the same conclusion? Why?

4. Did the content of the seminar play a part in the court's decision? Why or why not?

5. The legal assistant seemed to make the argument that, because other professionals such as financial planners were giving such advice, the legal assistant should be able to as well. Was the decision to create a different standard for legal assistants versus other professionals fair and consistent?

6. Read Footnote 2. How does the content of that footnote impact the rest of the decision? Why were the court's conclusions in Footnote 2 important to the case as a whole?

 For additional resources, visit our Web site at www.westlegalstudies.com

FILE AND LAW LIBRARY MANAGEMENT

Chapter Objectives

After you read this chapter, you should be able to:

- Discuss why file management is important.
- Explain centralized and decentralized filing systems.
- Discuss the importance of closing and purging files.
- Explain why library ordering should be centralized.
- Give examples of how law library costs can be reduced.

- For two hours I searched for our file on tax issues in the State of Maine. I found it under "S."

- We finally located the agreement with Boeing under "N." It was labeled "1979 Aircraft Contracts" by the lawyer and filed under "N" for "Nineteen" by the secretary.

- I waited two weeks for Alice to return to ask her about her previous work on a particular issue. She told me that Alan was the one who worked on it. He [Alan] said that his work would probably help me but that it wasn't the main issue in his case and he couldn't remember the file name.[1]

WHY LEGAL ASSISTANTS NEED AN UNDERSTANDING OF FILE AND LAW LIBRARY MANAGEMENT

Legal assistants work with hard copy and electronic files every single day. It is crucial that they know how to organize, track, and store client files. If a file or parts of a file are lost, misplaced, or misfiled, the effects can be devastating both to the office and to the client's case. Information must be stored so that it can be quickly found and retrieved. Legal assistants are responsible for organizing case files in many instances. In addition, many legal organizations are using automated file management systems. Legal assistants must have a good understanding of automated systems as law firms progress toward a paperless office.

Legal assistants also must have a basic understanding of law library management. Legal assistants use the law library to conduct legal research, so it is important that they know how libraries work and be familiar with electronic research resources. In addition, many legal assistants, especially in smaller offices, may actually be in charge of maintaining the library. Law libraries have changed drastically in recent years. More and more information is being stored electronically, so legal assistants must have a good understanding of how to access electronic information and research.

> I worked at a firm where the Records Department constantly struggled with proper maintenance of the files. Loose filing that was sometimes a year old stacked up in the file area. When an attorney needed something, hours if not days were spent looking for it. The alternative was to call cocounsel to request another copy, but we could only call so many times before the other attorney's office got frustrated. I ended up making working copies of important documents and stashing them in my office, but there was only so much room in my office. The Records Department was using bar coding technology, but when the documents themselves do not make it into the files, using a bar code to "find" material is moot.
>
> —Linda Rushton, CLA

INTRODUCTION TO FILE MANAGEMENT

Law offices of all types need a file system that allows them to store, track, and retrieve information about cases in a logical, efficient, and expeditious manner. The outcome of many legal matters depends on the case information gathered, including evidence, depositions, pleadings, discovery requests, and witness interviews. File information generally is worthless unless it is organized and available to the legal assistants and attorneys who will use it. File management is a large task, no matter the size of the law practice.

Figure 9-1 presents the characteristics of a good file system, whether the system is paperless or uses paper. Each of these areas is vital to a law office, and none can be compromised. A poor file system has some or all of the following problems:

1. Files (hardcopy and electronic) are lost and cannot be found.
2. Files are messy and disorganized.
3. Office staff is unclear about how the filing system works.
4. Attorneys and legal assistants do not trust the file system and keep their own files or keep the office's files in their possession.
5. Staff is constantly aggravated and frustrated over the file system.
6. Large amounts of time and money are wasted trying to find the file and information.
7. Poor-quality legal services are given to clients because of the poor filing system.
8. Electronic file systems are unreliable or do not work.

File management is an important topic because law office management is responsible for providing an effective system that adequately supports its attorneys and legal assistants. Files and file systems represent a tool that the attorney and legal assistant use to provide their services.

---

1. **Completeness**—The files (hard copy and/or electronic) are complete and contain all of the information relevant to the case or matter.
2. **Retention**—Filing procedures ensure that all items are retained for the appropriate length of time.
3. **Integrity**—Files are maintained so that they are accurate, sound, and reliable.
4. **Ease of Use**—The file structure and file access provide for quick and easy location of files. Electronic file systems are readily available to all staff.
5. **Security**—Files (hard copy and electronic) are maintained in a safe environment which prevents unauthorized access to the system as a whole or to individual files.
6. **Ease of Learning**—The file system is candid, straightforward, and easy for others to learn.
7. **Adaptability**—The file system is flexible and easy to modify if structural or functional changes in the organization are necessary.

Figure 9-1
An Effective File Management System[2]

◻

FILING METHODS AND TECHNIQUES

There are different variations or filing methods that accomplish the objectives in Figure 9-1. Which filing method is used depends on the particular needs of each law office. These needs may be based on such factors as the number of attorneys in the firm, the number of cases that will be tracked and stored, the type and power of computer hardware and software in use, the size and length of time typical cases are kept open or active, how much paper typical cases generate, the amount of space available for storage, whether the files will be kept in a central location, or whether departments or attorneys will keep their own files.

Each Legal Matter Is Maintained Separately

No matter which filing method is used in a law office, each case or legal matter must be maintained separately. Even if one client has several legal matters pending, each case/legal matter should have its own separate file and should be given its own file number. There is the danger that documents will be misplaced or lost if all documents are commingled.

When matters are commingled, it affects other law office systems, such as conflict-of-interest checking (which determines whether the law office has a conflict of interest), docket control, and billing. Each case should be checked for conflict-of-interest problems, should have its own distinct and separate deadlines entered into the docket control system, and should be billed to the client separately.

Alphabetic Systems

alphabetic filing system
Filing method in which cases are stored based on the last name of the client or organization.

In an **alphabetic filing system**, cases are stored based on the last name of the client or name of the organization. There is a natural tendency to alphabetize because it is a system that most people understand. In addition, staff members do not need to memorize case numbers or use numerical lists: a user knows exactly where the file should be in the drawer.

The larger the number of cases the law office is handling, the more problems it will experience with an alphabetical system. This is because names are not all that unique; many clients may have the same last name. It is not efficient to search through four or five file drawers or cabinets of "Smith" files looking for the right case. It also is not uncommon for clients to have the same first and last names. Other systems, such as a numerical or electronic system, can track an almost infinite number of cases with a unique number and will also protect the confidentiality of the client, because the client's name is not the identifier for the file and is therefore not written on all the files. In offices with a large number of cases, an alphabetic system may not be the best kind of filing system; they are difficult to expand and can require constantly shifting files to make room for more.

Numerical Systems

In a numerical filing system, each case or legal matter is given a separate file number. This is similar to when a case is filed with a court; a clerk assigns each action or lawsuit a separate case number. Case identifiers can be, but do not necessarily have to be, composed of all numbers (e.g., 234552). Variations can be used, such as alphanumeric, in which letters and numbers are used. For instance, a letter might be used in the case number to reflect which branch office is handling the case, and two of the numbers might reflect the year the case was filed, such as LA07-990004. The "LA" might stand for the office's Los Angeles location, and "07" stand for 2007, the year the case was initiated.

Letters also may stand for types of cases ("PB" for probate, "TX" for tax, etc.) or for a particular attorney— "Patricia Burns," and so forth. Even in a numerical system, however, legal matters for the same client can be kept together. For instance, in the example "LA07-990004," "99" could represent the client's personal number and "4" could mean that this is the fourth case that the office is handling for the client.

Another numerical filing method is to assign a range of numbers to a particular type of case, such as 000–999 for trusts, 1,000–1,999 for tax matters, and 2,000–2,999 for criminal matters.

A filing rule that sometimes bears out is that the longer the case number, the more misfiling and other types of errors occur; shorter numbers can also be remembered more easily. Numerical filing solves the shifting problems caused by alphabetical systems. When a new case is taken, the next sequential number is given to the file, and it is stored accordingly. This is different than the alphabetic system, where a new file is stored by the client's name. When the new file is added to the existing drawer in the alphabetical system, the drawer may be full, and then someone must shift or move files to make room for the new addition.

Bar Coding

Bar coding is a file management technique in which each file is tracked according to the file's bar code. Each time a user takes a file, the file's bar code and user's bar code are scanned into a computer. The computerized system then tracks which user checked out which file. When the file is returned, the file's bar code is scanned back into the computer. A report can be generated any time, listing what files are checked out and by whom. Using this system, it is possible to find the location of files quite easily. Bar codes are used in many libraries to track the library's collection. Bar coding of law office files works much the same way.

bar coding
A file management technique in which each file is tracked according to the file's bar code.

The "Paperless Office"—Electronic Document Management

Document management software organizes, controls, distributes, and allows for extensive searching of electronic documents, typically in a computer-networked environment. In a "paperless" office environment, all information is stored electronically. Document management software easily tracks and stores computer files that are already in an electronic format such as word processing, e-mail, and spreadsheet files. It allows a legal organization to file documents electronically so they can be found by anyone in the organization, even when there are hundreds of users spread across offices located throughout the world. Document management software can also accommodate hard copy documents through the use of imaging. **Imaging** uses a scanner to capture an image of a document. That image is stored electronically and

Document management software
Organizes, controls, distributes, and allows for extensive searching of electronic documents typically in a computer-networked environment.

Imaging
Uses a scanner to capture an image of a document. The image is stored electronically.

can be retrieved later. Given the enormous storage capacities of computers, document management software is the electronic equivalent of a filing room with thousands of file cabinets.

> *Our firm has been paperless for six years now. To start our paperless office, we installed two network copier/scanners. We developed handling procedures for all information that comes into the office, including the scanning of hard copy documents. Because all documents are stored electronically, we have quick access to them. Anyone in the office can find a file, no matter who created or filed the document. We encourage clients and opposing attorneys to e-mail and fax all communication for easy file maintenance. All attorneys and staff can work from home or other remote locations. We implemented a virtual private network, which, when used with any broadband Internet hookup, allows real-time direct access to our network from anywhere. Now, we are better organized and have better control of our information. With a paperless office we save money. We need fewer staff and we have reduced postage, paper, and storage costs. We also have better research capabilities and have quicker access to information.*[3]

Document management software provides for extensive searching capabilities and allows users to associate files with cases and create profiles of documents for easy retrieval. Document management software tracks files from the time they are opened until they are closed. It also allows many reports to be generated regarding the records that are being kept. Records can be printed regarding files assigned to specific attorneys, types of cases, and more. Many law offices have some kind of document management software; while many are not completely "paperless," most law offices use document management software to some extent. Document management software has many advantages, including the ability to share information across vast distances, excellent tracking and reporting capabilities, reduced instances of misfiling, ability to easily and quickly create a backup copy of information, reduced space and storage costs, and the ability to quickly search and sort information, among others.

Unfortunately, document management also has some down sides. The cost of technology can be substantial, and training of staff is essential. In addition, like any system, a document management system must be maintained and properly administered. Law offices must have procedures and rules for those documents that are saved long-term. Discussion drafts and unfinished documents may need to be stored in a different place. In addition, firms should have a document retention policy that includes both hard copy and electronic documents.

> *With the junk littered in the document management system, it is simply unsafe to rely on any document found there unless you wrote it, and you know it is the finished version.*[4]

Corporate, Government, and Legal Aid Filing Methods

Corporate law and government departments may arrange their matters differently. They may file matters by subject, by department, or by other means that suit their particular industry or need. Legal services/aid offices typically file cases alphabetically or even geographically, by city or county.

Centralized v. Decentralized

A fundamental law office filing consideration is whether the filing system will be centralized or decentralized. A **centralized file system** is where a file department or file clerk stores and manages all active law office files in one or more file rooms. In a **decentralized file system,** files are kept in various locations throughout the law office, such as each department storing its own files or each attorney keeping his or her own files.

A centralized system is typically used when the office has a complex filing procedure best handled by one department or file clerk staff; when the office wants a highly controlled system; or when several attorneys or legal assistants work on the same cases. Even though a law office may want a centralized system, the office must first have the physical space to accommodate it. Law offices in which a single attorney or legal assistant works on each case, such as real estate matters, or needs the case files for long periods of time may use a decentralized file system where the files are located in an individual's office or in a secretarial area. Some offices use a "pod," or team filing system, where several people—perhaps two or three attorneys, a secretary, and a legal assistant or two—have offices located close to one another and have their files stored next to them. Some offices may use a combination. Whether an office uses a centralized or decentralized system depends on the size of the office, type of cases handled, and the needs of the personnel involved. Closed files are almost always kept in a centralized location.

> *NEVER open a file without in some way placing it on the law office calendar or in a tickler system.*[5]

Opening Files

When a new or existing client comes into the office with a new legal matter, a new file should immediately be opened. The opening of a file should be standardized and requires certain information about the legal matter. A file-opening form or an electronic version (sometimes called a new client/matter form or case sheet) is customarily completed when opening a new file (see Figure 9-2).

The **file opening form** is used for a variety of purposes, including to check potential conflicts of interest, to assign a new case number and attorney to the matter, to track the area or specialty of the case, to set forth the type of fee agreement and billing frequency in the case, to enter the case in the timekeeping and billing system, to make docketing entries (such as when the statute of limitations in the matter

centralized file system
Method in which a file department or file clerk stores and manages all active law office files in one or more file rooms.

decentralized file system
System in which files are kept in various locations throughout the law office.

file opening form
A standardized form that is filled out when a new case is started. The form contains important information about the client and the case.

Figure 9-2   File-Opening Form

New File

Client (Check one)
_____ INDIVIDUAL

_____
Last   First   Middle Initial

_____ ENTITY _____
(Use complete name & common abbreviations; place articles [e.g., The] at end.)

_____ CLASS ACTION _____
(File Name, ex.: Popcorn Antitrust Litigation)

Matter (Check One)
_____ NON-LITIGATION
_____ LITIGATION
_____ Approved for litigation by—MUST BE INITIALED by submitting attorney!!

Nature of the Case
Area of law code: _____   Summary of work or dispute: _____

Client Contact (N/A for Class Actions)
Name: _____
Company: _____
Street: _____
City, State, Zip: _____
Telephone: _____
*New Adverse Parties:

_____
_____
_____

*New Related Parties (for Class Actions, Named Plaintiffs Only):

_____
_____
_____

*Will be entered into computer system by Bus. Dept. *AFTER* approval by Managing Partner.

Closed File

Date Closed: _____   **Atty. Or Sec. Initials:** _____
_____ Attach pleadings and/or file indexes. If indexes are not available, attach brief description of what is contained in the file(s). SEND FILES, THIS FORM, AND INDEX TO FILE ROOM.

Routing Lists
(Initial)

	New File:	Date:	Closed File:	Date:
Submitted by	_____	_____	_____	_____
Sec. of Submitting Person	_____	_____	_____	_____
Managing Partner	_____	_____	_____	_____
Business Department	_____	_____	_____	_____
File Department	_____	_____	_____	_____
Firm Newsletter	_____	_____	_____	_____
Docket for Litigation	_____	_____	_____	_____
EnviroLaw (Computer Center) Add?	_____			
IdeaLaw (Computer Center) Add?	_____			
JobLaw (Computer Center) Add?	_____			

Figure 9-2 *(Continued)*

Billing Address (N/A for Class Actions)
Name: _____
Company: _____
Street: _____
City, State, Zip: _____
Telephone: _____

Team Information (Use initials)
_____ _____ _____   Managing Attorney(s) (for non-litigation cases only)
_____ _____ _____   Bill Review Attorney(s)
_____ _____ _____   Originating Attorney(s)
_____ Calendar Attorney (for litigation cases only)
_____ Legal Assistant (for litigation cases only)
_____ Secretary to Calendar Attorney (for litigation cases only)

Referral Source (Check one)
_____ Existing Client   _____
     (Name)
_____ Non-Firm Attorney   _____
     (Name)
_____ Firm Attorney or Employee   _____
_____ Martindale-Hubbell   _____
_____ Other   _____

Fee Agreement (Check those that apply)
_____ Hourly
_____ Contingent _____ %
_____ Fee Petition
_____ Fixed Fee $ _____ or Fixed Range from $ _____ to $ _____
_____ Retainer $ _____
_____ Letter of Retainer sent by _____ on _____
     (Initials)   (Date)

Statement Format (Check those that apply)
Do you want identical disbursements grouped?   _____ Yes _____ No
Do you want attorney hours reflected on each time entry?   _____ Yes _____ No
Do you want fees extended on each time entry?   _____ Yes _____ No

Conflict Check

Conflict Check Completed By: _____   Date: _____
     (Initials)

Conflict Check Not Needed: _____
     (Initials of Submitting Person)

Check One:
_____ No conflicts
_____ Potential conflict with the following existing parties (from computer system):
_____
_____
(Or attach computer printout from Conflict Check System.)

**Figure 9-3
Typical Subcategories
of Files**

Accounting
Correspondence with Attorneys
Correspondence with Client
Deposition Summaries
Discovery
Evidence
General Correspondence
Investigation
Legal Research
Memorandums
Notes and Miscellaneous
Witnesses

might run), and to find out how the client was referred to the law office. Although file-opening forms are commercially available, most law offices choose to customize the form to reflect their own needs.

Copies of the file-opening form may be sent to the managing partner, other attorneys, accounting department, docket-control department, and the responsible attorney.

File Format and Internal File Rules

File format (or how case files are set up) and organization depend on the needs of each office. The type of file format will depend on the filing system that is used; for example, vertical file drawers require tabs in different places, while an open-shelf filing system requires tabs on the side.

Many offices use separate manila files as subdivisions in the same case to differentiate information in the same file, such as having files for "Accounting," "Discovery," "Pleadings," "Client Correspondence," and others (see Figure 9-3). The individual manila files are stored in one or more expanding files, so that all the files for one case are kept together. Many offices also use metal fasteners to hold the papers securely in place; original documents, however, should not be punched. Instead, they should be maintained separately and a copy put in the regular file. Finally, information is typically placed in each manila file in chronological order, with the oldest on the bottom and the newest on the top of the file. This gives the user a systematic way of finding information. It is routine to find duplicate and draft copies of documents in a file; however, this makes the organization process more difficult. If duplicates must be kept, they should be in a separate file folder labeled "Duplicates."

Color Coding

Color coding files is a simple but effective way to reduce the number of misfiled documents. Files can be color coded in a variety of ways; for example, red-labeled files may be used for probate and green files for criminal matters. Color coding can also be done according to the year the case was opened or according to the attorney handling the matter.

Color coding may used for cases that are especially sensitive or that need to be kept secure. For example, if the law office is trying to create a "Chinese wall" to keep a staff member from participating in a case, others can be alerted to the need for security by assigning a certain color of file label to the case. Finally, color coding can be used in an alphabetic filing system—for example, A–E equals blue, F–J equals green, and so forth.

Checking Files Out

In some law offices where many people have access to files, users are required to check out files electronically (in a process similar to one used in a public library) or to simply leave a large card where the file is stored, showing who checked out the file. It can be quite frustrating to search and search for a client file, only to discover that someone else took the file home to work on, or that the file is lost. Tracking the location of files is crucial to an effective file/record management system.

Closing, Storing, and Purging Files

After a legal matter has come to a conclusion and the final bill has been paid, the file is closed and taken out of the storage area of active files. It is boxed up and kept in the office's basement or an off-site storage facility for a certain number of years, until it is destroyed or put on microfilm, microfiche, or stored electronically on CDs or other storage devices.

A closed file is sometimes called a "dead file" or a "retired file." Some offices give the closed case a new number, to differentiate it from active cases. The closing of cases represents a problem for many law offices. Attorneys like to have access to closed files in case they someday need the information contained in them. Storage space can be quite expensive, however. Most law offices are continually opening and closing cases, which means that the flow of files never stops and that the required storage area gets larger and larger. Duplicate copies of documents should be removed in order to reduce file storage requirements.

A client must be made completely aware before his or her file is closed. It is strongly recommended that the law firm send a disengagement letter to the client, letting him or her know in writing that the file is being closed and that the client can have documents, evidence, or even the whole file returned to him or her. Electronic records also need to be purged or backed up at the same time the hard copy of the file is closed.

Most attorneys cannot rest comfortably knowing that closed client files have been destroyed, yet the actual frequency of need for a file that has been closed for more than one year is very low. Because of unwillingness to authorize file destruction, most law offices build up huge quantities of old paper that often end up in lofts, basements, barns, abandoned buildings, or, worst of all, on the office's premises in increasingly expensive space.

Figure 9-4
Sample Record
Retention Periods

Source: Adapted from
Association of Legal
Administrators. Reprinted
with permission.

Law Office Administration	Retention Period
Accounts payable and receivable ledgers	7 years
Audit reports	Permanently
Bank statement and reconciliations	3 years
Cash receipt books	Permanently
Canceled checks (except for payments of taxes, real estate, and other important payments—permanently)	7 years
Contracts, mortgages, notes, and leases (still in effect)	Permanently
Contracts, mortgages, notes, and leases (expired)	7 years
Correspondence, general (except important matters—permanently)	7 years
Deeds, mortgages, etc.	Permanently
Employment applications	3 years
Financial statements (year end)	Permanently
Insurance policies (expired)	3 years
Invoices	7 years
Minutes of directors' and stockholders' meetings	Permanently
Payroll records	7 years
Retirement and pension records	Permanently
Tax returns	Permanently
Time cards	7 years

Client Files and Documents

- Retention of client files and client-related documents depends on the ethical rules in your state.
- Before destroying a client file, contact the client to make sure he or she does not want the file or want something out of the file.
- When destroying client files, burn, shred, or recycle them to ensure client confidentiality.

One solution to storage problems is to purge or destroy files after a certain period of time (see Figure 9-4). Some state ethical rules also govern file retention. Some law offices purge all files after a certain number of years, such as seven or eight, while others purge only selected files. Destroying hard copy files usually means shredding, burning, or recycling them. Simply throwing them away does not protect the client's confidentiality and should not be done.

Organization of Files—A Major Legal Assistant Duty

File organization is a large part of what many legal assistants do. They must use files on a daily basis; therefore, for most legal assistants to become efficient at what they do, they must be able to organize and—in some cases—index case files in a logical and systematic fashion so they can quickly find information. Case material also must be organized in such a way that others, such as attorneys, can find the information quickly. A file that is a disorganized mess is useless in a law office. For instance, if the legal assistant is assisting an attorney at a deposition and the attorney asks him or her to find a specific answer in the discovery request, he or she must be able to locate it quickly. If the legal assistant is not familiar with the case, does not have the file organized, or misfiled the document, he or she will not have the ability to find the information quickly, and the client's case may suffer.

FILE MANAGEMENT AND ETHICS

There are several ethical questions that should be addressed when considering filing and filing systems. These issues include performing conflict-of-interest checks before a new case is taken, maintaining client-related property that is turned over to the law office during representation, maintaining trust- and client-related accounting records, returning a client's file to him or her if the client decides to change attorneys, and ensuring that the office's filing system and/or file destruction procedures maintain client confidentiality.

Client Property

Offices should be careful when closing files and especially when destroying files containing documents or other information that were given to the attorney by a client. Rule 1.15 of the *Model Rules of Professional Conduct* provides that a law office has a duty at the end of a case to give the client the option to pick up information that was delivered to the attorney for representation in the matter. Generally, unless the client consents, a lawyer should not destroy or discard items that clearly or probably belong to the client. In addition, an attorney should be especially careful not to destroy client information where the applicable statutory limitations period has not expired.

Duty to Turn Over File When Client Fires Attorney

An attorney also has a duty to turn over to a client his or her file when the client decides to fire an attorney and hire another one. What must be turned over to the client depends on the ethical rules and case law in each state. For example, Rule 3-700(D) of the *California Revised Rules of Professional Conduct* states:

(a) [An attorney] whose employment has terminated shall . . . promptly release to the client, all the client papers and property. Client papers and property include correspondence, pleadings, deposition transcripts, exhibits, physical evidence, expert's reports, and other items reasonably necessary to the client's representation, whether the client has paid for them or not.

In most states, the attorney must turn over any documents the new counsel will need to reasonably handle the matter. In some states, such as California, a law office cannot refuse to release a client's file just because the client still owes fees and expenses.

Destruction of Records of Account

Rule 1.15(a) of the *Model Rules of Professional Conduct* states that an attorney must maintain financial records related to a legal matter for five years after termination of representation. Law offices should carefully maintain accurate and complete records of the lawyer's receipt and disbursement of trust funds in every case.

Confidentiality

An attorney's duty to maintain the confidentiality of client-related matters should be a factor when considering a law office file management system. Files must be maintained so that sensitive information about a case or client is kept private. The confidentiality rule also does not stop once the case is closed. Law offices should be careful to destroy or dispose of files in a manner consistent with the confidentiality requirements.

INTRODUCTION TO LAW LIBRARY MANAGEMENT

> *Even though the library remains the single most valuable tangible asset of a law office or corporate legal department, it must justify the continuing investment that it requires.'*[5A]

Professional librarians may coordinate and manage the law library in medium- to large-sized law offices. In smaller law offices, however, legal assistants or associate attorneys may perform these duties. Figure 9-5 contains a list of librarian-related duties.

> *Today, only retired partners, law firm messengers, and people needing a quiet place to think or write can be find in law libraries, as virtually all legal resources have been digitized and made accessible through electronic data library services.*[6]

Law libraries are changing. The Internet, CD-ROM libraries, and data services such as Westlaw and LexisNexis have forever changed how and where lawyers and legal assistants access legal research. While hard copy books will probably never be completely replaced by their electronic counterparts, many libraries are going digital, and this has changed how libraries are managed. Library management used to be

- Trains and supervises staff
- Explains research techniques to lawyers and legal assistants, and answers questions
- Compiles legislative histories and bibliographies
- Selects and orders books, CD-ROM libraries, and other library resources
- Reviews and approves bills for payment
- Plans library growth
- Catalogs and tracks library resources using computerized methods
- Routes library-related materials to appropriate staff
- Files loose-leaf services and other library-related documents
- Manages check out of books and reshelves material
- Performs or assists legal professionals in legal research, particularly regarding computed-assisted legal research and legal and factual research on the Internet

**Figure 9-5
Librarian-Related
Duties**

centered around purchasing, maintaining, and storing shelf after shelf of books that constantly grew in number. This is no longer the case; many legal professionals do not even need a physical library at all. They can now access a host of electronic legal research at their desk. That said, law firms will always have to provide some type of "library" for their staff, but many firms have moved from the expense of hard copy books to electronic alternatives.

Depending on the structure of the law office, the library may be supervised by a library committee, a managing partner, or an office administrator, or all functions may be controlled by the librarian.

Law libraries generally are thought of as an overhead expense and, regardless of size, are costly to maintain. Proper library management can, however, reduce overhead expenses and increase the quality of services to clients at the same time.

Some legal assistants may be put in charge of the law library. Managing a law library may not seem at first like a difficult job, but in many instances it is. Books, periodicals, CD-ROM libraries, and other materials must be ordered on a regular basis to ensure the library is kept current; supplements to books (sometimes called "pocket parts") must be ordered and replaced regularly; the collection must be tracked using some type of computer or card catalog system (this requires quite a bit of time); books must be shelved and maintained; a library budget must be kept and tracked; and, from time to time, books must be tracked down and found. Many librarians perform legal research themselves, as well. Proper law library management can be a time-consuming task.

Developing a Library Collection

What distinguishes an excellent library from a mediocre one . . . is not its size but its usefulness to the practitioners who rely on it. Its worth depends not merely on the amount of information they can find there but on the quality of that information and the ease of gathering it.[7]

**Figure 9-6
Possible Holdings
in a Law Library**

• Case Law	• Statutes
• Citators	• Treatises
• Digests	• CD-ROM Libraries
• Encyclopedias	• Westlaw
• Index to Periodicals	• Internet Access
• Periodicals	• LexisNexis
• Reference Works	

There are many different types of materials that can be found in a law office library. The office's collection should mirror the type of practice and its specialties. As a law office's practice changes, the library also will need to change to keep information that is current with the needs of the law office. Figure 9-6 lists typical types of publications that are found in many law office library collections.

The extent of an office's collection will depend on many factors. Larger offices that have been in existence for many years will have much larger collections than will newer or smaller law offices. Some offices think that most, if not all, research should be performed in their own library, while other law offices that have large collections nearby, such as a law school or state or county law library, may want to keep their costs low and use these resources to the fullest extent possible.

A way to keep overhead costs low in the library is by purchasing CD-ROM libraries, including Internet access, maintaining Westlaw or LexisNexis, and keeping hard copy books and periodicals only as needed. This strategy limits the space requirements needed for most libraries and maximizes the use of computers already on the desks of most staff.

CD-ROM Legal Databases

CD-ROM legal database
A database like one found on Westlaw or LexisNexis, but packaged on CD-ROMs.

A **CD-ROM legal database** is a database like one found on Westlaw or LexisNexis, but packaged on one or more CD-ROMs. For example, the complete set of *Federal Reporters*, which contains federal appellate court decisions from 1880 to the present, takes up more than 150 linear feet of shelf space in a law library, and this does not count the indexes necessary to use the reporters. The same *Federal Reporters* come on 12 CD-ROM disks, take up a few inches of shelf space, and include a search engine that allows the user to search for needed material. Many CD-ROM publishers also offer connections to the Internet or online services so that research can be updated.

CD-ROM LEGAL LIBRARIES Hundreds and hundreds of CD-ROM legal libraries are currently available. Many books and periodicals published for the legal industry are also available on CD-ROM. This includes everything from criminal and family law to European tax laws, and everything in between. Most of the major legal book publishers, including West, BNA, Matthew Bender, and many others, offer a wide variety of CD-ROM products.

CD-ROM SEARCH ENGINES Searching CD-ROM legal databases is similar to searching on Westlaw and LexisNexis. Every CD-ROM legal database uses a search tool, typically either Premise or Folio Views, to perform the search. Users are able to utilize terms and connectors including proximity searches, wild card searches, and other searches similar to Westlaw and LexisNexis. Most search engines also have hypertext, which allows a user to go directly to another referenced document immediately (similar to the Internet). For example, if a user is reading a case and another case is referenced, the user can click the mouse on the reference to the second citation, and the computer will immediately take the user to the second case.

Advantages and Disadvantages of CD-ROM Legal Libraries

There are many advantages to using CD-ROM legal libraries, including the following:

- *Reduced space and expense considerations*—CD-ROM legal libraries take up a fraction of the space that similar information in book form would. While most law libraries will want some information in book form, there is much information that can be stored on CD-ROM. This has a tremendous impact on the annual operating cost of a law library for any legal organization. If a law firm or corporate law department can cut the size of its law library in half, it can save a tremendous amount on lease space, shelving, and other items. Because many legal organizations are in the business of making money, this is a very important consideration.
- *Portability*—Unlike rows and rows of books, CD-ROM legal libraries are inherently portable. Users can take the entire body of a state's case law into a courtroom on a laptop computer and have the information at their fingertips. This can prove extremely beneficial to the attorney or legal assistant.
- *Convenience*—Users can access information on their own computers without going to a library or even leaving their office. In addition, information on CD-ROM can be copied into a user's word processor, just like Westlaw and LexisNexis.
- *Cost*—The total cost of a CD-ROM legal library is often less than for hard copy books or for performing the research online using Westlaw or LexisNexis. It is also more cost effective for anyone who does a significant amount of legal research, because it can usually be done at the person's desk and, in many circumstances, electronic research is substantially faster than using books and indexes.
- *Maintenance*—The cost of maintaining books, and adding and deleting supplements and loose-leaf pages, should not be underestimated, particularly in a large law library. It takes library personnel numerous hours to do this, as compared to installing a new CD-ROM to replace an old one. As library personnel maintenance time lessens, productivity should increase in other areas, such as the amount of time library staff can spend to assist customers with research projects.

Disadvantages to CD-ROM legal libraries include the following:

- *Maintenance*—Maintenance of the computer software can be an issue: most CD-ROM databases have a monthly or quarterly subscription service that must be purchased to keep them up to date. New CD-ROMs and updates must be installed. In addition, search engines must be upgraded to new versions from time to time. Depending on the environment, such as whether the computers are networked or stand-alone, this can be quite time consuming. Keeping hardware requirements (including RAM and hard disk space) and networking requirements current can also take a great deal of time. In addition, sometimes the technology involved (including interfacing with a network) is a problem. The systems may not work, or they may be incompatible. Technical experts must be called in to make modifications, which can be both expensive and time consuming.

- *CD-ROM versus the Internet*—There is some question regarding the long-term validity of CD-ROMs, particularly when compared to the Internet. CD-ROMs must be continually updated, whereas Internet products never need to be updated because the product is always current.
- *Switching CD-ROMs*—While there are CD-ROM towers that can hold multiple CD-ROMs, many systems still require users or information system professionals to change CD-ROM disks. This can be inconvenient and time consuming. Some legal organizations copy all their CD-ROMs to large network servers so that CD-ROM towers are not necessary. This also makes accessing the information faster, as server access is much faster than CD-ROM access.
- *Training*—Training staff to use CD-ROMs legal databases can be a problem when different publishers or search engines are used.

Cataloging and Classifying the Collection

Proper classification and organization of a collection are imperative in order for the office to know what material it has and where it is located. If information is not arranged or organized in such a manner so that attorneys and legal assistants can easily find it without wasting time, the whole purpose of an in-house library is thwarted.

Cataloging is the process of listing and organizing the inventory of a library. This usually includes giving each book a separate call number and listing the book's author, title, publisher, subject, publication date, and so forth. Some offices classify and catalog their collections according to the Library of Congress classification system or the Dewey Decimal System. The Library of Congress system uses the alphabet for its general divisions. For instance, "K" is the letter that represents American Law. Figure 9-7 contains a list of selected Library of Congress legal classifications.

Figure 9-7
Modified Library of Congress Classification Numbers

Administrative Law	Constitutional Law
KF5401	KF4501
Agency	Consumer Law
KF1341	KF1601
Appellate	Advocacy Contracts
KF9050	KF801
Civil Procedure	Corporations
KF8810	KF1384
Commercial Transactions	Criminal Law
KF871	KF9201
Conflict of Laws	Criminal Procedure
KF8810	KF9601
Conservation of Natural Resources	Decedents' Estates and Trusts
KF5505	KF746

Other offices may simply group materials together, such as a tax section, labor section, or real property section. This is sometimes called a "neighborhood" classification system.

Computerized catalog systems can be created using almost any database management program. They are very easy to set up and are very flexible. There are also some commercially available library cataloging systems for many types of microcomputers.

Technology and the Law Library

Computer-Assisted Legal Research (CALR)

Computer-assisted legal research uses computers to search the words of cases, statutes, and documents themselves; two familiar legal-information services are Westlaw and LexisNexis.

Because CALR systems use the full text of the document, there is no need for indexes or digests. Instead, the user simply enters common words that describe the issue that might appear in the full text of the case or document, and the system retrieves all cases and documents that meet the request. Since the information is stored on large mainframes, the database can be searched and the documents quickly retrieved. The documents that are retrieved can be read on-line, can be sent off-line to a printer, or the full text can be downloaded to the user's computer. **On-line** means that the user is connected to an information system and is running up charges. **Off-line** means that a user is no longer connected to an information service and that no charges are accruing except possibly a printing or downloading charge. Alternatively, a list of the appropriate cases or documents can be printed or downloaded so that, if the user likes, he or she can go to a library and examine the full texts.

CALR can be significantly quicker than manual researching techniques. Further, when CALR is used correctly, it can also retrieve cases that might not otherwise have been found using manual methods because of poor indexing or other errors. CALR is faster than manual methods because it is possible to search many databases at once (e.g., searching the case laws of all 50 states on a specific subject). Using manual methods, the user would have to search through several sets of digests, supplements, and indexes.

CALR—in addition to being quicker and sometimes more accurate than manual researching—can also be more convenient. Nearly all legal-information services are available 24 hours a day, unlike many law libraries. Also, the research can be done from the legal professional's office. As mentioned before, when using a law library, it is possible that an important book might already be checked out or unavailable. Sources are always available on-line with CALR. Another important factor to consider is that new cases are entered into legal-information services usually within a few days of being handed down or decided. Therefore, the information that is available on-line is almost always more up-to-date than information available in books.

on-line
The user is connected to an information system and is running up charges.

off-line
The user is not connected to an information service and no charges are accruing except possibly a printing or downloading charge.

Although CALR is both fast and convenient, it is not free. Most legal-information services charge a yearly subscription fee, along with a fee based on the amount of time a user is connected to their system. Some services also charge a fee for every search that is done on their system. Some services have connect-time charges of more than $200 an hour. In addition, some services have a minimum monthly charge, even if the service is not used. Because CALR is so expensive, new users can run up large bills quickly. Therefore, it is particularly important that new users have a thorough understanding of the CALR system they will be using. This is usually not a problem, because most CALR systems have off-line training tutorials. On the average though, most legal issues take approximately 15 minutes to research. Most offices bill this expense back to their clients; some even do so at a higher rate than charged to help cover related expenses, such as long-distance charges. The office must be careful, however, to not bill the client for general overhead costs; general overhead costs should already be figured into the office's attorney and legal assistant billing rate, so it would be inappropriate for the client to be billed for them again.

Westlaw

Westlaw is a full-text legal information service provided by West Group. According to West, it is one of the largest law libraries in the world, with more than 10,000 separate databases available to its users. It contains cases from all West reporters as well as slip opinions, unreported cases, interactive databases from Dow Jones DIALOG databases, and much more. This site gives Westlaw users access to an enormous body of legal and nonlegal resources. Many of Westlaw's features are covered here, including its databases, types of search queries, and special features.

Westlaw can be accessed by using a microcomputer and Westlaw-specific proprietary software called Westmate, or by using a microcomputer and a standard Web browser to connect via the Internet.

LexisNexis

LexisNexis is a full-text legal information service. It was the first on-line, full-text legal information service and is one of the world's largest. LexisNexis and Westlaw are similar in many respects, with a few differences. LexisNexis can be accessed by using a microcomputer and specific proprietary software, or by using a microcomputer and a standard Web browser to connect via the Internet.

The Internet

Many, if not most, legal professionals are connected to the Internet and are using it in a variety of ways. Some of the most common include performing legal research, performing factual or business research, using e-mail to communicate with clients and colleagues, accessing court records, and performing marketing functions.

PERFORMING LEGAL RESEARCH ON THE INTERNET   Performing legal research on the Internet can be done, but it is not at all like researching on Westlaw or

LexisNexis. A user can look up, choose, and go to thousands of databases instantly using these two services; there is a uniform search engine and uniform Boolean language; and information is formatted neatly, succinctly, and uniformly. Even with all that, it still takes time, training, and experience to be proficient in Westlaw and LexisNexis.

Very little is uniform when performing legal research on the Internet. You must search for and find information where you can, and you must learn the nuances of many different searching techniques and languages. There is no one central depository of information. As with any kind of legal research, the more experience you have, the better, but it takes time, training, and experience to be good at it.

Following are some strategies to consider, adapted from *The Legal List— Research on the Internet*, when beginning an Internet legal research project:

1. **Is the Internet an appropriate place to find the legal information?** If the user is looking for historic documents, including articles and statutes, or a solid case law background that dates before 1990, the Internet is probably not the place to search. It is better suited for current law, or recent cases or information. In short, the Internet is not a replacement for a traditional law library. With that said, depending on the subject matter, the Internet can have rich treasures of information, but you have to look for them.

   A cost-conscience legal researcher should start by researching any CD-ROM databases and hard copy books that he or she has, since they are cheap and convenient. The user could then explore the Internet to see what is available on-line. Again, this is cheap (actually free) and handy. Finally, the user could go to Westlaw or LexisNexis to double-check and confirm the research, fill in any holes, and check citations (Shepardize).

2. **Understand your legal project and have a strategy.** It is important, when doing legal research on the Internet, to understand exactly what you are looking for and to have a strategy for finding it. The problem with searching for something on the Internet with no plan in mind is that you can easily spend three to four hours "surfing" from site to site without finding what you are looking for, because the amount of information available on the Web is so vast.

3. **Choose a finding tool.** Choose a finding tool or search engine that is suited to the type of information for which you are looking. Some tools are better than others for finding specific kinds of information. FindLaw and LawCrawler are usually good legal finding tools.

4. **To find precise legal information, use a guidebook.** If you are looking for precise information on the Internet, it is highly recommended that you purchase a legal guidebook. A guidebook will help you get an on-line starting point (lists of specific legal Internet sites by topic), which will greatly improve your ability to find the information you need. There are many Internet guidebooks published by most major legal publishers.

5. **Get help.** Not only is the Internet a good source for legal and nonlegal information, it is also a good resource for getting help. Belonging to listservs and discussion groups regarding the type of law in which you work is advantageous. When you get stuck or need help on a research project, ask for

help. It is possible, if not probable, that others have experienced the same problem you have. You must, of course, be discreet in how you ask for help.

6. **Use an on-line starting point.** It is important to have a starting point when performing legal research on the Internet. However, a good starting point for one type of legal research might be poor for others. Figure 9-8 provides a list of search engines, Figure 9-9 lists legal research starting points, and Figure 9-10 lists factual research starting points.

Figure 9-8
List of Search Engines/Gateways/Databases

Name of Site	Web URL (Address)
General Individual/Subject Directory Search Engines	
All The Web	<http://www.alltheweb.com>
AltaVista	<http://www.altavista.com>
Excite	<http://www.excite.com>
Google	<http://www.google.com>
Lycos	<http://www.lycos.com>
MSN Search	<http://search.msn.com>
Northern Light	<http://www.northernlight.com>
WebCrawler	<http://www.webcrawler.com>
Yahoo	<http://www.yahoo.com>
Specialty Search Engines	
Google U.S. Government	<http://www.google.com/unclesam>
SearchGov (Government)	<http://www.searchgov.com>
SearchEdu (Education)	<http://www.searchedu.com>
SearchMil (Military)	<http://www.searchmilcom>
Pandia Newsfinder (News)	<http://www.pandia.com/news>
Meta-search Engines	
Dogpile	<http://www.dogpile.com>
Ixquick	<http://www.ixquick.com>
Kartoo	<http://www.kartoo.com>
MetaCrawler	<http://www.metacrawler.com>
Profusion	<http://www.profusion.com>
qbSearch	<http://www.qbsearch.com>
Library Gateways	
Academic Information	<http://www.academicinfo.com>
Digital Librarian	<http://www.digital-librarian.com>
Infomine	<http://infomine.ucr.edu/>
Librarians' Index to the Internet	<http://www.lii.org>
The Internet Public Library	<http://www.ipl.org>
WWW Virtual Library	<http://www.vlib.org>
Subject-Specific Databases	
Monster.Com (employment)	<http://www.monster.com>
SearchEdu (college and university site)	<http://www.searchedu.com>
WebMD (health/medical information)	<http://www.webmd.com>

Figure 9-9 Legal Research Starting Points

Subject	Additional Information	Web URL (Address)
Legal Search Engine/Portal		
All Law	Legal search engine/portal	<http://www.alllaw.com>
FindLaw	Legal search engine/portal	<http://www.findlaw.com>
LawCrawler	Legal search engine/portal	<http://www.lawcrawler.com>
LawGuru	Legal search engine/portal	<http://www.lawguru.com>
General Starting Points (Including Federal and State Case Law and Statutes)		
CataLaw	General legal-related information	<http://www.catalaw.com>
HierosGamos	Large collection of links to legal resources	<http://www.hg.org>
Internet Legal Research Group	Large collection of links to legal resources	<http://www.ilrg.com>
Law & Politics Institutions Guide	Large collection of links to legal resources	<http://www.lpig.org/>
Legal Information Institute at Cornell	One of the best sources of legal information on the Web	<http://www.law.cornell.edu>
The Virtual Chase	Large collection of links to legal resources	<http://www.virtualchase.com>
WashLaw Web at Washburn University	Well-organized and comprehensive legal information	<http://www.washlaw.edu>
World Wide Web Virtual Library	General and legal-related information	<http://vlib.org/>
Law at Indiana University	Legal-related information	<http://www.law.indiana.edu/v-lib/>
Federal Government Information, Regulations, and Laws		
SearchGov	Government search engine	<http://www.searchgov.com>
FedWorld	Federal information	<http://www.fedworld.gov>
Google U.S. Government	Government search engine	<http://www.google.com/unclesam>
FirstGov	Government search engine	<http://www.firstgov.gov>
Legal Forms		
Internet Legal Research Group Forms	Free legal-forms database	<http://www.ilrg.com/forms/index.html>
Legal Encyclopedia		
Law About . . . (from Cornell Law School Legal Information Institute)	Legal encyclopedia	<http://www.law.cornell.edu/topical.html>

Figure 9-9 *(Continued)*

Subject	Additional Information	Web URL (Address)
Federal Regulations		
Code of Federal Regulations	Database for the code of federal regulations	<http://cfr.law.cornell.edu/cfr/>
News and Directories		
Chicago Tribune		<http://www.chicago.tribune.com>
Los Angeles Times		<http://www.latimes.com>
New York Times		<http://www.nytimes.com>
USA Today		<http://www.usatoday.com>
Wall Street Journal		<http://online.wsj.com/public/us>
Ultimate Collection of News Links	Contains thousands of news links	<http://www.pppp.net/links/news/NA.html>
NewsLink		<http://www.newslink.org/menu.html>
ARL Directory	Exhaustive list of publications available electronically	<http://www.arl.org/scomm/edir/archive.html>
The Virtual Chase News Sites	Links to news sites on the Web	<http://virtualchase.com/resources/news.shtml>
Researching Businesses		
The Virtual Chase	Links to sites with general business information	<http://virtualchase.com/resources/industry.shtml>
Business phone/address listings	Bigfoot	<http://www.bigfoot.com>
Yellow pages	BigYellow	<http://www.bigyellow.com>
Business fax lookup	555-1212	<http://www.555-1212.com/fax_us.htm>
Major Corporation Websites	Links	<http://www.cio.com/bookmark/>
Federal Securities and Exchange Commission	Required public filing for public companies	<http://www.sec.gov/cgi-bin/srch-edgar>
Annual reports for companies	Public Register's Annual Report Service	<http://www.prars.com>
Federal Securities and Exchange Commission	Electronic Data Gathering Analysis and Retrieval (EDGAR) Database Business Information	<http://www.sec.gov/edgarhp.htm>
Hoovers	Information regarding specific companies	<http://www.hoovers.com>
Public Records (Free)		
The Virtual Chase Public Records	Large list of links to finding public information on the Web	<http://virtualchase.com/people/public_records.html>
Vital Records Information	Births, marriages, deaths, divorces	<http://www.vitalrec.com/index.html>

Figure 9-9 *(Continued)*

Subject	Additional Information	Web URL (Address)
State Public Records	An excellent source of public records information is available from individual state Web sites. Many (but not all) states have a standard Web address,	
	<http://www.state.xx.us>,	
	Where "xx" is replaced by the state's two letter abbreviation.	
	Example: Florida = <http://www.state.fl.us> New York = <http://www.state.ny.us>	
The Public Records Resource Center	Large portal to many sites with public records	<http://www.access-central.com/>
BRB Public Information Records	Large portal to many sites with public records	<http://www.brbpub.com/pubrecsites.asp>
NETR online	Real estate public records	<http://www.netronline.com/public_records.htm>
Vendors of Public Records (Fee Based)		
CDB Infotek		<http://www.cdb.com/public>
AutoTrackXP		<http://www.dbt.com> <http://www.deepdata.com>
USDatalink Information Services		<http://www.usdatalink.com>
Westlaw		<http://www.westlaw.com>
LexisNexis		<http://www.lexisnexis.com>

PROBLEMS WITH RESEARCHING ON THE INTERNET There are inherent problems with researching on the Internet that legal professionals should consider before beginning.

- *Research on the Internet can take longer to perform.* This is especially true when looking for cases, statutes, and other primary information, because it is spread over so many different sites. Experience is required to know where certain kinds of information reside on the Internet and which sites are better than others, especially when looking for historical cases or data.
- *Research on the Internet must be checked for accuracy and given a citation.* Unlike Westlaw, LexisNexis, and other fee-based information services, you need to make sure that the data you have collected on the Internet is genuine. You must be able to cite the source of the information.
- *There are no added features to information.* The legal researcher needs to remember that cases and other material on the Internet are raw in nature. No additional features typically exist like the case synopsis and keynotes that Westlaw adds to the beginning of a case. For the most part, the information has not been managed, at least not to the extent that it is when using a fee-based service.

Figure 9-10   Factual Research Starting Points

Subject	Additional Information	Web URL (Address)
General Sites		
Maps	MSN Maps	<http://www.mappoint.com>
Maps	Mapsquest	<http://www.mapquest.com>
Case citation guide	The Bluebook	<http://www.law.cornell.edu/citation/>
Dictionary	Merriam-Webster	<http://www.m-w.com/netdict.htm>
Thesaurus	Merriam-Webster	<http://www.m-w.com>
Zip codes	U.S Postal Service	<http://www.usps.gov/ncsc/lookups/lookup_zip+4.html>
National lawyer directory	Martindale-Hubbell	<http://www.martindale.com>
National lawyer directory	FindLaw	<http://www.findlaw.com/14firms/index.html>
Finding Expert Witnesses		
Expert witnesses	Claims Providers of America	<http://www.claims.com>
Expert witnesses	Washburn University School of Law	<http://washlaw.edu/expert.html>
Expert Witnesses	Northern California Association of Law Libraries extensive expert list	<http://www.nocall.org/experts.htm>
Expert witnesses	Technical Advisory Service for Attorneys	<http://www.tasanet.com>
Expert witnesses	Expert Witness Directory	<http://www.expertpages.com/>
Expert witnesses	Expert Witness Network	<http://www.expertwitnessnetwork.com>
Expert witnesses	Jurispro Expert Witness Directory	<http://jurispro.com/>
Finding People, Addresses, Phone Numbers, and E-mail Addresses		
People, addresses, phone numbers, e-mail addresses, yellow pages	Yahoo	<http://www.people.yahoo.com/>
People, addresses, phone numbers	Database America	<http://www.databaseamerica.com/>
People, addresses, phone numbers, e-mail addresses, yellow pages	Bigfoot	<http://www.bigfoot.com>
People, addresses, phone numbers, e-mail addresses, yellow pages	InfoSpace	<http://www.infospace.com>
E-mail addresses	Internet Address Finder	<http://www.iaf.net>
People, address, phone number locator	The Virtual Chase White Pages and Phone Directories	<http://virtualchase.com/people/white_pages.html>

Figure 9-10   *(Continued)*

Subject	Additional Information	Web URL (Address)
Other Information About People		
PoliticalMoneyLine	Federal campaign donors	<http://www.tray.com/FECInfo/index.html-ssi>
Family Tree Maker's Genealogy Site	Family information from census, marriage, Social Security, and other sources	<http://www.familytreemaker.com/ffilink2.html>
Cyndi's List	Genealogy-related Web-site link	<http://www.cyndislist.com/>
Military City	Listing of military personnel	<http://www.militarycity.com> (small monthly cost)
Federal Bureau of Prisons	Federal prison inmates	<http://www.bop.gov>
American Medical Association	Physician list	<http://www.ama-assn.org/>
Ancestry Site	Ancestry database	<http://www.ancestry.com>
Government Record Search	Government records database for finding people	<http://www.governmentrecords.com>
Public Records (Free)		
The Virtual Chase Public Records	Large list of links to finding public information on the Web	<http://virtualchase.com/people/public_records.html>
Vital Records Information	Births, marriages, deaths, divorces	<http://www.vitalrec.com/index.html>
State Public Records	An excellent source of public records information is available from individual state Web sites. Many (but not all) states have a standard Web address, <http://www.state.xx.us>, Where "xx" is replaced by the state's two letter abbreviation. Example: Florida = <http://www.state.fl.us> New York = <http://www.state.ny.us>	
The Public Records Resource Center	Large portal to many sites with public records	<http://www.access-central.com/>
BRB Public Information Records	Large portal to many sites with public records	<http://www.brbpub.com/pubrecsites.asp>
NETR online	Real estate public records	<http://www.netronline.com/public_records.htm>

Figure 9-10 *(Continued)*

Subject	Additional Information	Web URL (Address)
Vendors of Public Records (Fee Based)		
CDB Infotek		<http://www.cdb.com/public>
AutoTrackXP		<http://www.dbt.com>
USDatalink Information Services		<http://www.usdatalink.com>
Westlaw		<http://www.westlaw.com>
LexisNexis		<http://www.lexisnexis.com>
News and Directories		
Chicago Tribune		<http://www.chicago.tribune.com>
Los Angeles Times		<http://www.latimes.com>
New York Times		<http://www.nytimes.com>
USA Today		<http://www.usatoday.com>
Wall Street Journal		<http://online.wsj.com/public/us>
ARL Directory	Exhaustive list of publications available electronically	<http://www.arl.org/scomm/edir/archive.html>
The Virtual Chase News Sites	Links to news sites on the Web	<http://virtualchase.com/resources/news.shtml>
Researching Businesses		
The Virtual Chase	Links to sites with general business information	<http://virtualchase.com/resources/industry.shtml>
Business phone/address listings	Bigfoot	<http://www.bigfoot.com>
Yellow pages	BigYellow	<http://www.bigyellow.com>
Business fax lookup	555-1212	<http://www.555-1212.com/fax_us.htm>
Major Corporation Websites	Links	<http://www.cio.com/bookmark/>
Federal Securities and Exchange Commission	Required public filing for public companies	<http://www.sec.gov/cgi-bin/srch-edgar>
Public Register's Annual Report Service	Annual reports for companies	<http://www.prars.com>
Federal Securities and Exchange Commission	Electronic Data Gathering Analysis and Retrieval (EDGAR) Database Business Information	<http://www.sec.gov/edgarhp.htm>
Hoovers	Information regarding specific companies	<http://www.hoovers.com>

Summary

Law offices of all types need a file system that allows them to store, track, and retrieve information about cases in a logical, efficient, and expeditious manner. When considering filing management techniques, each legal matter should be maintained separately and have its own case number. How a law office sets up its case numbering system is up to the office and its own needs. Alphabetical and numerical systems are common.

Some law offices are moving toward a "paperless" office, where all information is stored electronically. Document management software is a central part of any paperless office. Document management software organizes, controls, distributes, and allows for extensive searching of electronic documents, typically in a computer-networked environment. It can also accommodate hard copy documents through the use of imaging. Imaging uses a scanner to capture an image of a document. That image is stored electronically and can be retrieved later.

Law offices must also decide whether files should be kept in a central location in the office or whether they should be kept throughout the office using a decentralized approach.

Most law offices use a file-opening form to help track new cases. Because most offices cannot keep all files indefinitely, an office should close inactive files and destroy the closed files from time to time to reduce file-storage requirements. The *Model Rules* requires that attorneys safeguard client property. Many state rules require that attorneys turn over to a client his or her entire file when the client wishes to fire an attorney and retain new counsel.

Technology has greatly changed law libraries. Now, many legal resources are available on-line or in computer format. Most law libraries today include CD-ROM libraries, Westlaw or LexisNexis (or both), and the Internet.

Helpful Web Sites

Organization	Description	Internet Address
American Bar Association (ABA)	Association for attorneys. The site has a large amount of information and publications relevant to individuals working in the legal profession.	http://www.abanet.org
ABA Law Practice Today	ABA site devoted to law practice management issues, including file and records management.	http://www.abanet.org/lpm
Association of Legal Administrators	National association for legal administrators. Contains resources and information related to law office management and legal administration.	http://www.alanet.org
Law Office Computing magazine	Excellent magazine, but limited information on-line. The site has good links to manufacturers that offer law office software.	http://www.lawofficecomputing.com
Law Technology News	Excellent periodical for legal technology issues. Good white papers on technology issues.	http://www.lawtechnews.com and http://www.law.com/jsp/ltn/whitepapers.jsp

SUGGESTED READING

1. ARMA International. (2005). *Establishing alphabetic, numeric, and subject filing systems.*

2. ARMA International. (2002). *Information and documentation—records management.*

3. ARMA International. (2002). *Records center operations.*

4. ARMA International. (2005). *Retention management for records and information.*

5. Munneke, G. A., & Davis, A. E. (2003). *The essential form book—comprehensive management tools.* American Bar Association.

6. Levitt, C. A., & Rosch, M. E. (2004). *The lawyer's guide to fact finding on the Internet* (2nd ed.). American Bar Association.

KEY TERMS

alphabetic filing system
bar coding
centralized file system
CD-ROM legal database
decentralized file system

document management software
file opening form
imaging
off-line
on-line

TEST YOUR KNOWLEDGE

1. Name three attributes of an effective file management system.
2. Name two types of file systems.
3. What does document management software do?

4. What are three advantages of document management software/the "paperless office?"
5. Legal research comes in a number of formats; name two.

ON THE WEB EXERCISES

1. Go to the ABA Center for Professional Responsibility at http://www.abanet.org/cpr/home.html, find the *ABA Model Rules of Professional Conduct,* and read and print out the comments to Rule 1.15.

2. Using a general search engine, such as http://www.google.com or http://www.yahoo.com, find three manufacturers of legal document management software.

3. Visit five state bar association Web sites and find three articles on either filing, records management, record retention, law libraries, or opening/closing client files. The following link will take you to a Web site that connects to all state bar sites: http://www.abanet.org/barserv/stlobar.html.

PROJECTS

1. Research and write a paper on any subject related to law libraries. Many resources are available on-line or in most law libraries. Select a specific topic and cover it from a broad perspective. Your paper should cite at least five different resources.

2. Research and write a paper on any subject related to filing, records management, document management software, closing a law practice, or record retention. Many resources are available on-line or in most law libraries. Select a specific topic and cover it from a broad perspective. Your paper should cite at least five different resources.

QUESTIONS AND EXERCISES

1. Law libraries represent a large overhead cost to nearly every type of law office. List ways to reduce overhead costs of the library.

2. Your supervising attorney hands you a case file on which she would like you to do some work. It appears from the file that the client saw the attorney on two different cases: the purchase of a piece of property and a medical malpractice matter. When you ask the attorney, she states that the client has recently raised the medical malpractice matter, but that the client's primary focus is on the purchase of a piece of real estate. The attorney also states that she does not think the medical malpractice matter is significant, and that is why a separate file is not being opened. The attorney tells you not to worry about it. To your knowledge, the attorney is not doing any research on the malpractice matter. How would you handle the situation?

3. The solo practitioner you worked for is moving across the country and wishes to close his law practice. The attorney is going to destroy all files related to the law practice because he does not want to have to rent storage space in a city in which he will no longer live. The attorney is getting ready to dispose of the records by hauling them out to the dumpster. What is your advice to the attorney?

4. Your office represents a client who is suing his former partner in a business venture that went sour. Your office has represented the client for two years and has put about three hundred hours into the case. In addition, your office has taken five depositions and paid for the transcripts. Your office also has hired an expert witness. The expert witness prepared a report that supports your client's case. The office has about $30,000 worth of fees and expenses in the case. One afternoon, the client comes into the office and gives the receptionist a letter stating that he is terminating the relationship with the law office and that he wants his files returned to him within one week. The attorney in the case states that there is no way he is going to hand over anything until the client pays the office's expenses. The attorney states that because the client has not paid for any work, the files are not legally his, and because the law office fronted the expenses, the law office at least owns the deposition transcripts and expert witness report. How would you handle the matter?

5. You have known for several months that your office's filing system is terrible. Documents are routinely lost, files are misplaced, and information is never filed in a timely manner. From an ethics and malpractice perspective, discuss the problems that may arise if a client's file or a piece of evidence regarding a client file is lost and cannot be found.

6. The office you work for has recently added six attorneys and three legal assistants. The file system is no longer efficient. Finding files is time consuming. You have been asked to come up with a new filing system. The following are some details you should keep in mind when determining the new system:

- The three tax attorneys want to start their own department. The tax attorneys will shortly move their offices to the basement, and they want to keep their own files so they do not have to run up and down the stairs to get to them. None of the other attorneys use or need access to the tax files.

- Staff employees can be very reckless about the condition in which they leave files.
- When a case is opened, all the documents are kept in a large expanding file folder.
- Documents tend to fall out of the files, and there is little organization to the case files.
- Many of the attorneys work on cases together and need access to the cases.
- People are constantly looking through the office trying to find a file.
- Last week, the accounting department found out for the first time that the office has been handling a case for about four months. The client has never received a bill.
- The office wants a file system in which it can immediately tell when the case is filed, what type of case it is (the office mainly handles tax, probate, corporate, and general litigation matters), and which partner is responsible for the case (there are five partners).

Develop a strategy that will help eliminate these problems.

7. The partners in your office are displeased with the way the office's library is being maintained. They say that the library is hemorrhaging money with increased costs, which is crippling the office's profits. Your job is to draw up a plan to bring this situation under control. You have noticed the following:

- Several copies of books are purchased by different partners and placed on their bookshelves.
- The library is a mess most of the time. Books are kept in attorneys' and legal assistants' offices (they rarely check out the books and then fail to get them back to the library), there is not enough room for the materials the library does have, and books are stacked up on the floor.
- Many of the materials the library does have are outdated and no longer of use.
- You asked for several books, and, while you know they were ordered, you have not seen them yet.
- The library has no budget as such; purchases are made when the office thinks it needs them. In addition, when an attorney orders a book, the book is sometimes kept on the attorney's own bookshelf.
- All library costs, including Westlaw and LexisNexis, are absorbed by the office.
- The library has no Internet access, although it has been talked about.
- The library has one old desktop computer that has Westlaw and LexisNexis only.

NOTES

1. Heller, D., & Hunt, J. M. (1988). *Practicing law and managing people: How to be successful* (p. 60). Butterworth. Courtesy of Heller, Hunt, and Cunningham, Stoneham, MA.

2. Ibid., p. 62. Courtesy of Heller, Hunt, and Cunningham, Stoneham, MA.

3. Baird, T. (2005, July). Paperless and loving it. *Texas Bar Journal, 68*(7)591.

4. Parsons, M. (2003, September). Finishing Right. *Law Technology News,* 22.

5. Alabama State Bar Association. Organizing and maintaining files in a small law firm.

5A. Richard Sloane, "The Law Office Library," *The Lawyer's Handbook,* American Bar Association, 1983, B3-2. Reprinted by permission.

6. Quote attributed to Drexel University Law School Library.

7. Sloane, R. (1983). The law office library. *The Lawyer's Handbook* (p. B3-1). American Bar Association. Reprinted by permission.

ANSWERS TO TEST YOUR KNOWLEDGE

1. Completeness, retention, integrity, ease of use, security, ease of learning, and adaptability.
2. Alphabetical, numerical, electronic document management, bar coding, and color coding.
3. Organizes, controls, distributes, and allows for extensive searching of electronic documents, typically in a computer-networked environment.
4. The ability to share information across vast distances, excellent tracking and reporting capabilities, reduced instances of misfiling, ability to easily and quickly create a backup copy of the information, reduced space and storage costs, and the ability to quickly search and sort information.
5. Hard copy, CD-ROM, Internet, and on-line services such as Westlaw/LexisNexis.

CASE REVIEW

In re Cameron, 270 Ga. 512, 511 S.E.2d 514 (Ga. 1999).

Supreme Court of Georgia.

In the Matter of Johnnie CAMERON (Two Cases).

Nos. S99Y0257. S99Y0258.

Feb. 8, 1999.

*512 PER CURIAM.

The State Bar filed two Notices of Discipline against Respondent Johnnie Cameron alleging violations of Standards 4 (professional conduct involving dishonesty, fraud, deceit, or willful misrepresentation); 22 (withdrawal from employment without taking reasonable steps to avoid foreseeable prejudice to the rights of the client, including giving due notice to the client, allowing time for employment of other counsel, delivering to the client all papers and property to which the client is entitled, and complying with applicable laws and rules); and 44 (willful abandonment or disregard of a legal matter to the client's detriment) of Bar Rule 4-102(d). Upon Cameron's failure to respond to either of the Notices of Discipline within the time set by Bar Rule 4-208.3(a), Cameron was in default pursuant to Bar ***513** Rule 4-208.1(b) and subject to discipline by this Court. The State Bar

has recommended disbarment as an appropriate sanction for Cameron's violations of Standards 4, 22, and 44 of Bar Rule 4-102(d). We agree.

In one disciplinary matter, Cameron was hired by a client to represent him in a Social Security disability claim. The client gave Cameron documents pertaining to the claim and tried to reach Cameron by telephone numerous times. Cameron did not return the client's calls even when the client tried to reach Cameron regarding an appointment scheduled with a physician regarding the client's disability claim. On July 28, 1997, the client spoke with Cameron by telephone and Cameron promised to return the call on July 30, 1997 but failed to do so. After the Social Security Administration scheduled a disability hearing, the client again tried unsuccessfully to reach Cameron. Subsequently, the hearing was postponed when the hearing officer also could not reach Cameron. The client, in making additional attempts to reach Cameron, learned that Cameron's office had been vacated and his home telephone number disconnected. On September 5, 1997, the client wrote a letter to Cameron terminating Cameron's services and demanding the return of all documents. Cameron again failed to respond. Due to Cameron's failure to represent the client, the client was not able to present his disability case to the administrative law judge.

In a second matter, a client hired Cameron on or about November 14, 1997 to advise her on a will and property deeds and gave the original documents plus $50 to Cameron. Although Cameron stated that he would copy the documents and return the originals to the client, he failed to return the documents or to contact the client. The client made numerous attempts to call Cameron at his home and his office but was not able to reach him; she also learned that Cameron's fax number was disconnected. The client and the client's daughter contacted Cameron at his part-time job and requested the return of the original documents. Although in both instances Cameron promised to return the documents on the day of the telephone conversations, he did not keep the appointments or return the documents. In sum, Cameron did not do any work on the client's behalf, did not return any portion of the $50 fee, and failed to return the client's documents.

Although Cameron has no disciplinary history, the State Bar noted the pattern of dishonesty and abandonment evidenced by the two grievances filed and Cameron's failure to respond to the Notices of Investigation as aggravating factors in its recommendation for disbarment. Cameron has failed to respond to disciplinary authorities during the investigation of these matters and the Court finds no evidence of mitigating circumstances.

*514 We agree with the State Bar that disbarment is warranted as a result of Cameron's violation of Standards 4, 22, and 44 of Bar Rule 4-102(d). Accordingly, Cameron is disbarred from the practice of law in Georgia. He is reminded of his duties under Bar Rule 4-219(c).

Disbarred.

All the Justices concur.

END OF DOCUMENT

EXERCISES

1. List each act committed by the attorney that violated Standard 22 of the state bar rules regarding the "withdrawal from employment without taking reasonable steps to avoid foreseeable prejudice to the rights of the client. . . ."

2. If the attorney had argued that he should not be disciplined because the client had not paid him for the time spent on the case(s) (assuming it was true), would this have changed the outcome of the case?

3. What duty did the attorney have to his client(s) when he moved his office and had his home telephone number and office fax number disconnected?

4. Once the attorney took a part-time job, and assuming he quit the practice of law, what should the attorney have done?

5. Given the fact that the attorney had no prior discipline, do you think disbarment was appropriate?

 For additional resources, visit our Web site at www.westlegalstudies.com

Succeeding as a Legal Assistant

> The biggest reason we let legal assistants go is because they do not have the management skills necessary to perform adequately. They come out of school with a theoretical knowledge of law, but with few practical skills to manage themselves so as to succeed at our firm.[1]

Legal assistants must develop good management skills in order to succeed. They need to be accurate and thorough in everything they do. They must be routinely organized, prompt, and prepared. They must be team players and communicate effectively. These things do not come naturally; most are learned the hard, old-fashioned way: by trial and error over years. Read this section so that you can pick up some good ideas now that will save you many headaches once on the job. Some of the suggestions may sound simplistic, but they really are not. The suggestions in this chapter come from many legal assistants and from varied experiences. These suggestions really work, and while some are fundamental, all of them are important.

Accuracy, Thoroughness, and Quality

"Accuracy" and "thoroughness" are easy to say but hard to accomplish. However, high-quality work is vital to the performance of a professional. A law office is a team, and everyone must be able to rely on everyone else; each client is paying for and deserves the absolute best work product the team can provide.

One element of quality work is careful documentation. It is important that, when you talk to witnesses, clients, opposing counsel, or others, you keep written notes of your conversation and send a confirming letter that documents your conversation. Some cases can drag on for years; if proper notes are not kept in the file, vital information can be lost. Keeping proper documentation about the work you have done on a case is very important.

Mistakes happen. If something does slip by, do not try to cover it up. Admit and/or report the mistake, correct the mistake to the best of your ability as quickly as possible, take precautions to make sure it does not happen again, apologize, and go on. Because mistakes are natural and almost inevitable, being accurate and putting out quality work is a daily battle.

Ideas on how to improve the quality of your work include the following:

- **Create forms and systems.** If you do a job more than once, create a system using forms and instructions for yourself. This will evoke memories from the last time you performed the job and speed up the work.
- **Create checklists.** Make a checklist for the jobs you regularly perform. Checklists will keep you from failing to perform specific details of a job that otherwise might be forgotten. In this way, the high quality of your work is maintained.
- **Be careful and complete.** Be prudent and careful in your work. Do not hurry your work to the degree that accuracy and thoroughness are compromised. Your work should always be neat and complete.
- **Keep written documentation and notes.** Keeping proper documentation about work you have done on a case is very important.
- **Take pride in your work.** Do not let work that you are not proud to call your own go out with your name on it.
- **Work hard.** Accuracy and thoroughness are seldom reached by slothfulness. Work hard at what you do, and the quality of the work will always be better for it.
- **Ask for peer review.** If you have a particularly important project due and you have a question about the accuracy of your work, have another legal assistant or staff member look it over before it is turned in. While you do not want to become dependent on others or disrupt their productivity, sometimes a second opinion can really help, especially if you are new to the organization.
- **Never assume.** Do not assume anything. If you have the slightest doubt about something, check it out, conduct research, make sure that you pay attention to details, and double-check the accuracy of your work.
- **Use firm resources.** Use firm resources, like intranets, brief banks, and tools, to the fullest extent. You will learn from others and your work will be of higher quality if you use the collective knowledge of other experienced staff.

The Assignment

> *A senior partner thinks he has told a legal assistant to take care of an important filing. In actuality, all he told the legal assistant to do was to draft the necessary documents to make the filing. The legal assistant drafts the documents and puts them in the senior partner's box for review. The filing deadline is missed. The senior partner blames the legal assistant for the job not being done properly.*[2]

When a task is being assigned to you, make sure you understand exactly what the assignment is and what the supervising attorney wants. Be absolutely certain that you understand the whole assignment; do not guess or extrapolate. One of the most common mistakes a new legal assistant makes is to not ask questions. It takes a certain amount of maturity to say, "I do not understand," but it is absolutely critical. Your supervising attorney will not think any worse of you for it, and your chance of success on the task will be greatly enhanced. It is also a good idea to repeat the assignment back to the supervisor to make sure you understand all of the details. If a task is extremely complicated, ask the supervisor to help you break it down into smaller parts. You might say: "This appears to be a fairly good-sized job. Where do you recommend I start and how should I proceed; what steps should I take?"

It is also a good idea to write down your assignment. Have a pencil and a notebook or steno pad with you any time you talk to your supervisor about an assignment. A steno pad can serve as a journal, allowing you to keep all of your assignments in one place. If you record assignments, you will be able to refer back to them later if someone has a question or problem about work they gave you. Be sure to write down what the assignment is, who gave it to you, any comments the person made about the assignment, and when it is due. Always ask for the exact date an assignment is due, not "sometime next week" or "whenever you get to it." Also be sure to write down when you completed the assignment.

If an assignment gets a little fuzzy to you after you start it, ask the supervisor questions while you are still in the middle of it. Do not wait until the end of the assignment to realize you did something wrong; check in periodically and have the supervisor quickly review it. This is particularly important with large and complex tasks.

> *You start with real basic things, like you bring a pad and pencil with you. You don't get grabbed in the hallway and get an oral assignment of some significance and not write it down.*[3]

Do the following to communicate effectively when receiving assignments:

- **Ask questions when the assignment is given.** Ask questions about the assignment until you fully understand what you are being asked to perform. Be aware that miscommunication problems occur more frequently regarding assignments you have never done before.
- **Repeat the assignment to your supervisor.** Repeat the assignment back to the supervisor to make sure you understand all of the details.
- **Break down complex assignments into small tasks.** Ask the supervisor to help you break complex assignments down into smaller tasks and help you organize the priority of those tasks.
- **Have a pen and paper ready.** Always have a pen and paper (a steno pad works best) with you when you are being given as assignment. It allows you to remember when the assignment was given, by whom, any comments from the supervisor and when it is due.
- **Always ask for a due date.** Always ask for a specific due date. This prevents miscommunication regarding when an assignment should be completed.
- **Continue to ask questions and check in periodically.** As you work on the assignment, continue to ask clarifying questions and periodically check in with your supervisor to keep him or her updated on your progress.

Preparation and Organization

Successful legal assistants are organized and prepared for everything they do. Being organized is not hard; it just takes planning and time. Always have an appointment calendar with you so that you can record important appointments and deadlines. In addition, use a "things-to-do" list each day and try to plan and prioritize tasks so that assignments and projects are never late. Begin with the most important assignment you have to do or with the task that has the most pressing deadline. When you are working on projects for two or more attorneys, ask someone to prioritize the tasks for you. If you have a computer program that has organizational features, use it.

The following ideas will improve your preparation and organization:

- **Have an appointment calendar.** Carry an appointment calendar with you at all times or be sure to constantly update your computerized versions and print out hard copies regularly. This way, if you are caught in the hallway and given an assignment or meeting date, you will know if you have a conflict.
- **Make a "things-to-do" list.** Plan your day in advance, every day. Make a "things-to-do" list and try to complete your list every day, marking off items once they are completed.
- **Prioritize tasks.** When you are preparing your "things-to-do" list, always prioritize the tasks so that you turn in assignments on time. Give priority to assignments that have the most pressing deadlines. If you have a question about what assignment needs to be done first, ask your managing attorney for direction.

- **Be on time.** Always be on time when completing assignments and attending meetings, and always take good notes so that you will remember important facts or information provided in meetings.

Manage Your Time

Are you using your time effectively, or are you wasting it? Time management and organization go hand in hand.

The following ideas can help you manage your time effectively:

- **Set daily objectives.** Always plan your day by setting daily objectives and prioritizing them accordingly. Try to stick to your plan and achieve your objectives every day. Do the most important things first.
- **Do not waste your time on irrelevant tasks.** Do not waste your time on unimportant or unnecessary tasks. When someone walks into your office to talk about an irrelevant subject and you have a job due, politely ask him or her to come back another time when you are free.
- **Avoid procrastination.** Do not put off what you can do today. Procrastination is unprofessional and leads to dissatisfied clients. Stick to your daily schedule and do not put things off unless you have a good reason.
- **Avoid socializing in hallways.** Socializing is not only a waste of your time, it is also a distraction to others around you. In addition, it looks very unprofessional to clients.
- **Make a timeline or Gantt chart.** When you have a large project, take the time to make a Gantt chart. A Gantt chart is a plan or timeline of projected begin and end dates for the various parts of a project. A Gantt chart will help you plan how you will complete the project and will also allow you to track the progress of the work.
- **Have reference material close by.** Lay out your desk and office so that important reference materials are located within arm's reach to minimize time spent looking for things.

Effective Communication with Attorneys

One of your most important tasks will be to establish mutual confidence between yourself and your supervisor. Because legal assistants and attorneys must work together very closely, good communication is an absolute necessity.

If you want respect in this profession, you must command it. To command this respect, you must be an intelligent professional willing to take on responsibility without having to be asked. Find ways to make yourself even more valuable than you already appear to be. Don't sit and complain about the way things are. Take charge and change them.[4]

The following practices will help you maintain effective communication with your supervisor:

- **Always ask questions.** If you do not understand something, ask questions.
- **Listen.** Do not forget to listen carefully when communicating with your supervising attorney. Listen and make notes so that you remember the details you will need to complete assignments.
- **Be confident.** Do not be so intimidated by attorneys that you act timid and fail to communicate. Carry yourself with confidence and authority. When you talk, always make eye contact.
- **Check in.** Check in with your supervising attorney on a daily basis so that he or she is informed of your progress on assignments.
- **Do not make important decisions unilaterally.** Include the supervising attorney in the decision-making process.
- **Establish mutual confidence.** Establishing mutual confidence with your supervising attorney is crucial. Your supervising attorney needs to have confidence in your work, and you need to have confidence in his or her work.
- **Establish your limit of authority.** Ask your supervising attorney what your limit of authority is when making decisions. You need to know as clearly as possible when he or she should be involved in decisions and what types of decisions they are.

The Client Comes First

When you are with a client, he or she should be given your undivided attention. Do not take phone calls, allow interruptions, play with your nails, or do anything else that would take your attention away from the client. Treat each client courteously and respectfully, and as if he or she is the only client you have.

The following measures will help ensure that the client comes first:

- **Give clients your undivided attention.** When you are with a client, be sure that you give the client all of your attention. Do not take phone calls, open mail, or do anything else that would take your attention away from the client.
- **Give clients fast, courteous, respectful treatment.** Treat the client courteously and respectfully at *all* times. Always return client phone calls and e-mails as quickly as possible, but never later than the same day, and always try to answer their questions as soon as you can.
- **Treat each client as if he or she were your only client.** A client's case is very important to him or her and should be important to you. Let your clients know that their welfare genuinely concerns you.
- **Serve clients, but do not overstep your bounds.** Do not let your zeal to serve clients cause you to overstep your bounds. Let the attorney answer complex client questions and give legal advice.
- **Maintain client confidence.** Always maintain the strictest standards regarding client confidentiality.

Keep Accurate, Contemporaneous Time Sheets

Attorneys and legal assistants keep records of the amount of time spent on each case so that management will know how much to bill the client. Many firms require legal assistants to bill a certain number of hours to clients each year or each month, so when you start with a firm always be sure to ask how many hours of billable time you are expected to have per month and annually. Also ask when time sheets are due and when they are monitored for compliance (i.e., weekly, monthly, quarterly). Budget your time so that you know how many billable hours each month, week, or even day you will need to meet your goal, and then monitor yourself on your progress. Do not let yourself get behind, as you will not be able to make it up. If you are given a non-billable task, delegate the task as much as possible to secretaries and clerks. There are simple techniques to keeping accurate time sheets. Always record the necessary information on your time sheet *as the day progresses*. Do not try and go back at the end of the day or week and try to remember what you did; write it down as you perform the work.

Timekeepers, especially new timekeepers, have a tendency to subjectively discount their hours because they feel guilty for billing their time to clients. Record the time you *actually* spent working on a client's case: if it took six hours to research a legal issue, record the whole six hours. If your supervisor does not believe the finished product is worth that much, he or she can adjust the time billed. Simply put, it is not your call to reduce your hours. Record your actual time and go on.

To keep accurate time records, implement the following measures:

- **Keep track of budgeted and actual billable hours.** Your supervisor may tell you that you are responsible for billing 100 hours a month (i.e., 25 hours a week). You want to be sure every week that the time sheets you turn in to management show as close to the amount budgeted as possible. You need to track this.
- **Keep a time sheet near your phone and computer.** Always keep a time sheet next to your phone or computer so when you pick up the phone or prepare work on the computer, you can record the time for it.
- **Fill out the time sheet throughout the day.** Fill out your time sheet as you go throughout the day instead of trying to play the "memory game" to remember all the things you accomplished.
- **Record the actual time you spent on a case.** Always record the actual time it took you to perform the legal service. Let your supervisor make any decision to adjust or reduce time to be billed to the client.
- **Be absolutely honest and ethical.** Never bill a client for administrative tasks or for time you did not actually spend working on his or her case.

Work Hard and Efficiently

Everyone knows the difference between working hard and coasting. If you work hard, people will respect you and recognize you for it; if you do not, people will recognize this also and typically will resent you for it.

Do not be surprised if you must work overtime. The question as to whether legal assistants should be paid for overtime is a hot topic; some firms pay overtime compensation and some do not. In any event, if you have to work overtime, do it with a positive attitude. Be honest and sincere. Also try to work as efficiently as possible.

- **Pull your weight.** Do what is asked of you and produce quality work.
- **Put in overtime when required.** Be ready to put in overtime when it is required. Try to be pleasant and professional about it.
- **Work efficiently.** Work as efficiently as possible. If you have access to a computer, it makes sense to use it instead of doing something by hand.

Maintain a Positive Attitude and Team Spirit

The greatest key to success is something no one can give you—a good attitude! Enthusiasm has nothing to do with noise; it has more to do with motivation. It deals with our attitude. An attitude is something you can do something about. I can choose to be enthusiastic or I can choose not to be. Excitement is infectious; it's sort of like a case of the measles. You can't infect someone unless you have the real thing.[5]

A law office is a team that must rely on many different people to work together harmoniously in order to be successful. Approach your job with the goal of being a good team player and helping your team. Put the good of the firm above your own personal interest, and help the firm whenever you can, whether or not it is in your job description.

Good team players help other members of the team by passing along information and cooperating on tasks. They are able to give and receive help when it is needed. Another aspect of being a team player is knowing how to constructively criticize other players. First of all, be cordial and professional. Never criticize another staff member in front of a client, an attorney, or other staff members. Do not become emotional. Politely explain the problem and suggest a reasonable solution for solving it. Treat the other person as an equal. When you are the one being criticized, do not take the criticism personally; look beyond the finding of fault and try to make the adjustments suggested by the firm. Listen carefully and ask questions so that you understand the exact problem.

Your own effectiveness as a legal assistant may depend on how well you work with others at your level on the team. You may strongly dislike some people. You will need patience and interpersonal skills to learn to work with them and develop mutual trust and confidence.

- **Put the team first.** Always put the needs of the team before your own personal interests. In the long run, what is good for the team is good for you.
- **Delegate.** Delegate tasks to other team members when possible. Use the team.
- **Help other team members.** Always remember to take time to help other team members. Otherwise, they will not be willing to help you when you need it.
- **Share information.** Never hoard information. Pass information along to other staff members, remembering to put the team first.
- **Constructively and professionally criticize other team members.** Just because you are a team player does not mean you cannot constructively criticize others. Try to be respectful, professional, and nonemotional. Explain the criticism, then suggest ways to fix the problem. Treat others as equals.
- **Take criticism professionally.** Try to avoid becoming defensive and listen to what is being said. Try to implement the suggestions of the other party as soon as possible.
- **Get along with those you do not like.** You will probably not like everyone you work with. But, for the good of the team, work at relationships and treat all coworkers with courtesy and respect.

> *My secretary always backs me up, and she knows I'll back her up. One night she had a critical mailing to get out, and I stayed late with her so she could leave a little sooner. It's important to have a social relationship with her— you're concerned about her kids and she's concerned about how your weekend went.[6]*

- **Know the employees of your firm.** Get to know the employees of your firm and treat all employees as you would like to be treated.

Be a Self-Starter

> *In order to advance as a paralegal, you must prove that you are capable of taking on greater responsibility by performing your present duties exceptionally well. Show your initiative by anticipating the next stage of any assignment and completing it before you are asked to do it.[7]*

Self-starters are valuable employees. Self-starters are people who do not need to be told what to do; they see a job that should be done or a need that should be fulfilled and they do the job or meet the need without having to be told. They seek out and volunteer for new work, assume responsibility willingly, and anticipate future needs.

> *If you're in a meeting and everyone's talking about something, volunteer for it. Don't wait for them to point out, "That's something a paralegal could do."* [8]

Be flexible, open-minded, and creative; be a problem solver. Do not hesitate to courteously suggest new ways of doing things as long as the idea is well thought out (not off-the-cuff) and would provide the firm with a real benefit over the present way. However, before you try to implement a new idea or approach, be sure that you have researched, organized, and planned the project well in advance and have assessed the chances or risk of failure and the consequences of such a failure. Get others involved in the project, and ask for their help and input; this will help them accept the system later on.

Ideas on being a self-starter include the following:

- **Anticipate.** Anticipate what jobs need to be done or what need is unfilled, and then do the job or fulfill the need without being asked to do it.
- **Seek out and volunteer for assignments.** If a new assignment comes up (especially one with a lot of responsibility), volunteer for it.
- **Be flexible and open-minded.** Always be flexible and open-minded; have a positive attitude. All businesses must change with the times. Be adaptable.
- **Be aware of risk.** Before taking on a new assignment, research, organize, and plan. Assess your chances of success.
- **Get others involved.** Always include others in your development of new ideas. Get their thoughts and feedback. Not only is the information helpful, but people are far more willing to implement an idea to which they have contributed.

Stress Management

A law office is a very stressful place with a great deal of activities, deadlines, appointments, and problems. You must learn to manage your own stress, or it will manage you. Do not be so consumed with your work that you put it above your family or your own happiness. Learn to relax and participate in activities that allow you to do so. A healthy lifestyle and exercise can reduce your stress. You should also consider what causes your stress and how you can change your work environment to reduce it. Being a workaholic will only lead to burnout and frustration. Taking a vacation is also important; everyone needs an extended rest at least once a year.

To manage stress, follow these guidelines:

- **Remember your family.** Do not let your work rule your life. To be a complete person, you must work hard but you also have responsibilities to your family. Try not to go too far in either direction. You need a balance.
- **Participate in relaxing activities.** Learn to relax and participate in activities you enjoy.
- **Exercise.** A healthy lifestyle, with regular exercise, is another good way to reduce stress.

- **Consider your environment.** Consider where your stress comes from and how you can change your work environment to reduce the cause of your stress.
- **Take a vacation.** Take a vacation at least once a year. You need to rest and get away from the office from time to time.

CONCLUSION   A successful legal assistant must have many attributes in addition to good technical skills. Being a team player, having a positive attitude, working hard, and keeping accurate records are just a few of the skills that legal assistants must have.

Everything in this appendix must be considered in light of the corporate culture of the particular law practice in which you are working. **Corporate culture** refers to generally accepted behavior patterns within an organization; this will include the firm's values, personality, heroes, and mores. Most firms have written procedures or staff manuals that contain some of this information. Many policies, however, are never reduced to writing. Make it your business to understand your firm's position and how the firm views its clients, staff, and so on. Understanding how your particular firm looks at the world is very important.

NOTES

1. A legal administrator at a large Kansas City, Missouri firm.
2. Statsky, W. (1992). *Introduction to paralegalism* (p. 180). St. Paul, MN: West Publishing, citing Sgarlat. (1986, June). *The scapegoat phenomenon, The Journal,* 6(10) (Sacramento Association of Legal Assistants, June 1986).
3. Tokumitsu, C. (1991, November/December). How to avoid the top 10 mistakes paralegals make on the job. *Legal Assistant Today,* 31.
4. Statsky, W. (1992). *Introduction to paralegalism* (p. 192). St. Paul, MN: West Publishing, citing Roselle. (1984, November). *I don't get no respect!, National Paralegal Reporter,* 9(2).
5. Ibid., citing Johnson. (1998, July). President's message, *Arizona Paralegal Association Newsletter,* 1.
6. Tokumitsu, C. (1991, November/December). How to avoid the top 10 mistakes paralegals make on the job. *Legal Assistant Today,* 30.
7. Ibid.
8. Statsky, W. (1992). *Introduction to paralegalism* (p. 192). St. Paul, MN: West Publishing, citing Coyne. (1990, Winter). Strategies for paralegal career development. *National Paralegal Reporter,* 20.
9. Tokumitsu, C. (1991, November/December). How to avoid the top 10 mistakes paralegals make on the job. *Legal Assistant Today,* 29.

GLOSSARY

accounting software   Program that uses a computer to track and maintain the financial data and records of a business.

activity hourly rate   Fee based on the different hourly rates, depending on what type of service or activity is actually performed.

administrative management   Management decisions relating to operating or managing a law office, including financial and personnel matters.

administrative task   A task relating to the internal practices and duties involved with operating or managing a law office.

aged accounts receivable report   A report showing all cases that have outstanding balances due and how long these balances are past due.

Age Discrimination in Employment Act of 1967   Federal legislation that prohibits employers from discriminating against employees and applicants on the basis of age when the individual is 40 or older.

alphabetic filing system   Filing method in which cases are stored based on the last name of the client or organization.

Americans with Disabilities Act of 1990 (ADA)   Federal legislation that prohibits employers from discriminating against employees or applicants with disabilities.

application software   Instructs the computer to perform a specific application or task, such as word processing.

associate attorney   An attorney who is a salaried employee of the law firm, does not have an ownership interest in the firm, does not share in the profits, and has no vote regarding management decisions.

attorney-client privilege   A standard that precludes the disclosure of confidential communications between a lawyer and a client by the lawyer.

attorney/legal assistant hourly rate   A fee based on the attorney's or legal assistant's expertise and experience in a particular area.

attorneys   Attorneys counsel clients regarding their legal rights, represent clients in litigation, and negotiate agreements for clients.

bar coding   A file management technique in which each file is tracked according to the file's bar code.

Bates stamp   Stamps a document with a sequential number and then automatically advances to the next number.

billable time   Actual time that a legal assistant or attorney spends working on a case and that is directly billed to a client's account.

billing   The process of issuing invoices for the purpose of collecting monies for legal services performed and being reimbursed for expenses.

blended hourly rate fee   An hourly rate that is set taking into account the blend or mix of attorneys working on the matter.

bona fide occupation qualification   An allowable exception to equal employment opportunity; for example, for an employee to perform a specific job, the employee must be of a certain age, sex, or religion.

boutique firm   A small law office that specializes in only one or two areas of the law.

budget   A projected plan of income and expenses for a set period of time, usually a year.

calendar days   System for calculating deadlines that counts all days including weekends and holidays.

calendaring   A generic term used to describe the function of recording appointments for any type of business.

case management   A legal term that usually refers to functions such as docket control, things to do, contact information by case, case notes, document assembly, document tracking by case, integrated billing, and e-mail.

case retainer   A fee that is billed at the beginning of a matter, is not refundable to the client, and is usually paid at the beginning of the case as an incentive for the office to take the case.

case type productivity report   Report showing which types of cases (e.g., criminal, personal injury, bankruptcy, etc.) are the most profitable.

cash advance   Unearned monies that are an advance against the attorney's future fees and expenses.

CD-ROM   Peripheral device that uses optical technology, or laser beams, to store large quantities of data on a small laser disk.

CD-ROM legal database   A database like one found on Westlaw or LexisNexis, but packaged on CD-ROMs.

centralized file system   Method in which a file department or file clerk stores and manages all active law office files in one or more file rooms.

Certificate of Service   Establishes when a legal document was placed in the mail.

Chinese Wall   Term for a technique used to isolate the legal assistant or attorney with a conflict of interest from having anything to do with a case.

Civil Rights Act of 1964   Federal legislation that prohibits employers from discriminating against employees or applicants on the basis of race, color, national origin, religion, or gender.

clerks   Clerks provide support to other staff positions in a variety of miscellaneous functions.

client confidentiality   Keeping information exchanged between a client and law office staff confidential.

client hourly rate   Fee based on one hourly charge for the client, regardless of which attorney works on the case and what he or she does on the case.

coaching technique   Counseling that focuses on the positive aspects of the employee's performance and explores alternative ways to improve his or her performance.

communication   The transfer of a message from a sender to a receiver.

communication barrier   Something that inhibits or prevents the receiver from obtaining the correct message.

communication device   Device that allows computers to exchange information with one another. It is technically both an input and an output device.

computer   An electronic device that accepts, processes, outputs, and stores information.

computer programs   The step-by-step instructions that direct the computer to do certain tasks.

computer virus   A computer program that is destructive in nature and can bury itself within other programs.

conflict of interest   A competing personal or professional interest that would preclude an attorney or legal assistant from acting impartially toward the client.

contingency fee   A fee that is collected if the attorney successfully represents the client. The attorney is entitled to a percentage of the monies awarded to the client.

continuance   Rescheduling an appointment or court date.

contract attorney   An attorney temporarily hired by the law office for a specific job or period. When the job or period is finished, the relationship with the firm is over.

controlling   The process of determining whether the law practice is achieving its objectives, holding stakeholders accountable for their goals, and making strategy adjustments as necessary so the firm achieves its objectives.

court-awarded fees   Fees given to the prevailing party in a lawsuit pursuant to certain federal and state statutes.

criminal fraud   A false representation of a present or past fact made by a defendant.

cross-selling   Refers to selling additional services to existing clients.

database   A computer program that organizes, searches, and sorts data.

decentralized file system   System in which files are kept in various locations throughout the law office.

docket   A calendaring or scheduling system that tracks and organizes appointments, deadlines, and commitments.

docket control   A law-office-specific term that refers to entering, organizing, and controlling all the appointments, deadlines, and due dates for a legal organization.

document assembly software   Creates powerful standardized templates and forms.

document management software   Organizes, controls, distributes, and allows for extensive searching of electronic documents, typically in a networked environment.

earned retainer   Money the law office or attorney has earned and is entitled to deposit in the office's or attorney's own bank account.

electronic billing   When law firms bill clients using electronic means, such as the Internet.

employee attitude survey   A survey that is given to an organization's employees and asks the employees to rate the effectiveness of the organization in many specific areas.

employment-at-will doctrine   Doctrine that states that an employer and employee freely enter into an employment relationship, and that either party has the right to sever the relationship at any time without reason.

equal employment opportunity   Concept that requires employers to make employment-related decisions without arbitrarily discriminating against an individual.

Equal Pay Act of 1963   Federal legislation that prohibits employers from paying workers of one sex less than the rate paid to employee of the opposite sex for work on jobs that require equal skill, effort, and responsibility, and that are performed under the same working conditions.

escrow account   A separate bank account (also called a trust account), apart from a law office's or attorney's operating checking account, where unearned client funds are deposited.

essential job functions   Job duties or tasks that are necessary to the completion of the job and that will take up a significant part of the employee's time.

ethical rule   A minimal standard of conduct.

Ethical Wall   Term for a technique used to isolate the legal assistant or attorney with a conflict of interest from having anything to do with a case.

expense   A cost that the firm has incurred for the purpose of earning income.

expert witness   A person who has technical expertise in a specific field and agrees to give testimony for a client at trial.

extranet   A network designed to provide, disseminate, and share confidential information with clients.

facilities management   Refers to law office management's responsibility to plan, design, and control a law office's own building or office space effectively.

Fair Credit Reporting Act   A federal law that limits the use of consumer reports (including reference checks) in all employment decisions.

Fair Labor Standards Act (FLSA)   A federal law that sets minimum wage and overtime pay requirements for employees.

Family and Medical Leave Act of 1993   Federal legislation that allows employees in certain circumstances to receive up to 12 workweeks of unpaid leave from their jobs for family or health-related reasons.

feedback Information sent in response to a message.

file-opening form   A standardized form that is filled out when a new case is opened.

financial management   The oversight of a firm's financial assets and profitability to ensure overall financial health.

flat fee   A fee for legal services that is billed as a flat or fixed amount.

floor load capacity   Refers to the weight per square foot the floor can hold without collapsing.

FLSA exempt   The employee is not required to be paid overtime wages over 40 hours per week.

FLSA nonexempt   The employee is required to be paid overtime wages (time and a half) over 40 hours per week.

form file   A file that contains examples of documents used in a law office, including pleadings, contracts, wills, and discovery documents.

freelance/contract legal assistant   Works as an independent contractor with supervision by and/or accountability to an attorney; is hired for a specific job or period.

Gantt chart   A plan or timeline of the projected begin dates and dates of a project.

general counsel   The chief for a corporate legal department.

gross income   Monies that are received before expenses are deducted.

gross lease   The tenant pays only for base rent, and the landlord covers all other building-related expenses.

groupthink   The desire for group cohesiveness and consensus becomes stronger than the desire for the best possible decision.

hardware   The actual physical components of a computer system.

hourly rate fee   A fee for legal services that is billed to the client by the hour at an agreed-upon rate.

human resource management   Recruiting, hiring, training, evaluating, maintaining, and directing the personnel that will provide quality legal services to the clients.

imaging   The capture, retrieval, and storage of document images electronically.

income   Something of value that a law office receives from a client in exchange for the law office providing professional legal services.

income budget   Estimate of how many partners, associates, legal assistants, and others will bill for their time, what the appropriate rates of hourly charge should be, and the number of billable hours each timekeeper will be responsible for billing.

independent legal assistant   Provides services to clients in which the law is involved, but is not accountable to a lawyer.

integrated software   Software that combines several application functions into one.

Interest on Lawyers' Trust Account (IOLTA)   is an interest-bearing account set up specifically to hold trust funds. The interest that accrues on an IOLTA account is given to a state bar foundation or other nonprofit legal organization for the good of the public.

interior landscaping   Uses movable partitions or panels, and work surfaces, file cabinets, and drawers that attach to the partitions instead of interior walls.

internal control   Procedures that an organization establishes to set up checks and balances so that no individual in the organization has exclusive control over any part of the accounting system.

intranet   An internal information distribution system used only by a law firm staff.

just-in-time inventory   An inventory method that maintains minimum inventory levels to maximize cash flow.

law clerk   A law student working for a law firm on a part-time basis while he or she is finishing a law degree. Law clerk duties revolve almost exclusively around legal research and writing.

law librarian   A librarian responsible for maintaining a law library. Maintenance includes purchasing new books and periodicals, classifying, storing, indexing, and updating the holdings, and coordinating computer-assisted legal research (i.e., Westlaw, LexisNexis, and other services).

law office information system   A combination of human involvement, computer hardware and software, and raw information that work together to solve problems in a law office.

leadership   The act of motivating or causing others to perform and achieve objectives.

lease-to-purchase   A lease where the lessee agrees to make payments for a specific period of time, but at the end of the lease term the lessee is given the option to purchase the equipment.

legal administrator   Person responsible for some type of law office administrative system, such as general management, finance and accounting, human resources, marketing, or computer systems.

legal assistants   A distinguishing group of persons who assist attorneys in the delivery of legal services. They have knowledge and expertise regarding the legal system and substantive and procedural law that qualifies them to do work of a legal nature under the supervision of an attorney.

legal assistant manager   One who supervises, recruits, trains, distributes, sets priorities, and directs the overall management of a group of legal assistants.

legal malpractice   A claim that an attorney breached an ordinary standard of care that a reasonable attorney would have adhered to in that same circumstance.

legal marketing   The process of educating consumers on the quality legal services that a law office can provide.

legal secretaries   Employees who provide assistance and support to other law office staff by preparing documents, composing correspondence, scheduling appointments, and performing other tasks.

legal services office   A not-for-profit law office that receives grants from the government and private donations to pay for representation of disadvantaged persons who otherwise could not afford legal services.

legal team   A group made up of attorneys, administrators, law clerks, librarians, legal assistants, secretaries, clerks, and other third parties. Each provides a distinct range of services to clients and has a place on the legal team.

leveraging   The process of earning a profit from legal services that are provided by law office personnel (usually partners, associates, and legal assistants).

local area network   A multiuser system that links independent microcomputers together that are close in proximity for the purpose of sharing information, printers, and storage devices.

loss factor   The tenant's pro rata share of common space.

management   The administration of people and other resources to accomplish objectives.

management by objectives   A performance program in which the individual employee and the employer agree on goals for the employee.

management reports   Reports used to help management analyze whether the office is operating in an efficient and effective manner.

managing partner   An attorney in a law firm chosen by the partnership or the shareholders to run the firm on a day-to-day basis, make administrative decisions, and set policies.

marketing plan   Specifies a target audience the firm is trying to reach, the exact goals that the marketing program is to accomplish, and establishes a detailed strategy of how the goals will be achieved.

mission statement   A general, enduring statement of the purpose or intent of the law practice.

Model Code of Professional Responsibility   American Bar Association (ABA) code of ethics published in 1983 that are self-imposed ethical standards for ABA members but can also serve as a prototype of legal ethic standards for state court systems.

Model Rules of Professional Conduct   American Bar Association (ABA) code of ethics published in 1969 that are self-imposed ethical standards for ABA members but can also serve as a prototype of legal ethical standards for state court systems.

multitask operating system   System that allows the execution of several application programs at the same time.

negligent hiring   Hiring an employee without sufficiently and reasonably checking the employee's background.

net income   Monies that are left after expenses are deducted from gross income.

net lease   The tenant pays a base rent plus real estate taxes.

noise   Any situation that interferes with or distorts the message being communicated from the sender to the receiver.

non-billable time   Time that cannot be directly billed to a paying client.

nonequity partner   A partner who does not share in the profits or losses of the firm but may be entitled to certain benefits not given to associates.

of counsel   An attorney affiliated with the firm in some way, such as a retired or semiretired partner.

office manager   Manager who handles day-to-day operations of the law office, such as accounting, supervision of the clerical support staff, and assisting the managing partner.

office services management   The administration of a number of internal systems and services in a law office. These include mail, copy, fax, and telecommunication services, among others.

off-line   The user is not connected to an information service and no charges are accruing except possibly a printing or downloading charge.

on-line   The user is connected to an information system and is running up charges.

operating lease   A lease where the lessee agrees to make payments for a specific period of time.

operating system software   Instructs the computer how to operate its circuitry and how to communicate with input, output, and storage devices.

opportunity costs   Refers to the costs of forgoing or passing up other alternatives.

organizing   The process of arranging people and physical resources to carry out plans and accomplish objectives.

outside counsel   Refers to when a corporate or governmental law practice hires a private law office to help them with legal matters.

overhead   General administrative costs of doing business, including costs such as rent, utilities, phone, and salary costs for administrators.

partner   An owner in a private law practice (with the partnership form of business structure) who shares in the practice's profits and losses.

personal information manager (PIM)   Consolidates a number of different tasks into one computer program. Most PIMs include calendaring, things to do, a contact database that tracks names and addresses of people, note taking, and other tasks as well.

personnel handbook   A manual that lists the formal personnel policies of an organization.

planning   The process of setting objectives, assessing the future, and developing courses of action to achieve those objectives.

policy   A specific statement that sets out what is or is not acceptable.

powerful managing partner   A management structure in which a single partner is responsible for managing the firm.

practice management   Management decisions about how a law office will practice law and handle its cases.

pre-billing report   A rough draft version of billings.

prepaid legal service   A plan that a person can purchase that entitles the person to receive legal services either free or at a greatly reduced rate.

pro bono   Legal services that are provided free of charge to a client who is not able to pay for the services.

procedure   A series of steps that must be followed to accomplish a task.

pure retainer   A fee that obligates the office to be available to represent the client throughout the time period agreed upon.

rainmaking   The ability to bring in new clients to a law office.

reasonable accommodation   Accommodating a person with a disability, which may include making existing facilities readily accessible, restructuring the job, or modifying work schedules.

realization   Amount a firm actually receives in income as opposed to the amount it bills.

recurring entry   A calendar entry that recurs, typically either daily, weekly, monthly, or annually.

rental space   What rent is based upon; this includes usable space plus the tenant's pro rata share of all common space on the floor, such as hallways, stairwells, and bathrooms.

rephrasing   A technique used to improve communication by repeating back to a person your understanding of the conversation.

retainer for general representation   Retainer typically used when a client such as a corporation or school board requires continuing legal services throughout the year.

rule by all partners/shareholders   A management structure in which all partners/shareholders are included in decisions that affect the firm.

rule by management committee/board   Management structure that uses a committee structure to make management decisions for the firm.

settlement   A mutual agreement to resolve a dispute on specified terms.

sexual harassment   Unwelcome sexual advances, requests for sexual favors, and other verbal or physical conduct of a sexual nature that creates an intimidating, hostile, or offensive working environment.

shareholder   An owner in a private law practice (that is a corporation) who shares in the practice's profits and losses.

staff attorney   An attorney hired by a firm with the knowledge and understanding that he or she will never be considered for partnership.

staffing plan   Estimate of how many employees will be hired or funded by the firm, what positions or capacities they will serve in, what positions will need to be added, what old positions will be deleted, and how much compensation each employee will receive.

statute of limitations   A statute or law that sets a limit on the length of time a party has to file a suit. If a case is filed after the statute of limitations, the claim is barred and is dismissed as a matter of law.

storage capacity   The maximum amount of data that can be stored on a device.

storage device   Stores data that can be retrieved later.

strategic planning   The process of determining the major goals of a firm and then adopting the courses of action necessary to achieve those goals.

substantive task   A task that relates to the process of actually performing legal work for clients.

system   A consistent or organized way of doing something.

task lighting   Lights that are attached to work surfaces or furniture, or are free standing.

terminal   A keyboard and monitor that are used to communicate with computers.

timekeeper productivity report   Report showing how much billable and non-billable time is being spent by each timekeeper.

timekeeping   The process of tracking time for the purpose of billing clients.

timekeeping and billing service bureau   A company that—for a fee—processes attorney and legal assistant time sheets (usually on a monthly basis), generates billings, and records client payments for a law practice.

time sheet/time slip   A record of detailed information about the legal services professionals provide to each client.

time-to-billing percentage   System of adjusting downward the actual amount that will be billed to clients during the budget process, taking into account the fact that timekeepers are not always able to bill at their optimum levels.

total quality management A management philosophy based upon knowing the needs of each client and allowing those needs to drive the legal organization at all levels of activity, from the receptionist to the senior partner.

trust account A separate bank account (also called an escrow account), apart from a law office's or attorney's operating checking account, where unearned client funds are deposited.

unearned retainer Monies that are paid up front by the client as an advance against the attorney's future fees and expenses. Until the monies are actually earned by the attorney or law office, they belong to the client.

usable space Space that is actually available for offices, equipment, furniture, or occupiable area but does not include hallways, stairwells, and similar areas.

value billing A type of fee agreement that is based not on the time spent to perform the legal work but on the basis of the perceived value of services to the client.

word processing program Program used to edit, manipulate, and revise text to create documents.

workdays System of calculating deadlines that refers to only days when the court is open.

work letter The part of the lease that states what construction the landlord must perform before the tenant occupies the space.

wrongful termination A lawsuit in which a former employee alleges that an employer unlawfully terminated the employee.

zero-based budgeting system A type of budget that forces everyone in the organization to justify and explain his or her budget figures in depth without using prior year's figures as justification.

INDEX

ProLaw®

prolaw.thomsonelite.com

All-in-one software to automate the *practice* and manage the *business* of law.

The Engine to Power Your Practice

The Business Challenge

In today's competitive market, legal professionals are confronted with the rising need to deliver more value to clients while increasing productivity and efficiency. ProLaw was created with this mission in mind.

An Integrated Software Suite
Run all aspects of your practice from one place.

Traditionally, legal organizations have used several different applications to manage their business and practice activities. Separate software packages were used for accounting, bill generation, client development, case management, docketing, document management, time and expense tracking, and so on. ProLaw changed all of this by developing the first integrated solution designed to dramatically simplify the management and practice of law. Today, ProLaw from Thomson Elite leads the industry in providing everything needed to organize and automate your law practice or department.

From the convenience of a Microsoft Windows desktop environment or Web browser*, ProLaw automates case, relationship, and document management as well as time entry, billing, and accounting – all within one integrated solution. It provides comprehensive integration with Microsoft Outlook, Word, Westlaw research, court rules, and many other popular applications. Designed specifically for use in smaller and mid-size law firms, corporate legal departments, and government law offices, ProLaw matches the way legal offices actually work, so you can spend less time on administrative tasks and more time serving clients.

Leading Service Partner

ProLaw customers also benefit from convenient online, on-site and off-site training, cost-efficient support, maintenance and updates packages, a 24/7 self-support online knowledge base, and a growing selection of optional modules that allow you to add new capabilities as your needs change and your practice grows.

*Option available with ProLaw READY.

Corporate Office	Sales, Services and Support
5100 West Goldleaf Circle, Suite 100	4401 Masthead NE, Suite 100
Los Angeles, CA 90056-1271	Albuquerque, NM 87109
Phone: 323-642-5200	Sales: 800-977-6529
Support: 800-ELITEDP (800-354-8337)	Services and Support: 888-877-6529
Email: salesinfo@elite.com	Email: prolawinfo@thomson.com